SIXTH EDITION

W9-AWV-011

Work in Progress
A Guide to Academic Writing and Revising

LISA EDE
Oregon State University

BEDFORD/ST. MARTIN'S
Boston ◆ New York

For Bedford/St. Martin's

Developmental Editor: Stephanie Carpenter
Production Editor: Maria Teresa Burwell
Production Associate: Yexenia (Jessie) Markland
Production Supervisor: Pat Ollague
Marketing Manager: Brian Wheel
Art Director/Cover Design: Lucy Krikorian
Text Design: Wanda Kossak
Copy Editor: Rosemary Winfield
Photo Research: Martha Friedman
Cover Art: Emmett Williams "Robert Rauschenberg," 1992; plastic laminate, objects, acrylic paint, signed on reverse, 60 × 48 inches. Courtesy of the artist and Carl Solway Gallery, Cincinnati, Ohio. Photographer: Chris Gomien.
Composition: Stratford Publishing Services, Inc.
Printing and Binding: R. R. Donnelley & Sons Company

President: Joan E. Feinberg
Editorial Director: Denise B. Wydra
Editor in Chief: Nancy Perry
Director of Marketing: Karen Melton Soeltz
Director of Editing, Design, and Production: Marcia Cohen
Managing Editor: Erica T. Appel

Library of Congress Control Number: 2003107894

Manufactured in the United States of America.

9 8 7 6 5 4
f e d c b a

For information, write: Bedford/St. Martin's, 75 Arlington Street, Boston, MA 02116 (617–399–4000)

ISBN: 0-312-40650-9

Acknowledgments
Acknowledgments and copyrights appear at the back of the book on pages 508–09, which constitute an extension of the copyright page.

To my students
and
(of course)
to Gregory

Preface

With the first edition of *Work in Progress,* I wanted to write a theoretically sophisticated but commonsensical textbook, one grounded both in the centuries-old rhetorical tradition and in recent theoretical and pedagogical research on writing. I wanted to write a textbook that would enrich but not dominate the life of the classroom. Traditional textbooks too often place students and teachers in opposition: The teacher acts as the provider of knowledge, while students are positioned as passive absorbers of this wisdom. *Work in Progress* would, I hoped, foster the development of a genuinely collaborative community, grounded in mutual respect and a shared commitment to inquiry. Learning and teaching are, after all, both works in progress.

Fortunately, *Work in Progress* has been successful enough to warrant subsequent editions, and thus it continues as my own work in progress. With each new edition, I have attempted to build on the strengths of earlier editions and to respond to the needs and suggestions of instructors and students who have used the text. The fifth edition, for instance, added two new chapters — Chapter 4, "Understanding the Research Process" and Chapter 17, "Putting It All Together: Analyzing and Writing Academic Arguments" — designed to strengthen the text's emphasis on academic writing.

The most significant changes in this sixth edition are intended to build on and enrich the text's treatment of academic writing. *Work in Progress* has always provided a solid foundation for students entering the academy, for its rhetorical approach encourages students to learn how to analyze and address different disciplinary contexts and expectations. Now the discussion of academic analysis and argument has been significantly expanded from one to two chapters. In recognition of the increasing role that visual elements play in written texts, the sixth edition also includes a new chapter on document design.

These additions will, I hope, increase the usefulness and timeliness of *Work in Progress* — as well as reinforce the text's central goals. These goals continue to be reflected in a number of key features:

- a focus on the concept of the rhetorical situation (Chapters 5 and 6)
- explicit support for and reinforcement of collaborative learning and writing activities (Chapter 13)

- a broad range of examples of successful student writing in the disciplines (Chapter 17)

- attention to the impact of new technologies for student writers (Chapter 7)

- inclusion of a mini-anthology of readings focused on online writing technologies and situations (Chapter 3)

- extensive attention to the processes of reading and research, and to reading, writing, and research as dynamic, interdependent activities (Chapters 3 and 4)

- full discussion of the demands of academic writing and research (Chapters 4, 14, 15, 16, and 17)

- a strong emphasis on the importance of social context and textual conventions of writing (Chapter 6)

NEW TO THIS EDITION

Separate new chapters on analyzing and constructing arguments.   Extending the focus on academic writing, "Understanding Academic Analysis" (Chapter 15) guides students in thinking critically about how arguments work and in writing analyses across the curriculum. "Understanding Academic Argument" (Chapter 16) helps students construct their own arguments. Both chapters include new student models.

A new chapter on document design.   Practical advice for online and print document design is now the topic of a full chapter, "Strategies for Document Design" (Chapter 10), which includes several new examples. In keeping with the book's goals, the chapter encourages students to examine design principles in light of particular rhetorical situations.

More on avoiding plagiarism when working with sources.   The coverage of using sources in Chapter 4, "Understanding the Research Process," has been extended to focus more explicitly on avoiding plagiarism. The chapter builds on students' knowledge of rhetorical situations to help them understand citation conventions of the academic community, offering examples and guidelines for taking notes and using a working bibliography.

New help for multilingual writers.   Practical tips throughout the book, written with the help of a panel of experienced ESL instructors, guide multilingual students in editing their own work and understanding U.S. academic style.

ORGANIZATION

Part One is an introduction to the interdependent processes of writing, reading, and research. The four chapters in Part One approach these processes from a rhetorical perspective, one that calls attention to the situated nature of any act of communication. Rather than presenting students with formats or rules to follow, these chapters encourage students to build upon their commonsense understanding of communication through reading, writing, and researching. In keeping with this approach, detailed documentation guidelines have been provided in a separate section at the end of the book.

Part Two, which includes three chapters, focuses on the concept of the rhetorical situation. The first chapter in Part Two introduces students to the concept of the rhetorical situation and encourages them to take a strategic, situated approach to writing. Such an approach encourages students to ask questions about their role as writers, about their readers, and about the textual conventions that come into play in any particular rhetorical situation. The second chapter builds on the first by looking at textual conventions as socially constructed, socially negotiated understandings between readers and writers. It includes three articles on the same topic by linguist Deborah Tannen. Because these articles are directed toward quite different audiences, they provide a powerful case study of what it means to both address and invoke an audience. The final chapter in Part Two applies these understandings to online writing situations.

Part Three offers practical strategies for writing. The six chapters in Part Three cover the topics of invention, planning, drafting, document design, revision, and collaboration. These chapters introduce students to a variety of practical strategies they can use as they plan, draft, and revise. Rather than emphasizing a single, prescribed series of steps or strategies that students must follow, *Work in Progress* encourages students to develop a repertoire of strategies they can use (working alone and with others, on- and offline), depending on their purpose and situation.

Part Four initiates students into the reading and writing they will do as members of the academic community. The first of the four chapters in Part Four articulates a rhetorical approach to academic argument. This chapter offers suggestions for analyzing disciplinary conventions and for understanding what is expected for assignments. The second chapter helps students understand the demands of academic analysis, with a particular focus on analyzing academic arguments. The third chapter provides extensive information about writing academic arguments, and the final chapter presents an extended case study of one student's experience writing an essay on a poem by Emily Dickinson. It includes three drafts of the essay, as well as the student's analysis of her rhetorical situation and notes about her writing process. This chapter closes with a miscellany of examples of student writing across the disciplines.

I have attempted to make *Work in Progress* an innovative textbook — but also to be sure it remains a practical textbook. It provides a conceptual framework and activities that stimulate effective classroom instruction, yet it also offers teachers considerable autonomy and flexibility. Some teachers will particularly appreciate the book's emphasis on reading and on academic writing, for instance, while others may draw more heavily on its numerous interactive, collaborative, workshop-oriented activities. Still other instructors will appreciate the ways in which *Work in Progress*'s rhetorical approach supports an emphasis on cultural and/or literacy studies. The *Instructor's Notes* to *Work in Progress* provide further elaboration of ways in which the text can be used and the book's companion Web site offers additional resources.

ACKNOWLEDGMENTS

Before I wrote *Work in Progress*, acknowledgments sometimes struck me as formulaic or conventional. Now I recognize that they are neither; rather, acknowledgments are simply inadequate to the task at hand. Coming at the end of the preface — and hence twice marginalized — acknowledgments can never adequately convey the complex web of interrelationships that make a book like this possible. I hope that the people whose support and assistance I acknowledge here not only note my debt of gratitude but also recognize the sustaining role that they have played, and continue to play, in my life.

I would like to begin by thanking my colleagues at the Center for Writing and Learning at Oregon State University. I could accomplish little in my teaching, research, and administration without the support and friendship of Moira Dempsey, Saundra Mills, and Wayne Robertson. They, along with our writing assistants, have taught me what it means to collaborate in a sustaining, productive fashion. Others in the OSU English department, my second academic home, supported me while I wrote and revised this text. I am indebted to my colleagues Chris Anderson, Vicki Tolar Burton, and Anita Helle for their friendship and their commitment to writing over the years.

I have dedicated this book to my students, and I hope that it in some way reflects what *they* have taught me over the years. I also owe a great debt of gratitude to another friend and teacher, Suzanne Clark, who allowed me to persuade her to interrupt her own important works in progress to collaborate with me on the *Instructor's Notes*.

I also wish to acknowledge the students whose writing appears in this text. I am particularly grateful to Stevon Roberts, who wrote essays for the new chapters on academic analysis and argument. This edition of *Work in Progress* also includes an essay that Stevon coauthored with Julie Baird, as well as an additional new essay by Michelle Fuller. The companion Web site benefits from a new scientific essay by Christina Allen. I am also grateful to my colleague Wayne Robertson, whose memo requesting additional funds for Oregon State

University's Writing Center appears in Chapter 10, "Strategies for Document Design."

Colleagues and students play an important role in nurturing any project, but so do those who form the intangible but indispensable community of scholars that is one's most intimate disciplinary home. Here, it is harder to determine who to acknowledge; my debt to the composition theorists who have led the way or "grown up" with me is so great that I hesitate to list the names of specific individuals here for fear of omitting someone deserving of credit. I must, however, acknowledge my friend and frequent coauthor Andrea Lunsford, who writes with me even when I write alone.

I would also like to thank the many dedicated teachers of composition I have worked and talked with over the years. By their example, comments, suggestions, and questions, they have taught me a great deal about the teaching of writing. A number of writing instructors took time from their teaching to look carefully at the fifth edition. Their observations and suggestions have enriched and improved this new edition. These reviewers include the following instructors: Kathleen Ashman, Florida State Universitiy; Ivana Banks, University of Miami; Julie Sloan Brannon, Jacksonville Universitiy; Thomas Burkedall, Occidental College; Joy A. Burnett, Wayne State University; David Custer, Boisie State University; Anita Lee Daniels, University of Miami; Andrea Feldman, University of Colorado at Boulder; Burton Hatlen, University of Maine; Debra S. Knutson, Dakota State University; Kendra L. Matko, Western Michigan University; Lisa J. McClure, Southern Illinois University; Wendy McLallen, Florida State University; Rebecca Luginbuhl Mills, California State Polytechnic University, Pamona; Linda B. Moore, University of West Florida; Rolf Norgaard, University of Colorado at Boulder; Tim Peoples, Elon University; Glorida Shearin, Savannah State University; Joshua Sunderbruch, Southern Illinois University; Cynthia Walker, Faulkner University; Kris Walker, Tennessee Technological University; Maria N. Warren, University of West Florida; and Lisa M. Wilson, Winona State University.

Special thanks go to LuMing Mao at Miami University, Christina Ortmeier-Hooper at the University of New Hampshire, and Jan Frodesen at the University of California–Santa Barbara, who helped me develop the boxed suggestions for multilingual writers.

I wish to thank the dedicated staff of Bedford/St. Martin's, particularly Stephanie Pelkowski Carpenter. Working with Stephanie has been a joy from start to finish. Stephanie moves effortlessly from macro-level suggestions for revision to micro-level editorial queries: this edition of *Work in Progress* is stronger because of her influence. In addition, I want to thank project editor Maria Burwell, whose patient attention to detail proved especially valuable.

Finally, I want to (but cannot adequately) acknowledge the support of my husband, Gregory Pfarr, whose passionate commitment to his own creative endeavors, and our life together, sustains me.

Lisa Ede

Brief Contents

Contents

PART TWO

RHETORICAL SITUATIONS   155

5. Analyzing Rhetorical Situations   157

WRITING, READING, AND RESEARCH: AN INTRODUCTION

PART ONE

On Writing

A *college student in mathematics education* decides to keep a journal during his student-teaching practicum. He uses his journal to reflect on his students' problems, to record observations about the school where he is teaching, to analyze the effectiveness of his lesson plans, and to cope with the inevitable highs and lows of his first experience in the classroom. At the end of the term, for an advanced seminar in his major, he draws on the journal to write an essay on the relationship between theory and practice in mathematics education. "It's a good thing I kept that journal," he tells a friend. "It helped me get beyond clichés about teaching to what I really know works in the classroom."

A *businessperson* who is chairing his local school board learns that a group of parents plans to petition the board to have several young adult books removed from the middle-school library. Aware that petitions such as this can develop into major controversies if not handled properly, he decides to ask others how they have responded on similar occasions, so he logs into SchoolBoard, an electronic bulletin board for members of school boards and others interested in local educational issues, and types his query. His question provokes a lively exchange. After reading the responses, he prints a number of suggestions, types his thanks, and adds his own comments to the ongoing conversation.

Two *students in an introduction-to-literature class* learn that they must write an analysis of Mrs. Ramsey, a character in Virginia Woolf's *To the Lighthouse.* They meet to discuss possible essay topics. At first their conversation moves slowly; they both liked the novel and found Mrs. Ramsey interesting, but they're not sure how to move from a general response to a specific topic. Finally one of them suggests that they write down all the questions they have about Mrs. Ramsey. They do so and are reassured by their list. But what to do next? Why not try to imagine how different characters in Woolf's novel might respond to their questions, one of them suggests. Perhaps the characters' responses will help them see something that they might otherwise overlook. They quickly make a list of characters, divide them up, and agree to email their responses to each other and meet over the weekend for further conversation. As they say goodbye, they comment with relief on how good it feels to have gotten started.

A *consulting engineer* meets with colleagues to begin work on a proposal for a major construction project. Knowing they have just a month to meet the deadline, she assigns duties to group members. Some will begin research on technical issues; others will consult with resource people within the firm; and still others will begin writing nontechnical sections of the draft. Her role will be to organize and monitor the group effort and edit the final proposal. After the meeting, she works out a schedule for preliminary reports, emails it to her colleagues, and reminds them that thanks to their new groupware computer program, they will be able to generate, revise, and edit text together. This will be much more efficient, she observes, than their former practice of sending sections of text via email.

A *student from Chile* participating in an exchange program in the United States wants to apply for a scholarship that would allow her to spend an additional year studying abroad. After reviewing the scholarship application, she decides to spend the next two hours writing a rough draft of her autobiographical statement. Because she realizes that thoughts come more easily to her when she writes in her first language, she opts to compose in Spanish. "This way I won't have to worry if I've gotten every idiom or verb tense right," she thinks. "Later on I can translate this and have a friend look for language problems."

A *grandmother* realizes that her grandchildren know very little about their family's history, so she embarks on a family genealogy project. She begins by writing all that she remembers about her parents and grandparents. After printing and reading her first draft, she realizes that over the years she has forgotten many details, so she emails her draft to her brother and sister and asks for corrections and additions. Then she begins searching the World Wide Web for genealogy sites. Who knows? She might unearth some information about their family. And even if she doesn't, she is sure to locate both images and information that will enrich her project. She's tried to tell her grandchildren about her father's experiences in the war — but World War II is hard for twenty-first-century children to grasp. She feels that if she can find a photograph of the bombing of Pearl Harbor, which her father experienced firsthand, she might be able to make the war, and her father, more real to them. Thank goodness she invested in a new desktop publishing program and color printer recently! She'll need them for this important project.

A *senior majoring in sociology* meets with her adviser to discuss her senior honors thesis. The student is interested in the relationship of rap and hip-hop music to recent cultural, political, and economic developments in North America. The student and her adviser talk about the lengthy process involved in writing a thesis. The adviser recommends a two-pronged approach. "Look inward at your own interests and understandings by keeping a notebook of ideas and reading notes about your project," the adviser recommends. "Eventually, this notebook will lead to a proposal for your thesis — but for now just explore your ideas and respond to things you read. Be sure to look outward also. Obviously, you'll be collecting resources in the library, but you should also gather information online." They move to the adviser's computer and begin to surf the Web, looking for sites and bookmarking several that look promising. As they wrap up their conference, the adviser reminds the student that at the end of her project she'll give an oral presentation on her thesis. "As you look at Web sites, be sure to look for multimedia clips that you can use in your presentation," the adviser recommends.

People write for a variety of reasons. Many people write because they are required to. Term papers, business letters, reports, proposals, magazine articles — most are written by a person or a group asked to take on the responsibility for the project. Sometimes this writing simply reports the results of analysis or observations. But often the writing functions as a means for solving problems, making decisions, or coming to understand complex situations.

People also write to fulfill important personal needs. The grandmother describing her parents, bringing them to life for her grandchildren, writes because she wants to record her family's history. The student teacher uses his journal to help make sense of — and survive — his first year in the classroom. People write to solve problems and to communicate with others, but they write to look inward as well.

NOTE FOR MULTILINGUAL WRITERS

Multilingual writers write for a variety of reasons and often use more than one language to do so. As a multilingual writer, you may write in a first or home language other than English when you communicate with family and friends, keep a journal, write poetry or fiction, and so on. You might write first drafts of formal documents, such as academic essays or professional reports, in your first language and then translate these drafts into English. You might even "code switch," using your native or home language and English within the same text.

■ ■ ■

FOR EXPLORATION

What do you typically write, and why? Make a list of all the kinds of writing you regularly do — shopping lists, class notes, whatever. What kinds of writing do you do most often? Least often? What are your usual reasons for writing? If you write in more than one language, how does this influence your experiences as a writer? Which of your writing experiences are generally productive and satisfying? Unproductive and unsatisfying? In a paragraph or two explore why some writing experiences are productive and satisfying while others are not.

UNDERSTANDING HOW WRITING WORKS

At first glance, the writers described at the beginning of this chapter might seem to have little in common. But if you look more closely, you can see a number of similarities — similarities that can tell you something about how writing works.

- The writing that these people do matters; it helps determine how successful they are in school, on the job, or in their communities.

- None of these writers works in isolation. They may spend some time thinking and writing alone, but all interact regularly with others. Sometimes they do so to generate ideas or to get responses. On other occasions, they actually write with others.

- Whether writing alone or collaboratively, they all write in a specific context or situation. As writers, they are influenced by such factors as these:

   Their reason for writing and the nature of their writing project

   The issues they want to explore and the points they want to make

   The readers for whom they are writing

   The language in which they are composing

   Textual conventions, like report or business letter formats, that help define the form their writing takes

   Their feelings about their writing

   The amount of practice they have had with a particular kind of writing

External factors, such as deadlines and access to computers and online technologies

- No matter what they write, from the moment they begin to think about their writing, these writers face a complex series of *choices.* Some of these choices will involve the writing process. To make practical decisions about their writing, these writers ask themselves questions such as

Do I know enough about my subject? Do I need to do additional research? Should I consult online as well as print sources? Interview authorities on my topic?

When should I begin writing? How much time should I spend planning, drafting, and revising?

Should I compose in my first or home language and translate my text into English, or should I compose in English from the start?

How might I benefit from working with others?

- Other questions involve the writing itself:

What do I hope to accomplish? Are my goals realistic, and do they meet the needs and expectations of my readers?

How can I organize and develop my ideas most effectively?

How much supporting detail do I need to provide?

What tone or style is appropriate, given my subject, purpose, and audience?

How can I most effectively share my ideas with others? Through a conventional printed essay or report? Through a PowerPoint presentation? Or should I consider putting this online via the World Wide Web?

- They all recognize the significant role that writing plays in their personal and professional lives. Writing doesn't necessarily come easily, but they willingly spend the time and energy necessary to write well. Writing, they know, is important *work in progress.*

■ ■ ■

FOR EXPLORATION

Recall a particular successful writing experience. (Don't limit yourself to academic writing, by the way.) What factors enabled you to complete this writing successfully? Write a paragraph or more describing this experience and analyzing the reasons you consider it successful.

DEVELOPING RHETORICAL SENSITIVITY

How do writers make choices as they compose? Experienced writers like those described at the beginning of this chapter draw on *all* their resources when they write. They learn about writing from their reading, and they also analyze their own situation as writers. They think about their writing purposes — the meaning they wish to communicate, their reasons for writing — and their readers. They explore their own ideas, challenging themselves to express their ideas as clearly and carefully as possible. They play with words and phrases, sentences and paragraphs, to make their writing stylistically effective. And they take advantage of the resources available to them thanks to online technologies. In all of these activities, experienced writers practice *rhetorical sensitivity* — even though they might not use this phrase to describe their thinking and writing.

You may not be familiar with this phrase, either. It derives from the word *rhetoric,* the art of effective communication. Rhetoric is one of the oldest fields of intellectual study in Western culture; it was first formulated by such Greek and Roman rhetoricians as Isocrates (436–338 B.C.), Aristotle (384–322 B.C.), Cicero (106–43 B.C.), and Quintilian (A.D. 35–96). Originally developed to meet the needs of speakers, rhetoric quickly came to be applied to written texts as well.

In your daily life, you already practice considerable rhetorical sensitivity. As you make decisions about how you wish to interact with others, you naturally (if unconsciously) draw on your commonsense understanding of effective communication. Imagine, for instance, that you are preparing to interview for a job. In deciding what to wear, how to act, and what to say during the interview, you will make a number of decisions that reflect your rhetorical sensitivity. Much of your attention will focus on how you can present yourself best, but you also recognize the importance of being well prepared and of interacting effectively with your interviewers. If you are smart, you will consider the specific situation for which you are applying. Someone applying for a position in a bank might well dress and act differently than someone applying for a job as a swim coach. Successful applicants know that all that they do — the way they dress, present themselves, respond to questions, and interact with interviewers — is an attempt to communicate their strengths and persuade their audience to employ them.

As a "reader" of contemporary culture, you also employ rhetorical sensitivity. As a consumer, for instance, you are bombarded with advertisements urging you to purchase various products or services. How you respond to these advertisements will depend primarily on how you "read" them. Wise consumers know that advertisements are designed to persuade, and they learn ways to read them with a critical eye (even as they appreciate, say, a television commercial's humor or a magazine ad's design). You read other aspects of contemporary culture as well. Much of the time you may do so for entertainment: While watching sports or other programs on television, for instance, your primary goal may be to relax and enjoy yourself. If you find the plot of a detective show implausible or the action of the Monday night football game too slow, you can easily click to a more interesting program.

At times, however, you may choose to take a more critical, distanced perspective on such forms of popular culture as television, music, and magazines. After arguing with a friend about whether Eminem advocates homophobia and violence, you may well watch his videos with a careful eye, comparing him with other rappers. When you compare different musicians' lyrics, type of dress, and movements, you are considering the ways in which these groups attempt to appeal to and communicate with their audience. Though you probably would not have used this term to describe your analysis, you are analyzing the rhetoric of their performances.

When you think rhetorically, you consider the ways in which words and images are used to engage — and sometimes to persuade — others. Writers who think rhetorically apply their cultural understanding of human communication in general, and of written texts in particular, to the decisions that will enable effective communication within a specific writer-reader situation.

Seeing the Key Elements of Rhetoric in Context

As applied to written texts, rhetoric involves three key elements:

- One or more *writers* who have (or must discover) something to communicate

- One or more *readers* with whom the writer would like to communicate

- A *text* — an essay, poem, Web site, report, email, or other verbal (and, increasingly, also visual) communication — that makes this exchange of information possible

The relationship among these three elements is dynamic. Writers select and arrange language to express their meanings, but readers are equally active. Readers don't simply decipher the words on the page; they draw on their own experiences and expectations as they read. As a student, for instance, you naturally read your economics textbook differently than you read a popular novel. You also know that the more experience you have reading certain kinds of writing — science fiction novels or the sports or financial pages of the newspaper, for example — the more you will get out of them.

And what about the third rhetorical element, the text? As Chapter 7, "Negotiating Online Writing Situations," explains more fully, changes in the technologies of writing — the technologies that writers use to share their writing with readers — hold powerful implications for contemporary writers. A Midwestern farmer writing to a parent in the mid-nineteenth century would have had few choices to make about his text. He would have known that he would write a letter (following the conventions of that genre) by hand to his parents. Students living in the Midwest in the twenty-first century who wish to communicate with their parents have many more options. They could still write a letter by hand — for even in our technologically advanced culture handwritten letters are still highly valued. (Indeed, the infrequency with which we write letters makes them all the more prized.) But students could also call, email, fax, or exchange instant messages with their parents. If the student has constructed a Web site, his parents might interact with him by visiting his site. If they have their own site, they could acknowledge their connection with their son by linking their two sites. Such a link is quite different from the letter that nineteenth-century parents might send to a child, but in its own way it still communicates important information to readers (in this case, the parents, their children, and those surfing the Web).

As this example indicates, writing and reading do not occur in a vacuum. The language you grow up speaking, the social and cultural worlds you inhabit, the technologies of writing available to you: These and other factors all play important roles in your writing. Even native speakers of English who have been educated in the United States sometimes find certain aspects of standard written English to be puzzling or difficult. Those who have grown up speaking a different first or home language almost always do so. If you grow up speaking a language other than English, for instance, you may find English speakers' direct, concise prose style puzzling. Communication is central to all human cultures, but the form that this communication takes can vary in significant ways: What feels natural to a member of one community may feel strange or even uncomfortable to someone else.

Precisely because writing is a distinctly human activity, writers can sometimes experience difficulties and dilemmas. Students whose first language is not English often must work hard to understand and adapt to North American oral and written communication preferences. Even those who have grown up in American culture may find that the writing they are asked to do in college differs considerably from the language they use in their everyday lives. The United States is, after all, a country of many cultures, ethnic groups, languages, and dialects. The language that feels comfortable and natural to you when you speak with your family and friends may differ considerably from that required in academic reading and writing assignments.

■ ■ ■

FOR EXPLORATION

Take a few moments to write about the language that you speak in your home community and the language that you use at school. If you speak several dialects or languages, feel free to include this in your reflection. To

NOTE FOR MULTILINGUAL WRITERS

If English is not your first or home language, you may sometimes feel frustrated when teachers ask you to adapt to the conventions of academic writing in the United States. You may feel that you are being asked to stop speaking and writing in a way that feels natural to you. Although conflicts sometimes occur between first or home languages and those of the U.S. academy, your goal as a writer should not be to abandon your first or home language. Instead, as you become more fluent in the conventions of standard written English, you should try to develop a rhetorical sensitivity that allows you to write effectively in both languages and communities.

what extent do academic forms of writing feel comfortable or uncomfortable? Why? If you have found academic writing difficult or uncomfortable, what steps, if any, have you taken to meet this challenge?

Here is a second option for your consideration. Instead of writing about the relationship between your home and school languages, take this opportunity to reflect on your feelings about and uses of recent online writing technologies, such as email, the Web, and multimedia. How comfortable are you with these technologies? Has it been a struggle to learn to use them, or have they come more or less naturally to you? Do you find yourself missing such older writing practices as handwriting letters? Spend a few minutes writing about these and related questions.

Many writers whose first language is not standard written English (that is, the formal English that is used for academic writing in the United States) prefer to freewrite in their home language. If you are more comfortable writing in your first or home language than in standard written English, feel free to respond to this — and every other "For Exploration" throughout *Work in Progress* — in your first or home language.

Like life, writing involves negotiation. When you prepare for a job interview, you must decide how much you are willing to modify your everyday way of dressing to meet the expected demands of the situation. Similarly, when you write — whether in college, at work, or for civic or other activities — you must consider the expectations of others. At times it can be difficult to determine, let alone meet, these expectations. In your first weeks at a new job, for instance, you probably felt like the new kid on the block. Gradually, however, you became sensitive to the expectations of those with whom you worked. Likewise, as a college student you may at times feel like a new *writer* on the block. Both *Work in Progress* and your composition course will help you build on the rhetorical sensitivity that you already have, so that you can successfully complete your reading and writing assignments.

As you develop this rhetorical sensitivity, you will understand that writing offers many opportunities for self-expression. Unless you are writing entirely for yourself, however — as you do when you are writing in a journal — you must always consider the situation in which you are writing. Neither students nor businesspersons, to cite two examples, are free to write whatever they wish. Their participation in larger institutions brings constraints, just as it also provides opportunities for communication with others. A student writing an essay about a controversial issue and a middle-level manager writing an annual sales report are both taking advantage of institutionally sanctioned opportunities to communicate their own ideas. If the student and the manager wish to have their ideas taken seriously, if they wish to be effective with their intended audience, they must write in a form acceptable to their readers.

How do forms become "acceptable" to readers? Such forms as the essay, business letter, scientific report, and email develop over time, responding to the needs of readers and writers. The scientific report and the business letter, for instance, evolved along with and in response to the rise of modern science and of Western capitalism. Different forms of writing thus have histories, just as languages and countries do.

As a writer, you cannot ignore the situation within which you are writing or the forms and conventions that your readers expect you to follow. But unless you are writing a legal contract or filling out a renter's agreement, you also have considerable flexibility and opportunities for self-expression. An example from my experience writing *Work in Progress* may help clarify this point. When I started, I knew that I needed to follow certain conventions. Some of these conventions — such as the requirement that a textbook have headings, subheadings, and activities at the end of each chapter — are very general; others are more specific to composition textbooks. I didn't feel burdened or limited by these conventions; in fact, they reassured me, for they provided a framework that helped me develop my ideas. When you write, you, too, must work within conventions appropriate to your situation, purpose, and subject, but these conventions are generally enabling.

Demonstrating Rhetorical Sensitivity

Writers who demonstrate rhetorical sensitivity consider all the elements of rhetoric when they compose. They think about their own purposes and intentions — the meanings they want to convey to readers. They reflect on the image of themselves, the writer's *persona,* that they want to create in their writing. They consider the needs, interests, and expectations of their readers. And they draw on the knowledge they have gained about language through speaking, listening, reading, writing, and interacting with online technologies.

All writers — you included — have some degree of rhetorical sensitivity. Because you learned language as a child and have used it in your daily life ever since, you have already developed sensitivity to oral language. When you converse with others, you automatically adjust your language to the situation. (Indeed, you may even use one language or dialect with some speakers and another with others.) You naturally speak differently when you chat with friends than when you talk with your minister, employer, teacher, or family.

If you are like many students, you may be more confident of your ability to communicate effectively through oral language than through written discourse. How can you increase your rhetorical sensitivity as a writer? You can do so by reading broadly, writing often, and discussing your writing with others. Helping you achieve this rhetorical sensitivity is a major goal of this textbook and of your composition course.

■ ■ ■

FOR EXPLORATION

Take a few moments to reflect on your understanding of the terms *rhetoric* and *rhetorical sensitivity*. You may find it helpful to recall and describe an incident in your daily life when you were called on to demonstrate rhetorical sensitivity. Then write a paragraph or so stating your current understanding of these terms. Finally, write one or two questions that you still have about *rhetoric* and *rhetorical sensitivity*.

UNDERSTANDING WRITING "RULES"

Writing is hard but rewarding work. Sometimes people think that they can make that hard work just a little easier by establishing rigid rules. You may have been warned, for instance, never to use the pronoun *I* in your college writing. This rule may have confused you; you may have wondered what's so terrible about having a few *I*'s sprinkled throughout your essay.

If you think commonsensically about how language works, drawing on the rhetorical sensitivity you have developed as a reader and a writer, you can begin to understand how rules like this got established. You can also decide when this and other rules make sense and when they are overly rigid or unnecessarily limiting.

Let's look at the rule just mentioned: "Never use *I* in your writing." Teachers sometimes discourage students from using *I* because most academic writing is intended to focus on the subject being discussed, on arguments and evidence, rather than on the writer's individual experiences and opinions. A history professor who assigns an essay exam on the causes of the U.S. civil rights movement of the 1950s and 1960s will want you to demonstrate your ability to define and explain those causes rather than to express your personal feelings about the movement.

There's a kernel of commonsense wisdom, then, in the prohibition that some teachers have against using *I*. The problem is that there are times when *I* is exactly the right pronoun to use — when you're describing a personal experience, for example, or when you want to show that an observation truly is your own opinion. Rather than adhering rigidly to rules like this one, you can use your rhetorical sensitivity to decide what makes sense in a specific situation.

■ ■ ■

FOR EXPLORATION

Think of several writing "rules" that you've never understood or fully accepted. List as many of these rules as possible, and then choose one rule and write a brief explanation of why you question it.

NOTE FOR MULTILINGUAL WRITERS

Group or collaborative activities are common in North American classrooms. If you were educated in a country other than the United States or Canada, you may have had little experience with these activities. You may even question their usefulness and prefer a traditional, teacher-centered classroom.

 If you approach group activities with an open mind, you will soon discover that you can learn a good deal from your peers. Later in this chapter, you will find guidelines for collaborative work. Read these with care. You may also want to consult Chapter 13 of *Work in Progress*, "Strategies for Successful Collaboration." Even if this chapter is not required reading for your course, it will help you get the most out of both in- and out-of-class collaborative activities.

FOR COLLABORATION

Bring your response to the preceding "For Exploration" to class. Working with a group of classmates, discuss your lists, and select one writing rule that you all question. Consider the following questions, with one person recording all your answers:

1. Why do you all think that this writing rule may be questionable? Identify a situation when following this rule might not be preferable or wise.

2. What arguments in favor of this rule can your group identify? At what times would following this rule make good sense?

Be prepared to discuss your conclusions with your class.

THINKING — AND ACTING — LIKE A WRITER

As you've just seen, thinking commonsensically about writing can help you understand some of the basic conventions of writing. Later chapters focus more specifically on ways to increase your rhetorical sensitivity and thus become a more *effective* writer. But you may also wish to improve your *efficiency* as a writer — your ability to manage your time well, to cope with the inevitable frustrations of writing, and to use all your personal energies and resources when you write. How can commonsensical thinking about writing help you in that respect as well?

Writing is a *process,* and stopping to think about how your own writing process may affect the quality of your writing can prove illuminating. One of my students, for example, formulated an analogy that helped us all think very fruitfully about how the writing process works. "Writing," he said, "is actually a lot like sports."

Writing — like sports? Let's see what this comparison reveals about the writing process.

Writing and sports are both performance skills. You may know who won every Wimbledon since 1980, but if you don't actually play tennis, you're not a tennis player — just somebody who knows a lot about tennis. Similarly, you can know a lot about writing, but to demonstrate (and improve) your skills, you must *write.*

Writing and sports both require individuals to master complex skills and to perform these skills in an almost infinite number of situations. Athletes must learn specific skills, plays, or maneuvers, but they can never execute them routinely or thoughtlessly. Writers must be similarly resourceful and flexible. You can learn the principles of effective essay organization, for instance, and you may write a number of essays that are, in fact, well organized. Nevertheless, each time you sit down to write a new essay, you have to consider your options and make new choices about your writing. This is a primary reason that smart writers do not rely on formulas or rules but instead use rhetorical sensitivity to analyze and respond to each particular situation.

Experienced athletes and writers know that a positive attitude is essential. Some athletes "psych" themselves up before a game or competition, often with the help of a sports psychologist. But any serious athlete knows that's only part of what having a positive attitude means. It also means running five miles when you're already tired at three or doing twelve repetitions during weight training when you're exhausted and no one else would know if you did only eight. A positive attitude is equally important in writing. If you approach a writing task with a negative attitude — "I never was good at writing" — you create obstacles for yourself. Keeping a positive, open attitude is essential in tennis, skiing — and writing.

To maintain a high level of skill, both athletes and writers need frequent practice and effective coaching. "In sports," a coach once said, "you're either getting better or getting worse." Without practice — which for a writer means both reading and writing — your writing skills will inevitably slip (as will your confidence). Likewise, coaching is essential in writing because it's hard to distance yourself from your own work. Coaches — your writing instructor, a tutor (or writing assistant) at a writing center, or a fellow student — can help you gain a fresh perspective on your writing and make useful suggestions about revision as well.

Experienced athletes and writers continually set new goals for themselves. Athletes who believe that they are either getting better or getting worse continually set new challenges for themselves and analyze their performance. They know that coaches can help them but that they are ultimately the ones performing. Experienced writers know this too, so they look for opportunities to practice their writing. And they don't measure their success simply by a grade. They see their writing always as work in progress.

■ ■ ■

FOR EXPLORATION

Freewriting is a technique used to generate and explore ideas. Here is a description of freewriting by Peter Elbow, the professor who created this technique:

> To do a freewriting exercise, simply force yourself to write without stopping for [a certain number] of minutes. . . . If you can't think of anything to write, write about how that feels or repeat over and over "I have nothing to write" or "Nonsense" or "No." If you get stuck in the middle of a sentence or thought, just repeat the last word or phrase till something comes along. The only point is to keep writing.*

---

*This description is adapted from Peter Elbow, *Writing with Power: Techniques for Mastering the Writing Process* (New York: Oxford UP, 1981), 13.

Use the technique of freewriting that you learned earlier in this chapter to explore your attitude toward writing. Write for five or ten minutes, perhaps beginning with one of the following phrases:

When I write, I feel. . . .

Writing means. . . .

Writing is like. . . .

BECOMING PART OF A COMMUNITY OF WRITERS

For many people, one big difference between writing and sports is that athletes often belong to teams. Writers, they think, work in lonely isolation. But does writing actually require isolation and loneliness? Let's go back to the writers described at the beginning of this chapter. Like many in business, industry, and the professions, the consulting engineer works as part of one or more teams. Much of the time she composes alone, but her work is part of a group effort: Her drafts will be responded to, and perhaps changed, by members of the group. Several of the other writers talk extensively with friends and coworkers — sometimes in person and sometimes via email — before and while writing. And the businessperson takes advantage of an electronic bulletin board as he considers how the school board might best respond to a request to remove several books from a school library. Later, he and other school board members will work collaboratively to draft a response to the petition.

As these examples indicate, the romanticized image of the writer struggling alone until inspiration strikes is hardly accurate. Most writers alternate between periods of independent activity, composing alone at a computer or desk, and periods of social interactions — meeting with friends, colleagues, or team members for information, advice, or responses to drafts. They may also correspond with others in their field, or they may get in touch with people doing similar work through reading, research, or online writing technologies.

Finally, people who take their writing seriously are just like other people who share an interest. They like to develop social relationships or networks with others who feel as they do. They realize that these networks will help them learn new ideas, improve their skills, and share their interest and enthusiasm. Sometimes these relationships are formal and relatively permanent. Many poets and fiction writers, for instance, meet regularly to discuss work in progress. Perhaps more commonly, writers' networks are informal and shifting, though no less vital. A new manager in a corporation, for instance, may find one or two people with sound judgment and good writing skills to review important letters and reports. Similarly, students working on a major project for a class may meet informally but regularly to compare notes and provide mutual support.

Unfortunately, college life generally does not encourage the development of informal networks like these, especially among undergraduates. Students juggling coursework, jobs, families, and other activities can find it difficult to get together or to take the time to read and respond to one another's writing. Luckily, many colleges and universities have established writing centers, where you can go to talk with others about your writing. If your campus has a writing center, take advantage of the opportunity to get an informed response to your work.

■ ■ ■

FOR EXPLORATION

If your campus has a writing center, make an appointment to interview a tutor (sometimes also called a writing assistant or peer consultant) about the services the center provides. (If you are a multilingual writer, be sure to ask if the center has tutors who have been specially trained to work with writers like yourself.) You may also want to ask the tutor about his or her own experiences as a writer. Your instructor may ask you to present the results of your interview orally or to write a summary of your discussion.

Whether or not you have access to a writing center, you can still participate in an informal network with others who, like you, are working to improve their writing skills. Because you are in the same class and share the same assignments and concerns, you and your classmates constitute a natural community of writers. The following guidelines can help you participate effectively in group activities. These suggestions apply whether you work with the same group of students all term or participate in a variety of groups.

■ GUIDELINES FOR GROUP WORK

1. *Develop Effective Team-Working Skills.* Good teamwork doesn't come naturally; you may need to develop or strengthen the skills that will contribute to effective group work. As you work with others in your class, keep these suggestions in mind:

   ■ *Remember that people have different styles of learning and interacting.* Some of these differences represent individual preferences: Some students work out their ideas as they talk,

(continued)

(continued)

for instance, while others prefer to think through their ideas before speaking. Other differences are primarily cultural and thus reflect deeply embedded social practices and preferences. Effective groups value diversity and find ways to ensure that *all* members can comfortably participate in and benefit from group activities.

■ *Balance a commitment to "getting the job done" with patience and flexibility.* Time is usually limited, and responsible group members will recognize the need to "get the job done" but will also be flexible and patient.

■ *Work with your peers to articulate group goals and monitor group processes.* To work together successfully, group members must take the time to clarify goals and procedures; otherwise, valuable time is wasted. Similarly, effective groups develop some means (formal or informal) of evaluating group activities. If you are part of a group that is meeting regularly, you might decide to begin meetings by having each person state one way in which the group is working well and one way in which it could be improved. The time spent discussing these comments and suggestions could contribute to better group dynamics.

■ *Deal immediately and openly with any problems in the group process, such as a dominating or nonparticipating member.* It's not always easy to discuss problems such as these openly, but doing so is essential to effective group work.

2. *Take Time at the Start to Review Your Assignment and to Agree on Relevant Procedures.*

■ *For brief collaborative activities,* such as a fifteen-minute group discussion in class, you may need to spend only a few minutes reviewing your teacher's instructions and establishing basic ground rules.

■ *For more extended projects* — particularly those that will involve group meetings outside of class — plan to spend the first ten or fifteen minutes of your meeting reviewing your assignment and setting goals for your meeting. Begin by having group members discuss the assignment and the tasks it

(continued)

(continued)

involves. Which tasks need to be accomplished now, and which ones can wait until later? How should these responsibilities be divided among group members? (If your group is completing a good deal of work electronically via email or synchronous communications, be sure to build in time for regular review of goals, tasks, and accomplishments.)

3. *Be Ready to Assume Various Roles.*

   ■ Sometimes you may function as your group's leader, either informally or formally. At other times you may be called on to act as a mediator, to help the group reach a consensus. Or your main responsibility may be keeping the group on task so that you can achieve your goals in the time allotted. Effective group members assume the roles necessary to a specific task and situation, and they recognize the need for flexibility and variety.

4. *Develop Ways to Encourage Productive Conflict.*

   ■ "Two heads are better than one," the proverb reminds us — and that's because when two or more people get together to discuss an issue or solve a problem, they naturally have different ways of analyzing a topic or of approaching a problem. The diverse perspectives and strategies that people bring to a problem or task are one of the main reasons why group activities are so productive. Capitalize on these differences. Encourage the discussion of new ideas. Consider alternative approaches to your subject. Don't be afraid to disagree; doing so may enable your group to find a more creative solution to a problem, to discover a new and stimulating response to a question. Just be sure that your discussion remains both friendly and focused on the task at hand.

   Not all conflict is productive, of course. If personality conflicts prevent effective discussion about the writing to be done, your group is wasting time that could be better used for writing. Unproductive conflict erodes the effectiveness of your group; productive conflict enables your group to maximize your creativity and draw on all of your shared resources.

5. *Be Realistic about the Advantages and Disadvantages of Group Learning Activities.* No method is perfect, and group work is no exception. But group learning does bring many benefits:

(continued)

(continued)

- Groups have greater resources than individuals.

- Groups can employ more complex problem-solving methods than individuals.

- Working in groups can help you learn more effectively and efficiently.

- Participating in group activities can help prepare you for on-the-job teamwork.

- By responding as writers and readers, groups can give members immediate and meaningful responses to their writing and helpful suggestions for revision.

Group learning also brings potential disadvantages:

- It can take longer to achieve consensus or solve a problem, usually because members of a group examine more options and look at a problem from more angles than a single person would.

- Individual group members may not always be prepared, or they may try to dominate or withdraw from discussion.

- Group members may not share responsibility for a project equitably.

Most problems can be avoided if all participate fully in group activities and respond to problems when they occur. Groups are, after all, a bit like friendships or marriages: They develop and change; they require care and attention. Problems can arise, but if you're committed to keeping the group going, alert to signs of potential trouble, and willing to talk problems out, you can all benefit from group work.

FOR COLLABORATION

If your instructor has divided your class into groups, meet with your group to discuss how you can most effectively work as a team. Begin your meeting by exchanging names, phone numbers, and email addresses; take time just to get to know each other. You might also see if your group can formulate some friendly rules to guide group activities. You might all agree, for instance, to notify at least one member if you can't make a group meeting. Try to anticipate some of the problems you may have working together, such as coordinating schedules, and discuss how to resolve them.

FOR THOUGHT, DISCUSSION, AND WRITING

1. Now that you have read this first chapter, set some goals for yourself as a writer. Make a list of several goals you'd like to accomplish in your composition class this term. Then write a paragraph or more discussing how you plan to achieve these goals.

2. Interview one or more students in your current or prospective major. Ask about student writing in this field:

   What kinds of writing are students required to do in classes in this field? Is this writing similar to the writing done professionally in this field? If not, how is it different?

   How is their writing evaluated by their professors?

   How well do the students interviewed feel that their composition classes prepared them for the writing they now do?

   What advice about writing would they give to other students taking classes in this field?

   Your instructor may ask you to report the results of this interview to your class. Your instructor may also ask you to write an essay summarizing the results of your interview.

3. Reflect on your past experiences with group activities, and then freewrite for five to ten minutes in response to these questions: How much experience with collaborative activities in academic classes do you have? If you have little experience with these activities, what assumptions about their potential advantages and disadvantages do you bring to them? If you have participated in collaborative activities, how would you describe these experiences? What factors contribute to making group activities successful or unsuccessful? What strengths do you feel you bring to group activities? What weaknesses? Your freewrite should give you valuable information that you can draw on when you work with others in your class or that you might share with other members of your group. Discussion of these questions should enable you to work together more productively and efficiently.

Understanding the Writing Process

Writing is hardly a mysterious activity, yet it is sometimes viewed as if it were. Many people seem to think that those who write well possess a magical power or talent. According to this view, people are either born with the ability to write well or not, and those who do write well find writing easy. They just sit down, and the words and ideas begin to flow.

My own experiences as a writer, and those of my students, indicate that this popular stereotype simply isn't accurate. Successful writers work as hard on their writing as anyone else does. Unlike less accomplished writers, however, successful writers develop strategies that enable them to cope with the complexities of writing and thus to experience the satisfaction of a job well done.

Here are two essays, one by a student writer, Mary Ellen Kacmarcik, and one by a professor of English, Burton Hatlen. In different ways, Kacmarcik and Hatlen discuss what it means to be a writer and comment on their own development as writers. They also each make the point that, as Hatlen says, "writing is a craft, which can be learned by anyone willing to work at it." As you read their essays, ask yourself to what extent your own assumptions about writing and experiences as a writer resemble theirs. How are they different? See if you can recall specific experiences, such as those Kacmarcik and Hatlen describe in their essays, that played a critical role in your development as a writer or your understanding of writing.

A WRITER IS FORMED
by Mary Ellen Kacmarcik

The woman at the front of the room hardly resembled my idea of an English teacher. Her raggedy undershirt, heavy flannel jacket, disheveled pants, and braided, stringy hair gave her the appearance of having just returned from a backcountry expedition. And she was huge; she must have tipped the scales at well over two hundred pounds.

"My name is Harriet Jones," she said, "and this is English 111."

This was my introduction to college writing. Ten students had enrolled in this beginning composition class at Islands Community College. Like most of my classmates, I was returning to education after a period in the work force. I had spent one year at Western Washington University but had avoided writing classes. I discovered later, when I sent for my transcripts to apply to Oregon State University, that I had withdrawn from a writing course at Western. I have no memory of this. Did I drop it the first day, or did I struggle with an essay or two before giving up?

At any rate, I went to Alaska that summer to work in the seafood canneries. It was a trip I had planned with two friends during my senior year in high school. I expected to return to college in the fall with thousands of dollars in my bank account. The work was miserable, but I fell in love with remote Sitka, and I stayed. Time passed with adventures enough to fill a novel. I eventually landed a job I really wanted at Northern Lights Natural Foods, a small, family-owned natural foods store. That job inspired me to take a nutrition course at the community college. I realized during the course that some biology would help me understand nutrition, so I took biology the following semester. I began to consider a career in nutrition, which led me to apply to the Department of Foods and Nutrition at OSU. I wasn't ready to leave Sitka, however; I would work one more year and take a few more classes on the side.

That is how I came to be sitting in Ms. Jones's class, preparing myself for a relationship with an English grammar handbook. We were to respond to short stories, an exercise which in my experience was limited to junior high school book reports. Although I have always been an avid reader, I had given little thought to characters, conflicts, plots, and settings. So those early essays were on topics that did not interest me. I had never heard of a comma splice either, but Ms. Jones assured us that any paper containing one would be promptly rewarded with an E grade. I would agonize over blank pages, afraid to begin, afraid of saying the wrong thing, afraid of committing some technical error. I somehow managed to fill up the pages and hand in those early essays. Fortunately, Ms. Jones encouraged us to revise after she had graded our papers.

It turned out that she was also very willing to talk with us about writing. I discovered that this formidable woman was actually a caring, humorous person. The writing did not instantly become easier, though. During the second term, we worked on longer papers that required some research. We also did in-class assignments such as freewriting and essay exams. By the end of the term, I had finally become comfortable with putting my ideas on paper.

The year with Ms. Jones was great preparation for my studies at OSU. I learned the importance of editing my work and following conventions. I gained confidence in stating my views. I also learned that teachers are human and that most of them enjoy discussing projects with students outside of class.

In thinking about my history as a writer for this essay, I realized that I have always been a writer — even when I felt unconfident and out of practice. Letters to aunts, uncles, and grandparents were my earliest writings outside of schoolwork, and they have been the main link between my parents' families on the East Coast and my nuclear family here in the Northwest. These letters followed a set format for years:

Dear Aunt _____ (or Grandma),

How are you? I am fine. Thank you for the _____
_____ .

> Love,
> Mary Ellen

My letters have matured with me, and I consider them a sort of journal except that I mail this journal off in bits and pieces instead of keeping it to read later. My letters describe what I have been doing, how I feel about things, and what I plan to do. When I lived in Alaska, letters were my link to family and friends in Washington.

Another early writing experience was an expanded form of passing notes in school. A friend and I wrote notes to each other that often went on for pages, much of it nonsense and gossip. We would work on these packets for days before exchanging them. Now I can see that we were flexing and developing our writing muscles as well as building our friendship through the sharing of ideas.

Currently, I write the newsletter for a club I belong to, an activity I volunteered for to gain experience and to stay involved with writing. I would like to combine writing with nutrition as a career. (I considered a major in journalism, but I have a strong desire to learn everything I can about nutrition.) I would like to help people improve their health by sharing this knowledge with them. I still think of myself as someone who is going to write someday. But I have been writing because I wanted to ever since I learned how.

WRITING IS A CRAFT THAT CAN BE LEARNED, NOT AN EFFORTLESS OUTPOURING BY GENIUSES
by Burton Hatlen

A writer — that's what I would be when I grew up. I made that decision in 1952, when I was 16, along with what now seems to be half the people I knew at the time. We were all going to be "writers," whatever we meant by that.

I can't speak for my friends, but in my case, at least, being a writer meant living a certain kind of life. The setting would be Paris, *la rive gauche:* a sidewalk café. A man (with a beard, a beret dropping over his right eye, a turtleneck sweater, sandals, a pipe) is seated at a round table, a half-empty glass of red wine before him. There are other people around the table, but they are a little dim. And there is talk. Jung. Kafka. Anarchism. The decline of the West. But mostly there is that man. Me. Someday.

I didn't need anyone to tell me that the road from a dusty farming town in the Central Valley of California to that Paris café would be a long and difficult one. In fact, it was *supposed* to be long and difficult. "You must suffer, suffer" — so said a cartoon character of my youth to a would-be artist. And I had a real-life example of such suffering. When I was 10, my cousin brought her new husband, George, to town. George had actually been to Paris, and he was going to write a novel before returning there. Later, I heard my aunt tell my mother that she had read the manuscript of his novel. According to her, it was "filthy," and what was more, she whispered, she was sure George "drank." In any case, his novel remained unpublished and George never made it back to Paris. At some level I realized that his sad story augured ill for my own dreams of living the life of a writer in a 1950's version of Paris in the 20's.

Nevertheless, in 1956, after my junior year at Berkeley, I decided that if I was ever to become a writer, I'd better try to write. I spent five months working at various jobs, and when I had saved $500 I moved into a one-room apartment in San Francisco. By then the "renaissance" there was in full flower, and the city seemed to me a reasonable facsimile of Paris. In North Beach there were real cafés, where real poets — Kenneth Rexroth, Robert Duncan, Lawrence Ferlinghetti (who actually wore a beret) — sat around and talked. If location had anything to do with becoming a writer, San Francisco seemed the right place to be.

For three months, until my money ran out, I spent my evenings in North Beach and my days at the oilcloth-covered kitchen table in my apartment, writing. Or at least that's what I told myself I was doing. In fact, in those three months I managed to write only about three pages of what I called a novel. It was about a young man living alone in a San Francisco apartment, who looked into the sky one day, saw it split open, and went mad. I fussed for the first week or two over those pages, making sure that every word was *juste*. But I had never worked out a plot, and once the young man went mad, I didn't know what else to do with him.

I stopped writing, and devoted my days to reading — all of Dreiser, among other things. What I remember best about that time is not the few paragraphs I wrote, but the wonder I felt as I read the yellowing pages of my second-hand copy of *The Genius*.

In January I went back to Berkeley, and that spring, at the suggestion of one of my teachers, applied to graduate school. Over the next few years, the sidewalk café began to seem no more than an adolescent fantasy, and, before I knew it, I had become not a writer in Paris, but a teacher entangled in committee meetings and bureaucratic infighting.

What brought all this back to me was a conversation I had earlier this year with a one-time colleague of mine, the author of a respectable university-press book on Sir Thomas Browne and, in the days when we taught together, a tenured associate professor and a popular teacher of Shakespeare. A few years ago, at 44, he suddenly resigned his teaching position and moved to Boston, where, I heard later, he was working a couple of days a week as a waiter and spending the rest of his time writing. When I went to Boston last winter I looked him up.

We talked about his novel and my work. Then the conversation turned to our respective children, all of whom, we realized, had not only decided to become artists of one sort or another but, unlike us at their age, were actually *doing* so. I thought about the Paris café, and then I asked him what he had wanted to do with his life when he was 20.

"Actually," he said, "I wanted to live the way I'm living now — working at a nothing job that doesn't take anything out of me, and writing."

That was a pretty fair description of my own dream when I moved to that apartment in San Francisco. What had happened to it? I think the main reason that I never realized the dream was my mistaken notion of what it means to be a writer, which I had picked up partly from media images of Hemingway and Fitzgerald, Sartre and Camus, and partly from my teachers. Those influences had suggested that writing was something geniuses were somehow able to do without thinking about it; ordinary people dabbled at their peril. That writing is also a craft that can be learned, that a young person might decide to write and then systematically learn how to do so, was never so much as hinted at by anyone I knew. So, when the words for my novel did not automatically come pouring out of me, I had concluded that I must not be a writer.

In fact, I have over the years written enough poetry to make a good-sized book, and enough prose — if it were all gathered together — to make two or three. Yet I feel uncomfortable saying I'm a writer who teaches, preferring instead to see myself as a teacher who writes. Nevertheless, writing is clearly a major part of my life. Yes, I do feel some envy of my friend in Boston, who is at last doing what he dreamed of when he was 20. And no, I've never written that novel, because I still don't know how to go about it. If most of what I write is about other people's writing, that's all right, because through it I've found a way to share with others the wonder I felt 30 years ago as I read Dreiser.

Since then, I have gradually come to see that writing takes manifold forms, that the conception of writing as a hermetic mystery, which I picked up from my reading and my teachers in the 1950's, is not only wrong, but pernicious. It dishonors the writing that nongeniuses do and denies the hard work at the craft that is essential to all writing, even the writing of "geniuses." It caused my cousin's husband to decide that if he couldn't be a writer, he didn't want to be anything, and I think it caused me to waste several years chasing illusions.

The myth that real writing is the effortless outpouring of geniuses did not die in the 1950's. There is abundant evidence that it still persists — at least among my students, most of whom also dream that someone, some-day, will find a spark of "genius" in what they write. As a teacher who writes (or a writer who teaches), I am becoming more and more con-vinced that it's my job to nurture the writer in every student, while at the same time making it clear that writing is a craft, which can be learned by anyone willing to work at it.

■ ■ ■

FOR EXPLORATION

After reading Kacmarcik's and Hatlen's essays, reflect on your own assumptions about writing and your experiences as a writer. To do so, set aside at least half an hour to respond (either by freewriting or jotting down notes) to the following questions:

1. What are your earliest memories of learning to write? Of reading?

2. How was writing viewed by your family and friends when you were growing up?

3. What role did reading play in your development as a writer?

4. Can you recall particular experiences in school or on the job that influenced your current attitude toward writing?

5. If you were to describe your history as a writer, what stages or periods in your development would you identify? Write a sentence or two briefly characterizing each stage or period.

6. What images come to mind when you hear the term *writer*?

7. What images come to mind when you think of yourself as a writer? You may find it easiest to draw up a list of metaphors, such as "As a writer, I'm a turtle — slow and steady" or "As a writer, I'm a race-horse — fast out of the gate but never sure if I've got the stamina to finish." Write two or three sentences that use images or metaphors to characterize your sense of yourself as a writer.

8. What kinds of writing have you come to enjoy? To dislike?

9. What do you enjoy most about the process of writing? What do you enjoy least?

10. What goals would you like to set for yourself as a writer?

FOR EXPLORATION

Using the information generated by the previous Exploration, write a letter to your classmates and teacher in which you describe who you are as a writer today — and how you got to be that way.

FOR COLLABORATION

Bring enough copies of the above letter to share with members of your group. After you have all read one another's letters, work together to answer the following questions. Choose one person to record the group's answers so that you can share the results of your discussion with the rest of the class.

1. To what extent are your attitudes toward writing and experiences as writers similar? List three to five statements about your attitudes toward and experiences as writers with which all group members can agree.

2. What factors account for the differences in your attitudes toward writing and experiences as writers? List two or three factors that you agree account for these differences.

3. What common goals can you set for yourselves as writers? List at least three goals you can agree on.

MANAGING THE WRITING PROCESS

Writing is not a magical process. Rather, it is a craft that can indeed be learned. But how do writers actually manage the writing process? Notice how differently the following six students say that they proceed.

> My writing starts with contemplation. I let the topic I have chosen sink into my mind for a while. Then I brainstorm, coming up with words, phrases, and sentences that relate to my topic. It is usually during the brainstorming process that I find whether I have chosen the right topic.

If I am not satisfied with my topic, I start over. Then I make a simple plan for my essay, and then I start on my rough draft. Peer responses, final drafts, and revisions follow, sometimes with more brainstorming in between.

— EDITH CASTERLINE

I have to sit down at the computer and just write whatever comes out naturally. I then go back and work with what I've written.

— MICHELLE COLLUM

I have to think my ideas out in detail before I begin drafting. Only then can I begin writing and revising.

— MARSHA CARPER

When I write, I first brainstorm for an idea. This may take only a few minutes or days, depending on the kind of paper I'm working on. Once I get an idea, I sit down and start writing. This seems to be the best way for me to get started. After I've written the rough draft, I then go back and do some major revision. I revise and have others check for mistakes I might have missed, and then I print it out.

— DAVE GUENTHER

I write by coming up with a sketchy rough draft and then filling it in or changing it.

— PAUL AUSTIN

As a writer, I am first a thinker and then a doer. I first think about my ideas in my first language, which is Chinese. I work out my most important ideas — and also how best to organize and present them — in this way. Only when I feel sure that I know what I want to write do I begin drafting in English.

— HUAN LI

On the surface, these students' writing processes seem to have little in common. Actually, however, all involve the same three activities: planning, drafting, and revising. These activities don't necessarily occur in any set order. Michelle Collum postpones most of her planning until after she has generated a rough draft, for example, whereas Marsha Carper plans extensively before she writes her first word. To be successful, however, all these writers must sooner or later think critically and make choices about words, ideas, and anticipated responses of readers. Then they must try out these choices in their heads, on paper, or at the computer, evaluate the effects of these choices, and make appropriate changes in their drafts. Rather than being a magical or mysterious activity, then, writing is a process of planning, drafting, and revising.

Identifying Composing Styles

The preceding description of planning, drafting, and revising may make writing sound neater and more predictable than it actually is. Writing is, in fact, a messy and often unpredictable process. Even though all writers engage in planning, drafting, and revising, they do so in a variety of ways. Furthermore, no one approaches every writing task in the same way. (For this reason, it is more accurate to refer to writing *processes* rather than the writing process.) Instead, a writer will decide how to approach a writing assignment based on such factors as the nature and importance of the writing task, the schedule, the experience the writer has with a particular kind of writing, and so on.

Most experienced writers do, however, have a preferred way of managing the writing process. Some writers devote the most energy to planning, while others focus more on revising. Still others focus equally on planning, drafting, and revising.

Heavy Planners   Like Marsha Carper and Huan Li, heavy planners generally consider their ideas and plan their writing so carefully in their heads that their first drafts are often more like other writers' second or third drafts. As a consequence, they often revise less intensively and frequently than other students. Many of these students have disciplined themselves so that they can think about their writing in all sorts of places — on the subway, at work, in the garden pulling weeds, or in the car driving to and from school.

Some heavy planners write in this way because they prefer to; others develop this strategy out of necessity. Marsha Carper, for instance, says that she simply has to do a great deal of her writing "in her head" rather than on paper because she lives fifty miles from the university and must spend considerable time commuting. In addition, she's a mother as well as a student, and at home she often has to steal spare moments to work on her writing. As a result, she's learned to use every opportunity to think about her writing while she drives, cooks, or relaxes with her family.

Heavy Revisers   Like Michelle Collum and Paul Austin, heavy revisers need to find out what they want to say through the act of writing itself. When faced with a writing task, they prefer to sit down at a desk or computer and just begin writing.

Heavy revisers often state that writing their ideas out in a sustained spurt of activity reassures them that they have something to say and helps them avoid frustration. These students may not seem to plan because they begin drafting so early. Actually, however, their planning occurs as they draft and especially as they revise. Heavy revisers typically spend a great deal of their writing time revising their initial drafts. To do so effectively, they must be able to read their work critically and be able, often, to discard substantial portions of first drafts.

As you've probably realized, in both of these styles of composing, one of the components of the writing process is apparently abbreviated. Heavy planners don't seem to revise as extensively as other writers. Actually, however, they plan (and, in effect, revise) so thoroughly early in the process that they often don't need to revise as intensively later. Similarly, heavy revisers may not seem to plan; in fact, though, once they write their rough drafts, they plan and revise simultaneously and often extensively.

Sequential Composers   A third general style of composing is exemplified by Dave Guenther and Edith Casterline. These writers might best be called sequential composers because they devote roughly equivalent amounts of time to planning, drafting, and revising. Rather than trying out their ideas and planning their writing mentally, as heavy planners do, sequential composers typically rely on written notes and plans to give shape and force to their ideas. And unlike heavy revisers, sequential composers need to have greater control over form and subject matter as they draft.

Sequential composers' habit of allotting time for planning, drafting, and revising helps them deal with the inevitable anxieties of writing. Like heavy revisers, sequential composers need the reassurance of seeing their ideas written down: Generating a volume of notes and plans gives them the confidence to begin drafting. Sequential composers may not revise as extensively as heavy revisers, for they generally draft more slowly, reviewing their writing as they proceed. But revision is nevertheless an important part of their composing process; like most writers, sequential composers need a break from drafting to be able to critique their own words and ideas.

Each of these composing styles has advantages and disadvantages. Heavy planners can be efficient writers, spending less time drafting and revising than do other writers, but they must have great mental discipline. An unexpected interruption when they are working out their ideas — a child in tears, a phone call — can cause even the most disciplined thinker to have a momentary lapse. Because so much of their work is done in their heads, heavy planners are less likely to benefit from the fruitful explorations and revisions that occur when writers review notes and plans or reread their own texts. And because heavy planners put off drafting until relatively late in the composing process, they can encounter substantial difficulties if the sentences and paragraphs that had seemed so clearly developed in their minds don't look as coherent and polished on paper.

Heavy revisers experience different advantages and disadvantages. Because they write quickly and voluminously, heavy revisers aren't in danger of losing valuable ideas. Similarly, their frequent rereading of their drafts helps them remain open to new options that can improve their writing. However, heavy revisers must learn how to deal with emotional highs and lows that occur as they discover what they want to say through the process of writing itself. They must be able ruthlessly to critique their own writing, discarding large portions of text or perhaps starting over if necessary. And because they revise so extensively, heavy revisers must be careful to leave adequate time for revision or the quality of their work can suffer.

What about sequential composers? Because they plan to spend time planning, drafting, and revising — and do so primarily in writing — they have more external control over the writing process than heavy planners and revisers have. Sequential composers are also unlikely to fool themselves into thinking that a quickly generated collection of ideas is an adequate rough draft or that a plan brainstormed while taking the subway is adequate preparation for writing. Sequential composers can, however, develop inefficiently rigid habits — habits that reflect their need to have external control over their writing process. They may, for instance, waste valuable time developing detailed written plans when they're actually ready to begin drafting.

Good writers are aware of their preferred composing style — and of its potential advantages and disadvantages. They take responsibility for decisions about how to manage their writing, recognizing the difference, for instance, between the necessary incubation of ideas and procrastination. Good writers are also flexible; depending on the task or situation, they can modify their preferred approach. A person who generally is a heavy reviser when writing academic essays, for instance, might write routine business memos in a single sitting because that is the most efficient way to get the job done. Similarly, heavy planners who prefer to do much of the work of writing mentally must employ different strategies when writing collaboratively with others, or when engaged in research-based writing.

There is one other common way of managing the writing process — though it might best be described as management by avoidance — procrastination. All writers occasionally procrastinate, but if you habitually put off writing a first draft until you have time only for a *final* draft (and this at 3 A.M. on the day your essay is due), your chances of success are minimal. Though you may have invented good reasons for putting off writing — "I write better under pressure"; "I can't write until I have all my easier assignments done first" — procrastination makes it difficult for you to manage the writing process in an efficient and effective manner.

Is procrastination always harmful? Might it not sometimes be a period of necessary incubation, of unconscious but still productive planning? Here's what one thoughtful student writer discovered about her own tendency to procrastinate:

> For me, sometimes procrastination isn't really procrastination (or so I tell myself). Sometimes what I label procrastination is really planning. The trouble is that I don't always know when it's one or the other. . . .
>
> How do I procrastinate? Let me count the ways. I procrastinate by doing good works (helping overtime at my job, cleaning house, aiding

and abetting a variety of causes). I procrastinate by absorbing myself in a purely selfish activity (reading paperbacks, watching TV, going to movies). I procrastinate by visiting with friends, talking on the telephone, prolonging chance encounters. I procrastinate by eating and drinking (ice cream, coffee, cookies — all detrimental). Finally, I procrastinate by convincing myself that this time of day is not when I write well. I'd be much better off, I usually conclude, taking a nap. So I do.

Part of my difficulty is that I can see a certain validity in most of my reasons for procrastinating. There are some times of day when my thoughts flow better. I have forced myself to write papers in the past when I just didn't feel fluid. Not only were the papers difficult to write, they were poorly written, inarticulate papers. Even after several rewrites, they were merely marginal. I would much rather write when I am at my mental best.

I need to balance writing with other activities. The trouble is — just how to achieve the perfect balance!

— HOLLY HARDIN

Holly's realistic appraisal of the role that procrastination plays in her writing process should help her distinguish between useful incubation and unhelpful procrastination. Unlike students who tell themselves that they should never procrastinate — and then do so anyway, feeling guilty every moment — Holly knows that she has to consider a variety of factors before she decides to invite a friend to tea, bake a batch of chocolate chip cookies, or take a much-needed nap.

NOTE FOR MULTILINGUAL WRITERS

The composing process of planning, drafting, and revising may not be as familiar to you as it is to other members of the class whose first or home language is North American English. Educational systems throughout the world have different approaches to writing and to the teaching of writing. In thinking about your writing process as a student in an American college, reflect on how your previous experiences as a writer in your home culture or country enhance or interfere with your efforts to compose in standard written English. (Differences in approaches to revision may be especially relevant.) You may want to discuss the results of your reflection with your teacher or your tutor in the writing center.

Analyzing Your Composing Process

The poet William Stafford once commented that "a writer is not so much someone who has something to say as he is someone who has found a process that will bring about new things he would not have thought if he had not started to say them." Stafford's remarks emphasize the importance of developing a workable writing process — a repertoire of strategies that you can draw on in a variety of situations.

■ GUIDELINES FOR ANALYZING YOUR COMPOSING PROCESS

The following guidelines provide questions you can use to describe and evaluate your current composing strategies. Respond in writing to each of these questions.

1. What is your general attitude toward writing? How do you think this attitude affects the writing you do?

2. If your first or home language is not standard written English, how does knowing two or more languages influence your writing process? What language do you typically think in? Do you free-write, brainstorm, or make notes in your first language or in standard written English?

3. Which of the composing styles described in this chapter best describes the way you compose? If none seems to fit you, how do you compose?

4. How do you know when you are ready to begin writing? Do you have a regular "start-up" method or ritual?

5. How long do you typically work on your writing at any one time? Are you more likely to try to write an essay in a single sitting, or do you prefer to work on your writing over a number of days (or weeks)?

6. Have word processing and online technologies (such as the Internet and the World Wide Web) influenced your composing process? How?

7. What planning and revising strategies do you use? How do you know when you have spent enough time planning and revising?

(continued)

(continued)

8. What role do exchanges with others (such as conversations about your writing or responses to work in progress) typically play in your writing?

9. How do you procrastinate? (Be honest! All writers procrastinate occasionally.)

10. Are you aware of having preferred writing habits and rituals? What are they? Which are productive and supportive? Which interfere with or lessen the efficiency of your writing process?

11. Thinking in general about the writing you do, what do you find most rewarding and satisfying about writing? Most difficult and frustrating? Why?

FOR COLLABORATION

Meet with classmates to discuss your responses to the composing process questions. Begin your discussion by having each person state two important things he or she learned as a result of completing the analysis. (Appoint a recorder to write down each person's statements.) Once all members of your group have spoken, ask the recorder to read their statements aloud. Were any statements repeated by more than one member of the group? Working as a group, formulate two conclusions about the writing process based on your discussion that you would like to share with the class. (Avoid vague and general assertions, such as "Writing is difficult.") Be prepared to discuss your conclusions with your classmates.

Keeping a Writer's Notebook

Many writers keep journals or notebooks. Some writers may focus on work in progress, jotting down ideas, descriptions, or bits of conversation. Others use their journals or notebooks to reflect on their own experiences as writers. Holly Hardin's discussion of procrastination was, in fact, an entry from her notebook. You may want to record your responses to the Exploration exercises in this book in your own writer's notebook. Your teacher may also ask you to include entries from your writer's notebook in a portfolio of your written work.

Whatever is recorded, a writer's notebook serves a single purpose — to help the writer — so if you keep a notebook, it should reflect your own interests and needs. Your notebook may be a nicely bound blank book or a spiral notebook, whatever seems most inviting to you. If you compose at a computer, you might want to keep your notebook on a disk and print copies at regular intervals. The following guidelines suggest possible uses for your writer's notebook.

■ GUIDELINES FOR KEEPING A WRITER'S NOTEBOOK

Use your writer's notebook to

- Ask yourself questions
- Reflect on your writing process
- Record your thoughts about current writing projects
- Brainstorm in response to an assignment
- Record possible ideas for future writing projects
- Note details, arguments, or examples for particular writing projects
- Try out various introductions or conclusions
- Play with imagery or figurative language such as similes or metaphors
- Map out a plan for a writing project or its visual design
- Express your frustrations or satisfactions with your writing
- Keep schedules for writing projects
- Preserve random thoughts about work in progress
- Freewrite about an idea or a topic
- Copy phrases, sentences, or passages that impress you as particularly effective models for imitation or analysis
- Think about what you have learned about writing
- Reflect on the relationship between your reading and writing processes

FOR EXPLORATION

If you are not already doing so, try keeping a writer's notebook for two weeks. At the end of this period, consider the following questions: Did keeping a notebook help you come up with ideas for writing? (Can you find two or three entries that you could possibly develop into an essay?) Has your notebook given you any insights into how you manage the writing process? Did you enjoy writing in your notebook?

Developing Productive Writing Habits and Rituals

Professional writers are often particularly conscious of their writing habits and rituals. All writers, however, have some predispositions that affect their writing. Some people write best early in the morning; others, late at night. Some require a quiet atmosphere; others find the absence of noise or music distracting. Some people can compose only by writing longhand; others can't imagine writing without a computer. People have different ways of telling themselves that they are ready to write. Clearing my desk of its usual clutter is one way that I tell myself it's time to get serious. Here is how two students describe their start-up writing rituals:

> Exercise immediately before working on a paper seems to provide me mental, as well as physical, stimulation. After I run, I tackle a first draft with incredible PMA (positive mental attitude). The head of steam I build during my run (the natural "runner's high") tides me over to at least the second or third page of my first draft. Finishing most papers after that point is usually not a big problem. While I exercise, I spend as much time as I can thinking about new analogies or visualizing the paper's organization and flow. I think about the most basic message that I want my reader to get. If I were to summarize each paragraph in one sentence, I think to myself, what would the sentence say? Is there anything I can eliminate?
>
> Sometimes I think about a chosen audience for the topic. If I were to tell them about the subject face-to-face would my message change? What would I say? What would they most easily understand?
>
> Near the end of my run, I think about how good the paper will be — I hone my expectations. This cheerleading pushes me through the front door and straight to my desk. I can hardly wait to get started. I'm almost afraid the ideas I generated will escape me before I can corner them on paper.
>
> I don't know whether the final product of this process is any better than it might otherwise have been, but it eases the pain of first-draft compositions. I produce a draft more confidently and more quickly than I would by sitting down and hacking away at it.
>
> — HOLLY HARDIN

Most of my writing begins at the kitchen sink. After the dishes are drying in the rack and the living room is in order, I head for my bedroom — where I do my writing — and make the bed, fold socks, empty the trash, and straighten anything that looks at all out of order. Throughout the final stage of this ritual I am spiraling inward toward my writing desk, the last place I clean. When the desk is bare except for my computer, a handbook, and two dictionaries (a paperback for quick spelling references and a hardcover for bigger jobs), I sit down and begin contemplating the task at hand. Following the premise that the mind will take up the discipline put on the body and surroundings, the process of organization moves from the outside inward until I'm sitting in front of the computer sharpening a pencil with my pocketknife. Cleaning house is also a good way to work out the "prewrite jitters" and let me think casually about what I want or need to write. With the house straight at a quiet hour, I start on the first drafts of an introductory paragraph. Now the process has moved out again in a form that I can store, mull over, scribble on, and type again in a new draft. I'm off!

— Tom Grenier

Though Holly and Tom take two very different approaches, they both emphasize the ways in which their particular rituals help them cope with the "prewrite jitters." Productive writing rituals like these are a positive way of pampering yourself — of creating the environment most conducive to writing.

WRITING IN AN AGE OF COMPUTER AND ONLINE TECHNOLOGIES

As a student, you are undoubtedly already aware of the many ways that electronic technologies are influencing our lives. Chapter 7, "Negotiating Online Writing Situations," discusses some of the opportunities and constraints inherent in such media as email and hypertext. You may be aware, for instance, that users of email have developed an elaborate "netiquette" to guide their communications. Chapter 7 helps you understand the *rhetorical* reasons why these conventions have developed and provides guidelines you can employ as you take advantage of these new opportunities to communicate with others.

Whether you prefer to do much of your writing longhand or at the computer, you have probably already benefited from computers' word processing capabilities. Those who find pen or pencil drafting a slow process often marvel at the ease with which word processing enables them to generate text. Many writers report that composing at the computer encourages them to be creative and to revise more easily and effectively. And as companies produce increasingly sophisticated and powerful computers and software, word processing programs offer a variety of options in addition to such traditional features as a spellchecker and a thesaurus. Programs with window or split-screen capability, for instance, allow you to look at two sections of a text at the same time, and computer graphics programs allow you to include computer-generated charts, graphs, diagrams, photographs, and so on in your writing. The following suggestions will make the process of writing with a computer especially productive.

■ GUIDELINES FOR WRITING WITH A COMPUTER

1. *Find Your Own Best Way.* Some people reserve the computer for typing up and printing documents that they have already written by hand. They may make minor revisions at the computer, but they generally make major revisions on their printed texts by hand and then enter the changes into the computer. Others actually compose at the computer. A writer might brainstorm at the computer, for instance, and then use the word processing program's split-screen option to keep these notes onscreen as a guide while writing. As you might expect, heavy revisers adapt particularly easily to composing at the keyboard. Take the time to explore the options available to you and find those best suited to your own needs.

2. *Recognize the Limitations of Onscreen Revision.* Computers can make revision easier and faster, but they have potential limitations as well. Sometimes writers, seduced by the ease with which they can change things on the computer, focus too much on making minor stylistic modifications instead of organizing or developing ideas. Many writers find that to evaluate these more global aspects of their writing, they must work with hard copy. Because of the small size of the computer's screen, it can be difficult to grasp the big picture — yet effective writing depends on just this ability.

   When you print drafts of an essay to read and revise, be sure to save these earlier versions and keep track of their order by titling both computer and print drafts. (You might title different versions of a research paper on beekeeping "bee1," "bee2," "bee3," and so on.) You may decide that an introduction that you rejected in favor of a later version was best after all. Leaving a "paper trail" makes it easy to reinsert your original introduction.

(continued)

(continued)

3. *Take Advantage of the Useful Features That Many Word Processing Programs Provide.* Some writers use their computers' word processing programs as glorified typewriters, primarily to ease the burden of producing neatly printed texts. But most computer programs offer a number of functions that can make writing easier and more productive:

   ■ WINDOW or SPLIT-SCREEN functions allow you to work on multiple documents (or multiple versions of a single document) at the same time.

   ■ MARK UP, COMMENT, and TRACK CHANGE functions allow you to write notes or track changes that appear onscreen but not in the printed text. These features allow you to interact with your own writing and that of others without cluttering drafts with comments that must be deleted later.

   ■ CUT and PASTE functions enable you to move sections of text easily.

   ■ A SEARCH function makes it possible to locate every instance of a word or phrase. You can use this function when editing to check that you haven't overused a word or to correct a misspelled word used several times in a draft.

   ■ SAVE AS functions enable you to try a potentially risky revision without endangering your original.

4. *Use the Resources Available to You on the World Wide Web — but Use Them Responsibly.* Fifteen years ago, most personal computers were used primarily for word processing, desktop publishing, and related activities. But with the rise of the Internet and World Wide Web, computers increasingly serve as information conduits, bringing previously unimaginable resources to writers and readers. A student writing an essay on the Pre-Raphaelite painter Dante Gabriel Rossetti can easily locate a reproduction of one of his paintings on the Web, download it, and include it in an essay. If a group of students is constructing a Web site on this topic, they have access to even greater resources. They could, for instance, find a multimedia presentation on the textile workshop of William Morris, a fellow Pre-Raphaelite and friend of Rossetti's, download this presentation, and include it on their site.

(continued)

(continued)

The students could do this — but *should* they? To answer this question, writers need to understand that just as print texts can be — and often are — protected by copyright laws, so are online texts and multimedia documents. The exact nature of this protection is still unclear: The development of the Web has raised many questions about the applicability of copyright laws to Web-based materials. These questions will be addressed by the courts in coming years. For the present, you should probably assume that most materials on the Web fall under copyright protection — unless the site clearly indicates otherwise.

Does this mean that you can't include a film clip or a reproduction of an artwork in your writing after all? Not necessarily. Some Web sites, including many government sites, specifically state that information and images presented therein can be downloaded and used. Moreover, just as print documents and images that are more than seventy-five years old are considered to be "in the public domain" and can be used by anyone, so too is the case for such materials reproduced on the Web. The Web includes also many sites devoted to "clip art" — icons, backgrounds, and textures. These items are designed specifically for others to use, though some require acknowledgment of the source. Finally, if a site contains information or images that may be copyright-protected but could enrich your writing, you always have the option of writing to the person or organization that has posted the Web site and requesting permission to use the items in which you are interested.

The development of online technologies provides new opportunities, as well as potential dangers and difficulties, for writers. But has it changed the essential nature of writing or simply provided new possibilities for and means of expression? To answer this question, I contacted Mary Ellen Kacmarcik Gates and Burton Hatlen, the authors of the essays you read at the start of this chapter. I asked these writers to reflect on the ways in which computer and online technologies have changed their writing practices — and their sense of themselves as writers. Here are their responses to this question. (Before presenting their comments, I should note that after graduating from Oregon State University, Mary Ellen married, had two daughters, and worked for a time in the field of foods and nutrition. Most recently, Mary Ellen has been a stay-at-home mother homeschooling her daughters and participating in a variety of volunteer activities. Burton Hatlen continues to teach at the University of Maine.)

WRITING IN THE AGE OF THE INTERNET
by Mary Ellen Kacmarcik Gates

I think of a dozen beginnings for my first formal essay since college. Then I get stuck, so I sit down at the keyboard and jot ideas. Over the next week or two I open up the document and add to it — deleting this, moving that. As I do so, I become increasingly aware of how dependent I have become not only on word processing but on having access to the Internet and the World Wide Web. In my daily life, I do a fair amount of writing, including editing a monthly newsletter for a homeschool support group. Producing the newsletter has challenged me to increase my computer and online skills. Now I can send attachments via email, download materials from the World Wide Web, and insert them into word processed texts. I've become acquainted with folders, jpeg files, and hyperlinks.

Reading and writing email has become an essential part of my daily routine. Early in the morning, when my husband has left for work and the girls are still asleep, I turn on my computer. "Would you like to check to see if you have any new mail now?" the computer asks me. I click yes and wait eagerly for the messages. Email is great — it's like a post card. I can write a few sentences or a one-word reply and send it off. I worry sometimes, though, that email is too easy. I read a message, write a reply, send it — and it's out there for all the world to see. Sometimes after sending a message I realize that I didn't say what I meant to or that I said something that I really wouldn't want anyone else but the person I'm emailing to read, but it's too late. Of course, when I write to my mother, other family members, and friends, the stakes aren't too high. When I'm participating in an online discussion among members of my La Leche League group or some other sort of public forum, I try to be much more careful.

Email has become an essential part of my life, but I also do a good deal of reading online. I subscribe to an online newsletter for homeschoolers. The hostess of my monthly book club has a Web site where she sells discussion guides for members. I appreciate getting her guides online — but I appreciate even more getting together with the other members of my group to talk about the book we're discussing. I like the fact that when we get together there is no right or wrong answer. (What is the significance of the snow in *Snow Falling on Cedars*? I don't know. I don't care!) We use the discussion guides as springboards for discussion; it is assigned reading I look forward to.

Thinking about my book club reminds me that although reading and writing online have become central to my life, I have hardly abandoned print texts. At home there is so much to read — books, journals, newsletters (not to mention the ever present junk mail) — that it piles up everywhere. I am usually reading two library books at a time, one by the bed and another on the coffee table. My daughters don't know how to fall asleep without having a story read to them. I read some things — like the two bimonthly journals I receive from the La Leche League — with great care. Others, such as the newspaper, are skimmed. A letter from a friend is always a treasured gift.

When I think of letters, I think of my grandmother — and of a very special gift she left me. My grandmother died a few months ago, and when I learned that she had left me money in her will, I decided immediately to use the money to buy a better computer. This gift allows me to work faster and more efficiently online and to keep in touch with family and friends through email. Sometimes when I'm at the computer, I think of my grandmother. Snail mail letters, not emails, were the link that kept our relationship going. I'd seen my grandmother only once since 1962, so it was our letters over the years that created a bond between us.

What would my grandmother think of email? In recent years she was aware of computers, but she preferred not to learn how to use them. It would have been convenient to be able to email my grandmother, rather than writing my thoughts out longhand. But I don't think it would have changed our relationship or the thoughts I shared with her. For as much as having access to computer and online technologies has affected who I am as a writer and the processes I use when I write, some things remain the same. Whether I'm emailing a friend or writing a handwritten letter, what is most important to me are the ideas I am sharing.

Recently, a friend asked me to write words of wisdom for her daughter Brittany. She is collecting them in a special book to present to her daughter on her thirteenth birthday. My friend is younger than I am, yet she is years ahead of me in her parenting journey. I look to her as a mentor in my mothering. What will her daughter think of my advice? I struggle to think of what to say and how to say it. The pressure of writing something not just clever but wise hangs over me. That is when I remember that I don't have to get my writing perfect the first time. I just have to think, write, think, write, produce a draft, revise, think some more, write some more. Some writing takes more time, more drafts. (In situations like this, I'm especially grateful for word processing.) Some texts — like most of my emails — are written quickly. But despite computers, despite the Internet and all that it allows me to do, the basic process hasn't changed that much. The things that are are difficult about writing, like struggling to articulate my ideas in the clearest and most persuasive way, remain difficult. And the pleasures of accomplishing the task remain as well.

FROM OLIVETTI TO iMAC: TECHNOLOGY AS MEANS, NOT END
by Burton Hatlen

In 1953, when I left home for college (home was a farmhouse in the Central Valley of California, and college was Occidental College in Los Angeles), my parents gave me an Olivetti portable typewriter. I wrote all my college papers on this typewriter, along with weekly letters home to my parents, always composing directly on the machine; and five years later, I carried my Olivetti with me when I went east to graduate school, first at Columbia and then at Harvard. The Olivetti was a state-of-the-art machine in 1953, but it regularly jammed up when one of my large and clumsy fingers hit two keys simultaneously, and over the years the "e" wore away until it was almost illegible. Eventually, therefore, other typewriters entered my life. In the late 1960s I acquired an IBM electric typewriter, which employed a then-revolutionary technology: rather than a separate arm for each type slug, all the letters were on a single round ball, which spun and danced across the page, in response to my keystrokes. Between 1967 and 1971 I wrote my doctoral dissertation on this machine, at a desk in the living room of a farmhouse in Maine. And yes, the writing process extended to four years, at least in part because I found it impossible to let go of a page until it was free of all typing errors: if I chanced to hit the "r" when I was aiming for the "t" key, I compulsively retyped the entire page. I managed to finish the dissertation, eventually, and in the early 1970s I got tenure in the English department of the University of Maine. But for several years thereafter I wrote little prose because it was simply too much work. Instead I wrote poetry, where my typing habits actually served me well, as I carefully weighed each keystroke.

Somewhere around 1975, however, the English department secretary, Marilyn Emerick, let it be known that she was willing to type manuscripts for faculty, and suddenly I was liberated from the typewriter. She had a miraculous new machine, a correcting typewriter. And she was willing to decipher page after page of my handwritten scrawl. I can type, whether on a typewriter or on a computer, much faster than I can write by hand, but Marilyn's assistance meant that I no longer needed to worry about producing immaculate pages of text. Furthermore, the sheer muscular experience of propelling the ballpoint pen across the page seemed gloriously liberating, and the words began to pour out of me. I still had a typewriter in my office, but I rarely used it. For nearly ten years, Marilyn, who could type 140 words per minute, served as the essential intermediary for everything that I wrote.

And then, in 1983, during a summer of teaching at the Bard College Institute of Writing and Thinking, I met my first computer. Macintosh had donated a dozen or so computers to Bard, to be used for writing instruction; and, of course, if we on the faculty were to teach our students how to use these machines, we ourselves had to learn how to write on them. Within three weeks I was hooked, and I returned to the University of Maine that fall as a dedicated apostle of the computer revolution. Quite simply, the computer allowed me to write at full speed, without the hand cramps that would sometimes afflict me in my handwriting period, but it *also* allowed me to correct freely: not merely to clean up typos but also to engage in real revision, as I added, deleted, or moved about entire blocks of text. By 1985 I was doing all of my writing on a computer, and my writing habits have not changed significantly since then. Occasionally, I will still make a few notes in longhand, but these days when I am moved to write, I shift over almost immediately to the computer: at the moment, an iMac at home and a Macintosh G4 in the office.

And then there's email. Today, a Sunday, I've sent off three personal email messages, responded to three inquiries from students, and posted a boilerplate letter of invitation to twelve potential participants in a conference that I am organizing. Now, as the day draws to a close, I'm writing a few paragraphs on my writing habits, in response to a request from the author of this book, and I'll post these comments to her via email. That's a relatively light email day for me: I estimate that I normally spend at least two hours a day on email, sending and receiving from ten to twenty messages. I organize email conferences in all of my courses; and in one course that I am currently teaching, a distance education course, I communicate with the students largely by email. I edit a scholarly journal, and I communicate with contributors largely via email. As secretary of the Ezra Pound Society, a group devoted to the study of this poet's work, I am the "owner" of a listserv that generates from three or four to a dozen or so postings every day. I chair two university committees, and I organize our meetings via email. I regularly use email to organize panels at national conferences. These days, when I write an article, I often send it to an editor via email. Email has brought about a communications revolution, radically increasing the speed at which we can communicate information, person to person, around the world.

But has email changed the way I write? I don't believe so. In fact, I find myself resisting certain modes of discourse that seem to me too characteristic of the email culture: a tendency to shoot from the hip, a failure to think through issues carefully. Still, every day I'm online, trying to keep up with a world that seems to be spinning faster and faster.

Trying to keep up — that, I suppose, is what I've mostly been doing, all along. That Olivetti typewriter on which, almost fifty years ago now, in a dormitory room at Occidental College, I typed out letters to my parents back on the farm or essays that tried to puzzle out why Raskolnikov murdered those old women, seems today like a quaint relic of a world before the flood. (And what *did* happen to that typewriter, anyway? Did I give it away? Abandon it in a closet, when I left Boston for basic training at Fort Dix? I can't remember.) Still, the young man who wrote those letters and essays wasn't, as far as I can tell, so very different from the students who arrive, year after year, in my classrooms. Like them, he was trying to figure out how to do the right thing, in a world where that's never easy. Technology is always a means, never an end. Email can send our words around the world in a flash, but it cannot ensure that these words will be worth reading. "Ripeness is all," says Edgar to his dying father in Shakespeare's *King Lear,* and it still takes a lifetime to ripen into something like wisdom.

As these two writers' essays suggest, though computer and online technologies certainly offer many new opportunities for writers, they do not change the basic facts of a writer's life. Whether you are writing a letter by hand, word processing an essay, or composing an email message, as a writer you still need to take responsibility both for your writing process and for the results of that process. By reflecting on your own writing process and developing productive writing habits and rituals, you can meet the challenges you will face as a writer. As you do so, you will have the satisfaction of knowing (as Burton Hatlen observed earlier in this chapter) that writing is indeed a craft that can be learned, not an effortless outpouring by geniuses.

■ ■ ■

FOR THOUGHT, DISCUSSION, AND WRITING

1. You can learn a great deal about your own composing process by observing yourself as you write. To do so, follow these steps:

   Choose an upcoming writing project to study. Before beginning this project, reflect on it and its demands. How much time do you expect to spend working on this project, and how do you anticipate allocating your time? What challenges does this project hold for you? What particular strengths and resources do you bring to this project?

   As you work on the project, keep track of how you spend your time. Include a record of when you started and ended each work session as well as a description of your activities and a paragraph commenting on your process. What went well? What surprised you? What gave you problems? What might you do differently next time?

   After you have completed the project, draw on your prewriting analysis and process log to write a case study of this specific project. In developing your case study, consider questions such as these: To what extent was your prewriting analysis of your project accurate? How did you actually allocate your time when working on this project? What strategies did you rely on most heavily? What went well with your writing? What was difficult? Conclude by reflecting about what you have learned from this case study about yourself as a writer.

2. All writers procrastinate occasionally — some just procrastinate more effectively than others. After brainstorming or freewriting about your favorite ways of procrastinating, write a humorous or serious essay on procrastination.

3. You can learn a great deal about writing by reading interviews with professional writers. Choose one of the following collections, and read two interviews. While reading them, try to think of the ways the statements these writers make might — and might not — apply to your own writing.

> *The True Subject: Writers on Life and Craft.* Edited by Kurt Brown. St. Paul: Greywolf Press, 1993.

> *The Writer on Her Work.* Edited by Janet Sternburg. New York: Norton, 1980.

> *The Writer on Her Work.* Vol. 2, *New Essays in New Territory.* Edited by Janet Sternburg. New York: Norton, 1991.

> *Writers at Work: The Paris Review Interviews.* First series. Edited by Malcolm Cowley. New York: Viking, 1958.

> *Writers at Work: The Paris Review Interviews.* Subsequent series edited by George Plimpton. New York: Viking, 1963, 1967, 1976, and 1981.

> *The Writer's Craft.* Edited by John Hersey. New York: Knopf, 1974.

4. The Exploration activities on pp. 28 and 29 encouraged you to reflect on your assumptions about writing and your experiences as a writer. Drawing on these activities and on the rest of the chapter, write an essay in which you reflect on this subject.

Understanding the Reading Process

W hy do people read? Not surprisingly, people read for as many different reasons and in as many different contexts as they write. They read to gain information — to learn how to program their VCR or to make decisions about whether to attend a movie or purchase a new product. They read for pleasure. Whether surfing the Web or reading a novel, people enjoy immersing themselves in the lives and words of others. They read to engage in extended conversations with others about issues or questions of importance to them, such as ecology, U.S. foreign policy, or contemporary music. In all of these ways, people read to enlarge their world, to experience new ways of thinking and also of being and acting.

Recent developments in such online technologies as email and the World Wide Web provide a striking confirmation of the preceding observation. As anyone who has ever participated in the whirl of instant message or a chat-room conversation knows, those communicating online can — and some-times do — use the anonymity of email to try out new identities, including genders. Many find that the experience of reading online differs considerably from that of reading print texts. In the intense exchange characteristic of online conversations, for instance, the conventional distinction between read-ing and writing almost blurs. This blurring also characterizes the experience of reading hypertext documents on the Web, for the Web provides new opportu-nities for readers to take charge of — or "author" — their reading.

In one sense, of course, readers have always been free to move around in traditional print texts: They could choose to read ahead to the conclusion of a mystery novel, for instance, or to skim a single section of a how-to book. But the physical structure of most print texts encourages a linear reading, either of the entire text (as is the case with novels and of many nonfiction books) or of sections within the larger text (as occurs with car and home repair manuals). Such is not the case with the Web. Although Web sites do have homepages that provide an introduction to the site, they offer readers a multitude of options for both entering and navigating the site. You might begin a period of Web reading by entering the Web address (or URL — Uniform Resource Locator) of a site for those interested in the sport of spelunking, or exploring underground caves. But perhaps a link to a site on the Mammoth Cave in Kentucky will catch your eye, and before you know it, you're reading about its early exploration and development. And then a link to a company advertising a sale on spelunking equipment might draw your attention. As you move from site to site, you — not the creators of the Web sites — are determining what and how you read.

Online technologies provide new opportunities for readers to interact in powerful and exciting ways with texts. But experienced readers and writers have always understood that reading and writing are mutually reinforcing acts. Both are acts of *composing*, of constructing meaning through language.

When you first read an essay for an anthropology class, for instance, you engage in a preliminary or "rough" reading. The process of grappling with an essay for the first time — of attempting to determine where the writer is going and why — is similar to the process of writing a rough draft. When you reread an essay with an eye on the strategies used, or the arguments, you are "revising" your original reading, much as you revise a draft when you write.

Both writing and reading challenge you to construct or compose the meaning of a specific text; both also engage you in dialogue with others, even if you are reading alone at the computer or in the library. Precisely because they involve dialogue, reading and writing are best understood as rhetorically, culturally, and socially situated activities. The purposes you bring to your reading, the processes you use to engage with a text, your understanding of the significance of your reading: These and other aspects of your reading grow out of your understanding of your particular situation as a reader.

An example might help to clarify this point. Imagine two people sitting in a café reading and drinking tea. One person is reading an accounting textbook; the person at the next table is reading a zine (an informal, self-published poem, text, or magazine) he picked up from a bench by the cash register. Both persons are reading texts — but they are undoubtedly reading them in quite different ways. The differences reflect these readers' social and cultural understanding of the texts they are reading. The student reading the accounting textbook for a course in which she is enrolled has many reasons for believing the textbook is authoritative. As a result, the student reads the textbook slowly and with care. If asked what she is doing, the student might say that she is studying rather than reading — a statement that reflects both the attentive nature of her reading and her relationship with her text.

The person reading the zine is reading with a different set of understandings and expectations. He knows that zines represent a backlash against the typical magazines that characterize popular culture. Some zines are hand drawn and lettered rather than word processed, for instance. And even if word processed, they often have an intentionally crude, in-your-face design. Whereas textbooks go through a multilevel review process, one that adds to their credibility, anyone with the time and inclination can "publish" a zine. A zine found in a café could be a well-written and thought-provoking reflection on a contemporary issue, a poorly written diatribe — or simply boring. So the reader of the zine quickly skims the text to see if the topics are interesting and the writing worth reading.

Two readers surfing the Web might also read in quite diverse ways. Imagine a reader who has just learned that she has an illness and wishes to gather information about her illness online. This reader is likely to approach her online reading with seriousness and to search systematically for sites, such as the federally supported National Institutes of Health, that contain authoritative, scientifically supported studies. Though she is reading on the Web, she is approaching this online reading in the same way that she might read an important print text. And, in fact, she may well print many of the texts that she locates for more careful reading.

Contrast her situation with that of a second person who is also reading online. This person has recently taken up mountain biking and is interested in identifying possible places to vacation. Arriving at work a few minutes early, he decides to ease into his day by surfing the Web for possible vacation spots. This reader might move quickly — even almost randomly — from official sites, such as that of the American Mountain Biking Association, to homepages of mountain bikers (where he quickly scans for links to favorite vacation spots), to business and community sites, such as the visitors' information site for Moab, Utah, a hot vacation destination for mountain bikers.

As these examples indicate, whether you are reading traditional print texts or online texts, you are making cultural and rhetorical judgments about what you read. These judgments are often unconscious and intuitive. A businessperson who is offended by deviations from standard written English in professional memos and reports but who enjoys reading the magazine *Slam* — a magazine for obsessive fans of basketball — for pleasure might find nothing wrong with a headline that says simply "He Ready" or a paragraph that begins "Holla at a player, yo." In this and other ways, our participation in diverse cultures (such as the culture of business and the culture of basketball) influences the expectations that we bring to our reading.

Another powerful influence on our reading is genre. When we recognize that a text belongs to a certain genre — a genre such as the textbook, the special-interest magazine, the business report, or the newspaper — we make assumptions about the form that the writing will take and about the writing's purposes and subject matter. The businessperson reading a company's annual report understands that this is a serious document that must follow specific conventions, including those of standard written English. When he reads *Slam,* a magazine for basketball "insiders," he brings quite different expectations to his reading. *Slam* uses a good deal of specialized jargon, including the street and hip-hop language of some urban African Americans. Even though the businessperson would find this language inappropriate in business writing, he not only accepts but enjoys its use in *Slam.* He would be outraged, however, if he identified an error of accuracy in a story, for he reads *Slam* to learn the kind of current news and obscure historical facts that serious fans crave. While someone uninterested in basketball might wonder who could possibly be interested in a story about the six players in National Basketball Association history whose careers lasted only one minute of game time, this is the kind of obscure tidbit that the passionate fan craves.

Because writing requires the physical activity of drafting, you may be more aware of the active role you play as writer than as reader. Reading is, however, an equally active process. One of the pleasures of reading, in fact, is the way in which different texts encourage readers to play different roles and to emphasize different interests. As we do so, we expand not only our own experiences and understandings but our world as well. In this sense, reading is an intensely active process of making meaning. For instance, look at the "Harper's Index" for December 2002 (see Figure 3.1 on p. 53). As you read, notice how you forge connections among the items listed. If you are like most readers, you will discover that certain themes or issues emerge from your reading.

■ ■ ■

FOR EXPLORATION

Freewrite for five minutes about the experience of reading the "Harper's Index" (p. 53). What strategies did you use as you read these "telling facts"? Reread the "Index," and list the major themes that your reading stimulated. Reviewing this list, consider the extent to which your own background and experiences influenced your reading.

NOTE FOR MULTILINGUAL WRITERS

If you have recently begun studying in an English-speaking environment, you may find it difficult to interpret texts because you lack cultural knowledge about American history, literature, religions, and other experiences. You may also bring different rhetorical and cultural expectations to your reading. To better understand how you approach reading, reflect on how your own multilingual and multicultural background has influenced your expectations. You may find it helpful to discuss these expectations with your teacher, your classmates, or a tutor in your writing center. You can also ask these people about references or expressions that you don't understand. They will be happy to explain them to you.

HARPER'S INDEX

Number of names on the State Department's list of "suspected terrorists": 70,000

Number of times George W. Bush has said Osama bin Laden's name in public since July 8: 0

Hours after Defense Secretary Donald Rumsfeld learned Bin Laden was a suspect that he sought reasons to "hit" Iraq: 2.5

Percentage by which the Pentagon's September order for sunblock exceeded its last largest such order: 70

Rank of Israel and Turkey among nations in violation of the largest number of U.N. Security Council resolutions: 1, 2

Number of Kurdish members of Turkey's parliament jailed in 1994 when their party was declared illegal there: 7

Number still in prison: 4

Number of Turkish college students detained in the last year for requesting Kurdish-language classes: 1,146

Organizers' estimated attendance at this fall's largest peace rallies in London and New York, respectively: 400,000, 25,000

Estimated attendance according to police in each city: 150,000, 12,000

Number of estimates cited in each rally's coverage in the London *Times* and the *New York Times,* respectively: 2, 0

Minutes that service on two New York subway lines was halted this fall after a Sikh worker was seen emerging from a hatch: 92

Amount Colombia paid civilians for informing on rebels in its first five weeks of recruiting this year: $340,000

Percentage of the 223 trade unionists reported murdered or missing worldwide last year who worked in Colombia: 88

Number of "sub-harm" suicide "gestures" made this year by detainees held at the U.S. military base at Guantanamo Bay: 30

Minimum number of times the United States has deployed troops abroad in its 226-year history: 277

Number of days that the CIA's museum is open to the public each year: 0

Number of countries that use the U.S. dollar as currency: 10

Number of other countries whose currency is effectively pegged to the dollar: 34

Ratio of the annual tariffs that developed nations impose on one another to those they impose on developing nations: 1:4

Minimum percentage change since last year in Afghanistan's opium production: +1,000

Pounds of weapons-grade uranium reported to have been seized in September from a taxi in Turkey: 33

Ounces of black sand that the container — labeled "primarily youranuom" — actually contained: 0.2

Factor by which the cruising speed of NASA's new hypersonic cruise-missile engine exceeds that of previous missiles: 9.5

Percentage by which the speed of light has decreased in the last 20 billion years, according to Australian scientists: 0.0007

Average number of miles by which the magnetic North Pole moves each year: 25

Year in which the ozone hole over Antarctica is expected to close as a result of reduced chlorofluorocarbon use: 2050

Percentage change since 1980 in the per-watt cost of solar energy in the United States: −87

Days it takes an adult in Los Angeles to breathe in more air pollution than EPA guidelines recommend for a lifetime: 25

Average number of people killed per week by a sniper operating in suburban Maryland and Virginia this fall: 3

Average number of homicides per week during the same period in Washington, D.C.: 7

Percentage of Americans surveyed who say they refused to participate in a survey during the past year: 44

Percentage of those contacted for this survey who refused to participate in it: 60

Fee that Sprint PCS charges its "credit-challenged" customers each time they speak with a live representative: $3

Chances of getting a hotel room in Bethlehem on Christmas in 2000 and 2001, respectively: 0, 9 in 10

Chance that a Bethlehem hotel expects to be open this Christmas: 1 in 5

Rank of a burning Yule-log video loop among the top-rated 8–10 A.M. TV shows in New York City last Christmas: 1

Price of a child's personal ATM from FAO Schwarz last year: $20,000

Chances that a child fed "booger"-flavored jelly beans at a trade show this fall said they tasted like the real thing: 4 in 5

Figure 3.1

This "Harper's Index" appeared in the December 2002 issue of *Harper's Magazine.*

Reading, like writing, is a *situated* activity. When you read, you draw not only on the words on the page but on your own experiences as well. The connections that you perceived among the first twelve items in the "Harper's Index," for instance, were undoubtedly influenced by your views on responses to the attacks that took place on September 11, 2001. Reading is situated in additional ways. Just as you approach different writing tasks in different ways depending on your rhetorical situation, your approach to reading varies depending on the specific relationship of writer, reader, and text. Consider, for instance, how you read the introduction to a psychology text differently than you read a mystery novel or the sports page.

■ ■ ■

FOR EXPLORATION

Read the following two texts. The first, "Girl," is a brief short story set in the Caribbean by the contemporary writer Jamaica Kincaid. The second is the first two paragraphs of the introduction to *Language and Woman's Place,* a scholarly work by the linguist Robin Lakoff.

GIRL
by Jamaica Kincaid

Wash the white clothes on Monday and put them on the stone heap; wash the color clothes on Tuesday and put them on the clothesline to dry; don't walk barehead in the hot sun; cook pumpkin fritters in very hot sweet oil; soak your little cloths right after you take them off; when buying cotton to make yourself a nice blouse, be sure that it doesn't have gum on it, because that way it won't hold up well after a wash; soak salt fish overnight before you cook it; is it true that you sing benna in Sunday school?; always eat your food in such a way that it won't turn someone else's stomach; on Sundays try to walk like a lady and not like the slut you are so bent on becoming; don't sing benna in Sunday school; you mustn't speak to wharf rat-boys, not even to give directions; don't eat fruits on the street — flies will follow you; *but I don't sing benna on Sundays at all and never in Sunday school;* this is how to sew on a button; this is how to make a buttonhole for the button you have just sewed on; this is how to hem a dress when you see the hem coming down and so to prevent yourself from looking like the slut I know you are so bent on becoming; this is how

Jamaica Kincaid, "Girl." *At the Bottom of the River* (New York: Farrar, Strauss, Giroux, 1983).

you iron your father's khaki shirt so that it doesn't have a crease; this is how you iron your father's khaki pants so that they don't have a crease; this is how you grow okra — far from the house, because okra tree harbors red ants; when you are growing dasheen, make sure it gets plenty of water or else it makes your throat itch when you are eating it; this is how you sweep a corner; this is how you sweep a whole house; this is how you sweep a yard; this is how you smile to someone you don't like too much; this is how you smile to someone you don't like at all; this is how you smile to someone you like completely; this is how you set a table for tea; this is how you set a table for dinner; this is how you set a table for dinner with an important guest; this is how you set a table for lunch; this is how you set a table for breakfast; this is how to behave in the presence of men who don't know you very well, and this way they won't recognize immediately the slut I have warned you against becoming; be sure to wash every day, even if it is with your own spit; don't squat down to play marbles — you are not a boy, you know; don't pick people's flowers — you might catch something; don't throw stones at blackbirds, because it might not be a blackbird at all; this is how to make a bread pudding; this is how to make doukona; this is how to make pepper pot; this is how to make a good medicine for a cold; this is how to make a good medicine to throw away a child before it even becomes a child; this is how to catch a fish; this is how to throw back a fish you don't like, and that way something bad won't fall on you; this is how to bully a man; this is how a man bullies you; this is how to love a man, and if this doesn't work there are other ways, and if they don't work don't feel too bad about giving up; this is how to spit up in the air if you feel like it, and this is how to move quick so that it doesn't fall on you; this is how to make ends meet; always squeeze bread to make sure it's fresh; *but what if the baker won't let me feel the bread?;* you mean to say that after all you are really going to be the kind of woman who the baker won't let near the bread?

LANGUAGE AND WOMAN'S PLACE
by Robin Lakoff

Language uses us as much as we use language. As much as our choice of forms of expression is guided by the thoughts we want to express, to the same extent the way we feel about the things in the real world governs the way we express ourselves about these things. Two words can be synonymous in their denotative sense, but one will be used in

Robin Lakoff, *Language and Woman's Place* (New York: Harper Collins, 1975).

case a speaker feels favorably toward the object the word denotes, the other if he is unfavorably disposed. Similar situations are legion, involving unexpectedness, interest, and other emotional reactions on the part of the speaker to what he is talking about. Thus, while two speakers may be talking about the same thing or real-world situation, their descriptions may end up sounding utterly unrelated. The following well-known paradigm will be illustrative.

(a) I am strong-minded.

(b) You are obstinate.

(c) He is pigheaded.

If it is indeed true that our feelings about the world color our expression of our thoughts, then we can use our linguistic behavior as a diagnostic of our hidden feelings about things. For often — as anyone with even a nodding acquaintance with modern psychoanalytic writing knows too well — we can interpret our overt actions, or our perceptions, in accordance with our desires, distorting them as we see fit. But the linguistic data are there, in black and white, or on tape, unambiguous and unavoidable. Hence, while in the ideal world other kinds of evidence for sociological phenomena would be desirable along with, or in addition to, linguistic evidence, sometimes at least the latter is all we can get with certainty. This is especially likely in emotionally charged areas like that of sexism and other forms of discriminatory behavior. This book, then, is an attempt to provide diagnostic evidence from language use for one type of inequity that has been claimed to exist in our society: that between the roles of men and women. I will attempt to discover what language use can tell us about the nature and extent of any inequity; and finally to ask whether anything can be done, from the linguistic end of the problem: Does one correct a social inequity by changing linguistic disparities? We will find, I think, that women experience linguistic discrimination in two ways: in the way they are taught to use language, and in the way general language use treats them. Both tend, as we shall see, to relegate women to certain subservient functions: that of sex object, or servant; and therefore certain lexical items mean one thing applied to men, another to women, a difference that cannot be predicted except with reference to the different roles the sexes play in society.

Now use the following questions to analyze your reading experience.

1. What were your expectations when you began to read each of these texts? Did you expect to find one or the other easier or more interest-

ing to read? Why? To what extent did your expectations derive from your own previous experiences as a reader?

2. Each of these texts comments on the situation of women in society and the role that language plays in women's lives. How did your assumptions and values about these issues influence your reading? Did you approach these texts as a sympathetic reader, or were you resistant to the general subject at the start? Why?

3. Just as writers often shift goals and strategies while writing, readers too sometimes revise their goals and strategies while reading. Did you find yourself doing so while reading either passage? Why? What caused these shifts, if they occurred?

4. How would you describe each author's relationship with her readers? Did each of these texts invite you to play a different role as reader? Describe your role as you read these texts. How did your awareness of this role influence your reading? List several features of each text that encourage readers to adopt a particular role.

5. What factors made each of these texts more or less difficult to read? Did the two texts require you to draw on different skills and different prior knowledge about the subject matter? How?

6. If you found reading either of these texts difficult or unenjoyable, can you imagine someone else who would find them easy and pleasurable to read? What values, knowledge, and skills would this person have? In what ways would this person differ from you? If you found one of these passages easy and enjoyable reading, can you identify the reasons why?

Now reread these two texts. How did this second reading differ from your first? To what extent do you find yourself "revising" your first reading? List several ways that the second reading differed from the first.

FOR COLLABORATION

Meet with a group of classmates to discuss your responses to the preceding Exploration. (Appoint a member of the group to act as a recorder so you can share the results of your discussion with the rest of the class.) Begin by comparing your answers to each of the preceding six questions. Formulate two or three responses to the following questions:

1. In what ways do your answers to these questions differ?

2. What do these differences reveal about the reading process?

3. What do these differences reveal about the different expectations and experiences that you brought to your reading of these texts?

You can strengthen your reading and writing skills by taking time to reflect on how you read various texts. Periodically, you may want to take an inventory of your reading process. Such an inventory can give you valuable information about your strengths and limitations as a reader. It can also help you determine how best to approach unfamiliar texts. The following guidelines provide questions that you can use in an informal or a formal reading inventory to consider what you bring to the reading of a particular text, what the text brings to you, and where possible differences lie. The point of this inventory is not to determine if you are reading a text correctly. (If you read a poem that invites contemplation and interpretation in the same way that you read a chemistry textbook, however, there is a significant mismatch between what the text is bringing to you and what you are bringing to the text.) Your goal should be to understand both the text and your reading of the text.

■ GUIDELINES FOR CONDUCTING A READING INVENTORY

To reflect on your reading of a particular text, ask yourself these questions:

1. What were your initial thoughts about the text? Did you expect to find it easy or difficult? Interesting or boring? Were you looking forward to reading the text, or were you reading it primarily because it was assigned by a teacher or supervisor?

2. How would you describe your reading process for this text? What story would you tell about your reading?

3. Find and respond to one passage that is important to you and one passage that you believe is important for the author. Try to put yourself in the author's shoes. Do you think that the author would feel that your passage is important? How important is the author's passage to you? What can you learn about the text and your reading of it by comparing similarities and dissimilarities between the author's and your own expectations?

4. Next, ask yourself the following questions: What is this text reminding you of? What question is this text answering? What

(continued)

(continued)

problem is it addressing? What is left unsaid in the text? What is the text refusing to consider?

5. What major questions do you have about this text? To what extent does the text attempt to address these questions? If it does not address your questions, why might this be the case? (You might be an undergraduate reading a text written primarily for specialists in a particular field, for instance.)

6. What happens when you focus on your body's response to the text? How is your reading a performance that you make and do? What can your body's response to this text tell you about your experience of reading it?

7. Finally, how would you characterize your reading of this text — as a conversation? A lecture? Did your reading take you deeply into the text (as might be the case if you are reading an academic argument)? Or did it encourage you to relate your personal experience to the text (as might be the case if you are reading a poem or song lyrics)?

8. What have you learned from undertaking this inventory of your reading of a particular text? Take five minutes to freewrite about this experience.

READING VISUAL TEXTS

As the discussion thus far has emphasized, reading is as active — and as rhetorically, socially, and culturally situated — a process as writing. Skimming a popular magazine certainly demands less of our attention than reading a textbook full of complex calculations and scholarly references, but in either case the reader is intentionally (if often intuitively) choosing to engage a text in a specific manner. For just as writers draw on their rhetorical sensitivity when writing — sensitivity that they have gained in their years of reading, writing, speaking, and listening — so too do readers draw on their rhetorical sensitivity when reading.

But what role does *looking* — at texts, images, movies, television shows — play in the development of rhetorical sensitivity? As an experiment, turn back to the "Harper's Index" presented on p. 53. When you originally looked at this, did you notice the varying line indentations? Even if you were aware of them in your first reading, take a few moments to reread this text, taking particular care to observe the role that the indentations play in helping to define relationships among the statements included in the "Index." Notice, for instance, the sharp contrast between the sixth and seventh items. The sudden shift in level of indentation between these two statements emphasizes this contrast.

If something as simple as the indentation of a line can influence our response to and interpretation of a text, imagine the important role that images (such as photographs and drawings) and such design features as color, font size, and graphics can play in human communication. Think about the full range of reading that you do. If you are like me, you can easily identify a number of texts, such as magazines and Web pages, where visual elements are at least as important as the words on the page. If you want to be an engaged and critical reader, then, you must develop the ability to read visual texts with the same insight you bring to written texts.

For instance, look at the black-and-white reproductions of two magazine covers on pp. 61 and 62. (I will describe the use of color in the original covers as I discuss them.) The first cover, Figure 3.2, is from the February 2002 issue of *Wired* magazine. As you may already know, *Wired* is a nationally distributed, advertisement-filled magazine for those interested in online, wireless, and other newly developed information technologies. The second cover, Figure 3.3, is from the December 2002 issue of *The Co-op Thymes*, the monthly newsletter of the First Alternative Co-op in Corvallis, Oregon.

Each cover provides important cues that attentive readers will notice as they read both image and text. Each cover also assumes that whoever looks at the cover will "read" the images and words that are presented there in sophisticated ways. The *Wired* cover, for instance, assumes that readers will immediately associate the Disney characters (Goofy, Peter Pan, Donald Duck, and Mickey Mouse) who are raising a flag on a pile of rubble with the famous photo of an American flag being raised on a hill on Iwo Jima, a Japanese island, during World War II. The colors of the magazine's cover are the red, white, and blue of the American flag—blue figures raising a blue flag against a white background with primarily red type — which further reinforces this association. In case you are not familiar with the original photograph of the flag raising at Iwo Jima, see the reproduction of it, Figure 3.4, on p. 63. Many people have argued that the February 23, 1945, photograph of five marines and one navy corpsman raising the flag on the top of Mount Suribachi after one of the most brutal battles of World War II is the most memorable photograph of the war. It is almost certainly the most reproduced image in the United States from both World War I and World War II. This image — which was photographed by Joe Rosenthal, a photographer covering the Pacific war for the Associated Press — has appeared on a postage stamp and on the cover of countless magazines and newspapers. It also served as the model for the Marine Corps War Memorial in Arlington, Virginia.

Despite its popularity, this photograph has always been surrounded by controversy. When the photograph was first published, viewers assumed that it

THE NAKED TRUTH ABOUT INTERNET PORN: SEE PAGE 100

WIRED

FEBRUARY 2002

SMALL WORLD

SPECIAL GLOBALIZATION REPORT

DISNEY INVADER

INSIDE THE ULTIMATE CULTURE MACHINE

MELTDOWN
Big Steel In The
Borderless Economy

OPT OUT
The 4 Corners Of
The Unwired World

PLUS
→ After Enron
→ The Fertility Cops
→ Reengineering
  The Everglades

Figure 3.2   Cover from February 2002 issue of *Wired* magazine.

was taken during the original postbattle flag raising. In fact, the initial flag raising was interrupted by a brief mortar attack, and Rosenthal photographed a
second (somewhat staged) raising of the flag. For many in the United States,
however, this photograph serves now — as it did during the war — as an
image of American determination and of hope for the future at a time of great

Figure 3.3 Cover from *The Co-op Thymes*, the monthly newsletter of the First Alternative Co-op in Corvallis, Oregon.

uncertainty. In fact, after the attacks on the World Trade Towers and Pentagon on September 11, 2001, many saw a resemblance between the Iwo Jima photograph and a much-reproduced photograph of New York City firemen raising the United States flag over the rubble of the Towers.

So why did the editors of *Wired* choose to design a cover that shows Disney characters and alludes to a famous and, for many, beloved photograph?

Figure 3.4   **Joe Rosenthal's "Flag Raising on Iwo Jima." (February 23, 1945)**

The cover's headline gives an important clue: it informs readers that this issue of *Wired* includes a special globalization report on "Disney, Invader: Inside the Ultimate Culture Machine." Observant readers of the cover will note that the biggest and most emphatic word in the title is "Invader."

Clearly, this cover draws on international debates about what some have characterized as American cultural imperialism. Protests against this Americanization have taken multiple forms — from demonstrations at meetings of the World Trade Association to the "slow food" movement in Europe, which is sometimes billed as an effort to resist the "McDonaldsization" of Europe. The article that is featured on the cover of this issue of *Wired* — "The Ever-Expanding, Profit-Maximizing, Cultural-Imperialist, Wonderful World of Disney: The Serious Business of Selling All-American Fun" by Jonathan Weber — considers these issues. (For an online version of this article, see <http://wired .com/wired/archive/10.02/disney>.)

Although both the image on the cover and the title of the feature article seem to suggest that Disney has been victorious in its effort to expand its domain around the world, the article portrays a complex relationship between corporations that are attempting to export American culture and the people in other countries who may — or may not — be eager to consume this culture.

Complex political, economic, cultural, and technological factors are at play in any such effort. In fact, the author of this article argues that companies like Disney are as likely to fail as to succeed in their interactions with other cultures — or to be changed in significant ways by them. Here, for instance, is the concluding paragraph of the article:

> Disney's challenges both at home and abroad illustrate just how hard it is for even the biggest of American brands to keep growing — and give lie to many of the fears people have about cultural imperialism. Unlike other industries — oil, say, or agriculture, or even technology — cultural businesses depend on giving people what they want, as opposed to what they need. It is true that the giant media conglomerates can sometimes suffocate competition and choice. But in television and theme parks in most of the world, there has never been much competition anyway, and in the sale of plush toys it is hardly an issue. For the most part, people will decide what elements of American culture they want. The Disneys of the world are slaves to the tastes of Chen Ping and Wei Qing Hua [a Chinese man and woman who are interviewed as they visit a theme park at the start of the article], not the other way around. (p. 79)

What, then, is the relationship between the bold, provocative cover of the February 2002 issue of *Wired* and the feature article to which it alludes? Clearly, the cover is deliberately designed to catch the attention of those glancing at the magazine at a store or newsstand and to raise questions. Why are the Disney characters posed like the soldiers in the Iwo Jima photograph? Who is Disney invading, and why? Publishers want to raise these kinds of questions in the minds of people who might purchase their magazines — and hope that a provocative cover will persuade an indecisive consumer to pick up a magazine and head for the checkout stand. Granted, the editors of *Wired* took a potential risk in parodying a photograph that is revered by many. But as readers of *Wired* are aware, this magazine delights in flaunting conventional expectations through cutting-edge internal design features, such as unusual colors, fonts, margins, photographs, and images. The designers of this cover of *Wired* clearly believed that those reading the magazine would view this parody as thought-provoking rather than as disrespectful of the photograph on which it is based.

Just as writers of traditional print texts must consider the needs, interests, values, and assumptions of their readers, so too must those composing visual texts. This was true of the cover of *Wired* showing the Disney characters raising the American flag, and it is equally true of the cover of the December 2002 issue of *The Co-op Thymes*. Unlike *Wired*, which is a nationally distributed, mass-market magazine, the *Thymes* is a locally distributed newspaper for shoppers at the First Alternative Co-op in Corvallis, Oregon. The *Thymes* is mailed to member-owners each month; it is also available for free at checkout stands in the Co-op.

If *Wired* covers are designed to project the magazine's hip, urban, with-it technological focus, the cover of the *Thymes* reflects the focus of both the newspaper and the First Alternative Co-op. According to the mission statement of the Co-op, as presented in the first page of the newsletter,

> First Alternative is a community market aspiring to be a model for environmental sustainability through our purchasing and workplace practices. We

- Seek to honor our traditions and build upon our potential.
- Are committed to cultivating tolerance and diversity in our operations.
- Strive for excellence in our products and services. . . .
- Will act ethically and appropriately in our pricing practices.
- Seek to provide a democratic business climate, fostering worker and member participation, according to cooperative principles.

Although the cover of the December 2002 issue of the *Thymes* evokes the holiday traditions that readers associate with that month, it also reflects the Co-op's mission statement. The illustration that is the primary feature of the cover, for instance, evokes both tradition and potential, tolerance and diversity. As the original cover (which is printed in warm colors of blue, green, yellow, and related tones) makes clear, the individuals who have gathered to celebrate the holiday season represent multiple ages and ethnicities. They are clearly celebrating a holiday, as the candles, party hats, wine, and food suggest. The illustrator, Lucinda Kinch, has taken care, however, not to suggest a particular winter holiday, such as Christmas, Hannukah, or Kwanza. Instead, she evokes the cooperative spirit that the First Alternative Co-op and the Co-op's *Thymes* hope to encourage. The illustrator also evokes countless photographs, paintings, and drawings of holiday celebrations. She does not allude to any particular image, but she clearly assumes that readers will recognize that this is not just an ordinary gathering of friends but a special holiday celebration.

Although the cover of the February 2002 issue of *Wired* serves primarily to catch the consumer's attention and to provoke thought, the cover of the *Thymes* is designed not to encourage potential sales but to reflect the mission of the Co-op and to provide information about items of interest to readers and customers. Thus the text on the left side of the *Thymes* cover is divided into two sections of white text printed on a blue background: The top section lists the principles that guide the Co-op, while the bottom section lists the articles in this month's newsletter. Even though the *Thymes* is a free publication, the editors and designers want to encourage Co-op members and visitors to the Co-op to read the newsletter. Doing so is one way of becoming more involved with the Co-op — and this, of course, is what supporters of the First Alternative Co-op want to encourage.

As publications, *Wired* magazine and the *Thymes* differ in significant ways. Their missions are different, as are the images they project and the readership they hope to attract. These differences are reflected even in such apparently trivial features as the paper they are printed on: *Wired* is printed on expensive glossy paper, and the *Thymes* is printed on inexpensive newsprint. Nevertheless, the covers of these publications demonstrate great sensitivity to the needs and expectations of their readers and to their larger rhetorical situations. Both covers also assume that readers will bring both cultural knowledge and well-developed interpretive and analytical skills to their reading of these visual texts.

Not all magazine covers invite the kind of in-depth reading that I have just given these covers. Readers familiar with such weekly news magazines as *Time* and *Newsweek* know that these magazines' covers generally present a photograph of a person or persons or of a news event such as a natural disaster. The familiarity of such design features helps reassure readers that they know what to expect in these magazines. If the photograph of a person appears on the cover of *Newsweek,* for instance, readers know that one of the issue's major stories — perhaps even the cover story — focuses on this person. Such knowledge increases the readability of the cover and of the following story. The implicit message that the cover sends to readers is this: If a person or event is important in the United States or to Americans, our magazine will feature it.

Why is it important to be able to "read" visual images and to understand the potentially powerful role that design and visual elements can play in written texts? Perhaps the most important reason has to do with the increasingly pervasive role that images have come to play in modern life. Driving down the street, watching television, skimming a magazine: In these and other situations we are continually presented with images and texts — many of which are designed to persuade us to purchase, believe, or do certain things. Often these images can be a source of pleasure and entertainment. But given the persuasive intent of many images, critical readers will develop ways to not just "read" but "read into" these images. The following guidelines present questions you can ask to analyze any visual text.

■ GUIDELINES FOR ANALYZING VISUAL TEXTS

1. How would you characterize your overall impression of the general design and presentation of words and images in this visual text? Is the presentation cluttered or spare? Colorful or subdued?

(continued)

(continued)

Carefully organized or (apparently) randomly presented? Calm or "busy"? Traditional, contemporary, or cutting-edge?

2. What images or design features play a particularly important role in this piece? Does it present a single dominant image or a variety of images? If the latter, how are these images related? What is your eye drawn to when you first look at this piece? Why?

3. In what ways do the design and presentation of words and images in this piece appeal to logic and to reason? To emotion? What role (if any) does the credibility of a company or individual play in this piece? Does the piece assume that readers would recognize a trademark or corporate name, for instance, or recognize a photograph or drawing of a well-known figure?

4. What is the relationship between image and text in this piece? Does one predominate? Is their relationship explicit or implicit? Does the text function primarily to present information or to reinforce or extend — or even to subvert or undermine — the image?

5. Does the visual text assume prior knowledge about an image (as was the case with the *Wired* cover)? What sort of knowledge? Historical? Artistic? Cultural? Political? What role does this prior knowledge play in helping the visual text to achieve its impact? Does it work differently depending on the reader's prior knowledge?

6. If you were to translate the impact or message of the visual text into words, how would you describe it? What do you think that those who constructed this piece intend, in other words, for its visual impact to be? Do you believe that it achieves its intended impact? Why?

FOR EXPLORATION

Look at the advertisements presented on pp. 177–79 at the end of Chapter 5. Choose the ad that most intrigues, moves, or puzzles you, and analyze it according to the questions presented above, writing your responses to each question. Finally, write one or two paragraphs about what you have learned as a result of this analysis.

RECOGNIZING THE NEED FOR DIVERSE READING STRATEGIES

As a college student, you read many different kinds of texts for a wide variety of purposes. You may skim a magazine or surf the Web for fun and relaxation. You may read a novel for pleasure and for its insight into human emotions. When you read a textbook for, say, your Introduction to Western Civilization class, you may read primarily for information. On other occasions, you read not simply to gain information but to engage in the process of inquiry. Professors David Bartholomae and Anthony Petrosky call this kind of reading "strong reading":

> Reading involves a fair measure of push and shove. You make your mark on a book and it makes its mark on you. Reading is not simply a matter of hanging back and waiting for a piece, or its author, to tell you what the writing has to say. In fact, one of the difficult things about reading is that the pages before you will begin to speak only when the authors are silent and you begin to speak in their place, sometimes for them — doing their work, continuing their projects — and sometimes for yourself, following your own agenda.
>
> — DAVID BARTHOLOMAE AND ANTHONY PETROSKY,
> *WAYS OF READING*

Strong readers evaluate their reading in terms of what they are able to *do* with their reading. As they read they engage in active dialogue with the author of their text, posing questions and raising potential counterarguments to these presented by the author. If you are like many students, you may feel more confident reading for information than engaging in a strong reading of an essay, advertisement, poem, political treatise, engineering report, or Web site. Yet gaining the ability to "make your mark" on a verbal or visual text, rather than simply allowing the text to make its mark on you, is one of the most important goals of a college education. Such critical reading is intrinsically satisfying, for it enables you to engage in genuine inquiry. Strong reading naturally leads to — and benefits — writing; one of the best ways to strengthen your writing ability is thus to become adept at strong reading.

In Part Four of *Work in Progress*, "Analyzing and Writing Academic Arguments," you will learn more about how to become a strong reader — and writer — of academic texts. The following guidelines provide general suggestions that you can draw on in reading a wide variety of print and online texts.

■ GUIDELINES FOR EFFECTIVE READING

1. *Recognize That Effective Readers Are Flexible Readers.* Effective readers understand that different reading situations and mediums call for different reading strategies — and that their purpose in reading should help them determine how to approach a text. If you are researching an essay on the homeless in urban centers in the northeast, for instance, you might skim a number of print and online studies to become familiar with resources available on the subject. Once you have clearly defined your topic and purpose, you would then begin reading in a more focused and critical manner.

2. *Analyze the Text That You Are Reading for Clues about Its Rhetorical, Social, and Cultural Contexts.* Earlier in this chapter, you looked at the cover of the *Thymes,* a monthly newspaper published by the First Alternative Co-op in Corvallis, Oregon, with which you were almost certainly unfamiliar. You saw that by moving back and forth among the cover, mission statement, and table of contents — and possibly drawing on your general knowledge about cooperative grocery stores — you could begin to understand and evaluate the cover. A similar process of inquiry can help you to better understand the rhetorical, social, and cultural contexts of print and online texts. Here are some questions that you can ask yourself:

   ■ *Questions about the author, editor, or (in the case of Web sites) Webmaster* What did this person (or persons) hope the text would accomplish? How might those goals have influenced the form, content, and design of the text? To what extent does the text call attention to the role that the author, editor, or Webmaster played? Is it an obvious role, as is the case with personal essays and homepages? Is it a more distanced and even hidden role, as is the case with editors and Webmasters?

   ■ *Questions about readers* Who are the intended readers of this text? A general audience (of a magazine, for instance, or a Web site)? An audience of specialists (as for scientific or professional journals and industry-specific publications)? Or is the audience composed of students (as is the case with college textbooks)? What role does the text invite readers to

(continued)

(continued)

adopt as they read (study, surf, scan, or otherwise engage with) this text? Does the text assume that readers will bring considerable prior knowledge to their reading? What cultural or social understandings and preferences does the text assume? Does it assume, for instance, that readers won't read large passages of prose unless they are interrupted by images or other design features? That they will recognize a person whose photograph appears in an ad? That readers will share certain values and beliefs?

- *Questions about the text* When was this text published — and where? In a traditional print publication? (The comparison of the *Wired* and the *Thymes* covers should remind you that print publications are anything but equal.) On the Web? On an institutional site? A business site? A personal site? What can you infer about the reasons for publication? To inform? Entertain? Persuade?

3. *Develop Strategies for Reading against the Grain of a Text.* To read critically and actively, it sometimes helps to deliberately resist a text or to read "against the grain." For example, while reading an essay on abortion intended for a general audience, you might consider the essay from the perspective of a health-care provider or from that of a woman who has experienced an abortion. How would those readers respond to the author's arguments and strategies? You might read the essay paying particular attention to issues or examples that the author *doesn't* mention. Or you might focus on your own experience and how it supports or does not support the author's arguments. Such probing, resistant readings can help you determine not only what an essay says and does but also what it doesn't say and do and can thus provide an opening for fruitful questioning and analysis.

4. *Find Productive Ways to Respond to Challenging Texts.* As a college student, you will inevitably find some reading challenging. You may be unfamiliar with the research discussed or with the vocabulary or methodology used. You could have trouble determining what exactly is at stake in a particular argument. The following strategies will help you work through these and similar difficulties:

(continued)

(continued)

- *Identify reason(s) that a text seems difficult,* and then turn these reasons into questions that you can use as you read the text. Rather than becoming frustrated when a writer is commenting at length on an issue that seems unimportant to you, for instance, ask yourself *why* scholars in this field might find this issue worthy of attention.

- *Interact with the text.* Pose questions. Speculate about the implications of a line of argument. Look for gaps or absences in the presentation of evidence or ideas. Use your personal experience as a lens to consider the issues raised by a text — and then imagine how someone quite different from you might approach this issue or topic.

- *Be patient.* Just as the process of writing often requires rough drafts, so too can the process of reading require "rough readings." A text that on first reading seems difficult will often, on rereading, prove rewarding or more engaging.

DEVELOPING CRITICAL READING STRATEGIES

Reading critically means reading *actively,* reading not just to gather facts or information but to evaluate, analyze, appreciate, understand, and apply what you read. As a critical reader, you engage in a dialogue with the author. Rather than automatically accepting the author's perspective or arguments, you subject the author's ideas to careful examination.

To read critically, you need to develop a repertoire of reading strategies. The following discussion presents a number of strategies for critical reading and provides an opportunity for you to apply these strategies to a specific text, an article that considers the significance of the Internet.

Previewing

When you preview a text, you survey it quickly to establish or clarify your purpose and context for reading, asking yourself questions such as those included in the following guidelines. As you do so, recognize that print and online sources may call for different previewing strategies. With print sources, for instance, it is easy to determine the author and publisher. To learn the author of a homepage on the World Wide Web, however, you need to know how to read Web addresses. You also need to recognize that homepages include links to many disparate materials and that materials on the Internet and World Wide Web can appear, and disappear, with disconcerting frequency. Hence, determining the accuracy, authority, and currency of online resources can prove challenging. Whereas such print texts as scholarly journals and books have generally undergone extensive review and editing, such may not be the case with online sources.

■ GUIDELINES FOR PREVIEWING A TEXT

1. Where and when was this text published? If this text appears on the World Wide Web, how recently was it updated? What do this source and date suggest about the accuracy, authority, and currency of this text?

2. What, if anything, do you know about the author of this text?

3. What can you learn from the title?

4. What can you learn by quickly surveying this text? Is the text divided into sections? If so, how do these sections appear to be organized? What links does a Web site provide? How useful do these links seem to be? Can you easily perceive the general approach the author is taking? What predictions about this text can you make on the basis of a quick survey? What questions can you now formulate to guide your subsequent reading of this text?

5. What is your personal response to the text, based on this preview?

NOTE FOR MULTILINGUAL WRITERS

All readers benefit from previewing texts, but if you are a multilingual reader and writer, you will find previewing particularly helpful. When you preview a text, you gain valuable information that can help you read the text efficiently and effectively. As you preview the text, be sure to formulate questions that you have about specialized terms or about its general approach.

FOR EXPLORATION

Using the preceding guidelines, preview the following article.

NO "THERE" THERE

WHY CYBERSPACE ISN'T ANYPLACE
by Jonathan G. S. Koppell

I'm a pretty Net-savvy guy. I read my morning newspaper online. I buy discount airline tickets online, I participate in animated sports banter online. I even manage my finances online (if transferring money to cover checks qualifies as "managing my finances"). Still, I have never been to the magical land called cyberspace.

Cyberspace isn't on any map, but I know that it must exist, because it is spoken of every day. People spend hours in *chat rooms*. They visit *Web sites*. They travel through this electronic domain on an *information super-highway*. The language we use implies that cyberspace is a place as tangible as France or St. Louis or the coffee shop on the corner. But why, exactly, should we think of the Internet as a geographic location? I recently partic-ipated in a telephone conference call with people in several other states and countries. Were we all together in another "place"? I doubt that any of us thought so.

Many would say that it isn't just the act of communicating that makes cyberspace a place but the existence of a community consisting of broadly dispersed people. But that characteristic is not particularly distinc-tive. There are communities big and small that do not exist within any physical jurisdiction. Professional associations, alumni groups, and reli-gious orders are among them. Members of such groups feel a kinship with other members with whom they have never interacted, in either the real or the virtual sense.

Some would respond, "Those people all had something in common before they forged connections across boundaries. But cyberspace com-munities were created online. There were no prior affinities to bring them together. That's unique." Is it? Ham radio operators have a global network of friends and acquaintances who came together solely through their use of that instrument. Do they exist in "hamspace"? And why is the manner in which people make first contact so significant? Do pen pals exist in "penpalspace"?

One reason that cyberspace is described as a place is to avoid down-grading it to the status of a mere medium, and perhaps especially to avoid comparisons with television. Those who would distinguish the Internet from television point out that Web denizens are not mere passive recipi-ents of electronic signals. That may be (partly) true. But telephones and the postal system are also communications media that allow two-way communication. We don't regard them as places.

Jonathan G. S. Koppell, "No 'There' There." *Atlantic Monthly,* August 2000, 16, 18.

Thinking of the Internet as a place certainly makes it seem more intriguing. The idea of logging on and entering another space is suggestive in all sorts of ways. It raises issues of consciousness, allows us to think of ourselves as disembodied cybernauts, and sets us apart not just from our primitive ancestors but also from our recent ones. Not incidentally, representing the home computer and AOL membership as a gateway to another dimension helps to sell home computers and AOL memberships. The various Web sites, IPOs, and dot-coms-of-the-day feed on the fervor surrounding our exploration of this strange new land. By morphing the Internet into a destination, cyberspace has become the Klondike of our age. (Curiously, Seattle is reaping the benefits this time around, too.)

■ ■ ■

Metaphors matter: they can help to shape our views and actions. Consider the widespread acceptance of the term "marketplace of ideas" as a metaphor for free speech. This representation emphasizes one's freedom to enter the arena of discourse, rather than one's ability to be heard. Thus, in the context of campaign-finance regulation, protection of free speech means that unlimited campaign expenditures are sacrosanct, but guaranteeing equal opportunities to reach the electorate is not a consideration. If, in contrast, we imagined not a marketplace but a classroom, enabling the quietest voice to be heard would be more important than protecting the rights of the loudest. Another example is the ill-fated "war on drugs." By conceiving of drugs as an enemy to be defeated in combat, we blind ourselves to many potential solutions. In the context of war the legalization of drugs amounts to capitulation to the enemy — even if it might address many of the problems, such as crime, disease, and chronic poverty, that were used to justify the war in the first place.

For its part, the cyberspace-as-place metaphor raises issues of logic and psychology that may ultimately impede wise management of the Internet. Lawrence Lessig, of Harvard Law School, argues in his book *Code and Other Laws of Cyberspace* (1999) that the government should not sit by while private code (software) writers define the nature of the Internet. Such a seemingly neutral stance, Lessig says, is not neutral but irresponsible. In the case of cyberspace, laissez-faire government simply defers decision-making authority to profit-seeking companies. Guided only by commercial interests, the development of the Internet is skewed to favor the corporation rather than the individual or society as a whole.

The problem, Lessig explains, is that legislatures and courts are reluctant to regulate the Internet. He lays out some compelling reasons why this is so, but he skips a crucial one. Because we think of the Internet as a place, the prospect of "going there" takes on an extra dimension. Legislatures are wary of bringing government to cyberspace — as if it somehow existed in some pure state beyond ordinary society. Judges are reluctant to bring law into this "new" arena, as if applying existing laws to Internet transactions would be tantamount to colonizing Antarctica or the moon. In the context of legal discussions, cyberspace is seen not as a potentially anarchic realm but as a virginal Eden; the introduction of law would not so much bring order as corrupt utopia. Republicans in Congress have vowed to "stand at the door to the Internet" to defend its sanctity. Their "E-Contract 2000" would, for example, prohibit sales taxes in cyberspace for at least five years — as if such a moratorium were needed to nurture the most dynamic sector of the economy. Many Democrats, equally eager to win favor in the industry, also support the concept of an online duty-free "zone."

As it happens, Lessig himself reinforces cyberspace-as-place thinking. He argues that the Internet user exists simultaneously in two "places," a physical location and cyberspace — thus making the application of law somewhat difficult. In reality, the problems created by Internet transactions simply involve making decisions about jurisdiction. Should a criminal computer user, for example, be subject to the laws of the state in which he resides, or to the laws of the state in which the victim resides? This can be a knotty question, but it is not a new problem — not a "cyberspace problem." Such determinations are made every day with respect to telephone and postal transactions. Are these problems more common because of the Internet? Yes. Do they involve more jurisdictions because of the Internet? Yes. But they do not involve their own jurisdiction, any more than matters initiated or conducted through the mails involve "postalspace."

That is not to say that the Internet will have no consequences for governance. The growth of the Internet may gradually shift the locus of authority upward, from local and state governments to the federal government or even international institutions, because as human interactions transcend political boundaries, only governments with broad jurisdictions will be able to monitor certain kinds of behavior and enforce certain kinds of laws. Law and government will adapt accordingly.

The cyberspace-as-place metaphor is probably here to stay. And it has its uses, as do the many other fanciful metaphors we use in everyday speech. But let's not be misled. The regulation of cyberspace — in areas from copyright to taxation to privacy — hardly represents the spoliation of a pristine and untamed land.

Annotating

When you annotate a text, you highlight important words or passages and write comments or questions that help you establish a dialogue with the text or remember important points. Different readers have different styles of annotating. Some people are heavy annotators, highlighting many passages and filling the margins with comments and questions. Others annotate more selectively, preferring to write few comments and to highlight only the most important passages or key words. In thinking about your own annotating strategies, remember that your purpose in reading should influence the way you annotate a text. You would annotate a text you are reading primarily for information differently than you would an essay you are reading for an assignment or a poem you are reading for pleasure.

Many readers annotate directly on the text as they read. If you have borrowed the text or prefer not to mark up your own book, however, you can use a separate piece of paper or computer file to copy important passages and to write questions and comments.

How can you know the most effective way to annotate a text? The questions provided in the following guidelines can help you make appropriate choices as you read — and annotate — texts.

■ GUIDELINES FOR ANNOTATING A TEXT

1. What is your purpose in reading this text? What do you need to annotate to accomplish this purpose?

2. Where does the writer identify the purpose and the thesis (or main idea) of the text?

3. What are the main points, definitions, and examples? Would it be useful to number the main points or make a scratch outline in the margin?

4. What questions does this text suggest to you?

5. Can you identify key words that play an important role in this discussion? Does the text provide enough information so that you can understand these key words and appreciate their significance, or do you need to get further explanation?

6. Can you identify passages that seem to play a particularly crucial role in this text? What is your response to these passages?

7. Can you identify passages where your personal experience and values or knowledge of the subject cause you to question the author's assertions, evidence, or method?

FOR EXPLORATION

Annotate "No 'There' There: Why Cyberspace Isn't Anyplace" (pp. 73–75) as you would if you expected to write an essay responding to it for your composition class.

Summarizing

Never underestimate the usefulness of writing clear, concise summaries of texts you read. Writing a summary allows you to restate the major points of a book or essay in your own words. Summarizing is a skill worth developing, for it requires you to master the material you are reading and make it your own. Summaries can vary in length, depending on the complexity and length of the material being summarized. Ideally, however, they should be as brief as possible. Here are suggestions to follow as you write your own summaries.

■ GUIDELINES FOR SUMMARIZING A TEXT

1. Reread the material, trying to identify the main ideas.

2. Highlight or number the main points.

3. Generally stick to main points. Leave out examples and anecdotes.

4. Before writing, try to form a coherent mental outline of the most important ideas.

5. State the main ideas in your own words, as briefly and clearly as you can.

FOR EXPLORATION

Following the preceding guidelines, write a brief summary of "No 'There' There: Why Cyberspace Isn't Anyplace" (pp. 73–75).

Analyzing the Argument of a Text

Previewing, annotating, and summarizing can all help you determine the central informative or argumentative points made in a text. Sometimes, the central argument of a text is explicitly stated. Robin Lakoff begins her introduction to *Language and Woman's Place*, for instance, with this assertion: "Language uses us as much as we use language." Similarly, in his *Atlantic Monthly* article, Jonathan G. S. Koppell asserts that "the cyberspace-as-place metaphor raises issues of logic and psychology that may ultimately impede wise management of the Internet."

Not all authors are so direct. Someone writing about the consequences of contemporary feminism for life in North America may raise questions rather than provide answers or make strong assertions. Whether an author articulates a clear position on a subject or poses a question for consideration, critical readers attempt to determine for themselves if the author's analysis is valid — if the author provides good reasons in support of a position or line of analysis.

The following brief guidelines provide an introduction to analyzing the argument of a text. For a fuller discussion of this and related issues, see Part Four, "Analyzing and Writing Academic Arguments."

NOTE FOR MULTILINGUAL WRITERS

The questions posed below reflect one approach that you can use to analyze the argument of a text. If your first experience of reading is grounded in a language and culture other than English, some of these questions may strike you as odd. In many cultures, for instance, the major claim or thesis of a text is not announced explicitly: Doing so may seem overly obvious or even rude. Instead, readers may expect to grasp a text's argument "between the lines." There may be other differences, too. In some cultures, for instance, arguments from authority — from previous writers and thinkers — are particularly highly valued. Indeed, writers may assume that readers will recognize references to earlier texts and thus may not identify them explicitly. They may even weave words from these writers' texts into their own writing, assuming that readers will recognize the source. This is not an acceptable practice in North America.

As you read the questions below, consider the extent to which these questions are culturally grounded. As a student in North America, you want to become more comfortable with North American writing practices — so that you can learn from these differences. But this does not mean that you have to abandon the preferences that you bring from your home community or culture. You, your classmates, and your teacher will all benefit if you discuss these differences in class.

■ GUIDELINES FOR ANALYZING THE ARGUMENT OF A TEXT

1. What is the major claim or thesis of this text? Is it explicitly stated at any point, or is it implicit, requiring you to "read between the lines"?

(continued)

(continued)

2. What interests or values may have caused this writer to support this particular thesis? (Information about the writer from other sources, as well as clues from the writing itself, may help you determine this.)

3. What values and beliefs about this subject do you bring to your reading of this text? How might these values and beliefs affect your response to the writer's argument?

4. Does the writer define key terms? If not, what role do these unstated definitions play in the argument?

5. What other assumptions does the writer rely on in setting up or working through the argument? In texts on the World Wide Web, for instance, what choices and organizing principles do the links provided by the writer suggest?

6. What kind of evidence does the writer present? Is the evidence used logically and fairly? Has the writer failed to consider any significant evidence, particularly evidence that might refute his or her claims?

7. In what ways does the writer try to put the reader in a receptive frame of mind? Does the writer attempt to persuade the reader through inappropriately manipulative emotional appeals?

8. How does the writer establish his or her credibility? What image or *persona* does the writer create for himself or herself?

FOR EXPLORATION

Using the guidelines for analyzing the argument of a text, analyze the argument of "No 'There' There: Why Cyberspace Isn't Anyplace" (pp. 73–75). Be sure to answer all of the questions for analyzing an argument.

FOR COLLABORATION

By comparing your responses to the previous Explorations with those of your peers, you can gain a helpful perspective on the effectiveness of your critical reading strategies. You can also better understand how different purposes and practices influence the reading of and responses to texts.

Bring your responses to the previous four exploration activities in this chapter to class. Meeting with a group, compare your responses. After you have shared your responses, work together to describe briefly the extent to which your responses were similar or dissimilar. Then discuss what these similarities and differences have helped you understand about the process of critical reading, coming to two or three conclusions to share with your classmates.

FOR THOUGHT, DISCUSSION, AND WRITING

1. Analyze the first chapter of two textbooks you are reading this term (including this one, if you like). Do these textbooks share certain textual conventions? How do you think that the writers of these textbooks have analyzed their rhetorical situation? These textbooks are written for you and other students. How effective are they? How might they be more effective?

2. Earlier in this chapter you read "No 'There' There: Why Cyberspace Isn't Anyplace" by Jonathan G. S. Koppell (pp. 73–75). The readings at the end of this section focus on the benefits and limitations of the Web and of the Internet, the worldwide network of computers that support the Web and a variety of online forums. These readings, which have been selected from a number of print and online sources, range from the serious to the humorous. First skim the various texts, and then read them more carefully. Afterward, answer the following questions:

   ■ As you skimmed these texts, what were your expectations? To what extent did the form of a text and your knowledge of its original means and place of publication influence your expectations?

   ■ After reading each text more carefully, what was your response? To what extent did this response represent a deepening of or shift from your earlier expectations?

   ■ How did your own assumptions and values about the Web and the Internet influence your readings of these texts?

   ■ How would you describe the author's stance or relationship with readers in each of these texts? What role does each text invite you to play as reader? Did you find yourself reading the downloaded Web texts differently from texts first published in traditional print form?

   ■ How did the fact that you were reading these texts together, rather than separately, influence your reading process? Did you find that you substantially revised your goals and strategies as a reader as you moved from text to text? In what ways? Did some of these texts invite or elicit stronger reading than others? Why or why not?

- How did you respond to the content of these texts? Which texts did you find more or less persuasive? Why?

- How did reading these texts influence your own views about the Internet?

- What other observations about reading or about the subject of the Internet and the Web did these texts stimulate in you?

3. After reading the selections on the Internet and the Web, reread Koppell's *Atlantic Monthly* article. How has your reading of these additional texts influenced your response to Koppell's article?

4. Once you have read the following selections, you will have read a number of texts that focus on the Internet and the Web. Write an essay articulating your own views on this subject. Alternatively, write an essay that responds to one or more of the previous readings.

LAWRENCE LESSIG: THE "DINOSAURS" ARE TAKING OVER

Who should control the Internet? If Stanford University law professor Lawrence Lessig is right, the Internet will soon belong to Hollywood studios, record labels, and cable operators — corporate giants that he says are trying to cordon off chunks of the once-open data network. Lessig's mission is to stop them. At age 40, he's already the Net's most famous freedom fighter. Since 1995, he has been a seminal thinker on many of the Digital Age's most important battles — the AOL-Time Warner merger, Napster, and the Microsoft antitrust case.

In his latest book, *The Future of Ideas: The Fate of the Commons in a Connected World*, Lessig argues that imminent changes to Internet architecture plus court decisions that restrict the use of intellectual property will co-opt the Net on behalf of Establishment players — and stifle innovation. On April 29, Lessig spoke with *Business Week Online* technology reporter Jane Black about what he sees as some disturbing trends. Here are edited excerpts of that conversation:

Q: You argue that the Internet's popularity as a new medium is a result of its open architecture. How do you see this changing? And are the changes a threat to e-business?
A: There are two places where it's changing. One is at the physical level of the network. As we move from narrowband to broadband [access to the

"Lawrence Lessig: The 'Dinosaurs' Are Taking Over." *Business Week Online,* May 13, 2002.

Net], broadband operators are developing technology that gives them control over applications and content on the network.

Cable companies, for example, have a view of what the network should be used for. And they're beginning to pick and choose what kinds of content will flow quickly as a way of favoring — or not favoring — content providers. For instance, perhaps cable companies can make it more difficult [for Web sites] to use streaming video if that interferes with their video business. It's your father's AT&T all over again: They, not the user, decide what the network should be.

Q: What's the result of a controlled network?
A: The cost of innovation goes up significantly. Before, you just had to worry about complying with basic network protocol. Now you have to worry about making your program run on the full range of proprietary systems and devices connected to the network. Before, the network would serve whoever and whatever people wanted it to. Soon, you will need the permission of network owners.

Think about other platforms in our lives, like the highway system. Imagine if General Motors could build the highway system such that GM trucks ran better on it than Ford trucks. Or think about the electrical grid. Imagine if a Sony TV worked better on it than a Panasonic TV. The highway and electricity grids are all neutral platforms — a common standard that everyone builds on top of. That's an extraordinarily important feature for networks to have.

Q: And the second change that threatens e-business?
A: Dominant media is a huge threat. [Record labels and Hollywood studios] make their money because of the control they assert over the production and distribution of artists' work. In the music business, a handful of companies control more than 80 percent of the music in the world. These companies control not just distribution but a market where artists have to sell their souls to a record label just to have a right to develop music that can be distributed.

That's the model for the last century. The economic reasons that might have justified that tightly controlled structure have disappeared. The Internet can support much greater competition in production and distribution than [is possible with] the dominant five companies. The record labels have launched lawsuits against every company that has a model for distributing [music and entertainment] content they can't control. That has sent a clear message to venture capitalists: Don't deploy a technology that we don't approve of, or we will sue you into the Dark Ages.

The result is that the field has been left to dinosaurs. There would have been more chips, computers, and devices to deliver content if Congress had been more keen to allow innovation to occur. We've given control over the future to exactly the wrong people. And before we know it, the possibility for innovation will have disappeared.

Q: Why is it so difficult to head off these moves?
A: One reason is that Washington surrounds itself with the same people all of the time — [Motion Picture Association of America President] Jack Valenti and [Recording Industry Association of America President] Hillary Rosen. They've succeeded in making Washington believe this is a binary choice — between perfect protection or no protection. No one is seriously arguing for no protection. They are arguing for a balance that avoids the phenomenon we are seeing now — one where the last generation of technology controls the next generation of industry.

In fact, there are lots of solutions that would promote innovation. For example, Congress could do what it has always done — establish a flat compulsory licensing fee [such as the one radio stations pay to music publishers for playing their songs] so that any company can compete in the marketplace. That's what Napster [the free-music sharing Web site the recording industry sued out of existence] asked Washington for all along — a compulsory license. That could deal with 80% of the problem of existing content.

But these solutions are never recognized because, while the future under perfect competition would produce an industry with much greater income to artists and greater opportunities to consumers, the fact is that the concentrated players are going to lose.

The problem is, we've given control of the future to the people who will lose even under [the] best possible plan. It's like giving the communists control over the future of the new Russia. Congress continues to have them come down and testify. And they step forward and say they want communism to be protected for the next 100 years.

Q: The current debate over Web radio is a good example. New fees that the U.S. copyright office has mandated threaten to put small Webcasters out of business.
A: Web radio is a perfect example. In the course of its testimony before the CARP hearings [the Copyright Arbitration Royalty Panel, the government group responsible for setting compulsory license fee for Webcasters] the RIAA argued that higher rates would reduce the number of competitors to four or five big players. That's their model: To wipe out diversity and get back to a place where only a few people control delivery.

I understand why they want that. But I don't understand why Congress is giving it to them. And it's not just the fees that are ridiculously high — it's the data collection that has been mandated [by CARP and is awaiting approval]. If the RIAA has its way, Webcasters would have to report every song that every listener heard. In essence, it asks to create a national police state of music listening by forcing Webcasters to collect data and turn it over to copyright holders. My question is: Why? It kills competition and the development of niche markets. This is a classic example where the legal process is being used to destroy creativity and innovation.

Q: What should Washington do?
A: First in context of copyright, Congress should pass low fixed compulsory license fees for distribution of [music and entertainment] content on the Web. Those fees should not be tied to reporting every usage on the Web. They should be determined the same way they are now for radio — according to a sampling that gives some idea of what music is being played.

Second, Congress should repeal the 1998 DMCA [Digital Millennium Copyright Act, which, among other things makes it a crime to circumvent copyright-protection technology]. We have no reason to believe that the market won't work well enough to prevent abuse. We don't need the federal government threatening prosecution.

Finally, Congress needs to not pass new legislation, like the [recently introduced] Hollings' bill that would mandate a police state in every computer [by requiring that copyright-protection mechanisms be embedded in PCs, CD players, and anything else that can play, record, or manipulate data]. . . .

Q: Do we need a new definition or vision of copyright and intellectual property in order for e-business to move forward?
A: We don't need a new vision. We just need to recognize what the traditional vision has been. The traditional vision protects copyright owners from unfair competition. It has never been a way to give copyright holders perfect control over how consumers use content. We need to make sure that pirates don't set up CD pressing plants or competing entities that sell identical products. We need to stop worrying about whether you or I use a song on your PC and then transfer it your MP3 player.

WOW! OR MAYBE JUST SORT OF
by George F. Will

Victoria Will, Princeton sophomore, is in her dormitory room noodling on her computer when it says "ding." Glancing at its screen, she says, matter-of-factly, "Bettina is sending me a message." Ms. Will's father,

---

George F. Will, "Wow! Or Maybe Just Sort Of." *Newsweek*, April 16, 2001, 64.

assuming Bettina is a friend e-mailing from another college, asks, "Where is Bettina?" Ms. Will points to the wall in front of her: "Next door." Why, asks her father, doesn't Bettina just walk the 10 feet to Ms. Will's room? Ms. Will's answer, a look of bemused condescension, expresses her opinion that the question betrays an antiquated person's incomprehension of the New.

How much does all this new stuff matter? Have new information and communication technologies really produced a "new economy" and "changed everything"?

Cisco, which makes communications equipment, handles 68 percent of its orders online and 70 percent of its service calls are completed online, saving $1.4 billion annually, a sum equal to 7 percent of Cisco sales. This is a nice efficiency, but hardly evidence of a fundamentally new economic order. Or even a decisive business advantage. Cisco stock is down 83 percent from its peak last March.

Some say, perhaps rightly, that the information technologies produced revolutionary advances in productivity in recent years. However, these advances may be a statistical sleight-of-hand. Most of the increase in nonfarm productivity has been in the manufacture of durables. Now, suppose much of the increase in productivity ascribed to computers has been an increase in productivity in the production of computers, and that accounting practices record a better computer at a constant price as an increase in manufacturing volume and a decline in price.

Timothy Taylor, managing editor of the *Journal of Economic Perspectives*, writing in The Public Interest quarterly, notes that with a "humble" 2 percent annual per capita economic-growth rate, the average standard of living doubles in 36 years, quadruples in 72 years and rises about 50-fold in two centuries. The Industrial Revolution raised the growth rate approximately 2 percentage points — from essentially zero to 2 — and if the Information Revolution were to raise it an additional 2, the result would be "a phenomenal shift in the human condition" — per capita growth of 4 percent per year over two centuries would increase the standard of living 2,500-fold. If new technologies produce that result, they will have been revolutionary. Until then . . .

Given the magic of compounding, old-fashioned but steady can produce gaudy results. Under Warren Buffett's guidance over the past 36 years, Berkshire Hathaway's per-share book value has grown from $19 to $40,442 (23.6 percent compounded annually). In his "chairman's letter" for the company's 2000 report, Buffett includes this drollery: "We have embraced the twenty-first century by entering such cutting edge industries as brick, carpet, insulation and paint. Try to control your excitement." Berkshire Hathaway's cutting-edginess also includes See's Candies and Dairy Queen. It seems there is still money to be made in old things.

One hundred years ago, around 10:30 A.M. on January 10, 1901, near Beaumont, Texas, on a hillock called Spindletop, the first great gusher of the East Texas oil fields roared in. Before long, the population of Beaumont was such that water was selling for $6 a barrel while oil was selling for 3 cents a barrel. *That* was something new, and it led to a lot of new things, including the petroleum and vulcanized rubber and internal combustion energy New Economy. Which also was a poured concrete New Economy.

Robert Shiller is the Yale economist whose book *Irrational Exuberance* was published last March, just as the stock market began to vindicate the book's warnings about a burst bubble to be followed by a freefall. (Nasdaq's apogee was on March 10, 2000 — 13 months and $4 trillion ago.) Shiller argues that the Interstate Highway System has been more consequential than the Internet. The interstate led to low-density suburban living, the revolution in retailing called the mall, "greenfield" office and production facilities, distribution efficiencies that make possible just-in-time manufacturing that minimizes destabilizing run-ups and run-downs of inventories. Has the "information superhighway" done as much?

The quantifications and computations required to make such judgments are, to say no more, problematic, but consider: Have the new technologies, with their admittedly spectacular reductions of "information costs," really been more revolutionary, either in reducing costs or altering lives, than Britain's early nineteenth-century rapid development of cheap postal services made possible by railroads and macadamized roads?

Timothy Taylor, who is 40, notes that his grandmothers, who were born around 1900 and lived into the 1990s, were born into a Midwest still largely drawn by horses and lit by kerosene. In their lifetimes they experienced the coming of electrification and plumbing, machines for washing clothes and dishes and refrigerating food, automobiles and highways, telephones, antibiotics, air travel and home entertainments, including radio and recorded music to television and movies. Taylor says that based on a comparison of the first 40 years of his grandmothers' lives and the first 40 of his life — "what they saw between 1900 and 1940 and what I have lived through since 1960" — it is not clear that he will experience more technological, social, and economic change than they did.

The new information and communication technologies have contributed much to, among other things, the repose, convenience and amusement of Bettina and many others. Including Ms. Will, who, to amaze her father, caused her computer to break into song by finding her father's requested song in someone's "file" (it was not in Ms. Will's computer's file of 900 songs) in Spokane, Washington. Impressive. But has this impressive — what? — jukebox "changed everything"? Doubtful.

HOW THE WEB DESTROYS THE QUALITY
OF STUDENTS' RESEARCH PAPERS
by David Rothenberg

Sometimes I look forward to the end-of-semester rush, when students' final papers come streaming into my office and mailbox. I could have hundreds of pages of original thought to read and evaluate. Once in a while, it *is* truly exciting, and brilliant words are typed across a page in response to a question I've asked the class to discuss.

But this past semester was different. I noticed a disturbing decline in both the quality of the writing and the originality of the thoughts expressed. What had happened since last fall? Did I ask worse questions? Were my students unusually lazy? No. My class had fallen victim to the latest easy way of writing a paper: doing their research on the World Wide Web.

It's easy to spot a research paper that is based primarily on information collected from the Web. First, the bibliography cites no books, just articles or pointers to places in that virtual land somewhere off any map: http://www.etc. Then a strange preponderance of material in the bibliography is curiously out of date. A lot of stuff on the Web that is advertised as timely is actually at least a few years old. (One student submitted a research paper last semester in which all of his sources were articles published between September and December 1995; that was probably the time span of the Web page on which he found them.)

Another clue is the beautiful pictures and graphs that are inserted neatly into the body of the student's text. They look impressive, as though they were the result of careful work and analysis, but actually they often bear little relation to the precise subject of the paper. Cut and pasted from the vast realm of what's out there for the taking, they masquerade as original work.

Accompanying them are unattributed quotes (in which one can't tell who made the statement or in what context) and curiously detailed references to the kinds of things that are easy to find on the Web (pages and pages of federal documents, corporate propaganda, or snippets of commentary by people whose credibility is difficult to assess). Sadly, one finds few references to careful, in-depth commentaries on the subject of the paper, the kind of analysis that requires a book, rather than an article, for its full development.

Don't get me wrong, I'm no neo-Luddite. I am as enchanted as anyone else by the potential of this new technology to provide instant information. But too much of what passes for information these days is simply

David Rothenberg, "How the Web Destroys the Quality of Students' Research Papers." *Chronicle of Higher Education,* August 15, 1997.

advertising for information. Screen after screen shows you where you can find out more, how you can connect to this place or that. The acts of linking and networking and randomly jumping from here to there become as exciting or rewarding as actually finding anything of intellectual value.

Search engines, with their half-baked algorithms, are closer to slot machines than to library catalogues. You throw your query to the wind, and who knows what will come back to you? You may get 234,468 supposed references to whatever you want to know. Perhaps one in a thousand might actually help you. But it's easy to be sidetracked or frustrated as you try to go through those Web pages one by one. Unfortunately, they're not arranged in order of importance.

What I'm describing is the hunt-and-peck method of writing a paper. We all know that word processing makes many first drafts look far more polished than they are. If the paper doesn't reach the assigned five pages, readjust the margin, change the font size, and . . . *voilà*! Of course, those machinations take up time that the student could have spent revising the paper. With programs to check one's spelling and grammar now standard features on most computers, one wonders why students make any mistakes at all. But errors are as prevalent as ever, no matter how crisp the typeface. Instead of becoming perfectionists, too many students have become slackers, preferring to let the machine do their work for them.

What the Web adds to the shortcuts made possible by word processing is to make research look too easy. You toss a query to the machine, wait a few minutes, and suddenly a lot of possible sources of information appear on your screen. Instead of books that you have to check out of the library, read carefully, understand, synthesize, and then tactfully excerpt, these sources are quips, blips, pictures, and short summaries that may be downloaded magically to the dorm-room computer screen. Fabulous! How simple! The only problem is that a paper consisting of summaries of summaries is bound to be fragmented and superficial, and to demonstrate more of a random montage than an ability to sustain an argument through 10 to 15 double-spaced pages.

Of course, you can't blame the students for ignoring books. When college libraries are diverting funds from books to computer technology that will be obsolete in two years at most, they send a clear message to students: Don't read, just connect. Surf. Download. Cut and paste. Originality becomes hard to separate from plagiarism if no author is cited on a Web page. Clearly, the words are up for grabs, and students much prefer the fabulous jumble to the hard work of stopping to think and make sense of what they've read.

Libraries used to be repositories of words and ideas. Now they are seen as centers for the retrieval of information. Some of this information comes from other, bigger libraries, in the form of books that can take time to obtain through interlibrary loan. What happens to the many students (some things never change) who scramble to write a paper the night before it's due? The computer screen, the gateway to the world sitting right on their desks, promises instant access — but actually offers only a pale, two-dimensional version of a real library.

But it's also my fault. I take much of the blame for the decline in the quality of student research in my classes. I need to teach students how to read, to take time with language and ideas, to work through arguments, to synthesize disparate sources to come up with original thought. I need to help my students understand how to assess sources to determine their credibility, as well as to trust their own ideas more than snippets of thought that materialize on a screen. The placelessness of the Web leads to an ethereal randomness of thought. Gone are the pathways of logic and passion, the sense of the progress of an argument. Chance holds sway, and it more often misses than hits. Judgment must be taught, as well as the methods of exploration.

I'm seeing my students' attention spans wane and their ability to reason for themselves decline. I wish that the university's computer system would crash for a day, so that I could encourage them to go outside, sit under a tree, and read a really good book — from start to finish. I'd like them to sit for a while and ponder what it means to live in a world where some things get easier and easier so rapidly that we can hardly keep track of how easy they're getting, while other tasks remain as hard as ever — such as doing research and writing a good paper that teaches the writer something in the process. Knowledge does not emerge in a vacuum, but we do need silence and space for sustained thought. Next semester, I'm going to urge my students to turn off their glowing boxes and think, if only once in a while.

OMG, I'VE GOT S2PID DZS!
by The Daily Telegraph

Education experts in Scotland say literacy could be damaged by text messaging after a pupil handed in an essay written in text shorthand. The 13-year-old girl submitted the essay to a teacher, saying she found text messaging to be "easier than English."

"I could not believe what I was seeing," said her teacher. "The page was riddled with hieroglyphics, many of which I simply could not translate."

"OMG, I've got s2pid dzs!" *The Oregonian,* March 11, 2003, B01.

The teenager's essay began: "My smmr hols wr CWOT. B4, we usd 2go2 NY 2C my bro, his GF & 3 :- kds FTF. ILNY, It's a gr8 plc."

[*Translation:* "My summer holidays were a complete waste of time. Before, we used to go to New York to see my brother, his girlfriend and their three screaming kids face to face. I love New York, it's a great place."]

TIME TO DO EVERYTHING EXCEPT THINK
by David Brooks

Somewhere up in the canopy of society, way above where normal folks live, there will soon be people who live in a state of perfect wirelessness. They'll have mobile phones that download the Internet, check scores and trade stocks. They'll have Palm handhelds that play music, transfer photos and get Global Positioning System readouts. They'll have laptops on which they watch movies, listen to baseball games and check inventory back at the plant. In other words, every gadget they own will perform all the functions of all the other gadgets they own, and they will be able to do it all anywhere, any time.

Wireless Woman will do a full day's work on the beach in her bikini: her personal digital assistant comes with a thong clip so she can wear it on her way to the piña colada stand. Her phones beep, her pagers flash red lights; when they go off, she looks like a video arcade. Wireless Man will be able to put on his performance underwear, hop in his SUV and power himself up to the top of a Colorado mountain peak. He'll be up there with his MP3 device and his carabiners enjoying the view while conference-calling the sales force, and playing MegaDeath with gamers in Tokyo and Sydney. He'll be smart enough to have enough teeny-tiny lithium batteries on hand to last weeks, and if he swallows them they'd cure depression for life. He's waiting for them to develop a laptop filled with helium that would actually weigh less than nothing, and if it could blow up into an inflatable sex doll he'd never have to come down.

So there he sits in total freedom on that Rocky Mountain peak. The sky is blue. The air is crisp. Then the phone rings. His assistant wants to know if he wants to switch the company's overnight carrier. He turns off his phone so he can enjoy a little spiritual bliss. But first, there's his laptop. Maybe somebody sent him an important e-mail. He wrestles with his conscience. His conscience loses. It's so easy to check, after all . . .

Never being out of touch means never being able to get away. But Wireless Man's problem will be worse than that. His brain will have adapted to the tempo of wireless life. Every 15 seconds there is some new

David Brooks, "Time to Do Everything Except Think." *Newsweek,* April 30, 2001, 71.

thing to respond to. Soon he has this little rhythm machine in his brain. He does everything fast. He answers e-mails fast and sloppily. He's bought the fastest machines, and now the idea of waiting for something to download is a personal insult. His brain is operating at peak RPMs.

He sits amid nature's grandeur and says, "It's beautiful. But it's *not moving.* I wonder if I got any new voice mails." He's addicted to the perpetual flux of the information networks. He craves his next data fix. He's a speed freak, an info junkie. He wants to slow down, but can't.

Today's business people live in an overcommunicated world. There are too many Web sites, too many reports, too many bits of information bidding for their attention. The successful ones are forced to become deft machete wielders in this jungle of communication. They ruthlessly cut away at all the extraneous data that are encroaching upon them. They speed through their tasks so they can cover as much ground as possible, answering dozens of e-mails at a sitting and scrolling past dozens more. After all, the main scarcity in their life is not money; it's time. They guard every precious second, the way a desert wanderer guards his water.

The problem with all this speed, and the frantic energy that is spent using time efficiently, is that it undermines creativity. After all, creativity is usually something that happens while you're doing something else: when you're in the shower your brain has time to noodle about and create the odd connections that lead to new ideas. But if your brain is always multitasking, or responding to technoprompts, there is no time or energy for undirected mental play. Furthermore, if you are consumed by the same information loop circulating around everyone else, you don't have anything to stimulate you into thinking differently. You don't have time to read the history book or the science book that may actually prompt you to see your own business in a new light. You don't have access to unexpected knowledge. You're just swept along in the same narrow current as everyone else, which is swift but not deep.

So here's how I'm going to get rich. I'm going to design a placebo machine. It'll be a little gadget with voice recognition and everything. Wireless People will be able to log on and it will tell them they have no messages. After a while, they'll get used to having no messages. They'll be able to experience life instead of information. They'll be able to reflect instead of react. My machine won't even require batteries.

MASTERCARD ADVERTISEMENT

18 speed bike: $525

portable pup tent: $90

the longest paperback you could find: $9.99

seven days without email:

priceless

there are some things money can't buy.
for everything else there's MasterCard.®

WEB + LOG = BLOG

EVERYONE AND HIS DOG, IT SEEMS, IS PUBLISHING
PERSONAL OPINIONS ONLINE
by Christopher Elliott

Do you blog? Blogging — short for "Web logging" — is the latest online societal wrinkle: It's like keeping an opinionated journal on the Internet, but it's one that speaks to the greater affairs of the world. Is this just

Christopher Elliott, "Web + Log = BLOG." *USA Weekend,* December 27–29, 2002, 14.

another dot-com fad? Hardly. The University of California–Berkeley is offering the first-ever course on the phenom. Blogging is huge because, while we all have opinions, most of us can't press speed dial all day to express them on talk radio. Blogging has brought punditry to the people.

It calls to mind a funny, and now telling, remark made by journalist Jesse Oxfeld. He was enjoying his 15 minutes of fame in 1997 when, while attending Stanford University, he was sought out by the national press as the resident "expert" on school chum Chelsea Clinton. Oxfeld said he aspired to be a pundit but didn't know "where to find an entry-level job." Ahhh, Jesse, you were just a few years away from getting your wish.

Today, blogging welcomes all, from rookies, to pros, about a half-million people so far. It's the only way a guy like "Mr. Crunchy" (mistercrunchy.com) — a blogger named Chris (not me!) who lives in the suburbs and is married to "She Who Must Be Obeyed" — can claim to share a part of the universe with someone like Andrew Sullivan, the former *New Republic* editor and widely published pundit (andrewsullivan.com). Incidentally, Sullivan also shares the same pocket of cyberspace as a dog named Howard (littlehoward.com).

That's right, Pets are prolific bloggers. Babies, too. It's part of the "ain't this cute?" component of blogging: A person's view of the world washes down better with kitsch, so the opinion is imparted by a furry thing or infant who's clearly incapable of such thought. As a new dad, I confess: I've created such a blog for my son, Aren (elliott.org/aren). In a rational world, only my immediate family would call up Aren's latest salient words and chuckle among themselves. But this is not a rational world. No less than new-media guru JD Lasica, a columnist for the *American Journalism Review,* called Aren's site "really cool" in his own blog (jd.manilasites.com). And a Brazilian journalism site called my son "globally notable" for his blog. All that at 3 weeks old!

This free-for-all presents us with a quandary: How do you sort the professionally produced blogs from amateur musings? Should there be some kind of blogging bar that certifies legitimate bloggers, or blogging police that banish bad bloggers? The Web's founder, Tim Berners-Lee, said he intended to create something representative of the entire world, in all its glory and chaos. Fair enough. No George F. Will-ian bow tie required. But maybe a few minimal standards should be met by those seeking accreditation from the, let's say, Weblogging Authority on Seriousness, Truth and Excellence (WASTE). Any participant would be "de-blogged" for the following slights:

- *Excessive use of "z"*   For example, "resourcez" instead of "resources."

- *Failing to post new information*   A stale blog is not a blog; it's a bad Web site. So get over the 2000 election already.

- *Sucking away valuable bandwidth*   No one minds a thumbnail shot of your kitty, Buffy the Blogger. But don't force us to wait five minutes for your high-resolution Web cam show to pop up!

MISTER CRUNCHY BLOG

Today, blogging welcomes all, from rookies to pros, about a half-million people so far. It's the only way a guy like Mr. Crunchy — a blogger named Chris (not me!) who lives in the suburbs and is married to She Who Must Be Obeyed — can claim to share part of the universe with someone like Andrew Sullivan, the former *New Republic* editor and widely published pundit. Incidentally, Sullivan also shares the same pocket of cyberspace as a dog named Howard.

— Christopher Elliott,
USA Weekend magazine, 12/27/02

Tuesday, December 31, 2002

The *USA Weekend* piece is probably proof that there's no such thing as bad publicity. Somehow, despite the fact that I'm lucky to even share the Internet with Andrew Sullivan, traffic to this site has risen nicely since the weekend. Not as much as Little Howard's, most likely, but nicely nonetheless. Thanks to Mr. Elliott for that. . . . if I pick up a few more folks who find our little site here entertaining, it's all good. Coupla things: first of all, I'm also allowed to be in the same airports as Mr. Sullivan, and possibly even train stations. I hope that doesn't affect his travel plans too badly. Second thing: I have no idea how Mr. Elliott found me. We've never corresponded, despite the fact that he felt comfortable publishing my wife's given name in a national periodical. If we had, he would know that she recently changed it to She Who MUST Be Obeyed. Careful, Mr. Elliott. You do not want to piss this woman off. Somebody should talk to the fact checkers at *USA Weekend.* Capitalization counts, campers. Third, I think the remarkable thing about the Internet is not that Little Howard and I are on it, seeing how it's basically free and available to anyone, but that the heavily credentialed Mr. Sullivan is on it, without a salary, and unable to charge for subscriptions. Granted, he just did a begging drive and raised something like $70,000 from his visitors, but still . . . it's just not quite the same level of security and comfort. Little Howard and I are in it for the love. Fourth, I am in awe of the transformative powers of the oven, which can take something that looks like someone hurled in a cake pan and turn it into swmbo's carrot cake, which is just one of the reasons that tonight is going to be a pleasure.
Happy New Year, everybody.

Mister Crunchy Web log, December 31, 2002. Found at <mistercrunchy.com>.

PICTURE PAGES

WEB SITES FOR PEOPLE WHO HATE TO READ
by David F. Gallagher

In the movie *Smoke,* Harvey Keitel's character takes a picture of his Brooklyn cigar store every morning, a routine he has followed for 11 years. The resulting albums, which he mostly keeps to himself, form a photographic record of small day-to-day differences over time. "It's just one little part of the world," he tells a friend, "but things happen there, too, just like everywhere else."

Harvey has lots of kindred souls on the Web. Across the Internet and around the world, people are working on similar never-ending photographic projects. They are making photologs, a kind of Web site that is a combination of photo gallery and visual diary. Photologs, also known as photoblogs, are similar in format to Weblogs, but they are built around regular photo updates instead of commentary and links. Unlike standard Weblogs, they have been largely ignored, perhaps because they make no claims to revolutionary status. But photologs are a powerful idea in their own right — they combine some of the best aspects of Weblogs, such as instantaneous self-publishing, with a big dose of visual stimuli. As the concept catches on and the tools for making photologs become easier to use, they might just become the standard format for presenting personal photos on the Web.

How is a photolog different from a plain old Web page? Many people who have digital cameras find themselves churning out a constant stream of images because it is fun, easy, and cheap to do. Photologs are built to handle that stream, with the newest photos right up front and older ones receding into the background. Traditional online photo galleries lack this chronological structure and can be harder to update. And like Weblogs, many photologs are updated every day, making individual photos less important than the regular flow of images.

Photologgers tend to take their cameras with them everywhere, and this pays off most often in New York City, arguably the photolog capital of the world. Many of the city's photologs carry on the tradition of street photography, chronicling small things noticed amid New York's constant visual flux. Quarlo.com, for example, documents lonely urban landscapes inhabited by shadowy figures. Todd Gross, the man behind Quarlo, is one of the few photologgers with the patience to shoot his pictures on film and then scan them. Sometimes he even adds soundtracks, but there are no captions. In a similarly minimalist New York vein are Rion.nu and Slower.net, which focus on the colors and textures of the city's streets.

David F. Gallagher, "Picture Pages." *Slate.com,* November 18, 2002.

Unlike Weblogs, photologs leap over language barriers, which is a helpful thing when global log-hopping. The Beijing teenager behind Ziboy.com doesn't put captions on his photos in any language, but the faces in his shots say plenty without them. Fotodiario is a simple site that offers enigmatic glimpses of one man's life in São Paulo, Brazil.

In contrast to these mostly wordless sites, there is plenty of writing on Hunkabutta.com, a photolog by a Canadian expatriate in Tokyo named Mike Clarke. He specializes in surreptitious portraits of city dwellers and explorations of Japanese cultural quirks in journal-style entries.

All of the sites mentioned here have a certain aesthetic self-consciousness about them, but there are plenty of less artsy photologs whose creators are not much interested in attracting a global following. College kids and parents, for example, use them as a place for friends and family to check out their latest doings or their newest baby photos. As is the case with Weblogs, most of these sites will be of interest to only a few people. They document a very small part of the world — but things happen there, too, just like everywhere else.

WHY ARE ONLINE PERSONALS SO HOT?

MAYBE IT'S THE LINGERIE MODELS TROLLING FOR DATES
by Rufus Griscom

Twenty years from now, the idea that someone looking for love won't look for it online will be silly, akin to skipping the card catalog to instead wander the stacks because "the right books are found only by accident." We will be charmed, but helpless to point out that the approach isn't very pragmatic. After all, how likely is it that the book of your dreams will just fall off the shelf and into your arms?

Most of us who have found our soul mates relied on the randomness of the bar scene or the party circuit or life in general. This serendipity is culturally important — we have a collective investment in the idea that love is a chance event, and often it is. But serendipity is the hallmark of inefficient markets, and the marketplace of love, like it or not, is becoming more efficient.

TODAY, ONE IN FIVE SINGLES LOOKS FOR LOVE ON THE WEB
It's happened before: Monster and HotJobs rationalized the labor markets; eBay streamlined the collector markets. Online personals — which fundamentally sell people access to one another — are just now generat-

---

Rufus Griscom, "Why Are Online Personals So Hot?" *Wired.com,* November 2002.

ing the kind of growth metrics witnessed at the height of the dotcom frenzy. Dating and mating will never be the same.

I stumbled upon the online dating phenomenon after cofounding *Nerve.com* — a literary magazine with a personals section that became, almost by accident, a happening singles scene. The service now doubles in size every five months; a million people have signed on in the past year and a half alone. And it's not just my company. According to Jupiter Media Metrix, between November 2001 and April 2002, the online personals market grew 29 percent to 18.6 million users — a whopping 20 percent of the singles population.

More interesting and perhaps more telling than the growth rate is who's driving it. The people signing up at *Nerve* are, by and large, young, overeducated professionals. Newly minted doctors, lawyers, journalists, and media executives are flocking to these systems, and recently we saw an ad from our first Victoria's Secret model (she actually wrote, "if you wear J.Crew, don't bother to contact me"). Whereas the short format of print lent itself to desperate, transactional relationships (DJM SEEKS BI-CURIOUS SWF), the endless space afforded online personals is perfect for the legions of smarties who cruise there. They can show off their fancy language skills and quickly cut through a broad pool with Boolean searches. After all, things are left to chance when people don't have the tools to find what they are looking for.

WOMEN PAY TO CONTACT MEN AS OFTEN AS THE REVERSE
But most fascinating are the new courtship patterns the medium is creating. Eighteen months ago, traffic in our system was strongest on weekdays, with daily peaks at lunch and between 5 and 6 P.M.; now it surges on Thursdays and Fridays, with hits climbing throughout the day to a first peak at around 5:30 P.M., followed by a second between 11 and midnight. What we are seeing is that browsing e-personals is becoming a social activity in itself. Furthermore, women pay to contact men as often as the reverse, which is quite different from behavior in, for example, telephone-based dating systems. It's more evidence that the virtual dating world (like the more traditional bar, nightclub, and party) is a social environment — and not just the means to an end.

In 20 years we'll look back fondly on this era as the gilded age of twenty-first-century dating, a computer-enabled love-letter renaissance. Alexander Graham Bell certainly meant the lovers no harm, but his invention has taken a toll on romance. By the same token, it's safe to assume that the federal government had no romantic agenda when it launched the Arpanet, the Internet's precursor. At this point in their short history, online personals are long on wit and charm, the breeding ground for a reinvigorated epistolary tradition. For now, the literate have the run of the place.

So get in there while you can, because early next year, our instant-messaging client will have video capability. Technology marches on, thank goodness. But live video is likely to make the online dynamic a little more like the offline one, with cheerleaders and jocks reascendant.

DIGITAL LAND GRAB
by Henry Jenkins

Between 1869 and 1930, some 200 writers imitated, revised or parodied Lewis Carroll's *Alice in Wonderland*. Some sent Carroll's plucky protagonist into other imaginary lands; others sent different protagonists to encounter the Mad Hatter or the Cheshire Cat. Some promoted conservative agendas, others advocated feminism or socialism. Among Carroll's imitators were literary figures such as Christina Rossetti, Frances Hodgson Burnett and E. Nesbit. Literary critic Carolyn Sigler argues that Alice parodies contributed considerably to Carroll's subsequent reputation. Today, after Shakespeare's work and the Bible, Lewis Carroll's writings are the most often cited in the English-speaking world.

Now try a thought experiment. Imagine that the Wonderland stories were first appearing in 2000 as products of Disney or Viacom, and Rossetti, Burnett and Nesbit were publishing their parodies on the Internet. How long would it be before they were shut down by "cease-and-desist" letters? How many people would download "A New Alice in the Old Wonderland" before a studio flack asserted Disney's exclusive control over Humpty Dumpty™, The Cheshire Cat™ or The Red Queen™?

Rossetti's descendants, now called "fans," borrow characters, situations and themes from pre-existing works (more often television series than novels) and use them as resources for their own stories. Sometimes, such stories offer ideological critiques. Other times, fans recenter the plots around secondary characters or simply provide back story. These modern-day "scribblers" are housewives, secretaries, librarians, students, average citizens; their parodies are labors of love, paying public tribute to popular narratives that capture their imagination.

These fans are also shock troops in a struggle that will define the digital age. On the one hand, the past several decades have seen the introduction of new media technologies (from the VCR to MP3) that empower consumers to archive, annotate, appropriate and recirculate cultural materials. On the other, the emergence of new economic and legal structures makes tight control over intellectual property the basis for the cross-media exploitation of "branded" materials. We can already see bloody skirmishes

Henry Jenkins, "Digital Land Grab." *Technology Review*, March/April 2000.

over intellectual property as these two trends collide. Not long ago, Fox's lawyers took down dozens of *Buffy the Vampire Slayer* fan sites, and nobody even blinked because such saber rattling has become a regular occurrence.

A year or so ago, J. Michael Straczynski, executive producer of the cult television series *Babylon 5,* was speaking to the students in my science fiction class at MIT. One student asked him what he thought about "fans," and after a pause, he replied, "You mean, copyright infringers." The remark was met with nervous laughter and mutual misunderstanding.

So far, most discussions of intellectual property in cyberspace are preoccupied with calming corporate anxieties about controlling the flow of images and information. Technologists have touted new automated enforcement mechanisms that allow owners to ferret out infringements, and digital watermarks for tracing the precise origins of appropriated images. Yet we rarely ask whether such tight regulation of intellectual property is in the public interest. Who speaks for the fans? No one.

That doesn't mean they don't have a case. Indeed, there's much to be said on the scribblers' behalf. Fan critics might be covered by the same "fair use" protections that enable journalists or academics to critically assess media content, or by recent Supreme Court decisions broadening the definition of parody to include sampling. Fans don't profit from their borrowings, and they clearly mark their sites as unofficial to avoid consumer confusion. Fan sites don't diminish market value, often actively organizing letter-writing campaigns to keep floundering programs on the networks.

Sadly, none of this matters. If you are a housewife in Nebraska and you receive a letter from Viacom's attorneys telling you to remove your Web site or they will take away your house and your kid's college fund, you don't think twice about your alternatives. You fold.

As a result, although cease-and-desist orders are routine corporate practice, not a single case involving fan fiction has ever reached the courts. No civil-liberties organization has stepped forward to offer pro bono representation. Presumably, the right to free expression doesn't extend to the right to participate in your culture. As currently understood, the First Amendment protects media producers, but not media consumers. Copyright and trademarks are legal "rights" granted to property owners, while fair use is a "defense" which can only be asserted and adjudicated in response to infringement charges. And most of the people being caught in these battles lack the financial resources to take on a major corporation in court.

Disney, Fox and Viacom understand what's at stake here. The proliferating media mergers attest to their recognition that media convergence transforms intellectual property into solid gold. Viacom calls a television series like *Star Trek* a franchise that can generate a seemingly infinite number of derivative products and revenue streams in many media channels. What they can't produce and market directly, they license to another company.

Preparing for this new era, media companies are expanding their legal control over intellectual property as far and as wide as possible, stripmining our culture in the process. They have made inventive uses of trademark law to secure exclusive rights to everything from Spock's pointy ears to Superman's cape, pushed policies that erode the remaining protections for fair use, and lobbied for an expansion of the duration of their copyright protection and thus prevented works from falling into the public domain until they've been drained of value. In the end, we all suffer a diminished right to quote and critique core cultural materials. Imagine what our holiday season would look like if Clement Moore had trademarked Santa Claus!

For most of human history, the storyteller was the inheritor and protector of a shared cultural tradition. Homer took plots, characters, stories, well known to his audiences, and retold them in particularly vivid terms; the basic building blocks of his craft (plots, epithets, metaphors) were passed from one generation to another. The great works of the western tradition were polished like stones in a brook as they were handed off from bard to bard. This process of circulation and retelling improved the fit between story and culture, making these stories central to the way a people thought of themselves. King Arthur, for example, first surfaces as a passing reference in early chronicles and only over the course of several centuries of elaboration becomes complex enough to serve as the basis for *Le Morte D'Arthur*.

Contemporary Web culture is the traditional folk process working at lightning speed on a global scale. The difference is that our core myths now belong to corporations, rather than the folk.

And that kind of exclusive ownership cuts directly against the grain of the technology in question. From the start, computers were seen as tools of collaboration, designed to facilitate brainstorming and data sharing. If one follows the flow of ideas on a Web forum for more than a few posts, it becomes harder and harder to separate one person's intellectual property from another's. We quote freely, incorporating the original message into our own. When Netizens discuss television, we quote equally freely, pulling chunks of aired material into our posts, and adding our own speculations. Other people respond, add more material, and pretty soon the series as viewed by list participants differs radically from the series as aired. In other words, webbers approach television content as "shareware."

Still, what one originates, the law insists, one should have the right to control and profit from. The legal fiction is that no one is harmed by this land grab on the cultural commons. Tight control over intellectual property isn't ultimately a question of author's rights, because without much discussion, control has shifted from individual artists to media corpora-tions — authors now have little say over what happens to their creations. The corporate attorneys rule.

If trademarks are used too broadly and without a history of legal enforcement, companies will lose exclusive claims to them — so Coca-Cola sends out spies to make sure nobody gets served a Pepsi when they order a Coke, Xerox insists that we call a photocopy a photocopy and Fox scans the Web to make sure nobody puts an *X-Files* logo on an unautho-rized homepage. Attacking media consumers damages relationships vital to the future of their cultural franchises, but corporations see little choice, since turning a blind eye could pave the way for competitors to exploit valuable properties.

Copyright law was originally understood as a balance between the need to provide incentives to authors and the need to ensure the speedy circulation and absorption of new ideas. Contemporary corporate cul-ture has fundamentally shifted that balance, placing all the muscle on one side of the equation. Media companies certainly have the right to profit from their financial investments, but what about the "investments" — emotional, spiritual, intellectual — we consumers have made in our own culture?

Through its "associates" program, the online book dealer Amazon.com encourages amateur critics to build book-oriented Web sites. If they link back to Amazon's homepage, they will get profit points from every sale made to consumers who follow that link. Amazon has discovered that revitalizing a grassroots book culture increases public demand for books. Perhaps media producers should follow Amazon's example and find ways to transform media consumers from "copyright infringers" into niche marketers, active collaborators in the production of value from cultural materials.

Intellectual property law didn't matter much as long as amateur cul-ture was transmitted through subterranean channels, under the corporate radar, but the Web brought it into view by providing a public arena for grassroots storytelling. Suddenly, fan fiction is perceived as a direct threat to the media conglomerates.

One can, of course, imagine that fans should create original works with no relationship to previously circulating materials, but that would contradict everything we know about human creativity and storytelling. In this new global culture, the most powerful materials will be those that command worldwide recognition, and for the foreseeable future, those materials will originate within the mass media.

For the past century, mass media have displaced traditional folk prac-tices and replaced them with licensed products. When we recount our fantasies, they often involve media celebrities or fictional characters. When we speak with our friends, sitcom catchphrases and advertising jingles roll off our tongues. If we are going to tell stories that reflect our cultural experiences, they will borrow heavily from the material the media companies so aggressively marketed to us. Let's face it — media culture is our culture and, as such, has become an important public resource, the reservoir out of which all future creativity will arise. Given this situation, shouldn't we be concerned about the corporations that keep "infringing" on our cultural wellspring?

TWO DILBERT CARTOONS BY SCOTT ADAMS

Understanding the Research Process

The previous chapters have emphasized the mutually reinforcing nature of the processes of reading and writing. Although it is common to think of writing as a more active process than reading, both are acts of *composing* — of constructing meaning through language. When we write, we read and revise our text as we put words to paper. When we read, we construct the ongoing meaning of the text as our eyes move from word to word. The writing and reading relationship is a powerful example of synergy in action, for together these two processes accomplish results that neither could attain alone. Think of how much your writing depends on your reading. Much of your knowledge of the world — and also your knowledge of the structures of written language — is gained by reading. Through writing, you express that knowledge and share it with others.

Writing and reading are primary means of learning both new ideas and new skills, which is why they play such a central role in the work of the academy. But what role does research play in the reading and writing process? When you first think about research, you may think immediately of searching for articles and books in the library or of surfing the World Wide Web. Both libraries and the Web are valuable sources of information about many subjects, but research is actually a much more common activity in all of our lives — one that is an integral part of the writing and reading that we do. You are conducting research, for instance, if you consult a current issue of *Consumer Reports* before purchasing a new DVD player. You are conducting research if you read *Bride* magazine to help plan your own or a friend's wedding. You are conducting research if you use the World Wide Web to locate the Web pages of the American Kayaking Association so that you can find out about kayaking opportunities in your area.

Both writing and reading can stimulate research. While writing an essay on cloning, for instance, you may realize that you don't understand this process as clearly as you thought you did, so you consult a print or online source to clarify your understanding. Reading can also create questions for which we seek answers. While reading *The English Patient,* a novel by Michael Ondaatje set in Italy during World War II, I realized that I did not have a clear understanding of the relationship between Italy and Germany at the end of the war. Germany and Italy were allies in the war, so why were the Germans setting mines on Italian soil? Because I enjoyed reading the novel and wanted to be sure that I understood it, I consulted an encyclopedia and several online sources about this subject.

As these examples indicate, research is rooted in curiosity. We all conduct research to make decisions, enrich our understanding, and become better informed about the world around us. Research, then, is a natural human activity — one that complements and reinforces the processes of reading and writing as well as those of observing and listening. As a student, you may need to learn certain research techniques, such as using library databases or evaluating sources on the Web, but you already understand many basic principles of research.

This chapter provides strategies that you can use to become an effective researcher. These strategies will be helpful whether you are spending an hour or so gathering information to enrich an essay or undertaking a more substantial research paper. In either case you need to know three things: the kind of information you need for your project, the most efficient and productive way to locate that information, and how to make the most effective use of the information you have located.

■ ■ ■

FOR EXPLORATION

Think back to your previous experiences conducting academic research. First identify an experience that you found both satisfying and productive. Freewrite or brainstorm several paragraphs about this experience. What made this research satisfying and productive? Now identify an experience that was frustrating, unproductive, or in other ways difficult. Freewrite or brainstorm several paragraphs about this experience. Now stop to reflect on these two experiences. Write one paragraph reflecting on what you have learned by thinking and writing about them. Based on these reflections, articulate two or three suggestions you would give yourself to make future research more satisfying and productive.

ASSESSING YOUR GOALS AS A RESEARCHER

Like writing and reading, research is a goal-driven activity. In some cases, your goals as a researcher may be limited. You may simply need to clarify or confirm information that you already have or to gather some supplementary information. Perhaps you are writing an essay about your father's experiences in the military during the Vietnam War or in China during the Cultural Revolution. In writing your essay, your focus is primarily on your father's experiences. But you may want to gather information that will enrich your essay's historical and political context. This is very different from a formal research paper, which might focus, for instance, on the ethics of using Agent Orange to defoliate trees during the Vietnam War. A project like this, which could be addressed only in a paper of considerable length, would require an extensive research effort.

Whether you are writing an informal essay about your father's early experiences or a more formal research paper, you need to know how to locate, evaluate, use, and document sources: The basic knowledge of research required is the same. But the *process* you follow will differ according to your research goals. For instance, you may consult just three or four sources for information that will enrich your essay on your father's experiences, so the process of documenting your sources — presenting bibliographic information in an appropriate format — will be relatively simple. For more formal research papers, you'll need to keep track of a wide variety of sources: You might consult twenty to thirty print and online sources and perhaps also engage in field research (such as interviewing). Given these different levels of research, perhaps the most important things to keep in mind when you conduct research are the question you want to answer (your goal as a writer) and the scope and nature of your project. The following guidelines present questions that you can use to assess your goals as a researcher.

■ GUIDELINES FOR ASSESSING YOUR GOALS AS A RESEARCHER

1. What role does research play in this writing project? Will your research provide supplementary details and examples? Or will your research inquire in depth into a subject and present the results of that inquiry to readers?

2. What questions drive your research? How focused are these questions? Are you still at a relatively exploratory stage where you need to do some general reading, Web surfing, and talking with others to help narrow and focus your topic? Or are you prepared to engage in in-depth research?

3. Does the nature of your topic require you to use certain research strategies or explore particular sources? Someone writing about the evolution of guitar styles from the southern and country

(continued)

(continued)

blues musicians of the 1920s and 1930s to the rock 'n' roll gui-
tarists of today would certainly have to consult early recordings
of this music, for instance.

4. What "process" implications does your research topic or question
hold for you? A student who wants to gather information
through field research as well as through print and online
research must build in time for this activity.

DEVELOPING AN APPROPRIATE SEARCH STRATEGY

Whether you are conducting research to fill in a few holes in your understanding of a subject or are beginning a substantial research project, you need to
develop an appropriate search strategy, one that will enable you to gather the
information that you need and to do so in a timely fashion. If you are writing a
substantial research paper, you will undoubtedly begin with a general topic
that interests you, but your research will be more efficient once you have
turned the topic into a goal-driven question. If you are investigating the
media's coverage of AIDS, you will proceed differently than if you are investigating the adequacy of AIDS services provided in your community. The nature
of your project influences not only how you conduct your inquiry but also
what kinds of sources you consult.

Electronic technologies have dramatically increased the available sources
of information. If you are writing an essay on the French artist Paul Cézanne
for an art history class, for instance, you can use a search engine such as Google
to locate the Web site of the Louvre Museum in Paris. With just a few more
clicks you can view — and even download and print — reproductions of
some of Cézanne's best-known paintings, as well as commentaries written by
art historians. Opportunities such as these give you access to information that
might not otherwise be available. But there can be such a thing as too much
information, particularly if you are not sure whether it is authoritative and relevant to your project.

To make appropriate decisions about how best to research your topic, you
need to understand the strengths and limitations of the resources available to
you. Subscribing to a listserv or consulting an Internet newsgroup on your
topic can provide you with a broad and stimulating array of contemporary
views; a carefully worded online query may identify additional resources. But
to gain an adequate historical perspective on legislation governing water quality you would also need to consult scholarly books and articles as well as gov-

ernment documents. In addition, you might want to interview several scientists and legislators who are experts in this area. (Interviewing and other forms of field research are discussed later in this chapter.)

Particularly in substantial research projects, you may find it helpful to develop a multipronged research strategy. You might begin your research by reading postings to an Internet newsgroup, consulting your library's catalog (whether in print or online), and surfing the Web looking for sites on your subject. But you would also want to consult more specialized sources, such as electronic databases or primary documents relevant to your topic. The following guidelines will enable you to develop an appropriate research strategy.

■ GUIDELINES FOR DEVELOPING AN APPROPRIATE RESEARCH STRATEGY

1. *If You Are Not Already Familiar with Your Library's Resources, Take the Time to Learn about Them.* Many campus libraries and computer services programs offer workshops and online tutorials designed to familiarize users with print and electronic resources. You also may want to consult the research chapters of such writing handbooks as *The St. Martin's Handbook.*

2. *Make Appropriate Use of Primary and Secondary Sources on Your Topic.* Scholars distinguish between primary sources (such as diaries, letters, data from experiments, and historical documents) and secondary sources (such as encyclopedias, scholarly books, biographies, and scientific experiments). Depending on your purpose, a source may be either primary or secondary. If as part of your research for an essay on the Arctic you read contemporary writer Barry Lopez's *Arctic Dreams: Imagination and Desire in a Northern Landscape,* Lopez's book would be considered a secondary source. If, however, you were writing an essay about Lopez's prose style or career as a writer, then *Arctic Dreams* would serve as a primary source.

   Different kinds of writing projects require different kinds of sources. If you are researching a specific person or event, for instance, you would undoubtedly want to consult such primary sources as newspapers or magazines. Later in this chapter you will read an essay by Brenda Shonkwiler on the collapse of the Tacoma Narrows Bridge. Brenda's essay is enlivened by her use of

(continued)

(continued)

contemporary newspaper accounts of the disaster. Brenda knew, however, that given her interest in discovering why the bridge collapsed, secondary sources would play the most important role in her research. Her essay nicely balances the immediacy and power of primary sources with the perspective and insight of secondary materials.

For primary sources, you can also check into any special collections that your school houses. This is what Christina Allen did when researching the paper on Linus Pauling that appears in Chapter 16.

3. *Learn the Ins and Outs of Effective Keyword Searching.* Keyword searches — whether on electronic databases or catalogs in your library or on the Web — can be an efficient way to locate sources. Choosing appropriately narrow topics or keywords and experimenting with synonyms or other alternative terms for your topic can help you develop a manageable and relevant list of resources. If you are interested in the French Revolution, in other words, you might also search for "Marie Antoinette," "Louis XIV," or "Maximilien Robespierre." Often, a series of focused keyword searches can produce more helpful results than a single search using a broader term.

Be sure to take advantage of any advanced searching options offered. (Often, this option is given on a separate page.) Some search engines and library catalogs also allow for Boolean searches. These let you refine the ways that you look for information. You can use the term "and" to narrow and "or" to broaden a search, for instance. Most search engines use both "and" and "or" and such symbols as "+" and "−" to allow you to conduct more powerful and focused searches. Here is an example of the difference such a strategy can make. A search on Google for the phrase "suspension bridge" identified 105,000 Web sites, or "hits." When I narrowed the search by requesting information on "suspension+bridge+Washington," the number of hits was reduced to 58,000. This is still a large and unwieldy number of Web sites. You may be able to locate helpful information as a result of such a search — but you may also want to further limit your search. A search on Google requesting sites with "suspension+bridge+Washington+Tacoma+Narrows" generated 1,050 hits. An addi-

(continued)

(continued)

tional search with the added descriptor "reconstruction" (suspension+bridge+Washington+Tacoma Narrows+reconstruction) identified 100 sites. Because different search engines employ different keyword search strategies, it is a good idea to review the information they provide on conducting effective searches.

4. *Consult with Librarians, Teachers, and Others Who Can Help You in Your Inquiry.* Most college and university libraries employ both general and specialized (or subject matter) reference librarians. I have heard many librarians state that they wished that more students consulted them about ongoing research. The librarian will be better able to help you, however, if you pose specific questions. If you ask how to get information on a particular endangered species, the librarian at the reference desk can do little more than to suggest that you consult the library catalog or other databases. If instead you inform the librarian that you are looking for recent congressional reports on a particular endangered species, you are likely to get a more focused and helpful response.

Remember, too, that your instructor can be a source of information not only about your assignment but also about possible research strategies to investigate it. And teachers in other areas, as well as persons working in business and industry, are potential resources. While researching her essay on the Tacoma Narrows Bridge disaster, for instance, Brenda Shonkwiler interviewed professors in civil engineering and physics.

Managing the Logistics of Research Projects

Logistical problems can torpedo an otherwise feasible project. When you're working on an extensive research project — a fifteen-page paper for your political science class, for example — it's good to take the following as your motto: Anything that can go wrong will go wrong. I don't say this to discourage you but to remind you of some of the factors that are outside of your control or that require careful planning. Issues of access can play a critical role in research. If your project requires considerable work with primary sources, such as newspapers, do you have the time necessary to obtain microfiched copies and work your way through them? You will probably need to set aside an hour or more — while the library is open — for each research session. For that matter, are you sure that microfiched copies of the newspapers you wish to consult are readily available through your college library? If they are not, you will want to inquire at the start of your project about your library's interlibrary loan policies and request those items that are most central to your project at the earliest possible moment. Some colleges participate in consortiums that guarantee easy and quick access to shared resources; others require considerable time for interlibrary loan requests to be processed.

There are additional logistical issues to keep in mind. Suppose that you are writing a paper on current college students' attitudes toward body piercing and you want to survey the opinions of students in your sociology class. For your survey results to have merit — to contribute to your overall inquiry — you would have to spend five to six weeks developing, testing, implementing, and interpreting your survey. If you have only two weeks, perhaps you should conduct informal interviews with several students. These interviews would not give you as much information as a formal survey would — but they could add specificity and liveliness to your discussion.

Even in less complex situations where you are relying primarily on sources in your library and on the Web and are not engaged in field research, the demands of major research projects can seem overwhelming. Library books, photocopies of articles, printouts of Web sites, and notes you have taken can quickly accumulate into a mass of material that seems more like a confusing maze than an entryway to knowledge. As these examples demonstrate, time management and organizational skills are essential for research to proceed effectively. The following guidelines provide strategies you can use to make your research an enjoyable and exciting — rather than a frustrating and difficult — process.

NOTE FOR MULTILINGUAL WRITERS

If much of your experience conducting research is in a language other than English, you may find that managing research projects in English is particularly demanding. For this reason, you may want to work closely with general reference librarians and also with librarians who specialize in your subject area. (Most university libraries have librarians who specialize in such areas as the humanities, social sciences, sciences, education, and so on.) You may also find it helpful to set up regular weekly meetings with a tutor in your writing center. At these meetings, you can review both your work in progress and your research timetable.

■ GUIDELINES FOR MANAGING THE LOGISTICS OF RESEARCH PROJECTS

1. *Establish a Timetable for Your Research — and Review It Periodically to See If It Is Realistic.* One of the best ways to keep track of the work you need to do is to list the activities that are essential to your project in the order in which they should be completed. Here's what a sample list might look like:

   ■ Analyze the assignment and assess research goals.

   ■ Choose a preliminary topic.

   ■ Develop a preliminary search strategy.

   ■ Conduct the research needed to narrow the topic.

   ■ Finalize the topic.

   ■ Finalize a search strategy.

   ■ Conduct print and Internet research; start a bibliography.

   ■ Develop an outline for the paper.

   ■ Do additional research, if necessary.

   ■ Draft the research paper.

   ■ Get a response to the draft.

   ■ Revise the draft; prepare a list of works cited.

   ■ Proofread the final draft.

   Set tentative dates for each of these activities. If you regularly review your list and dates, you'll have a good sense of when you need to extend or limit the amount of time for a particular activity.

2. *Use a Research Log to Track What You Have Accomplished and to Make Notes.* A research log supplements the timetable that the previous guideline encouraged you to establish. You can keep a handwritten research log. Some writers prefer, for instance, to purchase a small pocket-sized notebook for each research project. In this notebook, you can record daily entries for work accomplished, keywords you have used in successful searches, to-do

(continued)

(continued)

lists, ideas to follow up, and so on. You can also use your computer for this purpose. In this case, set up a folder that can hold the kind of information suggested above. You could even establish subfolders about specific tasks or subjects. You could title these subfolders with such headings as "keyword searches," "books consulted," "articles consulted," "working bibliography," and so on. Whether you keep a handwritten or electronic research log, the point is to bring order to what can otherwise be a chaotic process.

3. *Build a Working Bibliography as You Go to Avoid Scrambling to Document All Your Sources at the End of the Project.* Sure, it takes time to create a complete bibliographic entry for each source as you consult it, but you'll be glad you did when you reach the final stages of your research project. Nothing is more frustrating than searching through a floor littered with books, photocopies of articles, and printouts of Web pages — particularly when it's 3 A.M., and your paper is due at 8 A.M.

When consulting sources on the Web, you will find that some information published there (such as government documents) is permanently available but that much is temporary. A Web site that you search Monday afternoon may be substantially revised by Tuesday morning — and the page that you wish to cite may be deleted. If you locate information of interest to you on the Web, be sure to download, save, and print it and also to gather all the information you will need to cite this source in your bibliography.

In the past, most writers kept entries for their working bibliography on three-inch by five-inch cards. Some writers still use these cards because they like the physical ease of manipulating the cards — by topic or by alphabetical order. But increasingly writers are using computer programs to organize their sources. Whichever method you use, be sure to check to see which documentation style your assignment requires before you begin your working bibliography so that you can be sure to record all of the information that style requires. The Writers' References Section of this book (see pages 465–507) provides essential information for the Modern Language Association (MLA) and American Psychological Association (APA) documentation styles.

EVALUATING SOURCES

The scholarly work of the academy is like an ongoing conversation. Even an apparently "original" discovery depends on the previous work of others. This is true whether that discovery involves identifying the molecular structure of DNA or developing a new reading of Freud's psychological theories. When scholars publish their research, they do so not to have the final word on their subject but to invite responses; it is through such responses that knowledge in the academy progresses.

The same holds true for other forms of inquiry. Discussions of political, environmental, cultural, economic, and other issues occur in many forums: in the popular press, special-interest groups, government and nonprofit educational bodies, and so on. These discussions, like those within the academy, can best be viewed as ongoing dialogues that occur in particular times and places. Contemporary debates over smoking differ in many ways from those that occurred in previous decades, for instance. In the 1980s, few tobacco companies were willing to state publicly that tobacco has harmful health effects. Now both those who wish to regulate or even ban tobacco in its various forms and those who grow tobacco and make cigarettes and other related products acknowledge tobacco's dangerous properties.

As these examples suggest, the question of what it means for a particular source to be authoritative is both complex and situated in a particular time and place. Although a scientist who in 1978 published a scholarly essay on the potential side effects of tobacco might well have been considered authoritative by his peers at that time, his or her research would likely have limited value to today's scientists.

Evaluating Print Sources

As a student, you already have considerable experience in evaluating print sources. You instinctively draw on this experience when you decide that a brief article in a popular magazine is less authoritative than one that appears in an encyclopedia or scholarly journal. You know also that the credentials of the author of a text are important. But to fully evaluate a source, you need to consider more than the credentials of the author and means of publication. You need to gain a sense of the "history" of the conversation that you seek (via your research) to enter. The following guidelines for evaluating print sources will help you achieve this goal.

■ GUIDELINES FOR EVALUATING PRINT SOURCES

1. *Begin by Considering the Traditional Criteria for Evaluating Print Sources.* These criteria are reflected in the following questions:

   ■ Who is the author? Is she or he a recognized expert on the topic? Have other sources referred favorably to this author's work? What biases might the source have?

   ■ Who published this source, and what can the means of publication tell you about the work's authoritativeness? Is this article or book published by a scholarly press? By a general or "trade" publisher? By a special-interest group, business, or industry?

   ■ What speaks for the accuracy of the information contained in this source? The reputation of the writer? The prestige of the press publishing it? The source's scholarly apparatus, such as footnotes and works cited? Scholarly or popular reviews? Citations found in other sources? Your own knowledge of the material?

   ■ For whom has the author written, and in what medium is the writing? Is this a work intended for general readers or specialists? How appropriate is the author's medium of publication for his or her audience?

   ■ When was this source published? If it was not published within the past five years, is it still current? Or might you have special reasons for wanting to consult an earlier source?

2. *If Your Initial Evaluation Is Positive, Continue to Assess the Source by Exploring It More Thoroughly.* You can accomplish this by reading the preface, foreword, table of contents, and abstract, if provided. You may also want to skim the introduction and conclusion of articles or first and last chapters of books.

3. *To the Fullest Extent Possible, Consider the "History" of the Source That You Are Evaluating.* To do so, ask questions like these:

   ■ What seems to be "at stake" in the issue or topic you are researching? Does this issue raise questions of policy? Fact? Value?

(continued)

(continued)

- Do those writing on this topic seem motivated primarily by a desire to understand their subject better, or do they seem intent on persuading others to do or believe something? Are those engaged with this topic specialists or generalists — or both? To what extent has the popular press focused attention on this topic?

- Whom do those writing on this topic seem to be addressing — the general public? A specific audience? Multiple audiences?

- Is this a contemporary topic or one with a long history — or both?

- How did you first learn about this topic? In what ways might your own introduction to and understanding of the topic influence your evaluation of your sources?

4. *Use a Good Source's Footnotes and Works Cited to Follow a "Paper Trail" That Will Lead You to Other Relevant Sources.* Most researchers have experienced what is sometimes called the Eureka moment — the moment when they find an article or book that is a particularly rich resource for their project. Perhaps the author articulates the issues at stake in ways that you've been trying to express but haven't quite succeeded in doing. Perhaps the author discusses a body of research that you had not previously been aware of — but that you can immediately see is relevant to your topic. Whatever the particularities of your Eureka moment, be sure to take full advantage of your discovery by reading the references in the list of works cited and footnotes with care. They will lead you to many additional useful sources.

Evaluating Web Sources

Evaluating information on the Internet can be a challenge. As Janet E. Alexander and Marsha Ann Tate observe in their book *Web Wisdom: How to Evaluate and Create Information Quality on the Web,* "Since the Web is such a new medium, many standards, conventions, and regulations commonly found in traditional media are largely absent" (2). Most television viewers, for instance, can easily distinguish an infomercial for a new cooking appliance — one that the announcer claims will produce tasty food *and* lower blood pressure and cholesterol — from a serious, scientifically grounded documentary on healthy cooking. But on the Web such distinctions can become murkier. While some Web sites, such as that of the Library of Congress, are clearly authoritative, others are much harder to evaluate.

When I searched the Web using the keywords "cancer+treatment," for instance, the American Cancer Society site and the Cancer Group Institute site appeared. You probably recognize the name of the first Web site — the American Cancer Society (ACS) (see <http://www.cancer.org>, shown in Figure 4.1). As one of the Web pages linked to the "About the ACS" section of its homepage reminds readers, the ACS is one of the oldest health organizations in the United States. The ACS homepage (reproduced on p. 117) provides links to a wide variety of resources — information about various kinds of cancer and their treatments, cancer survivors' networks, medical updates and activities, news, and resources in particular areas.

The second Web site is maintained by an organization that identifies itself as the Cancer Group Institute (see <http://www.cancergroup.com>). When I looked at the homepage of this Web site, I saw links to a number of other potentially useful sites. At the top of the page, for instance, are links to the following resources — "Reviews," "Clinical Trials," "Books," "Alternative," "Bulletin Board," "Drs. Page," "Survivors Club," "Children's Club," "Products," and "Ask Us." Next to these categories (each of which is a hotlink) is this statement: "We bring you the latest, unbiased medical information you have been searching for. Many health sites just give you general, outdated information. Cancer Group has the answers to most of your questions. In an easy to read and understandable format. . . ."

Which of these two sites seems to be more reliable for someone looking on the Web for information and resources about cancer? Does one site offer more authoritative and credible information than the other? The American Cancer Society site has a number of reassuring advantages. As mentioned earlier, the ACS is one of the oldest health organizations in the United States. Long before the World Wide Web existed, the ACS had earned the respect of doctors, researchers, and patients. The ACS is also a nonprofit association, so it does not intend to profit from product sales by offering information on the Web.

I decided to begin evaluating the Cancer Group Institute (CGI) by determining whether it is a nonprofit or profit-making association. When I clicked on the link to the CGI's mission statement, for instance, I learned that CancerGroup.com, the online home of CGI, characterizes itself as "the premier online cancer resource center for cancer patients, their families, and caregivers." Given the number of online cancer sites, including the ACS site, I realized that I should not accept this assertion without finding supporting information. Indeed, this sort of claim, with its air of self-promotion, raised my suspicions about the site's credibility.

I decided to investigate the CGI's Web site, which is several screens long and somewhat difficult to navigate. As I surfed the site, I made some potentially reassuring discoveries. The homepage for CGI states, for instance, that

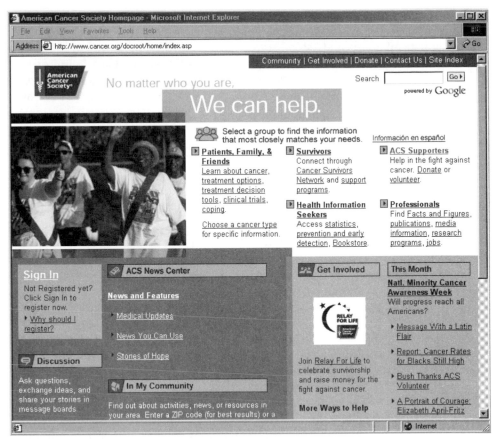

Figure 4.1   American Cancer Society Homepage.

teaching hospitals, such as those affiliated with Harvard, Yale, Columbia, and New York University, and other major medical centers use information provided by CGI. But it does not provide details about the nature of the information used or who has requested this information. The site also includes advertisements for "Connie's Beauty Products" and "Connie's Gift Ideas." My concerns about the CGI site were heightened when I clicked on a link that says "Physicians" and discovered the following introduction to pages titled "Physicians Reviews":

> Dear Drs.,
>   Exams are only round the corner. Do you want to pass them? Of course. Are you looking for current, easy to review reports that cuts out everything but the essential critical materials? We have been the secret weapon your colleagues don't want to tell you about.

I now understood that at least one major purpose of the CGI site is to sell exam review packets to medical students who are planning to take a state medical exam. I also understood something else — that the writing on the site is riddled with errors. I was willing to overlook the errors that I found early in my surfing of the site. (Did you notice that one of the site's links is missing an apostrophe? "Survivors Club" should be spelled "Survivors' Club." Moreover, the second sentence in this quotation from the Web site is a sentence fragment: "Cancer Group has the answers to most of your questions. In an easy to read and understandable format.") Since the "Dear Drs." letter quoted above also has a subject-verb error ("reports that cuts") and its link has a missing apostrophe ("Drs. Page"), it seems prudent to question whether site managers who are careless with grammar might also be careless with the information about cancer that they present.

This may be an overly harsh judgment: The CGI site may indeed sell exam review packets that provide accurate and helpful information for medical students who are preparing for board exams. After all, I have not compared the information about various cancers and their treatments that is presented on the CGI site with the information that is given by other authoritative sources, such as the ACS site and the U.S. National Institutes of Health. I do know enough to state that if I were researching a topic that was related to cancer, I would consider the ACS site to be considerably more authoritative and reliable than the CGI site.

Whether you are trying to learn more about potential treatments for a particular kind of cancer or about the problems that beset the steel industry in the United States in the 1970s and early 1980s, you can certainly find a plethora of materials on the Web. But as the previous example illustrates, you will have to evaluate these materials carefully before trusting their authority, objectivity, and accuracy. Many of the questions used to determine the authority of print materials can also be used to evaluate Web texts. But texts presented on the Web require some additional questions. Many Web sites, for instance, mix various kinds of pages.

In *Web Wisdom*, Alexander and Tate identify six different kinds of Web sites — advocacy, business, informational, news, personal, and entertainment — and they argue that each kind of Web site provides different challenges for those who wish to be critical readers and evaluators. Advocacy Web sites, for instance, seek to influence public opinion — to change people's minds and, possibly, encourage them to take action. The site for the Cancer Group Institute included both informational and business pages, which is why you cannot assume that information provided on a Web site's homepage is equally applicable to all pages on the site. This adds to the complexity of evaluating information presented on the Web. The following guidelines provide suggestions you can use to evaluate Web sites and Web pages.

■ GUIDELINES FOR EVALUATING WEB SITES
AND WEB PAGES

1. **Establish the Credibility of the Web Site or Page.** The first step in evaluating a Web site or page is to determine what person or organization stands behind the site — and thus takes responsibility for the authority and accuracy of the information presented therein. Sometimes this is easily determined. Even before I consulted the American Cancer Society's Web site, for instance, I knew that the ACS is a highly esteemed and well-established organization known for providing well researched, authoritative information. Had I not already known about the ACS, I could have arrived at the same conclusion by reading the "About the ACS" and "History and Mission" sections of the Web site, where the organization explains its history, mission, and procedures. In contrast, it was harder to determine the exact nature of the organization that stands behind the Cancer Group Institute.

In *Web Wisdom,* Alexander and Tate provide a series of questions that can be used to assess the authority of a site and also of a page on a site that contains mixed pages. Alexander and Tate point out that "the greater the number of 'yes' answers, the greater the likelihood that the quality of the information on the page can be determined" (54). The questions that Alexander and Tate list (pp. 55–57, excerpted here) are important for you to ask of any site you use as a source of information:

Authority of a Site

The answers to the following questions should be found either on a site's homepage or on a page directly linked to it.

- Is it clear what organization, company, or person is responsible for the contents of the site? This can be indicated by the use of a logo.

- If the site is a subsite of a larger organization, does the site provide the logo or name of the larger organization?

- Is there a way to contact the organization, company, or person responsible for the contents of the site? These contact points can be used to verify the legitimacy of the site. Although a phone number, mailing address, and email address

(continued)

(continued)

are all possible contact points, a mailing address and phone number provide a more reliable way of verifying legitimacy.

■ Are the qualifications of the organization, company, or person responsible for the contents of the site indicated?

■ If all the materials on the site are protected by a single copyright holder, is the name of the copyright holder given?

■ Does the site list any recommendations or ratings from outside sources?

Authority of a Page within a Site

■ Is it clear what organization, company, or person is responsible for the contents of the page? Similarity in page layout and design features can help signify responsibility.

■ If the material on the page is written by an individual author,

Is the author's name clearly indicated?

Are the author's qualifications for providing the information stated?

Is there a way of contacting the author? That is, does the person list a phone number, mailing address, and email address?

Is there a way of verifying the author's qualifications? That is, is there an indication of his or her expertise in the subject area, or a listing of memberships in professional organizations related to the topic?

■ If the material on the page is copyright protected, is the name of the copyright holder given?

■ Does the page have the official approval of the person, organization, or company responsible for the site?

2. **Evaluate the Quality of the Writing on the Site.** A Web site may be backed by an authoritative and well-established source, but if the quality of the writing is poor or the site is disorganized, the usefulness of the information it presents could be limited. Just as a print text should be free of grammatical, spelling, and other errors, so should a Web site. Web sites and pages should also provide sources for information they present — including information presented in graphs, charts, and tables.

(continued)

(continued)

3. **Determine the Ways in Which Individual, Corporate, or Organizational Biases Influence the Nature and Presentation of Information.** No Web site can be completely objective. In determining what treatments to discuss on its Web site, the American Cancer Society draws on carefully developed and clearly expressed assumptions about what does — and doesn't — count as valid scientific research. As a consequence, the site undoubtedly provides more information about treatments that have met established scientific protocols than about newer alternative treatments. Does this mean that the ACS site lacks credibility due to bias? No. The ACS takes care to describe and support its methodology, and it provides considerable support for its recommendations. Furthermore, the ACS has nothing to gain if those who visit the site are persuaded by the information it presents. The ACS is not selling this information or providing a profit-making service. It is a nonprofit organization.

The ACS constructed its Web site, in other words, solely for the purpose of providing helpful information for readers. Its interest is in education and not in promoting sales or services. While it would be a mistake to assume that any educational site automatically provides authoritative and accurate information, the fact that a site exists primarily to educate readers is important. In considering the objectivity of a Web site, then, be sure you understand why the site was constructed and what its goals are.

Does this mean that you should never consult a Web site that reflects a clear bias on a subject? That depends on the purpose of your research. If you are studying current debates on the regulation of tobacco, you may find it helpful to research a variety of position-oriented Web sites, from those of various tobacco company or industry organizations to those constructed by organizations that argue for tighter tobacco regulation. Doing so will help you examine how different parties in an issue represent information. In this case, your research will benefit from position-oriented information.

Whatever information you gather, you will always need to determine the ways in which individual, corporate, or organizational biases influence the nature and presentation of that information. You can use the following questions from *Web Wisdom* to evaluate the objectivity of any Web site or Web page:

(continued)

(continued)

Objectivity

- Is the point of view of the individual or organization responsible for providing the information evident?

- If there is an individual author of the material on the page, is it clear what relationship exists between the author and the person, company, or organization responsible for the site?

- Is the page free of advertising?

For pages that include advertising:

- Is a clear relationship drawn between the business, organization, or person responsible for the contents of the page and any advertisers represented on the page?

- If a page presents both advertising and information, are the two clearly differentiated?

- Is the site's policy relating to advertising and sponsorship explained?

For pages that have a nonprofit or corporate sponsor:

- Are the names of any nonprofit or corporate sponsors clearly listed?

- Are links included to the sites of any nonprofit or corporate sponsors so that a user may find more information about them?

- Is additional information provided about the nature of the sponsorship, such as whether it is nonrestrictive, educational, and so on?

4. **Be Sure to Check the Timeliness of the Information Presented on a Web Site.** One benefit of conducting research on the Web is that many sites offer up-to-date information. You can't assume, however, that a site that focuses on a timely topic, such as Palestinian-Israeli relations or the status of gun control legislation, is presenting current information. If a Webmaster temporarily or permanently stops maintaining a site, it can quickly become dated. For this reason, you should not assume that some-

(continued)

(continued)

thing found on the Web is up-to-date. When evaluating a Web source, think about whether the timeliness of the information is important for the topic you are researching. If it is, then ask the following questions from *Web Wisdom* to establish when the site that you are using was written and how recently it has been updated:

Currency

- Does the site show the date that the material was first created in any format?

- Does the site show the date that the material was first placed on this particular server?

- If the contents of the site have been revised, does the site show the date (and time, if appropriate) that the material was last revised?

5. **Consider the Information Presented on a Site in the Context of Its Intended Audience, Goals, and Purpose.** What should you do if you locate a Web site that contains technical information that is difficult for you to understand? If you apply Guideline 2 above (p. 120) for evaluating Web site writing, you might determine that the site is unhelpful since it lacks clarity. This could be a mistake. Readers with expertise in the subject area may find that a site with technical vocabulary is useful and informative. Moreover, the quality of the site's information may justify your efforts to understand it. Many Web sites designed for experts include pages with information for those with less knowledge. If you dismiss a site quickly because it appears too technical or complicated, you could miss out on a valuable source of information.

   The focus in this section of Chapter 4 is on providing basic information about evaluating Web sites. If you would like further information about Alexander and Tate's criteria for particular kinds of sites, you may wish to consult *Web Wisdom* or the Web site <http://www2.widener.edu/Wolfgram-Memorial-Library/webevaluation/webeval.htm>.

FOR EXPLORATION

Choose an interesting word or phrase, and use one or more search engines to search the Web. After reviewing the results of your search, choose two sites that interest you. Using the questions provided by Alexander and Tate, evaluate these sites. Write a paragraph or two for each site summarizing the results of your analysis.

USING SOURCES: QUOTING, PARAPHRASING, AND SUMMARIZING

Earlier in this chapter I said that the scholarly work of the academy is like an ongoing conversation. One writer argues that global warming may be influencing recent climate changes. Others respond to this argument — testing, elaborating, clarifying, questioning. Soon the issues at stake — the questions with which those addressing this subject are concerned — have evolved. The question of whether global warming is occurring becomes less controversial as evidence accumulates for its existence. In the meantime, other questions become more pressing. How concerned should scientists and the general public be about global warming? Can they do anything about it if, in fact, it is occurring?

As a student engaged in research, you are entering the scholarly (and, depending on your topic, also civic and popular) conversation on your subject. You probably can't participate in this conversation as an expert, but you can still "converse" with those whose words you are reading. Indeed, your instructors are not only interested in your ability to identify and locate information on your topic; they are also looking at how you make use of that information.

As this chapter has already emphasized, when you conduct research, you have (at least) two purposes. You want to learn something new about your subject by gathering information that helps you understand it. But you also want to understand the history of your subject — by learning what is accepted, what is not, who the experts are, what issues and questions they think are important, and whether you agree with them. The way that you use sources — the way that you integrate sources into your writing — tells readers whether you have accomplished these purposes.

As a writer, you have three options for integrating sources into your writing. You can quote your source's words exactly. You can paraphrase your source's words (by digesting the meaning stated in the source and representing it in your own language). And, finally, you can summarize the information presented in your source (by significantly abbreviating a text, whether a paragraph, a chapter, or even an entire book). How can you determine when to quote, paraphrase, and summarize? The following guidelines suggest criteria you can use to answer this question.

■ GUIDELINES FOR DETERMINING WHEN TO
QUOTE, PARAPHRASE, AND SUMMARIZE

1. *Quote Directly from Sources Only When You Have a Specific Purpose for Doing So.* Perhaps the language used in the source is so powerful — so pointed and memorable — that it expresses in a few words what you would take many words to express. Perhaps the author of the source is an authority whose expertise buttresses your own position. Perhaps you disagree with the source and want to play fair with it by allowing the author to speak in his or her own words. These are good reasons for including direct quotations in your writing.

2. *Paraphrase When You Want to Convey the Information in a Passage but Prefer to Represent the Ideas in Your Own Words.* When you paraphrase, you stay close to the meaning expressed in the original text, but you recast that language in your own words. You may paraphrase a source, for instance, because the author's words are not particularly memorable or because you do not want to interrupt your discussion with a direct quotation. Paraphrasing may strike you as the most efficient way to convey important information. Whatever your reason, when you paraphrase, it is important that you synthesize the original passage, present it in your own words, and acknowledge the source.

3. *Summarize When You Want to Present the Main Idea of a Text in Your Own Words.* Summaries are useful in many situations. You might be considering two book-length opposing arguments on a topic. If your purpose is to provide a context and not to discuss the arguments in great detail, a brief summary of each argument fulfills your purpose. When you summarize, you want to present the main points of the original text as succinctly as possible.

You may understand why you are quoting, paraphrasing, or summarizing a passage — and yet be unsure about how you should do so. When is a paraphrase just a paraphrase — and not plagiarism, or the inappropriate use of the words and ideas of another? What is the difference between paraphrasing and summarizing? My own use of Janet E. Alexander's and Marsha Ann Tate's *Web Wisdom: How to Evaluate and Create Information Quality on the Web* offers some examples. In discussing how to evaluate Web sources (pp. 115–23), I drew on Alexander's and Tate's work, for I recognized that their knowledge of and experience with evaluating Web sources was much greater than my own. When did I quote directly, paraphrase, and summarize? What logic guided these decisions?

If you look back at the "Evaluating Web Sources" section of this chapter, you will see that I quoted directly from Alexander and Tate for two general reasons. The first was when I felt that their words were more cogent or memorable than my own might be. This happened, for instance, when I quoted their statement that "since the Web is such a new medium, many standards, conventions, and regulations commonly found in traditional media are largely absent" (2). Here Alexander and Tate succinctly and memorably articulate an important point about the Web. I also quoted them directly when I included their questions for evaluating Web sites. I quoted their questions, rather than paraphrasing them, because I felt that the specific wording that they used was essential to their meaning.

On other occasions I paraphrased Alexander and Tate's wording. On page 58 of *Web Wisdom,* for instance, Alexander and Tate define *advocacy Web pages* as follows: "An advocacy Web page is one with the primary purpose of influencing public opinion. The purpose may be either to influence people's ideas or to encourage activism, and either a single individual or group of people may be responsible for the page." My paraphrase, which appears on p. 118 of this chapter, paraphrases their definition by stating that advocacy Web sites "seek to influence public opinion — to change people's minds and, possibly, encourage them to take action." This paraphrase remains true to the meaning expressed in Alexander and Tate's definition. (Because my purpose was to provide a broad characterization of advocacy sites, I didn't need to mention that advocacy Web sites can be sponsored by either individuals or groups.)

And I also summarized ideas presented at great length in *Web Wisdom.* In Alexander and Tate's book, for instance, the six kinds of Web sites are discussed in six separate chapters. I wanted readers to be aware of these distinctions among Web sites, but I could not go into similar detail. So on p. 118 of this chapter I simply note that the authors of *Web Wisdom* "identify six different kinds of Web sites — advocacy, business, informational, news, personal, and entertainment."

What other general information do you need to know about using sources? You should recognize that most often sources need to be introduced or contextualized. If you are writing an essay on the history of the concept of the aesthetic for a philosophy class, for instance, and want to include a quotation from Terry Eagleton's *The Ideology of the Aesthetic,* you might introduce this quotation as follows: "As British literary theorist Terry Eagleton observes, ..." It is also important to comment on the significance of quotations. Let's imagine that you want to quote Eagleton's observation that the body is "the enormous blindspot of all traditional philosophy" (234). You might follow this quotation with a sentence such as the following: "In calling attention to traditional philosophy's 'blindspot,' Eagleton challenges readers to place the work of such philosophers as Nietzsche at the center, rather than at the margins, of philosophy" (234). Comments like this demonstrate that you understand the implications of Eagleton's observation and can use it to develop your own analysis.

UNDERSTANDING AND AVOIDING PLAGIARISM

Plagiarism is, quite simply, the intentional or unintentional use of others' words or ideas as if they were your own. Whether you are a student, a scientist, an historian, or a politician, charges of plagiarism can have serious consequences. At some colleges, students who plagiarize fail not only the assignment but also the course; at colleges that have honor codes, students may even be expelled for plagiarism. Recently, two eminent historians — Stephen Ambrose and Doris Kearns Goodwin — acknowledged and apologized for plagiarism in their writing. Their professional credibility has been tarnished as a result of these admissions.

Some cases of plagiarism are intentional, such as when a student submits an essay written by a friend as his own, purchases a research paper from an online company, or copies a passage directly from source material without

---

NOTE FOR MULTILINGUAL WRITERS

The concept of plagiarism is central to the modern Western intellectual tradition. It rests on the notion of intellectual property — the belief that language can be "owned" by writers who create unique and original ideas. This concept was not always part of Western culture. It would have been foreign to both Chaucer and Shakespeare, for instance. Many forces — from the birth of the printing press to the development of capitalism and of modern notions of subjectivity — encouraged the formation of the concepts of intellectual property and of copyright in Western culture. But what seems obvious and commonsensical to many in the West sometimes looks quite different to those from other cultures. Indeed, in some countries, students are taught to use the words of others without attribution. Doing so is considered a sign of respect for one's cultural tradition. Moreover, writers in some countries assume that readers will recognize the words from other writers that are interwoven with the writers' own words. As a student in an American college, you need to follow Western documentation practices. They reflect Western understandings of subjectivity, language, and ownership.

providing attribution. These cases are rare, however. More often, plagiarism is unintentional and is the result of either sloppy note taking or lack of knowledge about the conventions of documentation. (Ambrose and Kearns Goodwin, for instance, cited problems with their note taking and that of their research assistants as the cause of their plagiarism.) You can avoid plagiarism if you understand the kinds of material that do and do not require documentation, you take systematic and accurate notes, and you give full credit to those whose words and ideas you use. The following guidelines provide suggestions that will help you to understand and avoid plagiarism.

■ GUIDELINES FOR UNDERSTANDING AND AVOIDING PLAGIARISM

1. *Be a Purposeful Note Taker.* The previous section of this chapter provided guidelines for determining when to quote, paraphrase, and summarize sources. You cannot follow these guidelines, however, unless you first take accurate and thorough notes. Your notes need to include sources and page numbers for all quotations, paraphrases, summaries, statistics, and graphics.

2. Whenever you quote directly from a source, be sure to use quotation marks. When you're in the midst of note taking, you may think that you'll remember which notes are and aren't direct quotes — but you probably won't. Similarly, if you write a close paraphrase of a passage, you should indicate that this paraphrase needs to be cited and is not a general note or summary. (When I paraphrase, for instance, I write "paraphrase: cite source" along with the page number in the margin.)

3. If you are copying a long passage and decide that several sentences are not relevant, you need to indicate that you have removed the sentences by including an ellipsis (three dots with a space between each dot). You also need to indicate any changed or added words to a quotation by enclosing them in square brackets.

4. If the passage that you are copying includes any quotations within it, be sure to note the quotations' source.

5. Keep a working bibliography either on your computer or in a notebook.

(continued)

(continued)

By following these suggestions, you will be able to understand what plagiarism is and avoid it. Even so, you may still encounter a problem from time to time. Sometimes you may wonder whether to give credit to an author. Have you written a passage that is so similar to its source that the author should be cited, or have you added enough of your own words and ideas that you do not need to cite the original author? What counts as common knowledge (and therefore does not need to be given a source) when you are writing a paper on recent studies on the decline of the stock market or the rings of Saturn? All writers find themselves facing dilemmas like these from time to time. If you find yourself wondering what to do, ask your teacher or a tutor in your writing center. When you do not have time to consult a teacher or a tutor, include a citation.

In thinking about how best to use sources, you might find it helpful to return to thinking about research as a conversation. A research-based essay is not a loosely related collection of quotations, paraphrases, and summaries from everyone who has written on your subject. Rather, your goal is to converse with other writers by analyzing and responding to their ideas. Sometimes you will hold the floor — for instance, when you advance your own arguments and analysis about your topic. At other times, the writers whose work you have read will lead the conversation, and you will reflect on their words and ideas. In so doing, you converse with others who have thought and written about your subject.

CONDUCTING FIELD RESEARCH

Thus far, this chapter has focused on locating, evaluating, and using print and online resources. But there are many additional ways to enrich your writing and research. You can find information through interviews, questionnaires, and firsthand observation.

If you are writing an essay on sexual harassment on college campuses, for instance, you will probably find it helpful to do some library research to get a broad perspective on the issue — national trends, the history of the present controversy, incidents on campuses other than your own, and so forth. But it might be especially helpful to interview an adviser or faculty member who is involved in setting or enforcing your own school's policy on the issue, as well as individuals who have publicly opposed that policy. You might distribute a questionnaire to other students designed to measure their opinions on the issue (asking, for instance, how they define sexual harassment; how prevalent they feel it is at your school; what, if any, policy they would like to see enforced; and so on). You might want to spend some hours closely observing the behavior of male and female students in a social setting. Even if these sources of information do not play a major role in your essay, they will enrich your understanding of your subject and help you to consider it from a variety of perspectives.

There are other advantages to this form of research, sometimes known as *field research* because it takes you out of the library or computer lab and puts you directly in the field. Many students find that field research helps them build enthusiasm for and commitment to their subject. Field research allows you to do original work — in effect, to *create* new information that no one before you has compiled in quite the same way.

This is not to say that traditional research is unnecessary. Even professional field researchers are careful to keep up with the work of other scholars, to compare their own findings with others', and to place themselves within the ongoing scholarly conversation. Effective mastery of library and Web research skills gives you access to the broadest, most comprehensive perspective on any topic. But depending on the topic you've chosen and the questions you are asking about it, field research can help you arrive at a fascinatingly detailed and particular *local* perspective on a subject.

Interviews

Interviews can often provide information that is unavailable through other kinds of research. Sometimes you may wish to consult an expert on the subject you are studying; on other occasions you may interview individuals to gain local perspectives on your issue, firsthand accounts of relevant experiences, or other information. A good interviewer is first of all a good listener — someone who is able to draw out the person being interviewed. Interviews are more formal and time-pressured than most conversations, so be sure that you do not underestimate the importance of carefully preparing for and conducting them. Here are some suggestions to follow when you interview someone for your writing.

■ GUIDELINES FOR CONDUCTING INTERVIEWS

1. Request an interview in advance. Explain why you want the interview, how long it will take, and what you hope to accomplish.

(continued)

(continued)

2. Come prepared with a list of written questions.

3. If you wish to tape the interview, remember to ask permission first.

4. Take notes during the interview, even if you use a tape recorder. Your notes will help refresh your memory later when you don't have time to review the entire tape; they can also help you identify the most important points of discussion.

5. Be flexible. Don't try to make the person you are interviewing answer all your prepared questions if he or she doesn't find some of them appropriate or interesting. If your interviewee focuses on one question or moves to a related issue, just accept this change in plans and return to your list of questions when appropriate.

6. Try a variety of questioning techniques. People are sometimes unable or unwilling to answer direct questions. Suppose that you want to write about your grandmother's experiences during World War II. If you simply ask her what life was like then, she may not respond very fully or specifically. Less direct questions may elicit more detailed answers.

Questionnaires

Distributing a questionnaire can be a good way to gain information about the attitudes, beliefs, and experiences of a large number of people. You might, for instance, question your fellow students on their career plans, their reading habits, or their opinions on your school's policy on hate speech.

A detailed discussion of the design and interpretation of questionnaires is beyond this book's scope. In some disciplines that deal extensively in questionnaire and poll data, such as sociology and political science, these matters are addressed in depth. For an English class, it may be best to use questionnaires as a rough indicator of broad trends and a source of differing perspectives on a topic rather than as a "scientific" measurement of the general population's views. Here are some guidelines for designing and using questionnaires. The suggestions assume that you have decided on a topic, determined an appropriate number of representative respondents, devised a way to distribute your questionnaires, and arranged to collect them when completed.

■ GUIDELINES FOR DESIGNING AND USING QUESTIONNAIRES

1. Treat the drafting of your questionnaire as you would any important writing project. In other words, keep your audience in mind, and be prepared to do more than one draft to make sure your questions are clear, easily answerable, and likely to solicit the information you seek.

2. Keep in mind that the longer and more difficult a questionnaire is, the fewer completed questionnaires you are likely to have returned. Yes-or-no and multiple-choice questions are the easiest to answer but restrict your respondent's freedom to give complex answers. Open-ended questions yield more nuanced answers but ask more work of your respondent and hence are best kept to a minimum.

3. Show a draft of your questionnaire to some friends before copying and distributing it. Seek feedback on the clarity and "user friendliness" of your questionnaire.

4. Include all appropriate demographic questions in addition to questions about your primary subject. Unless your respondents' names are vital, make clear that they have the option of remaining anonymous. You may want to ask for other personal characteristics, such as sex, income, marital status, age, or education, depending on the questions governing your research. If you are asking about attitudes toward sexual harassment, for instance, you may well want to be able to note differences between the answers given by men and women of various ages. Or if you are gathering opinions about the homeless, your respondents' income levels may be relevant.

5. You should write an explanation on the questionnaire of its purpose and the use you have in mind for it, and ask respondents to check off *yes* or *no* to indicate whether you have permission to quote them.

6. Distribute more copies than you need to have returned. The return rate will be well below 100 percent.

Unless you administer your questionnaire under tightly controlled conditions, you will not generate scientifically verifiable data. Still, there are good reasons for using questionnaires. Responses to questionnaires can prompt you to consider multiple perspectives on an issue; they can also provide illustrative examples and voices to bring into your essay. If, for example, in the course of an essay arguing for more child-care facilities on campus, you quote directly from statements made by single parents who are full-time students, your questionnaire will have contributed a good deal to your essay's persuasiveness.

Observation

Finally, don't overlook the kinds of information available by firsthand observation. Disciplines such as sociology and anthropology have long and rich traditions of case-study research in which "participant-observers" living in and moving among various communities attempt to observe and interpret social customs and patterns of behavior. Scholars using this methodology have gathered research data in twelve-step groups, day-care centers, crack houses, and corporate boardrooms.

Although you will probably not undertake full-scale case-study research, you can generate stimulating questions and gather interesting material for your writing assignments through close observation of various communities. If you are writing a paper on the effectiveness of your college or university's student government, you might interview members of that government (and those who have criticized it) and observe a variety of meetings — from the student senate to various subcommittees and working groups. You may already participate in activities that could contribute to your understanding of an issue. If you work as a restaurant waitperson, you might study the tipping practices of men and women to gain insight into gender differences and their social implications. As with other forms of field research, observation can enrich your understanding by generating questions and exposing you to multiple perspectives on a subject.

USING APPROPRIATE STYLES OF DOCUMENTATION

You may be surprised to learn that different disciplines use different documentation styles. Why can't all areas of scholarly work use the same style of documentation? The answer has to do with some of the assumptions and practices of the people who work in various disciplines. In the social sciences, for instance, scholars particularly value current scholarly work. The documentation style most widely used in the social sciences, APA (American Psychological Association) style, emphasizes a work's publication date by placing it immediately after the name of the author. In the humanities, where a Platonic dialogue may be as relevant today as it was in fifth-century B.C. Greece, publication dates are important but not as key as they are in the social sciences. As a consequence, publication dates appear at the end of citations in MLA (Modern Language Association) style.

MLA style and APA style are two of the most frequently required documentation styles for undergraduates. These styles specify the information that needs to be included in a reference and the format that needs to be followed for presenting that information. See the Documentation Guidelines at the back of this book for examples and explanations. MLA guidelines begin on p. 467 and APA guidelines begin on p. 486.

MLA and APA are not the only documentation styles used in the academy. Some disciplines in the humanities use the guidelines presented in the *Chicago Manual of Style* rather than MLA style. The Council of Science Editors, formerly known as the Council of Biology Editors (CBE), has created a documentation style for mathematics and the physical sciences. Additional documentation styles are used by scholars in various disciplines. You should never assume that an instructor will require a particular documentation style. If an instructor does not specify MLA, APA, Chicago, CBE, or some other style, be sure to ask him or her what style you should use.

SAMPLE RESEARCH ESSAY USING MLA DOCUMENTATION STYLE

Here is an essay by Brenda Shonkwiler, who is a preengineering student at Oregon State University. As a student in Carole Ann Crateau's first-year writing class, Brenda was asked to write a research-based essay on a subject of interest to her. Brenda chose to write about the 1940 collapse of the Tacoma Narrows Bridge. As a preengineering student, she was interested in learning more about the causes of the collapse and the steps that were taken to ensure that such a disaster would not recur.

Because her instructor requested it, Brenda created a title page (see p. 135). Title pages are not required by the MLA. Note also that, to annotate this essay, we have reproduced it in a narrower format than you will have on a standard (8½" × 11" sheet) of paper.

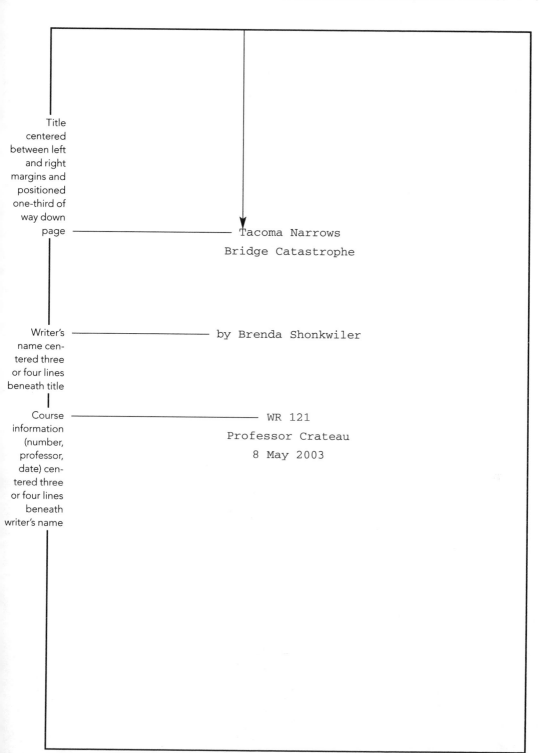

Title centered between left and right margins and positioned one-third of way down page ——————————— Tacoma Narrows
Bridge Catastrophe

Writer's name centered three or four lines beneath title ——————————— by Brenda Shonkwiler

Course information (number, professor, date) centered three or four lines beneath writer's name ——————————— WR 121
Professor Crateau
8 May 2003

½"

1"

Shonkwiler 1

Heading centered and positioned one inch from top edge of paper; announces topic

Writer's last name, followed by a space and the page number, in upper right corner, positioned one-half inch from top edge of paper

Tacoma Narrows Bridge Catastrophe

Millions of people cross bridges every day. Few
stop to worry that the bridge below them may collapse. On November 7, 1940, when the Tacoma Narrows
Bridge collapsed, three people and a dog were caught
on the bridge. Leonard Coatsworth, a Tacoma News
Tribune reporter who was on the bridge at the time
of collapse, tells his story:

Block quotation

Either just as I reached the towers or just as
I drove past them, the bridge began to sway
violently from side to side. This was something
new in my experience with the bridge. Hereto-
fore, the noticeable motion had been up and
down and undulating.

Before I realized it, the tilt from side
to side became so violent I lost control of the
car. [I] thought for a moment it would leap the
high curb and plunge across the sidewalk of
the bridge and into the railing.

I jammed on the brakes and got out of the
car, only to be thrown . . . again. Around me I
could hear the concrete cracking.

I started back to the car to get the dog,
but was thrown before I could reach it. The car
itself began to slide from side to side of the
roadway. I decided the bridge was breaking up
and my only hope was to get back to the shore.

On hands and knees most of the time, I
crawled 500 yards or more to the towers. Across
the roadway from me I became aware of another
man, alternately crawling and then running a
few steps in a crouched position.

My breath was coming in gasps, my knees

Shonkwiler   2

were raw and bleeding, my hands bruised and
swollen from gripping the concrete curb. But I
was spurred by the thought that if I could
reach the towers I would be safe. . . . Safely
back at the toll plaza, I saw the bridge in its
final collapse and saw my car plunge into the

Parenthetical citation ——— narrows. (Coatsworth 3)

This was a disastrous event that raised many ques-
tions. What factors led to this failure, and how ——— *These questions give readers a clear sense of the major issues that Brenda's essay will address*
could similar failures be prevented?

First-level subhead ——— Cause of Failure

The Tacoma Narrows Bridge was built to span
Puget Sound. It was the only fixed roadway connecting the Washington mainland and the Olympic Peninsula. At the time of construction, the bridge was
viewed as "the epitome of artistry in bridge construction" ("Tacoma Narrows"). However, the bridge
soon earned the nickname "Galloping Gertie" because
of its undulating motion. According to a Web site
sponsored by Underwater Atmospheric Systems, Inc.,
"thousands of people drove hundreds of miles to
experience the sensation of crossing the rolling
center span" of the bridge ("Galloping Gertie").
Despite the obvious oscillations of the bridge's
roadbed, bridge officials had confidence in the
structure. However, only four months after completion, the bridge collapsed during a windstorm. Wind-
induced vibrations made the oscillating and twisting
motions too extreme for the structure to withstand.
(See Figs. 1 through 3.) ——————————— *Parenthetical reference directs readers to figures*

Second-level subhead ——— Not Designed for Wind. At the time Galloping
Gertie was built, little was known about the effects
wind had on structures such as bridges. Thus, the

Shonkwiler   3

Fig. 1. <u>The Tacoma Narrows Bridge twisting</u>, 7 Nov. 1940, Tacoma Narrows Bridge Collection. Twisting just before failure.

Figure is positioned as soon as practical after paren-thetical reference

Credit line for image from Web source

bridge was designed without regard to vertical and torsional (twisting) motions caused by wind. Design-ers focused on stiffness under the traffic load and overlooked the role of stiffness in suppressing oscillations of bridges in wind (Koughan).

James Koughan notes that the bridge's flexibil-ity was its "fundamental weakness." Several factors led to this flexibility, including the bridge's nar-row deck, shallow solid girders, and thin support cables that were spaced far apart. According to Koughan, the decision to make the bridge narrow was "based on economic factors and transportation stud-ies," but it also left the bridge vulnerable to twisting.

Shonkwiler   4

Fig. 2. <u>Film still of the Tacoma Narrows Bridge twisting</u>, 7 Nov. 1940, Tacoma Narrows Collection. Twisting just before failure.

Suspension bridges, in general, are more flexible than other types of bridges. To decrease the flexibility, suspension bridges are typically stabilized with stiffening trusses. Such stiffening trusses are frameworks consisting of many interconnected braces that allow wind to flow through them with relatively little resistance, while diminishing (dampening) vertical and torsional motions. The Tacoma Narrows Bridge had been stiffened with solid girders (horizontal beams) instead of trusses. (See Fig. 4.) Koughan says that the girders "were unusually shallow, only [eight feet] deep, in comparison

Fig. 3. <u>Bridge midsection crashing into the waters of the</u> <u>Tacoma Narrows</u>, 7 Nov. 1940, Tacoma Narrows Bridge Collection. 600-foot section falling.

with their length," resulting in a depth-to-span ratio "over twice that of the Golden Gate Bridge" and making it "by far the most flexible design of its time."

Because the girders were solid, they did not allow wind to pass through them. This resulted in higher wind resistance than would be found in bridges with open stiffening trusses. Charles E. Andrew, chief engineer in charge of constructing the Tacoma Narrows Bridge, stated that in his opinion the collapse was due to the solid stiffening girders: "These caused the bridge to flutter, more or less as a leaf does in the wind. That set up a vibration that built up until the failure occurred.

Clear and helpful identification of the credentials of the person being quoted

Shonkwiler 6

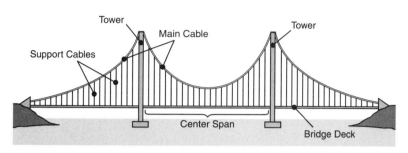

Tower

Main Cable

Tower

Support Cables

Center Span

Bridge Deck

Caption relates figure to text; clip art to which the writer has added her own labels—no credit needed

Fig. 4. Diagram Identifying Major Features of a Suspension Bridge. The bridge deck (roadway) is usually supported by stiffening trusses, but the Tacoma Narrows Bridge used solid girders instead.

. . . The Whitestone Bridge in New York is the only other bridge that has . . . stiffening girders of this type and we understand that it also has un-dulations in it, similar to the ones that occurred here . . ." (qtd. in "Big Tacoma Bridge Crashes" 5). The original plans drawn by Andrew and fellow engi-neers called for open trusses, but another engineer changed the plans.

In addition to these problems, the cables used to support the bridge were not large enough. Thin cables are easily stretched. This contributed to the bridge's inability to resist vertical and torsional motion. As Koughan observes, "All bridges are sub-ject to forces that cause torsion or lateral [side-to-side] lifting of the deck." He mentions a 1940 report by the Federal Works Agency that found such lifting insignificant in a suspension bridge that was vertically rigid and sufficiently wide.

Built for Aesthetics. Koughan argues that "the trend toward 'streamlining' in the 1930s took sus-pension bridge design away from the excessively stiff structures of the late nineteenth century and

back to the ribbon-like decks and aerodynamic problems of a hundred years earlier." Ever longer, slen-
derer, and lighter suspension bridges were being
conceived and erected. The Tacoma Narrows Bridge, a
prime example of this trend, was designed for a
"maximum of lightness, grace, and flexibility." However, in making the bridge aesthetically pleasing,
the designers unintentionally sacrificed much-needed
stiffness. Even though the design provided for sufficient strength as dictated by accepted practice at
the time, the bridge had been made too flexible to
withstand certain wind conditions.

Second-level   Overly Confident. Noticeable vertical undula-
subhead   tions of the bridge were witnessed even in the early
stages of construction. After being built, some
breezes as low as four miles per hour caused vertical oscillations (Moore). Motorists who crossed the
bridge felt that they were on a giant roller
coaster, watching the cars ahead disappear completely for moments at a time. Clearly, the Tacoma
Narrows Bridge was oscillating more than was
expected.

Although various concerns about the bridge's
stability had been expressed, many people were confident in the stability of the structure. The
motorists who traveled across the bridge daily were
not fazed by the bridge's motion. In fact, as indicated earlier, some people traveled large distances
just to cross the bridge and experience its rolling
motion. A bank near the Tacoma end of the bridge
even had a billboard advertisement boasting, "Safe
as the Narrows Bridge" (Gotchy 39). Officials were
even planning to save money by canceling the
bridge's insurance policies ("Bridge Facts and

Shonkwiler   8

Trivia"). Many people were shocked when the bridge collapsed.

First-level subhead — ## Prevention

Several things could have been done to prevent this catastrophe. By looking at past bridge failures and learning from them, the original plan could have been designed to account for wind-induced vibrations. The bridge could have also been strengthened while being constructed. Finally, after the bridge was built, research could have determined the problem and solutions could have been implemented.

Second-level subhead — ### Historical Precedent. Frederick B. Farquharson, a professor of civil engineering at the University of Washington, noted that the failure of the Tacoma Narrows Bridge "came as such a shock to the engineering profession that it is surprising to most to learn that the failure under the action of the wind was not without precedent" (Petroski 157). Had the designers of the Tacoma Narrows Bridge examined the historical failures (see Table 1), Galloping Gertie may have never galloped. In his book Design Paradigms, Petroski explains how historical precedent of failure could be overlooked:

Block quotation —
> It appears to be a trait of human nature to take repeated success as confirmation that everything is being done correctly. . . . The absence of dramatic failures can not only make designers complacent with regard to the genre of which they are so justifiably proud; a climate of success can also make designers react more slowly to warning signs that something is wrong. Even Farquharson, who personally observed the actual Tacoma Narrows Bridge and studied a model of it for three months, did not

Shonkwiler 9

expect the bridge to fail catastrophically the
way it did. (161)

Second-level subhead —————— <u>Actions Taken</u>. According to Koughan, engineers
tried several methods to minimize or eliminate the
motion of the Tacoma Narrows Bridge, without success. First, they had tie-down cables strung from
the plate girders to fifty-ton concrete blocks on
the shore, but the cables soon snapped. They then
installed inclined cables to attach the main cables
to the bridge deck in the middle of the long span,
but these cables failed to prevent the bridge from

Table positioned as soon as practical after paren-thetical ref-erence; table number on one line, table title on next line, both flush left; horizon-tal dividing lines as needed — Table 1
Suspension Bridge Failure Due to Wind

Bridge (location)	Span (ft.)	Failure Date
Dryburgh Abbey (Scotland)	260	1818
Union (England)	449	1821
Nassau (Germany)	245	1834
Brighton Chain Pier (England)	255	1836
Montrose (Scotland)	432	1838
Menai Strait (Wales)	580	1839
Roche-Bernard (France)	641	1852
Wheeling (United States)	1,010	1854
Niagara-Lewiston (USA--Canada)	1,041	1864
Niagara-Clifton (USA--Canada)	1,260	1889
Tacoma Narrows Bridge	2,800	1940

Source: Petroski 160.

Shonkwiler   10

vibrating. Finally, engineers relied on hydraulic
buffers placed between the towers and the deck's
floor system to reduce the longitudinal motion of
the main span, but scientists learned after the collapse that the sandblasting of the bridge had ren-
dered the buffers useless.

In addition, a fifty-foot model was constructed
at the University of Washington. Tests at certain
wind velocities showed that the bridge deck could
rise and fall as much as fifty inches ("A Great
Bridge Falls" 16). Unfortunately, by the time the
bridge collapsed, the studies had not progressed far
enough for a permanent stabilizer to be designed.

An effort was made to reduce the oscillations
of the bridge; however, all actions proved to be
ineffective. If the problem had been taken more
seriously, a greater effort would have been put into
finding a solution. Perhaps the failure could have
been prevented even after construction was complete.

Effects on Bridge Design

Research. The collapse of the Tacoma Narrows
Bridge initiated research on the aerodynamic stability of bridges. As bridge designer Mark Ketchum
explains, "The Tacoma experience taught engineers
that wind causes not only static loads on the
bridge, but also significant dynamic actions." After
the bridge failed, a new scale model of Galloping
Gertie was built and tested extensively in a wind
tunnel. According to Underwater Atmospheric Systems,
Inc., these tests "determine[d] the behavior and
stability of a physical model" and "had an important
effect on all suspension bridge designs that followed" ("Today's Tacoma Narrows"). Research on

Second-level
subhead

turbulence and eddies has led to fairly accurate predictions of wind effects and the ability to control a bridge's reaction to the wind.

Although there are several competing theories about the aerodynamic phenomena that caused Galloping Gertie's catastrophic collapse, research sparked by the disaster has taught designers to consider such varied forces as resonance, vortex shedding, and interactive self-excitation or negative damping (Koughan). Resonance, for instance, is a process in which an object's natural frequency of oscillation is amplified by an identical frequency. According to Albert Stetz, professor of physics at Oregon State University, resonance can occur when a small input force produces large deflections in a bridge. In Galloping Gertie's case, the resonant frequency may have been caused by strong wind gusts periodically blowing across the bridge, creating regions of high and low pressure above and below and thereby producing violent oscillations.

Galloping Gertie's oscillations may also be explained by the existence of vortices, or eddies, turbulent flows of air around the bridge structure. These flows of air create regions of alternating pressure on the side of the bridge that is sheltered from the wind, which in turn leads to resonance (Koughan). Long-span bridges are especially vulnerable to vortices, resulting in twisting and oscillating motions.

Another phenomenon, called interactive self-excitation, may have contributed to the bridge's violent motion and collapse. The difference between vortex-induced vibration and self-excitation is that in self-excitation, "the driving force for oscilla-

Shonkwiler   12

tion is not purely a function of time . . . but is
rather a function of bridge angle during torsional
oscillation and the rate of change of that angle"
(Koughan). According to this theory, the wind supplies the force, but as the bridge twists more and
faster, the effect of the wind becomes greater. A
bridge that starts twisting in a high wind can thus
begin to twist increasingly violently until it
becomes unstable and rips apart.

Second-level subhead ——————— New Tacoma Narrows Bridge. The research done
after Galloping Gertie collapsed enabled engineers
to design a more stable Tacoma Narrows Bridge. Built
in 1950, the second Tacoma Narrows Bridge replaced
Galloping Gertie and still stands today. (See Fig.
5.) This bridge was nicknamed Sturdy Gertie ("Tale
of Two Gerties").

Several changes had been made in the design.
Open trusses of greater depth replaced the stiffening girders of the original bridge that were solid
and too shallow. This added strength to the bridge
and reduced wind resistance. The design of the
bridge deck was also changed. (See Fig. 6.) The new
roadway was almost twice as wide as the old one,
49 feet 10 inches versus 26 feet ("Comparison of the
Bridges"). This increased the bridge's resistance to
torsion. According to Underwater Atmospheric Systems, Inc., "open steel grid slots . . . installed
between each of the four traffic lanes and both
curbs . . . function as vents to relieve oscillation" ("Comparison of the Bridges"). Hydraulic
energy absorbing and damping devices at the towers
and midspan also helped reduce oscillations by controlling self-excitation (Koughan).

Stability was also increased by strengthening

Fig. 5. <u>New Tacoma Narrows Bridge showing concrete construction</u>
<u>work, ca. 1950</u>, Tacoma Narrows Bridge Collection. Stiffening
trusses are along the sides of the bridge below the bridge deck.

the supports. The diameter of the main suspension
cable was increased from 17.5 inches to 20.25
inches. The number of wires in each of the support
cables was also increased. These changes strengthened the cables. In addition, the weight of each
shore anchor was increased by 13,500 tons, and the
weight of each main tower was increased by 748 tons
("Comparison of the Bridges"). These improvements
produced a structure of unprecedented function and
stability. Koughan sees the new bridge as "evidence
that the lessons learned about the collapse of 'Gal-

Shonkwiler 14

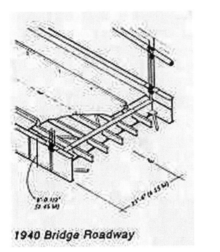

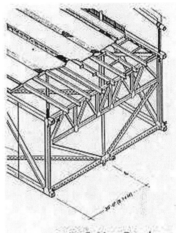

1940 Bridge Roadway

1950 Bridge Roadway

Fig. 6. Bridge Deck Comparison. At left, 1940 roadway; at right, 1950 roadway. Source: "Comparison of the Bridges."

loping Gertie' were being rigorously applied to new designs."

Second-level subhead ———— <u>New Designs</u>. The collapse of Galloping Gertie did have a positive side, initiating research that has proved beneficial to bridge designers everywhere. The need for engineers to have a complete understanding of nature's interaction with their designs has led to new problem-solving techniques. Now, designers still look at static loads but also review the implications of aerodynamic effects on the structures. The control of aerodynamic instabilities can be achieved by an aerodynamically shaped deck, stiffness, mass, and damping of the bridge system (Frandsen). After design, models are made and tested. Few bridges are currently constructed without first testing a model in a wind tunnel. Complex computer analyses are used as well. These steps are

Shonkwiler   15

taken to prevent catastrophes like Galloping Gertie's collapse from occurring again.

Conclusion

Clear summary of the major points made in this research paper

First-level subhead

The designers of the Tacoma Narrows Bridge did not anticipate the impact of wind. Historical examples of aerodynamic bridge failure were not well known or taken into account. The Tacoma Narrows Bridge oscillated in certain wind conditions from the start, but confidence in the bridge's stability was too high to invoke serious research. Efforts were taken to limit the oscillations, but proved ineffective. Owing to a combination of factors that is still debated today, only four months after its completion Galloping Gertie's motions became too violent, and the bridge ripped itself apart. The collapse initiated intensive research on bridge aerodynamics, and as a result bridges now are designed to resist wind-induced vibrations.

Today's motorists may grumble about traffic congestion on the Tacoma Narrows Bridge, but their experiences are certainly less harrowing than that of Leonard Coatsworth, who crawled off Galloping Gertie but lost his car and his dog on the fateful morning of November 7, 1940.

Works Cited list begins new page; heading centered and positioned one inch from top edge of page; all entries double-spaced

1"

Article in a newspaper

Sources listed alphabetically by author's last name; if author is unknown, listed by first major word used in title (excluding *a, an, the*)

Photograph from an online source

First line of entry aligns flush with left margin; subsequent lines indent one-half inch or five character spaces

Web site

Works Cited

"Big Tacoma Bridge Crashes 190 Feet into Puget
    Sound." <u>New York Times</u> 8 Nov. 1940: 1+.

"Bridge Facts and Trivia." <u>The Complete Tacoma Nar-</u>
    <u>rows Bridge Info Center</u>. 2003. Tacoma Area Citi-
    zens for Civic Pride and Friends of the Narrows
    Bridge. 27 Apr. 2003 <http://www.firebirdz.net/
    tnb/frames_text.htm>. Path: Did You Know?

<u>Bridge midsection crashing into the waters of the</u>
    <u>Tacoma Narrows</u>. 7 Nov. 1940. Tacoma Narrows
    Bridge Collection, University of Washington.
    29 April 2003 <http://www.lib.washington.edu/
    specialcoll/tnb>.

Coatsworth, Leonard. "Newsman Barely Escapes as
    Bridge Falls in Sound." <u>Oregonian</u> 8 Nov. 1940:
    sec. 1: 3.

"Comparison of the Bridges." Underwater Atmospheric
    Systems, Inc. 25 April 2003 <http://
    www.nwrain.com/~newtsuit/recoveries/narrows/
    comp.html>.

<u>Film still of the Tacoma Narrows Bridge twisting</u>.
    7 Nov. 1940. Tacoma Narrows Bridge Collection,
    University of Washington. 29 April 2003
    <http://www.lib.washington.edu/specialcoll
    /tnb>.

Frandsen, Jannette Behrndtz. "Research Projects in:
    Bridge Aerodynamics." 19 Dec. 2002. Louisiana
    State U. 27 Apr. 2003 <http://www.fsi.isu.edu/
    ~frandsen/bridge_projects.html>.

"Galloping Gertie." Underwater Atmospheric Systems,
    Inc. 25 Apr. 2003. <http://www.nwrain.com/
    ~newtsuit/recoveries/narrows/gg.html>.

Shonkwiler   17

Book —— Gotchy, Joe. <u>Bridging the Narrows</u>. Gig Harbor: Penin-
        sula Historical Society, 1990.

"A Great Bridge Falls." <u>New York Times</u> 9 Nov. 1940:
        16.

Ketchum, Mark. "Mark Ketchum's Bridge Aerodynamics
        Page." 26 Apr. 2003 <http://www.ketchum.org/
        wind.html>.

Koughan, James. "The Collapse of the Tacoma Narrows ——— Article in
        Bridge, Evaluation of Competing Theories of Its   an online
        Demise, and the Effects of the Disaster of Suc-   journal
        ceeding Bridge Designs." <u>Undergraduate Engineer-</u>
        <u>ing Review</u>. 1 Aug. 1996. U of Texas. 26 Apr.
        2003 <http:engineering.rowan.edu/~Kurz7668/
        FroshProj/Paper_jk.htm>.

Moore, Kristen. "The Tacoma Narrows Bridge Failure."
        U of Connecticut. 26 Apr. 2003 <http://
        www.math.uconn.edu/~kmoore/tacoma.html>.

<u>New Tacoma Narrows Bridge showing concrete construc-</u>
        <u>tion work, ca. 1950</u>. Tacoma Narrows Bridge Col-
        lection, University of Washington. 29 Apr. 2003
        <http://www.lib.washington.edu/specialcoll/
        tnb>.

Petroski, Henry. <u>Design Paradigms</u>. New York: Cam-
        bridge University Press, 1994.

Stetz, Albert. Personal interview. 29 April 2003.

"Tacoma Narrows Bridge." Underwater Atmospheric Sys-
        tems, Inc. 25 Apr. 2003 <http://www.nwrain.net/
        ~newtsuit/recoveries/narrows/narrows.htm>.

<u>The Tacoma Narrows Bridge twisting</u>. 7 Nov. 1940.
        Tacoma Narrows Bridge Collection, University
        of Washington. 29 Apr. 2003 <http://
        www.lib.washington.edu/specialcoll/tnb>.

Shonkwiler   18

"A Tale of Two Gerties." <u>Gig Harbor Peninsula Histor-</u>
     <u>ical Society and Museum</u>. 27 Apr. 2003 <http://
     www.gigharbormuseum.org/nbonlinexhibit.html>.
"Today's Tacoma Narrows Bridge." Underwater Atmo-
     spheric Systems, Inc. 25 Apr. 2003 <http://
     www.nwrain.net/~newtsuit/recoveries/
     narrows/cb.htm>.

■ ■ ■

FOR THOUGHT, DISCUSSION, AND WRITING

1. After reviewing this chapter's discussion of paraphrasing and summarizing, select one of the texts included as a reading at the end of Chapter 3, "Understanding the Reading Process." Choose a paragraph from the reading — one that strikes you as particularly interesting, thought-provoking, or informative. After reading this paragraph carefully, first write a paraphrase of it, and then summarize the same passage. Finally, write a paragraph explaining why your paraphrase and summary of this passage are effective.

2. Choose a topic that interests you. Using a Web search engine, do a general search on your topic, noting the number of hits that your search generates. Now develop a list of related terms, and use these to narrow your search. Run a keyword search for at least two items from this list, noting the number of hits for these searches. After reviewing the suggestions for advanced searching provided by your search engine, conduct an advanced search. Take a few minutes to write a paragraph reflecting on this search. What was productive? Unproductive? What would you do differently if you needed to search on this topic again?

3. Select two of the Web sites that you located in the previous activity. Using the suggestions for evaluating Web sites provided in this chapter, assess the quality of the information presented on each site. Write one or two paragraphs of evaluation for each site.

PART TWO

RHETORICAL SITUATIONS

Analyzing Rhetorical Situations

Whenever you write — whether you are jotting a note to a friend or working on a lab report — you are writing in the context of a specific situation with its own unique demands and opportunities. A management trainee writing a memo to her supervisor faces different challenges than an investigative journalist working on a story for the *New York Times* or a student writing a research paper for a political science class. Successful writers know that they must consider the situations in which they write; they can't rely on formulas or blind luck when they compose. They know they need to rely on their sensitivity — their understanding of the relationships among writers, readers, and texts — to help them make decisions as they write and revise.

NOTE FOR MULTILINGUAL WRITERS

The approach to rhetoric and rhetorical sensitivity that is advanced in this chapter is grounded in the Western rhetorical tradition. Other traditions hold different values and assumptions about communication. Your home culture, for instance, may value communal harmony as much as (or more than) individual self-expression, which is highly valued in Western rhetoric. It also may hold different stylistic preferences. For some writers from other communities, for instance, the English that is written by students, businesspersons, and others in North America seems abrupt and even rude. As a writer learning to communicate in different languages and communities, you need to understand the assumptions that are held by writers who are grounded in the Western rhetorical tradition — but you do not need to abandon your own culture's values. Your writing (and your thinking) will be enriched when you learn how to draw on *all* the rhetorical sensitivity that you have gained as a speaker, listener, writer, and reader.

In this section of *Work in Progress* you will learn how to use rhetorical sensitivity to analyze specific writing situations. In this chapter, for instance, you will learn to ask yourself questions about your rhetorical situation — questions that will enable you to determine the most fruitful way of approaching your topic and of responding to the needs and expectations of your readers. In Chapter 6, "Thinking about Communities and Conventions," you will learn how to read the forms and strategies of writing that characterize different communities of language users. This kind of rhetorically sensitive reading is particularly helpful when you are attempting to learn new forms of writing, as happens when students enter college or begin a new job. Finally, Chapter 7, "Negotiating Online Writing Situations," will help you apply what you know to the challenges — and opportunities — of writing online.

LEARNING TO ANALYZE YOUR RHETORICAL SITUATION

Rhetoric involves three key elements: a writer, a reader, and a text that makes communication possible. When you think about these elements, posing questions about the options available to you as a writer, you are analyzing your rhetorical situation. Such analysis will enable you to make decisions not only about the form and content of your writing but also about the medium of communication.

Imagine, for instance, that you have been meaning to write to a close friend. Now, you decide, is just the time to do so. But should you email or send a handwritten letter? The answer depends on your situation. If you are writing just to say hello and to let your friend know that you're thinking of him, you might choose email as your means of communication, for its ease and informality suit this purpose well. But suppose you are writing because you have just learned of a death in your friend's family. The seriousness of this situation and the more personal nature of a handwritten note might well prompt a letter.

As simple as it might seem, the question of whether to email or to send a handwritten letter is a rhetorical question, one that calls on you to consider all the elements of rhetoric. As a writer you have choices; the more fully you understand your situation, the better choices you can make. Even though people conventionally send handwritten letters of condolence, for instance, your relationship with your friend might in fact make you decide to email him. (You may be, for example, in the habit of emailing each other every few days, even about personal matters.)

■ ■ ■

FOR EXPLORATION

Imagine that you need to write the following texts:

> An application for an internship in your major
>
> A note to a friend whose parents have recently decided to divorce
>
> A posting to your class Web site that explains your reaction to a film that you viewed in class

Keeping the elements of rhetoric in mind, spend a few minutes thinking about how you would approach these different writing situations. Write a brief description of each situation, responding to the following questions:

1. What are your role as writer and your purpose for writing?

2. What image of yourself do you wish to present, and how will you vary your language accordingly?

3. How do the different readers of each text influence the form and content of your writing?

4. What medium of communication, email or print, is most appropriate? (In the third scenario, this has already been decided for you.)

5. What other factors, such as format and visual design, do you need to consider?

Using Your Rhetorical Analysis to Guide Your Writing

As the preceding example shows, writers naturally draw on their common-sense rhetorical sensitivity to determine the most effective ways to communicate with readers. The student deciding whether to email or to write a handwritten letter to his friend did not consciously run through a mental checklist of questions but rather drew on his intuitive understanding of his situation. When you face the challenge of new and more difficult kinds of writing, however, as you do in college, it often helps to analyze your rhetorical situation consciously. Such analysis encourages you to consider each of the elements of rhetoric when you write.

The following guidelines provide questions that you can use to analyze your rhetorical situation.

■ GUIDELINES FOR ANALYZING YOUR RHETORICAL SITUATION

Early in any writing project, you can lay a solid foundation by asking yourself the following questions:

Writer

1. Why are you writing?

2. What do you hope your writing will accomplish? Do you want to convey information? Change the reader's mind? Entertain the reader?

3. How might your goals as a writer influence the eventual form and content of your essay?

4. What role does this rhetorical situation invite you, the writer, to play? Is your role relatively fixed (as it is when you write an essay exam)? Or is it flexible to some extent?

5. What image of yourself (persona) do you want to convey to your readers? What "voice" do you want readers to "hear" when they read your writing?

Reader

1. Who is your intended audience? How have you envisioned this audience? Is it helpful to think of your readers as members of a specific audience (subscribers to a special-interest magazine, for instance) or as a general audience with a wide range of interests?

2. What role do you intend for readers to adopt as they read your writing? What kinds of cues will you use to signal this role to readers?

3. If you are writing to a specific audience, do those readers have any demographic characteristics that you need to consider — such as age, gender, religion, income, occupation, education, political preference, or something else?

4. How will your writing appeal to your readers' interests? Do you expect your readers already to be interested in the topic, or do you need to create and maintain their interest?

(continued)

(continued)

5. How might the needs and expectations of your readers influence the form, content, and style of your writing?

Text

1. If you are writing in response to an assignment, to what degree does the assignment specify or restrict the form and content of your text? How much freedom, in other words, do you, the writer, have?

2. What generic or stylistic conventions does your rhetorical situation require you to follow? Are these conventions rigidly defined (as in the case of lab reports) or flexible to some extent?

3. Does the nature of your subject implicitly or explicitly require that you provide certain kinds of evidence or explore certain issues?

4. Could you benefit by looking at models or other examples of the kind of writing that your situation requires, including models of document design?

5. What medium of communication (print, email, hypertext, and so on) seems the most appropriate means of conveying your message to readers?

As these questions indicate, the process of analyzing your rhetorical situation challenges you to look both within and without. Your intended meaning — what you want to communicate to your readers — is certainly important, as is your purpose for writing. But unless you're writing solely for yourself in your journal or notebook, you can't ignore your readers or other situational factors. Analyzing your rhetorical situation helps you to respond creatively as a writer and yet keeps you aware of limits on your freedom.

Setting Preliminary Goals

Before beginning a major writing project, you may find it helpful to write a brief analysis of your rhetorical situation, or you may simply review these questions mentally. This process of analyzing your rhetorical situation is an opportunity to determine your *preliminary* intentions or goals as a writer. (Your intentions will often shift as you write. That's fine. As you write, you will naturally revise your understanding of your rhetorical situation.) Despite its

---

NOTE FOR MULTILINGUAL WRITERS

As a multilingual writer, you may be unsure about how to answer the questions in the preceding Guidelines for Analyzing Your Rhetorical Situation. You might be unsure, for instance, about how best to appeal to your intended audience. Or you might be undecided about which stylistic and generic conventions you should follow in a particular rhetorical situation. When you have questions, don't hesitate to ask your teacher for clarification. Talking with a tutor at your writing center or with one or more students in your class about a particular writing assignment and situation can also be helpful.

---

tentativeness, however, your analysis of your situation will help you begin writing with a sense of direction and purpose.

Here is one student's analysis of her rhetorical situation. The student is Annette Chambers, and her rhetorical analysis is followed by her essay (p. 163).

> I am writing an essay about my hobby, fantasy role-playing: what it is, why I like it, how it works, how people tend to respond when I tell them about it — and why their responses bother me. I hope that those reading my essay will be entertained by and interested in my topic. But mainly I want them to understand that people who game are not all wild-eyed, psychologically damaged social misfits. I've been really frustrated with the way people respond when they learn that I participate in fantasy role-playing games. Most people make it clear that they think gaming is weird at best; some have gone so far as to ask me if I didn't fear for my soul since I "play" with "demons."
>
> My writing goals require both information and sensitivity to my audience. I need to provide enough information about gaming so people will understand what it is (and, just as important, what it is *not*) — but not so much that they get bogged down in unnecessary details. I also need to respond to the concerns people have about gaming. I want to show readers that the stereotypes they have about fantasy role-playing are just that: stereotypes. But I've got to be careful not to seem angry or defensive. I'm hoping that humor will help here.
>
> I'm writing this essay for an assignment in my composition class. The assignment is pretty general; it asks us to write an informative essay on a subject that we care about. So I have a fair amount of flexibility. I hope that a wide range of people might find my essay interesting and informative. I am directing this toward a general audience, even though

my teacher will be my immediate reader. Though I'm writing this essay for a class, I might submit it for publication to the student or local newspaper or to some magazines that publish brief, general-interest essays, such as airline magazines.

Writer: I've already explained why I'm writing and what I hope this essay will accomplish. Given my goals, I want to present myself as open, conversational, pleasant, and not at all defensive about my hobby. I want readers to see me as a bright, articulate person who likes to make believe but is firmly aware of the difference between reality and fantasy. This is really important to my credibility, since my major goal is to convince readers that game-players are normal people just like them.

Readers: I assume that most readers (especially my teacher!) will have little direct experience with fantasy role-playing, which they probably associate in a vague way with games like Dungeons and Dragons.™ Since some readers will believe the misconceptions about gaming I talk about, I need to be careful not to alienate them by portraying their concerns as stupid or silly. I hope to appeal to my readers by writing a vivid introduction that will draw readers in, and by using lively examples — and humor — to keep them interested. I hope that my use of humor and my general informality will tell readers that they should just sit back and enjoy the essay.

Text: Because my assignment is open-ended, I have quite a lot of freedom as a writer. But that doesn't mean that anything goes. Since I'm hoping to write a personal essay that will appeal to a broad range of readers, I need to make my essay interesting. I've read other personal essays, and we've talked about them in class, so I know that writers need to draw readers in. I can't assume that readers will care about my subject; I have to make them care. And I have to provide the kinds of details that will keep them interested as they read.

"SO, WHAT ARE YOU DOING THIS WEEKEND?"
by Annette Chambers

It's 2:45 in the morning, and I've just spent two and a half hours logged into email pretending to be an elfish woman on another planet. My name is Miri Ravan, and I'm something over 2,000 years old, though (as is the way of elves) I don't look much over thirty. At the moment, I'm having an uncomfortable discussion with my lover's daughter, D'versey, about relationships, which is hard because she's half succubus, spent her early life in Hell, and has a unique view of life. For example, she finds it odd that I don't casually become involved with anyone I find attractive, and has recently asked me to explain "just what *is* the difference between acquaintances and friends."

Or it's Saturday night, round 10:00, and I've been sitting in a stuffy little living room with five friends for about eight hours. This is how we've spent most Saturdays for almost ten years. I am Annabelle Jordan, a thirty-ish veterinarian with a photographic memory and a knack for "reading" people. I love dogs, hate rap, live in the suburbs of Tacoma, and just happen to hang out with a pack of vampires. Or I might be Maire Clare, an Irish woman living in twelfth-century London, who just happens to *be* a vampire. Or Silver, a former "personnel reclamation specialist" (read "kidnapper and sometimes assassin") who now runs the shadows of the mean streets of twenty-first-century Seattle.

I suppose I shouldn't be surprised that people look at me funny when I tell them about fantasy role-playing. After we get past the "you mean like Dungeons and Dragons™?" stage, their expressions usually range from curious, to wary, to alarmed. There is, I suppose, something odd, something not quite normal, about pretending to be somebody else for hours at a time, especially when that somebody may not even be human. But then, I've never really understood the attraction of staring at a television screen while grown men chase variously shaped balls around a field or court. Anyway, gaming is fun — as relaxing to me as watching sports is to others.

Of course there are other ways to relax that don't make people question your sanity or soul. Rock climbing, for instance. Though rock climbing seems pretty crazy to me, nobody stereotypes climbers as socially inept, psychologically warped, or morally questionable. No one suggests that climbing be banned as harmful to children. And nobody asks climbers if they don't worry about getting "too wrapped up in rock climbing" or wonders, in tones of sincere interest and concern, whether their hobby is "demonic." These are questions I've encountered more than once, and I always find myself pausing while I attempt to frame a reply.

However long the pause, the answer is always "Well, no." I don't worry about getting too involved. I don't spend my days fretting that I identify too strongly with Miri, or that Annabelle is becoming too great an influence on my thinking, or that if I'm not careful I might flip out and start randomly slaughtering innocent bystanders in the mistaken belief that they're monsters. As far as I can tell, no one who knows me well worries about these things either.

Is it possible to get too wrapped up? Yes, certainly; it's possible to take anything too far. It's also possible to fall off a mountain while you're climbing it, but that doesn't mean that all climbers have a death wish. I've been gaming for ten years or so and have encountered exactly one person who I thought allowed himself to get too caught up in the game. But he was like that about other things too. His obsessiveness colored his whole life, not just his role-playing. In some ways the game seemed to serve as a safety valve for him, a way of venting hostility he might otherwise have directed at real people instead of imaginary monsters.

Which brings me to demons. Yes, they do turn up in some of the games I play. So do elves and giants and centaurs and a whole host of other creatures. And, yes, they're powerful and evil and extremely dangerous. Since my group usually plays characters who at least try to be good, demons are popular enemies. But, no, role-playing isn't about summoning, communing with, speaking to, or even believing in demons. Mostly it's a way of being, for a few hours, someone you're not likely to get to be in real life — perhaps even someone you wouldn't want to be. It's a chance for you and some friends to make up imaginary people and see if you can make them work together toward a common goal.

In case you're unfamiliar with fantasy role-playing, here's how it works. Everyone in the group — usually between three and eight players — has a character, and each character has a defined set of skills and physical and mental characteristics, as well as a background including personality, goals, skills, and so forth. There's also a game master (GM) or storyteller who more or less (in my group it's mostly less) controls what's happening by setting up the scenarios to which the player characters respond. The goal is to get as deeply into character as possible, to speak, act, and react as though you are the person you're pretending to be, though the acting is usually limited to gestures and tones of voice.

If I want Annabelle to climb a fifteen-foot rock wall, something she's unlikely to be good at, given the background I've invented and skills I've chosen for her, I do not get up and start scaling the sofa. Instead, I tell the GM what I plan for her to do. Based on a combination of factors including her assigned strength and dexterity, the condition of the wall, and luck, the GM decides whether she manages to scramble over with a few seconds to spare, escapes because one of her companions distracts the werewolves, or falls to her doom.

Now, I don't believe in werewolves any more than I believe in demons, but part of the fun is that Annabelle does. Gaming is a chance to pretend, to play make believe, the way we all do as children. Perhaps it's this similarity to childhood games that makes people uncomfortable. After all, aren't we grown-ups now? Shouldn't we concern ourselves with grown-up things like work and money and having our own children? Well, maybe. But on the other hand, is getting together to play Dragonquest™ or Vampire: The Masquerade™ really so much weirder than getting together to watch football or play poker?

Besides, it's cheap therapy. Everyone in my group has at one time or another arrived looking exhausted, defeated, or just plain irritated, and growled, "I want to kill something." The rest of us sympathize, and then we let him kill something! This may not bring the long-term benefits of therapy, but role-playing is easy and inexpensive, and however much bloodshed our characters may be responsible for, none of us seems to have any trouble maintaining the fantasy–reality distinction. Our families, however irritated we may become with them, are alive and well. None of our coworkers seem worried that just because we spend part of our weekend waving swords or spells at the bad guys we're going to show up on Monday with a gun.

And yes, we do work, and go to school, and have, for the want of a better phrase, "real lives." Most of us have or are working toward college degrees. All of us have or are looking for jobs. Some of us are engaged or living together with another person. We pay our taxes and brush our teeth and can, with allowances for differing personalities and degrees of sociability, hold down our end of a "normal" conversation. Perhaps the real difference between us and rock climbers is that we spend our Saturdays with our feet planted firmly on the ground.

■ ■ ■

FOR EXPLORATION

To what extent does Annette Chambers's essay achieve the goals she established for herself in her analysis of her rhetorical situation? Reread Annette's analysis and essay. Keeping her analysis in mind, list three or four reasons that you believe Annette does or does not achieve her goals, and then find at least one passage in the essay that illustrates each of these statements. Finally, identify at least one way that Annette might strengthen her essay were she to revise.

THINKING ABOUT READERS

If you look again at Annette Chambers's description of her rhetorical situation (pp. 162–63), you will notice that concerns about her readers influence all aspects of her planning. Annette knows that if she wants to challenge readers' stereotypes about fantasy role-playing, it would hardly make sense to write an angry essay chastising readers for their misconceptions. Her situation invites a light, entertaining, informative approach, one that encourages dialogue and identification. Annette understands as well that the persona she projects will help determine how readers respond to her ideas. Consequently, she presents herself as open, pleasant, and friendly (note the role that humor plays in her essay, for instance) — and she invites readers to assume a similar stance. In so doing, she establishes common ground with readers and encourages them to be as open-minded about her hobby as she is about such hobbies as spectator sports and rock climbing.

Annette recognizes that she must do more than establish common ground with readers and project an inviting persona: She must respond to readers' misconceptions, and she must provide information they need to understand fantasy role-playing. If she provides too many details, readers may get bogged down; too few, and they will fail to understand how "normal" people could be drawn to her hobby. Annette also understands that she is writing for two potential audiences: for her teacher, who will actually read her essay, and for a more general audience of hypothetical readers. Negotiating this double audience could be tricky, but Annette understands that she can draw on her understanding of personal essay writing to make decisions as she writes. For Annette, the personal essay (an essay grounded in the writer's personal experience) is not an arbitrary form but a means of establishing a particular kind of relationship with readers, one that is conversational and informal. Annette understands that in evaluating her essay her teacher will consider the extent to which Annette has written an interesting, well-organized, personal essay, one that anticipates the needs and interests of a general audience of readers and that comments in significant ways on its topic.

In a different situation — writing an in-class essay exam, for instance — Annette would adjust her understanding of her reader accordingly. Teachers assign essay exams when they want to determine what students have learned about a subject and how effectively they can express this understanding to others. Given this expectation, a dramatic, attention-getting introduction might irritate, not entertain, her reader. A concise introductory paragraph, one that clearly specifies the writer's main point and indicates how the writer will support this point, would be more appropriate.

Here, for instance, is the introduction to an essay written by Elizabeth Ridlington, a student at Harvard. Elizabeth wrote this essay for an exam in her introductory political science class. The title of Elizabeth's essay is "Political and Economic Power."

Since the French Revolution, France has believed the state should be composed of citizens who voluntarily joined the nation because of their belief in certain ideals. The United States similarly believes that all citizens should agree with the principles formed at the time of the Revolutionary War and laid out in the Constitution. Despite this, neither country extends citizenship to everyone who agrees with these ideals and principles. Thus, other factors must influence these nations' understanding of — and laws regarding — citizenship. In this essay I argue that economic and political considerations have been more important in forming either country's understanding of citizenship than have been its founding ideals. Evidence of this can be found in the evolution of the understanding of citizenship, in the forces that initially pulled each nation into a single political unit, and in the outcome of specific crises.

In writing the above introduction to her essay, Elizabeth understood that in this rhetorical situation her reader, her political science teacher, is interested primarily in her understanding of her topic. Whereas Annette's introduction works hard to interest readers and to engage them with her topic, Elizabeth's introduction focuses on establishing a clear position on her topic and on identifying the most important arguments she will use to support this position. This introduction thus serves a dual purpose: It clearly articulates her position and also reassures her professor that the essay will be clearly organized and well supported.

As a writer, your relationship with your readers is always shifting and complex, not fixed and static; this relationship varies with your rhetorical situation. When you consider the expectations and interests of your readers, you naturally think *strategically* and thus build on the rhetorical sensitivity you have already developed as a speaker, listener, reader, and writer.

■ ■ ■

FOR EXPLORATION

Introductions often help signal the relationship the writer intends to establish with readers. The following excerpts introduce two different discussions of stress, both designed for a general audience. The first excerpt is from the introduction to *The Work/Stress Connection: How to Cope with Job Burnout*. The second is from the "Work and Stress" section in *The Columbia University College of Physicians and Surgeons Complete Home Medical Guide*. As you read these excerpts, think about the differing roles that they invite readers to assume.

> Sally Swanson, a thirty-eight-year-old mother of four, works as a bank teller in Des Moines, Iowa. Like many women, she feels the pressure of running a home, raising children, managing a job, and carving out leisure time for herself. "I did fine until we got a new supervisor last year," she says with an exhausted sigh. "Within two months I had started to burn out." Sally takes antacid pills several times a day. She worries that she may have an ulcer. "I feel as if he's looking over my shoulder all the time," she says. "He never has a good word to say to anyone. Sometimes the tension at the bank is so thick you could cut it with a knife."
>
> — *The Work/Stress Connection: How to Cope with Job Burnout*

Particular kinds of work seem to cause special stress, and the effects on health are manifested in an all-too-common pattern: fatigue, insomnia, eating disorders, nervousness, feelings of unhappiness, abuse of alcohol or drugs. Stress is often related to the nature of the job or imposed irregularities. Rotating shift work, in which hours are erratic or inconsistent with the normal sleep cycle, produces both physical and mental stress by constantly upsetting circadian rhythms that control specific hormonal and other responses. Jobs that involve little variation but require constant close attention, for example, assembly-line work or jobs requiring repetitive tasks with dangerous equipment, seem to be particularly stressful. In one study in a sawmill, people who ran the equipment had much higher levels of stress-related hormones than workers who did not come in contact with machinery, even though their jobs also may have been boring and repetitive.

— *The Columbia University College of Physicians and Surgeons Complete Home Medical Guide*

Now describe the writer-reader relationship established in each of these two introductions. What signals or cues do the authors provide for readers to enable them to recognize and adopt an appropriate role? Cite at least three examples of these signals or cues.

USING ARISTOTLE'S THREE APPEALS

Analyzing your rhetorical situation can provide information that will enable you to make crucial strategic, structural, and stylistic decisions about your writing. In considering how to use the information gained through this process, you may find it helpful to employ what Aristotle (384–322 B.C.) characterized as the three appeals. According to Aristotle, when speakers and writers communicate with others, they draw on these three general appeals:

Logos, the appeal to reason

Pathos, the appeal to emotion, values, and beliefs

Ethos, the appeal to the credibility of the speaker or writer

As a writer, you appeal to *logos* when you focus on the logical presentation of your subject by providing evidence and examples in support of your ideas. You appeal to *pathos* when you use the resources of language to engage your readers emotionally with your subject or appeal to their values, beliefs, or needs.

And you appeal to *ethos* when you create an image of yourself, a persona, that encourages readers to accept or act on your ideas.

These three appeals correspond to the three basic elements of rhetoric (writer, reader, and text). In appealing to *ethos*, you focus on the *writer's* character as implied in the text; in appealing to *pathos*, on the interaction of writer and *reader*; and in appealing to *logos*, on the logical statements about the subject made in your particular *text*. In some instances, you may rely predominantly on one of these appeals. A student writing a technical report, for instance, will typically emphasize scientific or technical evidence (*logos*), not emotional or personal appeals. More often, however, you will draw on all three appeals in your effort to create a fully persuasive document. A journalist writing an essay on child abuse might begin her discussion with several examples designed to gain the attention of her readers and to convince them of the importance of this issue (*pathos*). Although she may rely primarily on information about the negative consequences of child abuse (*logos*), she will undoubtedly also endeavor to create an image of herself as a caring, serious person (*ethos*), one whose analysis of a subject like child abuse could be trusted.

NOTE FOR MULTILINGUAL WRITERS

As noted earlier, the ideas expressed in this chapter — and throughout this text — are grounded in the Western rhetorical model. Aristotle's three appeals are examples of this model. If the Western rhetorical tradition is new to you, you will benefit from understanding its assumptions and practices. Try to identify ways in which these assumptions and practices compare with those of your home country or community. The Classical Chinese rhetorical tradition, for instance, does not separate mind and body. Instead, it uses the core concept of *xin* (heart-mind) to explain action. Instead of appealing to *logos* and *pathos* separately, Chinese students may simply want to appeal to their audience's *xin*.

In the following examples, Tova Johnson, a biology major at Oregon State University, and Brandon Barrett, a chemistry major at the same university, use Aristotle's three appeals to develop strategies for essays defining their major. Tova and Brandon were students in Carole Ann Crateau's first-year writing class when they wrote these essays. In presenting her assignment, Crateau informed students that their essays should include "information about your major that is new to your readers; in other words, it should not simply repeat the OSU catalog. Rather, it should be your unique perspective, written in clear, descriptive language." Crateau concluded her assignment with this advice: "Have fun with this assignment. Consider your audience (it should be this class unless you specify a different audience). And remember Aristotle's three appeals. How will your essay employ the appeals of *logos, pathos,* and *ethos*? As you write, keep these two questions in mind: What is your purpose? What do you hope to achieve with your audience?"

Tova's and Brandon's essays are preceded by their analyses of their rhetorical situations and of their essays' appeals to *logos, pathos,* and *ethos.*

Tova Johnson's Analysis of Her Rhetorical Situation and of Her Use of Logos, Pathos, and Ethos

I am writing this paper for my first-year writing class. My teacher has asked students to present our unique perspective on our academic majors. I see this as an invitation to be creative — to avoid catalog or textbook definitions of our majors and to instead explore our personal understandings. Given this expectation, my goal is to write an essay that conveys what I find exciting about biology and to do so in a way that my readers will find intriguing and accessible. I am not in an "anything goes" situation, however. This is a writing class, so my teacher will expect that my essay will follow the general conventions of English and of personal essay writing. I know from previous writing classes, for instance, that essays are most effective when you use specific examples, so I will try to do that.

Logos: I want readers to see the logical progression that I experienced from playing outdoors as a child to my pursuit of a biology major and to understand the pleasure that I experienced then and now in studying nature. To do this, I need to provide some specific examples that will both show my childhood interest in nature and connect that with the more formal study of biology. I can also help people understand my interest in biology by connecting it with something that most people are familiar with — reading. Perhaps if my readers see biology as connected to something they know, they will become enthused about it, just as I am. Or at least they will better understand why someone might want to major in biology.

Pathos: When I think about *pathos,* I realize that the introduction to my essay will be particularly important, for it's got to hook readers and convince them that this subject is accessible and interesting. Most of us have positive memories of childhood, so my hope is that by beginning with these memories I will connect with readers and encourage them to continue reading. I want readers to understand that there is beauty in biology, so I will need to use vivid details that engage the senses of my readers.

Ethos: For my readers to trust me, I must present myself as knowledge-able about and intimate with my subject. I want to convince my readers that I am genuinely in awe of and fascinated with life in general and biology in specific.

THE TEXTS OF LIFE
by Tova Johnson

I remember warm summer days when my younger sister Kelva and I watched ants that were making their homes in small holes in the cement behind our house. We watched in awe as the little brown scavengers emerged from their dark underground holes to meet the sunlight and to collect bits of grass and leaves that completely covered their backs as they returned to their holes to deposit their newfound treasures. My sister and I wanted desperately to enter their homes with them, to view their mag-nificent microdens, but our size prevented us. And so, our studies would end at their "doors."

My sister and I also found dried up earthworms, hard as sticks, in our backyard and attempted to hydrate them by putting them into small buckets full of water. Of course, we did not realize that the earthworms were already dead or that once they were dead, they could not be brought back to life. What we had realized, however, was that earthworms need moisture to survive, and we were attempting to satisfy that need for a few unfortunate crawlers. Our experiences with earthworms, along with our experiences with ants and other creatures that roamed the terrain of our yard, was, I believe, my first introduction to biology — the study of life.

Of course, we did not have texts, typically defined as books, but we had texts, nonetheless. The texts were the plants, bugs, worms, and other forms of life that we observed and, although not apparent to us at the time, studied. The life that we observed, that we "read," were our texts. This is the beauty of biology: We can wake up every day and be sur-rounded by texts waiting to be read, dissected, and engaged into our natu-ral inclinations to attempt to figure out one of life's greatest mysteries — life itself. What life is, what life consists of, what life exists in our universe, and how our own lives are situated in relation to these other forms of life are all issues that we can explore through biology. Indeed, by studying other forms of life, we grow to better understand ourselves.

The more I engage in biology, the more mysteries of life I uncover. And, like a young child looking into an ant hole, the deeper I want to probe. Majoring in biology works for me not just because of the back-ground working knowledge I will gain that will help me should I decide to pursue a career in medicine, but because it satisfies the awe-driven curios-ity that began enveloping my being as a child. Majoring in biology works for me because occasionally I find the golden key to one of life's mysteries. I learn more about myself and the world around me in the process, making me a more informed and whole individual.

"Reading" the texts of life that could only have been written with such beauty and perfection by the Divine Creator is a treasure, a gift, an honor, and a privilege. Through biology, I grab hold of this privilege every day.

Occasionally, I will stop once again to watch a little brown ant scouring the landscape for small pieces of grass and leaves to build its home. I will stop to watch a squirrel on the sidewalk flicking its tail like a big flagellum and then suddenly tense up and run up a tree as another squirrel comes along to chase it. I will stop to admire a tree that has fuzzy bell-shaped knobs extending from its branches. Sometimes, I will even stop to watch people like me, running on sneakered feet to make it to the next class, or laughing and teasing each other in the sunshine. I watch, I read, and I study. This is biology.

Brandon Barrett's Analysis of His Rhetorical Situation and of His Use of Logos, Pathos, and Ethos

I'm writing this essay to explain how I made the most important decision in my life to date: what to major in while in college. I want to explain this not only to my audience but to myself as well, for bold decisions frequently need to be revisited in light of new evidence. There are those for whom the choice of major isn't much of a choice at all. For them, it's a vocation, in the strict Webster's definition of the word: a summons, a calling. I'm not one of those people, and for me the decision was fraught with anxiety. Do I still believe that I made the right choice? Yes, I do, and I want my essay not only to reflect how serious I feel this issue to be but also to convey the confidence that I finally achieved.

This essay will be read by my professor and the other students in my class. Given this audience, I can speak in more conversational terms than I otherwise might. I can also be sure that all college students can relate to the topic at hand; therefore, the tone can be somewhat looser and less formal.

Logos: This essay is about my own opinions and experiences and therefore contains no statistics and hard facts. What it should contain, though, are legitimate reasons for choosing the major I did. If I seem insincere or uncertain, then my audience may question the honesty of my essay. My choice should be shown as following a set of believable driving forces.

Pathos: Since my audience is composed mostly of college students, I'll want to appeal to their own experiences regarding their choice of major and the sometimes conflicting emotions that accompany such a decision.

Specifically, I want to focus on the feelings of confidence and relief that come when you have firmly made up your mind. My audience will be able to relate to these feelings, and it will make the essay more relevant and real to them.

Ethos: The inherent danger in writing an essay about my desire to be a chemistry major is that I may be instantly labeled as boring or snooty. I want to dispel this image as quickly as possible in my essay, and humor is always a good way to counter such stereotypes. On the other hand, this is a serious subject, and the infusion of too much humor will portray me as somebody who hasn't given this too much thought. I want to strike a balance between being earnest and being human.

THE ALL-PURPOSE ANSWER
by Brandon Barrett

When I was a small child, I would ask my parents, as children are apt to do, questions concerning the important things in my life. "Why is the sky blue?" "Why do my Cocoa Puffs turn the milk in my cereal bowl brown?" If I asked my father questions such as these, he always attempted to provide detailed technical answers that left me solemnly nodding my head in complete confusion. But if I asked my mother, she would simply shrug her shoulders and reply, "Something to do with chemistry, I guess." Needless to say, I grew up with a healthy respect for the apparently boundless powers of chemistry. Its responsibilities seemed staggeringly wide-ranging, and I figured that if there was a God he was probably not an omnipotent deity but actually the Original Chemist.

In my early years, I regarded chemistry as nothing less than magic at work. So what is chemistry, if not magic — or a parent's response to a curious child's persistent questions? Chemistry is the study of the elements, how those elements combine, how they interact with one another, and how all this affects Joe Average down the street. Chemists, then, study not magic but microscopic bits of matter all busily doing their thing. When all those bits of matter can be coerced into doing something that humans find useful or interesting — like giving off massive quantities of energy, providing lighting for our homes, or making Uncle Henry smell a little better — then the chemists who produced the desired effect can pat themselves on the back and maybe even feel just a little bit like God.

Chemists solve problems, whether the problem is a need for a new medicine or a stronger plastic bowl to pour our Wheaties into. They develop new materials and study existing ones through a variety of techniques that have been refined over the decades. Chemists also struggle to keep the powers of chemistry in check by finding ways to reduce pollution that can be a by-product of chemical processes, to curb the dangers of nuclear waste, and to recycle used materials.

Chemistry is a dynamic field, constantly experiencing new discoveries and applications — heady stuff, to be sure, but heady stuff with a purpose. Chemistry isn't a static, sleepy field of dusty textbooks, nor does it — forgive me, geologists — revolve around issues of questionable importance, such as deviations in the slope of rock strata. Those who know little about chemistry sometimes view it as dull, but I am proud to say that I plan to earn my B.S. in chemistry. And from there, who knows? That's part of the beauty of chemistry. After graduating from college, I could do any number of things, from research to medical school. The study of chemistry is useful in its own right, but it is also great preparation for advanced study in other fields since it encourages the development of logical thought and reasoning. In one sense, logical thought (not to mention research and medical school) may seem a giant step away from a child's idle questions. But as chemistry demonstrates, perhaps those questions weren't so childish after all.

■ ■ ■

FOR EXPLORATION

In what ways do Tova Johnson's and Brandon Barrett's essays draw on Aristotle's three appeals? Write one or two paragraphs responding to this question. Be sure to include at least two or three examples in your analysis.

The strategies described in this chapter — analyzing your rhetorical situation and employing Aristotle's three appeals — are grounded in commonsense principles of communication, principles that date back at least to the time of Plato and Aristotle. Understanding these principles and knowing how to apply them will enable you to respond effectively in a variety of writing situations.

■ ■ ■

FOR THOUGHT, DISCUSSION, AND WRITING

1. Annette Chambers, Tova Johnson, and Brandon Barrett did a good job, you'll probably agree, in anticipating the expectations and interests of their readers. In writing their essays, they focused not just on content (what they wanted to say) but also on strategy (how they might convey their ideas to their readers). Not all interactions between writer and reader are as successful. You may have read textbooks that seemed more concerned with the subject matter than with

readers' needs and expectations. Or you may have received direct mail advertising or other business communications that irritated or offended you. Find an example of writing that in your view fails to anticipate the expectations and needs of the reader and write one or two paragraphs explaining your reasons. Your teacher may ask you to bring your example and written explanation to class to share with your classmates.

2. Analyze the ways in which the following three advertisements (pp. 177–79) draw on Aristotle's three appeals: *logos, pathos,* and *ethos.*

To my Children – David, Diana, Michael,
We're running out of tomorrows. I'm so proud of you!
I always *loved* you and always will.
Good bye my darlings.
                                    Mom

Dearest Jon,
I am so sorry my smoking will cheat us
out of 20 or 30 more years together. Remember
the fun we had every year at the lake. I will
ALWAYS love and treasure you.
                                    Linda

To the TOBACCO Companies,
    My name is Linda. I'm dying from emphysema
from **smoking**. We know you are in this for the
money. We are in it for our lives and the lives
of our loved ones. AND WE WILL <u>WIN</u>!

For information on quitting smoking,
call 1-800-4-A-LEGACY
or visit www.americanlegacy.org.
Time is **important**.

Legacy
American Legacy Foundation®

America's phone system.
A tradition of operating in the public trust.

Telephone service, a public trust

An Advertisement of the
American Telephone and Telegraph Company

237
July, 1928

The greatest phone system in the world started with a contract between a phone company and a nation.

AT&T was allowed to build and operate an integrated national telephone network. In return, AT&T held it in the public trust and managed it for the good of the entire nation. AT&T's mandate was to continuously improve the technology and make sure it was distributed universally – affordable and accessible to every American.

The Bell telephone companies inherited our nation's phone system and have a mandate from Congress to open the lines to competition and innovation.

The nation's phone system was built as a public trust – it's time for the Bell companies to work to restore it.

America deserves nothing less.

AT&T

"HOW MUCH LONGER?" "WHEN WILL THE MARKET RECOVER?"

"WHAT CAN I DO?"

WE AT LEAST HAVE AN ANSWER FOR THE LAST QUESTION.

There's never been a better time for Schwab Private Client.™

AN OBJECTIVE
PERSONAL RELATIONSHIP

Today, every investor is asking different questions. And there are no pat answers. That's where a Schwab Private Client Consultant can help. They'll work with you face to face to develop a personalized plan with your specific needs in mind. Your Private Client Consultant can also help you track your performance with periodic portfolio reports set against relevant benchmarks to help you keep on track.

GREG ROVENTINI
SCHWAB PRIVATE
CLIENT CONSULTANT

TOUGH MARKETS REQUIRE
THOUGHTFUL DIVERSIFICATION

Investing in the market should involve appropriate asset allocation and a long-term plan. Your Private Client Consultant can show you how to properly diversify across stocks, bonds and cash. Such diversification can help you weather fluctuations in the market. And for added expertise, your Schwab Private Client Consultant is backed by a dedicated team of specialists in areas like fixed income, global investing and retirement planning.

IDENTIFYING
POTENTIAL OPPORTUNITIES

The past few months have been painful for all of us. (After all, we're investors, too.) But there are things you can do, starting with a review of your current portfolio and asset allocation. Every day, we help investors reallocate certain assets to areas that may offer greater opportunities for returns or reduced risk in the year ahead. That may mean selling some stocks you're still hanging on to in hopes of a bounceback, taking the loss and potential tax write-offs and then reallocating that money to other investments or stocks. Your Private Client Consultant can help you find the customized solution that's right for you.

OBJECTIVE, EXPERT
ADVICE THAT'S NOT DRIVEN
BY COMMISSION

Schwab Private Client Consultants are paid as professionals, not commissioned brokers. You'll be charged a fee based on the assets in your portfolio. The consultants' compensation is linked to this asset amount, helping to ensure their focus is on achieving our clients' goals through objective advice.

EXPERIENCE A DIFFERENT WAY
TO MANAGE YOUR INVESTMENTS

To learn more about what a Schwab Private Client Consultant can do for you, call to schedule an initial consultation.

SCHEDULE AN APPOINTMENT
WITH A SCHWAB
PRIVATE CLIENT CONSULTANT.

CALL
1-800-761-5463.

THE PRINCIPLES OF SCHWAB

THE PRINCIPLE OF THE INDIVIDUAL INVESTOR · THE PRINCIPLE OF FACTS, NOT HYPE · THE PRINCIPLE OF ADVICE NOT DRIVEN BY COMMISSION

charles SCHWAB

| Call | 1-800-761-5463 | Click | schwab.com | Visit | 395 locations nationwide |

CHAPTER

6

Thinking about Communities and Conventions

Whenever you analyze a rhetorical situation, you ask yourself a number of commonsense questions about your writing purpose and situation. As you do so, you naturally draw on your previous experiences as a writer and reader and as a speaker and listener. No one had to teach you, for instance, that a letter of condolence to a friend whose mother recently died should be written differently than than an instant message asking a friend to drop by for pizza. Your general social and cultural understanding of the seriousness of your friend's bereavement would cause you automatically to write a formal, respectful letter. As Chapter 3, "Understanding the Reading Process," pointed out, readers often make similar rhetorical judgments. When you glance through your mail, tossing aside ads while eagerly searching for a letter from a friend, your actions are the result of a rhetorical judgment that you — perhaps unconsciously — are making about the nature and value of these texts. You may see a letter from a friend as an invitation to settle into a chair for welcome news. A sales brochure brings quite different expectations.

Whether you are reading or writing, you draw on your previous experiences to make a number of judgments about a text's purpose, subject matter, and form. When you are writing or reading familiar kinds of texts, these judgments occur almost automatically. In less familiar situations, you may have to work to understand the form and purpose of a text. I recently received a letter from a former student, Monica Molina, who now works at a community health center, where one of her responsibilities is to write grant proposals. In her letter, she commented as follows:

> It took quite a while before I could feel comfortable even thinking about trying to write my first grant proposal. Most of the ones at our center run 50 to 100 pages and seem so intimidating — full of strange subheadings, technical language, complicated explanations. I had to force myself to calm down and get into them. First I read some recent proposals, trying to figure out how they worked. Luckily, my boss is friendly and support-

ive, so she sat down with me and talked about her experiences writing proposals. We looked at some proposals together, and she told me about how proposals are reviewed by agencies. Now we're working together on my first proposal. I'm still nervous, but I'm beginning to feel more comfortable. When I feel stressed out about it, I try to tell myself that "firsts" are always difficult.

Most writers sooner or later face the challenge of writing (and reading) unfamiliar kinds of texts. Students entering a new discipline may find themselves puzzled by unfamiliar language or writing styles. And like Monica, those entering new professions often must learn new forms of writing.

Writers who wish to participate in a new community must strive to understand its reading and writing practices — to learn how to enter its conversations, as the rhetorician Kenneth Burke might say. For the forms and strategies of writing that characterize different communities are not arbitrary but rather reflect important shared assumptions and practices. These shared assumptions and practices — sometimes referred to as *textual conventions* — represent agreements between writers and readers about how to construct and interpret texts. As such, they are an important component of any rhetorical situation.

ANALYZING TEXTUAL CONVENTIONS

The notion of *textual convention* may be new to you, but you can understand it easily if you think about other uses of the word *convention*. For example, *social conventions* are implicit agreements among the members of a community or culture about how to act in particular situations. At one time in the United States, for example, it was acceptable for persons who chewed tobacco to spit tobacco juice into spittoons in restaurants and hotel lobbies. This particular social convention has changed over time and is no longer acceptable.

If social conventions represent agreements among individuals about how to act, textual conventions represent similar agreements about how to write and read texts. Just as we tend to take our own social conventions for granted, so too do we take for granted those textual conventions most familiar to us as readers and writers. When we begin a letter to our parents by writing "Dear Mom and Dad," for instance, we don't stop to wonder if this greeting is appropriate; we know from our experience as writers and readers that it is. When we read a text from another time or culture, we can sometimes see more clearly than in our own writing the extent to which such texts depend on shared understandings. During the Middle Ages, salutations (such as "Dear Mom and Dad") were much more formal and elaborate than contemporary greetings.

Here are two suggested salutations for teachers and pupils from *The Principles of Letter Writing,* a medieval guide for writers:

The Salutation of a Teacher to a Pupil

N —— , promoter of the scholastic profession, wishes N —— , his most dear friend and companion, to acquire the teachings of all literature, to possess fully all the diligence of the philosophical profession, to pursue not folly but the wisdom of Socrates and Plato.

The Salutation of a Pupil to a Teacher

To N —— , by divine grace resplendent in Ciceronian charm, N —— , inferior to his devoted learning, expresses the servitude of a sincere heart.*

The Principles of Letter Writing includes fourteen additional categories of salutations, including "Salutations of Close Friends or Associates," "Salutations of Subjects to Their Secular Lords," and "Salutations of Lords to Blamable and Offending Subordinates." The textual conventions governing these greetings reflect this period's attentiveness to differences in rank and station. Over time, such elaborate, ritualized salutations have been replaced by much simpler forms of address — thus, "Dear Mom and Dad."

Textual conventions are dynamic, changing over time as the assumptions, values, and practices of writers and readers change. Consider some of the textual conventions of email and other online writing. Emoticons, for instance — symbols such as **:-)** to indicate happiness, **:-(** to indicate sadness, or **:-O** to indicate shock or surprise — were developed by online writers who wished to express the kind of emotion often conveyed in face-to-face communication by such elements as voice, gesture, and facial expression. Not all who use email use emoticons, and those who do use them recognize that they may be more appropriate in some situations than others. But as a textual convention, emoticons clearly respond to the needs of some email users, writers, and readers.

■ ■ ■

FOR EXPLORATION

The transition from print to electronic writing technologies represents a significant change in the situation of writers and readers. Freewrite for five or ten minutes about the extent to which the textual conventions of online writing differ from those of traditional print communications.

---

*These salutations are excerpted from James J. Murphy, ed., *Three Medieval Rhetorical Arts* (Berkeley: U California P, 1971), 14–15. (The letter "N ——" in these salutations stands for "name.")

Making Appropriate Decisions about Your Writing

Whether you are entering a community of online writers or a new academic or professional community, analyzing your rhetorical situation will enable you to communicate effectively with others. Because they play such a critical role in making communication between writers and readers possible, textual conventions are an important component of the rhetorical situation. When you think about the kind of writing that you are being asked to do, for instance, you are thinking in part about the textual conventions that may limit your options as a writer in a specific situation. Textual conventions bring constraints, but they also increase the likelihood that readers will respond appropriately to a writer's ideas.

Some textual conventions are specific. Personal letters always begin with a greeting and end with a signature. Sonnets have fourteen rhymed lines, usually consisting of either an octave (eight lines) and sextet (six lines) or three four-line quatrains with a closing couplet. Similarly, lab reports usually include the following elements: title page, abstract, introduction, experimental design and methods, results, discussion, and references. Someone writing a sonnet or a lab report can deviate from these textual conventions, but doing so runs the risk of confusing or irritating readers.

Other textual conventions are much more general. Consider, for instance, the conventions of an academic essay:

Characteristics of an Effective Academic Essay

1. An effective essay is well organized and well developed. It establishes its subject or main idea in the introduction, develops that idea in a coherent manner in the body, and summarizes or completes the discussion in the conclusion.

2. An effective essay is logical. It supports its main points with well-chosen evidence, illustrations, and details.

3. An effective essay is clear and readable. It uses words, sentences, and paragraphs that are carefully crafted, appropriate for the writer's purpose and subject, and free of errors of usage, grammar, and punctuation.

These statements summarize some of the most general conventions that govern academic essays. But because these statements are so general and apply to so many different kinds of writing, you may not know just what they mean in specific situations and in your own writing.

Seeing Textual Conventions in Use

To see how textual conventions operate and to illustrate how you can analyze them, let's consider just one of the conventions of an effective essay: It uses an introduction to establish its subject or main idea. This particular textual convention is learned early, for even young children introduce stories (in Western cultures, at least) with the words *Once upon a time.* Most writers and readers can easily understand why an essay needs an introduction. No one likes to be thrown into the middle of a discussion without any idea of the subject. Still, writers are not always certain about what constitutes the best introduction for a specific essay.

Let's look at introductions to three articles by linguist Deborah Tannen to see how one writer tackles this problem. Each article is based on research that Tannen conducted on the limitations of what she describes as America's "argument culture." (In 1999, Tannen published a book titled *The Argument Culture: Stopping America's War of Words.*) You may be familiar with some of Tannen's work: Her book *You Just Don't Understand: Women and Men in Conversation,* published in 1990, was on the *New York Times* best-seller list for almost four years, including eight months at the top of the list. Tannen is not only a prolific writer — she has published nineteen books and nearly 100 articles — but she writes for unusually diverse audiences. If you visit her homepage at <http://www.georgetown.edu/faculty/tannend/index.htm>, you will notice that she lists the following categories for publications: books, academic publications, general audience publications, and creative writing (poetry, short stories, essays, and plays). Many links on Tannen's page allow you to access her complete texts if you wish to do so.

The first article that is excerpted here — "For Argument's Sake: Why Do We Feel Compelled to Fight about Everything?" (pp. 186–87) — appeared in the Sunday, March 15, 1998, edition of the *Washington Post,* a major newspaper with a large national distribution. The second article — "Agonism in the Academy: Surviving Higher Learning's Argument Culture" (pp. 188–89) — appeared in the March 31, 2000, edition of the *Chronicle of Higher Education.* This weekly newspaper is read by faculty, staff, and administrators who work in community colleges, four-year colleges, and universities. The final section of each issue of the *Chronicle* concludes with a one-page opinion column. Tannen's article appeared as such a column. The final article that is excerpted here — "Agonism in Academic Discourse" (pp. 190–91) — was published in 2002 in volume 34 of the *Journal of Pragmatics,* a scholarly publication that is read by people who are interested in such topics as pragmatics, semantics, language acquisition, and so on. Those who read this journal work in academic disciplines such as linguistics, sociology, psychology, anthropology, and philosophy. (The article follows the British style of punctuation.)

■ ■ ■

FOR EXPLORATION

Read the introductions to Tannen's three articles (pp. 185–90), and write three paragraphs characterizing their approaches — one paragraph for

For Argument's Sake

Why Do We Feel Compelled to Fight About Everything?

By DEBORAH TANNEN

I was waiting to go on a television talk show a few years ago for a discussion about how men and women communicate, when a man walked in wearing a shirt and tie and a floor-length skirt, the top of which was brushed by his waist-length red hair. He politely introduced himself and told me that he'd read and liked my book *You Just Don't Understand,* which had just been published. Then he added, "When I get out there, I'm going to attack you. But don't take it personally. That's why they invite me on, so that's what I'm going to do."

We went on the set and the show began. I had hardly managed to finish a sentence or two before the man threw his arms out in gestures of anger, and began shrieking — briefly hurling accusations at me, and then railing at length against women. The strangest thing about his hysterical outburst was how the studio audience reacted: They turned vicious — not attacking me (I hadn't said anything substantive yet) or him (who wants to tangle with someone who screams at you?) but the other guests: women who had come to talk about problems they had communicating with their spouses.

My antagonist was nothing more than a dependable provocateur, brought on to ensure a lively

show. The incident has stayed with me not because it was typical of the talk shows I have appeared on — it wasn't, I'm happy to say — but because it exemplifies the ritual nature of much of the opposition that pervades our public dialogue.

Everywhere we turn, there is evidence that, in public discourse, we prize contentiousness and aggression more than cooperation and conciliation. Headlines blare about the Starr Wars, the Mommy Wars, the Baby Wars, the Mammography Wars; everything is posed in terms of battles and duels, winners and losers, conflicts and disputes. Biographies have metamorphosed into demonographies whose authors don't just portray their subjects warts and all, but set out to dig up as much dirt as possible, as if the story of a person's life is contained in the warts, only the warts, and nothing but the warts.

It's all part of what I call the argument culture, which rests on the assumption that opposition is the best way to get anything done: The best way to discuss an idea is to set up a debate. The best way to cover news is to find people who express the most extreme views and present them as "both sides." The best way to begin an essay is to attack someone. The best way to show you're really thoughtful is to criticize. The best way to settle disputes is to litigate them.

It is the automatic nature of this response that I am calling into question. This is not to say that passionate opposition and strong verbal attacks are never appropriate. In the words of the Yugoslavian-born poet Charles Simic, "There are moments in life when true invective is called for, when it becomes an absolute necessity, out of a deep sense of justice, to denounce, mock, vituperate, lash out, in the strongest possible language." What I'm questioning is the ubiquity, the knee-jerk nature of approaching almost any issue, problem or public person in an adversarial way.

Smashing heads does not open minds. In this as in so many things, results are also causes, looping back and entrapping us. The pervasiveness of warlike formats and language grows out of, but also gives rise to, an ethic of aggression: We come to value aggressive tactics for their own sake — for the sake of argument. Compromise becomes a dirty word, and we often feel guilty if we are conciliatory rather than confrontational — even if we achieve the result we're seeking.

Here's one example. A woman called another talk show on which I was a guest. She told the following story: "I was in a place where a man was smoking, and there was a no-smoking sign. Instead of saying 'You aren't allowed to smoke in here. Put that out!' I said, 'I'm awfully sorry, but I have asthma, so your smoking makes it hard for me to breathe. Would you mind terribly not smoking?' When I said this, the man was extremely polite and solicitous, and he put his cigarette out, and I said, 'Oh, thank you, thank you!' as if he'd done a wonderful thing for me. Why did I do that?"

I think this woman expected me — the communications expert — to say she needs assertiveness training to confront smokers in a more aggressive manner. Instead, I told her that her approach was just fine. If she had tried to alter his behavior by reminding him of the rules, he might well have rebelled: "Who made you the enforcer? Mind your own business!" She had given the smoker a face-saving way of doing what she wanted, one that allowed him to feel chivalrous rather than chastised. This was kinder to him, but it was also kinder to herself, since it was more likely to lead to the result she desired.

Another caller disagreed with me, saying the first caller's style was "self-abasing." I persisted: There was nothing necessarily destructive about the way the woman handled the smoker. The mistake the second caller was making — a mistake many of us make — was to confuse ritual self-effacement with the literal kind. All human relations require us to find ways to get what we want from others without seeming to dominate them.

The opinions expressed by the two callers encapsulate the ethic of aggression that has us by our throats, particularly in public arenas such as politics and law.

Issues are routinely approached by having two sides stake out opposing positions and do battle. This sometimes drives people to take positions that are more adversarial than they feel — and can get in the way of reaching a possible resolution. I have experienced this firsthand.

For my book about the workplace, "Talking from 9 to 5," I spent time in companies, shadowing people, interviewing them and having individuals tape conversations when I wasn't there. Most companies were happy to proceed on a verbal agreement setting forth certain ground rules: Individuals would control the taping, identifying names would be changed, I would show them what I wrote about their company and change or delete anything they did not approve. I also signed confidentiality agreements promising not to reveal anything I learned about the company's business.

Some companies, however, referred the matter to their attorneys so a contract could be written. In no case where attorneys became involved — mine as well as theirs — could we reach an agreement on working together.

Negotiations with one company stand out. Having agreed on the procedures and safeguards, we expected to have a contract signed in a matter of weeks. But six months later, after thousands of dollars in legal fees and untold hours of everyone's time, the negotiations reached a dead end. The company's lawyer was demanding veto power over my entire book; it meant the company could (if it chose) prevent me from publishing the book even if I used no more than a handful of examples from this

Agonism in the Academy: Surviving Higher Learning's Argument Culture

By Deborah Tannen

A READING GROUP that I belong to, composed of professors, recently discussed a memoir by an academic. I came to the group's meeting full of anticipation, eager to examine the insights I'd gained from the book and to be enlightened by those that had intrigued my fellow group members. As the meeting began, one member announced that she hadn't read the book; four, including me, said they'd read and enjoyed it; and one said she hadn't liked it because she does not like academic memoirs. She energetically criticized the book. "It's written in two voices," she said, "and the voices don't interrogate each other."

Quickly, two other members joined her critique, their point of view becoming a chorus. They sounded smarter, seeing faults that the rest of us had missed, making us look naive. We credulous three tried in vain to get the group talking about what we had found interesting or important in the book, but our suggestions were dull compared to the game of critique.

I left the meeting disappointed because I had learned nothing new about the book or its subject. All I had learned about was the acumen of the critics. I was especially struck by the fact that one of the most talkative and influential critics was the member who had not read the book. Her unfamiliarity with the work had not hindered her, because the critics had focused more on what they saw as faults of the genre than on faults of the particular book.

The turn that the discussion had taken reminded me of the subject of my most recent book, *The Argument Culture.* The phenomenon I'd observed at the book-group meeting was an example of what the cultural linguist Walter Ong calls "agonism," which he defines in *Fighting for Life* as "programmed contentiousness" or "ceremonial combat." Agonism does not refer to disagreement, conflict, or vigorous dispute. It refers to retualized opposition — for instance, a debate in which the contestants are assigned opposing positions and one

party wins, rather than an argument that arises naturally when two parties disagree.

In *The Argument Culture,* I explored the role and effects of agonism in three domains of public discourse: journalism, politics, and the law. But the domain in which I first identified the phenomenon and began thinking about it is the academic world. I remain convinced that agonism is endemic in academe — and bad for it.

The way we train our students, conduct our classes and our research, and exchange ideas at meetings and in print are all driven by our ideological assumption that intellectual inquiry is a metaphorical battle. Following from that is a second assumption, that the best way to demonstrate intellectual prowess is to criticize, find fault, and attack.

Many aspects of our academic lives can be described as agonistic. For example, in our scholarly papers, most of us follow a conventional framework that requires us to position our work in opposition to someone else's, which we prove wrong. The framework tempts — almost requires — us to oversimplify or even misrepresent others' positions; cite the weakest example to make a generally resonable work appear less so; and ignore facts that supports others' views, citing only evidence that supports our own positions.

The way we train our students frequently reflects the battle metaphor as well. We assign scholarly work for them to read, then invite them to tear it apart. That is helpful to an extent, but it often means that they don't learn to do the harder work of integrating ideas, or of considering the work's historical and disciplinary context. Moreover,

it fosters in students a stance of arrogance and narrow-mindedness, qualities that do not serve the fundamental goals of education.

In the classroom, if students are engaged in heated debate, we believe that education is taking place. But in a 1993 article in *The History Teacher,* Patricia Rosof, who teaches at Hunter College High School in New York City, advises us to look more closely at what's really happening. If we do, she says, we will probably find that only a few students are participating; some other students may be paying attention, but many may be turned off. Furthermore, the students who are arguing generally simplify the points they are making or disputing. To win the argument, they ignore complexity and nuance. The refuse to concede a point raised by their opponents, even if they can see that it is valid, because such a concession would weaken their position. Nobody tries to synthesize the various views, because that would look indecisive, or weak.

If the class engages in discussion rather than debate — adding such intellectual activities as exploring ideas, uncovering nuances, comparing and contrasting different interpretations of a work — more students take part, and more of them gain a deeper, and more accurate, understanding of the material. Most important, the students learn a stance of respect and open-minded inquiry.

Academic rewards — good grades and good jobs — typically go to students and scholars who learn to tear down others' work, not to those who learn to build on the work of their colleagues. In *The Argument Culture,* I cited a study in which communications researchers Karen Tracy and Sheryl Baratz ex-

amined weekly colloquia attended by faculty members and graduate students at a large university. As the authors reported in a 1993 article in *Communication Monographs,* although most people said the purpose of the colloquia was to "trade ideas" and "learn things," faculty members in fact were judging the students' competence based on their participation in the colloquia. And the professors didn't admire students who asked "a nice little supportive question," as one put it — they valued "tough and challenging questions."

One problem with the agonistic culture of graduate training is that potential scholars who are not comfortable with that kind of interaction are likely to drop out. As a result, many talented and creative minds are lost to academe. And, with fewer colleagues who prefer different approaches, those who remain are more likely to egg each other on to even grater adversarial heights. Some scholars who do stay in acaceme are reluctant to present their work at conferences or submit it for publication because of their reluctance to take part in adversarial discourse. The cumulative effect is that nearly everyone feels vulnerable and defensive, and thus less willing to suggest new ideas, offer new perspectives, or question received wisdom.

Although scholarly attacks are ritual — prescribed by the conventions of academe — the emotions propelling them can be real. Jane Tompkins, a literary critic who has written about the genre of the western in modern fiction and film, has compared scholarly exchanges to shootouts. In a 1988 article in *The Georgia Review,* she noted that her own career took off when she published an essay that "began with a

journal of
PRAGMATICS

Journal of Pragmatics 34 (2002) 1651–1669

www.elsevier.com/locate/pragma

ELSEVIER

Agonism in academic discourse☆

Deborah Tannen

Linguistics Department, Georgetown University, Box 571051, Washington DC 20057-1051, USA

Abstract

The pervasiveness of agonism, that is, ritualized adversativeness, in contemporary western academic discourse is the source of both obfuscation of knowledge and personal suffering in academia. Framing academic discourse as a metaphorical battle leads to a variety of negative consequences, many of which have ethical as well as personal dimensions. Among these consequences is a widespread assumption that critical dialogue is synonymous with negative critique, at the expense of other types of 'critical thinking'. Another is the requirement that scholars search for weaknesses in others' work at the expense of seeking strengths, understanding the roots of theoretical differences, or integrating disparate but related ideas. Agonism also encourages the conceptualization of complex and subtle work as falling into two simplified warring camps. Finally, it leads to the exclusion or marginalization of those who lack a taste for agonistic interchange. Alternative approaches to intellectual interchange need not entirely replace agonistic ones but should be accommodated alongside them. © 2002 Elsevier Science B.V. All rights reserved.

Keywords: Academic discourse; Agonism; Disagreement; Ritualized opposition; Exclusion

☆ Varying versions of this paper were delivered at the Georgetown Linguistics Society 1995, Washington, DC; Georgetown University Round Table on Languages and Linguistics 1999, Washington, D.C.; Pragma99, Tel Aviv, Israel, August 1999; and as the Hayward Keniston Lecture, University of Michigan, October 27, 1999. A briefer account, written for a more general audience, appears as "Agonism in the Academy: Surviving Higher Learning's Argument Culture", The Chronicle of Higher Education March 31, 2000, B7-8. Some sections of the present paper are based on material that appears in my book The Argument Culture; most, however, is new. I would like to thank Elizabeth Eisenstein, Shari Kendall, Joseph P. Newhouse, and Keli Yerian for leading me to sources that I cite here. For thoughtful comments on an earlier draft, I am grateful to A.L. Becker, Paul Friedrich, Susan Gal, Heidi Hamilton, Natalie Schilling-Estes, Ron Scollon, Malcah Yaeger-Dror, and three anonymous reviewers. This contribution is dedicated to the memory of Suzanne Fleischman, whose death which occurred while I was working on the paper cast a shadow of sadness, and whose own work, like her article cited here, made such an enormous contribution to restoring the person of the scholar to scholarship.

E-mail address: tannend@georgetown.edu (D. Tannen).

1652   *D. Tannen / Journal of Pragmatics 34 (2002) 1651–1669*

1. Introduction and overview

In doing discourse analysis, we use discourse to do our analysis, yet we seldom examine the discourse we use. There are, of course, important exceptions, such as Tracy (1997) on departmental colloquia, Fleischman (1998) on the erasure of the personal in academic writing, Goffman (1981) on "The Lecture", Herring (1996) on e-mail lists, Chafe and Danielewicz (1987) who include "academic speaking" and "academic writing" in their comparison of spoken and written language, and Swales' (1990) study of academic writing as well as his recent examination of the physical and interactional contexts that give rise to it (1998). Perhaps most closely related to my topic is Hunston (1993), who examines oppositional argumentation in biology, history, and sociolinguistics articles (two each), and concludes that the less empirical disciplines are more 'argumentative'. Here I turn my attention to an aspect of academic discourse that, as far I know, has not previously been examined: what I call "agonism".

Ong (1981: 24), from whom I borrow the term, defines agonism as "programmed contentiousness", "ceremonial combat". I use the term to refer not to conflict, disagreement, or disputes per se, but rather to *ritualized* adversativeness. In academic discourse, this means conventionalized oppositional formats that result from an underlying ideology by which intellectual interchange is conceptualized as a metaphorical battle. In a recent book (Tannen, 1998), I explore the role and effects of agonism in three domains of public discourse: journalism, politics, and law. Here I turn to the discourse domain in which I first identified the phenomenon and began thinking about it: the academy.

My goal is to uncover agonistic elements in academic discourse and to examine their effects on our pursuit of knowledge and on the community of scholars engaged in that pursuit. In arguing that an ideology of agonism provides a usually unquestioned foundation for much of our oral and written interchange, I focus on exposing the destructive aspects of this ideology and its attendant practices. I do not, however, call for an end to agonism – a goal that would be unrealistic even if it were desirable, which I am not sure it is. Rather, I argue for a broadening of our modes of inquiry, so that agonism is, one might say, demoted from its place of ascendancy, and for a re-keying or 'toning down' of the more extreme incarnations of agonism in academic discourse.

In what follows, I begin by sketching my own early interest in agonism in conversational discourse. Then I briefly present some historical background, tracing the seeds of agonism in academic discourse to classical Greek philosophy and the medieval university. Against this backdrop, I move to examining agonistic elements as well as the cultural and ideological assumptions that underlie them in academic discourse: both spoken (at conferences, in classrooms, and in intellectual discussions) and written (in grant proposals, journal articles, books, and reviews of all of these). I demonstrate some unfortunate consequences of the agonistic character of these discourse types, both for the pursuit of knowledge and for the community of scholars and others who hope to gain from our knowledge. I then suggest that the existence and perpetuation of agonistic elements in academic discourse depends on each article. (Be sure to read the abstract and the footnote on the first page of the article from the *Journal of Pragmatics,* which provide important clues about Tannen's rhetorical situation and the interests and expectations of her scholarly readers.) How would you describe Tannen's tone in each article? What kind of language does she use in each article? What can you learn from your analysis about the differences among these articles?

Comparing and Contrasting Textual Conventions

By glancing at the first pages of Tannen's three articles, you will notice some striking differences among them. The first page of "For Argument's Sake: Why Do We Feel Compelled to Fight about Everything?" (pp. 186–87), has a good deal of white space and large illustrations. These illustrations, along with the title of the article, help draw readers into Tannen's text. After all, the *Washington Post* is a large multisection newspaper, and the Sunday edition is much larger than the daily edition. If Tannen and her editors hope to capture readers' interest, they must draw their attention in a dramatic way.

The incident that Tannen describes at the start of her article is certainly dramatic. She recalls her encounter with a strangely dressed man with waist-long red hair who, like her, is waiting to appear on a television show. After he praises her book *You Just Don't Understand,* the man nevertheless announces that "When I get out there, I'm going to attack you. But don't take it personally. That's why they invite me on, so that's what I'm going to do." After describing the rest of this incident and reflecting on her antagonist, Tannen moves to the major assertion of her article: "Everywhere we turn, there is evidence that, in public discourse, we prize contentiousness and aggression more than cooperation and conciliation." The rest of her article provides several examples of a widespread argument culture in America and suggests some of the limitations of such a culture.

The second article, from the *Chronicle of Higher Education* (pp. 188–89), is more visually dense than the first — though it does have some white space and a drawing of stylized boxers at the bottom of the page. Rather than having an attention-getting title that invites readers into the article with a question ("Why Do We Feel Compelled to Fight about Everything?"), the title of this article uses the scholarly term *agonism* to identify its subject. Tannen does appeal to her readers' interests, however, with her subtitle. Most readers would be aware that the academy can be a difficult and argumentative place, so they would appreciate knowing how best to *survive* in such a climate.

In the *Chronicle* article, as in the first article, Tannen begins by recounting an incident that suggests a culture of argument. Since her readers are educators, she focuses on an experience they might share — participating in a reading group whose members find it easier to criticize than praise a book (even when they haven't read it). After reflecting on this incident, she mentions her recently published book *The Argument Culture* and clarifies what she means by "agonism." After briefly describing her book, she sets out the thesis of her article: "The way we train our students, conduct our classes and our research, and exchange ideas at meetings and in print are all driven by our ideological assumption that intellectual inquiry is a metaphorical battle. Following from that is a second assumption, that the best way to demonstrate intellectual prowess is to criticize, find fault, and attack." In the remainder of her article, Tannen provides evidence to support these assertions, considers some of the negative consequences of agonism in the academy, and (in a brief closing paragraph) affirms the benefits of changing the culture of the academy. If the latter would happen, Tannen argues, academics "would learn more from each other, be heard more clearly by others, attract more varied talents to the scholarly life, and restore a measure of humanity to ourselves, our endeavor, and the academic world we inhabit."

An important difference between the *Washington Post* article and *Chronicle of Higher Education* article involves the examples and evidence that Tannen provides readers. In the *Post* article, Tannen focuses on examples that a broad range of readers can identify with, such as a phone call to a call-in talk show, the adversarial nature of the legal process, and the ritual attacks on politicians that often appear in the popular press. In the *Chronicle* article, Tannen provides a limited range of examples that involve academic life. She also supports her position by citing other scholars whose research supports her position. In these and other ways, Tannen adjusts her argument to address her particular rhetorical situation.

Tannen's third article (pp. 190–91) appeared in the *Journal of Pragmatics,* which is a specialized publication and presents the most cramped and least inviting first page. Rather than giving this article an attention-getting title, Tannen simply announces her subject: "Agonism in Academic Discourse." The article begins with a full page of prefatory material: the article title, the author's name and university address, an abstract, keywords, and a lengthy footnote that mentions previous versions of the article and makes extensive acknowledgments of people who assisted Tannen in writing the article.

The article itself is divided into sections with numbered headings. The first section, "Introduction and Overview," begins with a dense and heavily referenced discussion of the fact that "In doing discourse analysis, we [scholars] use discourse to do our analysis, yet we seldom examine the discourse we use." After acknowledging exceptions to this statement, Tannen stakes out a major claim for her article: "Here I turn my attention to an aspect of academic discourse that, as far . . . [as] I know, has not previously been examined: what I call 'agonism.'" (Because originality is highly prized in the academy, Tannen's claim that her subject "has not previously been examined" is particularly strong.) After providing further information about this term, Tannen establishes the framework for her article: "My goal is to uncover agonistic elements in academic discourse and to examine their effects on our pursuit of knowledge and on the community of scholars engaged in that pursuit." (Did you notice that in paragraph 2 Tannen cites her most recent book but does not mention its title or describe it, as she did in her article for the *Chronicle of Higher Education?*)

Unlike the *Post* and *Chronicle* articles, which are relatively brief, Tannen's article in the *Journal of Pragmatics* is eighteen densely argued pages long. In subsequent sections, she covers such topics as the roots of agonism in ancient Greek and medieval church discourse. Clearly, Tannen expects much more of readers of this scholarly article than she does of readers of the previous two articles. She assumes that readers will be familiar with the many references she cites or will at least appreciate their inclusion. She also assumes that readers who choose to read her article will bring considerable prior knowledge to this experience and will care deeply about her topic.

Analyzing the first few pages of each article supplies important clues about these three publications and about the expectations that Tannen holds about their readers. In the less specialized publications, Tannen seems to try harder to interest readers in the article. The publishers of those periodicals also seem to pay more attention to visual images and design elements like white space. People who read the *Washington Post,* the most general and least specialized of these publications, often don't have a clear purpose when they read. They read newspapers to learn about recent news and to "keep up" with recent intellectual, cultural, economic, and political developments. Even a person who spends a couple of hours reading the Sunday paper — and how many readers do that? — might well pass over Tannen's article. A writer will consequently attempt to gain the attention of these readers — and so will the editors who commission illustrations and design the visual look of the text.

Those who subscribe to the *Chronicle of Higher Education* represent a more homogeneous — though still diverse — readership. All who read this weekly newspaper either work or are interested in higher education. One reader might be a faculty member in the humanities; such a reader might well be interested in Tannen's essay. But other readers might work in admissions, financial aid, or athletics. For these readers, the term *agonism* might be unfamiliar. Moreover, just as readers skim daily newspapers like the *Washington Post,* so too do many readers skim this weekly publication. As a consequence, even though the readership of the *Chronicle of Higher Education* is less diverse than that of the *Washington Post,* Tannen uses a similar introductory strategy. She employs a catchy title or subtitle for each article, and she begins each article with an interesting anecdote that attempts to capture her readers' interest.

As you may have already realized, Tannen faces a different rhetorical situation in addressing readers of the scholarly *Journal of Pragmatics.* If readers of the *Washington Post* and the *Chronicle of Higher Education* read — or skim — these publications to keep current, those who subscribe to the *Journal of Pragmatics* read this journal to keep up with advances in their field. Readers of the *Journal of Pragmatics* undoubtedly subscribe to many professional publications. They don't have the time to read every article in these journals, so they skim the tables of contents, noting articles that directly affect their own research or have broad significance for their field. The prefatory material that appears in Tannen's third article matters very much to them. Readers of this journal don't have time to read every article in the journals to which they subscribe, so they review various articles' abstracts to determine not only *if* but also *how* they will read an article. Some will read only an article's abstract, others will skim the major points, and others will read the article with great care, returning to it as they conduct their own research. Readers of the *Journal of Pragmatics* would not want to encounter an engaging introduction like the ones that Tannen includes in the *Washington Post* and the *Chronicle of Higher Education*'s articles. Instead, they want a straightforward, concise approach. They value clear, specific headings and scholarly citations over inviting titles, illustrations, and opening anecdotes.

Although these three articles are grounded in the same research project, they differ dramatically in structure, tone, language, and approach to readers. Textual conventions play an important role in these differences. As shared agreements about the construction and interpretation of texts, textual conventions enable readers and writers to communicate successfully in different rhetorical situations.

■ ■ ■

FOR EXPLORATION

1. What kinds of examples are used in each excerpt? What function do they serve?

2. What relationship is established in each article between the writer and the reader? What cues help signal each relationship?

3. How would you characterize the styles of these three excerpts? Point to specific features that characterize each style. What is the effect of these stylistic differences?

4. What assumptions does Tannen make in each article about what readers already know? Point out specific instances that reflect these assumptions.

5. How would you describe the persona, or image of the writer, in each article? What specific factors contribute to the development and coherence of this persona?

UNDERSTANDING THE CONVENTIONS OF ACADEMIC WRITING

Some textual conventions are easy to identify. After reading just a few lab reports, for example, you recognize that this form of writing adheres to a set format. Other textual conventions are less easy to discern and to understand.

When you first read the introductions to Tannen's three essays, for instance, you probably noticed that the introduction to the *Journal of Pragmatics* essay differed considerably from the introductions to the other two, which were published in less scholarly periodicals. You may not, however, have noted the differences between the latter two introductions.

To recognize and understand these differences, you need some knowledge of the journals in which the essays were published and also of the readers of these journals. Tannen's decision to use a technical term, such as *agonism*, in the introduction to the *Chronicle of Higher Education* article reflects her assumption that readers would not only understand terms like this one but would expect them. Furthermore, using such terms subtly tells readers that the writer is an insider, privy to the terminology used by those in this field.

As this example indicates, recognizing and understanding textual conventions requires considerable knowledge not only of the forms of writing but also of the *situations* of writers and readers. When you join a new community of writers and readers, as you do when you enter college, you need to understand the demands of the writing you are expected to complete. Look again, for instance, at the characteristics of an effective essay on p. 183. When you first read these characteristics, they probably made sense to you. Of course, essays should be well organized, well developed, and logical.

When you begin work on an essay for history, sociology, or economics, however, you may find it difficult to determine how to embody these characteristics in your own writing. You might wonder about what will make your analysis of the economic impact of divorce on the modern family logical or illogical. What do economists consider to be appropriate evidence, illustrations, and details? And does your economics teacher value the same kind of logic, evidence, and details as your American literature teacher?

NOTE FOR MULTILINGUAL WRITERS

The conventions of academic writing vary from culture to culture. You may have written successful academic texts in your home culture that followed textual conventions that differ from those you are now being asked to follow. Conventions that can differ in various cultures include the rhetorical strategies that are commonly used to introduce essay topics, the kinds of information that qualify as "objective" evidence in argumentation, the use (or absence) of explicit transitions, and the use (or absence) of first-person pronouns. Given these and other potential differences, you may find it helpful to compare the conventions of academic writing in North America with those of your home culture.

■ ■ ■

FOR EXPLORATION

Freewrite for five or ten minutes about your experiences thus far with academic writing. What do you find productive and satisfying about such writing? What seems difficult and frustrating? Does your ability to respond to the demands of academic writing vary depending on the discipline? Do you find writing essays about literature easier, for instance, than writing lab reports and case studies? What do you think makes some kinds of academic writing harder or easier for you? If you are a multilingual writer, you may also want to consider how your involvement in multiple language communities influences your experiences as an academic writer of English.

Using Textual Conventions

You already know enough about rhetoric and the rhetorical situation to realize that there can be no one-size-fits-all approach to every academic writing situation. To respond successfully to the challenge of academic writing, you must explore rhetorical situations. You must also draw on the rhetorical sensitivity you have gained as a reader, writer, speaker, and listener.

What can you do when you are unfamiliar with the textual conventions of academic writing in general or of a particular discipline? A rhetorical approach to writing suggests that one important way to learn about textual conventions is to read examples of the kind of writing you wish to do. Discussing these models with an insider — your teacher, perhaps, or an advanced student in the field — can help you understand why these conventions work for these readers and writers. Forming a study group with others in your class or meeting with a tutor at a writing center can also help you increase your rhetorical sensitivity to the expectations of your teachers and the conventions of academic writing.

Finally, a rhetorical approach to writing encourages you to think *strategically* about writing — whether personal, professional, or academic — and to respond creatively to the challenges of each situation. As a writer, you have much to consider: your own goals as a writer, the nature of your subject and writing task, the expectations of your readers, the textual conventions your particular situation requires or allows. The rhetorical sensitivity that you have already developed can help you make appropriate choices in response to these and other concerns. But you can also draw on other resources — on textual examples and on discussions with teachers, writing assistants, and other students — as you work on a variety of writing tasks. As a writer, you are not alone. By reaching out to other writers, in person or by reading their work, you can become a fully participating member of the academic community.

■ ■ ■

FOR EXPLORATION

Interview a teacher in another course you are taking this term, preferably one in which you have done some writing, so that you can learn more about your teacher's expectations of student writing. You may wish to ask some or all of the following questions:

1. What do you look for when you read students' writing? How would you characterize effective student writing in your discipline?

2. In your discipline, what is the difference between an A and a C student essay (or lab report or case study)?

3. What are the major weaknesses or limitations of the writing produced by your students?

4. What advice would you give to students who want to understand how to write more effectively in introductory classes in your field?

5. Do you think your discipline values particular qualities in student writing not necessarily shared by other fields, or is good writing good writing no matter what the discipline?

6. Could you suggest some examples that I could read that would help me understand the conventions of effective writing in your discipline?

7. How would you characterize the differences between effective student writing and effective professional writing in your field?

8. What role do you see yourself playing when you read student writing?

9. Is there anything else you can tell me that would help me better understand the kind of student writing valued in your discipline?

After your interview, write a summary of your teacher's responses. Then write at least two paragraphs reflecting on what this interview has taught you about academic writing.

FOR COLLABORATION

Once you have completed the preceding Exploration activity, meet with a group of students. Begin by reading your summaries out loud. Working together (be sure to appoint a recorder), answer these questions:

■ Can you find three statements or beliefs shared by all the people interviewed?

- What were some major points of disagreement? Did some faculty members feel, for instance, that good student writing is good student writing whatever the discipline, while others believed that their discipline valued particular qualities in student writing?

- What surprised you in the interviews? Briefly explain why you were surprised.

- What did these interviews help you understand about academic writing? Include at least three statements that reflect your group's discussion of your interviews.

Be prepared to share your findings with the rest of the class.

FOR THOUGHT, DISCUSSION, AND WRITING

1. From a newspaper or a magazine, choose an essay, an editorial, or a column that you think succeeds in its purpose. Now turn back to the guidelines for analyzing your rhetorical situation on pp. 160–61, and answer the questions *as if you were the writer.* To answer the questions, look for evidence of the writer's intentions in the writing itself. (To determine what image or persona the writer wanted to portray, for instance, look at the kind of language the writer uses. Is it formal or conversational? Full of interesting images and vivid details or serious examples and statistics?) Answer each of the questions suggested by the guidelines. Then write a paragraph or more reflecting on what you have learned from this analysis.

2. Writers can follow appropriate textual conventions and still not be successful. Most textbooks follow certain conventions, such as having headings and subheadings, yet undoubtedly you have found some textbooks helpful and interesting, while others have seemed unhelpful and boring. Choose two textbooks — one that you like and one that you dislike — and make a list of at least four reasons that the former is successful and the latter is not.

3. Working with a group of students, write an essay that summarizes and reflects on what you have learned about academic writing as a result of completing the Exploration on p. 197 and the group activity on pp. 197–98.

Negotiating Online Writing Situations

As Chapter 6 emphasized, textual conventions are dynamic, changing over time as the values and situations of the writers and readers employing them change. Many factors played a role in the development of modern textual conventions. As medieval monarchies in Europe evolved into nations, and as these nations established democratic governmental and social structures, writers and readers moved away from the elaborate, status-conscious greetings typical of medieval salutations. As the daily lives of Europeans became less governed by rigid social and cultural hierarchies, so too did the texts they read and wrote change.

Significant cultural changes bring new opportunities and new challenges for writers. One of the most significant developments in the last thirty years has been the evolution of electronic technologies. From the development of the microprocessor in 1971 to the growth of the Internet, electronic technologies are providing new opportunities for writers to express their ideas. With new opportunities come new demands for writers.

There is a good deal you can do to understand the special demands of online writing. As we saw in Chapter 6, you can learn a great deal about textual conventions by reading examples of forms you wish to compose. Before developing your own Web site, for instance, you would want to spend considerable time exploring the Web as well as learning how to write and design Web pages. But you can also learn appropriate conventions for online writing situations by drawing on your commonsense understanding of how language works. Such a rhetorically grounded understanding will enable you to recognize that although email communications are generally much less formal than traditional print communications, you still need to consider your rhetorical situation. Though an email message to your supervisor at work might be less formal than a conventional print business memo, it should probably not be as informal and chatty as email to your friends or family. You would be naive not to recognize that since your supervisor has a printer and a back-up system, even the most ephemeral email is as permanent as any paper document. In the brave new world of electronic technologies, as in the world of print, you can and should draw on your rhetorical sensitivity to determine the best way to respond to specific online writing tasks.

■ ■ ■

FOR EXPLORATION

Take five or ten minutes to freewrite about your own experiences with online writing situations. How have you used electronic technologies such as email and the World Wide Web? What excites you about these technologies — and what questions or reservations about them do you have?

UNDERSTANDING WHAT'S AT STAKE IN THE TRANSITION FROM SCRIPT TO PRINT AND ONLINE TECHNOLOGIES

When you take a rhetorical perspective on communication, you consider the particular situation in which you are writing. One aspect of this situation involves the *medium* that you are using to convey your thoughts to readers. Throughout the centuries, people have relied on a variety of media — from stone, clay tablets, and papyrus to parchment, paper, and now electronic communication technologies — to capture their words and ideas. Each of these media has advantages and disadvantages. Compared with the clay tablets used by the Sumerians in the fourth century B.C., even high-quality paper is shockingly fragile. But thanks to printing and photocopying, paper holds significant advantages over clay tablets for mass production.

From carved symbols to movable type to email, what difference does it make to writers how and under what conditions they compose and reproduce their texts? To begin to answer this question, consider the following two messages to parents that were written by students living away from home. The first was written in France in the twelfth century by two brothers with a quill pen on parchment; the second was composed online on October 28, 2003, by Matthew Johnston, a student at the University of Oregon. You'll see other examples of Matthew's online writing later in this chapter.

A Letter to Parents: France, the Twelfth Century

To their very dear and respected parents M. Martre, knight, and Mme. his wife, M. and N., their sons, send greetings and filial obedience. This is to inform you that, by divine mercy, we are living in good health in the city of Orléans and are devoting ourselves wholly to study, mindful of the words of Cato, "To know anything is praiseworthy," etc. We occupy a good and comely dwelling, next door but one to the schools and market-place, so that we can go to school every day without wetting our feet. We have also good companions in the house with us, well advanced in their studies and of excellent habits — an advantage which we as well appreciate, for as the Psalmist says, "with an upright man thou wilt show thyself upright," etc. Wherefore lest production cease from lack of material, we beg your paternity to send us by the bearer, B., money for buying parchment, ink, a desk, and the other things we need, in sufficient amount that we may suffer no want on your account (God forbid!) but finish our studies and return home with honor. The bearer will also take charge of the shoes and stockings which you have to send us, and any news as well.

An Email to Mom: Oregon, 2003

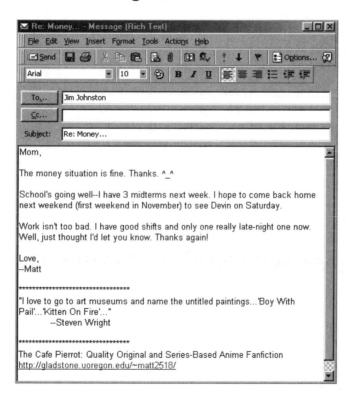

Although these messages share some features — both include greetings to the writer's parent or parents, for instance, and both attempt to give some sense of the students' daily life away from home — they differ in striking ways. The letter written in twelfth-century France uses formal diction and sentence structure. The brothers' frequent citation of ancient authorities, like their deferential salutation, reflects the textual conventions of their time, conventions that reflect that culture's veneration of authority. In contrast, Matthew Johnston's email message is informal. Matthew uses an emoticon to express emotion. And he has an elaborate signature line (or "sig") that includes a favorite quotation from comedian Steven Wright as well as the URL that was then current for "The Café Pierrot," a Web fanfiction site that he has created. Its tone is chatty and relaxed — almost as if the writer were speaking to his mother rather than writing to her.

Some of the differences between these two messages reflect broad cultural shifts that have occurred over the centuries. Today's family and social structures are much less hierarchical than those of medieval times, and this change has certainly influenced the ways in which modern writers address readers. But what role might differences in the written medium have played in the evolution of these textual conventions? What significance might the ease or difficulty and the financial cost of composing, reproducing, and sending texts hold for writers?

Consider the situation of the brothers in Orléans. To write to their parents, they had to purchase parchment and ink — expensive luxuries that the small percentage of the population who could read and write used only for important messages. When they did put pen to paper, medieval writers worked slowly and carefully, fearful of making an error and ruining their materials. Making even a single copy of an important document was time-consuming and costly. Since there was no regular postal service in medieval Europe, letter writers either had to carry letters themselves or pay a courier to do so. Conveying a letter from sender to receiver could take months. The decision to compose and send a letter was thus not made lightly. Once received, letters were considered important documents and were often retained indefinitely.

Matthew Johnston is writing at a time when reading and writing are common practices. Like many who have access to computers, Matthew has found email to be a particularly user-friendly means of written communication. Thanks to his school Internet account, Matthew pays only a modest technology resource fee to use email. He can email friends or family at any time of the day or night, and he knows that barring a system failure the message will be delivered almost immediately. Best of all, his email correspondents don't expect him to write the kind of formal prose that he associates with school assignments and conventional personal letters. After all, many messages are deleted immediately after they are read.

As these examples indicate, the medium that writers use to communicate their ideas can make a big difference in how they approach and experience the act of writing. Because of the high cost of materials, the labor involved with handwriting, and the difficulty of transporting their letter once written, the brothers writing in twelfth-century France took the act of writing a letter very seriously indeed. The nature of the written medium thus reinforced their culture's preference for elaborate and formal written communication. Because so many social and textual conventions have changed over the centuries, even if

Matthew Johnston were handwriting a letter to his mother, he would surely write much less formally than the brothers. But email's immediacy and ease — as well as the repertoire of abbreviations and symbols that have developed for use with this medium — encourage a particularly chatty and informal message.

Clearly, the new electronic technologies are providing exciting opportunities for communication. As anyone who has been flamed (verbally attacked online) knows, however, these technologies open the door to *mis*communication and *mis*understanding as well. Consequently, experienced writers understand that they must draw on their rhetorical sensitivity when composing online. Even though email communications are generally less formal than written communications, for instance, writers must still consider their audience. If Matthew Johnston were writing to his employer to explain why he could not attend a meeting, he would undoubtedly take a more formal tone than he did with his mother. Similarly, some of Matthew's emails are even looser and less formal than his already informal email to his mother. Here, for instance, is an email that Matthew sent to an electronic discussion group for people interested in the progressive rock group Dream Theater. Notice how in this email Matthew chooses not to follow a number of conventions of standard written English, such as putting quotation marks around song titles

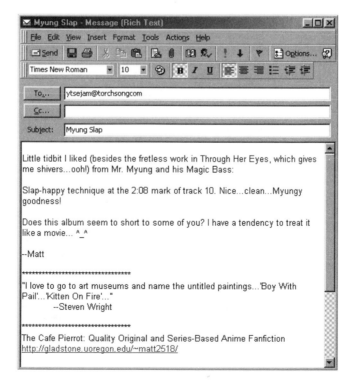

("Through Her Eyes") or using correct spelling ("Does this album seem to [instead of too] short to some of you?"). The voice here is of one fan speaking to another about very specific aspects of the music — such as a certain technique that appears "at the 2:08 mark of track 10."

When writing online, you can often draw on what you've learned from previous experiences with oral and written communication. But if you want to take full advantage of such new media as email and Web pages, you must understand the opportunities — and the constraints — they present to writers. The best way to become familiar with the new electronic technologies is, of course, to experience them. Although the following discussion is no substitute for participation on a listserv or for surfing the Web (activities described later in this chapter), it can remind you to some of the issues writers face when they go online.

CONSIDERING COMMON ONLINE WRITING SITUATIONS

Online technologies are providing new opportunities for communication — ones that have already influenced many reading and writing practices. Most writers have already experienced the benefits of email. Such electronic forums as mailing lists (sometimes also called listservs or discussion lists, where email is routed through a server program to subscribers) and *newsgroups* (electronic discussion groups anyone may visit) have brought new opportunities for communicating.

These and other online forums represent potentially — but not necessarily — radical innovations in the means of communication. All offer different opportunities and constraints.

Email

Email is sometimes characterized, for instance, as a medium that mediates between speech and writing. The ease and speed with which writers can compose, send, and receive email messages are remarkable. Yet depending on the situation, email can be as permanent as the most traditional printed text — and can have similar long-term consequences. Many in business, government, and industry both print and save important email messages, retaining them as evidence they may rely on later.

Electronic Discussion Groups

As was the case with Matthew Johnston's email to his mother, many email messages are person-to-person. But the Internet supports software programs that enable emails from individuals to be transmitted to many other people.

Many thousands of electronic discussion groups exist on the Internet, and they serve a variety of purposes. I have already mentioned newsgroups, which are topic-specific forums on the Internet that include personal postings on a particular subject as well as traditional kinds of information, such as that gathered from wire services like the Associated Press. You can log on to most newsgroups whenever you wish and take part in the electronic conversation. Mailing lists maintain lists of subscribers interested in discussing a specific topic. Once you subscribe to the list, you are automatically sent all the messages posted there. Some enthusiasts refer to these forums as the "Cafés of the Global Village," for they enable anyone who has access to the Internet — whether they live in Los Angeles or in an isolated outpost in Tonga — to converse with others who share their interest, whether <alt.exotic-music> or <misc.activism.progressive>. Matthew Johnston, for instance, subscribes to three mailing lists. The first, <emulab@lists.uoregon.edu>, is for students who work at a computer lab in the student union at the University of Oregon, while <blazers@interscapes.com> is, according to Matthew, a "mailing list for the Portland Trail Blazers and was set up as an alternative to the rah-rah attitudes of the newsgroup." The third, <ytsejam@torchsong .com>, is a mailing list for the music group Dream Theater. Matthew also sends emails to a related newsgroup for fans of Dream Theater, <alt.music .dream-theater>.

Not all those who subscribe to newsgroups or email lists participate actively in the electronic dialogue, however. Some "lurk" online, silently reading postings much as they read their newspaper. A number occasionally send messages — and others spend hours each day in online conferences. Whether just lurking or actively posting messages, those who participate in online discussion enjoy a freedom to exchange ideas that is generally not available in print. For though some online discussion groups are moderated (and thus do not accept all messages), most are open to anyone who wishes to log on or subscribe. Given the economic realities of such print media as newspapers, magazines, and books — almost all of which are controlled by corporations — this represents a considerable expansion of individuals' ability to publish their ideas to a broad audience.

Clearly, online forums have expanded the opportunity to exchange ideas. A posting to a newsgroup such as <sci.bio.ecology> could be from a biologist doing research, a gardener looking for advice on purchasing organic seeds, or a college senior looking for feedback on her ecological study of a nearby ecosystem. And therein, of course, lies a potential limitation of electronic discussion groups as sources of information. The same openness, freedom, and anonymity that characterize electronic discussion groups create potential difficulties for those who wish to use — and thus need to evaluate — information obtained online. To find a group that interests you, try searching a list of newsgroups, such as <www.groups.google.com>. (See Chapter 4 for help evaluating online sources.)

Real-Time Communication

Internet chat rooms (provided by some commercial services) and IRC (Internet relay chat) provide even greater openness and freedom. These applications enable writers to meet with others online at a given time and to "talk" with each other with almost the same ease and rapidity as if they were speaking over the phone. If you have not participated in this form of communication — often referred to as instant messaging or simply IM — you might imagine it as the Internet equivalent of a conference phone call.

Like newsgroups and email discussion groups, chat rooms and IRCs enable people who share an interest — or who just want to chat with others who happened to be logged on to their computers at that moment — to engage in real-time discussions. Often, those participating in these discussions choose to or are required to communicate under pseudonyms, or assumed nicknames. Some participants take advantage of the anonymity of the Internet to conceal or change such individual characteristics as age and gender. Many people find the opportunity to converse online with others who share their interests exciting; others find chat-room and IRC conversations repetitive, superficial, and even offensive — for those talking online will sometimes write things that they would never say in face-to-face conversations. Particularly when many people are participating in a single conversation, discussions or "chats" can be hard to follow. Only those with well-developed keyboarding skills can keep up with such conversations.

In case you haven't experienced chat-room conversation, here is a transcript of the first part of a conversation that Matthew Johnston had with two friends. As is often the case in chat rooms, Matthew and his friends have chosen pseudonyms. Since all three are fans of Japanese anime — animated figures, like those of Pokemon characters — their names draw on that culture.

```
Tanakahibiki Chat 10pm

You have just entered room "tanakahibiki Chat60."
MIzumi2 has entered the room.
Karigari Marie has entered the room.
MIzumi2:  HiHi
tanakahibiki:    'ello!
Karigari Marie:       Meow! =^.^=
tanakahibiki:    <blink blink>
Karigari Marie:       hehe
tanakahibiki:    You're feeling cute today, ne?
Karigari Marie:       too much caffiene . . .
tanakahibiki:    Any particular (Emily) Reason (EK)?
tanakahibiki:    Mr. Subliminal strikes again . . .  ^_^
Karigari Marie:       Emily? Dun know any Emily . . .  EK
  on the other hand . . . ^^;;;
tanakahibiki:    I thought that was her first name. My bad.
```

```
Karigari Marie:          Elizabeth. ^_^
tanakahibiki:    D'oh. I basically had a one in three
   chance, and I knew it wasn't Erin.
tanakahibiki:      ^_^
Karigari Marie:          hehe
tanakahibiki:    Strikeout!
Karigari Marie:          You on the Braves?
tanakahibiki:    I hate the Braves . . .
Karigari Marie:          ^^;;
Karigari Marie:          Exactly.
Karigari Marie:          Doesn't everyone?
tanakahibiki:    Yep.
Karigari Marie:          I dub this channel, the Braves
   Haters . . .
tanakahibiki:    Aye!
Karigari Marie:          I was hoping the Mets would beat
   the Braves and go to the Series . . . Mets vs.
   Yankees . . . woulda sucked to be in NY . . . ^^;;
tanakahibiki:    It woulda started a war.
tanakahibiki:    But it could have been classic.
Karigari Marie:          yup
MIzumi2:  Back! Told you the Yanks won, Rich!
Karigari Marie:          oro?
MIzumi2:  Yankees.
MIzumi2:  4-0!
Karigari Marie:          I didn't say the Yankees lost . . .
   only that they were losing in the 6th inning . . .
MIzumi2:  Ah, ok.
Karigari Marie:          And that was game 3 . . .
tanakahibiki:    hehehe . . .
tanakahibiki:    My how time flies.
Karigari Marie:          and lonly a 4 run deficit . . .
Karigari Marie:          Clean your ears Alex . . . ^^;;
MIzumi2:  Speaking of 3's . . . ^_^
tanakahibiki:    oh?
MIzumi2:  I noticed that your typo hasn't returned,
   Matt. ^^
```

As is often the case when an oral conversation is overheard, those not participating in this exchange can follow some — but not all — of this chat-room conversation. When tanakahibiki asks (twelve lines down) whether there is "Any particular (Emily) Reason (EK)?," readers not part of the conversation can only guess why tanakahibiki inserted "Emily" and "EK" into this conversational turn. Readers can catch the general drift of this conversation — those participating in this instant messaging session do not like the Atlanta Braves baseball team — but much remains unclear or obscure.

Real-time conversations can also take place in MUDS and MOOS — electronic spaces where participants can create text-based virtual environments. Some college teachers use MUDS (multiuser domains) to create virtual classrooms. Those logged into a MUD use commands to create or manipulate objects, enter or leave "rooms," comment on others' ideas, and so on. The first MUD was developed in 1979 to enable British students to play Dungeons & Dragons™ by computer.* MOOS (object-oriented MUDS) give participants the ability to create and manipulate their own virtual objects. There are hundreds of MUDS and MOOS in cyberspace. Some are designed entirely for play, as is the case with many fantasy and science-fiction MUDS. Others enable writers to engage in virtual scholarly conferences or similarly serious activities.

The World Wide Web

One of the most popular Internet applications is the World Wide Web, commonly known as the Web. Developed in the early 1990s at CERN, the European Particle Physics Laboratory in Geneva, the Web is based on hypertext, a system that links electronic texts. Unlike print texts, which are written to be read in a specific sequence, one page after another, hypertexts have links that allow readers to chart their own pathways through documents, clicking on *hyperlinks* to jump from one document to another.

Web pages include words — but they may also include such hypermedia as images, sound, and video. Imagine writing a paper on the role of music in Shakespeare's dramas. On the World Wide Web you could include recordings of the music, pictures of the instruments, and photos from several productions showing the musicians on stage.

Because the Web combines the powers of hypertext, hypermedia, and the Internet, it represents a powerful new way of organizing and conveying information — and a powerful new invitation to writers and readers. In the few years since its development, the Web has experienced phenomenal growth: One recent discussion of the World Wide Web claims, for instance, that "There are now more than a billion pages on the World Wide Web, all loosely tied together by seven billion annotated links, called hyperlinks, which is at least one link for each person on the planet. Each day, more than a million pages are added, and a page can appear in any language, written by any person, for any reason; it can be three lines long or the length of the Bible. For the first time in history, people everywhere have access to the thoughts, products, and writing of a large — and growing — percentage of the earth's population."† (For advice on constructing Web sites, see pp. 217–224.)

---

*Ellen Germain, "In the Jungle of MUD," *Time*, 13 September 1993, 61.
†Michael Specter, "Search and Deploy: The Race to Build a Better Search Engine," *The New Yorker*, 29 May 2000, 88.

■ ■ ■

FOR COLLABORATION

Meet with a group of students to discuss the advantages and disadvantages of online writing situations. Begin your discussion by having group members read their responses to the Exploration on p. 200. (If your group is typical, some members will have little or no experience in this regard, while others will have spent a good deal of time online.) Then respond to the following questions:

1. What personal, social, cultural, and economic factors have encouraged some of you to experiment with electronic technologies? Which factors have discouraged you?

2. To what extent do those who spend time online use these technologies to fulfill personal needs and interests? To complete academic assignments?

3. What advantages do these technologies offer? What disadvantages?

4. Looking beyond your own experiences, what larger ramifications do electronic technologies hold for our society? Consider, for instance, the unequal distribution of access to online resources. What other concerns do you all have about the ways that electronic technologies are influencing our society — and the world?

USING RHETORICAL SENSITIVITY IN ONLINE SITUATIONS

An example may help clarify how writers can use rhetorical sensitivity in online writing situations. A few years ago, WCENTER, an email discussion group for those who work at or are interested in writing centers, posted an interesting "thread" of related messages that demonstrates how such an analysis might proceed. The discussion addressed the question of why subscribers sometimes become irritated by "off-task" messages such as jokes and yet respond patiently when a new subscriber — generally a new writing center director — asks for the hundredth time how others keep writing-center records. Such a question might well prompt impatient or even angry responses, given the high volume of email messages that many subscribers to this list receive and the existence of a number of readily available print sources that address this and related questions. One subscriber, Carol Haviland, speculated that subscribers' differing responses had to do in part with the nature of WCENTER's email forum: "Email is virtually a different kind of text than either speech or book/journal print, but we tend to write it like the former and treat [or read] it like the latter."* Here is the response of another email discussion group subscriber, Sara Kimball:

> I agree, it's a medium in between speech and writing, and we sometimes write online like speech but react to it like writing -- and this can cause problems. Take, for example, the disputes we've occasionally had on this list when some people get a little playful and others get annoyed at "off-topic" threads. Quite a bit of f2f [face-to-face] conversation is . . . [talk] that establishes or maintains human relationships rather than conveying information. . . . Think of how much workplace talk is . . . chit-chat, joking, ritual greetings. For example, I'm currently in the midst of serving a two-year sentence on the English Department's Executive Committee. Most of our meetings begin with a few minutes of joking around and teasing each other. I've known playful speech to work wonders in bringing together people who are otherwise at odds with each other, at least to the point where we can work together. Mostly we're not aware of . . . [this kind of talk] until it's gone on for awhile, because it's ephemeral. I think one of the reasons this list works so well, normally, is that we do establish relationships with each other and with the list. Jokes about Harleys or crawfish and rounds of congratulations on births, promotions, new jobs, etc. are some of the ties that bind. *But* . . . . What might be play if it were speech becomes work if it's writing, something that might get tiresome to deal with if you're tired, distracted, or have a low message quota.
>
> BTW [by the way] Congratulations on the new babies!†

Sara Kimball's comment demonstrates that you can often draw on your general understanding of human communication to answer questions about online writing situations. In this instance, Kimball draws on her own work experience. In some situations — appropriate moments at work, parties — we

---

*Carol Haviland, <cph@wiley.csasb.edu>, "Re: Repeating," 20 August 1996, <wcenter@ttacs.ttu.edu> (20 August 1996).
†Sara Kimball, <skimball@uts.CC.utexas.edu>, "Re: Repeating," 21 August 1996, <wcenter@ttacs. ttu.edu> (21 August 1996).

all enjoy such ephemeral language play as chitchat and joking. In other situations, such conversation not only violates decorum but may even intrude on or interrupt our work or personal time.

In the case of WCENTER, those who subscribe to this email discussion group do so to interact with and learn from others who share their professional commitment. They are willing to go the extra mile when new subscribers ask questions that have been addressed many times in the past because they are aware of the demanding nature of writing-center work. Even though they enjoy the email discussion group's collegiality — as demonstrated in Sara Kimball's congratulations to the new parents — some may become irritated when the tenth or twentieth motorcycle joke appears onscreen.

Because WCENTER is a relatively small email discussion group, and because many on the list know one another personally through professional meetings, subscribers avoid flames or angry withdrawals from the list. When one or more posts elicit irritated responses, subscribers usually take time to reflect on the incident so that future postings can remain cordial. Subscribers to larger, more diverse email discussion groups might accept a more rough-and-ready atmosphere, where those who violate conventions are speedily flamed.

Whether you are emailing your supervisor or friend, posting a message to an electronic forum, or constructing a Web site, you can employ your rhetorical sensitivity to make appropriate decisions about online writing tasks. The following guidelines present general considerations to keep in mind as you navigate the multiple pathways of cyberspace.

■ GUIDELINES FOR WRITING EMAIL

1. *Consider Your Online Rhetorical Situation.* Some online rhetorical situations are more consequential than others. If you are "playing around" in an unmoderated chat room, the consequences for making a false step might be only wasting your time or being flamed. But if you are emailing someone important to you or are participating in a newsgroup or email discussion group discussion, you have more at stake. The following questions can help you to assess what's at stake in a given online situation:

   ■ What is your purpose in wanting to send or post this message? Relatively trivial? Serious?

   ■ If you are emailing one or more individuals, what is your relationship to this person or persons, and how might that influence the consequences of your message?

   (continued)

(*continued*)

- If you are posting a message to an online forum, what are the nature and purpose of this forum? To what extent does the discussion typically focus on a single topic? How long are most messages? Does the discussion emphasize the sharing of information, freewheeling debate, personal expression, or some combination thereof?

- Who typically participates in this online forum? A diverse, continually shifting group of individuals? A focused group of continuing subscribers?

- Have you taken advantage of opportunities to learn more about this forum? You can learn a good deal simply by lurking or listening online to electronic conversations. Most newsgroups and email discussion groups provide a list of FAQs (frequently asked questions) for new subscribers. Be sure to study the responses to these questions, if available, and to save them for future reference.

2. *Recognize That Electronic Messages May Circulate in Unintended Ways — and Have Unanticipated Consequences.* Due to the ease, speed, and apparent transience of email, writers sometimes forget that email messages are public, not private, in nature. As mentioned earlier, email messages are often printed and saved. Businesses, nonprofit organizations, and government agencies sometimes monitor email, and email messages (which many systems automatically archive) have been used as evidence in legal proceedings. When composing an email message to a friend, family member, or coworker, it's easy to imagine that your communication is private. Before you hit the SEND key, however, imagine that your message will appear in your daily newspaper or be forwarded to the worst possible person. If you have any hesitation, rewrite.

Be aware that inattentiveness to the address of a forwarded communication has caused many an online writer considerable embarrassment. If a coworker forwards a message from your supervisor to you and you accidentally respond by the REPLY to ALL command, your message will go to your supervisor, as well as to your friend. A humorous or critical comment intended for your friend but received by your supervisor could have unintended — and quite negative — consequences.

(*continued*)

(continued)

You should also consider your own ethical responsibilities before forwarding a message to another. Did the writer intend this communication to be private? Might forwarding this message embarrass or cause problems for the writer? Even if the answer to these questions is no, you should check with the writer before forwarding a message you have received.

3. *Consider the Needs of Your Readers and the Constraints of Online Communication.* What difference does it make whether a person reads text onscreen or on a piece of paper? According to research on this subject, those reading text onscreen often find it difficult to keep a message's "big picture" clearly in mind. As a consequence, those composing email messages need to pay particular attention to such matters as the length and structure of their message, the placement of important points, and the use of headings. The following suggestions — all of which assume that you are composing an important posting and not just "playing around" on the Internet — address these constraints.

   ■ *Be as concise as possible.* The relatively small size of most computer screens makes it difficult for readers to comprehend lengthy messages. Whereas someone reading a book can easily glance back to earlier sections, online readers must scroll through previous text — a more difficult and even disorienting process. If possible, try to limit your messages to two to three screens of text. If your purpose does require considerable development of ideas, break your text into brief paragraphs, and double the space between paragraphs. The appropriate use of space can also aid comprehension. Rather than string together a long list of items within a paragraph, for instance, put items on separate lines, using the * symbol or dashes (–) at the beginning of each item to create a bulleted list.

   ■ *Provide cues for your readers.* If you are emailing someone you do not know personally, begin your message with a brief introduction and statement of purpose. A simple "Dear Dr. Smith, I am a student in your history of Western civilization lecture class, and I would like to ask you about next week's assignment" should suffice. If you are posting to an online

(continued)

(continued)

forum, a similar contextualizing introduction will encourage readers to take you seriously.

If you find it necessary to post a lengthy message, be sure to use headings and numbered items to help your readers keep track of your ideas. If you desire a response to your message, you may find it helpful to place your most important point or request at the end of your message or to include the abbreviation "R.S.V.P." in your subject line.

Your subject line, in fact, is an important part of your message. Many writers simply reuse subject lines as they appear in the reply when a new heading might better reflect the purpose and content of their message. Subscribers to email discussion groups sometimes become irritated when a message under a thread's subject line has nothing to do with the thread. It takes just a moment to revise the subject line to fit your purpose. Doing so tells readers that you care about your message — and about their response to it.

- *Use shortened spellings, abbreviations, email jargon, and emoticons only in informal messages to individuals you know well or for electronic forums that regularly employ these devices.* It's fine for Matthew Johnston to use email jargon when writing to his mother. Many subscribers to electronic forums also employ these devices: By "listening in" to the conversation a while before posting a message, you can learn what's appropriate. But rhetorical common sense should tell you that in some situations, such as an important work- or school-related message, you would do well to use more formal and accessible language and style.

- *Use conventional capitalization and punctuation.* Don't make your readers go to extra trouble just to decipher your message. Sometimes online writers compose and send their messages so hurriedly that they type all words entirely lower case or entirely upper case. Some writers even omit all but the most essential punctuation marks. Given the challenges that onscreen reading already poses, time-saving practices such as these place extra burdens on readers, who may press their

(continued)

(continued)

DELETE key rather than struggle to decipher your text. You should be aware, as well, that some online readers experience the use of all upper-case letters as SHOUTING.

■ *When appropriate, include parts of the message to which you are responding.* Many email users have had the disconcerting experience of logging on to their computer after a weekend or a brief vacation and discovering a message such as this: "Great idea! Let's meet next Friday to discuss it." If they're lucky, their email program will enable them to retrieve previously sent messages, so they'll be able to discover just which "great idea" their correspondent is referring to. But how much easier it would have been if the person composing the message had included the relevant section from the previous message.

Most email programs have an option that allows you to include the message to which you are responding in your response. Particularly when the message to which you are responding is lengthy, or when you suspect the person to whom you are sending it may not open his or her email immediately, it can be both a courtesy and an aid to communication to include relevant portions of the original message. Doing so can help ensure that you get a speedy and positive response. When you are responding to lengthy messages, be sure to include only those parts of the message that pertain to your response. Here, for instance, is an email that Matthew Johnston sent me in response to an emailed query.

```
On Mon, 23 December 2002 Lede@orst.edu wrote:

>Hi Matt,
>If you don't mind, I'd like to ask you about
>the fanfiction on your Web site. How did you
>get interested in Japanese anime? And when you
>write fanfiction, are you basically extending
>an already developed plot and characters, or
>are you starting from scratch?
```

(continued)

(continued)

> I learned about anime through a friend who was
> in an anime club in Portland. Through him, I
> saw a number of titles in Japanese, and that
> got my interests going. College age students
> are more likely than not to have at least a
> cursory knowledge of anime (through Pokemon),
> though those of us who use computers are more
> likely to know more. All the labbies in the
> computer lab here at the U of O know a little.
> Also, interest in anime seems to be gender
> marked. Something like 80% of anime fans (don't
> quote me on that) are male.

By including in his email the section of my email to which he was responding, Matthew helped ensure that I would have the fullest — and quickest — understanding of the context for his response.

■ *Recognize that what you see onscreen as you type may not be what readers will receive.* Some email programs allow you to write in colors other than black, use indentation, and italicize or underline words. It's tempting to use these features because they can enliven or organize your text; unfortunately, only those readers who use the same email software that you do will receive the message as sent. Others may receive a confusing, weirdly indented mess. Since most people on email post messages to a variety of individuals and electronic forums, the best practice is to avoid using special formatting. That way you can ensure that all your readers will receive your text as written.

■ *Avoid elaborate sigs.* Many email programs enable users to develop a sig, or signature file, that automatically appears at the bottom of every email message. In some cases it's possible to develop elaborate sigs — including ones with visuals, mottos, or other individually devised features. But should you do so? Many users of email say no and suggest that sigs be kept to a maximum of five lines. Because of the limita-

(continued)

(continued)

      tions of reading onscreen text, an overly elaborate sig can actually detract from your message.

4. *Avoid "Flaming" — and Know How to Respond If You Are Flamed.* Email communications sometimes generate strong emotions, possibly because relationship cues (such as tone of voice) that might moderate hostility or suspicion are absent. In situations such as these, the ease and speed of responding to email can be a liability, rather than an asset, for an irate message composed in haste may be one you come to regret. If you get a message that angers you, count to ten, and ask yourself how many ways you might have misunderstood this message — or the person writing the message might have misunderstood you. Give yourself the time and distance needed to reflect on your situation and to ensure that you've read the message carefully.

      Be aware, too, that writers can unintentionally post messages that elicit flames. It can be particularly difficult to convey irony or wit online. Writers who post a message that they intend to be humorous or ironic are sometimes surprised to discover that readers interpret their post quite differently — and respond with a flame, rather than with appreciation. If you are flamed, resist the urge to counterattack. Depending on the nature of the flame, you might respond with a simple explanation or with silence.

The preceding guidelines should help you participate effectively in a variety of email writing situations. It is important to acknowledge, however, that the textual conventions governing email, newsgroups, email discussion groups, and instant messaging are still in flux and that many acceptable variations exist. The preceding guidelines offer a practical, conservative approach. After all, if you are at a social event and a person you don't know well makes a comment that may — or may not — be meant as a joke, you probably take the cautious step of waiting a moment to gather further information before responding. If you are in an unfamiliar online writing situation, similar caution may be justified. It takes only a minute to consider your audience or to tame an ironically barbed sentence; doing so may encourage a reader who might otherwise ignore — or flame — you to respond helpfully instead.

CONSTRUCTING PAGES ON THE
WORLD WIDE WEB

Though more people currently browse the Web than compose Web pages of their own, that situation is rapidly changing. You may only surf the Web now — but next year or next month you might wish or be asked to build a Web site.

In publishing your own pages on the World Wide Web, as with other forms of communication, you will do well to consider your rhetorical situation. Why do you wish to create a site on the Web? Is it an educational site designed to inform your audience about a particular topic? A personal site meant to reflect your interests and experiences? A professional or institutional site? Whom do you wish to visit your site? People seeking specific information about a topic or casual browsers? What kind of experience do you want your readers or "visitors" to have?

■ ■ ■

FOR EXPLORATION

On p. 219 is the homepage for Farhan Ahmed, a student at Lafayette College. From the homepage, visitors to the site can get to Farhan's other pages and to other Web sites that he likes.

Compare this homepage to your college's homepage. What differences do you observe in format and content? Spend five minutes writing about these differences. Now spend another five minutes writing about possible reasons for these differences. In doing so, consider such rhetorical issues as the purpose and audience for the two Web sites.

Writers who construct Web sites also need to consider the current constraints of Web technologies. At the present time, for instance, pages with many images can take a long time to download. Additionally, some browsers may not be able to access pages that include such graphic options as streaming video. How can you present innovative and interesting pages and also accommodate readers using a variety of browsers? How can you achieve the best balance between visual interest and textual information? All of these questions are *rhetorical* questions, for they require you to consider your own purpose in constructing a Web site, the audience for this site, and the most appropriate means (which in this case goes beyond words to include images, sounds, and video) of communicating with your intended audience.

It is beyond the scope of this chapter to provide detailed instructions for Web publishing — and even if it weren't, developments in scripting languages and Web browsers would quickly render such suggestions obsolete. Here are some general considerations to keep in mind when constructing a Web site.

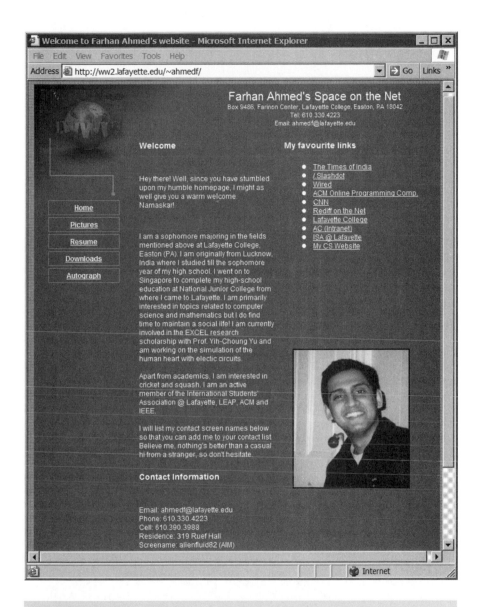

■ GUIDELINES FOR CONSTRUCTING A WEB SITE

1. *Just as Writers Develop Plans for Essays and Architects Draw Up Blueprints for Homes, So Too Should You Establish a Plan for Your Web Site.* In planning your Web site, remember that readers

(continued)

(continued)

access your site as a series of pages. How you organize these pages — the ways you relate them to each other both conceptually and through hyperlinks — can make your site an inviting, interesting, educational experience for readers or a confusing, irritating one. The most effective Web sites have an easily grasped organization that readers can move through easily. They also use a combination of links and menu bars to facilitate navigation within the site.

2. *As in Any Other Effort to Communicate with Readers, Consider Your Audience.* When considering the audience for a Web site, online writers face a rhetorical challenge — for in many cases their audience is both known and unknown. A collaborative team developing a site for a university theater program, for instance, would do well to keep its specific audience in mind. Reflecting on this audience will enable team members to make important decisions about the purpose, design, and structure of their Web pages:

> What should the University Theater Web site do? Hmmm . . . let's see. The immediate audiences will be students, faculty, alums, and people in our college's community. They'll want to know about this year's productions, current students and faculty, and ticket availability, box office times, and seating. There should be a link to the academic theater programs, and probably to other theater programs in the region. It would be nice to include some history of the program and a page of photos from past productions. How about some music from last summer's Gilbert and Sullivan operetta? And there should be a couple of email links to faculty and students — and a suggestion box as well.

Based on their own experiences on the Web, these team members would recognize that many unanticipated readers might be interested in accessing the site. Even if the theater program chose not to publicize its Web address, search engines such as Google or AltaVista might bring readers to the site. Accordingly, the team will attempt to construct a Web site that helps diverse readers with a variety of interests navigate its pages with ease.

If you are constructing a personal page, one designed primarily to present yourself to others, you may or may not have a specific audience of readers in mind. If you have a passionate interest in several specific subjects (rock climbing? environmental politics? something else?), you would certainly want to highlight

(continued)

(continued)

these interests by including links to other sites so that others can easily access more information on them. If you simply want to construct a Web site that expresses your individuality, a multi-dimensional presentation of yourself is likely to attract the broadest range of readers.

3. *As with Other Internet Applications, Consider the Needs of Your Readers by Working within the Constraints of Current Web Technologies.* In the years since the World Wide Web's inception, technologies have developed rapidly. Several years ago, those wishing to publish Web pages needed to learn HTML (hypertext markup language). Now commercial products make it possible to construct Web pages without knowing a lot about HTML. Because the Web has drawn such interest from the public and from commercial software developers, the conventions of Web publishing are very much in flux.

As you plan your Web site, remember that the presence of such features as sophisticated graphics will make a difference in the length of time it takes for pages to load on readers' screens. So you'll want to balance your desire for a sophisticated, image-enhanced Web site with readers' varying hardware and software capabilities. After all, you don't want people to decide that loading your site takes so much time that they'll just keep surfing.

4. *Recognize the Importance of an Inviting, Well-Organized Homepage.* In an issue of *The New Yorker,* writer John Seabrook posed the question "What exactly is a homepage?" Here is his response:

A home page is a reception area. . . . a way to meet people. You want guests to have a good time when they visit your home page, and you hope they will take away a favorable impression of you. You can link your home page to the home pages of friends or family, or to your employer's Web site, or to any other site you like, creating a kind of neighborhood for yourself. And you can design your page in any way you wish, and furnish it with anything that can be digitized — your ideas, your voice, your causes, pictures of your scars or your pets or your ancestors.*

---

*John Seabrook, "Home on the Net." *The New Yorker,* 16 October 1995, 66–76. (You may have noticed that while this chapter uses the spelling "email" and "homepage," Seabrook prefers "E-mail" and "home page." Here, as in other instances, conventions for online writing are still evolving.)

(continued)

(continued)

As Seabrook emphasizes, your homepage serves an important rhetorical purpose, for it determines whether readers will "take away a favorable impression of you." Depending on your purpose, your homepage may be relatively serious or humorous, complex or simple. But it should be suited to your intended audience.

5. *Remember That Basic Design Principles Apply to the Web as Well as to Print Materials.* In *The Non-Designer's Web Book,* Robin Williams and John Tollett remind readers that certain fundamental design principles are essential — whether you're writing a newsletter for a civic group or a Web page for that same organization. They define these principles as alignment, proximity, repetition, and contrast.

- A Web page is *aligned* if the items on the page are lined up either flush left, flush right, or centered. Keep in mind this does not mean you need to line up everything on the same side of the page: multiple columns in which each item is aligned within the column are fine, too. Williams and Tollett argue that "lack of alignment is the single most prevalent problem on web pages." Their advice to those constructing Web pages: "Don't mix alignments" (106).

- A Web page makes effective use of the design principle of *proximity* when the relationships between headings and subheadings, and between items in a list and other textual elements, are clear. An easy way to evaluate your Web page's use of proximity is to squint your eyes and see how your Web page looks. Does your eye move logically from one part of the page to another? If not, you will want to work on the internal relationships of items in your Web page.

- *Repetition* in Web design can involve elements that are visual, verbal, or both. Repetition is an important factor in tying your site together.

- A Web page effectively employs *contrast* when the design attracts your eye to the page and draws you in: "Contrasting elements guide your eyes around the page, create a hierarchy of information, and enable you to skim through the vast array of information . . . [to] pick out the information you

(continued)

(continued)

need" (118). Focal points play an important role in establishing contrast. A focal point — a point that the eye travels to first — may be an image or a logo. But it helps organize and orient readers' interactions with your Web site.

6. *Establish a Meaningful Visual Identity for Your Site.* Those surfing the Web have a particularly strong need to know where they are, where they came from, and where they are going. Establishing a clear and consistent visual theme for your site can help readers keep themselves on track as they navigate your site. There are other reasons for establishing a visual theme. Whether you are constructing a personal site or an institutional site, a visual theme — achieved through the use of photographs, images, and other aspects of design repeated on each page — creates an overall impression that will persuade readers that your site is (or isn't) worth visiting. It can also increase the rhetorical persuasiveness of your site. Farhan Ahmed, for instance, repeats the www and left-hand frame on each of his pages to create a visual identity for his site (p. 219).

7. *Keep the Demands of Online Reading in Mind as You Organize the Text on Your Site.* Most online readers find long stretches of unbroken text difficult to read at best. Often, those surfing the Web will simply move to another site rather than go to the trouble of reading large blocks of text. After all, most are reading on relatively small monitors. Furthermore, as the Web has developed, it has strongly emphasized visual as well as verbal content. Sophisticated readers of the Web expect sites to be constructed with online readers in mind. For these reasons, you will want to attend as closely to how you present the text you write as to the text itself. Chunking texts into small groupings, using bulleted lists, leaving plenty of white space, coordinating texts with relevant images: Through these and other means you can create a site that will make the process of reading online easy and enjoyable.

8. *Use Color to Increase Your Site's Visual Impact, but Keep Online Readers' Needs in Mind as You Do So.* Writers and designers have always understood that the effective use of color can significantly enhance a text's appeal. But the use of color in traditional print publications can be expensive; moreover, the range of colors that

(continued)

(continued)

can be achieved in print is limited. Those constructing Web sites have many more colors available to them. Surf the Web, and you'll discover that color is an important element of most Web sites. This does not mean, however, that just any use of color on the Web will enliven your site. Use too dark a background, for instance, and viewers will have difficulty reading your text. (This will be especially true if you use all caps or italics for your text.) Including too many colors can result in a page that feels "busy" and disorganized. Remember the basic principle of *contrast:* Readers looking at a Web page need a strong overall impression and pattern of movement to guide their eyes and help them understand how best to navigate your site. Too much color — used too many different ways — can make navigation difficult.

9. *Remember That Web Sites Are Always Works in Progress.* Those navigating the Web are almost by definition looking for timely information about a subject of interest to them. Whether they are interested in learning more about the situation in South Africa or the best places to mountain bike in Moab, Utah, those surfing the Web expect the information they locate to be timely and accurate. So those publishing Web pages should feel a particular obligation to keep their pages up-to-date. And because the Web itself is in continual flux — because Web sites constantly appear and disappear — conscientious Web publishers regularly update their pages and list the date on which they've most recently done so.

FOR EXPLORATION

Here are two Web sites. The first is for the Southern Poverty Law Center (p. 225). The second is for The National Audubon Society (p. 226). Study these Web sites carefully, and then analyze them according to the guidelines for Web sites presented earlier in this chapter (p. 219). To see the use of color on these sites or to navigate them yourself, you may want to visit them online. The URL for the Southern Poverty Law Center is <http://www.splcenter.org>; the URL for the National Audubon Society is <http://www.audubon.org>. To what extent do these sites model good Web design? Are there ways in which they might be improved? Write at least two paragraphs of analysis for each Web site.

FOR COLLABORATION

Meet with a group of peers to discuss your responses to the previous Exploration. Appoint a recorder to take notes about your discussion and to share the results of your analysis with the class. Be sure to consider the following questions. To what extent did group members agree in your analysis of each Web site? If there was disagreement, what points were most often sources of controversy? Did group members raise questions about these Web sites that were not covered in the preceding guidelines? What did your group learn about writing for the Web as a result of this analysis?

As with the guidelines presented earlier in this chapter for writing email to individuals, email discussion groups, or newsgroups (pp. 211–17), these guidelines represent a conservative approach to the Web. Depending on your own purpose and intended audience, you might reasonably choose to disregard one or more of these suggestions. Just as those writing essays can make appropriate decisions by considering such rhetorical considerations as their purpose, audience, and situation, so too should those writing for an online audience ask similar questions that will guide their writing.

■ ■ ■

FOR THOUGHT, DISCUSSION, AND WRITING

1. Subscribe for at least a week to an email discussion group of interest to you. Web sites such as <http://www.liszt.com> and <http://www.googlegroups.com> provide information about a number of email discussion groups. Your teacher or a college librarian may also have information about these forums. After monitoring this electronic conversation — and perhaps participating as well — write an analysis of this email discussion group. Be sure to consider the questions in Guideline 1 on pp. 211–12.

2. While monitoring an email discussion group's electronic conversation, identify at least five posts that you find particularly effective and five that seem ineffective. Save and print these posts, and write a brief explanation of why they are effective or ineffective, referring to the guidelines presented on pp. 211–17. Be prepared to discuss your conclusions with your classmates.

3. Spend at least an hour exploring as many Web sites (institutional, commercial, personal) as possible. Download several examples of sites that you find particularly successful or unsuccessful. Drawing on this chapter's discussion of the Web and on your own experience, identify three or four characteristics that successful sites share.

4. Write an essay considering one or more of the possible implications of the rapidly developing electronic technologies. As part of your research for this topic, you may wish to read the selections on this subject at the end of Chapter 3. You may also wish to consult a number of relevant online and library resources.

PART THREE

PRACTICAL STRATEGIES
FOR WRITING

Strategies for Invention

Writing is a complex, dynamic process, one that challenges you to draw on all your resources as you compose. As a writer, you don't need to wait in frustration at your desk or computer for inspiration to strike. By analyzing your rhetorical situation and by reflecting on your previous writing experiences, you can respond effectively and efficiently to the demands of writing.

Experienced writers are pragmatists. Understanding that different writing tasks call for different approaches, they develop a repertoire of strategies they can employ depending on the situation. They also tend to be flexible, recognizing that their writing may take unpredictable twists and turns. They know they may have to work their way through moments of frustration or difficulty to achieve the insights that make writing worthwhile. And they know, too, that they needn't work alone. Both informally and formally — from conversations with friends to collaboration with classmates, writing tutors, and teachers — successful writers benefit from the support and insights of others.

Like thinking, writing is too complex and situated a process to be reduced to rules or formulas. But even if writing can't be reduced to a set of directions, it does involve activities that you can understand, practice, and improve. In general, the writing process involves planning, drafting, and revising. Successful writers follow a variety of strategies as they work on these activities. Part Three presents a number of these strategies.

Read the chapters in Part Three with a writer's eye. Which of these strategies do you already use? Which ones could you use more effectively? What other strategies might extend your range or strengthen your writing abilities? As you read about and experiment with these strategies, remember to assess their usefulness based on your needs and preferences as a writer and your particular writing situation.

UNDERSTANDING HOW INVENTION WORKS

Like many writers, you may feel that discovering ideas to write about is the most mysterious part of the writing process. Where do ideas come from? How can you draw a blank one minute and suddenly know just the right way to support your argument or describe your experience the next? Is it possible to increase your ability to think and write creatively?

Writers and speakers have been concerned with questions such as these for centuries. The classical rhetoricians, in fact, were among the first to investigate this process of discovering and exploring ideas. The Roman rhetoricians called it *inventio*, for "invention" or "discovery." Contemporary writers, drawing on this Latin term, often refer to this process as *invention*. This chapter focuses on discovering and exploring ideas as part of the writing process.

In practice, invention usually involves both individual inquiry and dialogue with others. In writing this textbook, for instance, I spent a great deal of time thinking and working alone. I even experienced a few moments of what might be described as inspiration. As the acknowledgments in the preface of this book indicates, however, I could not have written *Work in Progress* without the help of many other people. In the earliest stages of this project I spoke with textbook editors and with other textbook authors. They helped me understand the demands of writing a textbook and the rhetorical situation to which a textbook generally responds. Once the project was under way, I spent many hours talking with both students and fellow composition instructors. By reading articles and books on the teaching of writing, I expanded these conversations. My silent dialogues with these writers were just as important as face-to-face conversations in helping me develop my ideas.

Most people don't write textbooks. But most writers generate and explore ideas by sitting quietly and thinking, brainstorming at the computer, reading, conducting research, and exchanging ideas with friends and colleagues. The following strategies aim to help you to invent successfully, whether you're working alone or with classmates or friends.

USING INFORMAL METHODS OF DISCOVERING AND EXPLORING IDEAS

You probably already use several informal methods of discovering and exploring ideas. You don't need extensive training to learn to brainstorm or cluster, for instance. Yet these methods can help you discover what you know — and don't know — about a subject. They can also enable you to explore your own ideas and to formulate productive questions that can guide you as you plan, draft, and revise your writing.

Most writers find that some of the following methods work better for them than others. That's fine, but be sure you give each method a fair chance. You may surprise yourself, as did Joanne Novak, a composition student in Professor Robert Inkster's composition class at St. Cloud State University. The following entry from her journal describes how her experience with informal invention methods taught her something new about writing.

> I began the process of using the informal methods thinking it was a waste of time because I just simply was not in the mood to write. I intended to try each of the informal methods to prove that they didn't work for me. I chose a topic I'd been thinking of writing about and tried freewriting. It was a jumbled mess. At that point I had trouble looping because I was embarrassed by the unorganized words that appeared on the paper, but I finally did come up with a shallow summarizing sentence. It sounded good, but it wasn't from the heart. It was something I knew I *should* feel. From the summarizing sentence I used the brainstorming method and came up blank.
>
> Feeling confident that my theory was correct and the text was wrong, I decided to prove it by clustering. As suggested, I put my topic in the center of the page and just drew in whatever came to mind around the outside. I saw some organization to this method. That started ideas coming faster than I could write. I jotted down a few words so I could remember the main idea, and before I knew it I was writing so small I could hardly form the letters as I was running out of space.
>
> I returned to brainstorming, which worked this time, and I ended up with a long list of things to write about. It was amazing. I reread my freewriting and found a few more ideas. I was shocked. I've always believed that I had to be in the mood to write or I couldn't come up with ideas. Now I see that that belief has in fact inhibited my writing.
>
> — Joanne Novak

Like Joanne Novak, you too may find informal methods of invention to be a productive means of discovering and exploring ideas.

Freewriting

Freewriting is the practice of writing as freely as possible without stopping. It is a simple but powerful strategy for exploring important issues and problems. Freewriting may at first seem *too* simple to achieve very powerful results — the only requirement is that you write continuously without stopping — but in fact it can help you discover ideas that you couldn't reach through more conscious and logical means. Because you generate a great deal of material when you freewrite, freewriting is also an excellent antidote for the nervousness many writers feel at the start of a project. (Freewriting can, by the way, be done quite effectively on the computer.) Finally, freewriting also encourages you to improve your fluency.

Freewriting is potentially powerful in a variety of writing situations. See how one student used freewriting as a means of exploring and focusing her ideas for a political science paper on low voter turnout.

> I just don't get it. As soon as I could register I did — it felt like a really important day. I'd watched my mother vote and my sisters vote and now it was my turn. But why do I vote; guess I should ask myself that question — and why don't other people? Do I feel that my vote makes a difference? There have been some close elections but not all that many, so my vote doesn't literally count, doesn't decide if we pay a new tax or elect a new senator. Part of it's the feeling I get. When I go to vote I know the people at the polling booth; they're my neighbors. I know the people who are running for office in local elections, and for state and national elections — well, I just feel that I should. But the statistics on voter turnout tell me I'm unusual. In this paper I want to go beyond statistics. I want to understand *why* people don't vote. Seems like I need to look not only at research in political science, but also maybe in sociology. (Check journals in economics too?) I wonder if it'd be okay for me to interview some students, maybe some staff and faculty, about voting — better check. But wait a minute; this is a small college in a small town, like the town I'm from. I wonder if people in cities would feel differently — they might. Maybe what I need to look at in my paper is rural/small town versus urban voting patterns.

This student's freewriting not only helped her explore her ideas but also identified a possible question to answer in her paper and sources she could draw on as she worked on her project.

Freewriting can also help you explore your personal experience, enabling you to gain access to images, events, and emotions that you have forgotten or suppressed. If you were writing an essay about your sense of family — how you developed this sense, what it is, and what it means to you now — freewriting could help you recall details and images that would lend a rich specificity to your essay. Here, for example, is my own freewriting about my sense of family. (You may understand this freewriting more easily if you know that I grew up in a family of twelve children, two of whom died in infancy.)

> Family. Family. So strong. So many children. Ten. But really twelve. Brian and Anthony dead, both babies. The youngest kids don't even remember — they know but don't remember. Odd. Our own family so enormous, but so little extended family. Mom's parents dead — I do remember Nana, though — one sister. Dad's parents dead too, one sister. Some of my brothers and sisters don't remember any grandparents. Now we're all spread out. Leni and Robin in Florida. Sara in Virginia. Andy in Mass. Laurie in Pennsylvania. Shelley and Jeff in Ohio, close to Mom and

Dad. Rob and me in Oregon, Julie in Washington — we're the farthest away. Have I forgotten anyone? The list, run down the list. (Memory: amazing friends with how quickly I could say the names, but only in order.) Leni, Lisa, Andy, Sara, Jeff, Robin, Michelle, Laurie, Julie, Robbie. The photo from last summer's reunion: fifty people, Mom and Dad, brothers, sisters, spouses, grandchildren. Could be a photo of a company's annual picnic — but it isn't. Families like this just don't exist anymore. When did it change? People used to smile at us when we all went out and ask how many. Now a friend with four children tells me people are shocked at the size of her family. I have no children, but I have family. Family — an invisible web that connects.

My brief freewrite did more than generate concrete images and details; it gave me a new insight into my own sense of family. Rereading my freewriting, I am surprised at the strong sense of loss that appears as I comment on my infant brothers' deaths and those of my grandparents. I also notice a potential contradiction between my strong sense of family and my recent experience of living a great distance from my parents and most of my brothers and sisters.

Looping

Looping, an extended or directed form of freewriting, alternates freewriting with analysis and reflection. Begin looping by first establishing a theme or topic for your freewriting; then freewrite for five or ten minutes. This is your first loop. After you have done so, reread what you have written. In rereading your freewriting, look for the center of gravity or "heart" of your ideas — the image, detail, issue, or problem that seems richest or most intriguing, compelling, or productive. Write a sentence that summarizes this understanding; this sentence will become the starting point of your second loop. In looking back at my previous freewriting, I can locate several potential starting points for an additional loop. I might, for instance, use the following question to begin another freewriting session:

> What does it mean that my family includes a number of people — my brothers and grandparents — that my younger brothers and sisters never knew, can't remember?

When you loop, you don't know where your freewriting and reflection will take you; you don't worry about the final product. My final essay on my sense of family might not even discuss the question generated by my freewriting. That's fine; the goal in freewriting and looping is not to produce a draft of an essay but to explore your own ideas and to discover ideas, images, and sometimes even words, phrases, and sentences that you can use in your writing.

■ ■ ■

FOR EXPLORATION

Freewrite for five minutes, beginning with the word *family.* (If you would prefer to write about another subject, simply choose a single word to begin your freewrite — sports, music, college, whatever — and continue this activity.) Then stop and reread your freewriting. What comments most interest or surprise you? Now write a statement that best expresses your freewriting's center of gravity or "heart." Use this comment to begin a second loop by freewriting for five minutes more.

After completing this second freewriting, stop and reread both passages. What did you learn from your freewriting? Does your freewriting suggest possible ideas for an essay? Finally, reflect on the process itself. Did you find the experience of looping helpful? Would you use freewriting and looping in the future as a means of generating and exploring your experiences and ideas?

Brainstorming

Like freewriting and looping, brainstorming is a simple but productive invention strategy. When you brainstorm, you list as quickly as possible all the thoughts about a subject that occur to you without censoring or stopping to reflect on your ideas. A student assigned to write an essay on child abuse for a sociology class would brainstorm by listing everything that comes to mind on this subject, from facts to images, memories, fragments of conversations, and other general impressions and responses. Later, the student would review this brainstorming list to identify ideas that seem most promising or helpful.

To brainstorm effectively, take a few moments at the start to formulate your goal, purpose, or problem. Then simply list your ideas as quickly as you can. You are the only one who needs to be able to decipher what you've written, so your brainstorming list can be as messy or as neat as you like. You can also brainstorm at the computer.

Brainstorming can enable you to discover and explore a number of ideas in a short time. Not all of them will be worth using in a piece of writing, of course. The premise of brainstorming is that the more ideas you can generate, the better your chances of coming up with good ones. Suppose that after freewriting about my family, I decided to explore the possibility of writing an essay about the potential contradiction between my sense that family is "an invisible web that connects" and the fact that I live so far away from my family. In the five minutes after I wrote that last sentence, I used brainstorming to generate the following list of ideas:

Think about role of place (geography) and family.

The house on Main St. — home since the 4th grade

Mom's letters: so important in keeping us all in touch!

Laurie, Shelley, and Sara all with new babies at Julie's wedding

Andy pulling the same joke on me for 30 years

The old house on Corey St. Why do I always remember the kitchen?

My sadness at missing Robin's, Shelley's, and Laurie's weddings because we were in Oregon

The wonderful, friendly, comfortable chaos at our reunion (the grandkids getting confused by all the aunts and uncles)

Am I fooling myself? Is the tie I feel with my family as strong as I think it is? Greeting-card sentiments versus reality?

Special family times: birthdays, Christmas, cooking and baking together. How to evoke these without making it all seem sentimental and cliché?

Maybe it's the difficult times that keep families together. The hard times that (especially when you're a teenager) you think you'll never get beyond.

Families change over time. So does your sense of family. How has mine changed?

I certainly would have a long way to go before I could write an essay about my sense of family, but this brief brainstorming list of ideas and questions has raised important issues I'd want to consider.

■ ■ ■

FOR EXPLORATION

Reread the freewriting you did about your sense of family (or about another topic of your choice), and then choose one issue or question you'd like to explore further. Write a single sentence summarizing this issue or question, and then brainstorm for five to ten minutes. After brainstorming, return to your list. Put an asterisk (*) beside those ideas or images that hadn't appeared in your earlier freewriting. How do these ideas or images add to your understanding of your sense of family?

Clustering

Like freewriting, looping, and brainstorming, clustering emphasizes spontaneity. The goal of all four strategies is to generate as many ideas as possible to discover what you know and what you might explore further. Clustering differs, however, in that it uses visual means to generate ideas. Some writers find that it enables them to explore their ideas more deeply and creatively.

Start with a single word or phrase. If you are responding to an assigned topic, choose the word that best summarizes or evokes that topic. Write this word in the center of a page of blank paper, and circle it. Now fill in the page by expanding on or developing ideas connected with this word. Don't censor your ideas or force your cluster to assume a certain shape. Simply circle your key ideas, and connect them either to the first word or to other related ideas. Your goal is to be as spontaneous as possible.

Figure 8.1 presents a cluster that I created shortly after freewriting and brainstorming about my sense of family. Notice that even though I wrote this only a short time later, the cluster reveals new details and images. After clustering you must distance yourself from the material you've generated so that you can evaluate it. In doing so, try to find the cluster's center of gravity — the idea or image that seems richest and most compelling.

NOTE FOR MULTILINGUAL WRITERS

When you practice informal methods of invention, you're focusing on generating ideas — not on being perfectly correct. If you are a multilingual writer, don't interrupt the flow of invention by stopping to edit grammatical forms, spelling, vocabulary, or punctuation. Feel free, in fact, to freewrite, brainstorm, and cluster in your first or home language if it increases your fluency and helps you generate ideas.

FOR EXPLORATION

Choose a word to use as the center of a cluster. Without planning or worrying about form, fill in your cluster by branching out from this central word. Just include whatever comes to mind.

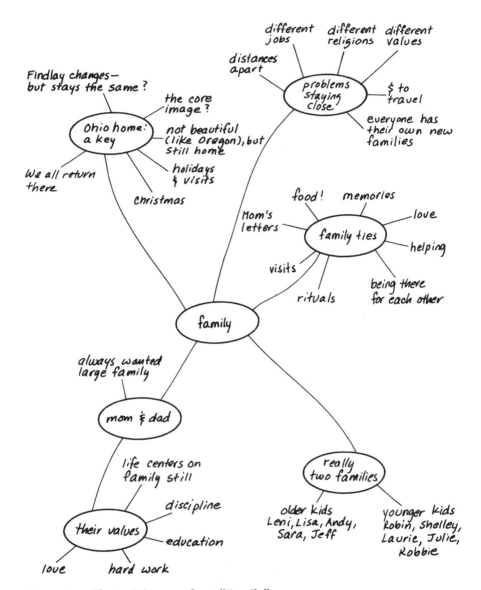

Figure 8.1   Cluster Diagram about "Family"

FOR COLLABORATION

Meet with a group of classmates to discuss informal methods of discovering and exploring ideas. Begin by having group members briefly describe the advantages and disadvantages they experienced with these methods.

(Appoint a recorder to summarize each person's statements.) Then, as a group, discuss your responses to these questions: (1) How might different students' preferences for one or more of these strategies be connected to different learning, composing, and cultural preferences? (2) What influence might such situational factors as the nature of the assignment or the amount of time available for working on an essay have on the decision to use one or more of these strategies? Be prepared to discuss your conclusions with your classmates.

USING FORMAL METHODS OF DISCOVERING AND EXPLORING IDEAS

The informal methods of discovering and exploring ideas have a number of advantages. They are easy to employ, and they can help you generate a reassuringly large volume of material when you're just beginning to work on a paper. These strategies also help you become interested in and committed to your work in progress. Sometimes, however, you may find more formal and systematic methods of discovering and exploring ideas helpful.

You are already familiar with one formal method of discovering and exploring your ideas: analyzing your rhetorical situation. The activities discussed in this section — asking the journalist's questions and the topical questions — provide a variety of strategies that you can use to explore a topic, consider it from diverse perspectives, and generate ideas about it. Because they *systematically* probe a topic, these strategies can help you discover not just what you know about a topic but also what you *don't* know and thus alert you to the need for additional reading and research.

The Journalist's Questions

The journalist's questions — *who, what, when, where, why,* and *how* — are perhaps the easiest of the formal methods to understand and apply. If you have taken a journalism class or written for a newspaper, you know that journalists are taught to answer these six questions in articles they write. By answering these questions, journalists can be sure that they have provided the most important information about an event, issue, or problem for their readers.

You may find these questions particularly useful when you are describing an event or writing an informative essay. Suppose that your political science instructor has assigned an essay on the recent political conflict between Israelis and Palestinians. Using the journalist's questions as headings, you could begin working on this assignment by asking yourself the following questions:

- *Who* is involved in this conflict?

- *What* issues most clearly divide those engaged in this dispute?

- *When* did the recent conflict begin, and how has it developed over the last few years?

- *Where* does the conflict seem most heated or violent?

- *Why* have those living in this area found it so difficult to resolve the situation?

- *How* might this conflict be resolved?

Although you might discover much the same information by simply brainstorming, using the journalist's questions ensures that you have covered all these major points. (Asking yourself who is involved in the Israeli/Palestinian conflict will remind you, for instance, that many countries and institutions currently play a role in this dispute.) Furthermore, using the journalist's questions as headings automatically organizes information as you generate it, whereas a brainstorming list would need to be analyzed and reorganized.

■ ■ ■

FOR EXPLORATION

Using the journalist's questions, systematically explore the subject that you have investigated in preceding Explorations in this chapter. (If you feel that you have exhausted this subject, feel free to choose a different topic.)

Once you have employed this method, take a few moments to reflect on this experience. To what extent did the strategy help you organize and systematically review what you already know, and to what extent did it define what you still need to find out?

The Topical Questions

The second formal method of discovering and exploring ideas is based on the topics of classical rhetoric. In his *Rhetoric*, Aristotle describes the topics as potential lines of argument or places (*topos* in Greek means "place") where speakers and writers can find evidence or arguments. Aristotle defined twenty-eight topics, but the list is generally abbreviated to five: *definition, comparison, relationship, circumstance,* and *testimony.*

The classical topics represent natural ways of thinking about ideas. When confronted by an intellectual problem, we all ask such questions as these:

- What is it? (definition)

- What is it like or unlike? (comparison)

- What caused it? (relationship)

- What is possible or impossible? (circumstance)

- What have others said about it? (testimony)

Aristotle's topics build on these natural mental habits.

You may use these questions to discover and explore ideas about a subject. To do so, simply pose each question in turn about your subject, writing down as many responses as possible. You may also find helpful the following list of topical questions.*

Questions about Physical Objects

1. What are the physical characteristics of the object (shape, dimensions, materials, etc.)?

2. What sort of structure does it have?

3. What other object is it similar to?

4. How does it differ from things that resemble it?

5. Who or what produced it?

6. Who uses it? For what?

Questions about Events

1. Exactly what happened? (who? what? when? where? why? how?)

2. What were its causes?

3. What were its consequences?

4. How was the event like or unlike similar events?

5. To what other events was it connected?

6. How might the event have been changed or avoided?

Questions about Abstract Concepts (e.g., democracy, justice)

1. How has the term been defined by others?

2. How do you define the term?

3. What other concepts have been associated with it?

---

*These questions appear in Edward P. J. Corbett, *The Little Rhetoric and Handbook* (Glenview, Ill.: Scott, Foresman, 1982), 38–39.

4. What counterarguments must be confronted and refuted?

5. What are the practical consequences of the proposition?

Questions about Propositions (statements to be proved or disproved)

1. What must be established before the reader will believe it?

2. What are the meanings of key words in the proposition?

3. By what kind of evidence or argument can the proposition be proved or disproved?

4. What counterarguments must be confronted and refuted?

5. What are the practical consequences of the proposition?

Like the other formal methods for discovering and exploring ideas, the topical questions can help you pinpoint alternative approaches to the subject or probe one subject systematically, organizing what you know already and identifying gaps that you need to fill.

■ ■ ■

FOR EXPLORATION

Use the topical questions to continue your investigation of the subject that you explored with the journalist's questions. What new information or ideas do the topical questions generate? How would you compare these methods?

NOTE FOR MULTILINGUAL WRITERS

What methods are used in your own writing culture to discover and explore ideas? Are they different from the informal and formal methods of invention that are discussed in this chapter? What rhetorical and cultural values are reflected by the methods that are used in your home writing culture? If significant differences exist between the methods of invention used in your own writing culture and those used in North American culture, how have you dealt with these differences?

INVENTING WITH OTHERS

Invention can be done collaboratively, in dialogue with others. Much of this dialogue occurs naturally as you go about your daily affairs. While riding the bus home after class, you might talk over a writing assignment with a friend, for example, or you might brainstorm about an essay topic with your spouse over dinner. The ideas you gain through such exchanges can contribute a great deal to your understanding of your subject.

This section presents two strategies you can use to learn with and from others as you write — group brainstorming and group troubleshooting — that build on the informal exchanges you already have with friends, class-mates, and family members.

Group Brainstorming

You have already experimented with brainstorming alone, so you are aware of its basic procedures and benefits. You can also brainstorm as part of a group. In fact, Alex Osborn, the person generally credited with naming this tech-nique, originally envisioned brainstorming as a group, not an individual, activity. Osborn believed that the enthusiasm generated by the group helped spark ideas. You will not be surprised to learn, then, that those who regularly write with teams or groups cite increased intellectual stimulation and improved quality of ideas as major benefits of collaboration.

Group brainstorming can be used for a variety of purposes. If your class has just been assigned a broad topic, for instance, your group could brain-storm a list of ways to approach or limit this topic. Or your group could gener-ate possible arguments in support of or in opposition to a specific thesis.

Because more than one person is involved, group brainstorming is more complicated than brainstorming alone. But it can be quite rewarding, as Johanna Wills, a student at Florida State University, indicates here: "I do like brainstorming alone, but group brainstorming is a terrific outlet for support as I face the challenges of writing."

■ GUIDELINES FOR GROUP BRAINSTORMING

1. At the start of your group session, carefully define the problem or issue that the group will address.

2. Appoint someone to act as a recorder. This person can write down everyone's ideas so that they can be reproduced and dis-tributed later.

(continued)

(continued)

3. Encourage group members to contribute freely and spontaneously to the discussion. Don't stop to discuss or evaluate ideas; your goal is to generate as many ideas as possible.

Group Troubleshooting

Group troubleshooting is a simple but often productive means of identifying and resolving writing problems by discussing work in progress with peers who respond with questions and advice. You will probably find group troubleshooting most productive in the early stages of writing when you are still working out your ideas and determining your approach to your subject. To troubleshoot effectively, follow this procedure:

■ GUIDELINES FOR
GROUP TROUBLESHOOTING

1. Decide how much time to spend on each person's writing. Appoint a timekeeper to enforce these limits.

2. Begin by having the writer describe the issue or problem that he or she would like to discuss. The writer also should try to identify particular questions for group response. These questions may be very general ("This is what I'm planning to do in my essay. Can you think of any problems I might run into?" "Do you have any suggestions about how I might develop my thesis?") or quite specific ("I've been able to think of two potential objections to my thesis. Can you think of others?" "I like these four ideas, but I don't think they fit together very well. What could I do?").

3. Let the writer facilitate the resulting discussion. If the writer needs a moment to write an idea down, for example, he or she should ask the group to pause briefly. The writer should also feel free to ask group members to clarify or elaborate on suggestions.

4. Try to respond to each writer's request for assistance as carefully and fully as possible.

FOR THOUGHT, DISCUSSION, AND WRITING

1. Early in this chapter you used freewriting, looping, brainstorming, and clustering to investigate your sense of family. Continue your exploration of this topic by drawing on the formal methods of invention. Then write an essay in which you explore just what the word *family* means to you. If you explored a topic other than family, write an essay on that subject.

2. Observe a group of your classmates as they brainstorm, and make notes about what you see. You may find it helpful to record how often each member of the group participates in the discussion, for example. Pay attention, too, to group dynamics. Is the group working effectively? Why or why not? What could group members do to interact more effectively? Summarize the results of your observations in a report addressed to the group. Be sure to suggest several ways that the group could work more effectively in the future.

3. Choose one of the strategies discussed in this chapter that you have not used in the past, and try it as you work on your current writing assignment. If you have time, discuss this experiment with some classmates. Then write a brief analysis of why this strategy did or did not work well.

Strategies for Planning and Drafting

Planning is an important part of the writing process. As the discussion of differing composing styles in Chapter 2 indicated, people plan in different ways. Some develop detailed written plans; others rely primarily on mental plans; others might plan by freewriting a draft and then determining their goals by rereading and reflecting on their own written text. Many other factors can affect the process of planning, from the time available to the complexity of the writing task. Nevertheless, planning always involves the following activities:

- Analyzing your rhetorical situation

- Discovering and exploring ideas

- Establishing a controlling purpose

- Formulating a workable plan

Earlier chapters have already discussed strategies that you can use to analyze your rhetorical situation and to discover and explore ideas. This chapter focuses on the remaining two activities in the list: establishing a controlling purpose and developing a workable plan. It also presents a number of strategies for effective drafting.

UNDERSTANDING THE PROCESS OF PLANNING

It may be helpful to think of planning as involving waves of "play" and "work." When you are discovering and exploring ideas, for example, you are in a sense playing. When you freewrite, loop, brainstorm, cluster, or engage in other creative blockbusting activities, your major goal is to be creative — to push your ideas as far as you can without worrying about how useful they may turn out to be later. Even more formal methods of invention, such as the topical questions, encourage mental play and exploration.

Most people can't write an essay based on a brainstorming list or thirty minutes of freewriting, however. At some point, they need to settle down to work, considering questions like the ones presented in the following guidelines.

■ GUIDELINES FOR PLANNING AN ESSAY

1. What main point do you want to make in this essay? How does this main point relate to your purpose — to what you want this essay to *do* for readers?

2. Who might be interested in reading this essay?

3. How might readers' expectations influence the form and content of this essay?

4. How can you structure your essay to communicate your ideas most effectively to readers?

5. What kinds of examples and details will best support your main point? What kind of evidence will your readers find most persuasive?

6. What textual conventions might you need or want to follow?

Questions such as these require you to determine what point you want to make and *can* make in your essay, to decide if you have all the information you need to support your assertions, and to consider the most effective way to present your ideas to readers. These planning activities generally require more discipline than the informal or formal play of invention. Because much of the crafting of your essay occurs as a result of these activities, however, this work can be intensely rewarding.

■ ■ ■

FOR EXPLORATION

How do you typically plan when you are working on a writing project? Do you rely on written plans, or do you use other means to determine goals and strategies for your writing? How might you make your process of planning more efficient and productive? Freewrite for five or ten minutes in response to these questions.

ESTABLISHING A CONTROLLING PURPOSE

The planning strategies discussed in this chapter are *goal-oriented*. You can't establish a controlling purpose or a workable plan for your essay without having at least a tentative sense of the goals you hope to achieve by writing. These goals may change as you work on your essay, but they represent an important starting point or preliminary set of assumptions for guiding your work in progress.

How can you determine appropriate goals for your writing? Whether you are writing a brief memo to your supervisor, a term paper for your history class, or an application for your first job, you can best understand and establish goals for writing by analyzing your rhetorical situation. This process, described in Chapter 5, encourages you to ask questions about the elements of rhetoric: writer, reader, and text. Once you have analyzed your rhetorical situation, you should have a clearer understanding of both your reasons for writing and also the most appropriate means to communicate your ideas to your readers.

Your *controlling purpose* reflects your essay's topic but differs from it in important ways. Unlike your topic, your controlling purpose is both action- and content-oriented. Your controlling purpose reveals not just what you want to write about, but also the point you wish to make and the effect you wish to have on your readers. It is an *operational statement of your intentions*.

Suppose that you are writing a guest editorial for your campus newspaper. "What are you going to write about?" a friend asks. "Library hours," you reply. You have just stated your topic — the subject you're going to write about — but this statement doesn't satisfy your friend. "What about library hours? What's your point?" "Oh," you say, "I'm going to argue that students should petition the vice president for academic affairs to extend the library hours. Current hours just aren't adequate." This second statement, which specifies the point you want to make and its desired effect on readers, is a good example of a clearly defined controlling purpose.

If you and your friend had time for a longer conversation, you could elaborate on the rhetorical situation for your editorial. You could discuss your own intentions as the writer more clearly, and you could note how you intend to anticipate and respond to readers' needs and interests. Your friend might be able to give you good advice about how your text should reflect one of the most important textual conventions of editorials — brevity.

An effective controlling purpose limits the topic and helps you clarify and organize your ideas. Once you have established a controlling purpose, you should be able to develop a number of questions that can guide you as you work on your writing. Here are some of the questions you might consider in response to the controlling purpose in the library editorial.

- What arguments will most effectively support my position?
- How can I focus my discussion so that I can make my point in the limited space typically given to editorials?

- Do I know enough about the reasons why current library hours are limited? Should I interview the director of the library or the vice president for academic affairs and ask them this question?

- Am I correct in assuming that other students find current hours a problem? Should I talk with some students to get their reactions to this problem? Should I develop a brief questionnaire that I could send to various campus Usenet and listserv groups?

- Should I find out how our library's hours compare with those at similar schools?

- Assuming that current library hours are a problem — and I'm convinced they are — how can I persuade students to sign a petition?

- Given my rhetorical situation, how formal should my language be? What image of myself should I try to create in my editorial?

As this example indicates, establishing a controlling purpose encourages you to be pragmatic and action-oriented. You may revise your controlling purpose as you work on your essay. In the meantime, you can use the insights gained by formulating and analyzing your controlling purpose to set preliminary goals for writing.

Once you have established a preliminary controlling purpose, you can test its effectiveness by asking yourself the questions listed in the following guidelines. (Or you may wish to discuss these questions with classmates.) If you can't answer one or more of these questions, you may not have analyzed your rhetorical situation carefully enough or spent adequate time discovering and exploring ideas.

■ GUIDELINES FOR EVALUATING YOUR CONTROLLING PURPOSE

1. How clearly does your controlling purpose indicate what you want this essay to do or to accomplish? Is your controlling purpose an operational statement of your intentions and not just a description of your topic?

2. How realistic are these intentions, given your rhetorical situation, the nature of the assignment, and your time and length limitations?

(continued)

(continued)

3. How might you accomplish this controlling purpose? Should you do additional reading? Talk with others? Spend more time discovering and exploring ideas?

4. In what ways does your controlling purpose respond to your understanding of your rhetorical situation, particularly the needs and expectations of your readers?

5. What questions, like those listed on pp. 249–50, does your analysis of your controlling purpose indicate that you need to consider as you work on your writing?

FOR EXPLORATION

For an essay that you are writing for this or another course, use the questions listed here to evaluate your current controlling purpose. Then write a paragraph evaluating the effectiveness of your controlling purpose and suggesting ways to improve it. Finally, list the questions that your evaluation indicates you need to consider as you work on this essay.

In some cases, you may be able to establish a controlling purpose early in your writing process. In many other instances, however, you will first have to think about your rhetorical situation and use informal and formal methods of

NOTE FOR MULTILINGUAL WRITERS

In the North American academic writing culture, the word *controlling* reflects the kind of control that writers wish to have over their writing and also the effect that they wish to have on readers. In your first or home culture, however, assumptions about writing may differ. Some cultures don't ask writers to "control" the effects of their writing; instead, they encourage writers to "invite" readers to engage in communication. If this is the case in your first or home culture, you may want to reflect on these differences. You may also want to share your reflections with your peers and invite their responses. Doing so can enrich both your and your peers' understanding of cultural differences in writing.

invention. You will, in other words, think and write your way into understanding what you want to say. You may even decide that the best way to determine your controlling purpose is to write a rough draft of your essay and see, in effect, what you think about your topic. This strategy, which is sometimes called *discovery drafting,* can work well as long as you recognize that your rough draft may need extensive analysis and revision.

You should always view any controlling purpose as preliminary or tentative, subject to revision. After you have worked on an essay for a while, your controlling purpose may evolve to reflect the understanding you have gained through further planning and drafting. You may even discover that your controlling purpose isn't feasible. In either case, the time you spend thinking about your preliminary controlling purpose is not wasted, for it enables you to begin the process of organizing and testing your ideas.

FORMULATING A WORKABLE PLAN

A written plan enables you to explore and organize your ideas and establish goals for your writing. Plans can take many forms. Some writers develop carefully structured, detailed plans. Others find that quick notes and diagrams are equally effective. The form that a plan takes should reflect your own needs, preferences, and situation.

As mentioned earlier, writers don't always make written plans. A very brief writing project or one that follows clearly defined textual conventions (such as a routine inventory update for a business) may not require a written plan. Nevertheless, as a college student, you will often find written plans helpful. Plans are efficient ways to try out your ideas. Developing a plan — whether a jotted list of notes or a formal outline — is also a good way to engage your unconscious mind in your writing process. Finally, many students find that by articulating their goals, by putting them on paper or onscreen, they can more effectively critique their own ideas, an important but often difficult part of the writing process.

There is no such thing as an ideal one-size-fits-all plan. An effective plan is a workable plan — one that works for you. Plans are utilitarian, meant to be used — and revised. In working on an essay, you may draw up a general plan only to revise this plan as you write. Nevertheless, if it helps you begin drafting, your first plan will fulfill its function well.

You may better understand how plans work by examining three students' actual plans. These plans vary significantly, yet each fulfilled the author's needs. The first plan is by Lisa DeArmand, a freshman majoring in business. It is a plan for a brief essay reviewing three popular pizza parlors near campus. As you can see, Lisa's plan is brief and simple. Lisa had already analyzed her rhetorical situation and recognized that the most effective way to organize her essay would be to compare the three restaurants. She also had detailed notes about these restaurants, including interviews with students, which she planned to use in her essay. Because Lisa had such a clear mental image of what she wanted to say and how she wanted to say it, she didn't need a complex or highly detailed written plan.

Lisa DeArmand's Plan

BOBBIE'S PIZZA	PIZZA-IN-A-HURRY	PIZZA ROMA
$8.00	$8.55	$9.10
close	coupons	best pizza!
limited hours	crust thin and soggy	unusual sauce
delivery charge	tastes like frozen pizza	two kinds of
pizza OK but not great		crust
little variety		more toppings

Now look at the plan by Dodie Forrest, a junior English major, for a take-home midterm in an American drama class (p. 254). It includes two diagrams that helped Dodie visualize how the essay might be organized, several quotes from the play that Dodie thought were important, reminders to herself, definitions of terms, and many general comments about the play. Dodie's task was more complex than Lisa's, so her plan needed to be more complex. Her task was also more open-ended. The question that Dodie was required to answer was this: "Explain why it is necessary for Arthur Miller to create wide sympathy for his character Willy Loman in *Death of a Salesman*. Does he create sympathy for Willy, or is the audience too tempted to judge him morally to be sympathetic?" Dodie used her plan to help explore her ideas and to determine the best organization for her essay. Although probably no one but Dodie could develop an essay from the various diagrams and notes she created, the plan fulfilled Dodie's needs — and that's what counts.

Here is a third plan, by Dave Ross, a returning student intending to major in natural resource economics. Dave began by writing about the "feel" he wanted his essay to have and then developed a detailed plan.

Dave Ross's Plan

This will be a personal essay about my experiences working at Urban Ore, a business that sells salvaged building materials. I want the reader to share my pleasure at working among all that great recyclable junk. The interesting "finds," the colorful characters, my own satisfaction at organizing the chaos. The essay should feel <u>crowded</u> with odds and ends, just like the salvage yard is: strange bits of description, stories, humorous observations. I guess "funky" is the word.

I. Description of the yard

Among one-family underclass homes, rusting railroad tracks, corrugated sheet metal auto body shops: a weedy, dusty scrapyard surrounded by

Dodie Forrest's Plan

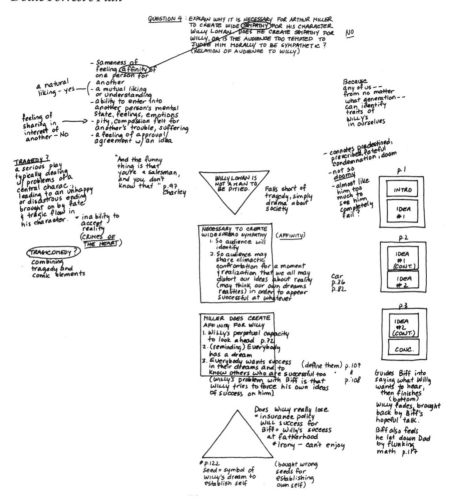

eight-foot cyclone fence, filled with doors, windows, kitchen cabinets, lamps, toilets, sinks, bathtubs, faucets, pipes, bricks, stoves, coils of wire.

A real business: this junk generates nearly $200,000 a year in sales to construction workers, contractors, or just weekend fixer-uppers.

II. People working there

Joe, the owner: Urban Studies Ph.D., abstract painter, two-time candidate for mayor.

Webb, looks like Jerry Garcia but with a rhino's strength.

Charles, lives on brown rice and has a passion for snakes.

Vagrant cats and a German shepherd named Ripthroat who melts when you scratch his butt.

III. Me working there

My first big job, organizing the windows and doors. First big rush of satisfaction: being able to tell a customer <u>exactly</u> where to find the bottom half of a double hung window, 36" by 28".

First Law of Urban Ore: "The more organized we are, the more we sell." But that's not the only reason I liked doing it. Bringing order out of chaos. An artist of the junkyard.

IV. Treasure island

Found among the weeds and blackberry brambles: Art Deco bathroom tiles, mint-condition platform heels, bottles of all shapes and colors, a Three Stooges coffee mug (think of more).

V. Not all fun

No electricity, heat, running water or toilet. Only one shack, crowded when it rains.

Winter: cold, stiff hands, wet gloves. Summer: pounding sun, dust.

Rusty nails, metal or glass edges

Hauling cast-iron bathtubs, six-burner ranges: hernia city!

VI. Conclusion

Honest, constructive work and creative in its way. Great when a customer found just what he/she wanted — or something they'd never dreamed of.

One evening, local skid-row types formed a band with stuff they'd found lying around. Played "Working on the Chain Gang" — sounded pretty bad, but a lot of spirit. A certain strange beauty amid the disorder — sums up Urban Ore for me.

Dave's plan is more detailed than Lisa's and more clearly organized than Dodie's. His approach to planning probably reflects his preference for detailed, well-organized plans. It also reflects the nature of the essay he had envisioned: He wanted to include such a profusion of material that a detailed plan would help ensure a coherent structure. Dave probably couldn't have worked efficiently from a freer, less clearly organized plan, like Dodie's — and Dodie might find Dave's approach equally difficult.

Plans play an important role in writing. They help you explore, organize, and try out your ideas; they also enable you to set goals for your writing. You might think of plans as notes, reminders, or directions that you write to yourself. No one else needs to be able to understand your plans, just as no one else needs to be able to shop from your grocery list. Through experimentation, you should be able to arrive at a style of planning that works for you.

NOTE FOR MULTILINGUAL WRITERS

You may find it helpful to consider how your knowledge of multiple languages or dialects affects how you formulate plans. Do you find it easier and more productive to formulate plans in your first or home language and then "translate" these plans into English? Conversely, do you find that formulating plans in English is helpful because it encourages you to keep North American rhetorical and cultural preferences in mind? You may want to experiment with both approaches so that you can determine the plan that works for you.

FOR EXPLORATION

What kinds of plans do you typically draw up? Do you formulate detailed, carefully structured plans, or do you prefer to develop less structured ones? Do you use diagrams or other visual elements in planning? Can you think of one or more suggestions that might enable you to develop more useful plans?

Use these questions to think about your plans. Then spend ten minutes writing down your most helpful observations about them.

FOR COLLABORATION

Meeting with a group of classmates, take turns reading your responses to the previous Exploration. After each person has read, work together to answer these questions. (Be sure to appoint a recorder.)

1. What planning strategies do the members of the group most often employ?

2. How often do you all develop written plans? What kinds of plans do you most often develop? How formal and detailed are your plans? Does anyone often use diagrams or other visual plans?

3. Did anyone suggest planning strategies that other members thought they might like to experiment with? If so, briefly describe these strategies and explain why they seem useful.

4. List three conclusions about planning with which all group members can agree. Make another list of at least three suggestions of ways to plan more efficiently and productively.

Be prepared to share the results of your discussion with your classmates.

DEVELOPING EFFECTIVE STRATEGIES FOR DRAFTING

Drafting is the point in the process when you write words on paper or online. You actually begin writing, of course, with your first freewriting or brainstorming in response to an assignment. Revision, too, often occurs before you complete a rough draft: If you make a list of possible titles for an essay, cross out two, and circle one as your best current choice, you have revised. Drafting itself is nevertheless an important component of the writing process, for it is through drafting that you create a text that embodies your preliminary intentions.

Overcoming Resistance to Drafting

When you first sit down at your desk or computer to begin drafting, it can be hard to imagine the satisfaction of completing a rough draft. Indeed, just picking up pen or pencil or beginning to type can seem daunting, leading you to think of a hundred things you'd rather do. All writers experience some resistance to drafting; productive writers, however, have developed ways to overcome this resistance.

Many writers rely on rituals to help them deal with what Tom Grenier calls the "prewrite jitters." There are other strategies you can use to overcome resistance to drafting. If you've already spent time discovering and exploring ideas and making one or more tentative plans, you will have the reassuring knowledge that you're not starting from scratch. Reading through early notes and plans is an effective way to begin a drafting session. You may find yourself turning hasty notes and fragments into full sentences or grouping them into paragraphs — drafting before you know it.

Another way to motivate yourself to start drafting is simply to remind yourself that you're working on a draft; it doesn't have to be perfect. When you begin drafting, your initial goal should simply be to *get the words down*. If you can't think of a way to open your essay, for instance, don't try to do so; simply begin writing whatever section you are ready to write. As you reread what you've written, you'll eventually discover an introduction that works.

Managing the Drafting Process

Once you pass the initial hurdle of getting started, you'll probably experience the drafting process as a series of ebbs and flows. You may write intensely for a short period, stop and spend time reviewing what you've written, make a few notes about how you might best proceed, and then draft again more slowly, pausing now and then to reread what you've written. The process of rereading your text as it develops is an important part of the drafting process. Research shows that experienced writers reread their writing often while drafting — and that they reread with an eye toward such major concerns as the extent to which their draft responds to the needs and expectations of readers. Chapter 12 presents a number of strategies that will help you read work in progress. Here are some suggestions that should help make the process of drafting efficient and productive.

■ GUIDELINES FOR DRAFTING AN ESSAY

1. *Don't Try to Correct — or Perfect — Your Writing as You Draft.* When you are drafting, your goal should be to put enough words on paper so that you can reflect on and revise your writing. The easiest way to produce a rough draft is to work at an even pace so the momentum of drafting can help you move steadily toward your goal. Stopping to worry whether a word is spelled correctly or to fiddle with a sentence can interrupt your momentum and throw you off balance. Furthermore, most writers find that it's easier to delete unnecessary or repetitive material when they revise than to add new material. When drafting, your goal should be to get words written, not to make decisions about revising. If you can't quite articulate an argument or formulate an example, write yourself a note and keep drafting. When you return to your draft, you can fill in these gaps and omissions.

(continued)

(continued)

2. *Try to Keep in Touch with Your "Felt Sense" — Your Awareness of What Your Writing Is Doing — as You Draft.* You attend to many things when you draft. You stop and reread the words on the page; you reflect about your topic and assignment; you think about your readers. If you are an effective writer, you look at what you have written not just to see what is on the page but also what *might be* there. Some writers call this kind of attention "keeping in touch with their *felt sense* as writers."*

You might think of felt sense as inspiration — and it is, in the sense that many writers would find it difficult to articulate why they are writing a particular sentence or paragraph. The ability to develop felt sense does not require magical or mysterious gifts, however. Writers develop felt sense when they are deeply immersed in their writing.

To develop and maintain a felt sense, you need to draft for long enough periods so that you can become immersed in your writing — an hour, minimally, but longer if possible. And as you write words, sentences, and paragraphs, you need to keep one eye on such global issues as the appropriateness of your organization. Reflecting on concerns such as these and jotting down notes about your current thoughts are good ways to keep in touch with your felt sense.

3. *Take Advantage of the Capabilities of Word Processing Programs.* Most writers find that computers make composing less frustrating and more productive. But if you are using a computer only to enter and change text, you are not taking advantage of its full range of options. One useful word processing feature allows you to write notes that appear onscreen but not on your printed text. If you are drafting quickly and wish to maintain your momentum but also remember a question or an idea, you can insert comments as you write and return to them in a later drafting session. Another common word processing feature, the split-screen or windows option, enables you to work with two texts at the same time. You might place a freewrite, outline, or plan in one window and write your draft in the other. Or you might keep

---

*Professor Sondra Perl discusses the concept of felt sense in "Understanding Composition," *College Composition and Communication* 31 (1980): 363–69.

(continued)

(continued)

your introduction in view as you write later sections. Always remember to protect your work by saving frequently, making backup copies of your drafts, and printing hard copies.

4. *Develop a Repertoire of Blockbusting Strategies.* All writers experience moments when the words won't come. Experienced writers don't just sit and bemoan their fate when this occurs. Instead, they draw on a repertoire of blockbusting strategies, including the following:

- Lower your standards. If you can't find the right words to express your ideas, get them down in any form you can. Write enough to remind yourself of the point you want to make; then move on.

- Stop trying to draft, and instead spend ten minutes freewriting or brainstorming.

- Switch to some writing task that you can do. If you can't determine how best to organize the body of your essay, for instance, spend some time revising your introduction or reviewing some background material on your subject. Or switch to another project you need to complete.

- Change strategies. If you've been trying to develop a written plan, try diagramming, clustering, or doodling instead.

- Talk out your ideas. Find a friend to talk with, or talk into a tape recorder. Begin by saying, "I've been trying to work on my essay, but I'm blocked. What I want to do is . . ."

- Take a few minutes to describe the difficulty you're experiencing; then take a break from writing to do something that will give you satisfaction — exercising, cooking, whatever.

5. *Learn When — and How — to Stop Drafting.* Ideally, you will come to a natural stopping point, a moment when you feel that you've solved a problem you've been wrestling with or concluded the section of your essay you've been working on. At this point it's a very good idea to take a few moments to jot down notes about what you've accomplished in that drafting session as well as about what you need to do when you return to your writing. You

(continued)

(continued)

may also wish to ask yourself a few questions: "What's the best transition here?" "Which examples should I use next?" If you're like many writers, your subconscious mind will reflect on these questions and present appropriate answers when you next sit down to draft.

6. *Benefit from the Process of Incubation.* Sometimes it helps to *stop* thinking consciously about your ideas and just let them develop in your mind while you relax, sleep, or occupy yourself with other projects. After this period of incubation, you will often spontaneously recognize how to resolve a problem or answer a question.

   You can't draw on your mind's subconscious powers, however, if you don't build in time for incubation. And don't confuse incubation with procrastination. Procrastination means avoiding the writing process; incubation means recognizing and using the fluctuations of the process to advantage.

FOR EXPLORATION

How do you typically draft an essay? How long do your drafting sessions usually last? What do you do when you run into problems while drafting? Could one or more of the suggestions presented here enable you to draft more productively? How might you best implement these suggestions? Spend five or ten minutes freewriting in response to these questions.

FOR COLLABORATION

Meeting with a group of classmates, take turns reading your responses to the preceding Exploration. After each person has read, work together to answer these questions. (Be sure to appoint a recorder.)

1. What drafting strategies do the members of your group most often employ?

2. How do group members overcome resistance to drafting? How long do drafting sessions typically last? How do you keep in touch with your felt sense while drafting?

3. Did anyone suggest drafting strategies that others might like to try? Briefly describe any such strategies, and explain why you believe they might be useful.

4. List three conclusions about drafting with which all group members can agree. Make another list of at least three suggestions on how you can draft more efficiently and productively.

Be prepared to share the results of your discussion with your classmates.

ORGANIZING AND DEVELOPING YOUR IDEAS

The British writer E. M. Forster once asked, "How can I know what I think until I see what I say?" By working through drafts of your work in progress, you gradually learn what you think about your subject. As you move from drafting to revising — a process that proceeds differently with each writing project — you also become increasingly engaged with issues of style and structure. "What do I think about this subject?" becomes less important than "How can I best present my ideas to my readers?"

This section presents guidelines for responding to the second question. These guidelines are only suggestions; your responses to these suggestions should be based on your understanding of your assignment, purpose, and rhetorical situation.

NOTE FOR MULTILINGUAL WRITERS

You may find it helpful to organize and perhaps even develop some of your thoughts in your first or home language.

■ GUIDELINES FOR ORGANIZING AND DEVELOPING YOUR IDEAS

1. *Check for Any "Code" Words That Mean Something to You but Not to Your Readers.* If you've spent time employing various invention strategies, begin your drafting session by reviewing the material you've already generated, looking for ideas and details you can use in your draft as well as for ones that need to be more fully developed. Often in rereading these explorations and early drafts, writers realize that they've relied on what Professor Linda Flower

(continued)

(continued)

calls "code words," words that convey meaning to the writer but not necessarily to readers.* Learning to recognize and expand or "unpack" code words in your writing can help you develop your ideas so that their significance is clear to readers.

Here is a paragraph one student did when freewriting about what the word *family* meant to her. Rereading the freewriting at the start of her drafting session, she recognized a number of code words, which she underlined.

When I think of the good things about my family, Christmas comes most quickly to mind. Our house was filled with such <u>warmth and joy</u>. Mom was busy, but she was <u>happy</u>. Dad seemed less absorbed in his work. In the weeks before Christmas he almost never worked late at the office, and he often arrived with brightly wrapped presents that he would tantalizingly show us — before whisking them off to their hiding place. And at night we <u>did fun things together</u> to prepare for the big day.

Words like *warmth* and *joy* undoubtedly evoke many strong connotations for the writer; most readers, however, would find these terms vague. By looking for code words in her freewriting, this writer realized that in drafting she would have to provide readers with plenty of concrete, specific details to enable them to visualize what she means.

2. *Share Your Controlling Purpose with Your Readers.* One way to help organize a draft is to share your controlling purpose with your readers. How to do so most effectively depends on a number of factors. If you are working on a take-home essay examination for your history class, for example, you may wish to include a *thesis statement,* a single sentence that states the main idea of your essay, in your introduction. You may also preview the main lines of argument you will use to support your position so that your instructor doesn't have to hunt for your main point.

    In other situations, including a specific thesis statement in the first paragraph of your essay may not be necessary or even desirable. If you are writing an essay about what the word *family* means to you, you might decide that you don't want to reveal the

---

*Linda Flower, *Problem-Solving Strategies for Writing in Colleges and Communities,* 5th ed. (Fort Worth: Harcourt Brace, 1996), 139.

(continued)

(continued)

main point of your essay at the start. Instead, you might begin with a specific example that will create interest in your essay and show, rather than tell, what *family* means to you.

North American readers quickly become irritated if they feel they're reading unorganized, disconnected prose or if their expectations about how a certain kind of writing should be organized are violated. For these reasons, sharing your intentions with readers and providing cues about how you will achieve them is essential. By analyzing your rhetorical situation and by studying how others engaged in similar writing tasks have fulfilled this obligation to readers, you can determine strategies to use to keep in touch with your readers.

3. *Take Advantage of Appropriate Methods of Organizing Information.* When you begin drafting, you don't have to come up with an organizational structure from scratch. Instead, you can draw on conventional methods of organization, methods that reflect common ways of analyzing and explaining information. Suppose that you are writing an essay about political and economic changes in Eastern Europe in the 1990s. Perhaps in your reading you were struck by the different responses of Russian and Czech citizens to economic privatization. You could draw on conventional methods of *comparing and contrasting* to organize your analysis. Or perhaps you wish to discuss the impact that severe industrial pollution in Russia could have on the development of a Western-style economy. After *classifying* the most prevalent forms of industrial pollution, you could discuss the consequences of this pollution for Russia's economy.

As these examples indicate, your subject may naturally lend itself to certain methods of organization. In some cases, you may be able to use a single method of organization — such as *comparison, definition, cause and effect,* or *problem-solution* — to organize your entire essay. More often, however, you will draw on several methods of organization to present your ideas. In considering how you can best draw on conventional methods of organizing information, remember that you should not impose these methods formulaically. Begin thinking about how to organize your writing by reflecting on your goals as a writer and your

(continued)

(continued)

rhetorical situation. If your analysis suggests that one or more methods of organizing information represent commonsensical, logical ways of approaching your subject, use them in drafting. But remember, form should grow out of meaning and not be imposed on it.

FOR THOUGHT, DISCUSSION, AND WRITING

1. Think of a time when you simply couldn't get started writing. What did you do to move beyond this block? How well did your efforts work — and why? After reflecting on your experience, write an essay (humorous or serious), about how you cope with writer's block.

2. Choose a writing assignment that you have just begun. After reflecting on your ideas, develop and write a workable plan. While drafting, keep a record of your activities. How helpful was your plan? Was it realistic? Did you revise your plan as you wrote? What can you learn about your writing process from this experience? Be prepared to discuss this experience with your class.

3. Interview someone who works in the field that you hope to enter after graduation, and ask how he or she plans and drafts on-the-job writing. What kinds of plans does this person typically construct? In what ways have electronic or other technologies (such as the tape recorder) influenced his or her planning and drafting strategies? Does this person experience writing blocks? If yes, what blockbusting strategies does he or she rely on? How do this person's profession and work schedule influence his or her planning and drafting? How often does he or she write alone? As a member of a group or team? What advice about writing would he or she give to a student, such as yourself, who hopes to enter this field? Write an essay summarizing the results of your interview.

Strategies for
Document Design

Electronic and digital technologies require communicators to make many more decisions about texts than they were required to do in the past. Someone who wants to share her passion for black Labrador retrievers, for instance, could create a research paper, an article, a Web site, or a video about this popular breed of dogs. Each medium would require her to be as concerned with the visual as with the verbal, for in all of these media the verbal and visual are interdependent.

Electronic and digital technologies are part of a larger historical trend toward increasing the role of visual elements in communication. Because of the dramatic proliferation of advertising in recent decades, consumers read hundreds of messages every week that attempt to persuade them to purchase products and services. Whether these messages take the form of magazine, television, or Web advertisements, visual elements play a critical role in their success. Television, video games, and movies have also created an appetite for visually sophisticated texts and images, and newspapers and magazines increasingly include complex graphics and color combinations in their articles and advertisements.

Until recently, few writers concerned themselves with the visual look of a text. Although advertising copy, magazines and newspapers, and business and technical texts have long been influenced by design concerns, just twenty years ago most writers composed either in longhand or at the typewriter. Students writing essays for college classes did have to use appropriate paper quality, margins, and (in the case of long, research-based essays) headings. And they also were often required to follow particular formats that specified the location of their name, course number, title of the essay, and so on. But these were the only visual elements that students needed to be concerned about in their papers.

Personal computers and word processing programs opened up a new world of options for writers, who can now easily vary text formats, print with color and multiple fonts, and develop sophisticated charts and graphs. Thanks to their large-capacity hard drives and fast processors, personal computers can now handle software programs with powerful graphics capabilities. With access to the World Wide Web, writers can easily (if not always legally) download texts, images, and even audio clips and integrate them into their own writing. It is increasingly common for students to develop texts that take full advantage of these options.

In word processing a document, for instance, writers need to consider such questions as these:

- What margins, spacing, and font should I use?

- Would my writing benefit from the use of special formats such as columns, bulleted lists, and text boxes?

- Should I use headings and subheadings to help organize my ideas?

- Would visual elements (such as a border, graph, chart, or some created or imported image) add to the effectiveness of my text?

- Would color make illustrations easier to interpret? Would color add to the overall effectiveness of my text?

Sometimes your instructor may specify a particular document design or format. (If you're unsure about instructors' preferences in this regard, don't hesitate to ask them.) On other occasions, you may have considerable flexibility in this regard.

■ ■ ■

FOR EXPLORATION

How attuned are you to the visual? Take a few moments to think about the many different texts that you read — from textbooks, magazines, newspapers, advertisements, and letters to Web sites, emails, and instant messages. How conscious are you of the ways that various design elements and images influence your response to and understanding of a text? (How does a magazine intended for twenty-somethings, for instance, use visual elements to differentiate itself from one intended for a different readership?) Do you have strong preferences about such visual features as type font, color, and images? Take five minutes to freewrite in response to these questions.

Looking at Document Design from a Rhetorical Perspective

Questions about word processing formats cannot be determined on a once-and-for-all basis. They are, in fact, rhetorical questions — questions that depend on your rhetorical situation. Just as you can analyze a rhetorical situation

NOTE FOR MULTILINGUAL WRITERS

Cultures have their own preferences about written texts, and they also have preferences about visual texts and visual design principles. If you are an international student, you may have noticed that the "look" of newspapers in your home country differs considerably from the look of most North American newspapers. These differences reflect cultural preferences about visual design.

Take a few moments to consider differences between North American visual design preferences and those of your home country or community. How might these design preferences influence the decisions that you need to make as a writer of academic texts? Which elements of your home community or culture's visual design preferences might enrich your academic writing, and vice versa?

to make decisions about your writing (see Chapter 5), so too can you analyze your situation to make decisions about document design and other visual elements of communication.

Imagine two students who are working on projects for a class. One student is taking an art history class: He is writing a twenty-page seminar paper on the nineteenth-century British artists who called themselves the Pre-Raphaelite Brotherhood. The second student, who is in an English class, is writing a four-page analysis of a poem by the contemporary American poet Mary Oliver. How should these students use visual elements in their writing? Both have access to computers and online technologies that allow them to import images (such as reproductions of paintings by various Pre-Raphaelites or photographs of Mary Oliver). But should they?

A rhetorical response to these questions would consider the students' particular situations. Though these two students are writing different kinds of essays for different classes, one aspect of their situation is shared. Both are writing academic essays, so both need to understand that any visual elements they use should reflect the seriousness and formality that generally characterize academic writing. Ideas are central in academic writing, so any image, chart, or other visual element that is used in a class assignment should be essential to the overall intellectual richness and impact of the writing.

As you have perhaps already realized, both students need to use visual elements. The student who is writing about the Pre-Raphaelites for an art history class is writing a long paper, so his headings will help orient readers to critical divisions within the writing. Even more important, however, is the role that reproductions of art by the Pre-Raphaelites could play in this student's analysis. Reproductions would enable readers to understand and evaluate the student's analysis of various paintings without having to refer to other sources. The art history student might also include photographs of the Pre-Raphaelites if he is sure that the photos will enrich his analysis, such as if he is discussing the historical, cultural, or social role that this movement played in nineteenth-century England.

The student writing on Oliver would also need to attend to visual elements. She would want to consider such visual issues as the use of white space, fonts, and headings, for instance, which are important for anyone writing an essay. But unless some aspect of the analysis requires visual support or clarification, the student writing about Oliver would probably not include photographs or other visual images. These images would add little to the development of her ideas and might even distract readers.

As these examples suggest, the role of document design in your writing process will vary depending on your situation. The student writing about the Oliver poem needs to follow her professor's requirements for basic essay format (margins, line spacing, titles, and so on). Concerns about document design, however, would play a relatively minor role in her writing process. The student writing about Pre-Raphaelites, on the other hand, needs to attend to document-design issues from the very start. He needs to select early on, for instance, the paintings by the Pre-Raphaelites that he will discuss at length. In making this decision, the student needs to focus on reproductions that are most relevant to his analysis, easily available, and legally reproducible.

As these examples suggest, a rhetorical approach to document design encourages you to ask questions about your audience, your text, and yourself. Let's consider several different situations.

- *The Audience*   If you are writing a take-home midterm for a political science class, your audience — your teacher — does not expect and probably does not want a visually complicated text to read. In a situation like this, you should follow traditional conventions of document design, which downplay the visual elements of communication. But suppose that you are a college senior writing an honors thesis, your subject cries out for illustration, and your audience is a committee of faculty members who are willing to discuss various visual elements with you. If you're writing about the therapeutic value of improvisational dance, for instance, or about the recent development of new techniques for ground-water purification, you might well decide to include illustrations, tables, and graphs in your thesis. Because you have worked intimately with your professors on this project, you can talk about these issues with them. You will have to meet the honors thesis format requirements, but anything else is up for negotiation with committee members.

- *The Text*   Textual conventions play a role in your design decision making. For instance, when Brenda Shonkwiler's teacher asked her students to write progress reports on their research projects, she specified that these reports should be written in memo format. In so doing, her teacher thereby defined much of the design of their documents. Memos are formatted in certain ways, and they often include headings. (As noted earlier, Brenda's teacher also provided the headings that students should use to organize and present their thoughts.) In many of the sciences, conventions about designing (and especially formatting) texts already exist, such as the headings used in lab reports and grant proposals. Brenda Shonkwiler's progress report appears on page 459.

■ *The Writer*   When you approach a writing assignment, you need to consider a number of issues and options. Perhaps the most important are the following: How much authority do you have in this particular situation? How knowledgeable are you about the textual conventions that inform the kind of writing you are undertaking? How much knowledge do you have of various technologies of writing that might visually enhance your text? And how much time do you have to take advantage of this knowledge?

As noted earlier, if you are writing a take-home midterm exam, the brief amount of time available to you and the emphasis on evaluation suggest a fairly traditional approach to document design. A neatly presented and correctly formatted essay is essential. In determining whether to include complex visual elements, your knowledge of the conventions of various disciplines comes into play. You may know that in some disciplines, such as geosciences, tables and figures are commonly used. In traditionally text-based disciplines such as English and philosophy, tables and figures are rarely included. If you are unsure of what is appropriate for a particular discipline, take a conservative approach — or ask your teacher.

■ ■ ■

FOR EXPLORATION

Chapter 17, "Putting It All Together: Writing Academic Arguments," concludes with a collection (or miscellany) of examples of student writing. This miscellany appears on pp. 438–62 of Chapter 17. Skim these essays, taking quick notes about each document's design and its effectiveness. When you look at the documents, note minor as well as major features. Monica Molina's essay, for instance (p. 451), uses asterisks to break her essay into three sections. This is not as obvious or strong a feature as the headings that Tara Gupta uses in her application for a summer fellowship (p. 443) — but it is still significant. Then, based on your notes, write two or three paragraphs about what you learned from this analysis.

FOR COLLABORATION

Bring your analysis to class, and meet with a group of students. Appoint someone to serve as recorder or reporter. Then have each student read his or her analysis. To what extent did group members agree and disagree about the effectiveness of the document designs used in the essays? Conclude by articulating two things you have learned as a result of this activity. Be prepared to share the results of your discussion with classmates.

Understanding the Basics of Document Design

Document design does not have to be a complicated process. If you know the basic principles of document design, you can create texts that will help readers get what they need from a printed page or a screen. The goal is to design accessible texts that share information and achieve their purpose, not to create elaborate documents with lots of bells and whistles. The following guidelines provide suggestions that can help you make effective decisions about document design for print- and Web-based texts.

■ GUIDELINES FOR EFFECTIVE DOCUMENT DESIGN

1. *Remember the Importance of Basic Design Principles.* Some basic principles of visual design — alignment, proximity, repetition, and contrast — are discussed in Chapter 7. If a text is *aligned,* similar items are placed consistently on the page. Lines of text and the edges of illustrations are usually aligned on the left side of the page. Occasionally, lines align on the right side or are centered. When relationships between text elements (such as headings, subheadings, and items in a list) and between text and visual elements (such as captions and photos) are clear, a page makes effective use of *proximity. Repetition,* if it is used appropriately, gives a page coherence. One example of repetition is the practice of indenting paragraphs.

   And, finally, when graphic designers ensure that white space is adequate in visual and verbal texts, they are recognizing the need for *contrast.* The white spaces around text — created by margins and double-spacing, for instance — frame the text and guide the reader's eyes through it. It is tiring to read a cramped text, whether that text includes only words or both words and visuals.

(continued)

(continued)

2. *Select an Appropriate Type Font and Type Size for Your Document.*
When writers composed texts on manual or electric typewriters,
they had few options for type font and type size. Today the computer presents writers with a dazzling — but potentially bewil-
dering — array of options. How can you make the best use of the
type fonts and sizes that are available to you?

This question is easily answered if you are writing a paper for
one of your college classes. For such writing, the easy-to-read 11-
or 12-point type size is best:

This is 11 point Times New Roman.

This is 12 point Times New Roman.

But what if you are composing a brochure, newsletter, or Web
site? In some situations, you may want to consider using an unusual font such as **Gill Sans Extrabold**, Avant Garde Gothic,
or **Heatwave**. Remember, though, that such fonts call attention
to themselves and should be used sparingly. Most writers limit
themselves to using two or at most three fonts in a document. If
you shift fonts and sizes too often within a document, you will
distract readers from focusing on your text.

3. *Know When — and How — to Use Color.* Color can add to a document's visual appeal and impact, so it can play an important
role in document design. Those who write brochures, Web pages,
newsletters, and similar documents often employ color in their
work. Those writing academic papers, however, usually compose
texts printed only in black ink. If you do use color, be sure to follow these design principles:

- Establish a plan for the use of color. How many colors will
  you use? Do you need to consider the costs of printing documents with color? What role do you want color to play in
  your overall design?

- Use color to emphasize key elements of your text — and do
  so consistently. If you are using color to emphasize subheads,
  for instance, use the same color throughout your text.

- Use two — or at most three — colors in your Web document. Depending on what browser readers are using, they

(continued)

(continued)

may not have access to the colors that you used to compose a document. Because downloading Web pages that rely heavily on color takes longer than downloading one-color pages, some readers may simply move to a site that is more speedily accessed. Given this situation, using fewer — rather than more — colors in Web-based documents makes sense.

4. *Use Visuals That Are Appropriate to Your Situation and Purpose.* Visuals can add to your text's persuasiveness. They are best used when your text truly *needs* them — that is, when a visual can present information more succinctly and clearly than words alone can. Visuals fall into two broad categories: tables and figures. Tables summarize data, usually by displaying information in clearly labeled horizontal rows and vertical columns. Figures include all other visuals: pie and bar charts, line and bar graphs, drawings, maps, photographs, and other illustrations.

Whether you are using tables or figures, common sense can help you make a number of important decisions. As noted earlier, you should use visuals only when they play a key role in communicating your ideas effectively. Never use visuals merely as decoration, particularly in academic writing. Be sure to number and title visuals and explain their significance in the body of your text. (A student who is writing about military deaths during the Vietnam war might introduce an important table by noting, "As Table 1 demonstrates, many more Vietnamese than American soldiers lost their lives during this war.") You may think that your visual's relevance to your discussion is obvious, but not all readers may find that to be the case. Finally, remember that different situations call for different visuals. Tables are especially effective at conveying numerical information, while graphs and charts call attention to relationships among data. Photographs, drawings, diagrams, maps, and other visuals should be chosen based on your purpose and audience.

5. *Be a Responsible User of Visuals Created by Others.* Whether you are using print- or Web-based visuals, take care to follow the conventions of copyright law. These laws are constantly being refined and revised — especially in the case of the Web. In general, the concept of "fair use" allows students to use brief excerpts of

(continued)

(continued)

copyright-protected material if they are using the material for a class and are not publishing it (in print or on the Web) or in some other way profiting from it. If you are downloading visuals from the Web, be sure to look for copyright notices and information about fair use. You will find that many sites will allow you to download information without requesting permission. If there is no such statement on a site, you should email the site's Webmaster for permission. (Figure 10.1 shows a sample permission request.) Of course, whenever you use visuals created by others, you should credit your source fully.

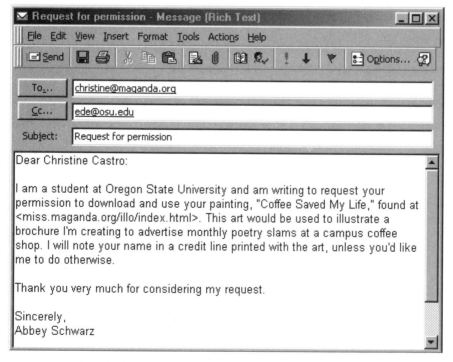

Figure 10.1   Sample Permission Request.

FOR EXPLORATION

In Chapter 4, you read Brenda Shonkwiler's research paper on the Tacoma Narrows Bridge catastrophe (pp. 135–53). Reread this paper, giving particular attention to its visuals. (Brenda's paper includes several photographs, as well as a diagram, a drawing, and a table.) How do these visual elements contribute to her paper's effectiveness? How does Brenda follow the conventions of copyright law in acknowledging the sources of these visuals?

Making Effective Decisions about Document Design

If you're like most readers, you'll agree that Brenda Shonkwiler's use of diverse visual elements enriches both the significance and impact of her research paper (pp. 135–53). A rhetorical understanding of document design emphasizes that what works well in one situation is not necessarily appropriate in another, however. For instance, in the progress report for her research paper project that Brenda wrote for her instructor, Brenda followed the traditional memo format and used significantly fewer visual elements — only headings and a table showing her work schedule. Brenda recognized that photographs and other figures were unnecessary — and, indeed, unhelpful — for this particular writing project.

One way to learn how to make effective decisions about document design is to study the decision-making process that others have followed in designing documents. Here are three versions of a memo that were written by my colleague Wayne Robertson, who coordinates Oregon State University's Writing Center and the writing assistants (undergraduate and graduate student tutors) who hold conferences with students about their writing. Toward the end of the fall 2001 term, Wayne realized that the Center did not have enough funds to provide its current level of service during the winter and spring terms. Although student enrollment at Oregon State had increased significantly over several years, the budgets of most units, including the Center, had been cut. University administrators had recently set aside money to provide one-time funds for units that provided essential educational services for students and established an Access Fund Committee to determine which units would receive additional resources.

Wayne knew that the Committee would have only a brief time to review the many proposals that various units would submit to it and that first impressions would be crucial. Because he had to keep his memo brief, focused, and visually persuasive, he decided to develop a table that would represent the Writing Center's significant increase in number of student contacts. Wayne wanted this increase to grab readers' attention the first time they looked at his proposal. This table needed to function as the persuasive "heart" of his memo.

Here is the first draft of Wayne Robertson's memo.

TO: The Access Fund Committee

FROM: Wayne Robertson, Coordinator
             Writing Center

DATE: December 3, 2001

SUBJECT: Writing Center Request for $8,000 of Student Pay

This request represents the inability of our current budget to meet increasing student numbers. During fall term 1999, we logged 1,094 student contacts (where each contact is a half hour individual session with a writing assistant). Last fall, we saw a 16% increase, logging 1,268 contacts. This fall, we have already recorded 1,593 contacts and expect to reach approximately 1,700 before the term is finished. This number represents a 34.1% increase over last year and a 55.4% increase over two years ago.

Year	Fall Term	% Increase	Entire Year	% Increase
1999–2000	1,094		3,423	
2000–2001	1,268		4,214	36.5%
2001–2002 projected	1,700		5,100	65.2%

The projection of 5,100 contacts for this coming year is conservative. As past years have demonstrated, more students come down to use the Writing Center as the year progresses. While we had 1,268 contacts during fall term of last year, we recorded 1,394 contacts winter term and 1,552 contacts in the spring. It is therefore a good possibility that our estimate of 5,100 may be low.

These severe increases have had a dramatic effect on the accessibility of our services for students. Even though we actively recruited over 10 new writing assistants and overspent our Fall budget by approximately 35%, we have operated at 100% capacity for the last two weeks and had to turn away over 70 students during dead week alone. Without being able to hire any more writing assistants, this situation will likely look worse over the next two terms.

Our budget for writing assistant salaries this year is $10,000. Already, we have spent nearly half of that amount this term. We estimate that in order for students to easily access our services, we will need to spend around $18,000 by the end of spring term. A grant of $8,000 will ensure that students looking for academic assistance will get it.

When Wayne reviewed this draft, he identified a number of problems. The first sentence, for instance, is awkward: Can a request represent an inability? Wayne knew that with time and effort he could revise his prose so that it was more effective. But he was more worried about developing a table that would persuasively convey information about student use of the Center. The table in the first draft certainly has problems. Not all cells in the tables include data, and the table is hard to read at a glance. The column headings do not identify the data, for instance, so committee members would have to read the memo's first paragraph to make sense of the table. But Wayne suspected that the table's visual prominence would draw readers' attention first. The first draft of this table would create confusion and a negative impression of the Center's request.

The second draft of the memo addresses these issues. Here is Wayne Robertson's second draft of his memo to the Access Fund Committee:

TO: Access Fund Committee

FROM: Wayne Robertson, Coordinator
                Writing Center

DATE: December 3, 2001

SUBJECT: Writing Center Access Fund Request for $8,000 Student Pay

In order to respond to the rapidly increasing number of students using the Writing Center's services, we are requesting an access grant of $8,000 to help pay writing tutors. As the following charts demonstrate, our number of student contacts[1] this Fall has increased 55% over Fall 1999, and we project that our total number of contacts for the year will show a 65% increase over 1999–2000.

Fall Term Student Contacts:

1999	2000	Projected 2001	Two-Year Increase
1,094 contacts	1,268 contacts	1,700 contacts	55.4%

Annual Student Contacts:

1999–2000	2000–2001	Projected 2001–2002	Two-Year Increase
3,423 contacts	4,214 contacts	5,100 contacts	65.2%

In order to keep up with student demand, the Writing Center hired 10 new work study students and increased the number of available appointments both for our daytime hours in Waldo Hall and our evening hours in the Valley Library. In order to make our services accessible for students, we spent nearly half our annual $10,000 budget for student pay during the fall term. Despite increasing the number of available appointments, however, the Writing Center has run at 100% capacity for the last two weeks of the term, and the Writing Desk in the Library has been full since the fifth

---

[1]One student contact at the Writing Center represents a half-hour individual tutoring session.

week of classes. During dead week alone, the Writing Center had to turn away over 70 students.

In order to keep tutors available for students the rest of the year, we estimate an additional $8,000 will be needed. This money will go directly into offering more tutoring sessions for students and will ensure that students can access the Center's services.

The first sentence of draft two is much more pointed than the first sentence of draft one. The nature of Wayne's request to the Access Committee is now much clearer. Table column headings now tell readers that the table demonstrates increases in student contacts. Each table cell now includes data, which reduces confusion.

If you compare the second paragraphs of each memo, you'll see an additional change. The first draft of that paragraph primarily explains the information that is provided in the table. But readers might find this explanation redundant if they're expecting the table to be self-explanatory. And why note that the estimate of 5,100 student contacts may be low, since it is the estimate that is included in the memo? In his second draft of this paragraph, Wayne makes a sophisticated rhetorical choice. Realizing that the access funds are limited and that many units across campus are requesting additional funds, Wayne emphasizes that the Writing Center has already done all that it could feasibly do to ensure that students will have access to Writing Center conferences.

Despite these significant improvements in his second-draft memo to the Access Fund Committee, Wayne nevertheless felt that the table was so crucial to his argument that it should be even more clear and persuasive. To highlight the extraordinary increase in student contacts at the Writing Center over the previous two years, Wayne made several crucial changes in his third and final draft.

December 6, 2001

TO: Access Fund Committee

FROM: Wayne Robertson, Coordinator
             Writing Center

SUBJECT: Access Fund Request

To provide essential educational services to the students who are using the Writing Center in rapidly increasing numbers, we are requesting access funds of $8,000 to help us pay the salaries of writing tutors. As the following charts demonstrate, the Center's number of student contacts[1] this fall

---

[1]One student contact at the Writing Center represents a half-hour individual tutoring session.

has increased 57% over fall 1999, and we estimate that our total number of contacts for the year will show a 65% increase over 1999–2000.

Fall Term Contacts		Annual Contacts	
Year	Number of Contacts	Year	Number of Contacts
Fall 1999	1,094	1999–2000	3,087
Fall 2000	1,268	2000–2001	4,214
Fall 2001	1,723	2001–2002	5,100 (estimate)
Two-year increase: 57.5%		**Two-year increase: 65.2%**	

Student demand this fall has required the Writing Center to increase appointments for our daytime hours at the Writing Center in Waldo Hall and for our evening hours at the Writing Desk in the Valley Library. By hiring a combination of students at work study and regular student wages, the Writing Center was able to offer 267 appointments per week compared to 171 per week in fall, 1999. Despite this increase, however, the Waldo Hall location ran at 100% capacity for the last two weeks of the term, and the Valley Library location was full from the fifth week of classes. During dead week alone, the Writing Center had to turn away over 70 students.

To meet these increasing demands, the Writing Center spent nearly half our annual $10,000 budget for student salaries during fall term. We will need an additional $8,000 to meet student needs for the winter and spring terms. The funds we are requesting will directly help pay for more tutoring sessions for students and will ensure that students can access the Center's services.

One third-draft change — placing the tables showing fall and annual student contacts next to each other rather than one following the other — reflects basic principles of design such as alignment, proximity, and contrast. Simply by changing the placement of the tables, Wayne uses headings, white space, and contrast more effectively. Since most North American readers read from left to right, this placement also helps readers grasp the essential information presented in the tables. The final touch is putting the fall and annual two-year increases at the bottom of each table: these bold figures call attention to the dramatic increase in student contacts that Oregon State University's Writing Center experienced in the years from 1999 to 2001–2002.

The third draft of his proposal is the one that Wayne submitted to the Access Fund Committee. Despite the large number of other proposals and the limited amount of available funds, the proposal for funds to pay student writing assistants was successful: the verbal argument and the visual presentation of supporting statistics were persuasive. Wayne attributed his proposal's success to several factors. "I think it helped that I worked on both the textual argument and document design from the start," he observed. "As a teacher of technical writing, I know the kind of problems that can occur when you develop these two sequentially, rather than together. When you do that, sometimes the visual and verbal arguments never do come together!" Wayne also avoided the urge to develop more complex graphics: "I played around with all sorts of ways of representing the increase in student contacts, including bar graphs and other visuals. Finally, I decided that simpler was better."

You can learn from Wayne's experiences in composing and designing a document that was important for him and the Writing Center. If you think that visuals or color could be incorporated into your own academic writing, include them in your planning and drafting. Early in your planning process, determine whether your technology is able to do what you need it to do. Don't wait until the night before your project is due to discover that your printer

Questions to ask your local beach health monitoring official:

- Which beaches do you monitor and how often?

- What do you test for?

- Where can I see the test results and who can explain them to me?

- What are the primary sources of pollution that affect this beach?

What to do if your beach is not monitored regularly:

- Avoid swimming after a heavy rain.

- Look for storm drains along the beach. Don't swim near them.

- If the waters of your beach have been designated as a no-discharge zone for vessel sewage, check to see if boat pumpout facilities are available and working.

- Look for trash and such other signs of pollution as oil slicks in the water. These kinds of pollutants may indicate the presence of disease-causing microorganisms that may also have been washed into the water.

- If you think your beach water is contaminated, contact your local health or environmental protection officials. It is important for them to know about suspected beach water contamination so they can protect citizens from exposure.

- Work with your local authorities to create a monitoring program.

In celebration of the 30th anniversary of the Clean Water Act, EPA presents

Before You Go to the Beach...

★ 2002 ★
THE YEAR OF
CLEAN WATER

can't print your tables or figures. Locate a printer that will do what you want it to do — with your first draft. Finally, recognize that both your written text and your visual elements will need to be revised several times.

FOR EXPLORATION

In the text discussion of Wayne Robertson's three drafts, I noted a number — but not all — of the changes that he made as he moved from draft to draft. Reread the three drafts, and identify at least two additional changes that improved the quality of Wayne's final proposal.

Wayne Robertson's memo is a good example of the persuasive use of visual design in writing. On page 282 is another example, a brochure developed by advocates of the Clean Water Act. Note how the creators use effective design elements to make their point.

FOR THOUGHT, DISCUSSION, AND WRITING

1. Turn back to the introductions to the three articles by Deborah Tannen that were presented in Chapter 6, "Thinking about Communities and Conventions," on pp. 185–90. The Chapter 6 discussion of these three introductions touched on issues of document design, noting, for instance, that the article intended for the broadest audience uses the most fully developed visuals in order to interest readers in Tannen's topic. But it did not discuss these visuals in depth. Drawing on the guidelines presented in this chapter, analyze the visual design of these documents and relate the elements of each design to the intended audience.

2. The textbook you are reading right now — *Work in Progress: A Guide for Academic Writing and Revising* — has, like most books, been designed by a team of editors, designers, and artists. This team has developed a design that is easy to read and attractive. It uses design elements such as type fonts and sizes, white space, headings, color, and visuals to increase the readability and effectiveness of the text. Drawing on the principles of design discussed in this chapter and also on your own design preferences, write a paragraph in which you evaluate the design of this textbook. Conclude your evaluation with one or two suggestions for improving the book's design in future editions.

3. For a community, church, civic, or other group project in which you are currently involved, develop a flyer, brochure, newsletter, or Web page that your group will use as an internal document or share with others. If you are not currently involved in such a project, develop a document that relates to a project that interests you.

4. The following text, "USA: The Way We'll Live Then," is from the January 1, 2000, issue of *Newsweek* magazine. As you may recall, the new

The 21st Century NATIONAL AFFAIRS

USA: The Way We'll Live Then

FIRST, THE GOOD NEWS: CHANCES ARE WE'LL LIVE LONGER and move somewhere warmer—probably California—where we'll shop online and chat on our tiny cell phones. Unfortunately, we'll also be fatter and more deeply in debt (your daughter's college education could cost about $250,000). But don't panic yet: these are only predictions, subject to unforeseeable innovations that will change the face of America. A best guess at the look of the nation in the next decades.

BRET BEGUN

Education

School enrollment
IN MILLIONS

K-8
9-12

1984 90 95 00 05 09

College enrollment*
IN MILLIONS

Women
Men

1984 90 95 00 05 09

Cost of 4-year college
IN THOUSANDS

Private
Public

1998 05 10 15 17

Occupations

Fastest-growing occupations
PERCENT CHANGE, 1994 TO 2005

Personal-care aides	118%
Home health aides	102
Systems analysts	92
Computer engineers	91
Other computer scientists	90
Physical therapists	79
Residential counselors	76
Human-services workers	74
Medical assistants	59
Paralegals	59

Job restructuring
IN PERCENT

Outer space
Leisure/ tourism
Info/ high tech
Services
Manufac- turing
Agriculture

1900 1930 1960 1990 2020 2050

Teleworkers
IN MILLIONS

Adults using the Internet for business from home

1995 97 99 01 03 04

Lawyers
IN THOUSANDS

1951 60 71 80 91 00

Gross domestic product
IN TRILLIONS

Value of goods and services

1997 10 20 30 40 50

Population

Race and ethnicity	1999	2050	PERCENT GROWTH
White	82.3%	74.8%	-9%
Black	12.9	15.4	19
Hispanic (any race)	11.2	24.5	119
Asian and Pacific Islander	4.0	8.7	118
Amer. Ind., Eskimo, Aleut.	0.9	1.1	22

Population by age
Each figure equals 1 million people

Population in July 1999: 272,330,000

July 1999

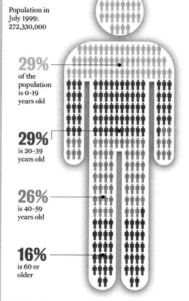

29% of the population is 0-19 years old

29% is 20-39 years old

26% is 40-59 years old

16% is 60 or older

Ratio of working-age population to the elderly
25 TO 64-YEAR-OLDS VS. 65 AND OLDER

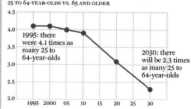

1995: there were 4.1 times as many 25 to 64-year-olds

2030: there will be 2.3 times as many 25 to 64-year-olds

1995 2000 05 10 15 20 25 30

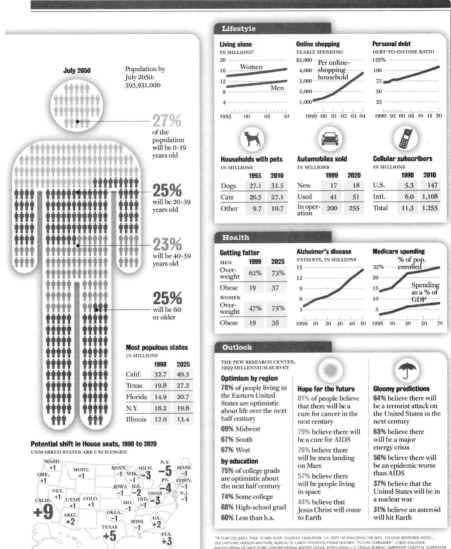

July 2050

Population by July 2050: 393,931,000

27% of the population will be 0-19 years old

25% will be 20-39 years old

23% will be 40-59 years old

25% will be 60 or older

Most populous states
IN MILLIONS

	1998	2025
Calif.	32.7	49.3
Texas	19.8	27.2
Florida	14.9	20.7
N.Y.	18.2	19.8
Illinois	12.0	13.4

Potential shift in House seats, 1990 to 2020
UNMARKED STATES ARE UNCHANGED

WASH. +1
ORE. +1
NEV. +1
CALIF. +9
UTAH +1
COLO. +1
ARIZ. +2
MONT. +1
MINN. -1
WIS. -1
MICH. -3
N.Y. -5
MASS. -1
PA. -1
CONN. -1
IOWA -1
ILL. -2
OHIO -4
N.J. -1
MO. -1
IND. -3
OKLA. -1
MISS. -1
GA. +2
TEXAS +5
FLA. +3

Lifestyle

Living alone
IN MILLIONS†

Women
Men

1995 00 05 10

Online shopping
YEARLY SPENDING

Per online-shopping household

$5,000
4,000
3,000
2,000
1,000

1999 00 01 02 03 04

Personal debt
DEBT-TO-INCOME RATIO

125%
100
75
50
25

1990 95 00 05 10 15 20

Households with pets
IN MILLIONS

	1993	2010
Dogs	27.1	31.5
Cats	20.5	27.1
Other	9.7	10.7

Automobiles sold
IN MILLIONS

	1999	2020
New	17	18
Used	41	51
In oper-ation	200	255

Cellular subscribers
IN MILLIONS

	1990	2010
U.S.	5.3	147
Intl.	6.0	1,108
Total	11.3	1,255

Health

Getting fatter

MEN	1999	2025
Over-weight	62%	73%
Obese	19	37
WOMEN		
Over-weight	47%	75%
Obese	19	35

Alzheimer's disease
PATIENTS, IN MILLIONS

15
12
9
6
3

1999 10 20 30 40 50

Medicare spending

% of pop. enrolled
Spending as a % of GDP

25%
20
15
10
5

1995 10 30 50 70

Outlook

THE PEW RESEARCH CENTER, 1999 MILLENNIUM SURVEY

Optimism by region
78% of people living in the Eastern United States are optimistic about life over the next half century
69% Midwest
67% South
67% West

by education
75% of college grads are optimistic about the next half century
74% Some college
68% High-school grad
60% Less than h.s.

Hope for the future
81% of people believe that there will be a cure for cancer in the next century
79% believe there will be a cure for AIDS
76% believe there will be men landing on Mars
57% believe there will be people living in space
44% believe that Jesus Christ will come to Earth

Gloomy predictions
64% believe there will be a terrorist attack on the United States in the next century
63% believe there will be a major energy crisis
56% believe there will be an epidemic worse than AIDS
37% believe that the United States will be in a nuclear war
31% believe an asteroid will hit Earth

*4-YEAR COLLEGES. †AGE 15 AND OVER. SOURCES: EDUCATION, U.S. DEPT. OF EDUCATION, THE NAT'L. COLLEGE RESOURCE ASSOC.; OCCUPATIONS, HUDSON INSTITUTE; BUREAU OF LABOR STATISTICS; FRANK FEATHER, "FUTURE CONSUMER"; CYBER DIALOGUE; ENCYCLOPEDIA OF THE FUTURE; CONGRESSIONAL BUDGET OFFICE; POPULATION, U.S. CENSUS BUREAU; AMERISTAT; LIFESTYLE, FORRESTER RESEARCH; EDWARD N. WOLFF, NEW YORK UNIVERSITY; AMERICAN DEMOGRAPHICS; THE POLK CO.; THE STRATEGIS GROUP; HEALTH; GEORGE L. BLACKBURN, BETH ISRAEL DEACONESS MEDICAL CENTER; ALZHEIMER'S ASSOC. GRAPHIC BY BONNIE SCRANTON—NEWSWEEK.

millennium inspired much speculation about the ways in which the twentieth and twenty-first centuries would differ from each other. Magazines and newspapers published many articles on this subject that relied on long verbal analyses of the challenges and opportunities facing humanity as it entered the new millennium. In this piece, however, *Newsweek* developed visual representations of "the look of the nation in the next decades." In what ways are these representations effective? What kind of information is missing from these representations? Your instructor may ask you to write an essay on this topic.

Strategies for Managing the Revision Process

In the broadest sense, revision occurs throughout the writing process. If you write a tentative first sentence, decide that it doesn't work, and cross it out, you have revised. Although revision can occur at any time, you will probably revise most intensively after you have completed a rough draft. At this point, you will have managed to articulate at least a preliminary statement of your ideas. Revision challenges you to look at your work from a dual perspective: to read your work with your own intentions in mind and also to try to consider your readers' perspectives.

Reading thus plays a crucial role in revision. When you read over your work, you attempt to discover strengths to build on and weaknesses to remedy. Consequently, you must think about not just what is actually in your text but also what is *not* there and what *could be* there. You must read the part (the introduction, say, or several paragraphs) while still keeping in mind the whole.

As a writer, you should have a healthy respect for the demands of revision, but you should not be overwhelmed by it. By studying both your own writing process and the products of that process (the essays and other papers that you write), you can develop an awareness of your strengths and weaknesses that will enable you to revise effectively and efficiently. As you write and revise, and as you read and respond to the work of others, you'll discover that revising can be the most rewarding part of the writing process. For when you revise, you have the satisfaction of bringing your ideas to completion in an appropriate form.

Here is how the popular columnist Ellen Goodman describes the satisfaction of revising.

> What makes me happy is rewriting. In the first draft you get your ideas and your theme clear, if you are using some kind of metaphor you get that established, and certainly you have to know where you're coming out. But the next time through it's like cleaning house, getting rid of all the junk, getting things in the right order, tightening things up.

> — Ellen Goodman

Christine Hoekstra, a junior English major, describes her experience of revision in very similar terms.

> Revision is an extremely important part of the writing process for me. It's really the part of writing where I feel the bulk of the work gets done — where the story takes shape, the essay is created. I couldn't imagine writing without revising.
>
> — CHRISTINE HOEKSTRA

For writers like Ellen Goodman and Christine Hoekstra, revision is the heart of the writing process.

Chapters 11 and 12 aim to help you experience the satisfaction of successful revision. Chapter 11 focuses on revision as a process, an activity. It answers questions like the following:

- What is revision? How does revision differ from proofreading, or correcting mistakes?

- How can you use responses to work in progress to help establish priorities for revision?

- How can you learn to read work in progress more objectively so that you can recognize strengths and weaknesses?

- How can you develop strategies that will help you revise more effectively and efficiently?

Chapter 12 discusses ways to improve your essay's structure and style. Together, Chapters 11 and 12 should help you understand why writers like Ellen Goodman and Christine Hoekstra can't imagine writing without revising.

REVISING THROUGH RE-VISION

You can learn a great deal about revision just by considering the word itself. *Revision* combines the root word *vision* with the prefix *re-*, meaning "again." When you revise, you "see again": You develop a new vision of your essay's shape or of the most emphatic way to improve the flow of a paragraph.

Revision is very different from editing, an activity that generally occurs at the end of the writing process. When you edit, you are concerned mainly with correctness. Does your essay have any errors of grammar, punctuation, or usage? Are your words spelled correctly? Do you need to fix any obvious problems of word choice or sentence structure? Editing is the tidying up that concludes the writing process.

NOTE FOR MULTILINGUAL WRITERS

For academic writers whose first language is standard North American English, revising is reshaping a piece of writing and editing is correcting individual sentences. These writers generally edit their writing after they draft and revise. If your first or home language is not standard North American English, however, you may find it helpful to correct some sentence-level problems during the revising process. You might want to do so, for instance, if errors distract you or if you are preparing an essay for peer response. Even in cases such as these, however, you should not let sentence correctness take more of your time than global issues such as the logic and structure of your paragraphs and of the essay as a whole.

FOR EXPLORATION

Using the preceding distinction between revision and editing, think back to some of your own writing experiences. When, and for what reasons, have you revised your work rather than just edited it? How would you characterize these revision experiences? Were they satisfying? Frustrating? Why? Freewrite for five or ten minutes about these revision experiences.

Unlike editing, revision is most typically a process of discovery where much more than correctness is at stake. Because it generates growth and change, revision sometimes requires you to take risks. Often these risks are minor. If you spend three or four minutes attempting to find just the right words to clarify an idea, for instance, you've lost only a little time if you're unsuccessful. Sometimes, however, when you revise, you make large-scale or global decisions with potentially more significant consequences.

After writing the first draft of an essay, for instance, Matt Brown, a first-year student planning to major in physics, met with members of his writing group to talk about his draft. He was unhappy with his essay, which argued that newspaper carriers work too hard and are paid too little, given the difficulty of their work. The members of his group were sympathetic to Matt's problems, but they couldn't help teasing him a bit. After all, how serious are a newspaper carrier's problems in the overall scheme of things?

Gradually, Matt recognized that he needed to take a different approach to his material. He realized that he could more effectively encourage his readers to empathize with carriers by taking a humorous approach, pointing out the problems carriers face in a lighthearted manner. Once he made this decision to revise his approach to his topic, Matt found that he was able to write and revise more quickly with much less frustration. In his case, taking the risk of trying a new approach paid off.

BENEFITING FROM RESPONSES TO WORK IN PROGRESS

As Matt Brown's experience indicates, you can draw on the responses of others to help you resee your writing. Talking with others can also provide crucial support. You may write alone a good deal of the time, but writing needn't be a lonely process.

When you ask others to respond to your writing, you are asking for feedback. Sometimes students confuse feedback with criticism. When you give writers feedback, you are attempting to help them see their writing in fresh and different ways. Providing feedback is thus not a negative process, and its goal is not to criticize but to help writers gain additional perspectives on their writing. Responses to work in progress can take a number of forms.

Eliciting Descriptive Responses Sometimes you may find it helpful to ask others to describe your writing for you. Professors Peter Elbow and Pat Belanoff suggest a number of questions you can ask readers to elicit descriptive responses to work in progress:*

Sayback "Say back to me in your own words what you hear me getting at in my writing."

Pointing "Which words or phrases stick in your mind? Which passages or features did you like best? Don't explain why."

Summarizing "What do you hear as my main point or idea (or event or feeling)? And the subsidiary ones?"

What's almost said or implied "What's *almost* said, implied, hovering around the edges? What would you like to hear more about?"

Center of gravity "What do you sense as the source of energy, the focal point, the seedbed, the generative center for this piece?"

Eliciting Analytical Responses On other occasions, you may find more analytical responses helpful. You might ask readers to comment on the organization of your essay or the extent to which it responds to the needs and interests

---

*Peter Elbow and Pat Belanoff, *A Community of Writers: A Workshop Course in Writing,* 3d ed. (Boston: McGraw-Hill, 2000). Excerpted from the appendix "Sharing and Responding."

of readers. Or you might ask readers to play what Elbow and Belanoff call "believing and doubting."

> *Believing*   Simply ask readers to *believe* everything you have written — and then tell you what that makes them notice. Even if they disagree strongly with what you have written, their job is to *pretend* to agree.

> *Doubting*   Now ask readers to pretend that everything is false, to find as many reasons as they can why you are wrong in what you say (or why your story doesn't make sense).

Eliciting Responses to Your Essay's Structure and Logic   Finally, if you are writing an argumentative essay, you might ask readers to respond to a series of questions designed to uncover potential weaknesses in your essay's structure or logic. The following "Skeleton Feedback" questions focus on three central issues:

1. Reasons and Support

    What is the main point, claim, or assertion of the paper?

    What are the main reasons or subsidiary points of the main point, claim, or assertion?

    Taking each reason in turn, answer these questions: What support, backing, or argument is given for it? What support *could* be given?

    What counterarguments could be made against this reason?

2. Assumptions

    What assumptions does the paper seem to make? What does the paper seem to take for granted?

3. Readers or Audience

    Who is the implied audience? Who is being addressed by the writer?

    Looking at the reasons, arguments, and assumptions, tell what kind of readers would tend to accept which ones (and what kind of readers would reject them).

    How does the writer *treat* the audience? As enemies? Friends? Equals? Children? What's the stance toward the audience?

To determine what kind of feedback is most helpful to you, think commonsensically about your writing. Where are you in your composing process? How do you feel about your draft and the kind of writing you are working on? If you have just completed a rough draft of an argument, for instance, you might find descriptive feedback most helpful. After you have worked longer on the essay, you might invite more analytical responses.

As a student, you can turn to many people for feedback. Some of these individuals, such as your instructor and classmates, can approach your writing as insiders. They know the assignment you are working on and the standards for evaluation. Others, such as your writing center tutor, friends, or family members, must approach your writing as outsiders. The differences in the situations of these potential respondents will influence how they respond; these differences should also influence how you use their responses. No matter who your respondent is, you must ultimately decide how to interpret and apply his or her comments and criticisms.

Responses from Friends and Family Members

You can certainly ask friends and family members to read and respond to your writing, but you should understand the strengths and weaknesses that they bring as readers. One important strength is that you trust them — otherwise, you wouldn't ask them to read your writing. Unless you spend time filling them in, however, friends and family members won't understand the nature of your assignment or your instructor's standards for evaluation. This lack of knowledge, as well as their natural desire to see you do well, may cause them to be less critical of your work than other readers might be. Still, friends and family members can provide useful responses to work in progress. When you are considering getting such responses, here are some suggestions to keep in mind.

■ GUIDELINES FOR GETTING RESPONSES FROM FRIENDS AND FAMILY

- Choose your respondents carefully. Is this person a competent writer? Have you benefited from his or her responses in the past?

- Recognize that friends and family members can't fully understand the assignment or situation, even if you take some time to explain it. Take this lack of knowledge into consideration when evaluating their comments.

- Draw on their strengths as outsiders. Rather than asking them to respond in detail to your essay, for instance, ask them to give a general impression or a descriptive response. You might also ask them to tell you what they think is the main idea or controlling purpose of your essay. If they can't identify one, or if their understanding differs substantially from your own, you've gained very useful information about your essay.

(continued)

(continued)

- Try asking them to read your work aloud to you *without having first read it silently themselves.* When you read your own work, you unconsciously compensate to reflect your intentions. Listening to someone else read your work can help you hear problems that you might not otherwise detect yourself. If your reader falters over a phrase or has to read a sentence several times before it makes sense, that may indicate a problem of style or logic.

- Don't rely solely on the response of friends or family members. Try to get at least one other informed response to your work.

Responses from Classmates

If you have been getting responses to your writing from fellow students, you know how helpful their reactions and advice can be. Here is a comment by education major Karen Boaz about her experiences with peer response:

> At first, I was wary of peer response to my writing. I was afraid of criticism and of exposing something as personal as writing to my classmates. Peer response turned out to be one of the most valuable aspects of my writing class. The members of my writing group were genuinely interested in my ideas, and they gave responses and suggestions I could really use.

Because your classmates know your instructor and the assignment as insiders, they can provide particularly effective responses to your writing. Students participating in writing groups typically form strong bonds; they genuinely want group members to do well, to develop as writers. Yet group members can often read work in progress more objectively than family members and friends can. When student writing groups function well, they provide a helpful balance of support and constructive criticism. To ensure that your writing group works well, follow these guidelines.

■ GUIDELINES FOR GETTING RESPONSES FROM A WRITING GROUP

Advice for Writers

- Learn to distinguish between your writing and yourself. Try not to respond defensively to suggestions for improvement, and don't

(continued)

(continued)

argue with readers' responses. Instead, use their responses to gain insight into your writing.

- Prepare for group meetings by carefully formulating the questions about your work that you most need to have answered.

- Always bring a legible draft to class.

- Be sure to bring a working draft, not a jumble of brainstorming ideas, freewriting, and notes.

- Provide information that will enable readers to understand your rhetorical situation. If you are addressing your essay to a specific audience — members of a certain organization, for example, or readers of a particular magazine — be sure classmates know.

- Remember that your fellow students' responses are just that: responses. Treat these comments seriously, for they are a potentially powerful indication of the strengths and weaknesses of your draft. But maintain your own authority as the writer. Your readers' responses may be useful evidence about the effectiveness of your essay, but you must always decide how to interpret these responses — what to accept and what to reject.

Advice for Readers

- Remember the golden rule: Respond to the writing of others as you would like them to respond to your work.

- Don't attempt to "play teacher." Your job is not to evaluate or grade your classmates' writing but to respond to it.

- Take your cue from the writer. If he or she asks you to summarize an essay's main point, don't launch into an analysis of its tone or organization.

- Remember that the more specific and concrete your response is, the more helpful it will be.

You don't need to be an expert to provide helpful responses to work in progress. You simply need to be an attentive, honest, supportive reader.

FOR COLLABORATION

Take five minutes to think about responses to your work that you have received from classmates. Freewrite for five or ten minutes about these experiences, and then draw up a list of statements describing the kinds of responses that you have found most helpful.

Meet with a group of your classmates. Begin by having each group member read his or her list. Then, working together, list all the suggestions for peer response. Have one student record all the suggestions and distribute them to everyone in the group for future use.

Responses from Writing Center Tutors

Many colleges and universities have writing centers staffed by undergraduate and graduate writing assistants or tutors. Sometimes students misunderstand the writing tutor's role. They may regard writing tutors as editors trained to correct their writing. Or they may think that they're faculty aides standing in for "real" instructors who are unavailable or too busy to meet with students. Neither view is accurate.

Writing tutors are simply good writers who have been trained to respond to peers' work. Like your classmates, a writing tutor's main job is to *respond* to your writing, not to analyze or critique it extensively. But unlike your classmates, a writing tutor has been formally trained in peer response methods. Because writing tutors work with many students, they are likely to have experience reading and responding to a broad range of writing. The following guidelines will enable you to make the most productive use of the time you spend with a writing tutor.

■ GUIDELINES FOR MEETING WITH A
WRITING TUTOR

- Before meeting with your writing tutor, reread your writing and identify your major goals. Would you benefit most from a discussion of your essay's organization, an examination of a section of your draft, or some other activity?

- Begin your conference by sharing these goals with your writing tutor. You might also find it helpful to give the writing tutor some sense of where you are in your process — in the early stages of drafting, for instance, or in the process of final editing.

(continued)

(continued)

■ Be realistic about what you can accomplish in the time available to you. Recognize, as well, that the writing tutor's job is to respond and advise, not to correct or rewrite your draft.

Responses from Your Instructor

Because your instructor is such an important reader for your written assignments, you want to be certain that you make good use of any written comments he or she provides. Use the following suggestions to help yourself benefit fully from an instructor's comments.

■ GUIDELINES FOR USING YOUR INSTRUCTOR'S RESPONSES

■ Read your instructor's written comments carefully. They are the clearest, most specific indication that you have of how well you have fulfilled the assignment.

■ Read your instructor's comments *more than once.* When you first read them, you will be reading mainly to understand his or her general response to your writing. That's a useful reading, but it does little to help you set goals for revision. Later, read the comments again several times, looking to establish priorities for revision.

■ Recognize the difference between your instructor's local and global comments. Local comments indicate specific questions, problems, or errors. For example, *awkward sentence* is a local comment indicating some stylistic or structural problem with a specific sentence. Global comments address broader issues, such as organization or the effectiveness of your evidence. The global comments in particular can help you set large-scale goals for revision.

■ Meet with your instructor if you don't understand his or her comments. Even if you do understand the comments, you may wish to meet to discuss your plans for revision.

Friends, family members, classmates, writing tutors, instructors: All can provide helpful responses to work in progress. None of these responses should take the place of your own judgment, however. Nor should you automatically accept responses, whether criticism or praise. Your job as the writer is to *interpret* and *evaluate* these responses, using them along with your own assessment of your rough draft to establish goals for revising.

BUILDING OBJECTIVITY TOWARD WORK IN PROGRESS

Because you must evaluate your own writing and interpret the responses of others, you will need to develop strategies for objectively viewing your own work in progress. Building such objectivity enables you to achieve the distance necessary to make the hard decisions that revision sometimes requires. The following suggestions should help you develop this objectivity.

■ GUIDELINES FOR REVISING OBJECTIVELY

1. *Plan at Least a Short Break between Writing and Revising.* It's difficult to critique your rough draft when you've just finished composing it. Your own intentions are still too fresh for you to be able to read your words as they are, not as you intended them to be. Read what one student, Audrey Meier, wrote in her journal about the importance of letting work in progress "sit a while":

   I can only do so much good thinking and writing at any one time. I need to work as hard as I can for a reasonable amount of time — say, two to three hours. But then I need to let go, shift gears. I call this the "baking" part of my writing process — it's when I put papers in my mental oven for a while. The result is almost always a better paper.

2. *Prepare Mentally for a Revising Session.* Taking a break from your writing before revising can help you gain distance from work in progress. But you also need to consider how you can best prepare for — and begin — revising. You may find it helpful to review your assignment and your analysis of your rhetorical situation before you reread your draft. As you do so, ask yourself the following questions:

(continued)

(continued)

- To what extent does your draft respond to the assignment?

- To what extent does your draft respond to your rhetorical situation as you have analyzed it and to the goals and objectives you established?

- What state is your draft in — how rough or near completion?

- What goals should you establish for this revising session, and how can you fulfill them? What should you work on first?

By preparing mentally before you begin revising, you will make the most efficient and most productive use of your time.

3. *Revise Work in Progress from Typed or Printed Copy.* We all grow used to our own handwriting, no matter how awkward or homely our scrawl. Even the letters on a computer screen can become overfamiliar after staring at them for hours. Perhaps for this reason, you may find that you're less critical of handwritten or electronically displayed texts than you are of printed drafts. To counteract this tendency, you may find it helpful to print your essays out as you write and revise. Once your words appear in print, you can often see problems that were invisible before. Revising from printed copy can help you detect local stylistic problems and also help you recognize global problems of organization and development.

4. *Use Descriptive Outlines to Help You "X-Ray" Your Draft.* Familiarity can make it difficult for you to evaluate your writing objectively. To gain distance from work in progress, you may find it helpful to "X-ray" your draft by developing what Professor Kenneth Bruffee calls a "descriptive outline."* To construct a descriptive outline, indicate the content and purpose of each paragraph in your essay — in other words, what each paragraph in your essay *says and does* for readers.

---

*Kenneth A. Bruffee, *A Short Course in Writing: Composition, Collaborative Learning, and Constructive Reading,* 4th ed. (New York: HarperCollins, 1993), 51.

To illustrate how you might use descriptive outlining when you revise, here is an essay by Rosie Rogel exploring what the word *family* means to her. She wrote this essay in response to the first activity on p. 236.

MEMORIES
by Rosie Rogel

My earliest memories are in Spanish. This seems a bit odd to me because I 1
no longer think in Spanish; English has long since prevailed in that
department. But, nonetheless, scattered images of my family replay themselves word for word in my first language. It's always been soothing for me
to hear my parents speak Spanish — those soft rolling R's can calm me
even today. These early childhood flashbacks have acted as a basis for what
my concept of a family truly is.

The word *family* causes my mind to flood with emotions and sensa- 2
tions straight out of my childhood. Images of my mother, the matriarch
of the small kingdom she and my father chose to create, fill my mind.
My mother's approval and support have always been very important to
my sisters and me. When we were small and contemplating behaving
poorly, one stern glance in our direction was (usually) enough to temper
the three-girl storm threatening to break. I recall somersaulting down the
grassy hill behind our home with my sisters, dizzy with delight at the in-
credible feeling of freshly cut grass against our skin. I remember warm
summer mornings when I'd brush my grandmother's hair in the early
morning sun. I'd stand on a chair, on the tips of my daintily painted pink
toes. How I loved to brush those thick locks. Before the brush reached the
ends of her hair, I'd pull it up and into the sun to admire the shimmering
fan of black strands, lightly threaded with silver, that I had created. I
remember my daddy trying to get me excited about my first day of kinder-
garten and how his strong, calloused hand knitted softly in mine miracu-
lously seemed to transfer his courage to me. These memories emerge from
some sweet corner of my mind, whispering to me just what the word *family* means. It means comfort, security, warmth, and happiness.

When I was small, my family was my entire world. As in most fami- 3
lies, the threads of our lives are entwined together. I learned everything
I know about relationships with other human beings from them. My
interaction with them has been the foundation for my ability to relate to
the rest of the world — whether I saw the world as good or bad largely
depended on how my parents taught me to view it. Thanks to my parents,
I saw the world as a beautiful garden with hundreds of flowers just waiting
to be admired and examined — each one different and each one equally
important.

My definition of the word *family* stretches much farther than simply 4
those people one lives with who are related (or not). As I got older, my
family stretched to include close friends. To me, a family member is someone who loves me unconditionally. It makes almost no difference to me
whether he or she is a blood relation. My definition of the word *family* also

includes the human race as a whole. We are family because we are here, together. I believe our humanity makes us family.

5   The word *family*, in every sense, is extremely important to me because of the huge impact our family (or lack of family) has on who it is we become. What we learn from the people who gave birth to us and raised us is something we'll carry with us always. Unfortunately, not everyone is lucky enough to be born among stable, loving families. There are those who are not, and entire communities are suffering because of it. This is where my far-stretching sense of the word *family* comes in.

6   The concept of the family unit has, of late, been furiously discussed in the media and in politics. The traditional, "typical" American family doesn't really exist anymore. To me, whether a family has one mother or one father (or two mothers, for that matter) doesn't matter. If there is love, acceptance, and trust swirling around, then it qualifies as a family. With these basic human needs met, a child can grow up, perhaps remembering somersaulting sisters, black-silver strands shimmering in the sun, or a reassuring hand-hold, to make a family of his or her own.

When Rosie Rogel asked members of her writing group to respond to this essay, they praised its vivid and moving examples, but they also indicated that the essay seemed to shift gears midway and that it covered quite a number of issues. To get a clearer sense of how her essay worked, Rosie decided to construct a descriptive outline. As she did so, she wrote comments she could use to establish priorities for revision; these appear in parentheses following her analysis of each paragraph.

Paragraph 1

What it says: This paragraph describes the importance of Spanish and of my earliest memories to my concept of family.

What it does for readers: This paragraph provides information readers need to know to understand my experience of family, and it emphasizes the importance of my early childhood experiences.
      (I like the way this paragraph emphasizes the importance of my heritage, but I wonder if the last sentence could be stronger.)

Paragraph 2

What it says: This paragraph presents a number of images and examples of my family life.

What it does for readers: By presenting vivid and concrete images, this paragraph will, I hope, create interest in my family and give readers a sense of what my family was like when I was growing up.

(I like this paragraph; my writing group also said this was one of the strongest paragraphs in the essay.)

Paragraph 3

What it says: This paragraph discusses several issues, such as the importance of my family to my development as a person and what I learned from my family.

What it does for readers: This paragraph continues to give readers information about what family means to me.
(This paragraph could be more focused. Also, I had a hard time determining what this paragraph does for readers.)

Paragraph 4

What it says: This paragraph presents my definition of family.

What it does for readers: This paragraph presents a new element in my understanding of family. Since most readers are likely to think of family as including their parents, sisters, brothers, etc., this paragraph asks readers to expand their understanding of family.
(I can see that this is quite a jump from the earlier paragraphs; this must be one of the places where my writing group started to feel I was switching gears. The early part of my essay is personal and concrete; this almost feels like it's from a different essay.)

Paragraph 5

What it says: This paragraph develops my argument that it's important to think of family as more than simply the people who are directly related to us. But it also goes back to the earlier topic of how much impact my immediate family had on me.

What it does for readers: ??
(I wanted this paragraph to bring together the early part of my essay, which focuses on my own experiences, and the expanded idea of family that I introduce in paragraph 4, but I'm not sure it really does this.)

Paragraph 6

What it says: This paragraph argues that the traditional American family doesn't exist.

What it does for readers: This paragraph raises a new issue and asks read-ers to agree with my position about this issue.

(Now that I'm summarizing each paragraph, I can see that this para-graph, like paragraphs 4 and 5, raises another new topic. Although the last sentence tries to remind readers of the first part of the essay, this paragraph doesn't really draw the essay together.)

After developing her descriptive outline, Rosie was able to see the kinds of shifts in purpose and tone that had concerned her readers. She also recognized that her draft attempted to cover too many issues. She couldn't both develop a rich and vivid portrait of her family and support several arguments about the nature and role of family in society today. By summarizing not only what each paragraph in her essay said but also what it did for readers, Rosie was able to establish priorities for revision.

■ ■ ■

FOR EXPLORATION

Choose an essay that you are currently working on, and develop a descrip-tive outline for each paragraph. Once you have done so, exchange essays with a classmate, and construct a similar outline for your classmate's essay. After you have completed this activity, compare the outlines of your essays. To what extent do your outlines coincide? To what extent do they differ? Did this exchange enable you to better understand the strengths and weaknesses of your essay? If so, in what ways?

REVISION IN ACTION: A CASE STUDY

What kinds of changes do writers make as they revise? The following case study, which chronicles the development of an essay by Kira Wennstrom, a first-year biology major, should give you a clearer, more concrete understand-ing of how revision works.

Kira's assignment was relatively open-ended: to write an essay describing some personal experience and explaining the significance of that experience. Kira had few problems coming up with a topic. During the previous summer she had cared for two children while their mother was in the hospital. The experience had taught her a great deal about herself and about the bond between parents and children. She wanted to explore her experience further and to share with others what she had learned.

Kira describes herself as a heavy planner, and her self-assessment seems accurate. She did much of the planning for this essay in her head rather than on paper. She thought for several days about her experience, and she also discussed it with friends and classmates. By the time she sat down to write the first draft, reproduced below, she had thought through her ideas so carefully that she was able to write using only a brief list of major ideas as a guide.

Kira's first draft is reprinted here. Its paragraphs are numbered for ease of reference. Also included are some of the written comments that members of Kira's writing group made in response to her draft.

Kira Wennstrom's First Draft

Can you do more to draw readers in?

While my friends swam and tanned at the lake, I ran a household with two incredibly rambunctious and mildly accident-prone children. However, I think in the long run my time was better spent than that of my peers. 1

When Josh and Timmy's mother had to go into the hospital, she asked me if I would be willing to stay with the boys until she could 2

Do you really want to emphasize these negative factors so strongly?

come home. I quickly accepted. However, the few days I had planned on became two weeks, and there was work and trouble and responsibility I never imagined.

Since the children were only five and eight, I couldn't leave them alone in the house; I had to be there or be with them 24 hours a day. In addition to the normal precautions of making sure I knew where they were, I also had to worry about their father. He and the boys' mother had divorced several years ago, and there were still problems with custody. 3

Nice concrete details in these, but do you need them all?

I spent my days as a housewife: planning meals, doing laundry, cleaning house. I handled all the typical minor emergencies. There were scraped knees to be washed and bandaged, fights to be settled, Kool-Aid to be cleaned out of the carpet, and once or twice I had to rescue pots and pans from the sandbox to cook dinner. 4

My evenings were spent preparing meals and dishes and settling disputes as to who was going to bed when and whose turn it was to choose the TV channel. After things settled down and the kids were in their rooms, I was finally left alone to read or watch Jay Leno before I hit my own pillow, exhausted. However, 5 my nights were seldom complete without being awakened to check out at least one scary noise or to deny a request for a midnight snack.

6   I had agreed to care for the kids knowing that it wouldn't be <u>all</u> fun, but I never dreamed the amount of laundry two active children can go through. I did a load of wash almost every other day and was just barely keeping up. I was also amazed by the complexities of working out a simple dinner schedule. There was no single entree that both boys liked. They would sooner have starved, I think, than eat anything that didn't come in a wrapper, a can, or a box. Gradually, as the days passed, however, I began to realize what it is about parenting that makes my mother's eyes bug out at the end of the day. I <u>loved</u> those children terribly.

The sentence structure flows smoothly here & during the rest of the essay, too.

Whew — this feels abrupt!

7   I discovered that perhaps the hardest part of parenting is the loss of privacy. I never had a moment to myself, completely to myself, when I could just let my mind catch up to the rest of me. Having always been used to spending hours alone and enjoying my own company, I found it incredibly difficult sometimes to force a smile when one of the boys interrupted a quiet minute with yet another demand on my time. I learned to treasure the ten or so minutes of silent darkness between the time I shut off the light and the time I went to sleep.

8   My own mother, whom I telephoned with great regularity, seemed to find enormous delight in the fact that I was going through the same thing that she had been trying (and failing) to explain for seventeen-odd years. She gave me marvelous advice and brilliant suggestions on how to cope with the whole mess and then, I am sure, hung up the phone and laughed her socks off in utter vindictiveness. But I can forgive her this because although I didn't realize it then, what I was experiencing would prove invaluable.

Now that I've read your essay twice, Kira, I can see that you want to balance the work of caring for Josh & Timothy with your love of them. Develop more fully?

9

Nice sentence structure

Your conclusion might have more impact if you helped readers understand how much you came to love Josh & Timmy.

I look at mothers, especially mine, with better understanding now, with less scorn. I look at children with a little more appreciation. I use my time alone more carefully now; I spend it wisely, now that I know how crucial it is. Most of all, I value my freedom more highly than ever because I know what it is to lose that freedom. As much as I cared about those children, it's not time yet to give up my claim to my life. I understand now how important it is to live for yourself before you live for anyone else.

Kira's first draft had many strengths, which members of her writing group acknowledged. But they had suggestions for improvement as well. A number of them commented that her abrupt shift in paragraph 6 to a strong statement of her love for Josh and Timmy confused them since it conflicted with her previous emphasis on all the "work and trouble" involved in caring for the two boys. This potential contradiction also made it difficult for Kira's readers to grasp the significance of her final paragraph; several commented that they weren't sure, finally, what point she was trying to make in this paragraph.

After Kira thought about her readers' responses to her draft, she met with a tutor and established the following priorities for revision:

To work on her introduction

To try to show more clearly why Josh and Timmy meant so much to her, despite all the work

To see if she could cut any of the housekeeping detail

To play with style a bit

Kira nicely identifies several ways that she could improve the focus, organization, and content of her essay. It's not possible to show all the stages that Kira's draft went through, for this process involved many scribbles, inserts, and crumpled papers. But the final draft (below) demonstrates that Kira's analysis enabled her truly to revise her essay, to "see again" how she could most effectively make her point. Here is Kira's revised essay with comments in the margin pointing out some of her most important changes.

THE BOYS OF SUMMER
by Kira Wennstrom

1   Few teenagers get the chance to be parents, and for those who do, it's usually too late to change their minds. One summer, though, I was given the opportunity to become a mother -- without the lifetime commitment.

New intro-duction gets the reader's attention.

2   When Josh and Timmy's mother had to go into the hospital, she asked me if I would be willing to stay with them until she could come home. I quickly accepted, envisioning a few days of playing "mommy" to the kids whose babysitter I had been for about two years. However, my visions of happy homemaking paled when the few days became two weeks and the trouble and responsibility of being a parent began to hit home.

3   Since the children were only five and eight, I couldn't leave them alone in the house; I had to be with them twenty-four hours a day. While my friends swam and tanned at the lake, I spent my days as a housewife: planning meals, doing laundry, cleaning house. I handled all the minor emergencies that seem to follow little boys around like shadows. There were fights to be settled, Kool-Aid to be cleaned out of the carpet, and once or twice pots and pans to be rescued from the sandbox to cook dinner.

Revised paragraph consolidates details about her situation from three draft paragraphs.

4   My days were whittled away with meals, dishes, and mountains of laundry. I did a load of wash almost every other day and just barely kept up. I was also amazed by the complexities of working out a simple dinner schedule. There was no single entree that both boys approved of, and it was like walking hot coals to try to serve anything new. They would sooner have starved, I think, than eat anything that didn't come out of a wrapper, box, or can. Most of all, though, I missed my privacy. Because the children were so dependent on me, I never had a moment to myself. I sometimes found it very difficult to force a smile when one of the boys

Concise and balanced paragraph combines details on routine work from three draft paragraphs.

interrupted a quiet moment with yet another demand on my time.

Paragraph prepares readers for the shift from responsibilities to emotions.

As the days passed and I became more pro- 5
ficient at running my little household, I began to realize a very surprising thing. Despite the trouble they caused, despite the demands they made, my two charges were becoming very special people to me -- people who needed me.

New dramatic scene shows readers Kira's deep feelings for the boys.

I remember taking the boys to the beach 6
one afternoon and buying them a corn-dog-and-soda lunch with Gummi worms for dessert. Josh, who was older than Timmy, loved the lake and delighted in swimming out just past the dock where the water was especially cool. Timmy was afraid to follow his brother and sat beside me on the sand, sucking on his last Gummi worm and looking wistfully out to where Josh was laughing and diving. After half an hour of this, Timmy touched me on the arm and said, "Take me to Josh, Kira."

"Are you sure, Timmy?" 7

"Mm-hm. But hold on tight to me." 8

So I held on tight to him, and we waded 9
into Rainy Lake's cool green water. When we got out past the point where Timmy could touch bottom, he locked his arms around my neck and pressed his face against my shoulder, but he didn't ask me to take him back. As we neared the spot where Josh was playing, I called, and he swam over to us. We splashed each other and giggled, and Timmy clutched me with one hand and Josh with the other. Their bodies were slick like seals, warm against me in the chill lake water. Together we swam along the shore, and they held on to me to keep afloat. They trusted me to keep them safe, and I would have drowned before I broke that trust. I loved them.

Paragraph adds detail that helps clarify Kira's feelings.

Because I loved them, the children had a 10
hold on me like nothing else I know. Simply by going out to play each day, they gave me more hours of worry than I like to admit. Every time one of them was late coming home, I imagined all the dreadful things that might be

happening -- an angry dog, a child molester, a car accident -- until he walked through the door, perfectly safe and wanting supper. When one of them was angry or hurt, I hurt. They were children, and it's so hard to be a child sometimes -- almost as hard as being a mother.

Mother is an effective new transition that connects paragraphs.

11   My own mother, whom I telephoned with great regularity, seemed to find enormous delight in the fact that I was going through the same things she had been trying (and failing) to explain to me for seventeen-odd years. She gave me marvelous suggestions on how to cope with the demands of my new family and then, I am sure, hung up the phone and laughed her socks off in utter vindictiveness. But I can forgive her this because, although I didn't know it then, what I was experiencing was invaluable.

12   I look at mothers, especially my own, with better understanding now, with less scorn. I look at children with a little more appreciation. I use my time alone more carefully now; I spend it wisely, now that I know how crucial it is. Most of all, I value my freedom more highly than ever because I know what it is to give up that freedom. As much as I cared about those children, it's not time yet to let others make such claims on my life. I understand now how important it is to live for yourself before you live for anyone else.

Conclusion now has greater impact and complexity.

Kira's revision is successful, I'm sure you'll agree. She combined and de-emphasized the details about how hard she worked — details that misdirected some of her readers and were also somewhat repetitive. She added paragraph 10 to explain her feelings for Josh and Timmy. And the scene at the beach, another important addition, gave concreteness and immediacy to these feelings. The resulting essay is a penetrating exploration of the rewards, and the demands, of caring for children.

■ ■ ■

FOR THOUGHT, DISCUSSION, AND WRITING

1. To study your own revision process, number and save all your plans, drafts, and revisions for a paper that you're currently writing or have written recently. After you have completed the paper, review these materials, paying particular attention to the revisions you made. Can you describe the revision strategies that you followed and identify ways to improve the effectiveness of this process? Your instructor may ask you to write an essay discussing what you have learned as a result of this analysis.

2. Ellen Goodman said that for her, revision is "like cleaning house." Take ten or fifteen minutes to make your own list of possible analogies for revision. Is revision for you like tuning a motor? Pruning a plant? Later, return to this list, and decide which analogy best expresses your process of revising. Develop this analogy in one or two paragraphs.

3. Interview two students in your class about their revision strategies. How do their revision strategies reflect their preferred composing styles? How are their strategies similar to and different from your own? How do these students feel about revising, and how do their feelings compare with your own? Can you apply any of the strategies they use in your own writing? What can you learn from these interviews about how revising works and about how you can improve your own revising process? Your instructor may ask you to write an essay summarizing the results of your interviews.

Strategies for Revising
Structure and Style

Revision is a demanding but rewarding process. Chapter 11 presented suggestions for *managing the process of revision* effectively and efficiently. Chapter 12 provides *strategies for revising* structure and style.

As you read this chapter, remember that decisions about structure and style, even about a single word, always require that you consider *context*. To decide whether a sentence is awkwardly written, for instance, you must look not just at that sentence but also at the surrounding paragraph.

From the moment you begin thinking about a writing project until you make your last revision, you must be an analyst and decision maker. Even though some decisions may seem minor, together they determine the character and the effectiveness of your writing.

ASKING THE BIG QUESTIONS: REVISING FOR FOCUS, CONTENT, AND ORGANIZATION

When you revise a draft, begin by asking yourself the big, important questions — questions about your essay's focus, content, and organization. These questions are big because they challenge you to consider the degree to which your essay has fulfilled its most significant goals. If you discover — as writers often do — that your essay has not achieved its original purpose or that your purpose evolved as you wrote, you will make major changes in your draft, changes that will significantly affect the meaning of your essay.

Asking the big questions first is a practical approach to revising. You don't want to spend an hour revising a paragraph that you will eventually delete because it doesn't contribute to your essay's main point. Furthermore, once you are confident that the overall focus, content, and organization of your essay are satisfactory, you will be better able to recognize less significant but still important stylistic problems.

Use the questions in the following guidelines to assess the effectiveness of your draft's focus, content, and organization.

■ GUIDELINES FOR EVALUATING FOCUS, CONTENT, AND ORGANIZATION

Focus

- What do you hope to accomplish in this essay? How clearly have you defined — and communicated — your controlling purpose?

- How does your essay represent an appropriate response to your rhetorical situation? If it is an academic essay, how does it fulfill the requirements of the assignment?

- Have you tried to do too much in this essay? Or are your goals too limited and inconsequential?

- How does your essay respond to the needs, interests, and expectations of your readers?

Content

- How does your essay develop or support your controlling purpose? How does it fulfill the commitment stated or implied by your controlling purpose?

- What supporting details or evidence have you provided for your most important generalizations? Are these supporting details and evidence adequate? Do they relate clearly to your controlling purpose and to each other?

- What additional details, evidence, or counterarguments might strengthen your essay?

- Have you included any material that is irrelevant to your purpose?

Organization

- What overall organizational strategy does your essay follow?

- Have you tested the effectiveness of this strategy by outlining or summarizing your essay?

- What is the relationship between the organization of your essay and your controlling purpose? Is this relationship clear to readers? How? What cues have you provided to make the organization clear and easy to follow?

(continued)

(continued)

■ Does your essay follow the general conventions appropriate for this kind of writing?

■ How could your introduction and conclusion be made more effective?

Here is how one student, Todd Carpenter, used these questions to establish goals for revision. Todd was responding to the following assignment: "Write a two- to three-page argumentative essay on a subject of your own choice. Consider your instructor and your classmates the primary readers of your essay." Todd described his rhetorical situation in these terms:

> I am writing an argumentative essay for my composition class. I want to convince my readers — my instructor and my classmates — that our government should institute a national bottle law. Oregon is one of the eleven states that currently have bottle laws, so most students in the class may already agree with me about this law's importance. (Because Oregon's bottle bill has been implemented since 1972, students may not realize how important it is.) But because this is an essay for my writing class, I've got to present an unbiased view. Even if my instructor agrees that there should be a national bottle law, she won't give me a good grade unless I write an effective argument. In class, my instructor has stressed the importance of looking at both sides of the issue and presenting evidence for my views, so I'll try to do that here.

Todd Carpenter's First Draft

WHY ISN'T THERE A NATIONAL BOTTLE LAW?

1   Our country faces an important problem, yet it's one that few people take seriously -- what to do with the bottles and cans we use daily. When thrown away, bottles and cans cause pollution, increase the volume of solid wastes, waste energy, and use up natural resources. To control these problems only eleven states have adopted bottle laws. What a shame.

2   If you're like me, you're tired of walking down streets and seeing fast-food wrappers, bottles, and cans. Last week I went to the coast and found a beautiful iso-

lated beach. It was great until I came upon some hamburger boxes and beer bottles. This happened with a bottle law. Think how much worse things would be if Oregon didn't have a bottle law.

Bottle laws are important because they require recycling, and recycling reduces pollution and solid waste. Recycling aluminum reduces air emissions associated with aluminum production by 96 percent. Solid waste would reduce as aluminum and glass are eliminated from landfills. Also, a large percentage of the pollution on and around streets and highways is bottles and cans. If these cans and bottles were worth some money, people would be less likely to throw them away.

Extracting aluminum ore requires twenty times as much electricity as recycling the metal. Therefore, if we recycled more aluminum, then less aluminum would have to be extracted. This would save enough energy to provide electrical power for at least two million people annually.

Bottle laws are currently effective in Oregon, Vermont, Maine, Michigan, Iowa, Connecticut, Delaware, Massachusetts, New York, California, and Hawaii. These laws work largely because of the legislation's support by the people. Of the Americans polled, 73 percent would support such bottle laws. Some people are getting tired of the environment being polluted and abused and now realize that this planet and its resources are finite. Aluminum is a natural resource and without recycling we will eventually run out.

With all the people in favor and the obvious environmental reasons supporting it, one would think that a national bottle law would have started long ago. But some people just don't want to bother with saving their containers, and it is a lot easier to just throw them away, despite the fact that they're worth five cents each. Steel and aluminum companies unfairly attack bottle bill laws -- and so do supermarkets. These biased efforts must be stopped now.

Although 54 percent of the aluminum beverage cans made and used in the U.S. are recycled at more than twenty-five hundred recycling centers, this could be increased to as much as 90 percent by requiring a national bottle law. Instead of considering unions' and companies' losses for a basis of decision on the bottle

```
law, we should consider the ecological gains. In the
future, a few dollars saved will mean nothing compared to
a polluted and destroyed environment society will face
without recycling.
```

Using the questions about focus, content, and organization earlier in this chapter, Todd analyzed his draft. His analysis revealed that his essay would be more effective if he made several important changes. Here is Todd's analysis of his essay.

Focus: My essay needs to be focused on a single subject, and I think it is, but I don't indicate my controlling purpose clearly enough at the start of my essay. I can also see that paragraph 2 gets off track because it talks about litter in general, not just the need for a bottle law. I should revise or drop this paragraph. I also may need to drop the last sentence of paragraph 6. It may get off track, too.

I tried to emphasize evidence in writing this draft, but I think I need to provide more. I need to talk more about the reasons why some companies and supermarkets attack bottle bills, and I should try to present their side of the issue also.

Content: The focus questions already helped me see that I need to revise paragraph 2 and add more evidence. I also don't describe how bottle laws work — and I should.

Organization: I think the basic organization of my essay is OK. I don't think that I have to make big changes in the structure of my essay. I just have to provide more information and take out some details that don't fit.

I'm not sure about my introduction and conclusion — maybe they could be better. I'll work on the rest of the essay and decide later.

By using the questions about focus, content, and organization to analyze his rough draft, Todd was able to set the following priorities for revising:

Stating his controlling purpose early in his essay

Cutting unnecessary material

Adding evidence in support of his position

Explaining how bottle laws work

Checking to be sure he's considered both sides of the argument

In analyzing his essay, Todd also realized that his introduction and conclusion might be made more effective. Given the importance of the other changes he needed to make, however, Todd put off working on the opening and closing paragraphs. Once he made the major changes his analysis called for, he could look again at his introduction and conclusion.

■ ■ ■

FOR EXPLORATION

Here is the revised version of Todd Carpenter's essay. Read the essay carefully, noting the major changes that Todd made as he revised. Write down the two or three most important changes. Finally, reread the essay with an eye for ways this essay could be improved further. Write down one or two suggestions for further revision.

WHY ISN'T THERE A NATIONAL BOTTLE LAW?
by Todd Carpenter

What do you do with your empty cans and bottles? There are two choices, throwing them away or recycling. Throwing away an aluminum beverage container wastes as much energy as filling a can with gasoline and pouring half out. Besides wasting energy, throwing away bottles and cans causes pollution, increases the volume of solid wastes, and uses up natural resources. To control these problems, only eleven states have adopted bottle laws. The United States government should require every state to have a bottle law or institute a national bottle law.

To understand how a bottle law can help, you must know how it works. When consumers buy canned or bottled beverages at the store, they pay deposits. This deposit can range from five to twenty cents per bottle or can. In order to get this deposit back, the bottles and cans must be returned to a supermarket after they are emptied. The supermarkets then return the bottles and cans to their manufacturers for either reuse or recycling.

Recycling plays a significant role in reducing pollution and solid waste. Recycling aluminum reduces air emissions associated with aluminum production by 96 percent. Solid waste is also reduced as aluminum and glass are eliminated from landfills. Finally, a large percentage of the pollution on and around the streets and highways is bottles and cans. If these could be returned to supermarkets for cash, people would be less likely to throw them away.

Extracting aluminum ore requires twenty times as much electricity as recycling the metal. Therefore, if we recycled more aluminum, less aluminum ore would have to be extracted. This could save enough energy to provide electrical power for at least two million people annually.

Bottle laws are currently in effect in Oregon, Vermont, Maine, Michigan, Iowa, Connecticut, Delaware, Massachusetts, New York, California, and Hawaii. These laws work largely because the general public supports them. A recent poll of Americans revealed that 73 percent support bottle laws. This support undoubtedly results from people's concern about pollution and our planet's limited resources.

Given the large number of people in favor of bottle laws, you might expect that we would already have a national bottle law. But a vocal minority of people don't want to bother with saving their containers, so they oppose such legislation. Some supermarket chains also lobby against bottle laws; they don't want to have to deal with all the cans that people would bring to them. I understand these individuals' concerns. Recycling bottles and cans does require extra effort from consumers and distributors. The larger economic and ecological issues indicate that this extra effort is worthwhile.

Finally, steel and aluminum companies and metal workers' unions oppose bottle laws because they fear they would cause cuts in their production and therefore affect jobs and wages. EPA and General Accounting studies estimate, however, that a national bottle law would produce a net increase of eighty thousand to one hundred thousand jobs, so these fears are misplaced.

Although 54 percent of the aluminum beverage cans made and used in the U.S. are currently recycled at more than twenty-five hundred recycling centers, we could increase this to as much as 90 percent by requiring a national bottle law. Instead of worrying about the inconvenience and possible economic consequences of instituting a national bottle law, we should consider the ecological gains. In the future, a little time saved will mean nothing compared to a polluted and destroyed environment.

■ ■ ■

FOR EXPLORATION

Use the guidelines for evaluating your focus, content, and organization to evaluate the draft of an essay you are currently working on. Respond as specifically and as concretely as possible, and then take a few moments to reflect on what you have learned about your draft. Finally, make a list of goals for revising.

KEEPING YOUR READERS ON TRACK: REVISING FOR COHERENCE

Most writers are aware that paragraphs and essays need to be unified — that they should focus on a single topic. You know, for instance, that if you interrupt a paragraph on the benefits of walking as a form of exercise with a sentence praising your favorite walking shoes, your readers will be confused and irritated. You may not be aware, however, that a paragraph or an essay can be unified and yet still present difficulties for readers. These difficulties arise when a paragraph or essay lacks coherence.

Writing is *coherent* when readers can move easily from word to word, sentence to sentence, and paragraph to paragraph. When writing is coherent, readers are often unaware that writers are giving them signals or cues that enable them to stay on track when they read; the writing just seems to flow. Writers have various means of achieving coherence. Some methods, such as *repeating key words and sentence structures* and using *pronouns* to refer to antecedent nouns, reinforce or emphasize the logical development of ideas. Another method is to use *transitional words*. Words like *but, although,* and *because* function as directions for readers; they tell readers what to do as they read. A sentence beginning with "For example" tells readers that this sentence will substantiate or exemplify a preceding point, not introduce a new idea or concept.

The following introduction to "Home Town," an essay by Ian Frazier, uses all of these methods to help keep readers on track. The most important means of achieving coherence are italicized. (As you read this paragraph, notice the unusual sentence structure that Frazier employs in the long fifth sentence, which describes the melting of a glacier. What stylistic reason might Frazier have had for constructing this sentence in this manner?)

> *When glaciers* covered much of northern Ohio, the land around Hudson, the town where I grew up, lay under one. *Glaciers* came and went several times, the most recent departing about 14,000 years ago. *When* we studied *glaciers* in an Ohio-history class in grade school, I imagined our *glacier* receding smoothly, like a sheet pulled off a new car. *Actually, glaciers* can move forward *but* they don't back up — *they* melt in place. *Most likely* the *glacier* above Hudson softened, *and* began to trickle underneath; rocks on its surface absorbed sunlight and melted tunnels into *it; it* rotted, *it* dwindled, *it* dripped, *it* ticked; *then it* dropped a pile of the sand and rocks *it* had been carrying around for centuries onto the ground in a heap. Hudson's landscape was hundreds of these little heaps — hills rarely big enough to sled down, a random arrangement made by gravity and smoothed by weather and time.
>
> — IAN FRAZIER, "HOME TOWN"

Most writers concern themselves with coherence *after* writing a rough draft and determining that the essay's focus, content, and organization are effective. At this point, the writer can attend to fine tuning, making changes that enable readers to move through the writing easily and enjoyably.

When you read work in progress to determine how you can strengthen its coherence, use your common sense. Your writing is coherent if readers know where they have been and where they are going as they read. Don't assume that your writing will be more coherent if you sprinkle transitions liberally throughout your prose. The logic of your discussion may not require numerous transitions; in such a case, adding them will only clutter up your writing. For example, the following introduction to an article published in *Yo! Youth Outlook,* a journal by and for youth in the San Francisco Bay Area, has relatively few explicit transitions. Rather, the author (who uses the pen name Atom) relies on logical relationships to keep the reader on track.

> The guy on the billboard looks like me: twentysomething; clad in baggy cut-offs, a T-shirt and tennies; scraggly hair hanging in his face. But he's not me. I'm a former bike messenger who's held onto the look but is trying to avoid the profession, due to its life-endangering aspects. He's a fashion model in a Calvin Klein ad, projecting a studied hip indifference while marketing upscale versions of my clothes that I couldn't possibly afford.
>
> Maybe Calvin and his peers in the fashion industry have noticed that a large percentage of young people today have jobs, not careers, and are sporting comfy, utilitarian togs in our pursuit of service sector nirvana. Or maybe the fashion industry is just moving on to the next slack thing, now that grunge is dead and flannel has been reclaimed by its traditional champions in agriculture and marketing.
>
> But marketing thrift-store clothes as high-priced high fashion is something of a paradox. Young folks who aren't proceeding directly to the boardroom don inexpensive apparel out of necessity rather than trendiness. Fifteen bucks for a white T-shirt that'll probably be stained with bike grease and spilled coffee within an hour? Calvin's gotta be kidding. Fifteen dollars is two or three hours' work for the average bicycle delivery specialist or espresso jockey.
>
> — ATOM, "THE BIKE MESSENGER LOOK GOES HIGH FASHION"

The logic of this essay's introduction is so clear that readers need relatively few explicit transitions: The first paragraph contrasts the "guy on the billboard" with the author of the essay; the second paragraph speculates on reasons why the bike messenger look has suddenly become fashionable; the third paragraph explores the paradox that most young people cannot afford to purchase the high-fashion versions of their own preferred dress. Such transitions as *but, or,* and *now* provide all the cues that readers need to keep on track.

Revision for coherence proceeds more effectively if you look first at large-scale issues, such as the relationship among your essay's introduction, body, and conclusion, before considering smaller concerns. When you revise for coherence, follow these steps.

■ GUIDELINES FOR REVISING FOR COHERENCE

- Read your draft quickly to determine if it flows smoothly. Pay particular attention to the movement from introduction to body and conclusion. How could you tighten or strengthen these connections?

- Now read slowly, paying close attention to the movement from paragraph to paragraph. How do new paragraphs build on or connect with previous paragraphs? Would more explicit connections, such as transitions, help readers better understand your ideas?

- Finally, read each paragraph separately. How do your word choice and sentence structure help readers progress from sentence to sentence? Would repeating key words or using pronouns or adding transitions increase a paragraph's coherence?

EXPLORING STYLISTIC OPTIONS

"Proper words in proper places" — that is how the eighteenth-century writer Jonathan Swift defined style. Swift's definition, though intentionally abstract, is accurate. Writing style reflects all of the choices that a writer makes, from global questions of approach and organization to the smallest details about punctuation and grammar. In this sense, *all* of the decisions that you make as a writer are stylistic decisions. When proper words *are* in proper places, readers are able to follow the writer's ideas with understanding and interest. In addition, they probably have some sense of the person behind the words, the writer's presence.

We often associate style with the personal, referring, for instance, to a person's style of dress or style of interacting with others. And a writer's style does reflect his or her individual taste and sensibility. But just as people dress differently for different occasions, so too do effective writers vary their style, depending on their rhetorical situation. As they do so, they are particularly attentive to the persona, or voice, they convey through their writing. Sometimes writers present strong and distinctive voices. Here, for instance, is the beginning of an essay by the novelist Ken Kesey on the Pendleton Round-Up, a Northwest rodeo.

> My father took me up the Gorge and over the hills to my first one thirty-five years ago. It was on my fourteenth birthday. I had to miss a couple of days' school plus the possibility of suiting up for the varsity game that Friday night. Gives you some idea of the importance Daddy placed on this event.
>
> For this is more than just a world-class rodeo. It is a week-long shindig, a yearly rendezvous dating back beyond the first white trappers, a traditional powwow ground for the Indian nations of the Northwest for nobody knows how many centuries.
>
> — KEN KESEY, "THE BLUE-RIBBON AMERICAN BEAUTY ROSE OF RODEO"

Kesey's word choice and sentence structure help create an image of the writer as folksy, relaxed, and yet also forceful — just the right insider to write about a famous rodeo.

In other situations, writers don't wish to present a distinctive personal voice, as in the following introduction to an article in *Sky & Telescope* that explores a cooperative effort being undertaken by software vendors.

> Not all astronomical software is created equal. Some have features that others do not. Consequently, much as a carless commuter may have to make multiple transfers with public transportation to arrive at a destination, performing all the actions desired for a night's observing may require several programs. Make your finder chart with one program, point the telescope with another, take some CCD images with a third, and process them with yet a fourth. Imagine how much more productive you could be if such steps could be performed in a seamless flow.
>
> — JEFF MEDKEFF, "THE ASCOM REVOLUTION"

■ ■ ■

FOR EXPLORATION

From a newspaper, magazine, or book that you are currently reading, choose one passage that presents a distinctive personal voice. Choose another passage that presents a more anonymous public voice. Then answer these questions in writing:

1. How would you describe the voice evoked by each passage?

2. How does the author of each passage succeed in creating this voice? (Cite specific examples to support your analysis.)

3. Write several sentences explaining how you respond personally to each of these passages.

If you think rhetorically, always asking yourself questions about your rhetorical situation, you will naturally consider such major stylistic issues as the voice that you wish your writing will convey to readers. Look again at the guidelines for analyzing a rhetorical situation on p. 160. These guidelines pose questions that can help you determine the appropriate style for specific situations. You may also find it helpful to review the discussion of Aristotle's three appeals — *logos, pathos,* and *ethos* on p. 169. Considering the degree to which you wish to draw on appeals to reason *(logos),* emotion *(pathos),* and your own credibility as writer *(ethos)* will help you consider your own voice and your relationship with readers.

REVISING FOR EFFECTIVE PROSE STYLE

In addition to considering such major stylistic issues as the voice you wish to convey to readers, you will also need to make a number of smaller but no less important stylistic decisions. Some of these decisions you will make consciously. When you study several sentences to determine which provides the most effective transition from one paragraph to the next, you are consciously considering an aspect of style. Other decisions are only partly conscious. When you write a word, strike it out, and write another, you are making a stylistic choice — even if you are only partly aware of the reasons why you prefer the latter word over the former.

The choices that you make as you draft and revise reflect not only your understanding of your rhetorical situation but also your awareness of general principles of effective prose style, principles that apply to much academic and professional writing. Perhaps the easiest way to understand these principles is to analyze a passage that illustrates effective prose style in action.

Here are two paragraphs from the first chapter of a psycholinguistics textbook. As you read these paragraphs, imagine that you have been assigned to read them for a course in psycholinguistics, an interdisciplinary field that studies linguistic behavior and the psychological mechanisms that make verbal communication possible. (For the purposes of our discussion, each sentence has been numbered.)

(1) Language stands at the center of human affairs, from the most prosaic to the most profound. (2) It is used for haggling with store clerks, telling off umpires, and gossiping with friends as well as for negotiating contracts, discussing ethics, and explaining religious beliefs. (3) It is the medium through which the manners, morals, and mythology of a society are passed on to the next generation. (4) Indeed, it is a basic ingredient in virtually every social situation. (5) The thread that runs through all

these activities is communication, people trying to put their ideas over to others. (6) As the main vehicle of human communication, language is indispensable.

(7) Communication with language is carried out through two basic human activities: speaking and listening. (8) These are of particular importance to psychologists, for they are mental activities that hold clues to the very nature of the human mind. (9) In speaking, people put ideas into words, talking about perceptions, feelings, and intentions they want other people to grasp. (10) In listening, they turn words into ideas, trying to reconstruct the perceptions, feelings, and intentions they were meant to grasp. (11) Speaking and listening, then, ought to reveal something fundamental about the mind and how it deals with perceptions, feelings, and intentions. (12) Speaking and listening, however, are more than that. (13) They are the tools people use in more global activities. (14) People talk in order to convey facts, ask for favors, and make promises, and others listen in order to receive this information. (15) These actions in turn are the pieces out of which casual conversations, negotiations, and other social exchanges are formed. (16) So speaking and listening ought to tell us a great deal about social and cultural activities too.

— HERBERT H. CLARK AND EVE V. CLARK, *PSYCHOLOGY AND LANGUAGE*

These two paragraphs, you would probably agree, do embody effective prose style. They are clearly organized. Each paragraph begins with a topic sentence, which the rest of the paragraph explains. The paragraphs are also coherent, with pronouns, key words, and sentence patterns helping readers proceed. But what most distinguishes these two paragraphs, what makes them so effective, is the authors' use of concrete, precise, economical language and carefully crafted sentences.

Suppose that the first paragraph were revised as follows. What would be lost?

(1) Language stands at the center of human affairs, from the most prosaic to the most profound. (2) It is a means of human communication. (3) It is a means of cultural change and regeneration. (4) It is found in every social situation. (5) The element that characterizes all these activities is communication. (6) As the main vehicle of human communication, language is indispensable.

This revision communicates roughly the same ideas as the original paragraph, but it lacks that paragraph's liveliness and interest. Instead of presenting vivid examples — "haggling with store clerks, telling off umpires, and gossiping with friends" — sentences 2, 3, 4, and 5 state only vague generalities. Moreover, these sentences are short and monotonous. Also lost in the revision is any sense of the authors' personalities, as revealed in their writing.

As this example demonstrates, effective prose style doesn't have to be flashy or call attention to itself. The focus in the original passage is on the *ideas* being discussed. The authors don't want readers to stop and think, "My, what a lovely sentence." But they do want their readers — students required to read their book for a course — to become interested in and engaged with their ideas. So they use strong verbs and vivid, concrete examples whenever possible. They pay careful attention to sentence structure, alternating sequences of sentences with parallel structures (sentences 2, 3, and 4 as well as sentences 9 and 10) with other, more varied sentences. They take care that the relationships among ideas are clear. In both paragraphs, for example, the first and last sentences (which readers are most likely to remember) articulate the most important ideas. As a result of these and other choices, these two paragraphs succeed in being both economical and emphatic.

Exploring your stylistic options — developing a style that reflects your understanding of yourself and the world and your feel for language — is one of the pleasures of writing. The following guidelines will help you revise your own writing for structure and style.

■ GUIDELINES FOR REVISING STRUCTURE
  AND STYLE

---

1. *Vary the Length and Structure of Your Sentences.* If you look again at the paragraphs from the psycholinguistics textbook (pp. 319–20), you will notice that the authors vary the length and structure of their sentences. In the first paragraph, for instance, the initial sentence is followed by a much longer sentence with multiple examples of the ways in which language "stands at the center of human affairs." The third and fourth sentences, while briefer than the second, are linked to it by their repetition of "it is" at the start of each sentence. Such repetition is helpful, for these sentences serve primarily to expand on the idea presented at the start of the paragraph. The authors are careful, however, to vary the structure of the fifth and sixth sentences, which emphasize the extent to which "language is indispensable."

   Now contrast this paragraph with the following excerpt from an essay urging students to use coupons when they shop:

   (1) Almost everywhere you look, there are coupons. (2) Daily newspapers are probably the best sources for coupons. (3) The *Oregonian* and the *Barometer* have coupons every day. (4) The *Gazette-Times* has

   (continued)

(continued)

coupons too. (5) The Sunday *Oregonian* is loaded with coupons. (6) Some of the sources that are not so obvious may be coupon trader bins in groceries and flyers handed out in dorms. (7) The backs of store receipts and coupons on boxes or other items you have previously purchased are also common.

The sentences in this paragraph lack variety. Sentences 2, 3, and 4 are all roughly the same length; they also follow the same subject-verb-object structure. (All also employ either "be" or "have" verbs.) Because the information they express is so obvious — each simply indicates a possible source of coupons — these sentences seem repetitive. The final two sentences break this pattern, but they are awkward and hard to follow.

See how this paragraph could be revised to be much more effective:

(1) You may be surprised by how easy it is to find coupons. (2) Daily newspapers, such as the *Oregonian,* the *Gazette-Times,* and the *Barometer,* are probably the best sources for coupons. (3) If you don't want to purchase a daily paper, the Sunday *Oregonian,* which is loaded with coupons, may be the next best choice. (4) Don't just look for coupons in newspapers, however. (5) You can also watch for special coupon bins in grocery stores and for flyers used to distribute coupons in dorms. (6) You can even discover coupons on the backs of store receipts or on the boxes or packages from other purchases.

You may have noticed that the revised paragraph changes more than sentence length and structure. The wording of the first sentence is now more emphatic. The final two sentences are more direct because they begin with *you,* the subject of the action. Finally, added transitions clarify the relationships among ideas in the paragraph. As this revision shows, even though you may be revising with a particular purpose in mind (in this case to vary the sentences), revision usually involves a multitude of changes.

When you revise, you generally want to achieve an appropriate variety of sentence lengths and structures, one that carries readers forward with a clear yet unobtrusive rhythm. The following paragraph from a student essay on salmon fishing illustrates this accomplishment.

Picture yourself in a scenic river setting. The fall colors are at their peak, and shades of burnt red and copper gold brighten up the shoreline. The

(continued)

(continued)

crisp, clean smell of fall is in the air, and a gentle breeze blows lightly against your face. Off in the distance you hear the sound of swift white water thundering over massive boulders until it gradually tames into slower-moving pools of crystal green. As you look out across the river, the smooth glassy surface is momentarily interrupted as a large salmon leaps free of its natural element.

You may at times want to use more dramatic sentence structures to emphasize a point. Here, for instance, is the first paragraph of Ian Frazier's book-length exploration of the heartland of America:

Away to the Great Plains of America, to that immense Western short-grass prairie now mostly plowed under! Away to the still-empty land beyond newsstands and malls and velvet restaurant ropes! Away to the headwaters of the Missouri, now quelled by many impoundment dams, and to the headwaters of the Platte, and to the almost invisible headwaters of the slurped-up Arkansas! Away to the land where TV used to set its most popular dramas, but not anymore! Away to the land beyond the hundredth meridian of longitude, where sometimes it rains and sometimes it doesn't, where agriculture stops and does a double take! Away to the skies of sparrow hawks sitting on telephone wires, thinking of mice and flaring their tail feathers suddenly, like a card trick! Away to the air shaft of the continent, where weather fronts from two hemispheres meet, and the wind blows almost all the time! Away to the fields of wheat and milo and sudan grass and flax and alfalfa and nothing! Away to parts of Montana and North Dakota and South Dakota and Wyoming and Nebraska and Kansas and Colorado and New Mexico and Oklahoma and Texas! Away to the high plains rolling in waves to the rising final chord of the Rocky Mountains!

— IAN FRAZIER, *GREAT PLAINS*

This dramatic paragraph encourages readers to abandon their conventional understandings of the Great Plains and reconsider this expansive region through Frazier's eyes. The contrast between Frazier's diction (which speaks of such mundane realities as "fields of wheat and milo and sudan grass") and his sentence structure, which is almost poetic in its intensity, establishes a tension that the rest of the book will explore.

Readers can hardly sustain such a dramatic and feverish pace, however, so just a few pages later Frazier's style shifts considerably:

(continued)

(continued)

> The Great Plains are about 2,500 miles long, and about 600 miles across at their widest point. The area they cover roughly parallels the Rocky Mountains, which mark their western boundary. Although they extend from the Southwestern United States well into Canada, no single state or province lies entirely within them.
>
> — IAN FRAZIER, *GREAT PLAINS*

This plainer, more conventional style is appropriate to Frazier's purpose, which is to provide readers with basic information about his subject.

2. *Use Language Appropriate to Your Purpose and Situation.* Look again at the two paragraphs from the psycholinguistics textbook on pp. 319–20. One of the strengths of these two paragraphs is the *specific, concrete words* and examples. Rather than writing that language "is a means of human communication," the authors say that language "is used for haggling with store clerks, telling off umpires, and gossiping with friends as well as for negotiating contracts, discussing ethics, and explaining religious beliefs." This sentence doesn't merely interest readers; it challenges them to pause and think about just how many ways they use language to communicate.

   Specific, concrete words can give your writing power and depth. Such language isn't always appropriate, however. Sometimes you need to use *abstract* or *general terms* to convey your meaning. Abstract words — like *patriotism, love,* and *duty* — refer to ideas, beliefs, relationships, conditions, and acts that you can't perceive with your senses. General words designate a group. The word *computer* is general; the word *iMac* identifies a specific machine within that group.

   Effective writing usually interweaves the specific and the concrete with the abstract and the general. In the first paragraph from the psycholinguistics textbook, for example, the authors specify and describe various ways people use language to communicate and then close with a much broader statement: "As the main vehicle of human communication, language is indispensable." Good writers use general and abstract language when appropriate — and for writing about intellectual problems or ideas or emotions, such language often is appropriate — but they balance

(continued)

(continued)

abstract generalities with concrete, specific words and examples that give their ideas force and vigor.

Some writers overuse abstract, general words, perhaps assuming that such words sound more intellectual, formal, or official. Here, for instance, is a paragraph from an essay analyzing *Sports Illustrated* (notice how vague much of the language is):

Sports Illustrated's articles are informative because its writers try to get information which nobody else knows. The articles explain how the subject is unique and how the subject became popular and successful. Articles are rarely negative. Most are positive and explain the good things in sports rather than emphasizing the negative aspects, such as drugs.

This paragraph leaves readers with more questions than answers. What does this writer mean when he calls articles "informative"? What kind of information that "nobody else knows" are writers for *Sports Illustrated* able to get? Just what kinds of subjects does the publication cover? (Many magazines feature articles about subjects that are "unique," "popular," and "successful.") Does the magazine emphasize the human drama of competition, for example, or strategy, techniques, and statistics? Readers familiar with *Sports Illustrated* can probably use their prior knowledge to interpret this paragraph; others can only guess at the writer's intentions.

3. *Reduce Wordiness.* Readers can be impatient. They are reading for a reason — their reason, not yours — and they may well become irritated by unnecessary words or flabby sentences. Experienced writers read their work carefully when revising to determine if they can prune unnecessary words and sentences.

In revising to eliminate wordiness, your goal is not necessarily to eliminate every possible word. Rather, your goal should be to ensure that *every word serves a purpose*. Words that are not strictly necessary can serve purposes of emphasis, rhythm, flow, or tone; the degree to which these are important to your writing is a question that can only be answered by considering your rhetorical situation and purpose.

Words and phrases that add unnecessary length to your sentences without serving any rhetorical purpose are known as *deadwood,* and deadwood turns up in the drafts of even the most

(continued)

(continued)

experienced writers. The revision phase is the time to concentrate on finding deadwood and clearing it out.

While rereading an early draft of the second chapter of this book, for instance, I noticed the following sentence:

Rather than *attempting to determine a sequence of activities that you always follow when you write,* you should develop a range of strategies that you can employ at any point in the writing process.

The deadwood is italicized; see now how I revised the sentence:

Rather than following a rigid sequence of activities, you should develop a range of strategies that you can employ at any point in the writing process.

This revised sentence communicates the same idea as the original but uses significantly fewer words (twenty-six rather than thirty-four). Like me, you will often discover wordy sentences when you reread your drafts. Don't be surprised at such discoveries. When you're struggling to express ideas, you can't expect to worry about being concise at the same time. Knowing this, however, you should be particularly alert for deadwood — words that clutter up your sentences and lessen their impact — when you revise.

Sometimes you can eliminate deadwood by deleting unnecessary words; in other cases, you may need to revise your sentence structure. The following examples of sentences clogged with deadwood are from early drafts of this textbook; I have italicized the unnecessary words. My revisions follow below the original sentence.

As you *work to improve your* writing, you can *benefit a great deal from* drawing on your *own* commonsense understanding of how people in our culture use language.

As you write, you can draw on your commonsense understanding of how people in our culture use language.

Your discussion with your instructor will be most profitable (for both of you) if you *have already done a fair amount of preparation before* the conference.

Your discussion with your instructor will be most profitable (for both of you) if you prepare for the conference.

(continued)

(continued)

> *One traditional way of viewing these disciplines is to see them as falling into* one of the following *major* categories: sciences, humanities, and social sciences.

> Most academic disciplines fall into one of the following categories: sciences, humanities, or social sciences.

> These examples emphasize that even experienced writers need to revise their writing to achieve an effective prose style. Placing "proper words in proper places" does require patience and commitment, but it is also one of the most rewarding parts of the writing process, for it ensures effective communication between writer and reader.

FOR THOUGHT, DISCUSSION, AND WRITING

1. From an essay you are currently working on, find a paragraph that lacks adequate coherence. Determine why the paragraph lacks coherence. Then use the strategies discussed in this chapter to revise your paragraph.

2. From the same essay, choose two or three paragraphs that you suspect could be more stylistically effective. Using this chapter's discussion of style as a guide, revise these paragraphs.

3. Here is an essay written by Ian Frazier, whose introduction to *Great Plains* you read earlier in this chapter. This essay was published in *The New Yorker* magazine. Read the essay, and then answer the questions that follow it.

TO MR. WINSLOW
by Ian Frazier

On June first, in the afternoon, four teen-agers approached a forty-two-year-old drama teacher named Allyn Winslow on Quaker Hill, in Brooklyn's Prospect Park, and tried to steal his new mountain bike. When he resisted and rode away, they shot him four times with a .22-calibre pistol. He rode down the hill to the cobbled path leading to the Picnic House, fell off his bike, and died. The TV news that evening showed the bike on the grass, and his body, covered by a sheet, next to it. I recognized the spot where he lay. I take my daughter to the pond nearby to throw bread to the ducks. She and I had sat there, or near there.

I walked by the spot the next day. It was marked by a wad of discarded surgical tape and an inside-out surgical glove. The day after, when I went by there I saw a Timberland shoebox with a bouquet of flowers in it, and a glass wine carafe with more flowers. In the shoebox was a piece of lined paper on which someone had written in blue ink: "To the biker Mr. Winslow, May you be in a better place with angels on a cloud." These words echoed in the media as reporters quoted and misquoted them. Men and women were carrying microphones and TV cameras in the vicinity, and if you weren't careful they would interview you. About a week later, an American flag had been stuck into the ground next to the shoebox. There was a bunch of papers in a clear-plastic envelope, and the one on top said, "AVENGE THIS ACT OF COWARDICE." In and around the shoebox were notes addressed to Mr. Winslow and his wife and their two children; a blue-and-white striped ribbon; a ceramic pipe; a bike rider's reflector badge in the image of a peace sign; a red-and-white bandanna; a flyer from the Guardian Angels organization; and an announcement of an upcoming service to be held in his memory.

The following week, the accumulation around the shoebox had grown. The flowers in it and in the wine carafe were fresh — roses, peonies, yellow freesias. Someone had arranged many pinecones and sprigs of oak leaves in a circle on the perimeter. In the ground by the flag was a cross made of wood, bound with red ribbon and draped with a string of purple glass beads, and, near the cross, a photocopy of a newspaper photograph of Allyn Winslow. A Dover edition of Shakespeare's "Complete Sonnets" rested on a pedestal made of a cross-section of a branch from a London Plane tree. There were also several anti-N.R.A. stickers, a blue candle in a plastic cup, and a five of spades from a pack of Bicycle playing cards. Chunks of paving stones held down a poster showing the number of people killed in 1990 by handguns in various countries: thirteen in Sweden, ninety-one in Switzerland, eighty-seven in Japan, sixty-eight in Canada, ten thousand five hundred and sixty-seven in the United States. A girl visiting the park on a class picnic asked another girl, "Is he buried here?"

A week or two later, many of the items had vanished. Someone had burned the flag, but the charred flagpole remained. The cross, broken off at the base, lay on the ground. The plastic cup with the candle was cracked. The grass around the spot was worn down in a circle and littered with dried flower stems. The carafe had a big chip out of the top. The shoebox had begun to sag. The papers were gone, except for a rain-stained sign saying, "To Honor, To Mourn Allyn Winslow," and a pamphlet, "Verses of Comfort, Assurance and Salvation."

By mid-July, the shoebox was in pieces. There were a few rocks, two small forked branches stuck in the ground, the ashes of a small fire, and a "You gotta have Park!" button. By mid-August, the tramped-down grass had begun to grow back. I noticed a piece of red-and-white string and a scrap from the shoebox. By September, so little of the memorial remained that the spot was hard to find. A closer look revealed the burned patch, some red-and-white string now faded to pink, and flower stems so scattered and broken you'd have to know what they were to recognize them.

Just now — a bright, chilly fall day — I went by the place again. Color in the park's trees had reached its peak. In a grove of buckskin-brown oaks, yellow shot up the fountain of a ginkgo tree. A flock of pigeons rose all at once and glided to a new part of the Long Meadow, circling once before landing, like a dog before it lies down. A police car slipped around the corner of the Picnic House, a one-man police scooter rode down the path, a police helicopter flew by just above the trees. At first, I could find no trace of the memorial at all: grass and clover have reclaimed the bared dirt. I got down on one knee, muddying my pants. Finally, I found a wooden stake broken off about half an inch above the ground: the base of the memorial cross, probably — the only sign of the unmeasured sorrows that converge here.

- How would you describe the general style of this essay? Write three or four sentences describing its style.

- How would you describe the persona or voice conveyed by this essay? List at least three specific characteristics of the writer's voice, and then indicate several passages that you think particularly exemplify these characteristics.

- Find three passages from this essay that you believe demonstrate the principles of effective prose style as discussed in this chapter. Indicate why you believe each passage is stylistically effective.

- What additional comments could you make about the structure and style of this essay? Did anything about the style of this essay surprise you? Formulate at least one additional comment about the essay's structure and style.

4. You can learn a great deal about the effective use of style by reading a variety of works by the same author. Here are references for several additional essays by Ian Frazier:

> Frazier, Ian. "Count on Crows." *The Utne Reader.* March–April 2001: 33+.
>
> ———. "Home Town." *The Atlantic Monthly.* Oct. 1994: 96+.
>
> ———. "Laws Concerning Food and Drink; Household Principles; Lamentations of the Father." *The Atlantic Monthly.* Feb. 1997: 89–90.
>
> ———. "Making Marks." *Audubon.* Nov.–Dec. 1996: 34+.
>
> ———. "On the Rez." *The Atlantic Monthly.* December 1995: 53+.
>
> ———. "Researchers Say." *The New Yorker.* 9 December 2002: 80–81.

Locate copies of three or four of these essays whose titles interest you, and read them with care. Once you have done so, write an essay discussing the relationship of style and content in Frazier's writing. In what ways does Frazier vary his style depending on the content of his article and his situation? What aspects of his style remain consistent?

CHAPTER 13

Strategies for Successful Collaboration

> Writing together has taught us a great deal. It has taught us how to read each other's illegible scrawls; how to be patient and flexible; how to listen to and criticize a draft; how to smile, not cry, when one of us announces that something the other has just written is not quite right. Most important, perhaps, it has taught us something we know as writers but can easily forget: that there is no simple, single, static writing process. Rather, there are writing processes — repertoires of strategies and habits that writers can learn, and change, if they have a strong enough motive for communicating.*

When Professor Andrea Lunsford and I wrote this statement in 1988, we had been writing regularly as coauthors for a number of years — and we had been studying collaborative writing practices for almost as long. In the mid-1980s, we surveyed fourteen hundred members of seven professional associations, including engineers, city planners, chemists, and psychologists.† Of the seven hundred professionals who responded to our survey, 87 percent indicated that they regularly wrote as members of a team or group. Since 98 percent of these same individuals also rated writing as important or very important to the successful execution of their jobs, it is safe to say that the writing they do as members of groups or teams matters a great deal to them. Later surveys and interviews with members of each organization only confirmed and enriched our understanding of the essential role that collaborative writing plays in these professionals' lives.

UNDERSTANDING COLLABORATIVE WRITING: INSIGHTS FROM THE WORLD OF WORK

The individuals Professor Lunsford and I studied are pragmatic, task-oriented writers: They engage in collaborative writing activities primarily because their

---

*Andrea A. Lunsford and Lisa Ede, "Collaboration and Compromise: The Fine Art of Writing with a Friend," *Writers on Writing*, Vol. 2, edited by Tom Waldrep (New York: Random House, 1988), 127.
†Lisa Ede and Andrea A. Lunsford, *Singular Texts/Plural Authors: Perspectives on Collaborative Writing* (Carbondale: Southern Illinois UP, 1990).

work requires them to do so. Sometimes the complexity and ambition of their project necessitates collaboration. This was certainly the case with Bill Qualls, a city planner working in a consulting engineering firm in the south, who heads a team responsible for designing and building large military installations. Albert Bernstein, a clinical psychologist in private practice in the northwest, gave other reasons, describing a collaborative effort to draft an informational brochure for a statewide organization. Although the brochure was a brief document, its development involved a time-consuming series of complex negotiations. Despite these difficulties, Bernstein characterized this and most other collaborations as effective — and as personally rewarding: "[When I write with others,] I do a much better job than I would have done alone. I extend myself further and I have a clearer idea of what we are trying to do."

People have many reasons for writing collaboratively — and an equally diverse number of ways for effectively negotiating the complex processes that such an effort involves. When you write with others, as when you write alone, there is no simple, single, static writing process that you can follow. You must consider each writing task you work on by analyzing your rhetorical situation and determining the most appropriate strategies to employ in a particular case.

Whether writing on the job or at school, writers face a number of challenges. Collaborative projects generally require more explicit planning, coordination, and monitoring of efforts than do individual projects. Melding a uniform style from the efforts of individual writers can require patience and a willingness to negotiate. Finally, collaborative writing efforts can engender the same kinds of difficulties that occur whenever human beings (with all our complexities and foibles) attempt to work together. Poor interpersonal communication, ineffective group dynamics, or inequitable sharing of responsibilities can turn a potentially productive group effort into a frustrating, time-consuming tug-of-war.

Collaborative writing does require sensitivity, patience, flexibility, and commitment. But the rewards of writing collaboratively with others can be substantial. Writers working collaboratively can, most obviously, take on projects that they would be unable to complete alone. If you're part of a group that wishes to study a complex issue or problem, such as the adequacy of your campus's computer services, you *have* to work together. Only by sharing responsibilities can you hope to do justice to your topic in the time available to you. Just as important, when you collaborate with others you can draw on group members' diverse interests, experiences, and capabilities. Group members will undoubtedly have had diverse experiences with your school's computer services, for example. These and other differences enable your group to examine all the issues at stake and thus can improve both your process of inquiry and the essay or report that will result from this process.

Collaboration can also bring individual satisfaction. Many of those Professor Lunsford and I interviewed commented on the ways in which working collaboratively with others on writing enabled them to "learn the ropes" and gain confidence. A number also emphasized that collaborative writing can bring personal rewards: When a collaboration works well, it becomes — as one city planner indicated — "as much a support group as a professional team."

RECOGNIZING THE DEMANDS OF ACADEMIC COLLABORATIVE WRITING PROJECTS

Like those in business and industry, many students find collaborative writing projects to be productive and personally rewarding. Here, for instance, is a journal entry by Latisha Armstrong, a sociology major, about one of her collaborative experiences:

> I was worried when I found out that the major project for my sociology class, an evaluation of a local social service agency, was a group project. My life is pretty complicated already — I didn't know how I'd find the time to meet. I wondered how we'd get along, divide up the work, keep track of who's doing what. Also, I'm really sweating it to do well in school, but not all students care. What if my grade suffered, or if I had to do most of the work to get the project done right? My group did have some rough moments, but we really pulled together. We were able to do a lot of library work *and* interview almost everyone at the agency. Sean did some fancy statistical stuff that really helped us analyze our data. And Sharon's final edit really worked out the kinks. Especially at the end of our project, when we were talking through our conclusions, I felt that I wasn't just studying sociology; I was doing it!

Latisha's comments suggest many of the rewards of collaborating on academic writing assignments. But they also call attention to some potential difficulties — difficulties that, while hardly unique to student collaborations, can prove troublesome: managing logistical and pragmatic matters, developing a shared commitment to the project and an equitable distribution of tasks, and negotiating interpersonal and group issues.

Those working collaboratively in business and industry also face these difficulties, of course, but they are often provided with support systems and incentives unavailable to students. A group of managers working on a report for their company often have the advantage of such in-house services as networked computers with shareware designed specifically for collaborative writing, photocopying services, conference rooms, and secretarial help. In addition, these managers may well have worked together on previous projects, so they will have had opportunities to get to know one another. Finally, teams in business and industry know that performance evaluations, as well as such incentives as salary increases, are directly tied to the success of their endeavor. Given this orientation, these managers are likely to understand the importance of subordinating their own interests or inclinations to the job at hand.

As you are aware, students lack a number of the advantages that I have just detailed. Students cannot count on the kind of support services available to those in business and industry. Most often, students writing collaboratively have not worked together previously. Finally, even though students may be assigned a group grade for a project, they receive an individual grade at the end of the term. Unfortunately, the individualistic, competitive nature of academic grading can work against the development of a strong identification with a team and its collaborative project.

The rest of this chapter suggests steps that you can take to address these and other potential difficulties inherent in collaboration. Collaborative writing does pose special challenges for students, but it can also help you improve your own writing skills. Here, for instance, is a comment by Andrea Barton, a student who is majoring in education at Oregon State University: "I have completed a few collaborative projects over the past several terms and now realize that is a superb way to approach writing. Collaboration is particularly helpful in my personal battle against procrastination. Collaborative writing also helps me tackle my fear of failure, which sometimes keeps me from writing altogether. Thanks to my collaborative projects, I feel I'm a stronger writer even when I'm working on individual projects."

■ ■ ■

FOR EXPLORATION

Think back to experiences you've had writing with others, whether in school, at work, or elsewhere. Recall one specific experience that you felt was particularly successful, and take five to ten minutes to freewrite or brainstorm a list of factors that made for a productive, satisfying collaboration. Now think of a less successful experience that involved collaboration on writing. Once again, freewrite or brainstorm a list of factors that played a role in the outcome of this collaboration. (If you haven't written collaboratively, recall experiences where you worked closely with others on extramural, civic, or similar projects.)

Developing Effective Interpersonal and Group Skills

The potential problems described in the previous section are just that — *potential* but not inevitable problems. What makes or breaks a group collaboration is the ability to develop effective interpersonal and group skills. If your group wastes time bickering over trivial matters or allows one or two members to dominate (or withdraw from) the project, you will not be able to take advantage of one of the major benefits of collaboration: the enriched understandings that develop when individuals with diverse experiences and skills jointly investigate a subject. In situations like this, morale falters and resentment grows. Your group should place a high priority on establishing a good working relationship. The following guidelines provide suggestions group members can use to ensure an efficient, congenial, and productive working relationship.

■ GUIDELINES FOR EFFECTIVE INTERPERSONAL AND GROUP SKILLS

1. *Understand the Importance of Attending to the Task and to the Group.* Whenever people work together, they are following at least two agendas: the explicit agenda of completing a designated project and the implicit and perhaps hidden agenda of developing a productive and rewarding working relationship with members of the group. To fulfill both agendas, group members need to adopt what Professors Linda Flower and John Ackerman refer to as task-conscious and interactive roles.* You are being task-conscious when you set deadlines, negotiate responsibilities, or argue for a particular approach or position. You are playing an interactive role when you encourage reserved group members to share their ideas, use humor to reduce a moment of tension, or praise a group member for a job well done. In effective groups, members know intuitively when they need to take on "task-conscious" and "interactive" roles; they also share responsibility for these roles so that all members can contribute as fully as possible to the group's effort.

2. *Find Ways to Acknowledge and Value Individual, Cultural, and Other Differences.* To succeed in any collaborative project, you need the good will and good work of every member of the group. And yet sometimes differences among group members can result in feelings of exclusion. Reserved students or those whose first

---

*The concepts of task-conscious and interactive roles are explained in Linda Flower and John Ackerman, *Writers at Work: Strategies for Communicating in Business and Professional Settings* (Fort Worth: Harcourt Brace, 1994).

(continued)

(continued)

language is not English may need more time to formulate and express their ideas. Students who in some way differ from the majority of group members — because of culture, race, age, or other differences — may wonder if other group members will understand and value their opinions. Effective groups find ways to demonstrate their respect for, and desire to learn from, all members. A simple request for additional perspectives ("Matt has made a good point here, but I wonder if others have different ideas") can encourage reluctant or uncertain members.

3. *Develop Your Active Listening Skills.* Many interpersonal and group problems can be avoided if participants regularly practice active listening. Active listening involves more than focusing on what others are saying; it includes being willing to engage with and credit their ideas fully — even (and especially) when you disagree with them. Imagine that your group is discussing an important aspect of a project and that one person begins to articulate an idea that strikes you as wrongheaded. An active listener resists the temptation to interrupt or discredit the speaker but instead concentrates with particular care on the ideas being expressed. If on reflection the ideas still seem problematic or confusing, an active listener paraphrases or "mirrors" the speaker's comments, perhaps saying something like "What I think I hear you suggesting is . . . " or "Am I right in thinking that you believe we should . . . ?" Rather than attacking ideas with which they disagree, active listeners ask questions that invite speakers to clarify or elaborate on their ideas. Many apparent disagreements turn out to be misunderstandings that are resolved in further discussion. Even where disagreements continue, active listening and "mirroring" enable you to demonstrate your respect for other group members.

4. *Recognize That How Your Group Handles Meetings Can Make or Break Your Collaborative Effort.* One question Professor Lunsford and I asked in our survey of collaborative-writing practices was this: "In your experience, what are the three greatest *disadvantages* of group writing in your profession?" One response aptly represented the views of many: "Time. Time. Time." Collaboration does take time — and when that time seems wasted, irritation and dissension can quickly develop. Here are some suggestions

(continued)

(continued)

for planning, conducting, and evaluating group sessions that will help you make the most of your time:

- *Spend your first meeting exploring your assignment, establishing basic ground rules, and encouraging the development of interpersonal trust and group identity.* No matter how elaborate and detailed an assignment is, students need to "read between the lines" to determine the processes and resources they should use to complete the assignment. When a group of students is working collaboratively on a major project, the need to talk explicitly and in detail about the assignment increases, for unless you develop a shared vision of its demands, the group is likely to waste time and effort. At the initial meeting, then, group members should spend a good deal of time discussing the assignment. Be sure to talk about both what the assignment requires and what processes and tasks are necessary to fulfill it. By the end of the meeting, you should have a preliminary or working consensus about how to proceed. This consensus may well include a number of alternate plans that you want to keep on the table; it might also include a list of questions for further discussion.

  You should also reserve time at your initial meeting to get to know one another — and to establish some ground rules for your collaborative effort. How will your group negotiate responsibilities? What will you do if a member is consistently late to meetings or does not follow through with tasks? How will you resolve conflicts or impasses? It's tempting to avoid questions such as these in the hope that your group will not need to address them. But discussing such issues up front is the best way to forestall later problems.

  If your meeting is effective, the process of discussing the assignment and agreeing on ground rules should have already laid the foundation for an effective group process. Nevertheless, you may find it helpful to conclude your meeting by encouraging members to discuss how they feel they can best contribute to the group effort and to raise any questions or reservations they have about the collaborative process.

- *Use an agenda to organize your meetings.* Once your project is under way, the structure of individual meetings may vary

(continued)

(continued)

considerably depending on the goals for each meeting. Whatever your purpose in meeting, however, you will find it helpful to follow an explicit — and written — agenda. This agenda need not be elaborate, but it should include specific goals to be accomplished and a plan for carrying them out. Conclude each meeting by reviewing the agenda, summarizing what you have accomplished, and assigning responsibilities for your next meeting. Save agendas from all meetings, so you can consult them if necessary.

■ *Supplement individual and group memory with written records.* When your group is engaged in an intensive, task-oriented discussion, it can seem tedious to make written notes summarizing your meeting. And yet both individual and group memory can be surprisingly brief — and varied. To ensure that all group members have the same understanding of group decisions, take turns keeping notes during your meetings. Conclude each meeting by reviewing (and, if necessary, revising) these notes, which should then be reproduced and distributed to all members of the group.

To facilitate communication among everyone in the group, you may find it useful to share regular progress reports. Members can also use such written reports to raise questions about current research or writing and to note issues for group discussion. At several points during your project, you may even find it helpful to devote all or part of a group meeting to generating a group progress report that summarizes what you have accomplished and lists tasks that still need to be completed.

5. *Develop Nonthreatening Ways to Deal with Problems.* All groups experience moments of difficulty. A brief flash of irritation between two group members may not merit attention, but significant interpersonal or group problems will worsen if not promptly addressed. Difficult as it can be, groups need to respond to such problems when they occur, and they need to do so in a way that encourages rather than diminishes group solidarity and effectiveness. But how? Whenever possible, avoid identifying problems with specific individuals. Even if you feel that a single group member has failed to carry out responsibilities, try to avoid directly accusing this person. You might suggest that it's an appropriate

(continued)

(continued)

time for the group to review what tasks have been completed, by whom, and when — with an eye to future assignments. Another strategy that is helpful when you wish to make a point but avoid conflict is to substitute "I" statements for "you" statements. Rather than saying to another student that "your ideas don't make sense," for instance, say "I'm having trouble following your point." By locating a problem in your understanding rather than in your group member's ideas, you avoid unnecessary conflict and encourage the clarification of ideas rather than anger.

6. *Know When You Should — and Shouldn't — Strive for Consensus.* The preceding suggestions aim to encourage cooperative, flexible, respectful working relationships. Placing too high a value on cooperation, however, can actually limit a group's effectiveness. Sometimes conflict can be productive. In a study of student collaborative writing groups, Professor Rebecca E. Burnett discovered that productive conflicts encourage groups to "re-examine opinions, share diverse ideas, and discover creative solutions."* A group cannot discover the most efficient way to divide responsibilities or to organize a group report without fully exploring all options. As a group, you should strive to avoid conflicts that interfere with your group's effectiveness, but you should encourage the free play of ideas. Premature consensus on such issues as the approach you should take to your topic or the most effective way to introduce your essay can work against decision-making.

7. *Build in Regular "Reality Checks" to Resolve Any Difficulties.* Even if you feel that your group is working well, it's helpful to schedule regular "reality checks." To do so, reserve time in meetings to discuss your collaborative process in a friendly, nonevaluative manner. You might conclude meetings, for instance, by freewriting about your group effort or about that particular meeting. Or you could respond to specific questions, such as the following:

What in our group process is working well?

How might we improve the productivity and efficiency of our collaborative effort?

---

*Rebecca E. Burnett, "Substantive Conflict in a Cooperative Context: A Way to Improve the Collaborative Planning of Workplace Documents," *Technical Communication* 38 (1991): 535.

(continued)

(continued)

> What about our group effort do we each find personally satisfying?
>
> What changes might make the group process more satisfying for me?
>
> Are there any issues, such as workload or deadlines, that we need to discuss or renegotiate?

If you regularly take time to raise questions such as these, your group should be better prepared to identify and resolve interpersonal or group problems.

8. *Expect the Unexpected.* Even with the best planning, most groups find that their work doesn't go quite as expected. One person's research may prove more time-consuming than anticipated, or it may uncover information that requires the group to rethink its approach to the topic. Illness or a family emergency may prevent another from completing work on time. As you organize and schedule your tasks, build in time for unexpected delays and problems. Recognize, too, that the group may need to redefine its goals or renegotiate the division of labor as you progress.

NOTE FOR MULTILINGUAL WRITERS

Students whose first or home language is not standard North American English sometimes worry about their ability to contribute to collaborative projects. In fact, diversity of experience and approach enhances collaborative efforts, for it encourages you to bring multiple perspectives to bear on your subject. You may find it helpful to review the following effective verbal strategies that were developed by Rebecca E. Burnett.

Acknowledge your collaborator's views or work.

"That's a convincing argument you're making."

"You've done some really good work so far."

(continued)

(continued)

Prompt your collaborator to clarify or elaborate.

"How does what you are planning to do relate to the assignment? It sounds to me like you're writing an argument, not a definition."

"That's interesting. Can you tell me more?"

"You've said a lot about the content that you plan to include. Can you tell me more about what you see as the purpose [or key points, audience reaction, or organization]?"

Direct your collaborator (infrequently!).

"You should reorganize these three points in order of importance if you want the reader to recognize their relative importance."

"Because the reader might be confused, I think that we should try another way of explaining this."

Contribute information to your collaborator.

"Let's organize this section by contrasting _____ with _____."

"I think that the best example would be _____."

Challenge your collaborator.

"I think that the audience already knows most of the things that you are planning to say. What will be new and interesting for them?"

"I don't think that your decision to leave out an example will work because the audience needs to see what you are saying."

Synthesize or consolidate plans about content and other rhetorical elements.

"Why do you think that _____ is a good way to appeal to this audience?"

"Will using a different example better support the point that we're making here?"

"Why do you like _____ better than _____ as a way to organize this information?"*

---

*Rebecca E. Burnett, "Decision-Making during the Collaborative Planning of Coauthors," *Hearing Ourselves Think: Cognitive Research in the College Writing Classroom*, edited by Ann M. Penrose and Barbara M. Sitko (New York: Oxford UP, 1993), 142.

As the guidelines on pages 335–40 suggest, when groups are working well, members share responsibilities, engage in an ongoing effort to analyze the group's effort, and make any needed modifications in process and product. As an example of such an analysis, here is an essay written by Merlla McLaughlin. Merlla and her classmates completed an investigative report on parking services at Oregon State University. After completing the collaborative report, they wrote individual essays analyzing their small-group dynamics. In her essay, Merlla refers to a personality assessment that she and other group members took in class. This assessment identified students as reds, blues, yellows, or whites. According to Merlla's instructor, Babette Bushnell, the significance of these colors is as follows: "Blues" are people-oriented and attend closely to interpersonal relations, "reds" are organizers and "take-charge" individuals, "whites" dislike conflict and thus often serve as peacemakers, and "yellows" are "fun" people who enjoy having a good time.

SMALL-GROUP DYNAMICS IN A CLASS PROJECT
by Merlla McLaughlin

College lectures provide learners with volumes of information. However, there are many experiences that cannot be understood well simply by *learning about* them in a classroom. Instead, these experiences can only be understood by *living* them. So it is with the workings of a small, task-focused group. What observations about small-group dynamics would I make after working with a group of peers on a class project? And what have I learned personally as a result of my involvement with our collaborative project?

LEADERSHIP EXPECTATIONS AND EMERGENCE
Our six group members were selected by our instructor; half were male and half female. Because we had performed personality assessments in class — and because these assessments identified most of us as "blues," concerned with intimacy and caring — I had expected that Nate, our only "red," might become our leader. (Kaari, the only "white," seemed poised to become the peacekeeper if need be.) However, after Nate missed the first two meetings, it seemed that Pat might emerge as leader. Pat had contributed often during our first three real meetings. More important, he has strong communications skills — and he is a tall male (and thus a commanding presence). Pat is also rhetorically sensitive. I was somewhat surprised, then, when our group developed a distributive type of leadership. The longer we worked together, however, the more convinced I became that this approach to leadership was best for our group.

ROLES PLAYED
Thanks in part to the distributed leadership that our group developed, the strengths of group members increasingly became apparent. While early in

our process Pat had been the key initiator and Nate had acted largely as information seeker, all group members eventually took on these task functions. We took turns serving as recorders, and we all gathered information and worked on our questionnaire. McKenzie, Kaari, Pat, and I all coordinated the group's work at some point. Joe was especially good at catching important details the rest of us were apt to miss. An example of this ability occurred at our second meeting when he asked us all to come to the third meeting with prepared questions. Later, he pointed out that parking problems on campus could affect surrounding businesses and that interviewing business owners and employees could be informative. Joe, McKenzie, Kaari, and I frequently clarified and elaborated information. Pat, Kaari, and Nate were particularly good at contributing ideas during brainstorming sessions. Nate and McKenzie kept humor in the group and in the project, with tension-relieving jokes.

Gender did seem to influence group members' approach to our project. For example, the women all seemed to take a holistic approach to the project and to make intuitive leaps in ways that the men generally did not. The men preferred a more systematic process. But our differing preferences complemented each other well and enabled us to conduct research effectively, organize the information we gathered logically, and prepare for, practice, and give a successful presentation.

DECISION-MAKING METHODS

Our decision to do an investigative report on Parking Services was not the result of a majority vote but was achieved instead through negotiated consensus. Nate was absent on the day that we made our decision, but we felt that we needed to move from brainstorming — which we had already done — to action. Several of us argued that a presentation on Parking Services at OSU would interest most students, and after discussion the others agreed. At our next meeting, Nate seemed happy to go along with our collaborative decision.

We spent a good deal of time negotiating the topic for our presentation. Once we did this, other, smaller decisions came naturally. At one point, for instance, we considered producing a videotape for part of our presentation. But after we discussed whether we had the resources and skills to shoot, edit, and produce a videotape, we quickly realized that it was not feasible. By using slides instead (which Pat and Nate prepared), we were still able to tie the whole presentation together through visual images.

SOCIAL ENVIRONMENT: HAPPY, HARMONIZING
INTIMACY-SEEKERS

As previously noted, our group primarily consisted of blues, and at least three of the four blues had white as their secondary color. (The other secondary color was yellow.) This partly explains why our group had little confrontation and conflict. Nate, the red, was most likely to be blunt in his speech, but everyone was rhetorically sensitive and self-monitoring during group interactions. The one time that Nate seemed put off, at the third meeting, it was not his words but his body language that expressed his discomfort. Nate sat on the far end of the group, leaned back in his chair, arms crossed, legs stretched out, ankles crossed. By contrast, everyone else in the group had scooted in close together. This was an awkward moment, but a rare one given our group's generally positive handling of conflict. This was not, I think, the result of groupthink, or of a fear of conflict. Instead, obstacles were treated not as one person's problems but rather as a group problem. As a consequence, we approached problems from a united position instead of forming "camps" and opposing each other.

LOOKING TOWARD THE FUTURE
Perhaps my most important personal understanding as a result of this project has to do with conflict. Although I personally find conflict difficult, I have found that some kinds of conflict are essential for increasing understanding between group members and creating an effective collaborative product. It was essential, for instance, that our group explore everyone's (well, everyone's but Nate's) ideas about possible topics for our presentation — and this inevitably required some conflict as one person suggested an idea and another said "But what about. . . . " Conflict (in the sense of discussion of multiple possibilities) is essential to the full exploration of ideas. When groups handle conflict positively, they increase the group's cohesiveness. I think all the members of our group felt, for instance, that their ideas about possible topics for our presentation were considered. Once we negotiated a topic, everyone could fully commit to it.

I think that as a result of this project I have a better sense of when conflict is — and isn't — productive. My group used conflict productively when we hashed out our ideas, and we avoided the kind of conflict that creates morale problems and wastes time. Each group operates somewhat differently, but with the grounding this class has provided I feel more prepared to understand and participate in future small-group projects.

■ ■ ■

FOR COLLABORATION

The Exploration on p. 334 encouraged you to reflect on previous collaborative writing experiences. Meet with the members of your writing group (or with other members of your class) to share your responses to these activities. What common factors did group members cite as leading to productive or unproductive collaborations? After listing these factors, look with particular care at those that led to unsatisfying, unproductive collaborations. To what extent do the guidelines on pp. 335–40 provide suggestions you can use to address these problems? Did your group identify problems not discussed in the guidelines? If so, make a list of these problems and of ways your group might anticipate or avoid them.

Planning, Drafting, and Revising Collaboratively

Many in business and industry know that when groups work well, they can produce better ideas — and better written products — than people working individually. To achieve this productivity, however, groups must learn how to maximize the benefits inherent in collaboration. Sometimes this involves taking the fullest possible advantage of group members' diverse experiences, interests, and ideas. Sometimes it involves finding effective and efficient ways to manage the collaborative process. If you're writing an essay alone, for instance, it doesn't matter if your plan is a jumbled, indecipherable mass of notes. As long as the plan makes sense to you, that's fine. When you write collaboratively, the development and maintenance of group "memory" requires more explicit, organized planning. The following guidelines provide suggestions for planning, drafting, and revising a collaborative work.

■ GUIDELINES FOR COLLABORATIVE PLANNING, DRAFTING, AND REVISING

PLANNING

1. *Take Advantage of Multiple Roles and Perspectives in the Planning Process.* When you plan collaboratively, you naturally draw on group members' varied experiences and perspectives. Researchers have identified several strategies that can maximize the effectiveness of this process. After studying student groups engaged in collaborative planning, for instance, Professor Rebecca E. Burnett discovered that students in the most effective groups regularly assumed a variety of roles. Sometimes they initiated ideas; in other instances they served as questioners, clarifiers, or recorders. As they worked together, they demonstrated a task-oriented, problem-solving approach to planning.

   Good questions are the heart of the collaborative planning process. To encourage her students to ask productive questions — questions that challenge them to look at their topic from

   (continued)

(continued)

multiple perspectives — Professor Burnett developed the following questions for collaborative planning.*

QUESTIONS FOR COLLABORATIVE PLANNING

Content Questions

What more can we say about _____?

What additional information might we include?

Have you considered including (excluding) _____?

Don't you think we should include (exclude) _____?

Purpose/Key Point Questions

What do we see as our main point (purpose)?

What did you mean by _____? Could you clarify the point about _____?

I can't quite see why you've decided to _____. Could you explain why?

I see a conflict between _____ and _____. How will we deal with it?

Audience Questions

Who is our intended audience? Why is this the appropriate audience?

What does the reader expect to read (learn, do)?

How will our reader react to _____? Connect _____ to _____?

What problems (conflicts, inconsistencies, gaps) might our reader see?

---

*Rebecca E. Burnett, "Benefits of Collaborative Planning in the Business Communication Classroom," *Bulletin of the Association for Business Communication* 53.2 (1990): 12.

(continued)

(continued)

Questions Relating to Conventions of Organization and Development

How can we explain _____?

How will we organize (develop, explain) this?

What support (or evidence) could we use? What examples could we use?

How does this (convention) let us deal with _____?

Questions Relating to Conventions of Design

Have you considered using _____? How do you think it would work?

Couldn't we also try _____?

How does this (convention) let us deal with _____?

Why do you like _____ better than _____ as a way to present this information?

Synthesis/Consolidation Questions

How does _____ relate to (develop, clarify) _____?

Given our purpose and audience, should we use _____?

Is there a conflict between using _____ and _____?

Why do you think _____ is a good way to explain our key point to this audience?

2. *Use Visual Representations to Develop and Clarify Your Group's Ideas.* When you're in an intense discussion, it can be easy to lose track of your ideas. Many collaborative writers have found that using such aids as chalkboards, large notepads of paper, or computers to record ideas can do a great deal to organize discussion — and also to clarify and stimulate ideas. It's much easier to determine how to organize a report, for instance, if the entire group can actually look at two or three possible organizational patterns, rather than trying to keep them in mind. Working with visual representations of ideas helps keep everyone on the same

(continued)

(continued)

mental page; it also encourages group, rather than individual, ownership of ideas. Recording ideas will help your group stay organized and on task.

3. *Be Prepared to Shift Gears as Work Progresses.* As a group moves from exploring ideas to planning and drafting, its understanding of the assignment and of the best ways to fulfill it may well change. Your group might begin a project assuming that you will present a strong argument for or against a specific issue, for instance, only to discover through reading and discussion that your arguments are in fact more complex. Be prepared to recognize — and act on — such shifts in position.

DRAFTING

4. *Take Time to Nurture a Collective "Felt Sense" of Your Writing.* Writers composing alone are often able to draw on their "felt sense" to make decisions as they write. While working on an essay for a women's studies class, for instance, you may suddenly realize that your introduction is too formal and may "see" how a more personal introduction would work better. Collaborative writers need to nurture a collective "felt sense." There are several strategies your group can use to do so. You might begin some of your group meetings, for instance, by having each member freewrite for five minutes in response to questions such as these: What are we trying to achieve in this essay or report? What is working well in our current draft? What seems rough or awkward? Or you might each respond in writing to the "Guidelines for Analyzing Your Rhetorical Situation" on pp. 160–61. Discussing group members' responses should enable you to articulate — and, if necessary, negotiate — a collective "felt sense" of your evolving text.

As your writing develops, you may occasionally find it useful to have one group member read the text aloud while others listen and make notes. The person reading should read the entire text without stopping; others should take notes quietly. Each group member should read his or her comments before you begin a general discussion of your responses. This activity can help you develop a holistic grasp of your text as it evolves and can generate responses you can use as you write and revise.

(continued)

(continued)

5. *Avoid a "Cut-and-Paste" Approach to Drafting.* Collaborative writers often find it efficient to take responsibility for drafting different sections of the text. This approach can work well — as long as you avoid a cut-and-paste approach to drafting. Such an approach assumes that once you have developed an outline or organization for your writing, individual members will work only on those portions of the text for which they are responsible. This approach has several negative consequences. For one thing, a cut-and-paste approach to drafting makes it difficult for group members to develop any felt sense about their work. Also, group members may develop such strong individual ownership of their writing that they resist changes to their drafts. Cut-and-paste approaches to drafting also make it difficult for group members to notice redundant sections.

   Even if group members initially assume responsibility for different sections of the text, you should begin exchanging and revising one another's drafts as soon as possible. (Be sure to keep a clear paper trail of all changes made, in case you ever wish to return to an earlier version.) The exchange of drafts will encourage group ownership of the text and make the process of developing a coherent and unified style much easier. It will also give you a head start on revising the final draft of your essay or report.

REVISING

6. *Maximize Your Group's Resources by Drawing on a Variety of Revision Strategies.* Collaborative revision presents a number of advantages over solitary revision. A group can draw on members' diverse perspectives to develop a richer, more detailed vision of its text's strengths and weaknesses. When your group meets to discuss alternative ways of organizing your essay, for instance, you can consider more options — and evaluate them more fully — than when you write alone. Group members can also function as a sample audience and as a peer response and support group. And once you articulate a shared understanding of the changes that need to be made, you can distribute tasks according to individuals' strengths and interests. One group member might agree to revise your essay's transitions so that they are more consistent and fluid, for example, while another rewrites the conclusion,

(continued)

(continued)

and a third checks all references to be sure they are accurate and in the correct form.

As your group revises its text, choose strategies appropriate for your situation and purpose. In some instances, it may be most efficient for members to trade drafts and revise one another's writing. At other times you may choose to work together in group revision sessions. To do so, have one group member function as recorder while others suggest changes. As your deadline nears, one or two members may take responsibility for a final revision to ensure consistency of style and tone. There is no one-size-fits-all way to approach the task of collaborative revision. Instead, your group should use strategies that are appropriate for your particular situation and purpose.

7. *Establish Explicit Goals for All Revision Sessions.* Whenever your group engages in revision activities, you should articulate specific, concrete goals; doing so will help keep you on track and enable you to make the best use of your time. If you agree to exchange rough drafts, for instance, you should decide whether members will simply comment on or actually revise one another's writing. Similarly, if you are engaged in a group revision session, you should begin by determining the issues you will focus on. As when you write alone, it is generally more efficient to consider global issues involving organization, focus, and content before spending time on such local concerns as sentence structure or word choice. Whether you are evaluating your current draft's organization or looking at the stylistic effectiveness of your essay's introduction, establishing clear goals will ensure a productive work session rather than an unfocused and frustrating free-for-all.

USING ELECTRONIC TECHNOLOGIES TO FACILITATE YOUR COLLABORATIVE EFFORT

Electronic technologies can help make collaborative writing more efficient and productive. Email, for instance, can enable members of your group to stay in touch between meetings, while networked computers can simplify drafting and revising. The following guidelines suggest ways your group can make the best use of the electronic technologies that are available to you.

■ GUIDELINES FOR USING ELECTRONIC TECHNOLOGIES IN COLLABORATIVE WRITING

1. *At Your First Meeting, Identify Group Members' Computer and On-line Skills — and Also the Hardware and Software You Will Use.* Depending on your personal situations and the resources of your college or university, members of your group may have excellent — or quite limited — access to electronic technologies. During your first meeting, take an inventory of your skills and resources. How many group members own computers or have convenient access to them? Do you all have email accounts? Do you have access to networked computers and to software programs that enable you to generate, revise, and edit text together? If you do not, what electronic resources will you use to share texts? (Will you share computer disks, for instance, or email texts to each other as attachments? If you plan to use attachments and you are not using the same server and email program, are you sure that attachments will be readable?)

2. *Agree at the Start on the Electronic Technologies That You Will Use and on the Ways That You Will Use Them. If Students in Your Group Vary in Their Computer Skills, Tutor Students Who Need to Learn Essential Procedures.* Electronic technologies can expedite your collaborative writing — but only if you take the time necessary to make sure that all members know how to carry out critical procedures. If one group member uses a particular program to produce or edit graphics to be used in the project and another does not have access to such software, problems can and probably will ensue. So first make certain basic decisions: What hardware and software will you use? Will your group set up an email list to facilitate communication? What common word processing features (such as the SAVE AS feature, which allows files to be saved in different versions and formats) should everyone use?

   All group members need to be able to use the electronic technologies and software programs that best support the project, so you may need to tutor those who need help coming up to speed.

3. *Take the Time to Make Basic Decisions about Document Format and Design.* When you're starting a collaborative project, margin size, font style, and font size can seem like low-priority issues for group discussion. But as group members begin exchanging drafts — and certainly when you begin working toward a final draft — you will be grateful that you made these decisions early on. For more information on document design, see Chapter 10.

(continued)

(continued)

4. *Recognize That Electronic Technologies May Require the Development of New Roles and Processes.* If your group is using email extensively, ask one person to serve as the team archivist. Everyone should save important messages, but someone should chronologically organize print and electronic copies of all communications. Group members may also want to take turns summarizing email discussions. After a series of messages on some issue, a summarizer might post a message along these lines: "We discussed the question of whether we should do X or Y. Susan and Jed argued that we should do X. Jason and Andrea recommended Y instead. The consensus seems to be leaning toward Susan and Jed's position, though I think that there might be a possible compromise." Taking time to summarize emails is important because a flurry of email can build up quickly and obscure the major point at issue.

   Similar issues can arise when a number of individuals share word processing responsibilities. As you move toward the final stages of your writing process, it becomes harder to keep track of the various drafts. For this reason, your group should agree to name files consistently. It should also appoint one member to keep track of file exchanges.

5. *Particularly Where Emails Are Involved, Remember to Practice Good "Netiquette."* This issue is discussed fully in Chapter 7, "Negotiating Online Writing Situations," so this guideline serves primarily as a reminder of that discussion. Doing something as simple as writing a subject heading that accurately reflects the content of your email can facilitate communications among group members.

6. *Anticipate — and Prepare for — Possible Electronic Failures and Glitches.* Technology, being a human invention, can and all too frequently does, fail. You will encounter power outages, difficulties getting online from a computer at home, accidental deletions of material, corrupted disks, and other problems. Given this fact, your group should plan ahead. Some of this planning represents little more than common sense: Back up copies in more than one location, save files often, and print hard copies of important communications and texts. But your group should also try to anticipate problems that are related to the technologies you are using and establish backup procedures in case the worst happens. If email is central to your collaborative process, for instance, you will want to share phone numbers as well as email addresses in case a server should experience major problems.

Successful collaborative writing, like writing in general, depends on neither luck nor magic. Just as individual writers can learn more efficient, productive, and satisfying ways of managing the writing process, so too can those working on group projects learn how to work — and write — together effectively.

■ ■ ■

FOR THOUGHT, DISCUSSION, AND WRITING

1. To learn more about your group's interactions, tape record a typical meeting. After you have done so, each group member should listen to the tape and respond in writing to the following questions:

   ■ How would you describe your group's interactions? Who spoke most often? Least often? Did gender differences appear in communication patterns (with men speaking more forcefully or frequently, for instance)? Were there cultural differences? What additional observations can you make about the group's conversational patterns and problem-solving strategies?

   ■ What behaviors seemed to be most productive for your group? Least productive? Why?

   ■ What one or two changes in conversational patterns or problem-solving strategies might improve your group's productiveness?

   ■ What most surprised you about your own contributions to the group?

   ■ What one or two changes in your own behavior might improve your group's performance?

   After you've all listened to the tape and responded to these questions, meet to discuss the group's responses. Be sure to focus your discussion on ways that the group could improve its interactions, and not on the strengths or weaknesses of specific group members.

2. While working on a collaborative writing project for your composition class — or for another class — keep detailed notes about your experiences. Drawing on these notes and on your analysis of a tape recorded group meeting (as described in the previous activity), write an essay that reflects what you have learned about yourself (as a writer and group participant) as a result of your collaborative experience.

ANALYZING AND WRITING ACADEMIC ARGUMENTS

PART FOUR

Understanding Academic Audiences and Assignments

A rhetorical approach to writing looks at the various contexts in which you write. As Part Two of this book emphasizes, even if you are writing alone at your computer, you are writing for a specific rhetorical situation. By analyzing that purpose, you can identify your situation as writer, choose a persona or "voice," and create a relationship with readers. You also can understand and implement the textual conventions that are appropriate for your writing.

Gaining an understanding of context is particularly important when you enter a new community of writers and readers. As a student entering the academic community, you need to develop an insider's understanding of the conventions that characterize academic writing. Some of these conventions are general and apply across the disciplines. Whatever their discipline, for instance, college teachers require students to earn the conclusions that they express in writing. Conclusions must reflect an open, unbiased intellectual engagement with the subject under consideration — whether that subject is a Renaissance painting by Leonardo da Vinci or a particular kind of fungus. Moreover, the logic behind these conclusions and the evidence for them must be provided in the writing so that readers can understand (and possibly question) the writer's assumptions and conclusions.

In an important sense, then, college instructors believe that all academic writing involves argument. But the specific model of argument that they have in mind is not about winning or losing a debate; it involves using evidence and reasoning to discover a version of truth about a particular subject. I use the words "a version" here to emphasize that the truth is always in process in academic writing and is always open to further discussion. A political scientist or economist who makes a convincing argument about federal policy on harvesting timber in national forests knows that others will add to, challenge, or refine that argument. In fact, having others respond to an observation is a sign that the writing has successfully raised questions that others consider important. In this sense, the scholarly work of the academy is like a conversation rather than a debate.

Part Four of *Work in Progress* will introduce you to the scholarly conversation of the academy and to the skills that you need to write the essays and reports that will earn approval from your instructors. This chapter describes the values and expectations of academic readers and shows you, as a writer, how to analyze academic writing assignments. Chapters 15 and 16 focus on two important skills required in all academic writing: analysis and argument. And Chapter 17 takes you through the process (via successive drafts of a student's essay) of writing and revising effective academic arguments. It concludes with a miscellany of examples of successful student academic writing.

UNDERSTANDING YOUR AUDIENCE: STUDENTS WRITING, INSTRUCTORS READING

Because your instructors are the primary readers of the writing you do in college, you need to understand their values and their goals for you and other students. As I have already indicated, your instructors share a commitment to the ideal of education as inquiry. Whether they teach in business, liberal arts, agriculture, engineering, or other fields, your instructors want to foster your ability to think, write, and speak well. When they read your papers and exams, your instructors are looking for both your knowledge of a specific subject and your ability to think and write clearly and effectively.

But your instructors will not necessarily bring identical expectations to your writing. Methods of inquiry and research questions vary from discipline to discipline, and textual conventions reflect these differing assumptions and practices. A lab report written for your chemistry class will use different kinds of evidence and be organized differently than an essay written for an American literature class. Stylistic expectations also vary among different disciplines. Passive voice (as in "It was discovered . . . ") is more commonly used in the sciences than in the humanities, for instance.

Despite these disciplinary differences, those who teach in colleges and universities generally agree that educated, thoughtful, and knowledgeable college graduates share certain characteristics. They believe, for instance, that perhaps the worst intellectual error is oversimplifying. They want their students to go beyond simplistic analysis and arguments to deeper and more complex understandings. Thus a historian might urge students to recognize that more was at stake in the American Civil War than freeing the slaves, and an engineer might encourage students to realize that the most obvious way to resolve a design problem is not necessarily the best.

Most college instructors want their students to be able to do more than memorize or summarize information. Indeed, they strive to develop students' abilities to analyze, apply, question, and evaluate information. They also want students to be able to consider issues from multiple perspectives, to recognize that nearly every issue has at least two sides. Because most intellectual issues are complex, instructors often teach students to limit the issue, question, or problem under discussion. They also believe that arguments should be supported by substantial and appropriate evidence, not emotional appeals or logical fallacies. Various disciplines accept different kinds of evidence and follow different methodologies to ensure that conclusions are as meaningful as possible. But all share the conviction that people who are arguing a point should support their assertions with more than just "in my opinion."

Such logical habits of mind are intrinsically rewarding. The knowledge that you can analyze a complex issue or problem, work through an argument, and develop your own position on a subject brings intellectual satisfaction and confidence. These same habits of thinking also bring extrinsic rewards, for as executives in business and industry emphasize, they are precisely the habits of mind that lead to success in positions of responsibility in any field. And they also enable you to participate effectively as a citizen of the world.

NOTE FOR MULTILINGUAL WRITERS

Whatever their home culture or community, all teachers value intellectual inquiry—but they all don't express this intellectual commitment in the same way. As a multilingual writer, you may at times feel uncomfortable with or not understand the expectations of North American educators. You may be used to different kinds of oral and written exchanges both in and out of class, for instance, or you may be unsure about the criteria that your teachers use to evaluate your writing. When you move among cultures and communities, such moments of difficulty are perhaps inevitable. You can make these moments productive, rather than disabling, by talking with your teachers about their expectations and by reflecting on differences between your prior and current educational experiences. You may also find it helpful to talk with classmates about these and related issues. Doing so will help you better understand the expectations of North American educators and also enrich the understanding of the students with whom you talk.

FOR EXPLORATION

Freewrite for five or ten minutes about your experiences as an academic writer. What has frustrated or confused you? What has excited you? What questions do you have about the academic rhetorical situation and the conventions of academic writing? If you are a multilingual writer, you might find it helpful to consider the expectations that you brought to academic writing in North America and your experiences thus far.

What do instructors look for when they read students' writing? Most broadly, your instructors want writing that demonstrates learning and a real commitment to and engagement with the subject being discussed. In many instances, particularly in the humanities, they want writing that reveals that you are making connections between the issues discussed in class and your life and personal values. And they always want writing that adheres to academic standards of clear thinking and effective communication. Specifically, most instructors hope to find the following characteristics in student writing:

- A limited but significant topic

- A meaningful context for discussion of the topic

- A sustained and full discussion, given the limitations of the topic, time, and length

- A clear pattern of organization

- Fair and effective use of sources (both print and online)

- Adequate detail and evidence as support for generalizations

- Appropriate, concise language

- Conventional grammar, punctuation, and usage

The following essay, written by Hope Leman for a class on politics and the media, meets these criteria. This essay was written in response to the following assignment for a take-home midterm exam:

> Journalists often suggest that they simply mirror reality. Some political scientists argue, however, that rather than mirroring reality journalists make judgments that subtly but significantly shape their resulting news reports. In so doing, scholars argue, journalists function more like flashlights than like mirrors.
>
> Write an essay in which you contrast the "mirror" and "flashlight" models of the role of journalists in American society. Successful essays will not only compare these two models but will also provide examples supporting their claims.

Since Hope was writing a take-home midterm essay, she did not have time to do a formal written analysis of her rhetorical situation. Still, her essay demonstrates considerable rhetorical sensitivity. Hope understands, for instance, that given her situation she should emphasize content rather than employ a dramatic or highly personal style. Hope's essay is, above all, clearly written. Even though it has moments of quiet humor (as when she comments on funhouses at the end of the second paragraph), the focus is on articulating the reasons why the "flashlight" model of media theory is the most valid and helpful for political scientists. Hope knows that her teacher will be reading a stack of midterms under time pressure, so she makes sure that her own writing is carefully organized and to the point. Here is Hope's essay.

THE ROLE OF JOURNALISTS IN AMERICAN SOCIETY: A COMPARISON OF THE "MIRROR" AND "FLASHLIGHT" MODELS
by Hope Leman

The "mirror" model of media theory holds that through their writing and news broadcasts journalists are an objective source of information for the public. This model assumes that journalists are free of bias and can be relied on to provide accurate information about the true state of affairs in the world. Advocates of the "flashlight" model disagree, believing that a journalist is like a person in a dark room holding a flashlight. The light from the flashlight falls briefly on various objects in the room, revealing part — but not all — of the room at any one time. This model assumes that journalists cannot possibly provide an objective view of reality but, at best, can convey only a partial understanding of a situation or event.

In this essay, I will argue that the "flashlight" model provides a more accurate and complex understanding of the role of journalists in America than the "mirror" model does. This model recognizes, for instance, that journalists are shaped by their personal backgrounds and experiences and by the pressures, mores, and customs of their profession. It also recognizes that journalists are under commercial pressure to sell their stories. News-papers and commercial networks are run on a for-profit basis. Thus, reporters have to "sell" their stories to readers. The easiest way to do that is to fit a given news event into a "story" framework. Human beings gener-ally relate well to easily digestible stories, as opposed to more complex analyses, which require more thought and concentration. Thus, reporters assigned to cover a given situation are likely to ask "What is the story?" and then to force events into that framework. Reality is seldom as neat as a story, however, and life does not always fall into neat compartments of "Once upon a time . . . " "and then . . . " and "The End." But the story framework dominates news coverage of events; thus, the media cannot function as a mirror since mirrors reflect rather than distort reality (except in funhouses).

The "mirror" model also fails to acknowledge that journalists make choices, including decisions about what stories to cover. These choices can be based on personal preference, but usually they are determined by editors, who respond to publishers, who, in turn, are eager to sell their product to the widest possible audiences. Most people tend not to like to read about seemingly insoluble social problems like poverty or homelessness. Thus journalists often choose not to cover social issues unless they fit a particular "story" format.

In addition to deciding what to cover, journalists must also determine the tone they will take in their reporting. If the "mirror" model of media theory were accurate, journalists wouldn't make implicit or explicit judgments in their reporting. But they do. They are only human, after all, and they will inevitably be influenced by their admiration or dislike for a person about whom they are writing, or by their belief about the significance of an event.

From start to finish, journalists must make a series of choices. They first make choices about what to cover; then they make choices about whether their tone will be positive or negative, which facts to include and which to omit, what adjectives to use, etc. Mirrors do not make choices — but a person holding a flashlight does. The latter can decide where to let the light drop, how long to leave it on that spot, and when to shift the light to something else. Journalists make these kinds of choices every day. Consequently, the "flashlight" model provides the more accurate understanding of the role that journalists play in American society, for the "mirror" model fails to take into account the many factors shaping even the simplest news story.

■ ■ ■

FOR COLLABORATION

Working with a group of classmates, respond to these questions about Hope Leman's essay. Appoint a recorder to write down the results of your discussion, which your instructor may ask you to present to the class.

1. Hope begins her essay not by attempting to interest readers in her subject but by defining the "mirror" and "flashlight" models of media theory. In a different context, Hope's introduction might seem abrupt. Given that Hope is responding to a midterm question and is writing under time pressure, why is this an effective way to begin her essay?

2. As Chapter 9 on planning and drafting explains, writers need to have a controlling purpose when they write. Sometimes they signal this purpose to readers by articulating an explicit thesis statement. Sometimes only subtle cues are necessary. In her essay, Hope includes an explicit thesis statement. Identify this statement, and then discuss the reasons that it is necessary in her particular situation.

3. In distinguishing between satisfactory and excellent responses to a question, instructors look for signs that a student has truly grasped the question and its implications. A satisfactory response provides the basic information necessary to address the question. An excellent response in some way reflects on or gives insight into the question itself. Hope Leman's instructors — and most academic readers of student writing — would characterize Hope's essay as excellent. What evidence for this assessment can you point to in her essay?

4. Academic writing is sometimes viewed as dull and lifeless — as, well, academic. And yet even in this essay written under time pressure Hope Leman's writing is not stuffy, dull, or pompous. Examine Hope's essay to identify passages where a personal voice contributes to the overall effectiveness of her essay. How does Hope blend this personal voice with the objective and distanced approach of this essay?

ANALYZING ACADEMIC WRITING ASSIGNMENTS

Understanding the values and goals of the academic community helps you to respond appropriately to the demands of academic writing. In addition, you must know how to analyze academic assignments because assignments (whether presented orally or in writing) provide concrete indications of instructors' expectations. You can improve your understanding of your academic assignments by analyzing each assignment, identifying its assumptions, and developing strategies to increase your commitment to it.

Analyzing an Assignment

All assignments are not alike. Some present broad, unstructured topics. A political science instructor might ask you to write a ten-page research paper discussing an important political consequence of the war in Iraq. Or a psychology instructor might ask you to write a four- to six-page essay exploring how your family background has influenced your attitudes about marriage or parenthood. Broad assignments like these call on you to choose a specific topic and to select an approach to analyzing and presenting your material.

In other instances, instructors offer quite specific assignments. Such assignments may substantially restrict your choice of a topic, and they may include a format or sequence of steps or activities that you must follow. Other assignments may fall halfway between these two extremes.

Whether instructors give broad or limited assignments, the words they use to describe these assignments, especially certain key words, can tell you a great deal about their expectations. These key words — *define, analyze, evaluate, defend, show, describe, review, prove, summarize, classify* — are crucial. An assignment that asks you to *summarize* Freud's Oedipal theory, for instance, is quite different from one that asks you to *criticize* or *evaluate* it. To summarize Freud's Oedipal theory, you need to recount its major features. Criticizing this theory challenges you to identify its strengths and weaknesses and to provide evidence for your assessment.

Identifying the Assumptions behind an Assignment

To complete an assignment effectively, you need to know more than whether it is broad or limited. You need to know the criteria your instructor will use to evaluate the assignment and the processes and resources that you can best use as you work on it. Some instructors provide information about these and related matters. If your instructor provides such suggestions, study them with care. If you don't understand how to act on your instructor's suggestions, make an appointment to speak with him or her. Discussing your assignment with other students in your class is another helpful way to test your understanding.

Not all instructors provide this kind of information about assignments, however. They may think that the criteria for evaluation and the processes and resources that students might best use to complete an assignment are so obvious that they need not be stated explicitly, or they may believe that students learn more effectively when they take full responsibility for all aspects of an assignment. For this reason, these instructors want students to discover for themselves how they can best work on an assignment and the features that characterize a successful response to an assignment.

You need to "read between the lines" of any assignment, for even detailed suggestions cannot tell you exactly what processes and resources you should use. One way to read between the lines is by thinking about the ways that your assignment relates to the objectives, class discussions, and readings for a course. Your instructor may not comment specifically on this connection, but you can be sure that one exists. Considering the questions in the following guidelines should help you recognize such connections and analyze the assumptions inherent in an assignment.

■ GUIDELINES FOR ANALYZING
   AN ASSIGNMENT

1. How does this assignment reflect the objectives of this course?

2. What general analytical and argumentative strategies does the instructor emphasize during class discussions? In discussions of

(continued)

(continued)

readings, what organizational, stylistic, and logical qualities does the instructor praise or criticize? How might this assignment represent the instructor's effort to help students develop the critical abilities that he or she emphasizes in class?

3. How much class time has the instructor spent on discussions of readings or on activities related to the content or form of this assignment? What has the instructor emphasized in these discussions or activities? How do these discussions and activities relate to this specific assignment?

4. Does this assignment call for a specific type of writing? How can you use your experience with previous writing assignments to help you complete this assignment?

5. To what extent does this assignment require you to follow the methodology and format characteristic of this discipline?

6. If this is one of several assignments for this course, can you apply comments the instructor has made about earlier essays to this current project?

Building Commitment to an Assignment

Most academic writing is, by definition, *required* writing — writing done to fulfill a requirement. As a student, you often find yourself writing not necessarily because you want to but because you have to. These conditions may make it hard for you to feel a strong sense of "ownership" of your writing. Furthermore, even if you're genuinely interested in your topic, you may feel so pressed by deadlines and other demands that all you can think is "I've just got to get this essay out of the way so I can get ready for biology lab." All writers face these problems.

Successful writers know, however, that they can't write well without being interested in and committed to their subjects. Consequently, they develop strategies to help them build this interest and commitment so that they can transform a required assignment (whether a research paper or a report for the boss) into a question or problem they care about and feel challenged to resolve. This is not to suggest that you must become passionately excited by every writing assignment. That would be unrealistic. But if you can't find some way to interest yourself in an assignment, to view it as an intellectual challenge you want to meet, you're going to have trouble getting beyond stale formulas.

Several strategies can help you build commitment to an assignment. You can, for instance, build your interest by using invention strategies, such as freewriting, looping, brainstorming, and clustering or the more formal journalist's questions and topical questions (see Chapter 8 for discussions of all these strategies). Keeping a writer's notebook may also help you generate interest in a topic that at first doesn't seem compelling. Suppose, for example, that your economics instructor has asked you to write an essay about the Great Depression. At first you might not find this subject interesting. After all, the Depression occurred decades ago. You'd rather evaluate some current economic policies. But after brainstorming, freewriting, or writing in your journal, you find that you keep coming back to a single image: the much-reproduced photograph of a businessman in a topcoat selling apples on a street corner. Did this actually happen? How often? How representative is this image of the Depression as a whole? Suddenly you've got a series of related questions — questions that you care about and that can help you limit and focus your topic.

When you build commitment to an assignment, you find reasons to want to write, reasons to "own" the assignment. The following guidelines can enable you to turn a required assignment into an interesting challenge that you want to complete.

■ GUIDELINES FOR GAINING COMMITMENT TO AN ASSIGNMENT

1. *Use Freewriting, Brainstorming, Journal Writing, or Other Informal Kinds of Writing to Explore What You Already Know about Your Assignment.* Freewriting and brainstorming can help you discover images, questions, contradictions, and problems that turn required assignments into questions you want to answer. You may also find it helpful simply to write or list what you already know about a subject. After doing so, you may be reassured to discover that you have a surprisingly large fund of information on your subject.

2. *Use the Same Strategies to Explore Your Feelings about an Assignment.* You may find it helpful to freewrite or brainstorm about your feelings concerning an assignment. While writing in her journal about a required assignment in a journalism class, for instance, Holly Hardin noted that she didn't want to work on a story about whether quarters or semesters are more conducive to learning because it was "just another dead issue." Once she understood the source of her resistance, Holly realized that she should see if her assumption was in fact correct. After interviewing several faculty members on campus, Holly discovered to her surprise that they held widely varying views on this subject. "Once I found a point of conflict," Holly wrote in a later journal entry, "I found a reason to write. From that point on, the story was not just easy to work on but interesting."

3. *Work Collaboratively with Other Students in the Class.* Any assignment can seem overwhelming — something to put off rather than to begin — when you're sitting alone in your room or the library thinking about it. A more productive strategy is to discuss the assignment, your approaches, and your available resources with other students in the class. I'm not talking about a gripe session or *only* a gripe session. You may want to spend a few moments commiserating with one another about how busy you are and how many assignments you need to do, but you should keep your primary goal in focus. By talking about your assignment and about your efforts to respond to it, you want to generate enthusiasm for this project and to help each other complete it more effectively.

(continued)

(continued)

> If you are enrolled in a course that you find difficult, you may wish to form a study group that meets on a regular basis. Simply meeting together with other students can provide discipline and intellectual and emotional reinforcement that you can use to your advantage. Your discussions and responses to works in progress can also help stimulate both your interest in the subject and your ability to respond successfully to assignments.

FOR EXPLORATION

Think back to an academic writing experience that was difficult or frustrating for you. To what extent did this problem result from your inability to build a genuine commitment to the assignment? How might you have responded more effectively to this problem? Freewrite for five or ten minutes about this experience.

FOR THOUGHT, DISCUSSION, AND WRITING

1. Interview an instructor who teaches a class you are taking this term or a class in your major area of study. Ask this person to describe his or her understanding of the goals of undergraduate education and the role that your particular class or field of study plays in achieving these goals. Discuss the special analytic and argumentative skills required to succeed in this course or field. Ask this person what advice he or she would give to someone, like yourself, who is taking a class in this field or planning to major in it. Be prepared to report the results of this interview to your group so that the group can present its collective findings to the class. Your instructor also may ask you to write an essay summarizing and commenting on the results of your interview.

2. Using the suggestions in this chapter, analyze a writing assignment that you are currently working on. Begin by analyzing the assignment as it is presented by your instructor. Then look for the assumptions behind the assignment, and develop strategies to help you build commitment to the assignment. Once you complete the assignment, try to determine if the analysis made your work easier or more productive. Would you follow this process again?

3. Take a few moments to think about your experiences with academic writing in college. Have certain kinds of writing assignments been

easy to complete successfully? Have any been difficult? Freewrite for five minutes in response to these questions. Then locate two assignments that you completed either for your composition class or for other courses. If possible, locate one assignment that your instructor evaluated as successful and another that your instructor was less satisfied with. After rereading the assignments and resulting essays, review the discussion of academic audiences and assignments in this chapter. Does the discussion help you better understand why your instructors evaluated your writing as they did? Freewrite for five minutes in response to this question.

Understanding
Academic Analysis

A s a student, you must respond to a wide range of writing assignments. For your American literature class, you may have to write an essay analyzing the significance of the whiteness of the whale in *Moby Dick*, whereas your business management class may require a collaboratively written case study. You may need to write a lab report for your chemistry class and to critique a reading for sociology.

Although these assignments vary considerably, a close look reveals that they all draw on two related skills: analysis and argument. This chapter will help you strengthen the first of these two important academic skills — analysis.

UNDERSTANDING HOW ANALYSIS WORKS

Analysis is the activity of separating something into parts and determining how these parts function to create the whole. When you analyze, you examine a text, an object, or a body of data to understand how it is structured or organized and to assess its effectiveness or validity. Most academic writing, thinking, and reading involve analysis. Literature students analyze how a play is structured or how a poem achieves its effect; economics students analyze the major causes of inflation; biology students analyze the enzymatic reactions that comprise the Krebs cycle; and art history students analyze how line, color, and texture come together in a painting.

As these examples indicate, analysis is not a single skill but a group of related skills. An art history student might explore how a famous painting by Michelangelo achieves its effect, for instance, by *comparing* it with a similar work by Raphael. A biology student might discuss future acid-rain damage to forests in Canada and the United States by first *defining* acid rain and then using *cause-and-effect* reasoning to predict worsening conditions. A student in economics might estimate the likelihood of severe inflation in the future by *categorizing* or *classifying* the major causes of previous inflationary periods and then *evaluating* the likelihood of such factors influencing the current economic situation.

Different disciplines naturally emphasize different analytic skills. But whether you are a history, biology, or business major, you need to understand and practice these crucial academic skills. You will do so most successfully if you establish a purpose and develop an appropriate framework or method for your analysis.

Establishing a Purpose for Your Analysis

Your instructors will often ask you to analyze a fairly limited subject, problem, or process: Mrs. Ramsey's role in Virginia Woolf's *To the Lighthouse,* feminists' criticisms of Freud's psychoanalytical theories, Mendel's third law of genetics. Such limited tasks are necessary because of the complexity of the material being analyzed. Whole books have been written on Woolf's masterpiece and Freud's theories, so you can hardly examine these subjects completely in a brief essay or a research paper. But though you are analyzing a limited topic, the purpose of your analysis is broad: to better understand the material examined. When you analyze a limited topic, you are like a person holding a flashlight in the dark: The beam of light that you project is narrow and focused and illuminates a much larger area.

Recognizing this larger purpose of analysis can help you make important decisions as you plan, draft, and revise. If your instructor has assigned a limited topic, for instance, you should ask yourself why he or she might have chosen this particular topic. What might make it an especially good means of understanding the larger issues at hand? If you are free to choose your own topic for analysis, your first questions should involve its larger significance. How will analyzing this topic improve your understanding of the larger subject? As you write, ask yourself regularly if your analysis is leading you to understand your topic more deeply. If you can answer yes to this question, you are probably doing a good job of analysis.

Even though the general purpose of your analysis is to understand the larger subject, you still need to establish a more specific purpose for your writing. Imagine, for instance, that your Shakespeare instructor has asked you to write an essay on the fool in *King Lear.* You might establish one of several specific purposes for your analysis:

To explain how the fool contributes to the development of a major theme in *King Lear*

To discuss the effectiveness or plausibility of Shakespeare's characterization of the fool

To define the role the fool plays in the plot

To agree or disagree with a particular critical perspective on the fool's role and significance

Establishing a specific purpose for your analysis helps you define how your analysis should proceed. It enables you to determine the important issues you should address or the questions you should answer.

There are no one-size-fits-all procedures you can follow to establish a purpose for your analysis. Sometimes your purpose will develop naturally as a result of reading, reflection, and discussion with others. In other instances, it may help to draw on the invention strategies described in Chapter 8; freewriting, brainstorming, and the topical questions can help you explore your subject and discover questions that can guide your analysis. You may need to write your way into an understanding of your purpose by composing a rough draft of your essay and seeing, in effect, what you think about your topic. Writing and thinking are dynamically interwoven processes.

Developing an Appropriate Method for Your Analysis

Once you have a purpose, how do you actually analyze something? The answer depends on the subject, process, or problem being analyzed; it also depends, in academic writing, on the discipline within which the analysis is done. The students studying *To the Lighthouse* and Mendel's third law may both use such analytic processes as definition, causal analysis, classification, and comparison to analyze their subjects. But the exact form of the processes that each uses — the way each organizes the analysis and the criteria each uses to evaluate it — may well differ. Despite these disciplinary differences, both students must establish some method for analysis if they are to succeed.

There are no hard-and-fast rules for establishing such a method. In general, however, you should look to the methods of inquiry characteristic of the specific discipline for guidance. The questions presented in the following guidelines can help you develop an appropriate method for your analysis.

■ GUIDELINES FOR DEVELOPING AN APPROPRIATE METHOD FOR ANALYSIS

- How have your instructors approached analysis in class? Do they rely on a systematic procedure, such as case-study or problem-solving methodology, or does their analysis vary, depending on the subject under discussion?

- What kinds of evidence and examples do they draw on?

(continued)

(continued)

- What kinds of questions do your instructors typically ask in class discussions? Why might people in the discipline view these as important questions?

- What kinds of answers to these questions do your instructors favor? Why might people in this discipline value such responses?

If, after considering these questions and reflecting on your experiences in a class, you continue to have difficulty settling on an appropriate method for analysis, meet with your instructor to get help. You might ask him or her to recommend student essays or articles from the field that you can read. Analyzing these texts can help you understand the analytical methods used in the field.

UNDERSTANDING THE RELATIONSHIP BETWEEN ANALYSIS AND ARGUMENT

As I mentioned at the start of Chapter 14, all academic writing has an argumentative edge. Sometimes that edge is obvious. If a student writes a political science essay arguing that the government should follow a particular environmental policy, that student is explicitly arguing that the government should do something. Essays that are organized around the question of whether something should or should not be done are easily recognizable as arguments — probably because they follow the debate format that many associate with argumentation.

But writers can express judgments — can present good reasons for their beliefs and actions — in other ways. A student analyzing the score of a Beethoven sonata for a music theory class may argue that it should be performed in a certain way but also may try to convince her reader, in this case her teacher, that she has a sophisticated understanding of the structure of the sonata she is studying. (She might do this by arguing that the second movement of the particular sonata is more daring or innovative than music historians have acknowledged.) Analysis will play a particularly central role in this student's writing: By identifying specific, concrete features of the score and positing relationships among these features, she will demonstrate her understanding of Beethoven's use of the sonata form.

As this example demonstrates, analysis and argument are mutually interdependent. Argumentation depends on analysis, for through analysis writers clarify the logic of their thinking and provide evidence for their judgments.

(The student arguing that the government should follow a particular environmental policy would certainly have to analyze the potential benefits and disadvantages of that policy and demonstrate that it is workable.) Similarly, analysis always carries an implicit argumentative burden. For when you analyze something, you are in effect asserting "This is how I believe X works" or "This is what I believe X means."

Academic analysis and argument call for similar habits of mind. Both encourage writers to suspend personal biases when they undertake academic inquiry. This is not to say that academic writers are expected to be absolutely objective. Your gut feeling that "workfare" programs may not provide single parents with adequate support for their children may cause you to investigate this topic for a political science or economics class. This gut feeling is a strength, not a weakness, for it enables you to find a topic of interest to you. Once you begin to explore your topic, however, you need to engage it dispassionately. You need, in other words, to be open to changing your mind.

If you do change your mind about the consequences of workfare programs for children, the reading and writing you have done probably have caused you to have a more detailed and specific understanding of the issues at stake in arguments over workfare programs. If the essay you write about this topic is successful, you will describe these issues and analyze their relationships and their implications. You will develop logical connections that make your reasoning — the logic behind your analysis — explicit. In these and other ways you are demonstrating to your readers that you have indeed understood your subject.

The following essay by Jacob Agatucci is a good example of academic analysis. In this essay, Jacob is not arguing that something should or should not be done. Rather, he is attempting to understand the roles that stage directions and cinematic technique play in helping contemporary audiences to better understand Shakespeare's plays. As a consequence, in his essay Jacob focuses on providing clear and specific examples and on analyzing the connections among and the implications of these examples.

DIALOGUE AS IMAGE IN *KING LEAR*
by Jacob Agatucci

What can theater and film directors do to help contemporary audiences appreciate the role of dialogue in Shakespeare's plays? What role can stage directions and cinematic technique play in helping audiences to understand the relationships among characters? These are important questions since contemporary audiences often find it difficult to follow the intricacies of Shakespearean dialogue. The language in which Shakespeare wrote is alien to many ears, and the lines are often delivered so quickly that the viewer finds it difficult to remember where a character stands in relation to other characters in a play. *King Lear* is a relevant example. Though the dialogue of the opening act defines the conflicts of the play — estranging loyal daughter from father and suggesting the deception of Goneril, Regan, and Edmund — important elements of this conflict could be lost to the untrained ear. The recent British Broadcasting Company (BBC) production of *King Lear* is a cinematic adaptation that honors Shakespeare's language and intentions but aids in its delivery through visual supplementation.

An example of this supplementation can be found during Act I, Scene 1. It occurs as King Lear derides Cordelia for not equaling her sisters' false expressions of love. The profiles of Lear and Cordelia, facing one another, fill the frame during the scene (see Fig. 1). Their faces are far enough apart to allow a space between them in which Kent is carefully framed — blurred and in the background. Thus the staging and cinematography, in addition to the dialogue, provide a visual representation of the disaffected parties (Lear and Cordelia) and the man (Kent) who seeks to alleviate their estrangement. This cinematic technique neatly encapsulates the relationship among these three characters and calls attention to an important feature of the plot.

Fig. 1 *King Lear:* Kent framed by Lear and Cordelia

A similar moment occurs when Scene 1 segues into Scene 2. Here, as in the earlier scene, essential characters in *King Lear* are brought together. In this case, however, it is the villains who are brought together. Here (see Fig. 2), the profiles of Regan and Goneril dominate the shot as they reflect on Lear's "long-ingraffed condition" (I. 1.330). Like Kent, Edmund is framed between them and in the background. Just as the former scene linked the protagonists of the play, this scene links its antagonists. This scene also emphasizes Edmund's role in the various deceptions that are central to the plot of *King Lear*. As Regan and Goneril end their exchange, they pull out of the frame to the left and right, and the camera focuses on Edmund, who is in the background (see Fig. 3). Since the next scene (Act I, Scene 2) begins with Edmund's soliloquy, Edmund's destructive ambition is visually linked with Goneril's and Regan's deceit.

Both of these scenes could easily have been shot with Kent and Edmund absent — but then viewers would have had to rely solely on dialogue to link characters and motives. Fortunately, the director chose to structure the play along visual as well as auditory lines. To do so, the director had to go beyond the stage directions included in *King Lear*, which revolve around entrances and exits, to consider the ways in which staging and cinematography could help clarify both the immediate dialogue and

Fig. 2 *King Lear:* **Edmund framed by Regan and Goneril**

Fig. 3 *King Lear:* **Edmund framed by Regan and Goneril**

future character relations. As a consequence, the BBC adaptation is especially sensitive to the needs of an audience that may not be familiar with Shakespearean dialogue.

Though Shakespeare's language is paramount within his plays, the BBC production of *King Lear* provides an innovative example of how the effective use of visual cues can supplement and clarify dialogue. Through both the physical placement of characters on the stage and careful cinematic technique, the BBC production uses visual cues to reinforce Shakespeare's dialogue. As a result, the experience of the audience is enriched, for they are left not simply with Shakespeare's words but with a synergistic combination of auditory and visual elements.

WORKS CITED

King Lear. Dir. Jonathan Miller. Prod. Shaun Sutton. Videocassette. BBC and Time-Life Films, 1987.

Shakespeare, William. *King Lear. The Complete Works of Shakespeare.* Ed. David Bevington. 4th ed. New York: Longman, 1997. 1167–1218.

■ ■ ■

FOR EXPLORATION

Reread Jacob Agatucci's essay, and then respond in writing to the following:

1. How would you describe the relationship between analysis and argument in Jacob's essay? To what extent does Jacob make a specific argument? What role does analysis play in the development of his ideas?

2. In academic writing, particular value is placed on explicitness and on developing logical connections among ideas. In what ways does Jacob's essay fulfill this expectation?

Analyzing Academic Arguments

Analysis plays a key role in all academic writing. It helps readers and writers to understand the world we live in and to recognize, examine, and formulate arguments about that world. As the discussion of visual texts in Chapter 3 demonstrates, analysis is not limited to written texts. Because we live in a media-saturated culture, we need to develop the ability to analyze visual texts—whether they are television ads or multimedia presentations on the Web. In colleges and universities in North America, however, the analysis of written texts is often particularly important.

The remainder of this chapter provides strategies that you can use to become a more sophisticated and critical reader of written texts. The key academic skill of analysis is central to literally all courses offered in the sciences, humanities, arts, and social sciences. It is also central to your effective participation in civic, cultural, political, and other affairs. Think of the debates that occurred throughout the world before the United States led a coalition of nations to war in Iraq on March 19, 2003. Some of the questions that were raised about this war were general: Should the United States and Great Britain attack Iraq? More often, however, the questions raised were more limited: Should United Nations approval be required for such an attack? What form should this approval take? Does a preemptive attack on Iraq meet the philosophical and religious criteria for a just war?

Arguments addressing these and related questions appeared in newspapers and magazines, on radio and television talk shows, and on the Internet in the days and months preceding the Iraq war. Writers developed complex arguments about the impending war that addressed a number of related issues. Someone arguing that a preemptive attack on Iraq does not meet the criteria for a just war, for instance, would have to examine various definitions of *just war* and present arguments about just war that have been developed in religion and philosophy.

An analysis of these and other arguments will feel less intimidating if you approach your evaluation of an argument by addressing three basic questions:

- What question is at issue?

- What position does the author take on this question?

- Do the author's reasons justify your acceptance of his or her argument?

By determining the question at issue, you get to the heart of any argument and distinguish major claims from minor elements of support. You can then identify the author's position on this question and evaluate whether he or she has provided good reasons for you to agree with this position.

■ ■ ■

FOR EXPLORATION

Take a few moments to freewrite about your previous experiences in analyzing academic arguments. Have you been more interested in analyzing some kinds of arguments than others? (You might enjoy analyzing political and historical texts, for instance, but find arguments in other areas less interesting.) Do these differences reflect personal preferences, cultural norms, or some other factors? What was your most positive experience with academic analysis, and what factors made it positive? What was your most negative experience with academic analysis, and what factors made it negative? What major questions and concerns do you have regarding the analysis of academic arguments?

Determining the Question at Issue: Lessons from Classical Rhetoric

When you determine the question at issue, you identify the main issue that is at stake in a particular argument. To argue that a preemptive war on Iraq meets the philosophical and religious criteria for a just war, for instance, you would have to *define* these criteria. To argue that the United States and its allies should have waited for a United Nations resolution before attacking Iraq, you would not be raising a question of definition but instead would be examining a question of *policy.*

Greek and Roman rhetoricians developed a method for determining the questions at issue in any particular argument. *Stasis theory* encourages readers to identify the major point on which a particular controversy rests. Since the classical period, scholars of rhetoric have presented a number of taxonomies for stasis theory. In this chapter, I employ the categories presented in John Gage's *The Shape of Reason.** Gage argues that six basic kinds of questions are at issue in argumentative writing:

■ *Questions of fact* arise from the reader's need to know "Does this [whatever it is] exist?"

■ *Questions of definition* arise from the reader's need to know "What is it?"

■ *Questions of interpretation* arise from the reader's need to know "What does it signify?"

■ *Questions of value* arise from the reader's need to know "Is it good?"

■ *Questions of consequence* arise from the reader's need to know "Will this cause that to happen?"

■ *Questions of policy* arise from the reader's need to know "What should be done about it?"

As Gage's categories suggest, when you attempt to determine the questions at issue in a particular argument, you draw on your rhetorical sensitivity (discussed in Chapter 5). You do so naturally in your everyday life. Imagine that a friend has urged you to drive with her to a concert that is being held in a city an hour from where you live—on a Tuesday night. Depending on your situation, the primary question at issue for you may be one of *value:* If, on the one hand, you value the concert enough, then you can justify the time, expense, and late-night bedtime that are involved in attending the concert. On the other hand, the primary question at issue for you may be one of *consequence:* If you first worry about the time involved in attending the concert, then you might not be able to justify the potentially negative consequences of taking time away from study, work, and family, especially on a weeknight.

Here is a brief argument by Amatai Etzioni about the advantages and disadvantages of traditional protections of privacy in North America; it is excerpted from his book *The Limits of Privacy* (1999). As you read Etzioni's analysis, consider which of the preceding six questions—fact, definition, interpretation, value, consequence, and policy—are most clearly at stake in his argument.

---

*John Gage, *The Shape of Reason: Argumentative Writing in College*, 3rd ed. (Needham Heights: Allyn and Bacon, 1991), 40.

LESS PRIVACY IS GOOD FOR US (AND YOU)*
Amitai Etzioni

Despite the fact that privacy is not so such as mentioned in the Constitution and that it was only shoehorned in some thirty-four years ago, it is viewed by most Americans as a profound, inalienable right.

The media is loaded with horror stories about the ways privacy is not so much nibbled away as it is stripped away by bosses who read your e-mail, neighbors who listen in on your cell phones, and E-Z passes that allow tollbooth operators to keep track of your movements. A typical headline decries the "End of Privacy" (Richard A. Spinello, in an issue of *America,* a Catholic weekly) or "The Death of Privacy" (Joshua Quittner, in *Time*).

It is time to pay attention to the other half of the equation that defines a good society: concerns for public health and safety that entail some rather justifiable diminution of privacy.

Take the HIV testing of infants. New medical data—for instance, evidence recently published by the prestigious *New England Journal of Medicine*—show that a significant proportion of children born to mothers who have HIV can ward off this horrible disease but only on two conditions: that their mothers not breast-feed them and that they immediately be given AZT. For this to happen, mothers must be informed that they have HIV. An estimated two-thirds of infected mothers are unaware. However, various civil libertarians and some gay activists vehemently oppose such disclosure on the grounds that when infants are tested for HIV, in effect one finds out if the mother is a carrier, and thus her privacy is violated. While New York State in 1996, after a very acrimonious debate, enacted a law that requires infant testing and disclosure of the findings to the mother, most other states have so far avoided dealing with this issue.

Congress passed the buck by asking the Institute of Medicine (IOM) to conduct a study of the matter. The IOM committee, dominated by politically correct people, just reported its recommendations. It suggested that all pregnant women be asked to consent to HIV testing as part of routine prenatal care. There is little wrong with such a recommendation other than it does not deal with many of the mothers who are drug addicts or otherwise live at society's margins. Many of these women do not show up

*Amitai Etzioni, *The Limits of Privacy* "Less Privacy Is Good for Us (and You)," *Current Issues and Enduring Questions,* ed. Sylvan Barnet and Hugo Bedau. Boston: Bedford/St. Martin's, 2002. 668–71. Amitai Etzioni is a professor at George Washington University and former senior adviser to the White House (1979–1980). Etzioni has written over a dozen books, including *The Limits of Privacy* (1999), from which this excerpt is taken.

for prenatal care, and they are particularly prone to HIV, according to a study published in the American Health Association's *Journal of School Health.* To save the lives of their children, they must be tested at delivery and treated even if this entails a violation of mothers' privacy.

Recently a suggestion to use driver's licenses to curb illegal immigration has sent the Coalition for Constitutional Liberties, a large group of libertarians, civil libertarians, and privacy advocates, into higher orbit than John Glenn ever traversed. The coalition wrote:

> This plan pushed us to the brink of tyranny, where citizens will not be allowed to travel, open bank accounts, obtain health care, get a job, or purchase firearms without first presenting the proper government papers.
>
> The authorizing section of the law . . . is reminiscent of the totalitarian dictates by Politburo members in the former Soviet Union, not the Congress of the United States of America.

Meanwhile, Wells Fargo is introducing a new device that allows a person to cash checks at its ATM machines because the machines recognize faces. Rapidly coming is a whole new industry of so-called biometrics that uses natural features such as voice, hand design, and eye pattern to recognize a person with the same extremely high reliability provided by the new DNA tests.

It's true that as biometrics catches on, it will practically strip Americans of anonymity, an important part of privacy. In the near future, a person who acquired a poor reputation in one part of the country will find it much more difficult to move to another part, change his name, and gain a whole fresh start. Biometrics see right through such assumed identities. One may hope that future communities will become more tolerant of such people, especially if they openly acknowledge the mistakes or their past and truly seek to lead a more prosocial life. But they will no longer be able to hide their pasts.

Above all, while biometrics clearly undermines privacy, the social benefits it promises are very substantial. Specifically, each year at least half a million criminals become fugitives, avoiding trial, incarceration, or serving their full sentences, often committing additional crimes while on the lam. People who fraudulently file for multiple income tax refunds using fake identities and multiple Social Security numbers cost the nation between $1 billion and $5 billion per year. Numerous divorced parents escape their financial obligations to their children by avoiding detection when they move or change jobs. (The sums owed to children are variously estimated as running between $18 billion to $23 billion a year.) Professional and amateur criminals, employing fraudulent identification documentation to make phony credit card purchases, cost credit card companies and retail businesses an indeterminate number of billions of dollars each year. The United States loses an estimated $18 billion a year to benefit fraud committed by illegal aliens using false IDs. A 1998 General Accounting Office report estimates identity fraud to cost $10 billion annually in entitlement programs alone.

People hired to work in child care centers, kindergartens, and schools cannot be effectively screened to keep out child abusers and sex offenders, largely because when background checks are conducted, convicted criminals escape detection by using false identification and aliases. Biometrics would sharply curtail all these crimes, although far from wipe them out singlehandedly.

The courts have recognized that privacy must be weighed against considerations of public interest but have tended to privilege privacy and make claims for public health or safety clear several high hurdles. In recent years these barriers have been somewhat lowered as courts have become more concerned with public safety and health. Given that these often are matters of state law and that neither legislatures nor courts act in unison, the details are complex and far from all pointing in one direction. But, by and large, courts have allowed mandatory drug testing of those who directly have the lives of others in their hands, including pilots, train engineers, drivers of school buses, and air traffic controllers, even though such testing violates their privacy. In case after case, the courts have disregarded objections to such tests by civil libertarians who argue that such tests constitute "suspicionless" searches, grossly violate privacy, and—as the ACLU puts it—"condition Americans to a police state."

All this points to a need to recast privacy in our civic culture, public policies, and legal doctrines. We should cease to treat it as unmitigated good, a sacred right (the way Warren and Brandeis referred to in their famous article and many since) or one that courts automatically privilege.

Instead, privacy should rely squarely on the Fourth Amendment, the only one that has a balance built right into its text. It recognizes both searches that wantonly violate privacy ("unreasonable" ones) and those that enhance the common good to such an extent that they are justified, even if they intrude into one's privacy. Moreover, it provides a mechanism to sort out which searches are in the public interest and which violate privacy without sufficient cause, by introducing the concept of warrants issued by a "neutral magistrate" presented with "probable cause." Warrants also limit the invasion of privacy "by specification of the person to be seized, the place to be searched, and the evidence to be sought." The Fourth may have become the Constitutional Foundation of privacy a long time ago if it was not for the fact that *Roe v. Wade* is construed as a privacy right, and touching it provokes fierce opposition. The good news, though, is that even the advocates of choice in this area are now looking to base their position on some other legal grounds, especially the Fourteenth Amendment.

We might be ready to treat privacy for what it is: one very important right but not one that trumps most other considerations, especially of public safety and health.

■ ■ ■

FOR COLLABORATION

After you have read Etzioni's argument, list the two most significant stasis questions at stake in his argument. Find at least one passage that you believe relates to each question. Then meet with a group of students, and share your responses to this assignment. (Appoint a timekeeper to ensure that all members of your group have a chance to share their responses.) To what extent did you agree or disagree with other group members on the stasis questions at stake in Etzioni's analysis? As a group, choose the two stasis questions that best apply to Etzioni's argument, and agree on two or three reasons why each question is central to his argument. Be prepared to share the results of your discussion with your classmates.

Identifying an Author's Position on a Question

You may find it helpful to identify an author's position in two stages. In the first stage of the process, you are reading the text carefully to determine the main question that the author has presented. If you review the first three paragraphs of Etzioni's argument, for instance, you will note that Etzioni observes in the first paragraph that privacy "is viewed by most Americans as a profound, inalienable right" and goes on to argue in the third paragraph that "It is time to pay attention to the other half of the equation that defines a good society: concerns for public health and safety that entail some rather justifiable diminution of privacy." The remainder of this excerpt from *The Limits of Privacy* clarifies and supports his position on this issue.

After you have identified the author's position on a question, you can use that knowledge to read his or her argument critically. Reading critically doesn't mean simply looking for logical flaws, poor evidence, and so on. Rather, critical readers shift stances as they read to develop a complex understanding of the issues at hand. In this sense, critical readers know how to play what Peter Elbow calls the believing and doubting game.[2] When you play the believing game, you attempt to *believe* the author's arguments by engaging these arguments sympathetically. For instance, you might try to put yourself in the position of the author or of someone who supports the author's position. What interests and experiences might cause the author to take this position? Simi-

---

[2]Peter Elbow, *Writing without Teachers* (New York: Oxford UP, 1973), 147–91.

larly, you might attempt to *doubt* his or her argument by making the objections that someone with a different position on this argument might make. Other ways of doubting an argument include examining the claims made in the argument and considering the evidence provided to support each claim.

When you read critically, your goal is not to demolish or disvalue the text you are reading. Rather, critical readers want to increase their understanding of the ideas being expressed. They also want to participate actively in the "conversation" of which any written text is a part. The following guidelines can help you become a more active and critical reader who reads both with and against the grain of an author's argument.

■ GUIDELINES FOR CRITICAL READING

1. Begin the process of reading by identifying the author's purpose or agenda. This may or may not be identical to the position that the author takes in his or her argument. A political columnist who writes an editorial arguing that the war in Iraq is a just war, for instance, may do so as part of a broader effort to support the Bush administration's foreign policies. Similarly, a Catholic commentator arguing against the war with Iraq may be attempting to support the strong stand that Pope John Paul II took against this war.

2. As the preceding guideline suggests, the more you can learn about an author—about his or her assumptions, beliefs, and experiences—the more you can bring to bear on your reading of his or her text. Is the author qualified to discuss the topic at hand? Why or why not? What unstated assumptions or underlying values and commitments does the author seem to hold? How might these influence the position that he or she takes in this particular argument? Your goal in asking these questions is to achieve the fullest possible understanding of the context in which a particular argument is written. As you do so, take care not to assume that an author continues to hold a position that he or she once held in the past. Understanding the general orientation that an author brings to an argument is helpful, but critical readers approach any argument with an open mind.

3. As you read, ask yourself what the author wants readers to do as a result of reading this text: Assent to the argument? Act on it? Gain

(continued)

(continued)

a richer understanding of a particular issue or problem? Does this purpose seem appropriate to the issues that are involved? How might this purpose influence the form and content of the author's argument?

4. If sources play an important role in the argument, what kinds of sources does the author rely on? How current and reliable do they appear? Are some perspectives on the argument included while others are left out?

5. Does this argument include any visual elements? What are they, and how have they been designed to appeal to readers? How do they contribute to the argument?

6. How open to persuasion are you with this particular topic? If you have already given considerable thought to the issues surrounding this topic, how willing are you to listen to another point of view? Similarly, if you agree with the author, can you maintain a critical distance so that you can examine the claims and support that the writer provides in this argument?

7. It is particularly important to be a critical reader of print and multimedia texts on the World Wide Web. For a fuller discussion of this subject, see Chapter 4's Guidelines for Evaluating Web Sites and Web Pages (pp. 119–23).

FOR EXPLORATION

Keep in mind the guidelines presented above as you reread the excerpt from Amitai Etzioni's *The Limits of Privacy* (pp. 381–84). After doing so, respond to the questions presented in these guidelines.

FOR COLLABORATION

After you have analyzed Etzioni's argument, meet with a group of peers to share the results of your analysis. Appoint a timekeeper so that all group members have an opportunity to share the results of their analysis. To what extent did other group members agree with your analysis of Etzioni's argument? To what extent did they disagree with your analysis? What did you learn as a result of this experience? Be prepared to share your responses to these questions with the rest of the class.

Determining Whether the Author Provides Good Reasons for His or Her Claims: Aristotle's Three Appeals and Stephen Toulmin's Framework for Analyzing Arguments

As the sixth item in the Guidelines for Critical Reading (pp. 385–86) suggests, you may agree with the position that a writer takes on a subject but nevertheless question the support that the writer provides for this position. One of the hallmarks of a critical reader, in fact, is the ability to maintain a critical distance from an argument, even when you have strong feelings for or against the position that the author takes. As mentioned earlier, critical readers move back and forth from believing to doubting an argument—even when they are predisposed to agree or disagree with it.

Two analytical frameworks—one ancient and one contemporary—can help you to evaluate the strengths and limitations of academic arguments. You have already been introduced to the first of these systems, Aristotle's three appeals, in Chapter 5 (pp. 169–76). As you may recall, in his *Rhetoric,* Aristotle determined that speakers and writers draw on three general appeals when they attempt to persuade others:

- *Logos,* the appeal to reason

- *Pathos,* the appeal to emotion, values, and beliefs

- *Ethos,* the appeal to the credibility of the speaker or writer

One way to analyze an argument is to determine the appeal that the author draws on most heavily and his or her degree of effectiveness in using it. When you consider an author's appeals to logos, ask yourself if the argument that you are reading is internally consistent and logical. Also ask yourself if the author has articulated clear and reasonable major claims and supported these claims with appropriate evidence. Appeals to pathos raise different issues: Here you identify the strategies that the author has employed to appeal to readers' values and interests. Finally, appeals to ethos encourage you to consider the credibility and trustworthiness of the author as demonstrated in the argument you are analyzing.

As you may be aware, appeals to logos—appeals that involve factual information and evidence—are often considered especially trustworthy by North American readers, particularly in the academy. Logical appeals include facts; firsthand evidence drawn from observations, interviews, surveys and questionnaires, experiments, and personal experience; and secondhand evidence drawn from authorities, the testimony of others, statistics, and other print and online sources. Critical readers understand that they should not automatically assume that support drawn from logical appeals is valid. After all, not all sources are equally valid, and facts can be out of date or taken out of context. (For a discussion of how to evaluate print and online sources, see pp. 113–23.)

As this example suggests, critical readers understand that they need to look at all three of Aristotle's appeals in context. Appeals to pathos—to the emotions, values, and beliefs that readers hold—can certainly be manipulative and inappropriate. We've all seen ads that seem to promise one thing (youth, beauty, fitness) to sell another. Nevertheless, emotional appeals play key roles in many kinds of arguments, including academic arguments. A student writing about humanitarian issues growing out of the war on Iraq might begin her essay by describing the loss of life, order, and basic material necessities that resulted from the war. In so doing, she would be appealing to readers' emotions and emphasizing the importance of her topic. The same is true for appeals to ethos. While we might well be skeptical when we see an ad where a movie star or sports hero praises this or that product, this does not mean that all appeals to ethos are suspect.

In this regard, let's return to the excerpt from Etzioni's *The Limits of Privacy* (pp. 381–84). The biographical information that accompanies this excerpt provides useful information about Etzioni's experience and qualifications; this information can help readers determine whether Etzioni is an authority on issues of privacy. Critical readers will keep this knowledge in mind as they read his argument, but they will also consider the credibility with which he makes his case. Does Etzioni use examples that are fair and reasonable? Does he attempt to develop a balanced, thoughtful argument? Does he seem to have society's best interest at heart, or does he seem to be pushing an agenda of his own personal assumptions and beliefs? By asking questions such as these, readers can determine whether they should trust Etzioni's credibility as a thinker and writer. Critical readers respect relevant experiences and qualifications that authors bring to various issues, but they are persuaded not by what an author has done or said in the past but by what the author does and says in the text that they are currently reading. In this regard, a thoughtful commentary by an average American in a newspaper may finally be more credible than a guest editorial column by a noted expert on a particular subject.

NOTE FOR MULTILINGUAL WRITERS

Are you familiar with appeals that are not included in Aristotle's three categories of appeals? If so, take the time to describe these appeals. Explain how they differ from Aristotle's appeals. Consider, as well, sharing this information with your classmates. Doing so would help your classmates to understand how rhetorical appeals are situated in particular cultural frameworks.

FOR EXPLORATION

Drawing on your understanding of Aristotle's three appeals, as explained in this chapter, analyze the excerpt from Etzioni's *The Limits of Privacy* (pp. 381–84). What appeals does he draw on most heavily? How effective is he in using these appeals? (Be sure to comment on each of the three appeals.)

FOR COLLABORATION

Meet with a group of peers to share your responses to the previous exploration. Appoint both a timekeeper and a recorder to summarize your group's responses. Begin by addressing this question: To what extent did members of your group agree—and disagree—on Etzioni's effectiveness in his use of Aristotle's three appeals? After responding to this question, develop a group position on Etzioni's use of Aristotle's three appeals. To do so, first agree on a statement that conveys your group's sense of how Etzioni employed each appeal. Then find one or two examples from his text that support your analysis. Be prepared to share the results of your discussion with your classmates.

Aristotle's three appeals comprise one framework that you can use to analyze academic arguments. Such a framework encourages you to step back from your commonsense understandings of—and immediate responses to—an argument. It enables you, in other words, to gain critical distance on your reading. A second framework that serves this purpose was developed by the British philosopher Stephen Toulmin; it is sometimes referred to simply as *Toulmin argument* or the *Toulmin system*. According to Toulmin, most arguments contain common features:

- *Claims* are statements of fact, opinion, or belief that provide the fundamental structure for arguments.

- *Qualifiers* are one or more statements that limit or clarify the claim in some way.

- *Warrants* are links from the claim to reasons and evidence. Warrants often take the form of assumptions and beliefs that may or may not be explicitly stated.

- *Reasons* are smaller assertions that support claims. They often begin with the word *because.*

- *Evidence* is examples, facts, statistics, statements by authorities, and personal experience used to back up reasons (and sometimes warrants).

Toulmin's framework for analyzing arguments encourages readers to consider every chain in an argument's development—including those aspects of the argument, such as warrants, that at times are left unstated. Sometimes a warrant is so self-evident writers do not state it explicitly. Few readers would object to the assertion that "Sylvia should make an excellent lawyer because she excelled in her classes in law school and in her early years of legal practice," even though the warrant for this claim ("Excelling in law school and in the early years of legal practice are good predictors of a person's success after law school") is missing. On other occasions, the absence of a warrant is a major flaw in the development of an argument. Many arguments about controversial subjects such as abortion and the environment flounder because the writers assume warrants (such as the warrant that endangered species should be protected despite financial considerations like real estate development and oil exploration) that others do not share.

With Toulmin's system in mind, consider Etzioni's discussion of HIV testing of infants. This discussion appears in the fourth and fifth paragraphs of his excerpt (pp. 381–82). Etzioni's major claim is clear. In the last sentence of paragraph five, he argues that "To save the lives of . . . children . . . [of women who have HIV, these children] must be tested at delivery and treated even if this entails a violation of mothers' privacy." Note that Etzioni's claim is qualified by his recognition that violating the mother's privacy is a serious matter. To meet his burden of proof, Etzioni must demonstrate that the benefits of testing infants for HIV outweigh the costs to new mothers, whose privacy rights will be violated.

Etzioni provides several reasons in support of his argument. He points out, for instance, that recent research by the *New England Journal of Medicine* shows that infants born with HIV can ward off the disease if they are tested at birth and treated immediately. As evidence of the need for such testing, he adds that "An estimated two-thirds of infected mothers are unaware" that they have HIV. Etzioni undertakes a second and related line of reasoning when he argues that efforts to address this problem without requiring the mandatory testing of all newborn infants have failed.

Etzioni's argument about HIV testing can be analyzed as follows:

- *Claim:* Testing newborn infants for HIV should be mandatory.

- *Qualifier:* Mandatory testing should occur even though this represents a violation of mothers' privacy.

- *Reasons:* (1) With testing and treatment, the lives of most infants who are born with HIV could be saved. (2) High-risk mothers who are particularly at risk of having infants with HIV are least likely to be aware that they have the disease and are least likely to agree to voluntary testing. (3) Efforts to increase the number of infants who are tested for HIV without requiring mandatory testing have failed.

- *Evidence:* (1) Authoritative medical data emphasize the benefits that can be gained by testing and treatment. (2) Data from such sources as the *Journal of School Health* confirm that high-risk mothers are particularly prone to HIV. (3) Unnamed sources estimate that two-thirds of infected mothers are unaware they have HIV.

- *Warrant:* Concerns for the health of newborn infants should take precedence over the need to maintain the privacy of their mothers.

This analysis outlines the basic structure of Etzioni's argument, but it still leaves room for readers to disagree about whether testing should be mandatory. Those who hold strong civil libertarian views may disagree with Etzioni's warrant, while others may question the reliability of the estimate that "two-thirds of infected mothers are unaware" that they have HIV. Etzioni's failure to provide evidence for this estimate—when he does provide evidence for other reasons that support his claim—might reasonably make some readers skeptical. They might argue that the number of women who are unlikely to know they have HIV and unlikely to be tested is much smaller than Etzioni suggests and that given this fact the need to protect mothers' privacy should take precedence. Finally, some readers might point out that Etzioni does not specify who should require mandatory testing (the federal government? the states?) or how it might best be carried out. Since Etzioni's discussion of mandatory HIV testing is part of a larger argument about privacy, it may be unrealistic to expect him to discuss issues of implementation, but critical readers would nevertheless note that these issues are unaddressed in Etzioni's text.

■ ■ ■

FOR EXPLORATION

Choose another section of Etzioni's argument (pp. 381–84), such as his discussion of biometrics, and analyze it according to Toulmin's system. What does this analysis reveal that you did not notice in earlier readings?

Recognizing Fallacies

When you analyze an argument, be aware of fallacies that may be at work. *Fallacies* are faults in an argument's structure that may call into question the argument's evidence or conclusions. Some fallacies are easy to recognize. If someone told you that anyone who doesn't like Eminem's music is an imbecile, you would recognize that this assertion is illogical and that rather than making a reasoned argument the speaker is unfairly attacking those whose taste in music differ from his own. (Such a statement is an example of an *ad hominem* fallacy.) At other times, fallacies can be harder to determine. After all, arguments always occur in some specific rhetorical situation: What looks like a fallacy in one situation may appear quite different in another. Sometimes judgments about a person's character or actions *are* relevant to an argument, for instance. Just because a writer or speaker grounds part of an argument in such a judgment does not mean that he or she is necessarily committing an ad hominem fallacy. To determine whether an argument is grounded in a fallacy, you need to consider it in the context of its specific rhetorical situation, including the place and time in which the argument was or is being made.

Since the time of Aristotle, rhetoricians have developed diverse ways of naming, describing, and categorizing various fallacies. Here I follow the categories presented in the fifth edition of Andrea A. Lunsford's *St. Martin's Handbook*.[3] Lunsford categorizes fallacies according to Aristotle's three major appeals of argument—ethical appeals (appeals to ethos), emotional appeals (appeals to pathos), and logical appeals (appeals to logos). As you read the following brief descriptions of these fallacies, remember that the point of studying fallacies is not to discredit the ideas of others. Writers who want to develop fair, well-reasoned arguments are concerned about fallacies because they realize that fallacies tend to shut down, rather than encourage, communication. The following guidelines for identifying fallacies list some of the most significant fallacies that appear in arguments.

■ GUIDELINES FOR IDENTIFYING FALLACIES

Ethical Fallacies

Those who employ ethical fallacies attempt to destroy the credibility of those who disagree with them. Examples of ethical fallacies include the following:

1. An *ad hominem* attack is an unfair attack on a person's character or actions, one that typically diverts attention from the issue at hand. An example of an ad hominem attack would be the statement that "Any American who opposed the war in Iraq is unpatriotic." A person's position on a war does not necessarily reflect his or her patriotism.

2. *Guilt by association* is an effort to damage a person's credibility by associating him or her with an unpopular or discredited activity or person. A student who argues that hip-hop music is bad because some hip-hop musicians such as Bobby Brown have

(continued)

---

[3]Andrea A. Lunsford, *The St. Martin's Handbook,* 5th ed. (Boston: Bedford/St. Martin's, 2003), 245–49.

(continued)

been involved in criminal activities is committing the fallacy of guilt by association. Some—but not all—hip-hop musicians have engaged in criminal activities, but their personal behavior is separate from the music that they create.

Emotional Fallacies

Emotional appeals can play a valid and important role in argumentation, but when these appeals are overblown or unfair, they distract readers from attending to the point that is being argued. Examples of emotional fallacies include the following:

1. A *bandwagon appeal* is the effort to argue that readers should support a person, activity, or movement because it is popular. This appeal is particularly common in advertising, where those promoting particular products often argue that "X is the best-selling product of its kind."

2. A *slippery slope* fallacy occurs when writers exaggerate the future consequences of an event or action, usually with an intent to frighten readers into agreeing with their argument. If someone who opposes censorship of pornography argues that "Once we start banning one form of literature, censorship will spread, and the next thing you know, we'll be burning books!," he or she is committing the slippery slope fallacy.

Logical Fallacies

Logical fallacies are arguments in which the claims, warrants, or evidence are invalid, insufficient, or disconnected. Examples of logical fallacies include the following:

1. *Begging the question* is stating a claim that depends on circular reasoning for justification. Arguing that "Abortion is murder because it involves the intentional murder of an unborn human being" is tantamount to saying "Abortion is murder because it is murder." This fallacy often detracts attention from the real issues at hand, for the question of whether a fetus should be considered a human being is complex.

2. A *hasty generalization* is drawn from insufficient evidence. If someone says, "Last week I attended a poetry reading supported

(continued)

> *(continued)*
>
> by the National Endowment of the Arts, and many of the speakers used profanity. Maybe the people who want to stop government funding for the NEA are right," this would be an example of a hasty generalization. One performance doesn't comprise a large enough sample for such a generalization.
>
> **3.** A *non sequitur* is an argument that attempts to connect two or more logically unrelated ideas. If someone states that "I hate it when people smoke in restaurants; there ought to be a law against cigarettes," this would represent a non sequitur, for eliminating smoking in restaurants and the negative effects of second-hand smoke does not require the elimination of legal tobacco sales.

Putting Theory into Practice: Academic Analysis in Action

As this chapter has emphasized, readers engage in academic analysis not to criticize or dissect another's argument but rather to *understand* that argument as fully as possible. When you analyze an academic argument, you attempt to go beyond your immediate response—which often takes the form of binary-driven observations ("I agree/don't agree, like/don't like, am interested/not interested in X")—to achieve a fuller, more complex understanding of it. Here is an example of a successful analysis of an academic argument. This essay by Stevon Roberts, a student at Oregon State University, analyzes the excerpt from Etzioni's *The Limits of Privacy* presented earlier in this chapter (pp. 381–84).*

THE PRICE OF PUBLIC SAFETY

Stevon Roberts

As a former senior adviser to the White House and author of *The Limits of Privacy* (1999), Amitai Etzioni is a formidable advocate for revision of one of America's most cherished luxuries: protection of personal privacy. In "Less Privacy Is Good for Us (and You)," an argument excerpted from the above volume, Etzioni urges Americans to look critically at traditional expectations for personal privacy and to be prepared to sacrifice those

---

*Citations refer to Amitae Etzioni. "Less Privacy Is Good for Us (and You)." *Current Issues and Enduring Questions: A Guide to Critical Thinking and Argument, with Readings.* Sylvan Barnet and Hugo Bedau, eds. Boston: Bedford / St. Martin's, 2002.

expectations for increased public health and safety. Although the volume was published before the terrorist attacks on September 11, 2001, and the essay makes no specific references to the tragedy, the events of that day give an increased sense of urgency to Etzioni's message and consequently might make Americans more receptive to protocols that afford protection from public risks in general.

In the interest of public health risks, Etzioni opens his argument with recent HIV testing procedures in hospitals that may infringe on the rights of pregnant women. He then shifts gears and takes a brief look at public outrage from the Coalition for Constitutional Liberties regarding driver's license availability. Next, he gives us a crash course in "biometrics," a controversial new technology that could save billions of dollars lost to fraud every year. Finally, Etzioni addresses our fears (and those of other civil libertarians) that these and other procedures that are designed to increase our public health and safety will not be implemented justly and ethically. Etzioni admits, however, that a growing number of people and interest groups are not convinced that old laws—such as the Fourth Amendment, which protects the United States from becoming a military state—can protect us from new technology. We are left to wonder: is Etzioni justified in making his unconventional claims despite such well-founded opposition?

After some brief media references, Etzioni's first substantial argument involves a real-world privacy dilemma facing pregnant women as well as various health and legal groups. Specifically, he focuses on HIV testing of newborns. This is an excellent place to start because the reactions of these groups help to shed light on our current attitudes toward privacy. Etzioni refers to the *New England Journal of Medicine,* which published evidence suggesting that infants born to HIV-infected women could ward off the disease with early diagnosis and treatment with AZT. In order for the infants to be treated, they must be tested. This becomes a privacy issue because testing infants for HIV also reveals whether "the mother is a carrier, and thus her privacy is violated" (669).

As Etzioni acknowledges, arguments in favor of required HIV testing of infants have met strong—and even vehement—opposition from civil libertarians, as well as from some gay activists. Indeed, the question of whether to test infants for HIV has been so contentious that most states, as well as the federal government, have avoided taking it on. In this regard, Etzioni chastises Congress for "pass[ing] the buck by asking the Institute of Medicine (IOM) to conduct a study of the matter." This effectively illustrates Congress's lack of willingness to become involved. IOM's solution suggests that all pregnant women should consent to HIV testing as part of their routine prenatal care. However, Etzioni feels this would leave out many women who "are drug addicts or otherwise live at society's margins" (669). Such women, he argues, "do not show up for prenatal care, and they are particularly prone to HIV, according to a study published in the American Health Association's *Journal of School Health*" (669). A succinct sentence sums up his solution: "To save the lives of their children, they [infants] must be tested at delivery and treated even if this entails a violation of mothers' privacy" (669).

This is a well-documented and compelling argument. Other parts of Etzioni's text, however, are not so well rounded. Instead of taking seriously the arguments forwarded by civil libertarians and others who raise concerns about privacy, Etzioni focuses on the media, which he believes tell "horror stories" about "The Death of Privacy" (669). When he does address the views of such groups, he represents their concerns by an inflammatory statement from the Coalition for Constitutional Liberties, which accuses those in favor of the plan of pushing the country "to the brink of tyranny" (669).

With this brief (and wholly unsuccessful) transition, Etzioni moves from the Coalition's alarmist complaints to Wells Fargo's introduction of "a new device that allows a person to cash checks at its ATM machines because the machines recognize faces" (670). These machines rely upon a new technology called biometrics, which, Etzioni explains, can use "natural features such as voice, hand design, and eye pattern to recognize a person with the same extremely high reliability provided by the new DNA tests" (670). Etzioni acknowledges that biometrics is a controversial technology, and he concedes that it will "practically strip Americans of anonymity, an important part of privacy" (670). With this new technology, people would find it difficult to change their names, move to another part of the country, and gain a fresh start in life. His solution is a hope that "future communities will become more tolerant of such people, especially if they openly acknowledge the mistakes of their past and truly seek to lead a more prosocial life" (670).

To his credit, Etzioni is quick to follow up the drawbacks of biometrics with compelling statistics about the potential benefits. He says, "Above all, while biometrics clearly undermines privacy, the social benefits it promises are very substantial" (670). He references $1 billion to $5 billion lost annually to tax fraud, $18 billion to $23 billion annually in lost child support, and $18 billion a year lost to fraud committed by illegal aliens with false IDs. In addition to the potential economic benefits, he says sex offenders who use false IDs would be more effectively screened, and would less easily find work for child care centers or schools (670).

Etzioni's presentation of biometrics is, ironically, both calculated *and* lacking in logistics. His predominantly economic appeal doesn't mention the cost associated with Wells Fargo's new face-recognizing ATM machines. Because he makes no attempt, even hypothetically, to weigh the cost of biometrics implementation against the savings from fraud protection or other liabilities, readers are left to assume that the overall results are beneficial, when that might not, in fact, be the case. For example, although he discusses credit card fraud, there is no mention of Internet credit card fraud. Biometrics countermeasures to combat this threat are likely to manifest as purchasable hardware devices, putting an unfair financial burden on lower-level consumers while taking the liability away from the credit card companies. It seems reasonable that while calculating the potential benefits, Etzioni should also calculate potential losses or system limitations, as he does when admitting that biometrics would not singlehandedly wipe out abusers from child care centers.

Additionally, the author's appeals to pathos are lacking substance. In fact, his only olive branch to the human condition is a concession that biometrics may make it difficult for criminals seeking a new life. His flaky solution to this problem is a touchy-feely dream in which everyone magically becomes more tolerant of criminals that repent and sin no more. Further, he makes no mention at all of persons seeking new lives for reasons other than legal trouble, such as women who have fled abusive husbands.

Etzioni concludes his argument by considering court trends in balancing the need to protect personal privacy with concerns about public health and safety. Although useful, this segment does not appear to lie in a strategic part of his argument. Court cases often set a context for interpretation and might benefit readers more in the beginning of an argument. He observes the courts have tended to "privilege privacy and make claims for public health or safety clear several high hurdles" (670). More recently, however, the courts are lowering these barriers with growing concern for public interest. For example, the courts have mandated drug testing for those who "directly have the lives of others in their hands, including pilots, train engineers, drivers of school buses, and air traffic controllers, even though such testing violates their privacy" (670). Etzioni reports that the ACLU feels these new laws "condition Americans to a police state" (671).

All of this, according to Etzioni, "points to a need to recast privacy in our civic culture, public policies, and legal doctrines. We should cease to treat it as an unmitigated good, a sacred right (the way Warren and Brandeis referred to in their famous article and many [other legal theorists have] since) or one that courts automatically privilege" (671). He feels that we should instead rely on the Fourth Amendment, which has built into its text safeguards that balance privacy and public security. His interpretation of the document's reference to "unreasonable" search protocols recognizes the difference between searches that "wantonly violate privacy," and those that "enhance the common good to such an extent that they are justified, even if they intrude into one's privacy" (671). Additionally, the amendment addresses sufficient cause by introducing warrants "issued by a 'neutral magistrate' presented with 'probable cause'" (671). Etzioni apparently believes interpretation of this document will be uniform from one court to the next. This assumption is problematic at best.

The author leaves us with a new vision of privacy as a "very important right but not one that trumps most other considerations, especially of public safety and health" (671). With this parting thought, the author packages a difficult and complex concept into a pill that is not terribly difficult to swallow. By the same token, however, his oversimplification may leave some readers feeling like something is missing.

Indeed, something *is* missing—the rest of Etzioni's book, from which this excerpt originates. Readers of this argument can only hope that Etzioni deals carefully and respectfully with the arguments of civil libertarians in other parts of his work, for he certainly does not do so here. His tendency to use only the most inflammatory statements from his opponents suggests he has no interest in fully addressing their respective concerns.

All things considered, Etzioni begins his essay with a clear purpose and a logical, tangible starting point. Through the inclusion of several diverse public-interest groups, health organizations, courts, and governmental bodies, he initially appears to address all aspects of the moral dilemma. This is especially true in the obvious benefit to newborns with HIV that are diagnosed early. But in this excerpt, he distracts readers from the true opposition by focusing primarily on the media, while turning the Coalition for Civil Liberties and the ACLU into radical doomsayers that jeopardize public welfare. He marginalizes their concerns, advocates for increased biometrics applications on the chance that billions of dollars might potentially be protected from fraud, and opposes legislation that would protect potential victims because society potentially could be more forgiving. Consequently, his venture into the hypothetical realm leaves opponents (and critical readers) unsatisfied.

■ ■ ■

FOR EXPLORATION

Now that you have read Etzioni's argument several times and have also read Stevon Roberts's analysis of it, reread Stevon's essay to determine its strengths and limitations. Identify two or three passages from the essay that struck you as particularly significant and helpful, and write several sentences of explanation for each passage. No essay, however successful, is perfect, so also identify one or more ways this essay might be even more successful.

FOR COLLABORATION

Bring your response to the previous Exploration to class to share with a group of peers. Appoint a timekeeper and a recorder. After all group members have shared their responses, answer these questions: (1) To what extent did other members of your group agree with your evaluation of Stevon Roberts's analysis? To what extent did they disagree? (2) Now that you have heard everyone's responses, what two or three passages in Stevon's essay does your group feel best demonstrates his analytical skills? (3) How might Stevon's essay be further strengthened? Be prepared to share the results of your discussion with your classmates.

FOR THOUGHT, DISCUSSION, AND WRITING

1. Chapter 3 presents a number of readings about cyberspace, including Jonathan G. S. Koppell's "No 'There' There." Choose two of the readings in that chapter that particularly interested you and analyze them to determine their strengths and weaknesses.

2. This chapter has focused on general strategies of analysis that apply across the curriculum. Some disciplines develop strategies for analysis that are particularly helpful to teachers and students who work in these disciplines. Interview an instructor who teaches a humanities, social sciences, natural and applied sciences, or business course that you are taking. Ask this teacher what methods of analysis he or she believes are particularly important in his or her discipline. Then write a brief summary describing what this interview helped you understand about analysis in this particular discipline.

3. The excerpt from Etzioni's *The Limits of Privacy* that is reprinted in this chapter also appears in Sylvan Barnet and Hugo Bedau's *Current Issues and Enduring Questions: A Guide to Critical Thinking and Argument, with Readings,* a first-year writing textbook. Here is another argument on privacy that appears in Barnet and Bedau's anthology. The author of this essay, Nadine Strossen, served as the president of the American Civil Liberties Union in 1998. Strossen published this essay on IntellectualCapital.com in that year. Drawing on the strategies discussed in this chapter, write an essay that analyzes the effectiveness of Strossen's argument.

EVERYONE IS WATCHING YOU
Nadine Strossen

In 1949, a young English author named Eric Blair opened his latest novel with a scene in an apartment building where on each landing, a poster with an "enormous face gazed from the wall. It was so contrived that the eyes follow you about when you move."

You probably know Blair better by his pen name—George Orwell.

The book, of course, was *1984,* and the poster bore the now-clichéd caption, "Big Brother is watching you." But even Blair's vivid imagination did not accurately predict the future. Today, the more appropriate caption would be, "Everyone Is Watching You."

"Everyone" includes banks, automated teller machines, parking lots, shopping centers, stadiums, and convenience stores. Also government offices, schools, businesses, and workplaces. Whether cruising through a toll booth, or buying a gallon of milk, or strolling in the park, private citizens increasingly are forfeiting their privacy whenever they venture out of their homes—or even, for that matter, while we are at home.

Consider the chilling story of Barbara Katende, who recently told the *New York Times* that she had spotted a camera on a rooftop about 200 yards from her apartment. A rooftop she had seen, but not thought about, every time she stood before her sixth-floor window with the blinds open, lounging around in her underwear or in nothing at all. The camera monitors traffic. But it has a powerful zoom lens and can turn in any direction. A technician who controls traffic cameras from a Manhattan studio told the *Times,* "If you can see the Empire State Building, we can see you."

Cities all over the country, including our nation's capital, are installing cameras to record citizens' every coming-and-going on the streets, sidewalks, and parks. In Tempe, Arizona, officials stuck a rotating camera—nicknamed "Sneaky Peak"—atop the municipal building.

Why? Why not? "It's the biggest hit on our Web page," a Tempe official told the *Washington Post.*

Even more chillingly, new "face recognition" technology makes it possible to instantly identify individuals who are captured on video through complicated searches of facial images stored in government databases. As CNN commented, this is "a wonderful way for government to spy on its citizens who went to the antigovernment rally."

Why the mania for surveillance? Many claim that we need to trade privacy for safety. But even many law-enforcement officials believe, based on their actual experience, that video surveillance does not effectively detect or deter crime.

A number of cities that previously used video cameras—for example, Miami Beach, Florida, Newark, New Jersey, White Plains, New York, and Fredricksburg, Virginia—have abandoned them, concluding that they were not worth the expense. Surveillance cameras that had been mounted for 22 months in New York City's Times Square led to only 10 arrests before they were dismantled, prompting the *New York Times* to dub them, "one of the greatest flops along the Great White Way."

Even in Blair's United Kingdom, where video-surveillance cameras are the most pervasive and powerful, the government itself has concluded that they have not demonstrably improved public safety. As noted by a report in the *Telegraph,* "A series of studies, including one by the Home

Office itself, suggest that" video surveillance "has merely pushed crime into other areas or that its initial impact fades rapidly."

Just last September, the police department in Oakland, California, urged the city council to reject a video-surveillance project that the police department itself initially had recommended, but about which it had second thoughts—in terms of both privacy and efficiency. As Oakland's police chief told the city council, "There is no conclusive way to establish that the presence of video surveillance cameras resulted in the prevention or reduction of crime."

Moreover, responding to a detailed letter of concern from the American Civil Liberties Union, the Oakland city attorney concluded that a "method of surveillance may be no greater than that which can be achieved by the naked eye. [T]he California Supreme Court has held that 'precious liberties' . . . do not simply shrink as the government acquires new means of infringing upon them."

I applaud the California supreme court's ruling, which echoes the pro-privacy principles first declared by U.S. Supreme Court Justice Louis Brandeis in a famous 1928 dissent. Unfortunately, the Brandeisian view of privacy—which he defined as "the right to be let alone, the most comprehensive of rights"—remains a minority position among current judges. The Supreme Court, for example, has held that the Constitution only protects expectations of privacy that society considers "reasonable." This creates a downward spiral: The more government and others invade our privacy, the fewer "reasonable expectations" of privacy we have, which means that government and others may intrude even further into our privacy, etc., etc.

Given the foreshortened view of constitutional privacy that is currently enforced by our courts, we have to develop other avenues of legal protection—most importantly, federal and state statutes. Here, too, we now have only a patchwork of protection.

We must, therefore, take political and other direct action to remedy the current lack of legal protection against the ubiquitous electronic "peeping Toms." Urge your community to oppose cameras in public places. If you notice a camera in an odd place, find out why it is there and what it is supposed to be recording. Tell businesses that record every transaction on camera that you will not be shopping there anymore. Before taking a job, let the employer know that you object to secret taping. And, most importantly, urge your elected officials to introduce laws limiting surveillance.

Understanding
Academic Argument

As Chapter 15 emphasizes, analysis and argument are linked in powerful ways. To write an effective argument, you must analyze both your own ideas and also those of others. Recognizing how other writers negotiate Aristotle's three appeals or how they establish appropriate chains of reasoning with a series of interconnected claims, qualifiers, warrants, reasons, and evidence will strengthen your ability to write academic arguments. Nevertheless, academic argument requires writers to have more than strong analytical skills. To write a successful academic argument, you must construct a carefully reasoned, well-supported essay and anticipate the interests and concerns of your readers.

Contextualizing Academic Argument

The first step in the process of writing a successful academic argument is to understand the ways in which academic arguments are similar to and different from other kinds of arguments. From one perspective, *all* language use is argumentative—or at least has an argumentative edge. If you say to a friend, "You've just got to hear Norah Jones's new CD!" you're making an implicit argument—even if neither you nor your friend views your statement that way. A sign that calls out "Best Deep-Dish Pizza in Chicago!" is similarly making an argumentative claim. Even prayers can be viewed as arguments. Some prayers represent direct appeals to God; others function as meditations directed toward self-understanding. In either case, those who pray are engaged in an argument for change—either in themselves or in the world around them.

As these examples suggest, arguments can serve many purposes beyond confrontation or debate. Sometimes the purpose of an argument is to change minds and hearts or to win this or that decision; this is particularly true in politics, business, and the law. But winning is not always the goal of argument— especially in the academy, where scholars focus on contributing to the scholarly conversation in their fields. Given this focus, students who bring a debate model of argumentation to academic writing often encounter problems. Think about the terminology used in debate: Debaters "attack" their "adversaries," hoping to "demolish" their arguments to "win" the judge's assent and claim "victory" in the contest. This model of argument may prevail in forensic and political debates but is less appropriate in academic arguments, where the goal is inquiry and not conquest. Your teachers are not interested in whether you can "attack" or "demolish" your opponents. Rather, they value your ability to examine an issue or problem from multiple perspectives. Their commitment is not to winning but to clear reasoning and substantial evidence. For these reasons, academic argument is best conceived of as inquiry—and not as debate.

Not all scholarly arguments are identical, however. Scholarly arguments reflect the aims and methods of specific academic disciplines and thus can vary in significant ways. Scholars in the humanities often write arguments that explore complex issues and ideas; interpretation—whether of literary texts, art works, or historical data—is central to arguments in the humanities. Scholars in the social sciences often argue about issues of policy; they also undertake studies that attempt to help readers better understand—and respond—to current issues and events. A sociologist might review recent research on the effects of children's gender on parents' child-rearing practices and conduct her own quantitative or qualitative study on this topic. The resulting argument would evaluate previous research and present conclusions based on the sociologist's own study. Argument is also central to research in the sciences and applied sciences. An engineer who argues in favor of one method of designing and building trusses for a bridge or a chemist who presents new information about a particular chemical reaction is making claims that he must support with evidence and reasons.

As these examples suggest, scholarly arguments grow out of and reflect disciplinary concerns. All scholars, however, agree that the best arguments explore ideas relevant to their subject as fully as possible—and from as many perspectives as possible. They also agree that arguments should be presented logically and should include relevant support for all significant claims. These preferences distinguish academic arguments from other kinds of arguments. You and your friend might spend an hour on a Saturday night arguing about the merits of Norah Jones's new album, but this discussion would undoubtedly be fluid and improvisational, with many digressions. In academic argument, great value is placed on the careful, consistent, and logical exploration of ideas.

Exploring Aristotle's Three Appeals

This does not mean that appeals to pathos and ethos—to emotion and to the credibility of the writer—have no role in academic argument. All writers—whether they are composing a letter to a friend, an editorial for the student newspaper, or an essay for a history class on the consequences of the Civil War in the South—need to establish their credibility, and they can accomplish this in many ways. In the academy, writers generally do so by demonstrating knowledge of their subject and of the methodologies that others in their field use to explore it. They reinforce their credibility when they explore their subject fairly and evenhandedly and show respect for their readers. Writers demonstrate this respect, for instance, when they anticipate the concerns that readers might hold and attempt to address any counterarguments that readers might make. In so doing, writers seek to establish common ground with readers rather than to win them over to a particular position.

Just as all writers appeal to ethos, so too do all writers appeal to pathos—to the emotions and to shared values. Sometimes this appeal is obvious and even manipulative. Print, radio, television, and Web requests for contributions to charitable causes use appeals to pathos. Even when writers compose texts that are relatively objective in tone and that emphasize appeals to logos, as much academic writing does, they nevertheless draw on and convey emotional appeals. An academic argument that is written with formal diction and an emphasis on good reasons and evidence is nevertheless sending readers a message: "This subject is much too important for me to treat it frivolously. This subject requires the attention that only reasoned argument can give."

Those who write academic arguments use appeals to pathos to emphasize the seriousness of the subject under consideration—but they also use other, more explicit appeals to the emotions. A writer who wants to emphasize the significance of a topic may employ concrete, specific information to convey just how much is at stake in understanding and addressing a problem or event. Scholars writing about the Holocaust, for instance, often use vivid and detailed descriptions to encourage readers to connect personally with the events about which they are writing. Those wanting to bring immediacy and impact to an argument also often employ figurative language, such as metaphors, similes, and analogies. When rhetorical scholar Edward P. J. Corbett wrote an article about the political protests of the 1960s, such as those associated with the Black Panthers and anti-Vietnam War movement, he organized his analysis around the metaphors of the open hand and the closed fist. The open hand, Corbett observed, "characterize[s] the kind of persuasive discourse that seeks to carry its point by reasoned, sustained, conciliatory discussion of the issues. The closed fist . . . signif[ies] the kind of persuasive activity that seeks to carry its point by non-rational, non-sequential, often non-verbal, frequently provocative means."[1] Corbett's essay was originally published in 1969—but it is still cited by other scholars, in large part because of the analogy he used to organize his argument.

---

[1]Edward P. J. Corbett, "The Rhetoric of the Open Hand and the Rhetoric of the Closed Fist," *College Composition and Communication* 20 (December 1969), 288.

■ ■ ■

FOR EXPLORATION

In Chapter 3, you read "No 'There' There," an essay by Jonathan G. S. Koppell on the metaphor of cyberspace (p. 73). Reread that essay and analyze the ways in which Koppel draws on appeals to ethos and pathos. You may find it helpful to know that Koppell's essay was published in *The Atlantic Monthly*. This is not a scholarly journal, but scholars often write for the journal, and the editors assume that their readers have a high level of education. How does Koppell provide good reasons and substantial evidence for his argument while also appealing to ethos and pathos? Write two or three responses to this question, and support each response with a representative passage from Koppell's text.

FOR COLLABORATION

Bring your responses to the previous Exploration to class, and meet with a group of peers. Appoint a timekeeper and a recorder. After each member of your group has had an opportunity to speak, agree on a statement that best describes your group's understanding of the appeals that Koppell makes to ethos and pathos. Be prepared to share this summary with your classmates.

UNDERSTANDING THE ROLE OF VALUES AND BELIEFS IN ARGUMENT

When you argue, you give reasons and evidence for your assertions. The student arguing against a Forest Service plan for a national forest might warn that increased timber harvesting will reduce access to the forest for campers and backpackers or that building more roads will adversely affect wildlife. This writer might also show that the Forest Service has failed to anticipate some problems with the plan and that cost-benefit calculations are skewed to reflect logging and economic-development interests. These are all potentially good reasons for questioning the proposed plan. Notice that these reasons necessarily imply certain values or beliefs. The argument against increasing the timber harvest and building more roads, for instance, reflects the belief that preserving wildlife habitats and wilderness lands is more important than the economic development of the resources.

Is this argument flawed because it appeals to values and beliefs? Of course not. When you argue, you can't suppress your own values and beliefs. Your values and beliefs enable you to make sense of the world; they provide links between the world you observe and experience and yourself (in Toulmin's terms, these links are *warrants*). They thus play an important role in any argument.

Suppose that you and a friend are getting ready to go out for breakfast. You look out the window and notice some threatening clouds. You say, "Looks like rain. We'd better take umbrellas since we're walking. I hate getting soaked." "Oh, I don't know," your friend replies. "I don't think it looks so bad. It usually rains in the afternoon in summer. I think we should risk it." Brief and informal as this exchange is, it constitutes an argument. Both you and your friend have observed something, analyzed it, and drawn conclusions — conclusions backed by reasons. Although you each cite different reasons, your conclusions may most strongly reflect your different personal preferences. You're generally cautious, and you don't like getting caught unprepared in a downpour, so you opt for an umbrella. Your friend is more of a risk taker.

If your individual preferences, values, and beliefs shape a single situation like this where only getting wet is at stake, imagine how crucial they are in more complicated and contested situations — situations where the central issue is not whether clouds will bring rain but whether a controversial proposal is right or wrong, just or unjust, effective or ineffective. Argument necessarily involves values and beliefs, held by both writer and reader. These values and beliefs cannot be denied or excluded, even in academic argument, with its emphasis on evidence and reasoned inquiry. The student arguing against the Forest Service plan cannot avoid using values and beliefs as bridges between reasons and conclusions. And not all of these bridges can be explicitly stated; that would lead to an endless chain of reasons. The standards of North American academic argument require, however, that the most important values and beliefs undergirding an argument be explicitly stated and defended. In this case, then, the student opposing the Forest Service plan should at some point state and support the belief that preserving wildlife habitats and wilderness lands should take priority over economic development.

It's not easy to identify and analyze your own values and beliefs, but doing so is essential in academic argument. Values and beliefs are often held unconsciously, and they function as part of a larger network of assumptions and practices. Your opinions about the best way for the government to respond to unemployed individuals reflect values and beliefs you hold about the family, the proper role of government, the nature of individual responsibility, and the importance of economic security. Thus if your political science instructor asks you to argue for or against programs requiring welfare recipients to work at state-mandated jobs in exchange for economic support, you need to analyze carefully not just these workfare programs but also the role your values and beliefs play in your analysis.

The following guidelines for analyzing your values and beliefs should enable you to respond more effectively to the demands of academic argument.

■ GUIDELINES FOR ANALYZING YOUR OWN VALUES AND BELIEFS

1. *Use Informal Invention Methods to Explore Your Values and Beliefs about a Subject.* To discover *why* you believe what you believe, you need to consider more than rational, logical arguments: You need to tap into your experiences and emotions. Freewriting, looping, brainstorming, and clustering are excellent ways to explore the values and beliefs that encourage you to adopt a particular stance toward an issue. (To review these strategies, see Chapter 8.)

2. *After Exploring Your Values and Beliefs, Consider the Degree to Which They Enable You to Argue Effectively about a Subject.* Exploring your own values and beliefs enables you to distance yourself from your habitual ways of thinking and thus encourages the analytical habits of mind your instructors want to foster. Such exploration can also help you discover ways to ground your argument in values and beliefs you share with your readers. (You may wish to review Todd Carpenter's essays, which appear in Chapter 12, to see how he achieves this goal.)

   Sometimes your exploration may enable you to realize that you face special challenges when it comes to writing an effective academic argument on a particular subject. For example, freewriting about your feelings about gun control may help you realize that your convictions about this issue are so deeply rooted in your beliefs and values that you will have to work hard to maintain academic standards of objectivity. You might do better, you realize, to choose a different subject for your argument.

3. *Imagine a "Devil's Advocate" Who Holds Different Values and Beliefs.* You may find it difficult to step outside your way of thinking to consider whether others might reasonably hold differing views — and yet much academic writing demands just this ability. Many writers find it helpful to engage in a silent dialogue with one or more "devil's advocates" — persons whose views differ considerably from their own. If you were writing an essay arguing that the federal government needs to increase funding for college student loans, you might engage in a mental or written dialogue with a hard-headed pragmatic congressperson or corporate

(continued)

(continued)

executive who might resist such an argument because of concerns about the national debt. Their challenges might help you recognize that your assumptions about the need for all students to have access to a college education are not universally shared and that other concerns — such as the need to reduce the national debt — might reasonably take precedence. Your dialogue has helped you learn that you must make your own assumptions explicit, provide good reasons why those assumptions are valid, and consider competing assumptions as well. Your dialogue might even help you realize that you need to limit or modify your goals for this essay.

4. *Engage in Discussions with Your Classmates.* You're probably already aware from informal discussions that even friends and family members can disagree about complex or controversial subjects. When you discuss current events with your friends or family, for example, they may naturally formulate questions that require you to reconsider not only your stance toward an issue or problem but also the assumptions, values, and beliefs that undergird this position. You can draw on this natural activity of mutual inquiry to help you explore your values, assumptions, and beliefs. This may take the form of informal dinner talk with friends or formal group discussions with classmates. Follow these steps for any formal discussions:

- Decide how much time each student will have to discuss his or her work. Appoint a timekeeper to enforce these limits.

- The writer should begin by describing the controlling purpose or thesis of the essay and then briefly list the values and beliefs that led to this position. The writer should then invite group members to ask questions designed to provide perspectives on these values and beliefs and to explain different views that others might reasonably hold.

- The writer should lead the resulting discussion, asking group members to clarify or elaborate on suggestions. Group members should remember that their goal is not to attack or criticize the writer's values and beliefs but rather to help the writer gain additional perspectives on them.

When you argue, you must consider not only your own values and beliefs but also those of your readers. The student writing about the Forest Service plan would present one argument to the local branch of the Sierra Club and a very different argument to representatives of the Forest Service. In arguing to the Sierra Club, the student would almost assuredly expect agreement and therefore might focus on how the group could best oppose the plan and why members should devote their time and energy to this rather than other projects. The argument to the Forest Service would be quite different. Recognizing that members of the Forest Service would know the plan very well, would have spent a great deal of time working on it, and would be strongly committed to it, the student might focus on a limited number of points, especially those that the Forest Service might be most able and willing to modify. The student might also take particular care to assume a tone that is not aggressive or strident to avoid alienating the audience.

In academic argument, of course, your reader is generally your instructor. In this rhetorical situation, the most useful approach is to consider the values and beliefs that your instructor holds as a member of the academic community. In writing for an economics or a political science instructor, the student arguing against the Forest Service plan should provide logical, accurate, and appropriate evidence for assertions. He or she should avoid strong emotional appeals and harsh expressions of outrage or bitterness, focusing instead on developing a succinct, clearly organized, carefully reasoned essay.

NOTE FOR MULTILINGUAL WRITERS

As I have mentioned before, the standards of academic argument that are discussed in this book reflect the assumptions and values of the Western rhetorical tradition—a tradition that you are learning. This tradition encourages writers to articulate and defend their values and beliefs. Non-Western rhetorical traditions, including your own, may operate within different values and beliefs. Some traditions, for instance, encourage writers to state their assumptions and values indirectly so that readers reach their own conclusions by uncovering them. Try to identify the differences between your home writing culture and the Western rhetorical tradition in the way each expects its writers to address their values and beliefs. If you share these differences with your teacher and classmates, you will enrich everyone's understanding of the way that rhetorical practices are linked to particular contexts.

FOR EXPLORATION

Think of an issue that concerns you. Perhaps you are involved with or have been following a campus controversy. You may oppose a decision made recently by your city council or some other elected body. Or you may be committed (or opposed) to broad national movements such as efforts to provide public child-care facilities, house the homeless, or improve public transportation. After reflecting on this issue, use the guidelines presented earlier in this section to analyze your values and beliefs. Then respond to the following questions.

1. Given your values and beliefs, what challenges would writing an academic essay on this subject pose for you?

2. To what extent did your analysis help you understand that others might reasonably hold different views on this subject? Make a list of the opposing arguments that others might make in response to your subject. Then briefly describe the values and beliefs that might lead readers to make these counterarguments. How might you respond to these arguments?

3. Now write the major assertions or arguments that you would use to support your controlling idea or thesis. Below each assertion, list the values or beliefs that your readers must share with you to accept that assertion.

4. How have the guidelines on pp. 407–08 and this application helped you understand how to write an effective academic argument? If you were to write an academic argument on this issue, how would you now organize and develop your ideas? What strategies would you now use to respond to the values and beliefs of your readers?

As these examples demonstrate, appeals to ethos and pathos play important roles in academic argument. For an academic argument to be effective, however, it must be firmly grounded in logos. The remainder of this chapter presents strategies that you can follow to meet the logical and evidentiary demands of academic writing. To meet these demands you need to (1) determine whether a claim can be argued, (2) develop an appropriately limited claim, (3) understand the role that values and beliefs play in your argument, (4) provide good reasons and appropriate evidence for your argument, and (5) acknowledge possible counterarguments.

DETERMINING WHETHER A CLAIM CAN BE ARGUED

You can't argue by yourself. If you disagree with a recent legislative decision reported in your morning newspaper, you may mumble angry words to yourself at breakfast — but you'd know that you're not arguing. To argue, you must argue with someone. Furthermore, the person with whom you wish to argue must agree with you that an assertion raises an arguable *issue.* If you like hip-hop music, for example, and your friend, who prefers jazz, refuses even to listen to (much less discuss) your favorite CD or tape, you can hardly argue about your friend's preferences. You'll both probably just wonder at the peculiarities of taste.

Similarly, in academic argument you and your reader (most often your instructor) must agree that an issue is worth arguing about if you are to argue successfully. Often this agreement involves sharing a common understanding of a problem, process, or idea. A student who writes an argument on the symbolism of Hester Prynne's scarlet A in *The Scarlet Letter,* for example, begins from a premise that she believes will be shared by the teacher — that Hester's A has significance for the meaning or theme of the novel. Another example of working from a shared understanding can be found in the essay about the Tacoma Narrows Bridge, reprinted in Chapter 4, in which student Brenda Shonkwiler takes a cue from the ongoing discussion that continues among engineers over sixty years after the bridge's collapse in 1940 and successfully argues that an understanding of the causes underlying the failure is important for preventing future engineering disasters.

How can you determine whether a claim is arguable? The following guidelines present the characteristics of an arguable claim:

■ GUIDELINES FOR DETERMINING WHETHER A CLAIM CAN BE ARGUED

Claims can be argued if they meet the following criteria:

■ *Arguable claims address issues that are debatable and have something significant at stake.* There's no point in arguing about matters of fact; there's also no point in arguing about matters of personal taste. Readers are likely to hold varying beliefs and opinions about a claim that is truly arguable.

(continued)

(continued)

■ *Arguable claims attempt to persuade readers to believe or do something.* The purposes and occasions for argument can vary. Some arguments attempt to convince readers that an act or a belief is right or wrong, helpful or unhelpful. Other arguments explore deeply complex issues and problems with a goal of understanding, not persuasion.

Developing an Appropriately Limited Claim

Arguable claims must meet an additional criteria: They must be sufficiently limited so that both writer and reader can determine the major issues at stake and lines of argument that might best address these issues. In a late-night discussion with friends, you may easily slip from a heated exchange over the causes of the current unrest in world affairs to a friendly debate about whether *Chicago* really deserved to win an Oscar as best movie of the year in 2002. In an academic argument, however, you must limit your discussion not just to a single issue but to a single *thesis,* a claim you will argue for. It is not enough, in other words, to decide that you want to write about nuclear energy or the need to protect the wilderness. Even limiting these subjects — writing about the Three Mile Island nuclear reactor or the Forest Service Land Management Plan for the White Mountain National Forest in New Hampshire — wouldn't help much. That's because your thesis must be an assertion — something, in other words, to argue about.

A clear, adequately limited thesis is vital for academic argument because it indicates (for you and for your reader) what's at stake. For this reason, many instructors and writers suggest that academic arguments should contain an explicit thesis statement — a single declarative sentence that asserts or denies something about the topic. The assertion "The United States Forest Service's land management plan for the White Mountain National Forest fails adequately to protect New Hampshire's wilderness areas" is an example of a thesis statement.

Thesis statements serve important functions for writers and readers. Developing a clear, limited thesis statement can help a writer stay on track and include evidence or details relevant to the main point rather than extraneous or only loosely related information. Readers — especially busy readers like your college instructors — also find thesis statements helpful. A clearly worded thesis statement in the introduction of an essay assures readers that the essay will be well organized and clearly written; it also helps them read your writing both more critically and more efficiently.

Here is the first paragraph of an essay written for a class on Latin American history. The student's thesis statement is italicized. Notice how this statement clearly articulates the student's position on the topic, the role of multinational and transnational corporations in Central America:

> Over the past fifty years, Latin American countries have worked hard to gain economic strength and well-being. To survive, however, these countries have been forced to rely on multinational and transnational corporations for money, jobs, and technological expertise. *In doing so, they have lost needed economic independence and have left themselves vulnerable to exploitation by foreign financiers.*

A clear thesis statement can help both writer *and* reader stay on track as they "compose" an essay.

■ ■ ■

FOR EXPLORATION

Look back at the rough draft and revised draft of Todd Carpenter's essay, "Why Isn't There a National Bottle Law?" in Chapter 12 (pp. 310–14). Reread both drafts, and then answer these questions.

1. The rough draft does not contain a clear thesis statement, but the revised draft does. What is the thesis statement in the revised draft? Does this thesis statement help make Todd's essay easier for you as a reader to follow?

2. Todd's analysis of his rhetorical situation, presented on p. 310, demonstrates his awareness of the academic rhetorical situation and of the demands of academic analysis and argument. Todd notes, for instance, that "even if my instructor agrees that there should be a national bottle law, she won't give me a good grade unless I write an effective argument. In class, my instructor has stressed the importance of looking at both sides of the issue and presenting evidence for my views, so I'll try to do that here." Review Todd's rough and revised drafts, paying particular attention to the ways in which the revised draft responds to these concerns. List at least three of these changes, and write a brief explanation of why they increase the effectiveness of Todd's essay as an academic argument.

3. Suppose that Todd wants to write an essay on bottle laws for members of an ecological group whom he hopes to persuade to support this effort. How might Todd revise his argument to meet the needs and

expectations of these readers, who are likely to support the idea of a national bottle law but may not view it as a priority for their particular organization?

If you are like many writers, you will at times have to think — and write — your way to a thesis. You may know the subject you want to discuss, and you may have a tentative or *working thesis* in mind from the start. Sometimes, however, you will find that only by actually writing a rough draft — by marshaling your ideas and ordering your evidence — can you determine what thesis you can support. In situations like this, you will revise your thesis as you write to reflect your increased understanding of your topic and your rhetorical situation.

Providing Good Reasons—and Supporting These Reasons with Appropriate Evidence

In Chapter 15, "Understanding Academic Analysis," you learned about stasis theory, Aristotle's three appeals, and the Toulmin system to analyze and evaluate arguments. You can use these analytical tools to construct and revise your own arguments. Let's say that you have drafted an argument challenging increased standardized testing in the public schools. You're majoring in education, and you have strong feelings about mandated assessments. Your draft explores your ideas as freely and fully as possible. Now it's two days later—time to step back and evaluate your draft's effectiveness. So you turn to Aristotle's three appeals.

As you reread your essay with the appeals of ethos, pathos, and logos in mind, you realize that you've marshaled a good deal of evidence about the limitations of standardized testing—and thus made good use of appeals to logos. Your argument is much less successful in employing the appeals of ethos and pathos, however. Rereading your essay with Aristotle's three appeals in mind, you realize that the passion that you bring to this subject caused you to write in a strident tone that might cause readers not to trust your credibility or sense of fairness. You haven't considered the advantages of standardized testing or the reasons that some might find such testing helpful and even necessary. Critical readers might well suspect that you've stacked the deck against standardized testing.

Clearly, you need to strengthen your argument's appeal to ethos. You revise your tone so that it is more evenhanded, and more important, you consider multiple points of view on this subject by presenting and evaluating possible counterarguments to your position. Perhaps in the process you'll discover some shared values and beliefs that can strengthen your argument. (You could acknowledge your opponents, for instance, for recognizing the importance of education as a national, and not just local, concern.) You'll want to find as many ways as possible to demonstrate to your readers that you realize the subject that you are discussing is complex and that reasonable people might well differ in their understanding of the best way to address it.

What about pathos? In rereading your essay, you realize that in gathering strong evidence about the dangers and limitations of standardized testing, you've failed to give your subject a human face. You've got plenty of statistics and expert testimony but little that demonstrates how standardized testing affects real students and teachers. Based on your own experiences and those of peers, you have good examples of this negative impact, so you write yourself a reminder to include at least one such example in your revised draft. You also look for other ways to remind readers that national debates over standardized assessment are not about decontextualized test scores but about the learning and teaching experiences of students and teachers across America.

As this example suggests, such analytical tools as Aristotle's three appeals, stasis theory, and the Toulmin system can play a key role in the construction of arguments. You may not use these analytical tools to write the first draft of your argument: The flow of your ideas might be limited if you constantly asked yourself, "Does Toulmin's system call this point a claim, reason, warrant, qualifier, or evidence?" while drafting. But once you have a rough draft, you can use these analytical tools to test your ideas and identify problems that you need to address and areas that you need to strengthen. The student who is arguing that recent increases in standardized testing threaten the quality of students' education, for instance, might find it helpful to identify the most important stasis questions at issue in her argument. Are they questions of fact? Definition? Interpretation? Value? Consequence? Policy?

In addition to employing the previously discussed analytical tools to evaluate your argument, you can also ask yourself commonsense questions about the evidence that you include to support your claims. These questions are presented in the following guidelines.

■ GUIDELINES FOR EVALUATING EVIDENCE

- *Questions about examples:* How representative are my examples? Will readers find these examples relevant to my argument? Do I provide enough examples to make my point? Too many? Is the significance of examples clear to readers?

- *Questions about statistical evidence:* Have I used statistical evidence compiled by a disinterested source? If not, do I have a good reason for presenting statistics from a source with an established position on my topic? (Such would be the case, for instance, if

(continued)

(continued)

you cited statistics from Planned Parenthood in an argument about the need for legal abortions.) Are the statistics based on an adequate sample, and have I drawn appropriate inferences from them, given the sample size? Have I considered multiple interpretations of the statistical evidence that I present?

■ *Questions about evidence provided by authorities:* Is this authority qualified to comment on my topic? Why? Is this authority likely to be biased? Are the comments of this authority timely? If they are not—if I am citing an ancient authority on a contemporary topic, for instance—do I have a clear reason for why I think that this authority's comment is relevant? Do I need to contextualize this authority's comments by sharing his or her credentials with readers, or can I assume that they already know and respect him or her?

FOR EXPLORATION

Think again about the issue you wrote about in response to the Exploration on p. 410. Formulate a tentative or working thesis statement that reflects your current position on this issue. Articulate two or three reasons or claims that support your thesis, and then list the major evidence you would use to support these claims. Finally, write a brief statement explaining why this evidence is appropriate, given your thesis statement and the reasons or claims that you have written.

ACKNOWLEDGING POSSIBLE COUNTERARGUMENTS

Since academic argument is modeled on inquiry and dialogue rather than debate, you must consider multiple "sides" of an issue. Discussing and responding to counterarguments in your essay are effective ways to demonstrate that you have seriously analyzed an issue from a number of perspectives — that you have drawn reasonable conclusions.

Earlier sections of this chapter provided a number of ways to discover counterarguments. For instance, you could dialogue with one or more "devil's advocates," or you could discuss your subject with a group of classmates. You might even decide to interview someone who holds a position different from your own. Being aware of your own values and beliefs can also help you identify possible counterarguments. The student arguing against the Forest Service plan might consider the views of someone with different values, perhaps someone who believes in the importance of economic development, such as the owner of a lumber company. Finally, reading and research (both print and online) can expose you to the ideas and arguments of others.

How you use the counterarguments that you identify will depend on your subject and your rhetorical situation. In some instances, these counter-arguments can play an important structural role in your essay. After introducing your essay and indicating your thesis, for example, you might present the major counterarguments to your position, refuting each in turn. You might also group these counterarguments, responding to them all at once at an appropriate point.

■ ■ ■

FOR COLLABORATION

This activity will help you recognize possible counterarguments to the thesis that you have been writing about in this chapter. To prepare for this group activity, be sure that you have a clear, easy-to-read statement of your tentative or working thesis and of the major evidence you would use to support this thesis in an academic essay. Now spend five to ten minutes brainstorming a list of possible counterarguments to your working thesis.

Bring these written materials to your group's meeting. Determine how much time the group can spend per person if each student is to get help. Appoint a timekeeper to be sure that the group stays on time. Then have each writer read his or her working thesis, evidence, and possible counterarguments, followed by members of the group suggesting additional counterarguments that the writer has not considered. Avoid getting bogged down in specific arguments; instead, focus on generating as many additional counterarguments as possible. Continue this procedure until each student's work has been discussed.

Putting Theory into Practice: Academic Argument in Action

One of the major tenets of this textbook is that written communication is *situated* within a particular context. Therefore, there is no one-size-fits-all form of argument—or of any other kind of writing. Instead, writers must respond to the specifics of their rhetorical situation. (To review the concept of the rhetorical situation, see Chapters 5 and 6.) As an example of such a response, look again at the rough and final drafts of Todd Carpenter's essay, "Why Isn't There a National Bottle Law?" in Chapter 12 (pp. 310–14). Note how Todd's revision strengthens his argument and addresses the specifics of his rhetorical situation.

Here is another example of an academic argument. This essay was written by Stevon Roberts, whose analysis of the excerpt from Etzioni's *The Limits of Privacy* you read in the preceding chapter (pp. 394–398). After analyzing Etzioni's argument, Steve decided that he wanted to explore his own views on privacy issues, particularly on the Internet and Web. The following essay is the result of that exploration.

MY IDENTITY CRISIS—AND YOURS
Stevon Roberts

My name is Steve. It is also Clint Eastwood, Harrison Ford, and George W. Bush. I have been known as One-two-three, Four-five-six, and Seven-eight-five-eight-three-one (I can't tell you the rest because that's private). I have lived in Springfield, Eugene, and Corvallis, Oregon—and in Singapore and the District of Columbia at 1600 Pennsylvania Avenue. Sometimes I make less than $20,000 a year, and sometimes my salary would make Bill Gates turn green with envy. Do I suffer from multiple personality disorder? No. But I have learned the hard way about the need to protect my privacy online. As a result, I now intentionally provide false information for businesses requesting my name, address, Social Security number, annual salary, marital status, music tastes, and weekend hobbies.

Am I paranoid? Maybe. But I have learned how to avoid having a telephone that rings off the hook with telemarketers peddling long-distance telephone or cable services and how to maintain multiple email accounts with various pseudonyms to keep marketers from bombing my primary inbox with mass mailings for loan refinancings and Viagra. You might be thinking that avoiding nuisances like these is simply not worth the hassle of managing multiple email accounts, logins, passwords, and so on. I encourage you to reconsider. There is a growing security risk associated with the mass distribution of information over computer networks. People who freely give out their names, numbers, or addresses are not just vulnerable to mass soliciting: they are targets for hackers and identity thieves.

Like me, your initial reaction to statements like these might be, "That would never happen to me. The chances of getting my computer hacked or having my identity stolen are minuscule." Besides, aren't there state and federal agencies as well as Internet service providers charged with protecting citizens from these crimes? What about all those businesses implementing increased security and privacy policies on their Web sites? These kinds of "protections" lulled me into a false sense of security. Then, in February 2003, "more than five million Visa and MasterCard accounts throughout the nation were accessed . . . after the system at a third-party processor was hacked" ("Millions of Visa, MasterCard Numbers Exposed"). One of those accounts was mine. This experience convinced me that there are some businesses I couldn't trust to protect my privacy and identity. I had to take a more active role in protecting myself, and I hope I can convince you to do the same.

Such an effort may sound daunting and unnecessary, given the number of institutions and legislative bodies trying to protect us. It's important to recognize, however, that the laissez-faire nature of the Internet—one of its great strengths—is also a limitation where privacy is concerned. The speed with which technologies develop comes at a great cost: those who we have traditionally relied on to protect us cannot anticipate emergent problems, so they are always one step behind. As a result, attention to our personal privacy often yields to more immediate problems, such as hacking and virus control. Given this situation, citizens need to develop habits and strategies that minimize the exposure of personal information.

Chances are good that you have already had at least some exposure to this topic. Awareness of the danger is an important first step to take. But how willing are you to act on this awareness? How many take the time to learn who's collecting information and what they're collecting it for? One of the fastest-growing channels for private information exchange has silently exploited an estimated 90 percent of all computers connected to the Internet. Appropriately, it's called "spyware." ZDNet's Robert Vamosi describes spyware (also known as adware) as a "hidden software program that transmits user information via the Internet to advertisers in exchange for free downloaded software." Let's say that you want to install a program—maybe a download manager. To do so, you register the software with your name, address, phone number, email, and various other kinds of information. What the software distributors don't always tell you during installation (or more often don't tell you in LARGE ENOUGH PRINT) is that while you're being a good citizen of the Internet and registering your download manager, a hidden program may be simultaneously installed that transmits this personal information to advertisers who can target you for advertisements (Vamosi).

This may not sound particularly problematic, but spyware can transmit personal information not only to advertisers (which is bad enough) but also to those who would use this information for illegal purposes. Think about it: every time private information is transmitted, the chance for unauthorized interception by hackers increases. Collection, pooling, and distribution of this data increase the number of repositories waiting to be hit by the next hacker or identity thief. Because many legitimate software programs are packaged together with spyware and installed by unwary users, Internet service providers and policymakers cannot police their installation and usage. Spyware has already infested a wide variety of programs, including password managers, download managers, messaging programs, screensavers, and peer-to-peer file sharing programs.

In addition to being a courier for spyware, peer-to-peer (also known as "P2P") software has other inherent risks. This software allows users to share selected contents of their hard drives (such as music and movies) over a network supported by other users, or "peers." In the wake of Napster's collapse, people have indiscriminately flocked to these alternative networks for music and video—perhaps without understanding that they are not as secure as Napster was. P2P networks are not organized around a central, regulated network, so there are no built-in safeguards against hackers. P2P software may give your Internet provider address (sort of like a long telephone number for your computer) to malicious users. "By using your unique IP address, someone can immediately begin attacking your computer, monitor or follow your online and computer activity, or steal your private information, such as occurs in identify theft ("IP Address"). P2P programs can also be reverse engineered—that is, "hackers [have] the ability to change the software code so that it can be used for other purposes" (Kabay). The software may be used, for example, to gain unauthorized access to your computer and plant viruses or steal sensitive information like private files and bank account numbers.

If you work online, you're undoubtedly familiar with the irritating bulk email that we refer to as spam, but you may not be familiar with its potential threats to privacy. Recent software innovations combined with lax attitudes toward protecting email addresses have led to an epidemic of spam for inboxes around the country. America Online (AOL) reported in 1997 that spam made up almost a third of its 30 million email messages (Bigelow). That was five years ago. Over just the last eighteen months, spam has increased fivefold (Vise). AOL alone "blocks 780 million pieces of junk e-mail daily, or 100 million more e-mails than it delivers" (Vise). Spam wastes time. It monopolizes bandwidth and time, costing corporations billions of dollars a year. And now, it poses a security risk. According to Infoworld.com's Heather Harreld, "Marketing companies have begun to embed invisible HTML [hypertext markup language] 'bugs' or 'beacons' in their e-mail. Because these tiny one-pixel images must be retrieved from the sender's server when the message is opened, they can tell the sender when and how often a recipient looks at a message." As Harreld points out, HTML code embedded in the message can "allow the sender to gather information like the recipient's IP address, the type of browser they use, and the Web sites they visit." Sharon Ward, director of enterprise business applications at Hurwitz Group, in Framingham, Massachusetts, believes "It's just a matter of time [before] someone [can] figure out how to use these things against people or corporations." Ward speculates that this latest marketing development might be a hacker's newest tool—a "tricky little Trojan Horse for getting viruses into unsuspecting people's e-mail" (Harreld).

With businesses and identity thieves becoming increasingly aggressive in trying to steal private information, you need to take preventative measures to avoid becoming a victim of identity theft or fraud. Install a firewall on your home computer. (Your school and your office probably already have firewalls.) Firewalls are user-configurable gateways that are designed to block information from going into or out of a computer on certain ports or from certain software. It is also important to spend more time choosing the software you run on your computer in the first place— all of it. By reading software reviews (which are abundant online), you may be able to keep your machine from getting spyware, which is often much easier than getting rid of it (although you can look into antispyware software now available). If you are averse to reading reviews for yourself, ask your favorite computer guru what software you should (or shouldn't) be running.

How much money you invest will probably depend on how you use your computer, but any firewall or antispyware program is better than none at all. Time spent installing and updating the software is well spent when you compare it with the processing time and Internet bandwidth that spyware can leech away from your computer. More important, it is far less time than you will spend on hold with your bank's customer service center if your credit card is illegally used. Some Internet service providers will even assist you with the installation of this software since it helps maintain their network security as well as yours. Although you are ultimately responsible for protecting your own personal information, it's nice to have allies who are willing to help.

Yahoo, one email provider, has been especially proactive in promoting public awareness and participation with a contest for people who report unsolicited email. It uses the information that you send to help protect against further spamming for you as well as others. This is a great alternative to blocking spam or sending a "do not send me any more mail" request, which (contrary to popular belief) only affirms the presence of a valid email account and makes you a likely candidate for continued spamming. But better than this is not giving out your email address (or any personal information) if you don't absolutely have to. When you fill out applications or registration forms, fill in only the required fields, and read privacy policies with careful attention to where your information may be sent. Be sure to deselect any checkboxes for newsletters, agreements to make your information available to others and so forth. It may also be in your interest to give businesses whose privacy policies you aren't satisfied with an alternative email address that doesn't include your real name. This will help to reduce pooling and distribution of your information, and it is time well spent when you compare it to the time spent wading through pages and pages of spam sent to your primary business or personal email accounts (is there an echo in here?).

These steps are relatively easy to take, and they can dramatically improve the security of your identity and privacy online. I would caution you, however, not simply to follow my advice and then forget all about it. It will always be tempting to let others work to maintain your privacy and identity. Recent history has demonstrated, however, that the rapid evolution of online technologies has presented new challenges as well as new opportunities, and those who use the Web must remain vigilant and evolve to meet those challenges or face ever-increasing threats to security. My solutions have evolved to include juggling multiple email accounts and offering intentionally false data to confuse information archives, but your solution may not need to be so complex. Perhaps you'll start with two email addresses—one you give to businesses and one you give only to your close friends or office. By taking responsibility with these steps and being on the lookout for new habits and strategies to improve your privacy and security, you can help thwart this crisis concerning peoples' identities.

WORKS CITED

Bigelow, Stephen. "CNET Teaches Self-Defense against Spam." *CNET* 27 Mar. 2001. 12 Oct. 2003 <http://www.cnet.com>.

"IP Address Hacking and Scanning: Internet Security Background Report." *Discount-Evidence-Eliminator.com* 28 Feb. 2003. 11 Oct. 2003 <http://www.discount-evidence-eliminator.com/articles /ip-address-hacking.htm>.

Harreld, Heather. "Embedded HTML 'Bugs' Pose Potential Security Risk." *Infoworld* 5 Dec. 2000. 8 Oct. 2003 <http://archive.infoworld .com>.

Kabay, M. E. "Peer-to-Peer Software and Security." *NetworkWorldFusion* 28 Aug. 2000. 12 Oct. 2003 <http://www.nwfusion.com/newsletters /sec/2000/0828sec1.html?nf>.

"Millions of Visa, MasterCard Numbers Exposed." *ZDNet* 18 Feb. 2003. 8 Oct. 2003 <http://zdnet.com.com/2100-1105-984842.html>.

Vamosi, Robert. "What Is Spyware?" *ZDNet* 28 June 2001. 12 Oct. 2003 <http://www.zdnet.com/products/stories/reviews /0,4161,2612053,00.html>.

Vise, David A. "AOL Joins Microsoft in a Reply to Spam." *The Washington Post* 21 Feb. 2003: EOI. *Washingtonpost.com.* 11 Oct. 2003 <http:// www.washingtonpost.com/wp-dyn/articles/A38150-2003Feb20 .html>.

■ ■ ■

FOR EXPLORATION

Once you have read Stevon's essay, reread it, annotating as you read. Can you identify a thesis? What major claims support this thesis? And what reasons and evidence support the claims? Finally, evaluate the overall effectiveness of Stevon's argument. What would you identify as particular strengths of his argument? What weaknesses, if any, can you identify?

FOR COLLABORATION

Meet with a group of peers to discuss your responses to the preceding activity. Appoint a timekeeper so that all have an opportunity to share their ideas. After all have done so, answer these questions: To what extent did you agree in your assessment of Stevon Roberts's essay? To what extent did you disagree? What did reading and evaluating his essay help you better understand about the demands of academic argument? Be prepared to share your ideas with your classmates.

When you enter a college or university, you join an academic community with unique values, beliefs, and methods of inquiry. Yet few members of that community will discuss these directly with you. Instead, your history instructor explores the impact of printing on the Renaissance imagination, and your political science instructor focuses on recent events in the Middle East. Your instructors leave it to you to understand the academic rhetorical situation and to master the skills necessary to succeed in their courses. You don't have to face this challenge alone, however. Your composition instructor and your classmates, acting as both coaches and supporters, can help you understand and develop the critical thinking, reading, and writing skills necessary for success in school. What is at stake in your composition course, then, is not just earning a passing grade or fulfilling a requirement but becoming a fully participating and successful member of the academic community.

■ ■ ■

FOR THOUGHT, DISCUSSION, AND WRITING

1. This chapter has presented activities designed to improve your understanding of academic argument. The Exploration on p. 410, for instance, asks you to identify the values, assumptions, and beliefs that have led you to hold strong views on an issue. The one on p. 416 asks you to formulate a tentative or working thesis and to list the major

evidence you would use to support it. Finally, the group activity on p. 417 encourages you to acknowledge possible counterarguments to your thesis.

Drawing on these activities, write an essay directed to an academic reader on the topic you have explored, revising your working thesis if you need to do so.

2. This chapter has focused on argumentative strategies that apply across the academic curriculum. While scholars in all disciplines would probably agree with the discussion of argument that is presented in this chapter, they might be quick to add that arguments in their own disciplines have unique features. Interview a teacher whose course you are currently taking in one of the following areas: the humanities, the social sciences, the natural and applied sciences, or business. Ask this teacher what characteristics he or she looks for in a successful academic argument in his or her discipline. Then write a brief summary describing what this interview helped you to understand about argument in this particular discipline.

3. Newspaper editorials and opinion columns represent one common form of argument. If your college or university publishes a newspaper, read several issues in sequence, paying particular attention to editorials and opinion columns that are published therein. (If your school does not publish a newspaper, choose a local newspaper instead.) Choose one editorial or opinion column that you believe represents a successful argument; choose another that for one or more reasons strikes you as suspect. Bring these texts to class, and be prepared to share your evaluations of them with your classmates.

Putting It All Together: Analyzing and Writing Academic Arguments

One of the best ways to understand a complex process is to see that process in action. An aspiring chef who wants to learn how to make croissants can read recipe after recipe and yet not quite grasp the technique required to make these rich, crescent-shaped rolls. Observing someone who is actually making croissants — someone demonstrating critical elements of the technique — can make a world of difference. So it is with writers. This chapter provides an opportunity for you to take an in-depth look at one writer's process in action. Though you will not be able to sit next to this writer as she composes, you will be able to observe — and learn from — the three drafts of a single essay that are presented here. With each draft, this writer clarifies and strengthens her argument.

The writer is Beth Runciman, a student at Smith College in Northampton, Massachusetts. For an American literature survey course, Beth was assigned to write an essay analyzing a poem by Emily Dickinson, a nineteenth-century American writer. As a first step in her composing process, Beth wrote an analysis of her rhetorical situation. Here is Beth's analysis:

> This assignment calls for a formal argument, so I will need to follow the conventions of an academic essay, with a clear introduction and conclusion and a logical order to the organization. The assignment asks us to demonstrate that we understand what's going on in the poem we choose to write about — that we locate the poem in its historical context and that we talk about the literary techniques the author is using to make her point. I'll want to make sure that the argument I present is grounded in evidence from the poem itself and that I'm able to quote specific lines from the poem to support what I say. I'll also want to use the vocabulary we've studied in class — terms like image, metaphor, meter, and line break.
>
> The audience for this essay is my professor. I know that she appreciates Dickinson's poetry, but what she'll be looking for in my essay isn't so much appreciation as understanding. To help convey that understanding, I need to adopt a tone of objectivity and authority.

Notice how in these comments Beth moves from a general assessment of her assignment — "I need to follow the conventions of an academic essay, with a clear introduction and conclusion and a logical order to the organization" — to consideration of the conventions of the discipline for which she is writing, in this case literary criticism. Beth understands that when instructors read student writing, they do so from the perspective of their disciplinary training. Given this, Beth recognizes that her goal is to demonstrate her ability to analyze and interpret Dickinson's poem and not to persuade her teacher to believe or do something.

Beth's understanding of her rhetorical situation will influence the choices she makes as a writer. To become more self-conscious about these choices, Beth concluded her analysis by considering how her essay might best address Aristotle's three appeals: the appeal to logos, or reason; to pathos, or emotion; and to ethos, or the credibility of the writer. (If you wish to review Aristotle's three appeals, see p. 169.)

> **Logos:** I'll appeal most strongly to logos when writing this essay. To be successful, I've got to show my teacher that I can analyze the poem in detail and draw conclusions from my analysis.

> **Pathos:** Emotional appeals won't play a strong role in my essay. Dickinson's poem is very emotional, but my analysis needs to focus on its technique and content. I do want to appeal to pathos in one way, though: I want to encourage the reader to appreciate Dickinson's skill and daring.

> **Ethos:** I want my teacher to see me as being fully in control of my ideas and their presentation. If my analysis (logos) is effective, my teacher will view me as a credible writer.

Beth's analysis has helped prepare her to meet the demands of her assignment. This analysis has reminded Beth that even when an assignment is relatively broad and open-ended, as hers is, her teacher nevertheless has specific expectations about how students can best complete it. In this instance, Beth's teacher expects that successful students will write essays demonstrating their ability to "talk the talk and walk the walk" of literary criticism.

BETH'S FIRST DRAFT: ANALYZING EMILY DICKINSON'S POEM #48

As mentioned earlier, Beth worked her way through three drafts before she arrived at an essay that satisfied her. According to Beth, each draft had a slightly different purpose. "In my first draft," she said, "I was trying to analyze the poem itself and understand how Dickinson's choices of meter, rhythm, imagery, and syntax made the poem what it was. I wrote this draft to talk to myself about all the ways the poem was working. I knew I would need to know it inside out to write a formal argument about it."

Beth wrote this comment, by the way, in a writing-process journal that she kept while working on her essay. Beth was taking a first-year writing class at the same time that she was enrolled in her American literature survey class, and her writing instructor had asked her students to choose a writing assignment from a different class and keep detailed notes about their writing process. You may find it helpful to undertake similar self-study. (See pp. 35–36 for directions for a case study of your own writing process.)

Here is Beth Runciman's first draft of her essay. It is preceded by the Emily Dickinson poem that Beth chose to analyze.

ANALYSIS OF EMILY DICKINSON'S POEM #48 [FIRST DRAFT]
by Beth Runciman

> Once more, my now bewildered Dove
> Bestirs her puzzled wings
> Once more her mistress, on the deep
> Her troubled question flings —
>
> Thrice to the floating casement
> The Patriarch's bird returned,
> Courage! My brave Columba!
> There may yet be Land!

In poem #48 ("Once more, my now bewildered Dove"), Dickinson talks about feelings of hope and feelings of desperation, and she uses the story of Noah and the end of the flood as a metaphor to do so. In the story, Noah releases a dove from the ark three times near the end of the flood. He knows that if the bird cannot see land, it will return to the ark. If land is in sight, however, the bird will fly toward it, showing Noah the direction in which to sail. Dickinson builds the whole poem around this image. She replaces "The Patriarch," Noah, with a female speaker; we know this from the word "mistress." This speaker's tone is desperate, as Noah's would be as well — an ark can hold only so much food, and if the bird does not direct Noah to land soon enough, all living creatures will perish.

Dickinson's rhythm and word choice create a frantic and desperate tone in the first stanza. We know this from the progression of the speaker's adjectives, from "bewildered" to "puzzled" to "troubled," in which each adjective is more severe than the preceding one. The verb "flings" at the end of the stanza is a desperate action as well, drawing attention to the speaker's urgency. Working against this urgency metaphorically, however, is the time the speaker has had to endure simply waiting. We get this sense in the poem's first phrase, "Once more," as well as in the stanza's rhythm. The speaker talks in iambs, making the reader wait for the stressed syllable. In this way, the speaker creates in the reader a feeling similar to what she is experiencing.

This desperation is not unchecked, however. The speaker's attention in the poem is focused on the dove, a symbol of hope. Here Dickinson uses the image of Noah releasing and waiting for the dove. From this image we infer that Noah is watching the bird carefully and earnestly as it flies. In the biblical story, if Noah loses sight of the bird and it does not return, he will not know which way to sail, and eventually everything on his boat will perish. The speaker in this poem is trying to ignore her own desperation and pay attention only to her hope, as symbolized by the bird. Dickinson's syntax as well as her imagery support this idea of hopeful attention. We know from the word "my" in the first line that this poem is written in the first person. In the second and third lines, however, the speaker refers to herself in the third person as "her mistress," the mistress of the dove. The speaker is so focused on the dove that the sense of the bird replaces the speaker's sense of self as a valid reference point. The bird is so important that it makes sense for the speaker to talk about herself only in relation to it.

The second stanza serves to clarify the speaker's imagery about the flood and to change the poem's tone. "Thrice to the floating casement / The Patriarch's bird returned," is a direct reference to Noah's experience as told in the Bible. In the last two lines of this stanza, the voice of the speaker and the voice of Noah merge together. Instead of desperation, both these voices encourage the dove in its search for land and thus encourage the spirit of hopefulness within themselves. By ending the poem with the assertion "There may yet be Land!" the speaker shows the reader that her circumstances have not gotten the better of her. In this way, Dickinson uses the poem as a way of presenting an emotional process or progression — in this case, from the heavy and urgent feelings of fear to the strong and self-assured experience of hope and faith.

Even in this early version, Beth Runciman's essay has a number of strengths. Perhaps most impressive is her ability to read Dickinson's poem with care and to make specific and detailed comments about the meaning of the poem and Dickinson's craft as a writer. Beth uses the vocabulary of literary criticism (terms like "stanza," "iambs," and "image") to good effect. And she draws on her previous knowledge of the Bible to clarify some of the references in the poem. Nevertheless, when Beth looked closely at her draft, she saw some limitations. "There's a lot of specific information in this draft," she wrote in her process journal. "But it doesn't add up. There's not a clear enough point. I end with a kind of assertion about how the poem works, but it's pretty general. It could probably apply to a number of other poems by Dickinson." Beth's last comment is particularly telling, for if her comments could apply to other Dickinson poems, then she is writing at a fairly general level and needs to sharpen both her analysis and her argument.

BETH'S SECOND DRAFT: DEVELOPING A THESIS

The next time Beth worked on her essay, she decided to begin by freewriting about her goals for this drafting session. Writing in her process journal, Beth commented, "I think I understand how this poem works, but I'm not doing enough with it. I've got to figure out exactly what I want to argue in my essay. I think that I could do more with the biblical references that Dickinson uses. In my first draft I talk about these references, but I don't really explain how important they are to the poem's meaning. I'll try to do that now." Here is the draft that Beth wrote in response to this goal setting.

AN EXPLORATION OF EMILY DICKINSON'S POEM #48 [SECOND DRAFT]
by Beth Runciman

Poets often write for an audience that shares a certain background or knowledge base. They build their poems assuming that readers will be familiar enough with their references to understand the work. Writing in the late nineteenth century, Emily Dickinson frequently used biblical allusions in her poetry. In this essay, I explore how such an allusion works in Dickinson's poem #48 ("Once more, my now bewildered Dove"). I closely read the poem, describing the poetic techniques Dickinson uses, and I demonstrate that the reader's knowledge of the story of Noah and the Ark plays a crucial role in the poem's communication with the reader.

According to the biblical story, Noah released a dove from the ark three times near the end of the great flood. Noah knew that if the bird could not see land, it would return to the ark. If land were in sight, however, the bird would fly toward it, showing Noah the direction in which to sail. Dickinson builds her whole poem around the image of this third release. In poem #48, she writes:

Once more, my now bewildered Dove
Bestirs her puzzled wings
Once more her mistress, on the deep
Her troubled question flings —

> Thrice to the floating casement
> The Patriarch's bird returned,
> Courage! My brave Columba!
> There may yet be Land!

The first and second lines of the second stanza refer directly to Noah's experience as told in the Bible. However, in this poem Dickinson also selectively edits this biblical scene, making the story her own. She replaces "The Patriarch," Noah, with a female speaker; we know this from her choice of the word "mistress." Throughout the poem, Dickinson draws on her readers' knowledge of the end of the flood to talk about the feelings of hope and feelings of desperation that belong to her unique speaker.

Dickinson's rhythm and word choice create a frantic and desperate tone in the first stanza. We know this from the progression of the speaker's adjectives, from "bewildered" to "puzzled" to "troubled," in which each adjective is more severe than the preceding one. The verb "flings" at the end of the stanza is a desperate action as well, drawing attention to the speaker's urgency. These choices underscore the desperation implicit in the biblical story. Noah's ark can hold only so much food, and if the bird does not direct Noah to land soon enough, all living creatures will perish.

Working against this urgency metaphorically, however, is the time the speaker has had to endure simply waiting. We get this sense in the poem's first phrase, "Once more," as well as in the stanza's rhythm. The speaker talks in iambs, making the reader wait for the stressed syllable. In this way, Dickinson creates in the reader a feeling similar to what her speaker is experiencing, waiting and watching for the bird.

The speaker's desperation is not unchecked, however. Her attention throughout the poem is focused on the dove, a traditional symbol of hope. Here, Dickinson draws on the image of Noah releasing and waiting for the dove; in the story, we infer that Noah is watching the bird carefully and earnestly as it flies. If Noah loses sight of the bird and it does not return, he will not know which way to sail, and eventually everything on his boat will perish. By structuring her poem around this image, Dickinson suggests that her speaker is trying to ignore her own desperation and pay attention only to her hope, as symbolized by the bird.

The syntax in the poem supports this idea of hopeful attention. We know from the word "my" in the first line that this poem is written in the first person. In the second and third lines, however, the speaker refers to herself in the third person as "her mistress," the mistress of the dove. The speaker is so focused on the dove that the sense of the bird replaces the speaker's sense of self as a valid reference point. The bird is so important that it makes sense for the speaker to talk about herself only in relation to it.

In the last two lines of this stanza, the voice of the speaker and the voice of Noah merge. Instead of desperation, both these voices seek to encourage the dove in its search for land and thus encourage the spirit of hopefulness within themselves. By ending the poem with the assertion "There may yet be Land!" the speaker shows the reader that her circumstances have not gotten the better of her.

In this poem, then, Dickinson uses the biblical image as a way of presenting an emotional progression within her speaker, from the heavy and urgent feelings of fear to the strong and self-assured experience of hope and faith. She draws on changes in tone, supported by her choices of rhythm and syntax, to support the emotional process the biblical scene suggests. She also edits the image to serve her purposes, and she depends on the reader's prior knowledge of the biblical version for her changes to be meaningful. Dickinson's poem is an excellent example of an author drawing on and interpreting a shared cultural story in a piece of poetry.

This second draft improves Beth's earlier effort in several important ways. The new introduction provides background information that leads directly to a statement of purpose: "In this essay, I explore how such an allusion works in Dickinson's poem #48 ('Once more, my now bewildered Dove'). I closely read the poem, describing the poetic techniques Dickinson uses, and I demonstrate that the reader's knowledge of the story of Noah and the Ark plays a crucial role in the poem's communication with the reader." Included in this statement of purpose is a thesis statement: "the reader's knowledge of the story of Noah and the Ark plays a crucial role in the poem's communication with the reader." Also helpful is Beth's comment that she will "closely read the poem" — for what those in the discipline of English studies call "close reading" is a specific way of reading texts. In using this term here, Beth is signaling to her teacher that she understands the importance of this method for analyzing literary texts and will employ it in her essay.

The next two paragraphs of Beth's second draft generally follow the lines of her first draft — but with one important difference. Beth revises the first draft's straightforward observation (that Dickinson "replaces 'The Patriarch,' Noah, with a female speaker") with the stronger and more pointed comment that "in this poem Dickinson also selectively edits this biblical scene, making the story her own." In addition to this change, Beth significantly develops the conclusion to her essay. Beth's first draft ended with the observation that "Dickinson uses the poem as a way of presenting an emotional process, or progression, in this case from the heavy and urgent feelings of fear to the strong and self-assured experience of hope and faith." This sentence now begins a new paragraph that builds on many of the observations Beth has made about how the poem achieves its effect. The final sentence of this draft — "Dickinson's poem is an excellent example of an author drawing on and interpreting a shared cultural story in a piece of poetry" — demonstrates that Beth not only understands the poem but can generalize from it to other literary efforts.

BETH'S FINAL DRAFT: CLARIFYING AND EXTENDING HER ARGUMENT

After completing the second draft of her essay, Beth waited a day before rereading it. "I need to have time between drafts," she wrote in her process journal. "I either love or hate my writing right after I've written something. Either way, there's no point in trying to work with it then." When Beth did return to her draft, she saw that she had improved her essay. But she was still dissatisfied with her overall argument. "What frustrates me," Beth wrote, "is that I haven't been able to convey how gutsy Dickinson is being in this poem." In an effort to clarify her ideas, Beth spent some time rereading Dickinson's poem and brainstorming and freewriting about it. She also reviewed notes she had taken during class discussions of Dickinson's poetry. And, finally, she returned to her original analysis of her rhetorical situation (p. 425). "There's nothing wrong with this analysis," Beth wrote in her process journal. "But it's pretty general. Maybe if I force myself to be more specific I can work out what I want to do." So Beth wrote a new second paragraph for her analysis:

> In class, we talked about how subversive Emily Dickinson's poetry was for her historical moment, and I remember being surprised at the critical edge that laced much of her work. For this assignment I want to explore not only how #48 works as a poem but also how it challenges certain norms of nineteenth-century New England society. I want my reader to come away from my essay with an appreciation of Dickinson's method for critiquing the culture in which she lived her life, as well as with an appreciation for her poetic skills and her use of biblical references.

As Beth noted in her process journal, this was a critical moment in her writing. She was finally able to see what she wanted to be at stake in her argument. She didn't want just to show that Dickinson was a good poet who knew how to use biblical allusions effectively. She wanted to demonstrate that Dickinson was a subversive poet. As Beth explained in her process journal, this insight was important in several ways. "I saw I had the hook that I needed to give my argument zip," she wrote. "But even better I reconnected with my passion for Dickinson. I'm a rebel, and I was really drawn to the rebel in Dickinson — but I couldn't find a way to get that into my writing. Now I can."

Did Beth succeed in demonstrating that Dickinson's poem #48 "challenges certain norms of nineteenth-century New England society"? You can decide for yourself as you read the third and final draft of her essay.

THE MATRIARCH'S BIRD [FINAL DRAFT]
by Beth Runciman

> Once more, my now bewildered Dove
> Bestirs her puzzled wings
> Once more her mistress, on the deep
> Her troubled question flings —
>
> Thrice to the floating casement
> The Patriarch's bird returned,
> Courage! My brave Columba!
> There may yet be Land!

Poets often write for an audience that shares a certain background or knowledge base, and they build their poems assuming that readers will be familiar enough with their references to understand their work. Writing in the late nineteenth century, Emily Dickinson frequently used allusions to biblical stories in her poetry. In this essay, I explore how such an allusion works in Dickinson's poem #48 ("Once more, my now bewildered Dove"). I closely read the poem, describing the techniques Dickinson uses to communicate through it, and I argue that the reader's knowledge of the story of Noah and the Ark plays a crucial role in this communication.

More is going on in this poem, however, than a simple reference to a shared cultural story. Dickinson selectively edits the details of this tale, and she retells it with her own unique and, I would argue, subversive slant. Instead of calling to mind the familiar story of Noah and reinforcing traditional nineteenth-century values, Dickinson changes the tale to suggest a radical revision of nineteenth-century ideals. The fact that the text she revises is held sacred by most of her audience makes this revision all the more startling and gives the poem its subversive appeal.

According to the Bible, Noah released a dove from the ark three times near the end of the flood. He knew that if the bird could not see land, it would return to the ark. If land were in sight, however, the bird would fly toward it, demonstrating to Noah the direction in which to sail. In poem #48, Dickinson builds her entire poem around the image of this third release. "Thrice to the floating casement / The Patriarch's bird returned" is a direct reference to Noah's experience as told in the Bible. Dickinson's poem depends on her readers' recognition of the biblical story from these brief lines. The tone in both of her stanzas — the tone she sets up to match Noah's emotional state during the releasing of the dove — reinforces this recognition.

In the first stanza, her rhythm and word choice create a frantic and desperate tone. We know this from the progression of the speaker's adjectives. Each adjective — from "bewildered" to "puzzled" to "troubled" — is more emphatic than the preceding one. The verb "flings" at the end of the stanza is a desperate action as well, drawing attention to the speaker's urgency. These choices underscore the desperation implicit in the biblical story. Noah's ark can hold only so much food, and if the bird does not direct Noah to land soon enough, all living creatures will perish.

Working against this urgency metaphorically, however, is the time the speaker has had to endure waiting for the dove to return. We get this sense in the poem's first phrase, "Once more," as well as in the stanza's rhythm. The speaker talks in iambs, making the reader wait for the stressed syllable. In this way, Dickinson creates in the reader a feeling similar to what her speaker is experiencing.

There is something unexpected about this speaker, however. Dickinson replaces the figure of "The Patriarch," Noah, with a female speaker; we know this from her choice of the word "mistress" and by the female possessive pronoun that appears in "*her* troubled question." To Dickinson's contemporaries, this would have been a scandalous revision indeed. At that time in New England, biblical laws were invoked to uphold the father as the rightful ruler of the family and to maintain separate spheres of work for men and women. Women were expected to be obedient wives, to stay home, and to raise children, and stories from the Bible were frequently told to ensure that they did so. To suggest that a woman could have done the work that Noah did — responding to the very voice of God and saving all living creatures from certain death — would disrupt the assumptions on which society was built. Not only was Dickinson suggesting that women could do men's work; she was using the same text her contemporaries frequently called on to suggest exactly the opposite.

So of course Dickinson takes particular care to ground the reader in the biblical tale, despite the fact that the speaker is female. While the poem opens with a desperate and frantic tone, the speaker's desperation is not unchecked. Throughout the poem, her attention is focused on the dove, a traditional symbol of hope. If Noah loses sight of the bird and it does not return, he will not know which way to sail, and eventually all living creatures on his boat will perish. Drawing on this shared cultural knowledge, Dickinson suggests that her speaker, like Noah, is trying to ignore her own desperation and pay attention only to her hope, as symbolized by the bird. By structuring her poem around the exact emotional dimensions of this moment, Dickinson reinforces the idea that her speaker is, in fact, the same Noah as in the biblical story.

Dickinson's syntax works to communicate her speaker's hopeful attention. We know from the word "my" in the first line that this poem is written in the first person. In the second and third lines, however, the speaker refers to herself in the third person as "her mistress," the mistress of the dove. The speaker is so focused on the dove that the bird replaces the speaker's self as a reference point. In the last two lines of this stanza, the voice of the speaker and the voice of Noah merge. Instead of desperation, both these voices seek to encourage the dove in its search for land and thus encourage the spirit of hopefulness within themselves. By ending the poem with the assertion "There may yet be Land!" the speaker shows the reader that her circumstances have not gotten the better of her. These are the most subversive lines in the poem: In them, Dickinson's speaker becomes Noah and speaks with his voice. There is no longer any room for doubt about who this speaker is or about the fact of Dickinson's substitution of a female for Noah. By speaking out in the voice of Noah, one of the most important men in the sacred biblical text, Dickinson's female speaker becomes impossible for her reader to dismiss.

Several things are going on in this poem, then. Dickinson presents her readers with a poem that documents an emotional progression, from the heavy and urgent feelings of fear to the strong and self-assured experience of hope and faith. She draws on changes in tone, supported by the careful use of rhythm and syntax, to support this progression. Dickinson builds this progression around a well-known biblical tale and depends on her readers' shared cultural knowledge of the Bible. However, she edits the tale to convey a more subversive message. By substituting a female speaker for Noah, Dickinson challenges fundamental assumptions of sex-segregated nineteenth-century society; further, her challenge is based in the very text on which those assumptions were thought to rest. Thus does Dickinson's poem quietly — but effectively — challenge the cultural norms of her day.

The first thing you might have noticed about Beth's draft is that it now has a title: "The Matriarch's Bird." This titles provides important cues to the reader about the focus of her essay, for the term "matriarch" calls to mind the related term "patriarch." This is a term used in the Hebrew Scripture to refer to such important male figures as Adam and Noah. A "matriarch," then, is a female figure of great importance in her society. Beth's title thus prepares readers for her discussion of Dickinson's subversion of the biblical story of Noah and the Ark.

There are other important additions to Beth's essay. After the introduction, which resembles that of the previous draft, Beth added a new second paragraph, in which she claims "More is going on in this poem, however, than a simple reference to a shared cultural story." This paragraph adds complexity and significance to Beth's interpretation of Dickinson's poem. While her earlier drafts focused primarily on how Dickinson's poem works — how it is put together and achieves its effect — this draft goes beyond analysis to argument. It demonstrates that Beth can read a poem with care, place that poem in its historical context, and make claims about its contemporary significance.

In the sixth paragraph, Beth further develops and supports her position. She does so by building on an observation that has appeared in all three drafts: that Dickinson replaces the figure of Noah with a female speaker. But here for the first time she considers the cultural context of this change and provides explicit links that connect evidence with larger generalizations:

> To Dickinson's contemporaries, this would have been a scandalous revision indeed. At that time in New England, biblical laws were invoked to uphold the father as the rightful ruler of the family and to maintain separate spheres of work for men and women. Women were expected to be obedient wives, to stay home, and to raise children, and stories from the Bible were frequently told to ensure that they did so. To suggest that a woman could have done the work that Noah did — responding to the very voice of God and saving all living creatures from certain death — would disrupt the assumptions on which society was built. Not only was Dickinson suggesting that women could do men's work; she was using the same text her contemporaries frequently called on to suggest exactly the opposite.

Here, and again in the closing paragraphs of her essay, Beth effectively argues that Dickinson not only grounds her poem in her readers' knowledge of the Bible but subverts the biblical story for her own purposes.

Thanks to her three drafts, Beth was able to write her way to an effective academic argument. In her final process journal entry, Beth commented on this experience, observing, "In this essay, I didn't know exactly what I was going to argue until the final draft — but I wouldn't have been able to see that argument and make it work if I hadn't studied the poem by writing the other drafts first." With each draft, Beth's argument became clearer, and the links between her evidence and her generalizations became both more explicit and more fully developed.

■ ■ ■

FOR EXPLORATION

The preceding analysis has focused primarily on global changes that Beth Runciman made as she worked on her essay. But in addition to revising the approach and organization of her essay, Beth made many small, local changes. After rereading the second and third drafts of Beth's essay, identify at least three local (word- or sentence-level) revisions that Beth made that in your view improved her writing.

LEARNING FROM YOUR READING OF BETH'S THREE DRAFTS

To write a successful essay on Dickinson's poem #48, Beth Runciman drew on her understanding of writing and of the writing process as well as on her rhetorical awareness of the demands of academic argument. By giving herself the time to write three drafts of her essay, Beth demonstrated her control over the composing process. But as Beth noted in her journal, this process was hardly perfect: Beth had hoped to arrange for a peer-response session with her study group — but she ran out of time. "I know my essay would be even better if someone else had been able to read it," Beth wrote in her process journal. "Once I've wrestled my way through to getting the big things working, I have a lot of trouble seeing smaller things like awkward sentences and errors."

As I'm sure you will agree, Beth did indeed do a good job of attending to "the big things." She took time at the start of her writing process, for instance, to think long and hard about the demands of her assignment. (Many students neglect to do this seemingly obvious step, and their writing often suffers as a result.) Because Beth's assignment was general and open-ended, she needed to make a number of inferences about her teacher's expectations. As her analysis of her rhetorical situation demonstrates, Beth drew both on her knowledge of the conventions of academic writing and her understanding of literary criticism to do so.

Once Beth began drafting, she moved back and forth from analysis to argument. Her first draft about Dickinson's poem was primarily analytical: It focused on how the poem "works," how it achieves its effect. But Beth quickly recognized that without an argumentative "edge" her observations lacked force. Once she was able to determine what was at stake in her analysis — in this case the subversiveness of Dickinson's poem — she was able to clarify and extend her argument. Equally important was Beth's exploration of her own values and beliefs as they relate to Dickinson. A bit of a rebel herself, Beth was emotionally as well as intellectually drawn to Dickinson's nonconformity. She was able to use that connection to her advantage in her writing.

In her second draft, Beth for the first time observes, for instance, that in poem #48 Dickinson "selectively edits this bibilical scene, making the story her own." In her third draft, Beth clarifies what she means by this statement and provides further examples in support of it, arguing that Dickinson's use of Biblical allusions is not only characteristic of her poetry but also intentionally subversive. As these examples suggest, Beth used the revision process to strengthen and enrich her draft. As a result, each draft of her essay became increasingly analytical and pointed. As Beth observed in her writing-process journal, she wrote her first draft primarily "to talk to . . . [herself] about all the ways the poem was working." By her third draft, Beth had composed a fully developed, well-supported, and interesting argument.

■ ■ ■

FOR EXPLORATION

Reread the final draft of Beth Runciman's essay, keeping the preceding analysis in mind. As you read, focus particularly on these questions: Would Beth's essay be stronger if she specifically acknowledged that she was undertaking a feminist reading of Dickinson's poem? Should Beth have addressed possible counterarguments to her reading more explicitly and fully, or does her brief allusion to possible counterarguments suffice?

FOR COLLABORATION

Bring your response to the previous Exploration to class. Working together with a group of classmates, discuss your response to the questions presented there. Be prepared to discuss your conclusions with your classmates.

FURTHER EXPLORATIONS OF ACADEMIC WRITING: A MISCELLANY OF STUDENT ESSAYS

One of the most important ways to learn about writing is through reading. As Chapter 6, "Thinking about Communities and Conventions," emphasized, you can learn a good deal by studying examples of various kinds of writing. In that chapter, for instance, you read three essays by linguist Deborah Tannen and observed the ways in which she adapted her writing to the needs and expectations of readers of three different publications, including the newspaper *The Washington Post* and the scholarly *Journal of Pragmatics.* In the final section of this chapter, you will read a variety of examples of student writing across the disciplines — from anthropology to chemistry to ethnic studies. These essays are not models in any strict or rigid sense, for assignments given in different disciplines can vary considerably. But they can give you a sense of the kinds of writing that you can expect to undertake as you continue your studies.

Before presenting these essays, I would like briefly to discuss other opportunities available to you as a beginning college writer. Almost certainly, for instance, your college or university offers writing classes in addition to the one that you are now taking. These classes may or may not be required — but if you are serious about writing, you should consider taking additional course work in this area. You may be able to supplement these classes by consulting with tutors at your campus writing center. Not all colleges and universities provide such centers, but many do.

Various departments across campus recognize how important writing is to student success and so are offering writing-intensive courses. Sometimes these courses are part of a writing-across-the-curriculum requirement. At

Oregon State University, for instance, students must take at least one writing-intensive course in their major before they graduate. If your school has such a requirement or offers such courses as electives, be sure to take this course sooner rather than later. Better yet, take several such courses in disciplines related to your major.

I hope you will both enjoy and learn from the examples of successful academic writing in the following collection of student writing in the disciplines.*

I *THINK* I AM, I *THINK* I AM
by Julie Baird and Stevon Roberts

> *The first essay in this section's miscellany of student writing was written for an introductory philosophy class titled Great Ideas in Philosophy. The essay's authors, Stevon Roberts and Julie Baird, were responding to the following questions on Descartes's* Meditations on First Philosophy: *(1) What is Descartes's method of doubt, and how does he use it? and (2) what kind of being is Descartes, and how does he establish his conclusion?*

In *Meditations on First Philosophy,* Descartes introduces to us the concepts of being and existence. Through his documented rationale, we are able to share some conclusions about the kind of being that Descartes establishes that he is. In the first meditation, he proposes doubt as a key to decoding the mystery of truth. In his second meditation, he refutes doubt for the existence of thought and therefore concludes that he himself must exist in some form or other. It is then that he begins to explore the nature of that form, consequently giving us the opportunity to follow his logic and reach the same conclusion.

Descartes first wets his philosophical feet (and ours) by creating a body of "knowledge" based on doubt. It is interesting to note that this knowledge is really derived from lack of knowledge since Descartes begins his meditations by discounting all of his previous knowledge as potentially untrue. Descartes claims, "Whatever I have up till now accepted as most true, I have acquired from either the senses or through the senses. But from time to time I have found that the senses deceive, and it is prudent never to trust completely those who have deceived us even once" (12). This suggests that Descartes is already preparing to divorce physical existence from a theoretical existence that is characterized by a thinking mind. But he's not certain of his existence at all up to this point.

In the second meditation, Descartes explores the possibility that there might exist a deceptive entity whose sole purpose is to deceive his senses. Descartes asserts that even if this were the case, the existence of the demon

---

*Citations refer to Rene Descartes. *Meditations on First Philosophy: With Selections from the Objections and Replies.* Translated and edited by John Cottingham. Cambridge: Cambridge University Press, 1996.

deceiving him necessarily requires his own existence. He says, "I too undoubtedly exist, if he is deceiving me; and let him deceive me as much as he can, he will never bring about that I am nothing so long as I think I am something" (17). This lays the foundation for Descartes's assertion that he is a thinking being because he persuades himself of, if nothing else, this one thing.

However, Descartes still believes he lacks a sufficient understanding of his existence. He uses his prior meditation on doubt to reason that he is not merely a human body or thin vapor. Instead, he is "a thing that thinks. . . . A thing that doubts, understands, affirms, denies, is willing, is unwilling, and also imagines and has sensory perceptions." Descartes illustrates these qualities by explaining to us the physical characteristics of wax. Because these physical properties can be altered by exposure to different physical environments, he calls them "accidental" properties. But the wax remains. Even though characteristics that can be perceived by the senses are all altered, the essence of the wax is unchanged. He feels that he is just like the wax in that he has intrinsic properties that are not influenced by external forces: His core being (like that of the wax) remains, despite potentially false sensory perceptions.

In the sixth and final meditation, Descartes further separates the mind from the body and ultimately decides that he is a thinking being who exists apart from the corporeal but is still intimately tied with the physical body. He says that material things are capable of existing (in theory) since they can be perceived clearly and distinctly. Descartes illustrates this concept with mathematics. He distinguishes between a pentagon, which can be both imagined and understood in "the mind's eye" and a chiliagon (a polygon with 1,000 sides), which might be understood but not imagined. He uses this comparison to illustrate the difference between the mind and the imaginative effort, suggesting that corporeal math exists in our minds as physical law, while imagination predicates a superreal soul apart from the mind, which is where Descartes believes he exists. His final step is to completely divorce this soul from his body in saying he is "distinct from [his] body and can exist without it" (54).

In following Descartes's progression of logic, it is easy to arrive at the conclusion about what kind of being Descartes believes he is. Descartes first recognizes the limitations of his physical being and establishes a body of knowledge based on empirical evidence. In so doing, he offers a caveat: There might exist a being whose purpose is to deceive his senses, in which case his own independent existence is unquestionably affirmed. With this confidence in his existence, he begins to explore the nature of that existence, explaining that any physical properties are merely "accidental" and that his true being exists apart from the physical world—but not completely. His core being (or soul) is still intimately tied with the physical body even though he can distinguish between them. Finally, Descartes arrives at the conclusion that he is a real, *thinking* being who exists apart from the entity that he had perceived via sensory experience.

"EVERYDAY EXPOSURE TO TOXIC POLLUTANTS"
by Hannah Grubb

The assignment to which Julie Baird and Stevon Roberts responded was quite specific (p. 439). Often, however, students are given much more general and open-ended assignments. This was the case with the essay by Hannah Grubb, presented below. Hannah was a student at the University of Oregon, and she wrote this essay for an introductory chemistry class. Hannah's teacher asked students to select an article from a recent issue of Scientific American *that in some way involved chemistry. Students were to demonstrate their understanding of the article by summarizing and responding to it. Hannah chose to write about an article titled "Everyday Exposure to Toxic Pollutants" by Wayne R. Ott and John W. Roberts. This article appeared in the February 1998 issue of* Scientific American.

Pollutants are everywhere. Walking down a busy street, I inhale car exhaust, gas fumes, secondhand smoke, and other toxic substances. Flying into Los Angeles to visit friends, I notice that the sky over the city is a distinctly different color than the beautiful clean air over the Pacific Ocean. Opening the newspaper, I read debates about the use of pesticides and news of the war on pollution. Like many people, I worry about the effects of pollution on my health. But rarely have I thought about the toxins that I could be breathing in my very own home.

"Everyday Exposure to Toxic Pollutants" examines those toxins and considers their relative concentrations indoors and outdoors. After reading this article by Wayne R. Ott and John W. Roberts, I now know that I have more to worry about sitting in my own home than when I go jogging through city streets. Their study discusses the presence of volatile organic compounds, carbon monoxide, pesticides, and dangerous particles within and outside of homes across America. One surprising finding is that even in cities where industrial and chemical processing plants have a major presence, the air outside is generally cleaner than the air indoors. The source of this indoor pollution, according to Ott and Roberts, is ordinary consumer products, such as air fresheners and cleaning compounds, and various building materials. Another major pollutant, tetrachloroethylene, is found on clothes that have been dry cleaned. This chemical has been found to cause cancer in laboratory animals. Chloroform, a gas that also causes cancer in laboratory animals, is a by-product of showers, boiling water, and clothes washers.

Dust particles, which are continually around us (whether we can see them or not), also carry toxic particles into our lungs. I might pick up particles of insecticides on my shoes, for instance, and carry these particles into my home where they can settle and mix in with other dust. This is especially dangerous for small children, who spend most of their time on or near the ground and who are still developing. But adults are at risk also.

Ott and Roberts state that "pesticides and volatile organic compounds found indoors cause perhaps 3,000 cases of cancer a year in the U.S., making these substances just as threatening to nonsmokers as radon . . . and second-hand tobacco smoke" (90). Ott and Roberts conclude that the main sources of indoor pollution are such run-of-the-mill products that most people don't even think to question whether they should or shouldn't use them. Because the effect of indoor pollutants is not as noticeable as, say, the exhaust from an old car, few people are aware of their dangers. But they should be, as this analogy from Ott's and Roberts's article suggests: "If truckloads of dust with the same concentrations of toxic chemicals as is found in most carpets were deposited outside, these locations would be considered hazardous-waste dumps" (91).

"Everyday Exposure to Toxic Pollutants" by Ott and Roberts is a relevant and informative discussion of problems that many people don't even realize exist. It certainly puts general concerns about pollution in perspective. Recently there have been campaigns about the use of pesticides in our residence hall cafeterias. And as I went jogging the other day, I cringed as I passed a smoker, and I purposely ran through quiet neighborhoods to get away from cars and their pollution. Perhaps I should have been worrying about inhaling chloroform every time I make a cup of tea.

FACULTY SHOW CRITIQUE
by Michelle Fuller

In an introductory art class, Michelle Fuller and other students were required by their teacher to attend a show of artwork by faculty members at Oregon State University. Their teacher asked students first to view the show and then to choose a particular piece of art to analyze. "Please write a two-page essay analyzing a painting, print, drawing, or sculpture," the teacher told the students. "Be sure to pay attention to the elements of composition we have been studying in class." Here is the essay that Michelle Fuller wrote in response to this assignment.

I viewed many diverse pieces of artwork at the Fairbanks Gallery Faculty show. I found the painting *Avocados and Parrot Tulips* by Shelley Jordan, a still life done in oil on canvas, particularly appealing. I enjoyed it not for what was painted but for how it was painted. Jordan employed an excellent use of composition, light, and brushwork.

One of the first things I noticed when viewing *Avocados* was that my eye continually moved around the canvas. I did not expect this to happen because I have seen many bland and static still lifes before. Items such as two vases with tulips, a glass plate, avocados, and fabric were arranged on a table in an almost circular composition. Not only did this motion lead the eye around the page, but it also led the eye to travel off the canvas and back on again. Lines created by the tulip stems aided this motion and drew the eye inward on the canvas. I also appreciated how the contrast between the straight tulip stems and the curving avocados and plates created compositional movement.

Another thing that kept my eye moving was the excellent use of light throughout *Avocados*. Highlights were painted in small, incompletely blended dabs whose repetition across the canvas greatly contributed to the visual interest of the work. In some areas, such as the avocados, highlights also illustrated the texture of objects. In addition, Jordan used color instead of relying on plain white highlights to create reflections and the appearance of falling light. These highlights reinforced the idea that objects like the vases and the glass plate had shiny, reflective surfaces. I felt the artist's use of light enlivened what I often consider to be a dull subject matter.

When inspecting the brushwork of the highlights, I also noticed the mastery with which the work as a whole had been painted. The brushstrokes had been confidently applied, and it seemed as if no area had needed reworking. This proficient application of paint was very important to the overall unity of the painting. Without it, the highlights and objects might have seemed disorganized—but the skillful painting technique helped unite the piece's different objects. Moreover, there was a pleasing variety of brushstrokes throughout the piece. The difference between the more softly blended background and the more impasto application of the highlights created a needed sense of depth in the still life.

Avocados and Parrot Tulips was one of the best still lifes I have seen in a long time. It appeared to me that Jordan had not intended this painting to be a political statement or some other kind of dramatic message. Instead, I felt that *Avocados* was simply intended to be a beautiful piece of art—and that Jordan did an excellent job fulfilling this intention.

FIELD MEASUREMENTS OF PHOTOSYNTHESIS AND TRANSPIRATION RATES IN DWARF SNAPDRAGON (*CHAENORRHINUM MINUS* LANGE): AN INVESTIGATION OF WATER STRESS ADAPTATIONS
by Tara Gupta

Here is another essay written by a student in the sciences. The student, Tara Gupta from Colgate University, wrote the following as an application for a summer research fellowship at her university. Note that Tara uses headings to mark the various sections of her application. She also uses the documentation style required by the Council of Science Editors, formerly the Council of Biology Editors. For details on this reference style, consult their handbook, Scientific Style and Format: The CBE Manual for Authors, Editors, and Publishers. *The current edition, the sixth, was published in 1994 (Cambridge).*

Specific and informative title, name, and other relevant information centered on title page

Field Measurements of
Photosynthesis and Transpiration
Rates in Dwarf Snapdragon
(*Chaenorrhinum minus* Lange):
An Investigation of Water Stress
Adaptations

Tara Gupta

Proposal for a
Summer Research
Fellowship
Colgate University
February 25, 2003

Water Stress Adaptations 2

Introduction

Dwarf snapdragon (*Chaenorrhinum minus*) is a weedy pioneer plant found growing in central New York during spring and summer. The distribution of this species has been limited almost exclusively to the cinder ballast of railroad tracks[1] and to sterile strips of land along highways.[2] In these harsh environments, characterized by intense sunlight and poor soil water retention, one would expect *C. minus* to exhibit anatomical features similar to those of xeromorphic plants (species adapted to arid habitats).

However, this is not the case. T. Gupta and R. Arnold (unpublished) have found that the leaves and stems of *C. minus* are not covered by a thick, waxy cuticle but rather with a thin cuticle that is less effective in inhibiting water loss through diffusion. The root system is not long and thick, capable of reaching deeper, moister soils; instead, it is thin and diffuse, permeating only the topmost (and driest) soil horizon. Moreover, in contrast to many xeromorphic plants, the stomata (pores regulating gas exchange) are not found in sunken crypts or cavities in the epidermis that retard water loss from transpiration.

Despite a lack of these morphological adaptations to water stress, *C. minus* continues to grow and reproduce when morning dew has been its only source of water for up to five weeks (R. Arnold, personal communication). Such growth involves fixation of carbon by photosynthesis and requires that the stomata be open to admit sufficient carbon dioxide. Given the dry, sunny environment, the time

---

Shortened title appears next to page number

Headings throughout help organize the proposal

Introduction states the scientific issue, gives background information, and cites relevant studies by others; CBE-style superscript number is shown

Unpublished source cited in parentheses within text but not included in references

Water Stress Adaptations   3

required for adequate carbon fixation must also mean a significant loss of water through transpiration as open stomata exchange carbon dioxide with water. How does *C. minus* balance the need for carbon with the need to conserve water?

States purposes and scope of proposed study

————————— Purposes of the Proposed Study

The above observations have led me to an exploration of the extent to which *C. minus* is able to photosynthesize under conditions of low water availability. It is my hypothesis that *C. minus* adapts to these conditions by photosynthesizing in the early morning and late afternoon, when leaf and air temperatures are lower and transpirational water loss is reduced. During the middle of the day, its photosynthetic rate may be very low, perhaps even zero, on hot, sunny afternoons. Similar diurnal changes in photosynthetic rate in response to midday water deficits have been described in crop plants.[3,4] There appear to be no comparable studies on noncrop species in their natural habitats.

Significance of the study noted

Relates the proposed research project to future research

Thus, the research proposed here aims to help explain the apparent paradox of an organism that thrives in water-stressed conditions despite a lack of morphological adaptations. This summer's work will also serve as a basis for controlled experiments in a plant growth chamber on the individual effects of temperature, light intensity, soil water availability, and other environmental factors on photosynthesis and transpiration rates. These experiments are planned for the coming fall semester.

Briefly describes methodology to be used

————————— Methods and Timeline

Simultaneous measurements of photosynthesis and transpiration rates will indicate the balance

Water Stress Adaptations   4

C. minus has achieved in acquiring the energy it
needs while retaining the water available to it.
These measurements will be taken daily from June 22 ——— Provides
to September 7, 2003, at field sites in the Hamil-   timeline for
                                                            the study
ton, NY, area, using an LI-6220 portable photo-
synthesis system (LICOR, Inc., Lincoln, NE). Basic
methodology and use of correction factors will be
similar to that described in related studies.[5-7]
Data will be collected at regular intervals throughout the daylight hours and will be related to measurements of ambient air temperature, leaf
temperature, relative humidity, light intensity,
wind velocity, and cloud cover.

Budget ———————————————— Budget pro-
                                                            vides item-
                                                            ized details

1 kg soda lime, 4–8 mesh	$70
(for absorption of CO_2 in photosynthesis analyzer)	
1 kg anhydrous magnesium perchlorate	$130
(used as desiccant for photosynthesis analyzer)	
SigmaScan software (Jandel Scientific Software, Inc.)	$195
(for measurement of leaf areas for which photosynthesis and transpiration rates are to be determined)	
Estimated 500 miles travel to field sites in own car @ $0.28/mile	$140
CO_2 cylinder, 80 days rental @ $0.25/day	$20
(for calibration of photosynthesis analyzer)	
TOTAL REQUEST	$555

Water Stress Adaptations   5

———————————————— References

[1]Wildrlechner MP. Historical and phenological obser-
    vations of the spread of *Chaenorrhinum minus*
    across North America. Can J Bot 1983;61:179–87.

[2]Dwarf Snapdragon [Internet]. Olympia, WA: Washington
    State Noxious Weed Control Board; [updated 2001
    July 7; cited 2003 Jan 25]. Available from:
    http://www.wa.gov/agr/weedboard/weed_info/dwarf
    snapdragon.html

[3]Boyer JS. Plant productivity and environment. Sci-
    ence 1982;218:443–8.

[4]Manhas JG, Sukumaran NP. Diurnal changes in net pho-
    tosynthetic rate in potato in two environments.
    Potato Res 1988;31:375–8.

[5]Doley, DG, Unwin GL, Yates DJ. Spatial and temporal
    distribution of photosynthesis and transpiration
    by single leaves in a rainforest tree. *Argyro-
    dendron peralatum.* Aust J Plant Physiol
    1988;15:317–26.

[6]Kallarackal J, Milburn JA, Baker DA. Water relations
    of the banana. III. Effects of controlled water
    stress on water potential, transpiration, photo-
    synthesis and leaf growth. Aust J Plant Physiol
    1990;17:79–90.

[7]Idso SB, Allen SG, Kimball BA, Choudhury BJ. Prob-
    lems with porometry: measuring net photo-
    synthesis by leaf chamber techniques. Agron
    1989;81:475–9.

Includes all
published
works cited;
numbers
correspond
to order
in which
sources were
first men-
tioned in the
text; CBE
citation-
sequence
format is
shown

LINCOLN'S PRESIDENCY AND PUBLIC OPINION
by Elizabeth Ridlington

In-class essay exams are a common form of academic writing. Essay exams pose special challenges for writers, for you must be able both to recall information and to present it in a clearly organized — and concise — manner. The following essay exam meets these goals. During a midterm for a course in American history at Harvard University, student Elizabeth Ridlington had fifty minutes to respond to this question: "During his presidency, did Lincoln primarily respond to public opinion, or did he shape public opinion more than he responded to it?" This is what she wrote.

This essay argues that Lincoln shaped public opinion more than he responded to it and examines the issues of military recruitment, northern war goals, and emancipation as examples of Lincoln's interaction with public opinion.

At the start of the war Lincoln needed men for the military. Because of this, he could hardly ignore public opinion. But even as he responded in various ways to public opinion, he did not significantly modify his policy goals. Lincoln's first call for seventy-five thousand soldiers was filled through militias that were under state rather than federal control. As the war progressed, the federal government took more control of military recruitment. The government set quotas for each state and permitted the enlistment of African American soldiers via the Militia Act. Kentucky, a slave state, protested, and Lincoln waived the requirement that blacks be enlisted so long as Kentucky still filled its quota. In so doing, Lincoln responded to public opinion without changing his policy goal. Another example of this strategy occurred when the first federal draft produced riots in New York City. When the riots occurred, Lincoln relented temporarily and waited for the unrest to quiet down. Then he reinstated the federal draft. Again, Lincoln responded to a volatile situation and even temporarily withdrew the federal draft. But he ultimately reinstated the draft.

Lincoln's efforts to shape public opinion in the north in favor of the war provides another example of his proactive stance. Whenever he discussed the war, Lincoln equated it with freedom and democracy. Northerners linked democracy with their personal freedom and daily well-being, and therefore Lincoln's linkage of the Union with democracy fostered northern support for the war even when the conflict was bloody and northern victory was anything but assured. After the emancipation, Lincoln continued his effort to influence public opinion by connecting the abolition of slavery with democracy. The image of a "new birth of freedom" that Lincoln painted in his Gettysburg address was part of this effort to overcome northern racism and a reluctance to fight for the freedom of blacks.

The process that led to the emancipation provides perhaps the clearest example of Lincoln's determination to shape public opinion rather than simply respond to it. Lincoln's views on slavery were more progressive than those of his contemporaries. These views caused him personally to wish to abolish slavery. At the same time, Lincoln knew that winning the war was his highest priority. Consequently, retaining the border states early in the war was more important to Lincoln than emancipation, and for this reason he revoked Freemont's proclamation in the summer of 1861. In explaining this decision privately to Freemont, Lincoln admitted that he was concerned about public opinion in Kentucky since it would determine if Kentucky stayed with the Union. However, in a letter that Lincoln knew might be made public, Lincoln denied that he had reacted to Kentucky's pressure and claimed that emancipation was not among his powers — a clear effort to gain public approval. Even when others such as Frederick Douglass (in a September 1861 speech) demanded emancipation, Lincoln did not change his policy. Not until July 1862 did Lincoln draft the preliminary emancipation proclamation. Rather than releasing it then, at the advice of his cabinet he waited for a time when it would have a more positive impact on public opinion.

Lincoln realized that the timing of the Emancipation Proclamation was crucial. While he was waiting for an opportune time to release the document, Horace Greeley published his "Prayer of Twenty Million," calling on Lincoln to abolish slavery. Lincoln's response, a letter for publication, emphasized the importance of the Union and the secondary importance of the status of slavery. By taking this position, Lincoln hoped to shape public opinion. He wanted northerners to believe that he saw the Union cause as foremost, so that the release of the proclamation would create as few racial concerns as possible. The Emancipation Proclamation was released on January 1, 1863. Once it was released, Lincoln stood by it despite strong public opposition. In 1864, when Democrats called for an armistice with the south, Lincoln stood by his decision to abolish slavery. He defended his position on military grounds, hoping voters would approve in the 1864 election.

As the examples I have just discussed indicate, Lincoln could not ignore public opinion, and at times he had to respond to it. But when Lincoln did so, this was always part of a larger effort to shape public opinion and to ensure Union victory.

BETWEEN CULTURES
by Monica Molina

The personal essay is another common form of academic writing, particularly in the humanities. Here is a personal essay written by Monica Molina, a student at Oregon State University. Monica wrote this essay for an ethnic studies class. Her assignment was to write an essay that in some way reflected on her ethnic heritage.

Opening the door and peering curiously around the room full of brown faces, I felt nervous and awkward. My fears were soon eased, however, as cheerful voices welcomed me to an Oregon State University Hispanic Student Union meeting. Although I wasn't sure what the meeting would be about, I felt suddenly comfortable — almost like I was among family. But then some students in the corner began speaking in Spanish, their crescendo building with excitement as they shared a story. Soon it seemed that everyone was adding bits of information. I sat quietly, just getting the gist of what they were saying. Then everyone broke into laughter. Everyone but me, that is; I had missed the punchline.

*   *   *

Spanish sounds like a song to me, one that is beautiful and rich, but one I can't quite catch the words to. I ache for the foreign sounds to roll off my tongue, but instead only a few words stumble out, flat and anglicized. I studied Spanish for three years in high school, and for one year in college, but learning a language in a classroom from textbooks is different from hearing it spoken by your parents at home. My father is Mexican, and his native language is Spanish. But he has never spoken anything other than English with my mother, sisters, and me.

I was surrounded by Anglo culture as I grew up, and I assimilated easily, not even knowing what I was missing. Educated in mainstream schools and raised in a predominantly white neighborhood, I accepted the images I saw on television and in the movies. Most of the time, I took it for granted that we would speak English at home. When my friends learned that my father was Mexican and asked me if I spoke Spanish, or if we spoke it at home, I always answered "no," feeling a sudden sense of confusion and loss.

At times as I was growing up, I wondered why my father never spoke Spanish with us. Recently, I decided to ask him about it. My dad seemed surprised by my question and replied that he didn't know; perhaps it was because he was too busy to teach us. He didn't seem to want to talk about this subject. I could tell that he didn't understand why I asked the question or what it might mean to me. I didn't push my question, for I realized that it really doesn't matter why my father didn't speak Spanish with us. What matters is how I feel about this now — now that I realize I know only the Anglo side of my heritage and not the Mexican side. What matters is my desire to connect with my father's culture, with the Mexican heritage that has been ignored and silenced.

When I was a child, I asked innocent questions about life in Mexico that annoyed my father, questions like "Do they have ice cream in Mexico?" My dad would shake his head in disbelief at these questions and not even answer. Now I realize that the questions reminded him too much of snobby Anglos asking if the water was OK to drink in Mexico. My father must have found it hard to realize how little I knew about Mexican culture. Moreover, he probably felt there was no point in teaching us about a culture we would never embrace as our own.

My father struggled to learn to speak English and to make a place for himself in this country. But my father's English reminds my mom, sisters, and me that he is different from us. Dad's English is distinct in that he has created his own pronunciations and vocabulary. His words and phrases have become part of our family language, and we sometimes tease him about them. One of his favorite phrases is "You crazy!"; now we all say that to each other. We also mimic the exasperated way he says "What?!" Sometimes my father realizes that we are teasing him and laughs, but other times he gets angry. His anger reminds me how easy it is to forget his struggles with English and with Anglo culture, just as it is hard for my father to sense my need to connect with his Mexican way of life.

As a fifth grader, I remember my father coming to me with business letters to check for grammar and spelling. As I gently explained to my dad why a tense was wrong or a word misspelled, I knew it must be hard for him to ask his daughter for help. My father's lack of English skills coupled with my limited knowledge of Spanish highlighted the gap between our Anglo and Mexican cultures. I felt this gap most strongly when my dad called his family in Mexico. Calling home was a pretty big event, and my mom would tell us to be quiet so dad could hear. We would sit listening to the unfamiliar language, fascinated with the quick sounds and changes in expression. After my father hung up, we would rush to him and ask what he had said.

As a teenager, and now as a college student, I have made attempts to learn about my father's culture. Sometimes I try to explain my longing to connect with my Mexican heritage to my father, but he doesn't seem to understand why this is important to me. He also doesn't understand why some people would question my identification with Mexico and its cultural heritage. When I told my dad that people sometimes ask whether I am Mexican and are surprised when I say "yes" since I can't speak Spanish very well, he says it's none of their business and "to hell with them." Lately

I'm beginning to think that my father may be right. Other people may worry if I don't fit into predetermined ethnic categories. But I think I can identify with both Mexican and Anglo cultures as long as I define what that means for me.

*   *   *

I come home from another Hispanic Student Union meeting, excited about the possibility of attending my first MECHA (Movimiento Estudiantil Chicano de Azatlan) conference. Entering my house, I notice that the answering machine light is on and push the button. My father begins the message he has left for me. Because his voice is so familiar, I don't usually hear my father's accent. But today it rings out as a reminder of the ways in which we're both similar and different. As I listen to my dad telling me what time he'll pick me up for a quick trip home, I think of how different my world is from his. My father came to a new country and had to work hard to support a family; he had to believe that he was gaining more than he was giving up. Because my father has struggled, I have more opportunities. In some ways, my success will be his. But unlike my father, I may not have to choose between two cultures. For me, gaining something new may not have to mean leaving something else behind.

THE HOPI WORLD VIEW: A CYCLIC MODEL OF BALANCE AND DUALITY
by Eric Hill

This essay was written by Eric Hill, a student at the University of Southern California. Eric wrote this essay as a take-home midterm for an anthropology class. The assignment to which he responded was as follows: "In a succinct and clearly organized essay, describe the Hopi world view, and relate it to other cultural world views." (In case you are not familiar with the term cosmography, it means a description of a particular world or universe.)

One of the most striking characteristics of Hopi myth and cosmography is the repetition of specific themes and metaphors. A theme that appears consistently throughout Hopi thought and that seems to be at the heart of their complex symbology is a cyclical view of the universe. This cyclical view is reflected not only in Hopi ceremonies and beliefs but also in their secular activities. It forms the basis of their culture and dictates much of their daily behavior — including rituals for birth and death.

The Hopi's cyclical view of the universe is both like and unlike Western views. It is like Western views in that it has a definite sense of duality. But it is not the kind of polarized duality found in most Western religious and cultural models, where body and soul, mind and spirit, are at odds. Reading about the Hopi, I was surprised to discover that much in Hopi thought seems essentially Taoist in nature. Like Taoists, the Hopi reconcile life and death by viewing them as two halves of the same whole. When a child is born into a Hopi household, a ritual is performed in which the infant is named and covered in corn meal. The ritual for the dead is carried out in much the same manner: the deceased is given a new name, and the body is washed and then covered in corn meal. In the Hopi's cyclical view of the universe, opposites exist to create a sense of balance *through* their polarization.

It is no coincidence that the Hopi view of life directly parallels the path of the sun across the sky. Just as the human emerges from the womb into this life, the sun emerges from the horizon in the east. Both the sun and human being enter this world via the navel or entrance from the underworld. Both must "set" at the end of their cycle and then enter once again into the underworld. This mythical image of emergence and reemergence gives Hopi thought a distinctly Eastern rather than Western flavor.

This cyclical dance of duality is made even more apparent by the significance of corn in Hopi life. Besides being the most important staple in their diet, corn is also essential to their ceremonial life. In nature, corn must die to seed the ground so that more corn can be produced. With the growing of corn, as with other aspects of Hopi life and culture, the life-death-life cycle is clearly delineated. As this example indicates, corn is the embodiment of many symbols, concepts, and practices essential to Hopi thought. This is evident in their view of the corn mother, who is androgynous: the tassel or pollen stem is male, while the ear is female. Here, as elsewhere in Hopi thought, the necessity of coexisting opposites is emphasized. Male and female qualities share equal importance in the life cycle.

As these examples indicate, from the Hopi perspective birth and death, male and female, are opposites (in the sense that they are two different ends or aspects of reality); yet they nevertheless emerge (and reemerge) together into life here, above, and below. The Hopi world view is unique; it reflects Hopi culture and history. But it also looks both to the East and the West. Like Western cosmographies, it is based on dualisms. But like Eastern cosmographies, it sees these dualisms as interdependent aspects of reality that emerge (and reemerge) as part of larger processes.

LAYING IT ON THE LINES
by Chris Bowman

College students are often asked to read and respond to one or more books. Chris Bowman, a student at Oregon State University, was asked to do just this in an ethnic studies course on narratives of Latino migration. Here is the essay that Chris wrote in response to her assignment. The book Chris read is Between the Lines: Letters between Undocumented Mexican and Central American Immigrants and Their Families and Friends. *This book was edited by Larry Siems and published in 1992 by the University of Arizona Press.*

To read *Between the Lines* is to begin to understand the *lives* of migrant Latinos in America. I emphasize the word *lives* because it is often automatic to think with singularity: *the* migrant worker. In this book, a collection of letters between immigrants to the United States and their families and friends in Mexico and Central America, multiple stories emerge. These stories provide powerful insights into the many complex relationships that are affected when Latinos come to the United States.

The letters collected in *Between the Lines* are from husbands and wives, daughters and sons, in-laws, nieces, uncles, sisters, fathers, and mothers. Friends write to friends. Priests write for those who cannot write themselves. Surprisingly, the letters from illiterate Latinos — letters that, in the case of those who speak indigenous languages, have been translated twice — have a refreshingly emotional style that feels like conversation. But whether the authors wrote or dictated their thoughts, through almost every letter there winds a thread of love and longing for those who are far away.

In many letters, writers implore their loved ones to write, send photos, send news. To encourage response, the writers send their own news — about health, children, finance. They also share gossip, advice, and hopes for the future. In this respect, these migrants and their families are like any other ordinary "American" family. And yet they are clearly not ordinary. These writers lead difficult lives, more difficult than those of many Americans. In the very first letter, the writer tells of his deep sadness when he realized how much he would have to endure to get to America. Another letter writer describes her disappointment when friends give her a chilly reception when she comes to the United States. Worried that she has done something wrong, she discovers that her friends were both sad and angry that she would now be subjected to the hardships that they had endured.

As these examples indicate, the letters in *Between the Lines* are very powerful. And they are powerfully arranged by Larry Siems, the editor of this collection. Siems has organized the letters to suggest the process that migrants and their loved ones experience as the migrants acculturate. The first letters are from those who have recently arrived in this country, and while they speak of hardship, there is an underlying tone of hopefulness. The next section is comprised of letters from those who have been left behind. These letters convey faith in and encouragement for the migrants, as well as fears and advice about how to negotiate new situations. The next three sections are from close friends, spouses, and families. It is clear from the letters in these sections that the writers have been apart for some time — but that the letters continue to nurture their relationships. The final section includes a mix of letters that emphasize the complexity and difficulty of the lives of migrants. They also demonstrate the reasons that people continue to risk these difficulties to come to the United States.

Between the Lines contributes to an understanding of the lives of Latino migrants in America because it tells a different story than that portrayed in the media. The media often portray migrants as people who impulsively leave one country for another. As these letters reveal, the decision to leave family and friends is heart-wrenching. One man writes of how he hid when his friend came to tell him goodbye because he could not bear the parting. Many apologize to their families for leaving but state that this is the only way that they can help their families.

Between the Lines also corrects many popular misconceptions about the lives of Latino migrants. These are not people on public assistance. These are workers who are sending money home to loved ones and saving what little they can for their future. The letters tell stories of migrants who are exploited by employers who refuse to pay them after a job has been completed, knowing full well that the undocumented worker has no recourse in such a situation. Letters also tell (time and time again) of migrants being scorned because they do not speak English. One writer describes how "here one feels like a sad lost dog. . . . [in Mexico] one has freedom even to scream in his house and do in his house whatever he pleases, and here if you do all this the first to arrive are the police because the neighbors call them" (299).

For most who come, the United States is not like they thought it would be. So maintaining a link with their families and friends is vital to their existence. Not that they entirely leave their past behind. The letters in *Between the Lines* indicate that many migrants move to neighborhoods where they know at least one person from their home country — or even village. The letters that go back and forth from the United States to home thus participate in an ongoing neighborhood grapevine that discourages misbehavior.

Clearly, as Larry Siems indicates in his comments on the letters in this collection, these are individuals attempting to lead ordinary lives. They are also people who are deeply misunderstood and shamelessly abused. It's heartbreaking to read of vigilante groups who look on border crossings as opportunities for target practice. How ironic that many citizens in the

United States are concerned about such practices as bilingual education but can't see the many ways that Latino migrants are mistreated in our country.

Between the Lines tells the story of human beings who are striving to provide for themselves and for their families. This should be a familiar story — but in this case it is not. These people know what it's like for their families to go hungry. Many know the horrors of war. And all know what it's like to be forced to leave the ones they love in order for them (and often for their families) to survive. That's what this book is about.

TACOMA NARROWS BRIDGE FAILURE: PROGRESS REPORT

by Brenda Shonkwiler

> *The final essay in this miscellany is by a student whose writing you have already read, Brenda Shonkwiler. Chapter 4, "Understanding the Research Process," includes a research paper that Brenda, a student at Oregon State University, wrote for her first-year writing class. Here is a report that Brenda wrote for her instructor, Carole Ann Crateau, when she was two-thirds of the way through her project. As the subject heading indicates, it serves as a progress report on her work.*

March 8, 2003

To: Carole Ann Crateau

From: Brenda Shonkwiler

Subject: Tacoma Narrows Bridge Failure — Interviews and Progress
            Report

The Tacoma Narrows Bridge was built to span Puget Sound. At the time, it was the only fixed roadway connecting the Washington mainland and the Olympic Peninsula. When it was built, the Narrows Bridge was praised as the epitome of artistry in bridge construction. However, the bridge soon earned the nickname "Galloping Gertie" because of its rolling, undulating motion. People drove hundreds of miles to drive across Gertie's center span. Despite the obvious oscillations of the bridge's roadbed, many people, including bridge officials, were confident in the structure. A bank near the Tacoma end of the bridge even had a billboard advertisement that boasted "Safe as the Narrows Bridge." However, in November 1940, only four months after completion, the bridge collapsed in a windstorm due to wind-induced vibrations. The oscillating and twisting motions had become too strong for the bridge to withstand.

The bridge failure initiated research on the aerodynamic stability of bridges. A special wind tunnel was built at the University of Washington to test three-dimensional models. Several years were spent researching and testing before the second Tacoma Narrows Bridge was constructed. Ten years after Galloping Gertie collapsed, the new bridge was completed. This new bridge is of major significance because of its numerous unique design features. This was the first time a research program was implemented to investigate the aerodynamic effects of wind action on a bridge. This effort provided significant information to suspension bridge engineers nation-wide and had an important effect on all suspension bridge designs that followed.

To learn more about the topic, I set up two interviews. One was with P. C. Klingeman, a professor in the civil engineering department at Oregon State University (OSU). The other interview was with Albert Stetz, a physics instructor at OSU. These interviews assisted in my research efforts.

In this report I summarize these interviews and describe my progress on my project.

STRUCTURAL ASPECTS
To learn more about Gertie's structural problems and how bridges are now designed to prevent problems from wind-related vibrations, I decided to interview my strengths-of-materials teacher, P. C. Klingeman. He is a pro-fessor in the civil engineering department and knows about structures, so I thought he would be a good resource. When I told Professor Klingeman about my project, he loaned me a three-minute video showing the col-lapse of the Tacoma Narrows Bridge. I could see how much the bridge twisted torsionally and oscillated vertically. In one clip, a person got out of his car and tried to run off of the bridge while it shook violently.

In the interview, I asked Professor Klingeman about the flexibility of the concrete. At maximum twisting, one side of the bridge deck was 28 feet above the other. I did not realize that concrete was that flexible. Professor Klingeman explained that there was a steel mesh within the concrete that helped hold the bridge together. The violent motion of the bridge had caused stress fractures in the concrete. This allowed the bridge deck to twist and oscillate as much as it did. The steel reinforcements are what kept the bridge from crumbling right away.

We then discussed the depth of the stiffening girders, which was eight feet. I wanted to know what this told us about the bridge and how it affected structural stability. Professor Klingeman said that it was the thickness of the center span. Because the stiffening girders were solid, no air could pass through them. This created a tremendous amount of wind resistance. The new Tacoma Narrows Bridge was built without solid stiffening girders. The depth of the girders was increased while the wind resistance was decreased, resulting in a more stable structure.

In my preliminary research, I discovered that the bridge was oscillating even while it was being constructed. I was curious as to why nothing had been done to stiffen the bridge before it collapsed. Professor Klingeman told me that at the time people did not know enough about wind's effect on bridges. As it turns out, a few modifications were made to the bridge, but they were not very effective. Many people believed that the bridge was safe and were confident that it would remain standing.

Then I asked how the collapse of the Tacoma Narrows Bridge has affected the way bridges were currently designed. I discovered that the collapse generated much research on aerodynamics. Bridge models were tested in wind tunnels. This helped bridge designers learn about the effects of wind on bridges.

Professor Klingeman spent the remainder of the time explaining to me how bridges are built. I had gone to the library before the interview. One of the books I checked out, *Bridging the Narrows,* had many pictures showing how the two Tacoma Narrows Bridges were constructed. Professor Klingeman explained the whole process, using the pictures to illustrate it.

This interview was very informative. Many of my questions were answered, and I learned about the process of bridge construction.

ROLE OF RESONANCE

To understand the role that resonance had in the collapse of the Tacoma Narrows Bridge, I interviewed Albert Stetz, a physics professor at OSU. I had read in my physics book that all structures have a natural frequency, so I asked Professor Stetz about that topic. He explained that a simple harmonic oscillator could be used as a base model. The equation to model simple harmonic motion can be derived from the Taylor series.[1] I had learned about the Taylor series last year in calculus, so I knew what he was talking about. When the oscillations are small, the first term of the Taylor series can be used for a fairly accurate approximation. However, as the oscillations increase, the approximation becomes less accurate. When the oscillations become violent, some of the other terms of the Taylor series start to apply. At this point, the motion is no longer simple harmonic motion. This explanation was interesting to me because it tied together things I had learned in calculus and in physics. Professor Stetz's explanation helped me understand how complicated Galloping Gertie's motion was, and why it was so difficult to predict. Professor Stetz used examples, such as the motion of earthquakes and metronomes, to illustrate the variety of applications of the Taylor series to physics.

---

[1]Taylor series: $f(x) = f(0) + \dfrac{f'(0)}{1!}x + \dfrac{f''(0)}{2!}x^2 + \ldots$

This interview was interesting and informative. I learned some fascinating things about resonance and oscillations and gained helpful background information on what happened to Galloping Gertie.

IMPACT OF INTERVIEWS

The information I gained from the two interviews increased my background knowledge of the subject. Because of my interview with Professor Klingeman, I have a much better understanding of the way bridges are put together, how wind causes torsion and oscillations, and how it is possible that problems with the bridge were overlooked. The interview with Professor Stetz helped me understand the impact of resonance.

The interviews helped me look at my topic from various perspectives and enabled me to widen my research. The cause of the Tacoma Narrows Bridge collapse is complicated. There were several factors that eventually led to the failure. After the interviews, I was able to conduct research on such topics as *suspension bridges, vortex-induced vibrations, long-span bridges, bridge aerodynamics, turbulence,* and *wind tunnels.*

WORK STATUS

My project is coming along nicely. I have been able to find a variety of sources, mostly from the Internet. Now it is just a matter of looking through the information, deciding what is important, and putting it all together. I still have not looked for newspaper articles from 1940 to see what was written when the bridge collapsed. That would be a good source that could add interest to my discussion of the collapse of the Tacoma Narrows Bridge.

I found a short video in the Valley Library that I plan to use in my oral presentation. The video is similar to the one Professor Klingeman loaned to me, but it includes a few more scenes. This video will be a great visual aid. I am glad I found it.

CONCLUSION

Through videos, research, and interviews, I have learned a great deal about the failure of the Tacoma Narrows Bridge. The two interviews I conducted were informative and helped me widen my research. I now better understand how such a catastrophe could have occurred and what is being done in current bridge design to prevent similar failures from happening in the future.

■ ■ ■

FOR EXPLORATION

As a college student you undoubtedly have more experience in some kinds of academic writing than in others. Think about a kind of academic writing that you feel particularly confident about. (This might be analyses of literary or historical texts, lab reports in the sciences, case studies in the social sciences, and so on.) Now take five minutes to freewrite about a specific analytical technique required in this kind of writing. What specific writing abilities does this technique call for?

FOR GROUP WORK

Meet with a group of classmates to discuss your responses to the preceding Exploration. (Appoint a member of the group to act as a recorder so you can share the results of your discussion with the rest of the class.) Begin by having each student read his or her freewriting. Then answer these questions:

1. How many different kinds of writing did group members write about?

2. Did some of these kinds of writing require similar analytical and writing skills?

3. In what ways did the demands of these kinds of writing differ?

FOR THOUGHT, DISCUSSION, AND WRITING

1. Take a few minutes to think about your work thus far in your writing course. With what aspects of this work are you most — and least — pleased? In thinking about this question, be sure to think about both product and process. You may feel that several of your essays could be stronger in one or another way, for instance, and yet you could feel satisfied about the effort you put into your writing. After some thought, freewrite or brainstorm a list of observations.

2. Now take a few minutes to look to the future. Think about the course of study you hope to undertake. If you don't know the specific major you will have, you probably have a sense of the general area of focus you wish to pursue. What writing demands will your studies make of

you? How prepared do you feel to respond to these demands? What additional steps can you take to become the strongest, most efficient writer possible? After reflecting on these questions, freewrite or brainstorm a second list of observations.

3. Drawing on the two previous activities, write an essay in which you consider your development as a writer. As you do so, consider both your development as a writer to this point and the future demands you face.

WRITERS' REFERENCES

MLA Documentation Guidelines

M LA documentation style, developed specifically for those writing about literature and related areas, is used in a number of other disciplines in the humanities as well. This section provides examples of the most common forms of documentation. For further information, consult the sixth edition of the *MLA Handbook for Writers of Research Papers* (published in 2003) or the MLA online style guide: <http://www.mla.org/style/style_index.htm>.

In-Text Citations

MLA style requires documentation in the text of an essay for every quotation, paraphrase, and summary as well as other material requiring documentation. In-text citations document material from other sources with both signal phrases and parenthetical citations. Signal phrases introduce the material, often including the author's name. Keep your parenthetical citations short, but include the information your readers need to locate the full citation in the list of works cited at the end of the text.

Place a parenthetical citation as near the relevant material as possible without disrupting the flow of the sentence, as in the following examples.

1. AUTHOR NAMED IN A SIGNAL PHRASE

Ordinarily, you can use the author's name in a signal phrase — to introduce the material — and cite the page number(s) in parentheses.

```
Herrera indicates that Kahlo believed in a "vitalistic
form of pantheism" (328).
```

2. AUTHOR NAMED IN PARENTHESES

When you do not mention the author in a signal phrase, include the author's last name before the page number(s) in the parentheses.

In places, de Beauvoir "sees Marxists as believing in subjectivity" (Whitmarsh 63).

3. TWO OR THREE AUTHORS

Use all the authors' last names in a phrase or in parentheses.

Gortner, Hebrun, and Nicolson maintain that "opinion leaders" influence other people in an organization because they are respected, not because they hold high positions (175).

4. FOUR OR MORE AUTHORS

Use the first author's name and *et al.* ("and others"), or name all the authors in a phrase or in parentheses.

Similarly, as Belenky, Clinchy, Goldberger, and Tarule assert, examining the lives of women expands our understanding of human development (7).

5. CORPORATE OR GROUP AUTHOR

Give the full name of a corporate author (or a shortened form of it if it is long).

Any study of social welfare involves a close analysis of "the impacts, the benefits, and the costs" of its policies (Social Research Corporation iii).

6. UNKNOWN AUTHOR

Use the full title, if it is brief, in your text — or a shortened version of the title in parentheses.

"Hype," by one analysis, is "an artificially engendered atmosphere of hysteria" ("Today's Marketplace" 51).

7. AUTHOR OF TWO OR MORE WORKS

If your list of works cited has more than one work by the same author, include a shortened version of the title of the work.

```
Gardner shows readers their own silliness in his de-
scription of a "pointless, ridiculous monster, crouched
in the shadows, stinking of dead men, murdered children,
and martyred cows" (Grendel 2).
```

8. TWO OR MORE AUTHORS WITH THE SAME LAST NAME

Always include the authors' first *and* last names in the signal phrases the first time you cite a source. For later references, just use the last name.

```
Children will learn to write if they are allowed to
choose their own subjects, James Britton asserts, citing
the Schools Council study of the 1960s (37-42).
```

9. MULTIVOLUME WORK

Note the volume number first and then the page number(s).

```
Modernist writers prized experimentation and gradually
even sought to blur the line between poetry and prose,
according to Forster (3: 150).
```

If you name only one volume of the work in your list of works cited, you need include only the page number.

10. LITERARY WORK

Because literary works are often available in many different editions, cite the page number(s) from the edition you used followed by a semicolon, and, in addition, give other identifying information that will lead readers to the passage in any edition — such as the act and scene in a play (37; sc. 1). For a novel, indicate the part or chapter (175; ch. 4).

```
In utter despair, Dostoyevsky's character Mitya wonders
aloud about the "terrible tragedies realism inflicts on
people" (376; bk. 8, ch. 2).
```

For poems, cite the part (if there is one) and line(s). If you are citing only line numbers, use the word *line(s)* in the first reference (lines 33–34).

```
On dying, Whitman speculates, "All goes onward and out-
ward, nothing collapses. / And to die is different from
what anyone supposed, and luckier" (6.129-30).
```

For verse plays, give only the act, scene, and line numbers.

```
As Macbeth begins, the witches greet Banquo as "Lesser
than Macbeth, and greater" (1.3.65).
```

11. WORK IN AN ANTHOLOGY

For an essay, short story, or other piece of prose reprinted in an anthology, use the name of the author of the work (not the editor of the anthology) and the page number(s) from the anthology.

```
Narratives of captivity play a major role in early writ-
ing by women in the United States, as demonstrated by
Silko (219).
```

12. SACRED TEXT

Identify quotations from sacred texts by giving the title of the edition used, the book, and the chapter and verse (or their equivalent) separated by a period. In your text, spell out the names of books. In parenthetical citations, use abbreviations for books with names of five or more letters (*Gen.* for *Genesis*).

```
He ignored the admonition "Pride goes before destruc-
tion, and a haughty spirit before a fall" (New Oxford
Annotated Bible, Prov. 16.18).
```

13. INDIRECT SOURCE

Use the abbreviation *qtd. in* to indicate that you are quoting from someone else's report of a conversation, interview, letter, or the like.

```
As Arthur Miller says, "When somebody is destroyed
everybody finally contributes to it, but in Willy's
case, the end product would be virtually the same" (qtd.
in Martin and Meyer 375).
```

14. TWO OR MORE SOURCES IN THE SAME CITATION

Separate the information with semicolons.

```
Economists recommend that employment be redefined to
include unpaid domestic labor (Clark 148; Nevins 39).
```

15. ENTIRE WORK OR ONE-PAGE ARTICLE

Include the reference in the text without any page numbers or parentheses.

```
Michael Ondaatje's poetic sensibility transfers beauti-
fully to prose in The English Patient.
```

16. WORK WITHOUT PAGE NUMBERS

If a work has no page numbers, you may omit the page number. If a work uses paragraph numbers instead, use the abbreviation *par(s).*

```
Whitman considered their speech "a source of a native
grand opera," in the words of Ellison (par. 13).
```

17. NONPRINT OR ELECTRONIC SOURCE

Give enough information in a signal phrase or parenthetical citation for readers to locate the source in the list of works cited. Usually give the author or title under which you list the source. If you are citing any specific section(s), include the page, part, paragraph, or screen number in parentheses.

```
Describing children's language acquisition, Pinker
explains that "what's innate about language is just a
way of paying attention to parental speech" (Johnson,
sec. 1).
```

Explanatory and Bibliographic Notes

MLA style allows explanatory notes for information or commentary that does not readily fit into your text but is needed for clarification or further explanation. In addition, MLA style permits bibliographic notes for citing several sources for one point and for offering thanks to, information about, or evaluation of a source. Use superscript numbers in the text to refer readers to the notes, which may appear as endnotes (typed under the heading *Notes* on a separate page after the text but before the list of works cited) or as footnotes.

1. SUPERSCRIPT NUMBER IN TEXT

```
Stewart emphasizes the existence of social contacts in
Hawthorne's life so that the audience will accept a dif-
ferent Hawthorne, one more attuned to modern times than
the figure in Woodberry.³
```

2. NOTE

> [3] Woodberry does, however, show that Hawthorne was often an unsociable individual. He emphasizes the seclusion of Hawthorne's mother, who separated herself from her family after the death of her husband, often even taking meals alone (28). Woodberry seems to imply that Mrs. Hawthorne's isolation rubbed off onto her son.

List of Works Cited

A list of works cited is an alphabetical list of the sources you have referred to in your essay. (If your instructor asks you to list everything you have read as background, call the list *Works Consulted.*) Here are some guidelines for preparing such a list.

- Start your list on a separate page after the text of your essay and any notes.

- Continue the consecutive numbering of pages.

- Type the heading *Works Cited,* not underlined, italicized, or in quotation marks, centered one inch from the top of the page.

- Start each entry flush with the left margin; indent subsequent lines one-half inch (or five spaces). Double-space the entire list.

- List sources alphabetically by author's last name. If the author is unknown, alphabetize the source by the first major word of the title.

The sample works cited entries that follow observe the MLA's advice to underline words that are often italicized in print. Although most computers can generate italics easily, the MLA recommends that "you can avoid ambiguity by using underlining" in your research essays. If you wish to use italics instead, first check with your instructor.

BOOKS

The basic entry for a book includes three elements, each followed by a period: the author's name, last name first; the title and subtitle, underlined or (if your instructor permits) italicized, with all major words capitalized; and the city of publication, a shortened version of the publisher's name, and the year of publication.

1. ONE AUTHOR

deCordova, Richard. <u>Picture Personalities: The Emergence
    of the Star System in America</u>. Urbana: U of Illi-
    nois P, 1990.

2. TWO OR THREE AUTHORS

Appleby, Joyce, Lynn Hunt, and Margaret Jacob. <u>Telling
    the Truth about History</u>. New York: Norton, 1994.

3. CORPORATE OR GROUP AUTHOR

American Chemical Society. <u>Handbook for Authors of
    Papers in the American Chemical Society Publica-
    tions</u>. Washington: American Chemical Soc., 1978.

4. UNKNOWN AUTHOR

<u>The New York Times Atlas of the World</u>. New York: New
    York Times Books, 1980.

5. TWO OR MORE BOOKS BY THE SAME AUTHOR(S)

Lorde, Audre. <u>A Burst of Light</u>. Ithaca: Firebrand, 1988.
---. <u>Sister Outsider</u>. Trumansburg: Crossing, 1984.

6. EDITOR(S)

Wall, Cheryl A., ed. <u>Changing Our Own Words: Essays on
    Criticism, Theory, and Writing by Black Women</u>. New
    Brunswick: Rutgers UP, 1989.

7. AUTHOR AND EDITOR

James, Henry. <u>Portrait of a Lady</u>. Ed. Leon Edel. Boston:
    Houghton, 1963.

8. WORK IN AN ANTHOLOGY OR CHAPTER IN A BOOK WITH AN EDITOR

Gordon, Mary. "The Parable of the Cave." <u>The Writer on
    Her Work</u>. Ed. Janet Sternburg. New York: Norton,
    1980. 27–32.

9. TWO OR MORE ITEMS FROM AN ANTHOLOGY

Include the anthology itself in your list of works cited. Also list each selection separately by its author and title, followed by a cross-reference to the anthology, alphabetizing all entries.

Donalson, Melvin, ed. <u>Cornerstones: An Anthology of African American Literature</u>. New York: St. Martin's, 1996.

Ellison, Ralph. "What America Would Be Like without Blacks." Donalson 737-41.

10. TRANSLATION

Zamora, Martha. <u>Frida Kahlo: The Brush of Anguish</u>. Trans. Marilyn Sode Smith. San Francisco: Chronicle, 1990.

11. EDITION OTHER THAN THE FIRST

Kelly, Alfred H., Winfred A. Harbison, and Herman Belz. <u>The American Constitution: Its Origins and Development</u>. 6th ed. New York: Norton, 1983.

12. ONE VOLUME OF A MULTIVOLUME WORK

Foner, Philip S., and Ronald L. Lewis, eds. <u>The Black Worker</u>. Vol. 3. Philadelphia: Lippincott, 1980. 8 vols.

13. TWO OR MORE VOLUMES OF A MULTIVOLUME WORK

Foner, Philip S., and Ronald L. Lewis, eds. <u>The Black Worker</u>. 8 vols. Philadelphia: Lippincott, 1980.

14. PREFACE, FOREWORD, INTRODUCTION, OR AFTERWORD

Schlesinger, Arthur M., Jr. Introduction. <u>Pioneer Women: Voices from the Kansas Frontier</u>. By Joanna L. Stratton. New York: Simon, 1981. 11-15.

15. ARTICLE IN A REFERENCE WORK

List the author of the article. If no author is identified, begin with the title. For a well-known encyclopedia, just note the edition and date. If the entries in the reference work are in alphabetical order, you need not give volume or page numbers.

```
Johnson, Peder J. "Concept Learning." Encyclopedia of
     Education. 1971.
"Traquair, Sir John Stewart." Encyclopaedia Britannica.
     11th ed. 1911.
```

16. BOOK THAT IS PART OF A SERIES

```
Moss, Beverly J., ed. Literacy across Communities. Writ-
     ten Lang. Ser. 2. Cresskill: Hampton, 1994.
```

17. GOVERNMENT DOCUMENT

Begin with the author, if identified. Otherwise, start with the name of the government, followed by the agency and any subdivision. Use abbreviations if they can be readily understood. Then give the title. For congressional documents, cite the number, session, and house; the type (*Report, Resolution, Document*), in abbreviated form; and the number of the material. If you cite the *Congressional Record,* give only the date and page number. Otherwise, end with publication information; the publisher is often the Government Printing Office (*GPO*).

```
United States. Cong. House. Report of the Joint Subcom-
     mittee on Reconstruction. 39th Cong., 1st sess.
     H. Rept. 30. 1865. New York: Arno, 1969.
United States. Census Bureau. Historical Statistics of
     the United States, Colonial Times to 1870. Washing-
     ton: GPO, 1975.
```

18. PAMPHLET

```
Why Is Central America a Conflict Area? Opposing View-
     points Pamphlets. St. Paul: Greenhaven, 1984.
```

19. PUBLISHED PROCEEDINGS OF A CONFERENCE

```
Martin, John Steven, and Christine Mason Sutherland,
     eds. Proceedings of the Canadian Society for the
     History of Rhetoric. Calgary: Canadian Soc. for the
     History of Rhetoric, 1986.
```

20. TITLE WITHIN A TITLE

Do not underline or italicize the title of a book within the title of a book you are citing. Underline and enclose in quotation marks the title of a short work within a book title.

Gilbert, Stuart. <u>James Joyce's</u> Ulysses. New York: Vintage-Random, 1955.
Renza, Louis A. <u>"A White Heron" and the Question of a Minor Literature</u>. Madison: U of Wisconsin P, 1984.

PERIODICALS

The basic entry for a periodical includes the following elements: the author's name, last name first; the article title, in quotation marks, with all major words capitalized; and the publication information, including the periodical title (underlined or italicized), the volume and issue numbers (if any), the date of publication, and the page number(s). Each of the three elements ends with a period (which in the article title goes *inside* the closing quotation marks).

21. ARTICLE IN A JOURNAL PAGINATED BY VOLUME

Norris, Margot. "Narration under a Blindfold: Reading Joyce's 'Clay.'" <u>PMLA</u> 102 (1987): 206–15.

22. ARTICLE IN A JOURNAL PAGINATED BY ISSUE

Follow the volume number with a period and the issue number.

Loffy, John. "The Politics at Modernism's Funeral." <u>Canadian Journal of Political and Social Theory</u> 6.3 (1987): 89–96.

23. ARTICLE IN A MONTHLY MAGAZINE

Weiss, Philip. "The Book Thief: A True Tale of Bibliomania." <u>Harper's</u> Jan. 1994: 37–56.

24. ARTICLE IN A WEEKLY MAGAZINE

Hillenbrand, Laura. "A Sudden Illness." <u>The New Yorker</u> July 7, 2003: 56–65.

25. ARTICLE IN A NEWSPAPER

After the author and title of the article, give the name of the newspaper as it appears on the front page but without any initial *A, An,* or *The.* Add the city in brackets after the name if it is not part of the title. Then give the date and edition if one is listed, and add a colon. Follow the colon with a space, the section number or letter (if given), and then the page number(s). If the article appears on discontinuous pages, give the first page followed by a plus sign.

> Riding, Alan. "Loss Estimates Are Cut on Iraqi Arti-
>   facts." New York Times 1 May 2003, late ed.: A1+.

26. EDITORIAL OR LETTER TO THE EDITOR

> Magee, Doug. "Soldier's Home." Editorial. Nation 26 Mar.
>   1988: 400-01.

27. UNSIGNED ARTICLE

> "Tipping the Balance." Time 25 June 2001: 34+.

28. REVIEW

List the reviewer's name and the title of the review, if any, followed by *Rev. of* and the title and author or director of the work reviewed. Then add the publication information for the periodical in which the review appears.

> Solinger, Rickie. "Unsafe for Women." Rev. of Next Time,
>   She'll Be Dead: Battering and How to Stop It, by Ann
>   Jones. New York Times Book Review 20 Mar. 1994: 16.

ELECTRONIC SOURCES

Electronic sources such as CD-ROMs, World Wide Web sites, and email differ from print sources in the ease with which they can be — and the frequency with which they are — changed, updated, or even eliminated. In addition, as the *MLA Handbook for Writers of Research Papers* notes, electronic media "so far lack agreed-on means of organizing works" so that it is often hard to identify information that can direct a reader to the source. In recommending the following guidelines for some of the most common kinds of electronic sources, the *Handbook* adds, "writers must often settle for citing whatever information is available to them." Further guidelines for citing electronic sources can be found in the *Handbook* and online at <http://www.mla.org>.

Note that MLA style requires that electronic addresses, or URLs, in a Works Cited list be broken only after a slash.

The basic entry for an electronic source includes up to five elements, each followed by a period: the author's name, if known; the title and subtitle in quotation marks of a part of a site, with all major words capitalized; any print publication information; the electronic publication information, including the title of the site (underlined or italicized), any editor(s) of the site, the version number, the date of electronic publication (or latest update), and the name of any sponsoring organization; and the most recent date you accessed the source, followed by its URL enclosed in angle brackets. The entry always includes the last two elements.

29. DOCUMENT FROM A WEB SITE

Scott, Walter. "Remarks on Frankenstein, or the Modern
    Prometheus: A Novel." <u>Romantic Circles</u>. Ed. Neil
    Fraistat, Steven Jones, Donald Reiman, and Carl
    Stahmer. 1996. 15 Apr. 1998 <http://www.udel.edu/
    swilson/mws/bemrev.html>.

If a source's URL is long and complicated, you may provide the URL of the site's search page. You may also provide the URL of the site's homepage followed by the word *Path,* a colon, and the sequence of links you clicked to reach the page, with links separated by semicolons.

"Important Dates in the Women's Rights Movement."
    <u>HistoryChannel.com</u>. 2003. History Channel. 13 March
    2003 <http://historychannel.com>. Path: Women's
    History; Special Feature -- Women's Suffrage; The
    History of Women's Suffrage in America; Timeline.

30. ENTIRE WEB SITE

<u>The Orlando Project: An Integrated History of Women's
    Writing in the British Isles</u>. 1997. U of Alberta.
    9 Oct. 1977 <http://www.ualberta.ca/ORLANDO/>.

31. COURSE, DEPARTMENT, OR PERSONAL SITE

For a course site, include the title of the course and a description such as *Course homepage.* For a department site, begin with the name of the department and a description such as *Dept. homepage.* Do not underline or italicize any items or enclose them in quotation marks.

```
Lunsford, Andrea A. Memory and Media. Course homepage.
    Sept.-Dec. 2002. Dept. of English, Stanford U.
    13 March 2003 <http://www.stanford.edu/class/
    english12sc>.
```

Underline or italicize the title of a personal site; if no title exists, include a description such as *Homepage.* Include the organization or institution associated with the site (if any) before the access date.

```
Lunsford, Andrea A. Homepage. 27 Mar. 2003. Dept. of
    English, Stanford U. 2 May 2003 <http://
    www.stanford.edu/~lunsforl/>.
```

32. ONLINE BOOK

```
Riis, Jacob A. How the Other Half Lives: Studies among
    the Tenements of New York. Ed. David Phillips. New
    York: Scribner's, 1890. 26 Mar. 1998 <http://
    www.cis.yale.edu/amstud/inforev/riis/
    title.html>.
```

If you are citing a poem, essay, or other short work within a book, include its title after the author's name. Give the URL of the short work, not of the book, if they differ.

```
Dickinson, Emily. "The Grass." Poems: Emily Dickinson.
    Boston, 1891. Humanities Text Initiative American
    Verse Collection. Ed. Nancy Kushigian. 1995. U of
    Michigan. 9 Oct. 1997 <http://www.planet.net/
    pkrisxle/emily/poemsOnline.html>.
```

33. ARTICLE IN AN ONLINE PERIODICAL

After the title of the work or material, in quotation marks, include the name of the periodical; the volume or issue number, if any; the date of publication; and the range or total number of pages, paragraphs, parts, or other sections, if they are numbered.

```
Gallagher, Brian. "Greta Garbo Is Sad: Some Historical
    Reflections on the Paradoxes of Stardom in the
    American Film Industry, 1910-1960." Images: A Jour-
    nal of Film and Popular Culture 3 (1997): 7 pts.
```

```
        7 Aug 2002 <http://imagesjournal.com/issue03/
        infocus.htm>.
Gawande, Atul. "Drowsy Docs." Slate 9 Oct. 1997. 10 Oct.
        1997 <http://www.slate.com/MedicalExaminer/
        97-10-09/MedicalExaminer.asp>.
```

34. WORK FROM AN ONLINE SUBSCRIPTION SERVICE

To cite a work from an online subscription service, follow the guidelines for the appropriate type of work and include the URL of the specific work, if possible, or the URL for the search page if the specific URL is long and complicated. If the service supplies no URL or one that will not be accessible to your readers, you must provide other access information.

To cite an article from an online service to which you subscribe personally, such as America Online, after the information about the work give the name of the database, if known, the title of the online service, the date of access and either the word *Keyword,* followed by the keyword used, or the word *Path,* followed by the sequence of links.

```
Weeks, W. William. "Beyond the Ark." Nature Conservancy
        Mar.-Apr. 1999. America Online. 2 Apr. 1999. Key-
        word: Ecology.
```

For a work from an online service to which a library subscribes, list the information about the work, followed by the name of the database (if known), the name of the service, the library, the date of access, and the URL of the service's homepage (if known).

```
"Breaking the Dieting Habit: Drug Therapy for Eating
        Disorders." Psychology Today Mar. 1995: 12+. Elec-
        tric Lib. Main Lib., Columbus, OH. 31 Mar. 1999
        <http://www.elibrary.com/>.
```

35. POSTING TO A DISCUSSION GROUP

After the document title, in quotation marks, include the description *Online posting* and the date of posting. For a listserv posting, then give the name of the listserv; the date of access; and the URL of the listserv or the email address of its moderator. For a newsgroup posting, end with the date of access and the name of the newsgroup, in angle brackets, with the prefix *news.*

```
Martin, Jerry. "The IRA & Sinn Fein." Online
        posting. 31 Mar. 1998. 1 Apr. 1998
        <news:soc.culture.irish>.
```

You should always cite an archival version of a posting, if one is available.

```
Chagall, Nancy. "Web Publishing and Censorship." 2 Feb.
    1997. Online posting. ACW: The Alliance for Comput-
    ers and Writing Discussion List. 10 Oct. 1997
    <http://english.ttu.edu/acw-1/archive.htm>.
```

36. EMAIL MESSAGE

Include the writer's name; the subject line of the message, in quotation marks; a description of the message that mentions the recipient; and the date of the message.

```
Lunsford, Andrea A. "New Texts." Email to Kristin Bowen.
    25 July 2002.
```

37. SYNCHRONOUS COMMUNICATION

In citing a posting in a forum such as a MOO, MUD, or IRC, include the name(s) of any specific speaker(s) you are citing; a description of the event; its date; the name of the forum; the date of access; and the URL. Always cite an archived version of the posting if one is available.

```
Patuto, Jeremy, Simon Fennel, and James Goss. The Myti-
    lene Debate. 9 May 1996. MiamiMOO. 28 Mar. 1998
    <http://moo.cas.edu/cgi-bin/moo?look+4085>.
```

38. OTHER ONLINE SOURCES

In citing other online sources, follow the guidelines given on pp. 477–81, but adapt them as necessary. Here are examples of citations for an interview, a film, and a photograph of a work of art, accessed online.

```
Dyson, Esther. Interview. Hotseat 23 May 1997
    <http://www.hotwired.com/packet/hotseat/97/20/
    index4a.html>.
Face/Off. Dir. John Woo. 1997. Hollywood.com. 8 Mar.
    2000 <http://www.hollywood.com/multimedia/movies/
    faceoff/trailer/mmindex.html>.
Lawrence, Jacob. Pool Parlor. 1942. Metropolitan
    Museum of Art, New York. 2 May 2003 <http://
    www.metmuseum.org/special/African_American_Artists/
    ma42.167.r.htm>.
```

39. CD-ROM, PERIODICALLY REVISED

Include the author's name; publication information for the print version, if any, of the text (including its title and date of publication); the title of the database; the medium (*CD-ROM*); the name of the company producing it; and the electronic publication date.

```
Natchez, Gladys. "Frida Kahlo and Diego Rivera: The
    Transformation of Catastrophe to Creativity."
    Psychotherapy-Patient 4.1 (1987): 153-74. PsycLIT.
    CD-ROM. SilverPlatter. Nov. 1994.
```

40. SINGLE-ISSUE CD-ROM, DISKETTE, OR MAGNETIC TAPE

```
"Communion." The Oxford English Dictionary. 2nd ed.
    CD-ROM. Oxford: Oxford UP, 1992.
```

41. WORK IN AN INDETERMINATE ELECTRONIC MEDIUM

If you are not sure whether material accessed through a local network is stored on a central computer's hard drive, on a CD-ROM, or on the Web, use the label *Electronic.* Include any publication information that is available, the name of the network or of its sponsoring organization, and the date of access.

```
"Communion." The Oxford English Dictionary. 2nd ed.
    Oxford: Oxford UP, 1992. Electronic. OhioLink. Ohio
    State U Lib. 15 Apr. 1998.
```

OTHER SOURCES

42. UNPUBLISHED DISSERTATION OR THESIS

Enclose the title in quotation marks. Add the identification *Diss.* or *M.A. thesis,* the name of the university or professional school and so on; and the year the dissertation or thesis was accepted.

```
LeCourt, Donna. "The Self in Motion: The Status of the
    (Student) Subject in Composition Studies." Diss.
    Ohio State U, 1993.
```

43. PUBLISHED DISSERTATION

Cite a published dissertation as a book, adding the identification *Diss.* and the name of the university. If the dissertation was published by University Microfilms International, add *Ann Arbor: UMI* and the year, and list the UMI number at the end of the entry.

Botts, Roderic C. <u>Influences in the Teaching of English,</u>
    <u>1917-1935: An Illusion of Progress</u>. Diss. North-
    eastern U, 1970. Ann Arbor: UMI, 1971. 71-1799.

44. ARTICLE FROM A MICROFORM

Treat the article as a printed work, but add the name of the microform and information for locating it.

Sharpe, Lora. "A Quilter's Tribute." <u>Boston Globe</u> 25
    Mar. 1989. <u>Newsbank: Social Relations</u> 12 (1989):
    fiche 6, grids B4-6.

45. INTERVIEW

Beja, Morris. Personal interview. 2 Oct. 1997.
Schorr, Daniel. Interview. <u>Weekend Edition</u>. Natl. Public
    Radio. WEVO, Concord. 26 Mar. 1988.

46. LETTER

If the letter was published, cite it as a selection in a book, noting the date and any identifying number after the title.

Frost, Robert. "Letter to Editor of the <u>Independent</u>." 28
    Mar. 1894. <u>Selected Letters of Robert Frost</u>. Ed.
    Lawrance Thompson. New York: Holt, 1964. 19.

If the letter was sent to you, follow this form.

Anzaldúa, Gloria. Letter to the author. 10 Sept. 2002.

47. FILM OR VIDEOCASSETTE

In general, start with the title; then name the director, the distributing company, and the date of release. Other contributors, such as writers or actors, may follow the director. If you cite a particular person's work, start the entry with that person's name. For a videocassette or DVD, include the original film release date (if relevant) and the label *Videocassette* or *DVD*.

<u>The Big Sleep</u>. Dir. Howard Hawks. Perf. Humphrey Bogart
    and Lauren Bacall. Warner Bros., 1946. DVD. Warner
    Home Video, 2000.
<u>The Star</u>. Dir. Lawrence Pitkethly. Videocassette.
    CBS/Fox Video, 1995.

```
Weaver, Sigourney, perf. Aliens. Dir. James Cameron.
     20th Century Fox, 1986.
```

48. TELEVISION OR RADIO PROGRAM

In general, begin with the title of the program. Then list the narrator, writer, director, actors, or other contributors, as necessary; the network; the local station and city, if any; and the broadcast date. If you cite a particular person's work, begin the entry with that person's name. If you cite a particular episode, include any title, in quotation marks, before the program's title. If the program is part of a series, include the series title (not underlined, italicized, or in quotation marks) before the network.

```
Box Office Bombshell: Marilyn Monroe. Narr. Peter
     Graves. Writ. Andy Thomas, Jeff Schefel, and Kevin
     Burns. Dir. Bill Harris. A&E Biography. Arts and
     Entertainment Network. 23 Oct. 1997.
```

49. SOUND RECORDING

Begin with the name of the composer, performer, or conductor, depending on whose work you are citing. Next give the title of the recording, which is underlined or italicized, or the title of the composition, which is not. End with the manufacturer and the year of issue. If you are not citing a compact disc, give the medium before the manufacturer. If you are citing a particular song, include its title, in quotation marks, before the title of the recording.

```
Grieg, Edvard. Concerto in A-minor, op. 16. Cond. Eugene
     Ormandy. Philadelphia Orch. LP. RCA, 1989.
Kilcher, Jewel. "Amen." Pieces of You. A&R, 1994.
```

50. WORK OF ART

```
Kahlo, Frida. Self-Portrait with Cropped Hair. Museum of
     Modern Art, New York.
```

51. LECTURE OR SPEECH

```
Lu, Min-Zhan. "The Politics of Listening." Conference on
     College Composition and Communication. Palmer
     House, Chicago. 3 Apr. 1998.
```

52. PERFORMANCE

List the title, other appropriate details (such as composer, writer, or director), the place, and the date. If you cite a particular person's work, begin the entry with that person's name.

Frankie and Johnny in the Clair de Lune. By Terrence
     McNally. Dir. Paul Benedict. Westside Arts Theater,
     New York. 18 Jan. 1988.
Watson, Emily, perf. The Mill on the Floss. Masterpiece
     Theatre. PBS. WNET, New York. 2 Jan. 2000.

53. MAP OR CHART

Pennsylvania. Map. Chicago: Rand, 1985.

54. CARTOON OR COMIC STRIP

Trudeau, Garry. "Doonesbury." Comic strip. Philadelphia
     Inquirer 9 Mar. 1988: 37.

55. ADVERTISEMENT

Dannon Yogurt. Advertisement. TV Guide 4 Dec. 1999: A14.

APA Documentation Guidelines

The APA documentation style was established by the American Psychological Association and is used broadly in the social sciences. For further information, consult the fifth edition of the *Publication Manual of the American Psychological Association,* published in 2001. The APA has also established a Web site with information about APA Electronic Style Guidelines: <http://www.apastyle.org/elecref.html>.

In-Text Citations

APA style requires parenthetical citations in the text to document quotations, paraphrases, summaries, and other material from a source. These in-text citations correspond to full bibliographic entries in a list of references at the end of the text.

1. AUTHOR NAMED IN A SIGNAL PHRASE

Generally, use the author's name in a signal phrase to introduce the cited material, and place the date, in parentheses, immediately after the author's name. For a quotation, the page number, preceded by *p.,* appears in parentheses after the quotation. For electronic texts or other works without page numbers, paragraph numbers preceded by *para.* or the symbol ¶ may be used instead. For a long, set-off quotation, position the page reference in parentheses two spaces after the final punctuation.

```
Key (1983) has argued that the placement of women in
print advertisements is subliminally important.

As Briggs (1970) observed, parents play an important role
in building their children's self-esteem because "chil-
dren value themselves to the degree that they have been
valued" (p. 14).
```

```
Denes (1980, ¶1) claimed that psychotherapy is an art
that is "volatile, unpredictable, standardless in its
outcome, subjective in its worth."
```

2. AUTHOR NAMED IN PARENTHESES

When you do not mention the author in a signal phrase in your text, give the name and the date in parentheses.

```
One study has found that only 68% of letters received by
editors were actually published (Renfro, 1979).
```

3. TWO AUTHORS

Use both names in all citations. Use *and* in a signal phrase, but use an ampersand (&) in parentheses.

```
Murphy and Orkow (1985) reached somewhat different
conclusions by designing a study that was less
dependent on subjective judgment than were previous
studies.
```

```
A recent study that was less dependent on subjective
judgment resulted in conclusions somewhat different
from those of previous studies (Murphy & Orkow, 1985).
```

4. THREE TO FIVE AUTHORS

List all the authors' names for the first reference.

```
Belenky, Clinchy, Goldberger, and Tarule (1986) have
suggested that many women rely on observing and
listening to others as ways of learning about
themselves.
```

In subsequent references, use just the first author's name plus *et al.*

```
From this experience, observed Belenky et al. (1986),
women learn to listen to themselves think, a step toward
self-expression.
```

5. SIX OR MORE AUTHORS

Use only the first author's name and *et al.* in *every* citation.

```
As Mueller et al. (1980) demonstrated, television holds
the potential for distorting and manipulating consumers
as free-willed decision makers.
```

6. CORPORATE OR GROUP AUTHOR

If the name of an organization or a corporation is long, spell it out the first time, followed by an abbreviation in brackets. In later citations, use the abbreviation only.

```
FIRST CITATION (Centers for Disease Control [CDC], 1990)
LATER CITATION (CDC, 1990)
```

7. UNKNOWN AUTHOR

Use the title or its first few words in a signal phrase or in parentheses (in this example, a book's title is italicized).

```
The school profiles for the county substantiated this
trend (Guide to Secondary Schools, 1983).
```

8. TWO OR MORE AUTHORS WITH THE SAME LAST NAME

If your list of references includes works by different authors with the same last name, include the authors' initials in each citation.

```
G. Jones (1984) conducted the groundbreaking study of
retroviruses.
```

9. TWO OR MORE SOURCES WITHIN THE SAME PARENTHESES

List sources by different authors in alphabetical order by author's last name, separated by semicolons: (Chodorow, 1978; Gilligan, 1982). List works by the same author in chronological order, separated by commas: (Gilligan, 1977, 1982).

10. SPECIFIC PARTS OF A SOURCE

Use abbreviations (*chap.*, *p.*, and so on) in a parenthetical citation to name the part of a work you are citing.

```
Montgomery (1988, chap. 9) argued that his research
yielded the opposite results.
```

11. EMAIL AND OTHER PERSONAL COMMUNICATION

Cite any personal letters, email, electronic bulletin-board correspondence, telephone conversations, or interviews with the person's initial(s) and last name, the identification *personal communication,* and the date. Note, however, that APA recommends not including personal communications in the reference list.

```
J. L. Morin (personal communication, October 14, 1999)
supported with new evidence the claims made in her ar-
ticle.
```

12. WORLD WIDE WEB SITE

To cite a source found on the Web, indicate the chapter or figure, as appropriate. If the source provides no date of publication, use the abbreviation *n.d.* To document a quotation, include the page or paragraph numbers, if available. You may omit them if they are not available.

```
Shade argued the importance of "ensuring equitable gen-
der access to the Internet" (1993).
```

Content Notes

APA style allows you to use content notes to expand or supplement your text. Indicate such notes in your text by superscript numerals. Type the notes themselves on a separate page after the last page of the text, under the heading *Footnotes,* centered at the top of the page. Double-space all entries. Indent the first line of each note five spaces, but begin subsequent lines at the left margin.

SUPERSCRIPT NUMERAL IN TEXT

```
The age of the children involved was an important factor
in the selection of items for the questionnaire.[1]
```

FOOTNOTE

```
    [1] Marjorie Youngston Forman and William Cole of the
Child Study Team provided great assistance in identifying
appropriate items.
```

List of References

The alphabetical list of the sources cited in your document is called *References.* (If your instructor asks that you list everything you have read as background — not just the sources you cite — call the list *Bibliography.*) Here are some guidelines for preparing such a list.

- Start your list on a separate page after the text of your document but before any appendices or notes.

- Type the heading *References,* neither italicized nor in quotation marks, centered one inch from the top of the page.

- Begin your first entry. Unless your instructor suggests otherwise, do not indent the first line of each entry, but indent subsequent lines one-half inch or five spaces. Double-space the entire list.

- List sources alphabetically by authors' last names. If the author of a source is unknown, alphabetize the source by the first major word of the title.

For print sources, the APA style specifies the treatment and placement of four basic elements — author, publication date, title, and publication information.

- *Author*   List all authors with last name first, and use only initials for first and middle names. Separate the names of multiple authors with commas, and use an ampersand before the last author's name.

- *Publication date*   Enclose the date in parentheses. Use only the year for books and journals; use the year, a comma, and the month or month and day for magazines; use the year, a comma, and the month and day for newspapers. Do not abbreviate.

- *Title*   Italicize titles and subtitles of books and periodicals. Do not enclose titles of articles in quotation marks. For books and articles, capitalize only the first word of the title and subtitle and any proper nouns or proper adjectives. Capitalize all major words in a periodical title.

- *Publication information*   For a book, list the city of publication (and the country or postal abbreviation for the state if the city is unfamiliar), a colon, and the publisher's name, dropping *Inc., Co.,* or *Publishers.* For a periodical, follow the periodical title with a comma, the volume number (italicized), the issue number (if appropriate) in parentheses and followed by a comma, and the inclusive page numbers of the article. For newspapers and for articles or chapters in books, include the abbreviation *p.* ("page") or *pp.* ("pages").

The following sample entries are in a hanging indent format, in which the first line aligns on the left and the subsequent lines indent one-half inch or five spaces. This is the customary APA format for final copy, including student papers. Unless your instructor suggests otherwise, it is the format we recommend. Note, however, that for manuscripts submitted to journals, APA requires the reverse (first line of each entry indented, subsequent lines flush left), assuming that the citations will be converted by a typesetting system to a hanging indent. Note that APA allows italics in student papers. Some instructors prefer underlining; check which format your instructor prefers.

BOOKS

1. ONE AUTHOR

Lightman, A. (1993). *Einstein's dreams*. New York: Warner Books.

2. TWO OR MORE AUTHORS

Newcombe, F., & Ratcliffe, G. (1978). *Defining females: The nature of women in society*. New York: Wiley.

3. CORPORATE OR GROUP AUTHOR

Institute of Financial Education. (1983). *Income property lending*. Homewood, IL: Dow Jones-Irwin.

Use the word *Author* as the publisher when the organization is both the author and the publisher.

American Chemical Society. (1978). *Handbook for authors of papers in American Chemical Society publications*. Washington, DC: Author.

4. UNKNOWN AUTHOR

National Geographic atlas of the world. (1999). Washington, DC: National Geographic Society.

5. EDITOR

Hardy, H. H. (Ed.) (1998). *The proper study of mankind*. New York: Farrar, Straus.

6. SELECTION IN A BOOK WITH AN EDITOR

West, C. (1992). The postmodern crisis of the black
    intellectuals. In L. Grossberg, C. Nelson, & P.
    Treichler (Eds.), *Cultural studies* (pp. 689–705).
    New York: Routledge.

7. TRANSLATION

Durkheim, E. (1957). *Suicide* (J. A. Spaulding & G. Simp-
    son, Trans.). Glencoe, IL: Free Press of Glencoe.

8. EDITION OTHER THAN THE FIRST

Kohn, M. L. (1977). *Class and conformity: A study in
    values* (2nd ed.). Chicago: University of Chicago
    Press.

9. ONE VOLUME OF A MULTIVOLUME WORK

Baltes, P., & Brim, O. G. (Eds.). (1980). *Life-span
    development and behavior* (Vol. 3). New York: Basic
    Books.

10. ARTICLE IN A REFERENCE WORK

Ochs, E. (1989). Language acquisition. In *International
    encyclopedia of communications* (Vol. 2, pp.
    390–393). New York: Oxford University Press.

If no author is listed, begin with the title.

11. REPUBLICATION

Piaget, J. (1952). *The language and thought of the
    child.* London: Routledge & Kegan Paul. (Original
    work published 1932)

12. GOVERNMENT DOCUMENT

U.S. Census Bureau. (1975). *Historical statistics of the
    United States, colonial times to 1870.* Washington,
    DC: U.S. Government Printing Office.

13. TWO OR MORE WORKS BY THE SAME AUTHOR(S)

List two or more works by the same author in chronological order. Repeat the author's name in each entry.

```
Goodall, J. (1991). Through a window. Boston: Houghton
     Mifflin.
Goodall, J. (1999). Reason for hope: A spiritual jour-
     ney. New York: Warner Books.
```

PERIODICALS

14. ARTICLE IN A JOURNAL PAGINATED BY VOLUME

```
Shuy, R. (1981). A holistic view of language. Research
     in the Teaching of English, 15, 101-111.
```

15. ARTICLE IN A JOURNAL PAGINATED BY ISSUE

```
Maienza, J. G. (1986). The superintendency: Characteris-
     tics of access for men and women. Educational
     Administration Quarterly, 22(4), 59-79.
```

16. ARTICLE IN A MAGAZINE

```
Quinn, J. B. (2002, September 16). Bonds for beginners.
     Newsweek, 45.
```

17. ARTICLE IN A NEWSPAPER

```
Browne, M. W. (1988, April 26). Lasers for the battle-
     field raise concern for eyesight. The New York
     Times, pp. C1, C8.
```

18. EDITORIAL OR LETTER TO THE EDITOR

```
Russell, J. S. (1994, March 27). The language instinct
     [Letter to the editor]. New York Times Book Review,
     27.
```

19. UNSIGNED ARTICLE

```
What sort of person reads Creative Computing? (1985,
     August). Creative Computing, 8, 10.
```

20. REVIEW

```
Larmore, C. E. (1989). [Review of the book Patterns of
    moral complexity]. Ethics, 99, 423–426.
```

21. PUBLISHED INTERVIEW

```
McCarthy, E. (1968, December 24). [Interview with
    Boston Globe Washington staff]. Boston Globe,
    p. B27.
```

ELECTRONIC SOURCES

The APA's Web site, <http://www.apastyle.org/elecref.html>, includes current guidelines for citing various electronic sources, updating the information given in the fifth edition of the *Publication Manual of the American Psychological Association.*

The basic entry for most sources you access via the Internet should include the following elements:

- *Author*   Give the author's name, if available.

- *Publication date*   Include the date of Internet publication or of the most recent update, if available. Use *n.d.* if the publication date is unavailable.

- *Title*   List the title of the document or subject line of the message, neither italicized nor placed in quotation marks.

- *Publication information*   For documents from databases or other scholarly projects, give the city of the publisher or sponsoring organization, followed by the name. For articles from online journals or newspapers, follow the title with a comma, the volume number (italicized), the issue number (if appropriate) in parentheses and followed by a comma, and the inclusive page numbers of the article.

- *Retrieval information*   Type the word *Retrieved* followed by the date of access, followed by a comma. End with the URL or other retrieval information and no period.

22. WORLD WIDE WEB SITE

To cite a document from a Web site, include information as you would for a print document, followed by a note on its retrieval.

```
Mullins, B. (1995). Introduction to Robert Hass. Read-
    ings in Contemporary Poetry at Dia Center for the
```

```
         Arts. Retrieved April 24, 1997 from:
         http://www.diacenter.org/prg/poetry/95-96/
         interhass.html
    Shade, L. R. (1993). Gender issues in computer net-
         working. Retrieved January 28, 2000 from
         http://www.0.delphi.com/woman/text3.html
```

If no author is identified, start with the title of the document.

```
    Media images can spur eating disorders in teens. (2000,
         February 16). InteliHealth. Retrieved June 29,
         2001, from http://www.intelihealth.com/IH/ihtIH/
         WSIHW000/333/8014/269144.html
```

23. ARTICLE FROM AN ONLINE PERIODICAL

If the article also appears in a print journal, no retrieval statement is required; instead, include the label *[Electronic version]* after the article title. However, if the online version differs from the print document (for example, if the online format is different or lacks page numbers), include the date of access and URL.

```
    Palmer, K. S. (2000, September 12). In academia, males
         under a microscope. Washington Post. Retrieved Jan-
         uary 23, 2001, from http://www.washingtonpost.com
    Steedman, M., & Jones, G. P. (2000). Information struc-
         ture and the syntax-phonology interface [Electronic
         version]. Linguistic Inquiry, 31, 649-689.
```

To cite an online article that did not appear in print, give the date of access and URL.

```
    Taylor, J. (1998, June). Constructing the relational
         mind. Psyche, 4(10). Retrieved August 11, 2001,
         from http://psyche.cs.monash.edu.au/v4/psyche
         -4-10-taylor.html
```

24. ARTICLE OR ABSTRACT FROM A DATABASE

List the date you retrieved the article and only the name of the database. If you are citing an abstract, end by typing *Abstract retrieved,* the date of access, and the name of the database. End with the document number in parentheses, if appropriate.

Hayhoe, G. (2001). The long and winding road: Technology's future. *Technical Communication, 48*(2),
133–145. Retrieved September 22, 2001, from Pro-
Quest database.

McCall, R. B. (1998). Science and the press: Like oil
and water? *American Psychologist, 43*(2). 87–94.
Abstract retrieved August 23, 2002, from PsycINFO
database (1988-18263-001).

25. ONLINE GOVERNMENT DOCUMENT

End with the date of access and the URL. If no date is given, use *n.d.*

Finn, J. D. (1998, April). *Class size and students at
risk: What is known? What is next?* Retrieved
September 5, 2002, from United States Department
of Education Web site http://www.ed.gov/pubs/
ClassSize/title.html

26. POSTING TO A DISCUSSION GROUP

List an online posting in the references list only if you are able to retrieve
the message from an archive. After the author's name and date, include the
subject line from the posting, with any information that further identifies the
message in square brackets. For a listserv message, end with the retrieval statement, including the name of the list and the URL of the archived message.

Troike, R. C. (2001, June 21). Buttercups and primroses
[Msg. 8]. Message posted to the American Dialect
Society's ADS-L electronic mailing list, archived
at http://listserv.linguistlist.org/archives/
ads-1.html

For a newsgroup posting, end with the name of the newsgroup. Use the
author's screen name if the real name is unavailable.

Wittenberg, E. (2001, July 11). Gender and the Internet
[Msg. 4]. Message posted to news://
comp.edu.composition

27. EMAIL MESSAGE OR SYNCHRONOUS COMMUNICATION

The APA's *Publication Manual* discourages including email messages or
synchronous communications (MOOS, MUDS) in a list of references and suggests citing them only in text as personal communication (p. 489).

28. FTP (FILE TRANSFER PROTOCOL), TELNET, OR GOPHER SITE

After the retrieval statement, give the address (substituting *ftp, telnet,* or *gopher* for *http* at the beginning of the URL) or the path followed to access information, with slashes to indicate menu selections.

```
Korn, P. (1994, October). How much does breast cancer
    really cost? Self. Retrieved May 5, 1997, from
    gopher://nysernet.org:70/00/BCIC/Sources/SELF/94/
    how-much
```

29. SOFTWARE OR COMPUTER PROGRAM

```
McAfee Office 2000. Version 2.0 [Computer software].
    (1999). Santa Clara, CA: Network Associates.
```

OTHER SOURCES

30. TECHNICAL OR RESEARCH REPORTS AND WORKING PAPERS

```
Wilson, K. S. (1986). Palenque: An interactive multi-
    media optical disc prototype for children (Working
    Paper No. 2). New York: Center for Children and
    Technology, Bank Street College of Education.
```

31. PAPER PRESENTED AT A MEETING OR SYMPOSIUM, UNPUBLISHED

Cite the month of the meeting if it is available.

```
Engelbart, D. C. (1970, April). Intellectual implica-
    tions of multi-access computing. Paper presented at
    the meeting of the Interdisciplinary Conference on
    Multi-Access Computer Networks, Washington, DC.
```

32. DISSERTATION, UNPUBLISHED

```
Leverenz, C. A. (1994). Collaboration and difference in
    the composition classroom. Unpublished doctoral
    dissertation, Ohio State University, Columbus.
```

33. POSTER SESSION

```
Ulman, H. L., & Walborn, E. (1993, March). Hypertext in
    the composition classroom. Poster session presented
    at the Annual Conference on College Composition and
    Communication, San Diego.
```

34. FILM OR VIDEOTAPE

```
Hitchcock, A. (Producer & Director). (1954). Rear window
    [Motion picture]. Los Angeles: MGM.
```

35. TELEVISION PROGRAM, SINGLE EPISODE

Begin with the names of the script writers, and give the name of the director, in parentheses, after the episode title.

```
Imperioli, M. (Writer), & Buscemi, S. (Director). (2002,
    October 20). Everybody hurts [Television series
    episode]. In D. Chase (Executive producer), The
    Sopranos. New York: Home Box Office.
```

36. RECORDING

Begin with the name of the writer or composer followed by the date of copyright. Give the recording date if it is different from the copyright date.

```
Colvin, S. (1991). I don't know why. [Recorded by
    A. Krauss and Union Station]. On Every time you say
    goodbye [Cassette]. Cambridge, MA: Rounder Records.
    (1992)
```

Web Resources

The World Wide Web hosts numerous sites useful to students. The following sites provide a starting point (and only a starting point) for exploring the riches of the Web. For live links to these resources, go to <bedfordstmartins.com/workinprogress>.

General Web Resources

The Library of Congress (LOC) homepage provides access to the catalogs, collections, exhibitions, special programs, and research services of the Library of Congress. The LOC's National Digital Library Program offers access to documents, films, photos, and sound recordings in the American Memory Historical Collections.
<http://lcweb.loc.gov>

The Internet Public Library Web site provides a large collection of easily searched online serials, newspapers, and texts. It also includes materials designed to encourage more effective and efficient searching of the Web.

Purdue University Libraries' Virtual Reference Desk provides an array of online resources, including dictionaries, thesauri, acronyms, and almanacs; general works on information technology; maps and travel information; phone books and area codes; selected government documents; and other reference sources.
<www.lib.purdue.edu/eresources/readyref/>

The WWW Virtual Library is a rich resource for information on the following subjects: agriculture, business and economics, computer science, communications and media, education, engineering, humanities, information management, international affairs, law, recreation, regional studies, science, and society. Tim Berners-Lee, who created HTML and the Web, founded this site.
<http://vlib.org/>

Refdesk.com includes links to media and a wide array of reference sources, from airline flight trackers to zip-4 look-up.
<www.refdesk.com>

The California State University System's Global Campus Web site contains a variety of materials (including images, sounds,

text, and video) to be used for educational purposes. Topics covered include business, fine arts, engineering, liberal arts, library, and science.
<www.csulb.edu/~gcampus/>

The Educational Resources Information Center, which is sponsored by the National Library of Education, provides access to the ERIC database, the largest source of educational information in the world. It also provides links to ERIC clearinghouse sites, resources, and special projects.
<www.eric.ed.gov/resources/index.htm>

Official U.S. Executive Branch Web Sites provide links to all existing Web sites of the executive branch of the U.S. government.
<http://lcweb.loc.gov/global/executive/fed.html>

The United States Legislative Branch Web Sites provide links to a number of sites directly or indirectly related to the U.S. Congress. They include links for congressional mega sites, which are rich resources for information on current legislative initiatives, as well as links to congressional members, committees, organizations, schedules, calendars, floor proceedings, records and journals, votes, and other information.
<http://thomas.loc.gov/home/legbranch/legbranch.htm>

The Federal Judiciary Homepage provides a variety of resources about the federal judiciary system. These include information about the U.S. courts and various judicial system publications and directions. Links are provided to current news releases and reports, as well as to items about the judiciary in various news sources.

Web Resources for Writers

The International Writing Center Association's Resources for Writers Web page is a rich source of online help for all aspects of writing. The page includes links to a grammar hotline directory, handouts, online tutoring, and miscellaneous resources, such as punctuation guides, MLA and APA citation formats, and tips for technical writers.
<http://iwca.syr.edu>

Bartleby.com offers resources for writing and literary study, including *The American Heritage Dictionary, Columbia Encyclopedia,* and *Roget's II* thesaurus.
<www.bartleby.com>

Online Writing Labs (OWLs) and Centers

The International Writing Center Association's Directory of Writing Centers Online provides links to the many online writing centers throughout North America. Some of these online writing centers will assist all writers; others provide services only to students at their university. These and other policies are clearly stated on each center's homepage.
<http://iwca.syr.edu/IWCA/IWCAOWLS.html>

The following list includes some particularly well-developed online writing centers. The first such center in the United States was developed by Muriel Harris at Purdue University. Purdue's center remains one of the most valuable online resources for writers.

Purdue University's Online Writing Lab
<http://owl.english.purdue.edu/>

The Writers' Workshop at the University of Illinois, Champaign–Urbana
<**www.english.uiuc.edu/cws/ wworkshop/index.htm**>

Washington State University's Online Writing Lab
<**http://owl.wsu.edu/**>

Oregon State University's Online Writing Lab
<**http://cwl.oregonstate.edu/owl.html**>

Writing@CSU: The Writing Center at Colorado State University
<**http://www.colostate.edu**>

Resources for Multilingual Writers

The Online English Grammar, maintained by Anthony Hughes, provides multiple resources for multilingual students, including extensive information about various aspects of English, practice pages, a grammar clinic, and a learning center.
<**www.eduFind.com/english/grammar/**>

Dave's ESL Café Web site provides a rich array of resources for multilingual writers — from a quiz center to handouts, message exchanges, and chat central.
<**www.eslcafe.com/**>

George Washington University's ESL Study Hall provides links to resources for reading, writing, vocabulary, conversation, grammar, and listening.
<**http://home.gwv.edu/~meloni/es/ studyhall**>

The Frizzy University Network Web site provides assistance with grammar and with online reference materials (both general and specific to ESL). It also provides links to ESL discussion lists, to information about studying in the United States, and Web site construction.
<**http://thecity.sfsu.edu/%7Efunweb/**>

Karin's ESL PartyLand Web site includes seventy-five interactive quizzes, fifteen discussion forums, interactive lessons on a variety of topics, a chat room, and links to a variety of resources for multilingual writers.
<**www.eslpartyland.com/**>

Resources for the Humanities and Fine Arts

The University of California's **Voice of the Shuttle,** which is maintained by Alan Liu, is a particularly rich site for humanities research. In addition to listing resources on a wide variety of topics in the humanities, it includes extensive information on Web searching. Other resources include lists of highly ranked Web sites; guides to evaluating Internet resources; and humanities texts, archives, journals, and discussion lists and newsgroups.
<**http://vos.ucsb.edu/**>

Project Gutenberg originated in 1971, when Michael Hart decided that the best use of the Internet was to make public domain works available to the public. Project Gutenberg provides access to hundreds of downloadable (and, in the case of public domain texts, reproducible) texts — from Shakespeare and Lewis Carroll to Poe and Dante.
<**http://promo.net/pg/**>

Worldwide Internet Music Resources is a service provided by the William and Gayle

Cook Music Library, Indiana University. The site includes links to a wide range of resources on both classical and contemporary music.
<**www.music.indiana.edu/ music_resources/**>

Valdosta University's Home Page of Philosophy Resources provides links to numerous and diverse resources related to all branches of classical and contemporary philosophy. Representative links include Tuft's Greek Library, the Internet Encyclopedia of Philosophy, the Markkula Center for Applied Ethics, and homepages sponsored by various teachers and students of philosophy.
<**www.valdosta.peachnet.edu/ ~rbarnett/phi/resource.html**>

Art History Resources on the Web, a site maintained by Chris Witcombe of Sweet Briar College, includes an extensive array of links. All periods of art history — from prehistoric to the present — are covered, as are all mediums. The site also includes links to general research resources and to museums and galleries around the world.
<**http://witcombe.sbc.edu/ ARTHLinks.html**>

The World Wide Virtual Library: History Index provides links to historical sites organized according to time, place, and area within history. It also lists online services about history, research tools, and general resources.
<**www.ku.edu/history/vl**>

Resources for the Social Sciences

The American Psychological Association homepage includes research links to news articles, publications, and a for-fee searchable database; guidelines on library research and tips on APA documentation style; and informational content on parenting, mental health, and other topics.
<**www.apa.org/**>

The American Psychological Society, an international association of professionals in psychology, publishes the APS *Observer* online, a bimonthly journal offering in-depth articles on current topics in psychological science, noteworthy research, and issues that are affecting the field. It also provides links to psychology departments, psychological societies and organizations, government agencies, and related sites.
<**www.psychologicalscience.org**>

Psych Web offers a wealth of information on psychology and the social sciences, including thousands of links to psychology homepages of universities around the world, journals in psychology and the social sciences, psychology-related Web sites, APA style guides, and even complete versions of two classic texts in psychology, Sigmund Freud's *The Interpretation of Dreams* and William James's *The Varieties of Religious Experience*.
<**www.psywww.com/**>

The Society of Professional Journalists, the largest journalism organization in the United States, offers a Web site with in-depth information on such issues as ethics in journalism, the Freedom of Information Act, student journalism, cameras in court, privacy, reporter's privilege, online challenges, the Supreme Court and the media, and trial coverage.
<**www.spj.org**>

IDEAS (Internet Documents in Economics Access Service) is a storehouse of articles

in the field of economics, including published articles from hundreds of journals, author information, institution homepages, software information, and papers in progress, all classified by journal title or by *Journal of Economic Literature* codes.
<http://ideas.repec.org>

THOMAS is a service of the Library of Congress that provides legislative information on the Internet, including the status and history of bills, the congressional record, committee information, background materials on the legislative process, copies of historical documents, and much more.
<http://thomas.loc.gov>

Foreign Government Resources on the Web, sponsored by the University of Michigan, provides links to foreign government Web sites and background information on foreign countries, including leader biographies, human rights records, politics and election data; information on constitutions, laws, treaties, and embassies; and current news via links to international newspapers.
<www.lib.umich.edu/govdocs/
foreign.html>

The U.S. Census Bureau, part of the United States Department of Commerce, offers census information from Census 2000 and earlier, including data on population size broken down by state, county, and city; business-related figures; and information on income, poverty, minorities, genealogy, housing, and foreign trade.
<www.census.gov>

The Department of History at Tennessee Technological University offers links to databases and sites related to issues in the social sciences, including international affairs, the global environment, the Internet, demographics, policy analysis, government, political organizations, and social development.
<www.tntech.edu/history>

The **SocioWeb** is an unaffiliated guide to Web resources in the field of sociology, with links arranged by the following topics: Net indexes and guides, commercial sites, giants of sociology, journals and zines, learning sociology, sociological associations, sociology in action, sociological theory, surveys and statistics, topical research, university departments, and writings.
<www.socioweb.com/~markbl/
socioweb>

A Sociological Tour through Cyberspace, hosted by The Department of Sociology and Anthropology at Trinity University, features opinions, data analyses, essays, and links arranged by the following categories: general sociological resources, sociological theory, data resources and Web tools, and methods and statistics.
<www.trinity.edu/~mkearl/>

The University of Iowa Department of Communication Studies **Links to Communication Studies Resources** is organized around the following subject areas: advertising; cultural studies and popular culture; digital media, hypertext, cybernetics, cyborgs, and virtual realities; film studies; gender, ethnicity, and race in mass communication; general communication resources; health and science communication; journalism and mass communication; media studies; political communication; rhetorical studies; social science resources; speeches and speechmakers; and visual communication/visual rhetorics.
<www.uiowa.edu/~commstud/
resources/>

Resources for the Sciences and Mathematics

The **Math Archives Undergrads' Page** provides links to the following topics: societies, undergraduate projects and research, summer programs, competitions, careers, undergraduate publications, and other Web sites.
<http://archives.math.utk.edu/undergraduates.html>

Math on the Web, maintained by the American Mathematics Society, includes links to the following topics: literature guides, mathematics online, mathematics organized, people, reference literature, servers, and related resources.
<www.ams.org/mathweb/>

Biology Links, maintained by Harvard University's Department of Molecular and Cellular Biology, provides links to resources on specific topics within molecular and cellular biology, as well as to general Internet resources for biology, banks and tables, selected model organism and biological databases, and biological software directories.
<http://mcb.harvard.edu/BioLinks.html>

The National Human Genome Research Institute Web site serves as a clearinghouse for research on this important project. Topics include the ethical, legal, and social implications of the human genome project; policy and public affairs issues; and genomic and genetic resources.
<www.genome.gov>

The National Institutes of Health (NIH) Web site includes news, health information, and links to scientific resources and to NIH suborganizations. The NIH is the central government organization dealing with health issues.

Indiana University's **ChemInfo** provides resources to a wide range of online resources in chemistry. The site offers both alphabetical and keyword searches.
<www.indiana.edu/~cheminfo/>

EEVL, The Internet Guide to Engineering, Mathematics, and Computing is a British site that includes links to a variety of sites for engineering and related disciplines.
<www.eevl.ac.uk>

Physics News, maintained by the Brown University Physics Department, presents news and information related to physics and public policy, current work in physics, science news from wire services, and links to other journals and magazines.
<www.het.brown.edu/news/>

The Virtual Library: Earth Science provides links to sites on cartography, geography, meteorology, oceanography, and other subjects within the earth sciences.
<http://vlib.org/EarthScience.html>

Developing a Portfolio of Your Written Work

Increasingly, writing teachers are integrating portfolios into course work. Sometimes, portfolios serve primarily to organize and store work in progress; such portfolios are often called *working* portfolios. In other cases, portfolios serve a more public purpose; these *presentation* portfolios highlight a writer's strengths and accomplishments. In writing classes, presentation portfolios often play a role in assessment, including end-of-term grading. Both types of portfolios can provide you with an excellent opportunity to reflect upon your writing process, progress, and future goals.

Whether your teacher asks you to develop a working portfolio or a presentation portfolio, the following guidelines can help you benefit from the process.

■ GUIDELINES FOR KEEPING A WRITING PORTFOLIO

1. *Understand the Purpose and Requirements of Your Portfolio.* The first thing you need to know is whether you are developing a working or a presentation portfolio — or both. A working portfolio exists primarily for your personal use, though your teacher may also ask to review it. A presentation portfolio serves a public function. Your teacher may ask you to develop both a working and a presentation portfolio. In this situation, your working portfolio serves as a source of materials for your presentation portfolio, which you will develop at the end of (and maybe during) the term. A presentation portfolio will include some or all of the materials in your working portfolio, organized according to a particular format. Your teacher may also ask you to write

(continued)

(continued)

additional commentary, such as a cover letter for your portfolio, introductions to individual projects, and analyses of your growth as a writer.

Portfolios can vary considerably in their purpose and requirements. If your teacher asks you to develop a portfolio, you should be sure you know the answers to the following questions:

What primary function does my portfolio serve? If I am developing both a working and a presentation portfolio, what is the relationship between them?

What should my portfolio include?

If I am able to select some or all of the materials in my portfolio, what criteria should govern my selection?

How should my portfolio be organized?

Will my portfolio be evaluated? When, by whom, and according to what criteria?

What role does this evaluation play in determining my final course grade?

Will I be asked to write descriptive or reflective statements about my portfolio? What kind of information might I need to gather during the term to prepare to write these comments?

Is there anything else I need to know to develop an effective portfolio? Do I need to use a specific binder, for instance? Do all materials need to be typed or printed, or are handwritten materials acceptable? What role do neatness and other aspects of visual presentation play in the evaluation of my portfolio? Are there any other requirements I must follow?

2. *Make the Fullest Possible Use of Your Portfolio.* Portfolio development takes time and care, so you might be tempted to look on it as a burden, something to expend minimal energy on. And yet the process of gathering, organizing, and reflecting on your writing can be a powerful aid to learning and can also help you gain confidence as a writer — if you take this process seriously. If you save drafts of your essays but never take the time to review them,

(continued)

(continued)

you may fulfill the minimal requirement for developing a portfolio, but you will have failed to take advantage of a valuable opportunity to learn more about your strengths and weaknesses as a writer.

3. *Organize Materials for Your Portfolio as You Produce Them.* A few simple but effective organizational strategies can help you to keep track of materials for a portfolio.

> Identify all drafts, whether print or electronic, with a date and with a brief heading.

> Develop a system for organizing your drafts. You may want to keep all drafts for a single project in one envelope. If you are composing on a computer, you might set up a directory or folder for each project, taking care to name and save all versions of drafts as you work on them. (In most cases, you will also want to print and organize electronically generated drafts. Even if you submit your portfolio on disk, you should still print backups in case of hardware or software problems.)

> Begin each drafting session by reviewing previous work on your project. Doing so will make it easier for you to keep your notes and drafts in order. This practice brings additional benefits, for it will help you reimmerse yourself in your project. It may also remind you that sections that you discarded from earlier versions might work well in your current draft.

> Organize your materials at the end of each drafting session. If you have been drafting on a computer, print the current version of your draft and clip or staple it together, then add it to earlier drafts of this essay.

4. *Keep Notes about Your Composing Process.* Teachers sometimes ask students to include reflections on their composing process in their portfolio. Sometimes these reflections are general; in other instances they focus on projects you have done during the term. Keeping process notes about your writing will enable you to respond to such an assignment and thus gain a richer understanding of yourself as a writer.

Acknowledgments

Index

Instructor's Notes

SIXTH EDITION

Work in Progress

A Guide to Academic Writing and Revising

a b c d e f g h i j k l m n o p q r s t u v w x y z

Lisa Ede

Suzanne Clark
Lisa Ede

Instructor's Notes

WORK IN PROGRESS

Instructor's Notes

WORK IN PROGRESS

Lisa Ede

SIXTH EDITION

Prepared by

Suzanne Clark
and
Lisa Ede

Bedford/St. Martin's
Boston ◆ New York

CONTENTS

Instructor's Notes

WORK IN PROGRESS

INTRODUCTION

A Few Words about *Work in Progress*

Work in Progress addresses students as writers in a rhetorical situation. Instead of assuming that they must learn to write by following directions from teacher and text, this approach locates students in the sphere of writing. They are apprentice writers, to be sure, but nonetheless fellow writers, ready to learn the secrets of the craft: its messiness, chaos, uncertainty, and ambiguity, as well as its shaping, transforming power.

Of course, as teachers of writing, we try to get our students to become writers, to take themselves seriously, and to become active problem solvers as they write. In that sense, this text has familiar, recognizable goals. What may seem new or perhaps unfamiliar is the way in which *Work in Progress* asks students to undertake their composition studies in the role of writers. The goal of becoming a better writer is punctuated by completed papers, but it is inherently work in progress. Such a goal is dynamic, not final.

From the beginning, *Work in Progress* asks students to see their writing as work in progress. They are led to investigate, describe, and question the rhetorical situation of their writing. They are encouraged to see themselves as part of a community of writers—to read each other's work, to exchange tips and ideas, to discover for themselves how they read and how their understanding of this process and of textual conventions can influence their own writing. They are encouraged to become aware of and respond to their intellectual and cultural circumstances, including in particular their situation as students writing in an academic environment. Their rhetorical situations may include various uses of electronic technologies and may open out to analyses of cultural context. They learn to take charge of their own writing processes, including evaluating and revising. Multilingual students are guided to consider cultural differences as part of the rhetorical situation.

Work in Progress is not a panacea, but it can have important consequences for you and for your students. Worried students will discover that their task has a human scale. And your familiar frustration with not being able to cure all your students' writing ills also can be relieved as students move from viewing themselves as patients suffering from linguistic dis-ease to regarding themselves as healthy (if beginning) writers, capable of learning to make their own diagnoses and to manage their own plans.

Work in Progress invites students into the collaborative circle of writers that we, as experts, know—where writing is always risky, uncertain, and sometimes painful but also a rewarding and highly social activity. This text teaches principles of writing not as certainties but as strategies, ways of going on despite encountering the inevitable problems. It will help you change the nature of your authority from isolated expert to advanced fellow participant. It will help you establish your class as a community of writers. We believe that writing is a powerful component in the work of both individuals and groups. So this text demonstrates not only how to write but how to make writing an instrument of learning.

We proceed, however, with a certain humility. Since teaching, like writing, is work in progress and classrooms present widely differing rhetorical situations, the possibilities for using this text are multiple and complex. Our aim in writing these Instructor's Notes was to give you as much help as we can about workable plans for teaching and as much information as we can about useful ideas and about our experiences teaching this text. As fellow teachers, we offer strategies, not certainties; we offer these Instructor's Notes as an act of collaboration.

HOW TO USE THESE INSTRUCTOR'S NOTES

These Instructor's Notes are designed to complement and support *Work in Progress*. In writing these notes, we were particularly aware of the needs of beginning teachers of writing—teachers who bring many strengths to the classroom but who lack extensive pedagogical experience and who may be just becoming acquainted with research in composition studies. We hope in this manual to provide concrete suggestions that will enable beginning teachers to teach confidently and effectively—to embark successfully on the work in progress that teaching always comprises. We also hope, however, to provide helpful, stimulating resources and suggestions for experienced teachers of writing.

This manual is divided into the following four sections:

- Section 1 provides an overview of and rationale for *Work in Progress*. It also discusses alternative ways of using this text and suggests course plans for quarter- and semester-long classes.

- Section 2 presents practical strategies for teaching using a rhetorical approach, including using research, addressing plagiarism, speaking to the needs of multilingual and multicultural students, reading and writing about visual texts, writing academic arguments, using online writing, learning collaboratively, handling the paper load, and responding to students' writing. It contains suggestions for teaching writing assignments, including freewriting, brainstorming, interviewing, the writer's notebook, essays, research, and writing online. There is a brief section on helping students plan and on using portfolios. Although your program probably includes some form of teaching evaluations, this section suggests some ways to include ongoing assessment as part of the collaborative processes of the course. It concludes with a brief bibliography designed to acquaint those unfamiliar with research in composition with some important resources for instructors.

- Section 3, the longest section of this manual, provides chapter-by-chapter suggestions for teaching the concepts and activities presented in each chapter of *Work in Progress*. Beginning instructors, in particular, should find this section helpful in preparing for class discussions and activities and in responding to students' writing.

- Section 4 includes sample assignments and student papers from instructors who have taught *Work in Progress*. These materials are included here so that you may reproduce them for use as class handouts.

We have made certain changes in the Instructor's Notes for this sixth edition of *Work in Progress:*

- We have added material on research, documentation, and plagiarism; on argument; and on the perspectives of multilingual writers.

- We have added the support for expanded chapters in this edition: a full chapter on document design, a full chapter on academic analysis, and a full chapter on argument.

- We have added further reading on multilingual writers and on argument.

- We have taken advantage of the responses from students and instructors who used the first five editions of *Work in Progress* to pass on suggestions to you.

We wrote these Instructor's Notes to be used by beginning and experienced teachers of writing. If you have suggestions about how this manual could be improved, please write to us in care of Bedford/St. Martin's, 75 Arlington St., Boston, MA 02116.

1. OVERVIEW AND COURSE PLANS

Rationale for the Basic Features of *Work in Progress*

Unlike longer and often more prescriptive texts, *Work in Progress* provides a conceptual framework that can stimulate effective classroom instruction while offering instructors considerable autonomy and flexibility. This approach reflects the author's belief that composition texts should support and enrich, but not dominate, the life of the classroom.

Work in Progress richly reflects recent research in composition and rhetoric, and yet as a practical, commonsensical textbook, it attempts to convey complex theoretical ideas without being intimidating or irrelevant to students. Its most distinctive features include the following:

- Full discussion of the concept of the rhetorical situation, including strategies that students can use to decide the most appropriate way of approaching any writing task, with increased attention throughout to academic contexts
- *New to this edition:* a full chapter on document design
- *New to this edition:* a full chapter on academic analysis
- *New to this edition:* a full chapter on argument
- *New to this edition:* a section addressing documentation and plagiarism in the chapter on research
- *New to this edition:* attention in every chapter to the perspectives of multilingual writers together with activities that encourage attention to cultural differences as part of the rhetorical situation
- *New to this edition:* additional examples of student writing, including many comments by students about their writing practices
- *New to this edition:* close analysis of a number of student texts used as models, and a "Miscellany of Student Essays" in Chapter 17
- attention to reading visual texts and using document design for writing assignments
- A rhetorical approach to the processes of reading, writing, and research that sees them as dynamic, interdependent activities
- A rhetorical approach that allows a better understanding of the nature and role of models, whether "expert" or student
- A rhetorical approach that helps students construct agency as well as deconstruct questions of convention and authority
- Full discussion of the demands of academic writing
- A chapter presenting a rhetorical approach to online writing and new applications to online writing throughout the text (Chapter 7)
- A chapter on strategies for successful collaboration, together with explicit support for and reinforcement of collaborative learning and writing activities throughout (Chapter 13)
- A strong emphasis on the importance of social context and of textual conventions of writing—that is, on writing within discourses
- Activities interspersed throughout the text, as well as at the end of each chapter, that encourage students to apply the concepts and strategies discussed in the text

How *Work in Progress* Is Organized

Work in Progress is divided into four major parts. Part One, "Writing, Reading, and Research: An Introduction," has the following chapters:

- Chapter 1:   On Writing
- Chapter 2:   Understanding the Writing Process
- Chapter 3:   Understanding the Reading Process
- Chapter 4:   Understanding the Research Process

These four chapters establish the conceptual and pedagogical framework for the text. Together, they enable students to develop a sophisticated yet commonsensical understanding of writing, reading, and research as fundamental processes. The discussion and activities in these chapters also encourage students to begin to think of themselves as writers and participants in communities of writers, particularly in an academic community. They prompt students to see writing, reading, and research as interconnected processes. New in this edition are "Guidelines for Conducting a Reading Inventory" and new readings about and from the Internet in Chapter 3, "Understanding the Reading Process," and a section on styles of documentation and on plagiarism in Chapter 4, "Understanding the Research Process." New in this edition as well are numerous notes and activities that address multilingual writers in particular.

Part Two of *Work in Progress*, "Rhetorical Situations," includes three chapters:

- Chapter 5: Analyzing Rhetorical Situations
- Chapter 6: Thinking about Communities and Conventions
- Chapter 7: Negotiating Online Writing Situations

These chapters show students how to use rhetorical analysis, a reading of audience and texts, to understand the framework for their own writing. They include the cross-cultural situation of multilingual writers as part of the rhetorical situation. This section of the text introduces students to the concepts of *ethos, logos,* and *pathos* in Chapter 5 through the models of other student writing and analysis. It shows students, in Chapter 6, how the content of writing may change in different situations through an analysis of three articles on the same set of psychological experiments that appeared in three very different journals. Finally, Chapter 7 applies rhetorical analysis to online situations, discussing the online writing of one student in emails, chat rooms, and a Web page, and showing how to approach the design of Web pages. This edition features new advertisements for analysis in Chapter 5, new online sites in Chapter 6, and notes for multilingual writers throughout.

Part Three of *Work in Progress*, "Practical Strategies for Writing," includes six chapters:

- Chapter 8: Strategies for Invention
- Chapter 9: Strategies for Planning and Drafting
- Chapter 10: Strategies for Document Design
- Chapter 11: Strategies for Managing the Revision Process
- Chapter 12: Strategies for Revising Structure and Style
- Chapter 13: Strategies for Successful Collaboration

As the title of Part Three suggests, these six chapters introduce students to a variety of practical strategies they can use as they plan, draft, and revise. Here, the text emphasizes not a single prescribed series of steps or strategies that students must follow but a repertory of strategies they can draw on, working alone and with others, depending on their purpose and situation. Throughout this edition there new discussions for multilingual writers about effective strategies using the first language and questions of translation. Chapter 10, now a full chapter on document design, includes a new "Guidelines for Effective Document Design" and an analysis of a new sample document with drafts. Chapter 13 has added particular help for multilingual writers on the collaborative process.

Part Four of *Work in Progress*, "Analyzing and Writing Academic Arguments," consists of the following four chapters:

- Chapter 14: Understanding Academic Audiences and Assignments
- Chapter 15: Understanding Academic Analysis
- Chapter 16: Understanding Academic Argument
- Chapter 17: Putting It All Together: Analyzing and Writing Academic Arguments

This final part of *Work in Progress* speaks to students about the reading and writing that they will do as members of the academic community. Students learn approaches to analyzing texts and writing arguments that will help them read and write more effectively in the disciplines. The sixth edition of *Work in Progress* has added substantial new material for this section. Chapter 14 offers suggestions for analyzing disciplinary conventions and for understanding what is expected in assignments, with a note for multilingual students. Chapter 15 includes new material on analyzing academic arguments: a discussion of the question at issue, of critical reading, of good reasons, Aristotle's appeals, Toulmin's framework for argument, and argumentative fallacies. There are new readings for analysis and new "Guidelines for Critical Reading." Chapter 16 is a new chapter on academic argument, discussing it as inquiry rather than as debate, together with a new example of student writing and new "Guidelines for determining Whether a Claim Can Be Argued" and "Guidelines for Evaluating Evidence." Chapter 17 is a close rhetorical analysis of an argument in progress, following the development of a student essay through three drafts, followed by "A Miscellany of Student Essays" in the disciplines that includes several new essays.

Following the last chapter is Writers' References, an easy-to-use reference section with MLA and APA documentation guidelines and instructions for preparing a portfolio.

Each chapter in *Work in Progress* includes activities designed to help students understand and apply the ideas presented in the text. New to this edition are notes and activities particularly addressed to multilingual writers. Two kinds of activities—explorations and group activities or collaborations—are interspersed throughout each chapter. At the end of each chapter are activities "For Thought, Discussion, and Writing." Activities designated as Explorations are designed primarily to stimulate students' understanding of and response to the text. Many Explorations ask students to reflect on previous writing experiences or to brainstorm, freewrite, or talk with others in response to discussions in the text. Others ask students to apply concepts or strategies presented in the text. Those designated for Group Work or Collaboration involve students in carefully designed collaborative learning and writing experiences. In general, assignments lead students to reflect on writing and the rhetorical situation of learning to write as the subject of a critical inquiry as well as the process they are undergoing.

This edition includes increased references to the use of computers and other technologies in connection with writing, and provides the site locations for many online references.

How to Take Advantage of the Flexibility of *Work in Progress*

Work in Progress is an innovative but practical textbook that can be used effectively by teachers employing diverse approaches to the teaching of writing. Instructors using this text can be assured that they will have time for a variety of classroom activities—from peer-response groups to the analysis of readings or discussions of writing in the disciplines. Students who have used *Work in Progress* have consistently praised the text as both easy and interesting to read. Consequently, instructors are not required to spend large amounts of class time explaining the basic concepts in the text. Instead they can engage the class in discussions of substantial rhetorical issues or of the numerous and diverse examples of student and professional writing. Furthermore, the text's many activities—more than any one instructor could assign—can stimulate discussions and interactions. Our point here is that instructors truly are free to decide the degree to which they want to tie classroom discussions or activities directly to the text. A recent discussion on a listserv related to writing pedagogy included the complaint that composition textbooks too often straitjacket instructors, limiting their options. *Work in Progress* gives you the rhetorical support you need without calling attention to a program that is not yours.

How can instructors who favor different approaches use *Work in Progress?* The sixth edition has particularly addressed the need to teach *academic writing and argument* across the disciplines but not to teach any method that is specific to only one discipline. Those who are emphasizing academic writing and argument will find substantial assistance in presenting the fundamentals of reading, research, and writing.

Instructors who are introducing increased use of *electronic technologies* to their writing classes will find suggestions throughout *Work in Progress* for ways to apply this rhetorical approach to writing and reading online. Chapters 2, 3, and 4 as well as Chapter 7 focus on helping students to think rhetorically about the writing that they themselves publish online and Internet sources they might use for research. The readings in Chapter 3 discuss the cultural questions posed by the increasing use of these new technologies. A rhetorical approach to document design allows students to use basic principles on both online and written texts. Because it explicitly teaches students to approach online writing with the knowledge gained from a rhetorical perspective—analyzing purpose, conventions, and audience— you will find that *Work in Progress* can be used effectively as the text for a class meeting in a computer classroom as well as for classes with more limited access to the Internet.

Those who wish to engage students with *collaborative learning* activities will find substantial support for these approaches in this text, based on the idea of writing as an interactive or dialogic process. Part One of *Work in Progress*, "Writing, Reading, and Research: An Introduction," devotes considerable attention to composing processes, a discussion reinforced in Part Three, "Practical Strategies for Writing." Furthermore, the For Exploration, For Group Work, For Collaboration, and For Thought, Discussion, and Writing activities interspersed throughout the chapters all reinforce a process-centered, collaborative emphasis. You may wish to use collaboration as a learning strategy and also to have students write some assignments in collaboration. *Work in Progress* devotes the entirety of Chapter 13 to collaborative writing, which should prove useful to teachers who wish to engage their students in a full range of collaborative activities.

Work in Progress lends itself very well to the *cultural studies* approach used by some institutions where it has been adopted. The emphasis on students and the rhetorical situation throughout the text shows students how to include cultural analysis in their approach to writing and reading. As students learn to think in more complicated ways about how audiences interact with writing and about how cultural conventions define what can be said, they can understand more and more specifically how writing must negotiate its claims and how the interpretations of readers arise out of contexts that require an analysis of culture. New in this edition, interspersed throughout the text, are specific notes and exercises directed toward multilingual and multicultural writers. These address the special concerns of such students, but also assume that cultural differences can become resources for understanding a rhetorical and situated approach to writing.

Instructors who favor using the *modes of discourse, writing across the curriculum,* or *thematic* approaches to the teaching of writing can also use *Work in Progress* effectively. (Of course, these approaches are often used in conjunction with collaborative, process-oriented teaching practices.) Like many traditional rhetorics, *Work in Progress* suggests topics in the text but does not require their assignment. Thus instructors wishing to base class discussions and topic assignments on the modes of discourse, disciplinary conventions, or specific themes or subjects can easily do so.

Although *Work in Progress* contains a number of essays by students and professionals and thus can be used as the only text for a course, it can be combined with other texts as well. Like most rhetorics, *Work in Progress* can be supplemented by a handbook, which can serve as a reference on grammar and usage for students. More important, perhaps, the *Work in Progress* approach to reading and academic writing more directly supports and reinforces the use of a reader than do many traditional rhetorics, which may contain brief examples of professional or academic writing but lack explicit comment on the reading process or the nature of academic writing. *Work in Progress* can thus be assigned very effectively with a traditional reader, a collection of readings exploring a particular theme or subject, a reader focusing on writing across the curriculum, or even a novel, a nonfiction work, or literacy narratives such as Richard Rodriguez's *Hunger of Memory,* Mike Rose's *Lives on the Boundary,* Keith Gilyard's *Voices of the Self,* Victor Villanueva's *Bootstraps,* or Natasha Lvovich's *The Multilingual Self.*

Finally, we would like to note that *Work in Progress* has most often been used in first-year writing courses but has also been used successfully with intermediate and advanced composition students, including a number of future writing instructors in courses on teaching writing. Students in these classes reported that the text enabled them consciously to recognize and discuss understandings that had largely been implicit, if present at all. In anonymous evaluations of the text, advanced students consistently recommended that *Work in Progress* be used in future intermediate and advanced composition classes.

Because we believe that *Work in Progress* can be used successfully with quite diverse approaches to the teaching of writing, as well as with different levels of students, we would appreciate hearing from instructors who have used *Work in Progress* in their composition classes, and we would particularly appreciate receiving copies of syllabi, assignments, or other handouts that indicate how teachers have integrated *Work in Progress* into their classroom practices.

Course Plans

In the following syllabi, we present possible ways of organizing your quarter or semester course using *Work in Progress* with or without an accompanying reader. Although these plans follow the sequence of the chapters in the textbook, you should feel free to vary the order of the chapters in ways that best suit your classroom. Following these syllabi are suggestions about variations in chapter order to accommodate the situation in your course.

Suggestions for Using *Work in Progress* without a Reader

There are many more suggested exercises and discussions in this text than one term's work can cover. The reflective approach to increasing rhetorical sensitivity means that students are increasingly independent, so that *Work in Progress* particularly lends itself to a class analyzing the development of the student writings produced within it. One of the strengths of *Work in Progress* is its close reading of student and professional texts. This analysis provides a model for the analysis of student writing in your class.

Work in Progress stimulates reflection on the processes of learning and writing that you may wish to explicitly make the subject of your course. The reading portfolio on electronic technologies can help such a reflective approach. If your students are making new transitions into the wired academic life, they may especially appreciate the opportunity to reflect critically on the institution and their experiences as writers within it.

This edition of *Work in Progress* lends itself to use with online readings, if you wish to have students learn to make use of research on the Web. Chapter 4, "Understanding the Research Process," includes "Guidelines for Evaluating Web Sites and Web Pages," and Chapter 7, "Negotiating Online Writing Situations," focuses on composing for email and Web sites.

Plan to take advantage of class time to develop collaborative learning activities. In addition to the group activities described in the text, you can regularly have group members brainstorm in response to assignments, analyze readings, and respond to *Work in Progress*. The inclusion of multicultural perspectives in collaborative activities will help students understand the importance of different perspectives for a rhetorical analysis.

Use the writing assignments suggested in *Work in Progress*, or design your own series of assignments. If you have students keep a writer's notebook and write responses to all the prompts as they work through the reading, they will amass an impressive amount of material appropriate for reflection. Professor Bob Inkster at St. Cloud University had students write about their reading, about learning in other classes, about observations from field trips—all as a basis for drafts and finished papers.

You may wish to develop assignments based on strands or linked to a specific theme or issue. This is the approach used by instructors in the writing program at Florida State University, for example, led by Professor Wendy Bishop. They developed several different approaches to *Work in Progress*, working collaboratively on different strands to differentiate their teaching. Kathy Burton used a packet of media readings from magazines and newspapers for a public-media approach. Kim Haimes-Korn and Gay Lynn Crossley suggested authority as a topic, using a packet of various academic pieces together with student papers to help students explore finding their voice in an academic setting, and Ron Wiginton used a personal-discovery approach. Cindy Wheatley-Lovoy had students explore the characteristic style of three disciplines for a research-oriented approach featuring their investigation of writing across the disciplines.

Many instructors wish to photocopy packets of materials for use in their classes. Sample essays written by previous students in response to assignments can be particularly helpful. The "Miscellany of Student Essays" that ends Chapter 17 will give you student writing to analyze and use as models. See also Section 3 of this manual for sample assignments and student essays available for your use.

Quarter Syllabus for *Work in Progress*

Major Assignments
Five essays, developed from invention through rough and final drafts

Week 1
Work in Progress, Preface and Chapter 1
Assign essay 1

Week 2
Work in Progress, Chapters 2 and 3
Rough draft of essay 1 due: in-class peer response

Week 3
Work in Progress, Chapter 4
Final draft of essay 1 due
Assign essay 2

Week 4
Work in Progress, Chapters 5, 6, and 7
Rough draft of essay 2 due: in-class peer response
Additional online peer response by email

Week 5
Work in Progress, Chapters 8 and 9
Final draft of essay 2 due
Assign essay 3
Turn in all work to date in a folder
Midterm course evaluation

Week 6
Work in Progress, Chapters 10 and 11
Class meetings canceled: conferences (may be with individuals or with groups)

Week 7
Work in Progress, Chapters 12 and 13
Rough draft of essay 3 due: in-class peer response
Collaborative exercise

Week 8
Work in Progress, Chapters 14 and 15
Final draft of essay 3 due
Assign essay 4

Week 9
Work in Progress, Chapters 16 and 17
Rough draft of essay 4 due

Week 10
Final draft of essay 4 due in folder with all written work from the quarter
Assign essay 5, or prepare students to write essay 5 as a final examination

Finals Week
Essay 5 written in class as final examination
Or essay 5 due

Semester Syllabus for *Work in Progress*

Major Assignments
Eight essays, developed from invention through rough and final drafts

Week 1
Work in Progress, Preface and Chapter 1
Assign essay 1

Week 2
Work in Progress, Chapters 2 and 3
Rough draft of essay 1 due: in-class peer response

Week 3
Work in Progress, Chapter 4
Final draft of essay 1 due

Week 4
Work in Progress, Chapter 5
Rough draft of essay 2 due: in-class peer response

Week 5
Work in Progress, Chapter 6
Final draft of essay 2 due
Assign essay 3
Turn in all work to date in a folder
Course evaluation

Week 6
Work in Progress, Chapter 7
Class meetings canceled: conferences (individual or group)
Discussion of revision in conferences

Week 7
Work in Progress, Chapter 8
Rough draft of essay 3 due: in-class peer response
Discussion of revision

Week 8
Work in Progress, Chapters 9 and 10
Final draft of essay 3 due
Assign essay 4

Week 9
Work in Progress, Chapters 11 and 12
Rough draft of essay 4 due: in-class peer response

Week 10
Work in Progress, Chapter 13
Final draft of essay 4 due
Assign essay 5

Week 11
Work in Progress, Chapter 14
Discuss collaboration
Rough draft of essay 5 due: in-class peer response
Turn in all work to date in a folder

Week 12
Work in Progress, Chapter 15
Final draft of essay 5 due
Assign essay 6

Week 13
Work in Progress, Chapter 16
Rough draft of essay 6 due: in-class peer response
Assign essay 7

Week 14
Work in Progress, Chapter 17
Review and practice
Final draft of essay 6 due
Rough draft of essay 7 due

Week 15
Completion of activities, reflections on writing and group procedures
Final draft of essay 7 due in folder with all written work from the semester
Assign essay 8, or prepare students to write essay 8 as a final examination

Finals Week
Essay 8 written in class as final examination
Or essay 8 due

Suggestions for Using *Work in Progress* with a Reader

In selecting a reader, you might choose from several excellent texts, use a collection that you gather yourself, or consider other kinds of reading appropriate to a composition class, ranging from anthologies of materials for writing across the curriculum to collections of short stories and interviews with writers. If you are interested in emphasizing the reading-writing connection, you might want to use a collection of essays gathered around a single theme. Whatever your choice, *Work in Progress* allows you great flexibility and freedom in developing your course.

You might make essay assignments from the suggestions in *Work in Progress* or from assignments accompanying the reader. You might also wish to develop your own essay assignments to suit your situation. Many activities and essays in the text can readily be adapted for use with readings. Section 4 of this manual also supplies sample assignments accompanied by student essays.

When you construct your course schedule, you might want to alternate days when students respond to reading with days when they write and work in groups. This pattern is especially useful during the beginning weeks of the class when students are reflecting about their own histories as writers and the kinds of writing processes they might use.

Consider regularly using writing as a way to help students respond to their reading and learn the material it covers. For example, have students write opening and closing summaries of class discussions, responses to discussions, and questions or issues they wish to raise.

Quarter Syllabus for a Class Using *Work in Progress* with a Reader

Major Assignments
Eight reading assignments
Five essays, developed from invention through rough and final drafts

Week 1
Work in Progress, Preface and Chapter 1
Read and discuss assignment A from reader
Assign activities from *Work in Progress*

Week 2
Work in Progress, Chapters 2 and 3
Read and discuss assignment B from reader
Assign essay 1

Week 3
Work in Progress, Chapter 4
Read and discuss assignment C from reader
Rough draft of essay 1 due

Week 4
Work in Progress, Chapters 5, 6, and 7
Read and discuss assignment D from reader
Final draft of essay 1 due
Assign essay 2

Week 5
Work in Progress, Chapters 8 and 9
Read and discuss assignment E from reader
Rough draft of essay 2 due
Midterm evaluation of the course

Week 6
Work in Progress, Chapters 10 and 11
Class meetings canceled: conferences (with individuals or groups)
Final draft of essay 2 due
Assign essay 3

Week 7
Work in Progress, Chapters 12 and 13
Read and discuss assignment F from reader
Rough draft of essay 3 due

Week 8
Work in Progress, Chapters 14 and 15
Read and discuss assignment G from reader
Final draft of essay 3 due
Assign essay 4

Week 9
Work in Progress, Chapter 16
Read and discuss assignment H from reader
Rough draft of essay 4 due

Week 10
Work in Progress, Chapter 17
Completion of activities, reflections on writing and group processes
Final draft of essay 4 due

Finals Week
Essay 5 written in class as final examination

Semester Syllabus for a Class Using *Work in Progress* with a Reader

Major Assignments
Thirteen reading assignments
Seven essays, developed from invention through rough and final drafts

Week 1
Work in Progress, Preface and Chapter 1
Read and discuss assignment A from reader
Assign activities from *Work in Progress*

Week 2
Work in Progress, Chapters 2 and 3
Read and discuss assignment B from reader
Assign essay 1

Week 3
Work in Progress, Chapter 4
Read and discuss assignment C from reader
Rough draft of essay 1 due

Week 4
Work in Progress, Chapter 5
Read and discuss assignment D from reader
Final draft of essay 1 due
Assign essay 2

Week 5
Work in Progress, Chapter 6
Read and discuss assignment E from reader
Rough draft of essay 2 due
Midterm course evaluation

Week 6
Work in Progress, Chapter 7
Class meeting canceled: conferences (with individuals or groups)

Week 7
Work in Progress, Chapter 8
Read and discuss assignment F from reader
Final draft of essay 2 due
Assign essay 3

Week 8
Work in Progress, Chapters 9 and 10
Read and discuss assignment G from reader
Rough draft of essay 3 due

Week 9
Work in Progress, Chapters 11 and 12
Read and discuss assignment H from reader
Final draft of essay 3 due
Assign essay 4

Week 10
Work in Progress, Chapter 13
Read and discuss assignment I from reader
Rough draft of essay 4 due

Week 11
Work in Progress, Chapter 14
Read and discuss assignment J from reader
Final draft of essay 4 due
Assign essay 5

Week 12
Work in Progress, Chapter 15
Read and discuss assignment K from reader
Rough draft of essay 5 due

Week 13
Work in Progress, Chapter 16
Read and discuss assignment L from reader
Final draft of essay 5 due
Assign essay 6

Week 14
Review *Work in Progress,* Chapter 17
Read and discuss assignment M from reader
Rough draft of essay 6 due

Week 15
Completion of activities
Reflections on writing and group processes
Final draft of essay 6 due
Prepare for essay 7

Finals Week
Essay 7 final draft written in class as final examination

Suggestions for Assigning Chapters Out of Numerical Sequence

Work in Progress has seventeen chapters, arranged in four sections, which you can use in various sequences to suit the aims of your course. When you follow the order given in the book, you begin by orienting students to writing, to their own composing processes, to reading as a writer, and to research as a process. The second section introduces students to the rhetorical situation in greater depth, extending it to writing and reading online. The third part introduces students to strategies for writing, moving from invention and planning through drafting to revision, and including collaboration. In the last section, students look specifically at academic writing and argument. Many instructors will find that proceeding through the text as organized supplies the logical order that they wish. However, *Work in Progress* has worked well for instructors using other kinds of orders, including the following three examples.

Beginning a class with Part Three makes sense if you wish your students to start thinking about and experimenting with writing strategies immediately, reserving reflection on concepts such as the rhetorical situation and the writing process until later in the term. An assignment sequence with this emphasis would look like this:

Chapter 8: Strategies for Invention
Chapter 9: Strategies for Planning and Drafting
Chapter 10: Strategies for Document Design
Chapter 11: Strategies for Managing the Revision Process
Chapter 12: Strategies for Revising Structure and Style
Chapter 13: Strategies for Successful Collaboration
Chapter 1: On Writing
Chapter 2: Understanding the Writing Process
Chapter 3: Understanding the Reading Process
Chapter 4: Understanding the Research Process

Chapter 5: Analyzing Rhetorical Situations

Chapter 6: Thinking about Communities and Conventions

Chapter 7: Negotiating Online Writing

Chapter 14: Understanding Academic Audiences and Assignments

Chapter 15: Understanding Academic Analysis

Chapter 16: Understanding Academic Argument

Chapter 17: Putting It All Together: Analyzing and Writing Academic Arguments

If you choose to emphasize the reading-writing connection, particularly if you wish students to think in terms of academic writing in their first assignments, begin the class with Chapters 3 and 5 (and perhaps 7, for online situations), so that students understand the concept of the rhetorical situation, then go to Chapters 14 through 17.

Chapter 3: Understanding the Reading Process

Chapter 5: Analyzing Rhetorical Situations

Chapter 6: Thinking about Communities and Conventions

Chapter 7: Negotiating Online Writing Situations

Chapter 14: Understanding Academic Audiences and Assignments

Chapter 15: Understanding Academic Analysis

Chapter 16: Understanding Academic Argument

Chapter 17: Putting It All Together: Analyzing and Writing Academic Arguments

Finally, should you have a two-term composition sequence, consider using *Work in Progress* as one of your textbooks for both terms. A logical arrangement would be to choose for the first term a reader that emphasizes either individual or cultural narrative and analysis or writing that reflects the students' situation and community. One of the multicultural readers now available would be very suitable. Accompany reading assignments with Parts One, Two, and Three of *Work in Progress*. In the second term, choose a reader organized around issues or a theme, or select a collection of academic essays and arguments. Begin by having students review Part Three on writing strategies, and then move to Part Four.

Term One
- Chapter 1: On Writing
- Chapter 2: Understanding the Writing Process
- Chapter 3: Understanding the Reading Process
- Chapter 4: Understanding the Research Process
- Chapter 5: Analyzing Rhetorical Situations
- Chapter 6: Thinking about Communities and Conventions
- Chapter 7: Negotiating Online Writing Situations
- Chapter 8: Strategies for Invention
- Chapter 9: Strategies for Planning and Drafting
- Chapter 10: Strategies for Document Design
- Chapter 11: Strategies for Managing the Revision Process
- Chapter 12: Strategies for Revising Structure and Style
- Chapter 13: Strategies for Successful Collaboration

Term Two
Review *Work in Progress,* Chapters 1–12, and ask students to use the chapters on strategies as a reference for this term (Chapters 8–12).

- Chapter 14: Understanding Academic Audiences and Assignments
- Chapter 15: Understanding Academic Analysis
- Chapter 16: Understanding Academic Argument
- Chapter 17: Putting It All Together: Analyzing and Writing Academic Arguments

Using *Work in Progress* with a Cultural Studies Approach

It is easy to use *Work in Progress* with a cultural studies approach to writing. The material on the rhetorical situation will help students to understand the social nature of discourse and to analyze the intertextuality of culture. Some programs use a cultural studies reader with *Work in Progress*. Salt Lake Community College uses Kathleen Cain's *Living in the USA* or John Trimbur and Diana George's *Reading Culture* together with *Work in Progress* for their English 101 course. Southern Illinois University at Carbondale uses Gary Colombo's *Rereading America* as a choice for its English 101 with *Work in Progress*. The integration of multilingual and multicultural students into the class offers a possibility for enriching this approach.

Using *Work in Progress* to Teach Academic Discourse

We believe that *Work in Progress* works very well to combine an academic orientation, demanding reading assignments, and the rhetorical approach to reading and writing. We have experimented with using online material in a class oriented to thinking about technology from a cultural studies perspective. A sample syllabus from such a course will suggest how online elements might be integrated into a class emphasizing argument: using email to correspond with students, using links as resources, using a class mailing list for discussion and exchange of exercises, using email and disks to turn in essays electronically, using email for students to exchange peer reviews, and using online research as part of the reading assignments.

WR xxx: COLLEGE COMPOSITION
Writing, Culture, and the New Technologies

INSTRUCTOR
Suzanne Clark: 523 PLC, Phone: 6-5819
Office hours: W 1–4
Email: sclark@darkwing.uoregon.edu
- *Texts and Online Resources*
- *Requirements*
- *Schedule*

TEXTS
Required
Lisa Ede, *Work in Progress*
Bartholomae and Petrosky, *Ways of Reading*
Class listserv: rhetoric@lists
Recommended
The Everyday Writer
Online! A Reference Guide to Using Internet Sources
A good dictionary
Handy links to other sites

YOUR EMAIL ACCOUNT

To access the class account and the instructor's email from outside the classroom, you will need to have your university email account set up. The class will require—and help to develop—basic familiarity with email, newsgroups, and the World Wide Web. You will be given some opportunities in class to take advantage of the access to instructions and materials made available on the Web. However, you will need to locate other modes of access to the network as well—in the library or other computer labs on campus or via modem.

REQUIREMENTS

1. *Essays:* Write four essays of 4 to 6 pages (or 1,000 to 1,500 words), typed double-spaced. Bring to class two printed copies of your first draft for peer review (essays 1.1, 2.1, 3.1). Submit the first draft to the instructor by email. Revise after workshop discussion. Resubmit the first draft together with the revised final version: 1.2, 2.2, and 3.2 by email, or to the class folder as a printout. Submit the final draft on paper as well.

2. *Reflective essay:* Your fourth essay should be a reflective essay about your collected writing, due at term's end. In this essay, you will have a chance to review your own progress in writing and your developing sense of your rhetorical situation in a writing world changed by online communications. Your drafting of this essay needs to include small-group discussion with other members of the class (scheduled for the last two days of the quarter). Submit your draft, their comments, as well as your final essay.

3. *Readings:* Prepare to discuss assigned material before coming to class. Read material in Ede's *Work in Progress,* and write out assigned exercises. Raise questions on the class mailing list for discussion. Your classmates will either be able to help you or will share your questions and welcome the responses. Post selected writing exercises on the mailing list.

   The essays in *Ways of Reading* demand a strong reading style: You will need to work actively to make meaning, often going back over parts or even all of the essay several times. I expect you to raise questions, seek out more information about aspects of the material that puzzle or interest you, and rely on discussions and disagreements with classmates to help you decide the meaning for yourself. Read the introductory material in *Ways of Reading* to help you understand the kind of reading required for this material. Post your questions and your responses for discussion on the mailing list.

4. *Email discussion:* Reflect on the reading and on class discourse, and use the class email list to submit emails at least once a week before class on Wednesday. These weekly postings may include questions about writing, questions about the reading, your disagreements with the reading, summaries of questions that arise during class discussion, ideas for developing questions, and responses to other postings. You are required to post a selected response to the exercises in Ede for each chapter. You are responsible for reading your classmates' postings. Your email contributions should average at least 250 words a week, and you will receive credit weekly for them: pass or not pass. If you have questions for me about your work, please direct them to my email and not to the class email list.

5. *Class participation:* Discuss readings in class, and participate in writing groups. These activities are so central to the development of your understanding of argument that I will base 15 percent of the total grade solely on your careful and thorough contributions to them. This is in addition to the written record of your exchanges. In other words, your class participation could potentially raise or lower your course grade by almost a whole point (such as from B to C+).

6. *Attendance:* More than two absences will lower your grade.

   Notes: I do not accept late work. No grades of incomplete will be given for the course.

Grades: Grades are based on essays (with drafts and peer evaluations), 60 percent; on-line writing, 25 percent; class participation and presentations, 15 percent.

Plagiarism: All work submitted in this course must be your own and written exclusively for this course. Sources must be properly documented. Academic dishonesty will result in your failing the class.

SCHEDULE

Reading assignments are from *Work in Progress* and *Ways of Reading*.

Week I
Introduction to Technologies and Each Other
Introduction. Key terms
"Panopticism" (225): discipline and the space of writing
Read *Work in Progress*, Chapters 1–2

Week II
Reading and Research
"Panopticism" (225)
Discovering the issues: Discussion, Web searches
Workshop and peer review
Read *Work in Progress*, Chapters 3–4

Week III
Discovering Your Rhetorical Situation
Discuss email responses on the class listserv
Essay 1.1 due by the start of class (bring a disk or submit by email)
Peer review
Read *Work in Progress*, Chapters 5–7
Discuss exercises from *Work in Progress*

Week IV
Culture, Rhetoric, and Technology
Writing and researching online
Evaluating WWW sources: paper 1.2 due
"Ways of Seeing" (50)
Read *Work in Progress*, Chapters 8, 9, 10

Week V
Culture and History in Your Writing
"Ways of Seeing" (50)
The visual as part of an argument: revision
Workshop on collaboration and culture
Read *Work in Progress*, Chapters 11, 12, 13

Week VI
Questions at Issue
Locating debates through collaborative process
Read *Work in Progress*, Chapter 14
Essay 2.1 due by the start of class: peer review
"Indians" (617)

Week VII
The Rhetoric of Critique
Critical argument
Work in Progress, Chapter 15
Essay 2.2 due by the start of class
"Indians" (617)

Week VIII
Refutation and Counterarguments
Counterarguments in peer review and discussion
Using counterarguments for inquiry and academic writing
Work in Progress, Chapter 16
Using the WWW to expand a sense of questions at issue
Paper 3.1 due: peer review

Week IX
The New Economy of Argument: Earning Your Conclusions
Using detail: presentations on the anthropology of the Web
Work in Progress, Chapter 17
"Deep Play" (228)
Paper 3.2 due

Week X
Earning Our Conclusion
Presentations on rhetoric and the Web
Small groups

Final Week
March 21: Final date for turning in essay 4.2. This essay must include a reflective component that looks at your writing in this class together with its rhetorical situation in culture
and technology.

Work in Progress for Advanced Courses

Work in Progress also lends itself to use in upper-division advanced courses. More advanced
students can usefully make a much more extensive commitment to analyzing and exploring the rhetorical situation of their writing. Here is the syllabus constructed by Lisa Ede for
one such class, a workshop in advanced composition taught at the senior level.

WR 416/516: ADVANCED COMPOSITION
DR. LISA EDE
FALL TERM

ENGLISH OFFICE: Moreland 236, 737-1636
CWL OFFICE: Waldo 125B, 737-3710
EMAIL: LEde@orst.edu

OFFICE HOURS (ENGLISH)
Monday & Wednesday, 3–4 P.M.
Tuesday, 3:30–4 P.M.

I'm generally on campus all day Monday through Thursday. Students are my highest priority, so I'd be happy to meet with you outside my scheduled office hours. Feel free to drop by my CWL office or to call or email me for an appointment. I spend most of my on-campus time at the CWL, so that's the best number to call if you're trying to reach me. I check my email regularly when I'm on campus. I don't have email at home, however, so keep that in mind if you're emailing me on a Friday, Saturday, or Sunday.

TEXTS

Lisa Ede, *Work in Progress: A Guide to Academic Writing and Revising* (sixth edition)
Photocopied professional and student essays. I will provide copies of the professional essays as a "payback" for my *WIP* royalty; you will provide copies of your own writing for group and/or class members, as indicated on the syllabus.

COURSE OVERVIEW

This class provides an opportunity for students to refine their writing skills while also exploring a number of important questions about writing. What does it mean to be a writer? How do writers learn to negotiate the diverse (and sometimes conflicting) expectations of different discourse communities? What role do textual conventions, and the assumptions underlying them, play in this process? What options do writers have if they wish to resist these conventions? How can writers know when it's safe to compose alternate or experimental forms—and how can they learn the conventions that underlie these (seemingly conventionless) texts? In this class we'll consider questions such as these as we work together on a series of writing projects.

COURSE POLICIES

Attendance: Since WR 416/516 is a writing workshop, attendance and participation are essential. More than two unexcused absences provides grounds for lowering your final course grade.

Due dates: Reading and writing assignments are due on the date indicated on the syllabus. Unless I have granted you an extension, I cannot accept late assignments.

Errors: As its title indicates, Advanced Composition is an advanced writing course. Students entering the class should thus have mastered the conventions of standard written English (SWE). As a consequence, I expect all drafts submitted for evaluation—as opposed to in-class or other informal writing—to be relatively free of major errors. I'm aware that even good writers can benefit from reviewing the conventions of SWE, so I've devoted a class to this topic. I'll also be happy to work with you individually on grammar, punctuation, and usage—and of course you can meet with a writing assistant at the CWL's Writing Center as well. By the end of the term, students who wish to do well in this course should be submitting essays that are free of significant errors.

Revision: You may revise any of the essays for this class. To submit a revision, however, you must
- Provide evidence that you have met with either a peer or a writing assistant to work on your essay after I returned it to you. If you meet with a writing assistant, ask him or her to give you a blue slip, which you can attach to your essay. If you meet with one or more peers, either include a copy of their comments or a signed statement written by the student(s) with whom you met. This statement should provide basic information about your meeting—such as date, time, length of meeting—and summarize your work together.
- Write a two- to three-paragraph statement describing the major revisions you have made and commenting on the reasons that you made these changes. You should also include a brief reflection about what you have learned as a result of the process of revising.

- Include all previous drafts of your essay with your revised draft, clearly indicating the order in which they were composed.

COURSE REQUIREMENTS

Essay 1: Literacy narrative, 1 single-spaced page (10 percent of grade)

Essay 2: Response essay, 2 to 4 double-spaced pages undergraduate/4 to 6 pages graduate (20 percent of grade)

The worksheet for essay 2 addresses these questions:

- Which of the literacy narratives do you plan to respond to?
- Why did you choose this literacy narrative? Emotional engagement or dislike? Strong agreement or disagreement with the author? Some other reason?
- How do you plan to focus your response?
- What concerns do you bring to this assignment?

Groups will have the last 10 minutes of the class to arrange for out-of-class responses to essay 2; these responses should occur during the fourth week of class.

Essay 3: Open topic, 3 to 5 pages double-spaced undergraduate/5 to 8 pages graduate (30 percent of grade)

Essay 4: Open topic, 3 to 5 pages undergraduate/5 to 8 pages graduate (30 percent of grade)

Final examination: Essay reflecting on what you have learned about writing—and about yourself as a writer (10 percent of grade)

A FEW MISCELLANEOUS COMMENTS AND SUGGESTIONS

Any of the four major essays may be written collaboratively. I strongly encourage you to take advantage of this opportunity to experience the satisfactions, and the challenges, of collaborative writing.

I encourage you to follow the practice of professional writers and acknowledge the contributions of others to your writing process. You can include a brief statement of acknowledgments at the bottom of the final page of your essay.

When you turn in formal writing assignments, please use a pocket folder to organize your materials. Put all notes, rough drafts, and peer responses in one pocket of the folder and your draft in the other. Please also include a writing process analysis for each essay. This analysis should (1) briefly describe how you wrote the essay (how long you worked, how difficult or easy you found the process, etc.), (2) characterize the strengths and weaknesses of your current draft as you perceive them, and (3) indicate several issues or questions you'd particularly like me to consider as I read your essay.

OSU's Writing Center, located in Waldo Hall, represents an important resource for writers of all levels. I urge you to take advantage of this important resource. In the past, many WR 416/516 students have set up weekly appointments with a writing assistant and have found this ongoing collaboration to be tremendously helpful. To make a half-hour appointment, call 737-5640.

COURSE SCHEDULE OVERVIEW: MAJOR DUE DATES

Week 3
Tuesday, October 15, essay 1 due

Week 4
Friday, October 25, essay 2 due

Week 5
During week 5, I will meet individually with students. We will discuss your general progress in the course and any other concerns you may have. In preparation for our conference, please write a proposal for your third essay, using the questions for analyzing your rhetorical situation listed on pages 78–84 in *WIP*. Bring this proposal to our conference. We should also have time to work on individual essays, so be sure to bring drafts (a revision of your first essay? a draft of your third essay?) you'd like me to look at.

Week 6
Tuesday, November 12, essay 3 due

Week 7
Group workshops for essay 4 (In preparation for this workshop, please write a proposal for your essay, using the questions for analyzing your rhetorical situation listed in *WIP*. In addition, respond to these questions: What strengths do you bring to this writing project as you currently visualize it? What challenges does it pose for you? Finally, pose three troubleshooting questions you would like your group to address. Be sure to bring a copy for me.)

Week 8
Group workshop for essay 4 (Bring two copies of no more than two double-spaced pages of your essay—the first two pages might be logical—to class for response. In looking at the essays, you will be focusing primarily on style. Your purpose: to apply our recent discussions of style to your writing.)

Week 11 (Finals Week)
Monday, December 9, essay 4 due

2. TEACHING PRACTICES

This section of the Instructor's Notes discusses a number of effective teaching practices. These approaches to teaching have in common an emphasis on the reading and writing relationship and the rhetorical situation. The class itself involves the rhetorical situation. Our Instructor's Notes focus in particular on the following:

Academic writing

Argument

Research

Documentation and plagiarism

Visual texts

Writing online

Using collaborative practices

Multilingual and multicultural writers

Community service writing

Handling the paper load

Responding to student writing

Using writing assignments

Evaluating your teaching

Further reading in composition studies

Academic Writing

Even though there are real differences among disciplines, there are certain common assumptions in academic writing that your students can identify as they develop their "rhetorical sensitivity." You may find, as some studies have shown, that students entering higher education do not have very much experience with what we are calling "academic writing." The careful processes of reflection, analysis, search for evidence, weighing of reasons, and the efforts to be understood clearly that students experience in your class will gradually begin to clarify the method—your classroom itself will serve as the model of inquiry. You can help by repeatedly calling attention to the process and by monitoring your students' understanding. In particular, you can point out that their opinions are important, and that the process of discussing and listening to differing opinions gradually establishes a context for them that serves as a rhetorical situation. How are classroom opinions different from nonacademic expressions of opinion? When opinion becomes part of a process of inquiry rather than a conversation-ending generalization, it begins to take on a characteristic of academic writing. As another example, you can note that evidence and reasons become as important as conclusions, in classroom discussions as in academic writing. Keep the uniqueness of academic inquiry in mind—by comparison, for example, with "discussions" students may have heard on television, where an attitude of conclusiveness trumps the search for knowledge.

Students may find it especially difficult to write in ways that seem overly formal or distant from their cultural traditions, and you may be sympathetic. International students testify that academic writing in North America sometimes seems to them "rude" or insulting to the reader. It's helpful for other students in your class to know about these differences, since they may inadvertently violate cultural sensibilities if they are writing for international readers (and in these days of the Internet, the possibilities are immediate.)

Many professors encourage their students to intertwine the personal with course content, to argue from their own sense of values, or otherwise to challenge the assumption that academic discourse tries to avoid personal preferences. Postfoundationalism or social construction has challenged the very idea that such purity is possible. However, even social construction can generate arguments divorced from the speaking person. Finally, an abstract situation of arguments is not more important than whether the argument matters to the writer and the reader. Patricia Bizzell says, "What I really care about is what my students believe, how they will conduct their lives, and not just whether they have learned to analyze beliefs or lives in correct postmodern fashion" (*Academic Discourse and Critical Consciousness* 279).

The subject of "academic discourse" has itself been widely discussed in rhetoric and composition scholarship. Here are some selected titles that may be of interest:

Bartholomae, David. "Inventing the University." *When a Writer Can't Write*. Ed. Michael Rose. New York: Guilford, 1985. 134–65.
Bizzell, Patricia. *Academic Discourse and Critical Consciousness*. Pittsburgh: U of Pittsburgh P, 1992.
Chiseri-Strater, Elizabeth. *Academic Literacies: The Public and Private Discourse of University Students*. Portsmouth: Boynton/Cook, 1992.
Geisler, Cheryl. *Academic Literacy and the Nature of Expertise*. Hillsdale: Erlbaum, 1994.

Argument

This edition of *Work in Progress* has added a new chapter on writing arguments as well as new material on critical reading and on analyzing academic arguments. Students who have learned to analyze their rhetorical situation will be helped in these chapters to clarify and formalize the understanding they have developed and to write more logically and forcefully in the tradition of Western rhetoric. These chapters draw on theories of argument that include Aristotle's analysis of rhetorical appeals, John Gage's analysis of questions at issue, and Stephen Toulmin's descriptions of the elements of argument. The text explains to students that there is, in fact, a continuum of "argument" in academic writing, and that from one perspective, everything written is an argument. However, some kinds of writing call for a more focused, conscious structuring as an argument, with a recognizable thesis, a "question at issue," and careful articulation of reasons and evidence. These arguments enjoy a privileged status in academic reasoning because Western culture endorses these forms of inquiry. Even if students in your classes come from cultures that prefer, perhaps, less direct or pointed forms of reasoning, they may need to master these approaches in order to write successfully in their future courses. They may find it useful to think in terms of the conventions of genre and code-switching. If poets can learn to write sonnets, scholars can learn to write arguments that will earn them success and a hearing for their ideas.

At the same time, however, academic argument is not separable from the open-ended processes of inquiry—from the pursuit of knowledge rather than persuasion, taking account of counterarguments, and admitting uncertainty. One student, deeply involved in animal rights activities, explained that she composed her arguments by imagining opposition—beginning with the conclusion she wanted her audience to arrive at and then trying out all the ways she could to persuade them to agree with her, refuting any possible rebuttal they could find. Failing to include the possibility to changing her own mind, or of discovering knowledge that would modify her ideas, she developed an idea of argument as persuasion that is not academic inquiry in the sense presented here.

Your students' "rhetorical sensitivity" can help them understand how to approach an academic argument by analyzing the context of their writing and by developing arguments through attentive analysis. In academic writing, argument is both more pervasive and less combative than the opinion columns that students are perhaps reading in newspapers. The rhetorical situation of academic arguments depends on conversations among scholars and in students' classes that determine what's at stake, what issues are significant, and what the context for those issues might be. Analysis is central to the process. Careful reading of primary material or sources, careful observation, and careful listening are the first steps to writing. The acts of interpretation that such reading, observing, and listening require may themselves generate an argument—one others might not agree with—that requires analysis and evidence. This is often the substance of classroom discussions. Even science, Donna Haraway has argued, produces "situated knowledges."

Research

Chapter 4, "Understanding the Research Process," follows logically from the chapter on reading and shows how reading, research, and writing are interdependent activities—and that research is integral to the writing process, especially for academic writing. Many students assume that all writing is creative or personal unless research is specifically assigned. However, this assumes a very limited and perhaps romantic view of rhetorical invention. Writing requires knowledge about context, other debates, audience, evidence, and details, and so writing needs the knowledge that research—formal or informal—provides. "Understanding the Research Process" approaches research as a part of most writing tasks that students undertake and not as something they do only for formal research papers.

Understanding how to use research means that students will gradually form the habit of reaching out to other sources to help them write all kinds of texts. You can add research exercises to your teaching to help them see research as another aspect of the writing process. For example, if you point out to them that interviewing other class members about their views is a form of research, you can also help them see that such inquiries can be done responsibly and carefully—by giving proper credit to sources. The separation of informal methods of invention from formal logic and later from scientific research is a historical phenomenon that dates from Peter Ramus in the late sixteenth century. Discipline-specific research methods, such as the close reading of literary analysis or the experimental method of science, have specific steps and rules, but the rise of interdisciplinary work has made it especially clear that research is a more general part of inquiry too and that separating it from writing is artificial.

Since your students will begin thinking about research early, you can ask them to include that step in their writing assignments. Students may be becoming more habituated to doing so because they frequently and easily turn to the Web for an answer to questions. However, they are not often in the habit of documenting such research, and that informality could become troubling. To help students understand ways to enhance their own credibility and to acknowledge their debts to others, ask them to make such consulting explicit, referring them to the Documentation Guidelines at the back of the book and to see the following section on documentation and plagiarism. For instance, when you are having students write an analysis of their rhetorical situation, you may ask them to make research an explicit part of their invention process: to track or even, as an exercise, to write documentation for a brief survey of Web sites, of library sources, or of other people's opinions. Professional researchers call this the "survey of the literature," but it is a process that students also undertake, much less deliberately.

In planning class time for discussions of research, you may want to include time to address the following issues that often come up for student research papers. Help students understand the importance of the following guidelines:

- Be precise about possible counterarguments.

- Use the words of the writer by taking them into your own vocabulary to make a literary argument. Be careful that the text is integrated into the argument so that a paper is not interrupted by unassimilated quotations or so other-text-centered that it loses your voice and argument and becomes only commentary.

- Focus on getting to the argument as economically and dramatically as possible.

- Eliminate whatever looks like filler, vague gestures toward a background, or abstractions that are not going to play a role in the development of the major point. Note that this may violate multilingual students' sense of "good writing"—be ready to explain.

- Use summarizing statements both to inform and to argue.

- Start paragraphs with their own voice or argument rather than a quotation or another critic's argument that confuses readers about your authority.

- Provide a context for quotations, and identify the relevance of those quoted.

- Pay attention to the structure of comparison-contrast analysis.

- Carefully format in-text citations and lists of works cited per MLA or APA documentation guidelines, as discussed in the easy-reference section at the back of the book.

Documentation and Plagiarism

This edition of *Work in Progress* has added material on documentation and a section on plagiarism to Chapter 4, "Understanding the Research Process." The two topics are, of course, related, because students get into trouble with plagiarism when they do not properly document their sources. Here are some of the problems with documentation you may encounter:

1. Students may not understand that slightly changing the original words of a source does not eliminate the necessity of documenting it—and indeed, that it is important to quote accurately! The section on plagiarism in this chapter emphasizes carefulness. Such plagiarism is partly a problem of note taking.

2. Sometimes students do not realize that they gain credibility by using quotations and sources, when it is relevant and appropriate. They may be confused about the value of originality and their lack of familiarity with academic discourse means that they may not associate invention with research.

3. Most students do not know how to integrate quotations into their texts gracefully. Spend some time on the mechanics of this. Working on paraphrasing, summarizing, and so forth can help address the problem created by using large chunks of quotation. There are, in other words, reasons why students do not know how to use documentation effectively that you can address directly with some practice.

4. You may encounter several levels of plagiarism. It is clearly academic dishonesty and not academic ignorance when students simply copy someone else's work and call it their own—downloading a paper from the Internet, copying a paper written by another student, or copying from printed works, perhaps from more than one. The technique of "collage," pasting together quotations from a number of sources without acknowledgment, also seems a violation that all students should understand. However, this is a matter of a cultural understanding particular to our laws about intellectual

property as well as to our practices of quotation. You should explain as clearly as possible that collage is plagiarism. Most professors count as plagiarism any use of a source without acknowledgment. You may find that you must teach your students exactly what this means.

5. Surveys suggest that plagiarism is very widespread, not (for the most part) innocent, and often not detected. A clear announcement on your syllabus and in your class, some time spent in explanation, and follow-up detection work will help ensure that your students do not practice plagiarism in your class. Online sources may seem tempting for plagiarists, but Web search engines have made it very much easier to find plagiarized sources: simply type into Google or other search engines several words in a sentence to locate its source.

6. Be ready to spend extra time explaining documentation to any multicultural writers who are violating the rules since there are cultural differences in how quotations and traditional sources are used in texts.

Visual Texts

The sixth edition of *Work in Progress* can help you integrate visual texts into your work on both reading and writing. Chapter 3, "Understanding the Reading Process," leads students carefully through a process of reading visual texts; Chapter 7, "Negotiating Online Writing Situations," summarizes some principles of design for Web sites. This edition includes a completely new chapter on "Strategies for Document Design"—Chapter 10. Furthermore, the concept of a visual rhetoric is integrated throughout the book, especially in references to online situations.

You can take advantage of this addition by including visual texts in your assignments. If you assign the composition of Web pages, attention to design elements will be part of the conventions students already understand, even if they don't know how to use them. You can also help them to use visual elements in other writing assignments, not as decoration but as an integral part of the rhetorical task. For an example, see the student texts in *Work in Progress* by Brenda Shonkwiler (in Chapters 4 and 9) or by Jacob Agatucci (in Chapter 15). You may wish to help students make this connection by having them describe in words the analytic or persuasive work that the visual elements contribute.

For an approach to visual rhetoric online, see "Visual Rhetoric," available at

http://www.sla.purdue.edu/dblakesley/visual/

For further reading, see

McQuade, Donald, and Christine McQuade. *Seeing and Writing.* Boston: Bedford/St. Martin's, 2000.

Writing Online

Writing classes are making increased and diverse uses of electronic technologies. How can you incorporate these new possibilities into your writing course? Many writing programs have developed ways to enable students to write together in computer labs and interact with the instructor. However, with increasingly widespread use of computers, classroom use of online writing has gone beyond methods that are specifically tailored to individual institutions and assume class access to a computer lab.

In *Work in Progress* and in these Instructor's Notes, we focus on a discussion of writing online. How can you integrate the various modes of communication made possible by the Internet into your teaching practices: email, mailing lists, newsgroups, online discussions or chats, Web research, and publication on the Web? What forms of online writing will your students most need to learn to read, evaluate, and write effectively? And how can you take into account, additionally, the differences in your students' previous experiences and in their access to an Internet connection?

If your classroom has an Internet connection and you have access to a projector, you may use the Internet as a basis for class discussions and analyses. You may, for example, look at several Web sites in class, using the "Guidelines for Evaluating Web Sites and Web Pages" from Chapter 4. Even without an Internet connection, if you have access to a laptop computer and a projector, you can bring examples into class to demonstrate.

Your institution may have a number of resources for you to draw on in deciding how your classes will be involved in online writing. Workshops offered by the computer center, the library, the teaching resources center, or the writing program itself may range from the basic uses of email and Web browsers to more advanced Web publishing, discussion groups, and collaborative writing programs. There is also a great deal of help available online. Here are some links to sites that will get you started:

> **http://english.ttu.edu/kairos** (*Kairos*: A Journal for Teachers of Writing in Webbed Environments)
>
> **http://www.powa.org** (Paradigm Online Writing Assistant)

Kinds of Online Writing

1. *Email:* Your students are more likely to know how to use email than any other form of online writing; national publications increasingly note that most college students send email messages to friends and family. Emailing for personal uses can easily be expanded into emailing for classroom purposes—with classmates, with you, the instructor, with members of mailing lists, and with Web site monitors. Many institutions provide email accounts for students and the wiring or modem call-in lines for students to access their accounts from dorm rooms and apartments. Tell students who do not have email accounts how to get them on your campus, and suggest available options.

Instruct your students about how you would like them to use email to interact with you—for example, to ask questions, find out about assignments, inform you of emergencies when they must miss class, or send other messages that they might otherwise have telephoned you about. Inform them as well about when they can expect you to have read and replied to email (some students have unreasonable expectations about how quickly you can get back to them). You may wish to set up a separate email account just for your classes or make arrangements with your computer center for sufficient space to deal with the increased message load. Current versions of mail software on Internet browsers and Eudora will allow you to filter messages so you can view and organize class messages. Some instructors hold email office hours, encouraging students to send and receive emails during a specific time period.

An additional use for email from students is to submit writing assignments. Informal For Exploration assignments can be sent to you before class, giving you a moment to glance over them before you hold a discussion. These can probably be sent as ordinary messages, without word processing. You can also comment on drafts of essays via email. Your students can even send you the drafts as attachments. Given the problems with viruses connected to attachments, you may wish to be careful about using them, however. Students can send you a rough draft that is simply copied and pasted into a regular email rather than sent as an attachment. If you decide to handle drafts or papers online, think about how you will organize these email exchanges ahead of time. Having drafts on your computer instead of on paper can be confusing if you don't have a recording system that accounts for this. And when you go to class with your class file, you will not have paper copies of student work with you. Finally, you may find, as we have, that an email conference does not substitute for face-to-face meetings but rather acts as a supplement. Therefore, email conferencing will add to your "paper load." The advantage to email is that it permits you more precise, more convenient, and more individualized interaction with students. The disadvantage is that your overall time spent interacting may very well increase. Take the extra time required into account when you plan.

2. *Mailing lists, listservs, or email discussion groups:* Mailing lists are widespread, but even the public lists require that you subscribe to participate. You can find lists of interest to you at the following Web site:

http://www.ifla.org/I/training/listserv/lists.htm (The International Federation of Library Associations and Institutions has Internet discussion lists, Usenet resources, Netiquette, and other guides.)

You may wish to make assignments for your class to participate in public mailing lists (as suggested in Chapter 5). Students may also subscribe to mailing lists that might help them with research projects or to extend inquiry that began with one of your readings.

Besides having them participate in public mailing lists, you may decide to set up a list just for your class. Many of the For Exploration and For Group Work exercises in *Work in Progress* lend themselves nicely to being posted on a class email discussion group so that responses can be read before an in-person discussion. Your computer center or technicians will help you with the details at your institution. It is not particularly complicated, and such a class discussion list can be a productive addition to your class if it is working well. All the members of the class will need to subscribe to your class list (or you can subscribe them, if they give you their email addresses). You can also use it for certain kinds of discussions (of readings, for example) and for announcements (extremely handy). If you want students to post additional comments beyond their responses to assignments, instruct them about what kind of interaction you are looking for. You may, for example, tell them not to use the class email discussion group for informal or personal exchanges but rather to limit posts to class work. If you want a high level of participation, you will need to tell students how to get started and to involve everyone at the beginning. Many students will not post work or comments on a class list until it is specifically assigned. In our experience, such class email discussion groups are often more vigorous if the instructor's contributions are kept to a minimum. You will need to control the list carefully in other ways, however. Don't let the volume of messages become excessive, for example, because it will overload student emails. Don't let a flame war get overheated. Be careful that student exchanges remain productive and academic. It is all too easy to stir up an "incident" with careless language, insulting terms, and so forth.

3. *Newsgroups:* Newsgroups belong to a network called Usenet that makes them accessible on a news server. They are older online functions than the Web; interest groups increasingly start up new Web sites with a discussion group rather than newsgroups. Nevertheless, newsgroups offer a fascinating panoply of topics that groups of people have found interesting to write about. Because it is easier for students to *lurk* in a newsgroup than on a mailing list (they don't have to subscribe to read the current posts), you may wish to have students look at a number of newsgroups as a way to examine the culture and rhetorical conventions of Internet communities. The Usenet can be easily accessed from browsers. Google has a "Groups" site that enables access to Usenet discussion forums: <http://groups.google.com>.

4. *The World Wide Web:* What people mean by online or Internet writing is dominated by the Web. Your class may use the Web both to read and research topics and to write Web pages themselves. Students may also use these sites as a starting point for their own input, to participate in online discussion in the rapidly multiplying chat rooms made available at many sites, or to email their comments and questions.

Your students will need help conducting searches and evaluating Web sites for your class. Your campus may offer workshops on effective searching or may have a librarian, computer technician, or teaching center associate who can come to your classroom and give a presentation for your students: it will be worth the time spent. Or you yourself can go through some of the most common tools for searching and help students distinguish kinds of searches and how to refine search terms. Online writing labs (OWLs) on the Web include the one at Purdue: <http:owl.english.purdue.edu>.

Evaluating sites is the second important issue for your students in using the Web for coursework. Chapter 4 of *Work in Progress* has "Guidelines for Evaluating Web Sites and Web Pages" to help your students. Students need to assess carefully the rhetorical situation of a site and its use of rhetorical conventions. The assignments in Chapter 4 will help them develop the ability to be critically evaluative in their assessment of Web sources. For an additional excellent overview and discussion of evaluation criteria, see Elizabeth Kirk's "Evaluating Information Found on the Internet" <http://www.library.jnu.edu/elp/useit/evaluate>.

In addition to the dizzying array of sites available on the Web, your students may also participate in some of the many chat groups attached to sites. The homepages of many news networks, television stations, and newspapers now offer message boards or chat rooms on current events that are good resources for rhetorical analysis as well as opportunities for your students to write online informally in a public setting.

Basic Guidelines for Introducing Online Writing into Your Classroom

1. *Assess the knowledge and access your students have as soon as possible.* If you make assumptions without checking, you may waste class time explaining what everyone knows. Or you may face a class of frustrated and demoralized students who have not been able to follow your instructions.

2. *Point to help or to resources—such as computer labs and workshops—for students who do not know how to do what is required for online assignments.* You may even want to provide a small amount of such instruction in class. It is particularly useful to teach students to find online information about how to work on the Internet: you may want to set aside a day for it.

3. *Realize that using electronic technologies requires extra time—of you as well as of your students, both in class and outside class.* Be sure to plan accordingly. We estimate that adding significant amounts of online writing, particularly if you meet in a computer classroom, may cut your time for class activities by as much as one-third—even though your reading and writing assignments have not increased.

4. *Give your students explicit directions about using email to interact with you.* Don't forget to include your email address on your syllabus. Then specify: What kinds of email do you want? Will you comment on drafts and papers?

5. *Plan how you will organize the submission of online assignments from the beginning of class.* The more work you accept online, the more critical it becomes to think about how you will keep track of it and ensure access when you need it. While it is wonderful to be able to eliminate paperwork and easier to keep and store disks than paper files, you will

probably not move entirely to electronic submissions. Therefore, you will have to maintain student files both on your computer and in paper files.

6. *Remember that you are teaching writing, not technology.* You are not expected to be an expert, although you should not ask students to do what you do not understand well enough to explain briefly. The simplest functions (use of email and use of Web sites) have interesting and extensive rhetorical implications: there's no need to add technological complexity to the coursework. Above all, keep in view your central purpose. *Work in Progress* emphasizes the rhetorical situation of online writing, not the technology needed to do it. You may even find you wish to work at times from paper copies of online writing to focus your class and avoid issues of technological complications.

Using Collaborative Practices

Writing classes increasingly make use of collaborative practices, some as supplements to a traditional, instructor-centered classroom and others as the informing principle of the course. What choices might you make? Instructors plan their writing classes with very different goals in mind, which increasingly may include writing collaborative assignments, so the project from start to finish is done by a group or team. Students enter college writing classes with widely differing kinds of previous experience with collaboration. In this section of the Instructor's Notes, we make suggestions that should help you discover the collaborative practices that are most appropriate to your situation. *Work in Progress* has a full chapter that focuses specifically on helping your students to write collaboratively: Chapter 13, "Strategies for Successful Collaboration."

In one sense, writers cannot avoid collaboration because they must incorporate other points of view into their discourse to be rhetorically effective: writing is dialogic. Collaboration can enhance this process and take advantage of the learning fostered by explicitly taking other views into account. Conflict as well as cooperation is at the heart of effective collaboration. Class discussions that articulate multiple points of view and the possibilities of differences as well as agreements provide one important benefit of collaboration. Increasingly, collaboration is emerging as an important writing practice for multicultural literacy, in discussions of using computers to write collaboratively across distances, and in thinking about the relationships of oral and written (and electronic) literacies.

The collaborative practices described in *Work in Progress* help students to work together on the goal of learning to write. When students collaborate in your writing class, their primary job is to produce knowledge about their writing, not friendship or even knowledge about other areas, although those may be important extra benefits. In addition, this text supports specifically collaborative writing assignments, which may include having groups write entire essays together. Collaboration works best if you can shift student attention so that they see how their first task is implicated with the work in progress of learning to write rather than the short-term goals of producing papers with good grades. You may need to make this explicit on your syllabus and in your grading procedures.

To ensure effective collaborative learning experiences, instructors must pay as much attention to group dynamics as to content. Though the role of the instructor moves out of the spotlight, your *collaborative* role as structurer, responder, consultant, and facilitator demands great skill and remains chiefly responsible for the success or failure of the class. Collaborative classes do not teach themselves. In the final part of this section, we provide some ways of evaluating your teaching success in such a classroom.

Additional Suggestions for Using Collaborative Learning Groups in Classes

1. *Recognize that collaborative learning challenges both you and your students to learn new roles.* Instructors need to learn to trust the collaborative learning process. They have to be able to exchange the certainty of a well-prepared, well-delivered lecture for the uncertainty of peer interactions. They have to be able to put aside the hierarchies of expertise to make time for apprentice writers to talk about their craft. Instructors also need to recognize that their general pedagogical assumptions and practices will influence students' perceptions of collaborative learning. Those who tend to be authoritarian in most of their dealings with students, for instance, or who obviously value the instructor's wisdom over students' inexperienced opinions may find it difficult to convince students that they genuinely want them to collaborate with one another. Additionally, the writing program needs to support collaboration. Evaluations of instructors should acknowledge the importance of collaboration and look specifically for good collaborative practices.

Students will enter college writing classes in the context of an academic community that tends to favor competition, not cooperation, so students may be suspicious of group activities. At the same time, the most competitive disciplines may demand that students work with others in teams. Some may have no experience with collaborative groups, while others may imagine that working in groups is interesting but doesn't really count. Many will be used to focusing on short-term goals and assignments, so that they prefer tasks oriented toward solving specific problems rather than toward the long-term goal of progress in writing. *Work in Progress* mediates this problem by integrating group activities with the topics of each chapter so that students can see how their work is related to the concepts they are learning. In Chapter 13, students will focus specifically on learning to collaborate more effectively.

2. *Acknowledge the importance of resistance.* Collaborative practices need to make a place for students' resistance, which may very well mark a problem that needs to be recognized. You can ask your students to write about resistance to discover the forms it takes in your class. Resistance to collaboration may reflect ongoing problems in relations among students that they are reluctant to address. Group activities in *Work in Progress* carefully define tasks so students can choose the amount of personal exposure they want to risk. Since the institution defines the instructor as an authority who insists on certain points of view or procedures or due dates or standards, you may find resistance to all of these appearing as resistance to you. You will make such resistance more productive if you ensure that students understand you want *diverse* responses and expect the assertion of differences.

3. *Remember that collaborative learning can involve more than the use of peer response groups.* Many instructors use peer response groups in their writing classes. Such groups enable students to read and respond to work in progress, and we strongly recommend their use. Collaborative learning groups can function in other ways, however. Group activities suggested in *Work in Progress* utilize a number of approaches. Students brainstorm together, compare responses to checklists and guidelines, analyze responses to readings, and write and revise together. Collaborative learning activities need not be time-consuming. An instructor might want to have students spend ten minutes in groups discussing a question generated by a reading, for instance, before leading a full class discussion on the same issue.

4. *Develop ways to foster students' collaborative learning skills.* Instructors can improve students' ability to work collaboratively in the following ways:

Using collaborative practices from the very first day of the term

Demonstrating a collaborative approach through participation and example

Observing and interacting with groups as they work together

Demonstrating through grades and other means that collaborative learning counts in your class

Taking class time to discuss effective group dynamics and to respond to students' questions about group work

Encouraging students to monitor their group's effectiveness through self-evaluations and peer evaluations

Instructors might allocate time during the first two or three classes to help students learn to work collaboratively with each other. Students need to develop a willingness to explore a topic, to discover disagreements, and to negotiate the making of meaning. Beginning groups will benefit from heterogeneity and from assignments that encourage diverse responses, since the greatest threat to effective collaboration is a premature shutting down of differing perspectives.

It is especially important to start with what students know. On the first day students can freewrite their responses to a question like "How can writing help you succeed in college?" and collect their responses in small groups. Such a question could be simply boring and predictable if there were a right answer, but encouraging students to come up with unpredictable answers will set another, more productive kind of standard for group activities. Next the groups could try to write a collaborative answer to the question "Why write?" taking the various responses into account, and report to the class as a whole. Such a sequence establishes from the first that group work is work, not a break, but also that it requires heterogeneity to be productive. If students go on to do the activities in Chapter 1, they may compare responses to the question about college writing with their answers to the first question about their own previous experiences with writing. *Work in Progress* begins with commonplace understandings about writing. The "Guidelines for Group Work" in Chapter 1 provide specific suggestions to help students orient themselves.

Talking about writing and writing about talking, students begin to weave a network of connections between speech and the written language—connections that for many students have been hard to make or nonexistent (writing is someone else's language, probably the teacher's, or maybe Shakespeare's, or Melville's, or Alice Walker's). Talking makes the community of student writers literate about their shared experiences.

Talking also leads students to collaborate with one another, to be excited about one another's work, and to see writing as a social act rather than a solitary one. The scene of writing enlarges from the garret to include parts of the world—class, library, fields, stores, family, work.

After talking, the activities should return to writing, and the text has a number of suggestions about essays students might write as the result of their inquiries. These essay assignments ask students to synthesize what they have learned through writing exercises, exploration, reflection, and discussion. Students put into writing what they have learned about writing.

5. *Structure groups and collaborative activities carefully.* There are some advantages to allowing students to form their own groups, but in general you should structure groups yourself, especially at the beginning of the class. In so doing, remember that groups work most effectively when members bring a variety of strengths and experiences to group activities. Alternatively, you could form groups for most activities randomly (counting off students in groups of three or four, for instance) but allow students to choose long-term peer response groups of five. You might want to think about including a technologically adept class member in a group when they are using online resources.

How are collaborative assignments different from others? When you assign groups to collaborate on substantial projects (activities that involve more, for instance, than responding to a reading or a series of questions and then reporting back to the class), you should structure your assignments with particular care. Effective collaborative learning assignments share the following characteristics:

- They *require* collaboration for the project to be completed successfully. Otherwise, they may seem like a waste of time to some students.
- They are explained in writing so students don't have to begin by arguing about the assignment.
- They suggest how the project or activity is to be completed, and they suggest how the group should approach each stage of the assignment. They may also suggest possible roles for group members (recorder, timekeeper, reporter, and so on).
- They build opportunities for self-evaluation and peer evaluation into the assignment.
- They encourage group members to negotiate issues of authority and responsibility; they also encourage creative conflict while protecting minority views.

How can collaboration be graded? Simple check-off systems can provide the basis for a grade on collaborative work, using records submitted by groups at the end of each class. For important, lengthy collaborative learning projects, students can receive a group grade. You can incorporate feedback generated by troubleshooting and self-analysis in the determination of this grade. Students can submit individual portfolios reflecting their participation in a group project to help demonstrate excellence in leadership and good citizenship. Finally, students can submit peer evaluations in the form of letters assessing the contributions of other group members.

6. *Take advantage of the differences among students that collaboration can help to address.* Working together requires careful leadership by the teacher to successfully organize group work, to initiate dialogue and provide a model of interaction, to keep the class as a learning community focused on its specific goals of studying writing, and finally, to establish the basis for a sense of community and for good citizenship within that community.

What worries some instructors are the problems students might encounter working together. Sometimes students simply have not had enough experience with collaborative learning, and so the course will be useful for them in this respect. But what about the moments when students encounter conflict? You as instructor can help here not by lecturing but by providing a model of nondivisive responsiveness. What you show them is how to engage in a dialectical exchange, which takes the other person's point of view into account without abandoning one's own. One of the reasons a teacher-centered classroom limits the possibilities for learning is precisely that it avoids or even represses conflict. Such a discussion is made much easier by the fact that everyone has a stake in the dialogue: everyone has writing that is under discussion.

To ensure that everyone has a stake in the group process, as well as to make sure students do their work, you may want to make it a prerequisite of participating in collaborative groups that each member has brought the needed assignment. Those who have not done the writing can work alone or in a separate group.

7. *Assign multivocal as well as univocal collaborative essays.* Rather than working in the group to produce a seamless document projecting agreement, your groups might try a collage or collection of their various texts, simply juxtaposed or else assembled with connecting explanations and transitions. Highlighting rather than smoothing over the differences in voices, styles, and perspectives has been an increasingly popular practice among feminists and others

who want to keep cultural characteristics distinct, a way to honor differences as well as to suggest the collective mode of some groups' decision making. Sometimes texts are even written in different languages. Of course, it would be an illusion to suggest that such documents reflect a total lack of hierarchy or selection, since someone must make choices at some point. Nonetheless, they allow groups another option besides imposing a consensual style or argument on members who see the consensus as a distortion. They also allow groups to explore ways that differences in vernacular language and culture may enhance knowledge.

Further Reading

This discussion of collaborative writing and learning is necessarily brief. For further information see the following:

Brooke, Robert, Ruth Mirtz, and Rick Evans. *Small Groups in Writing Workshops: Invitations to a Writer's Life*. Urbana, IL: NCTE, 1994.

Buranen, Lise, and Alice M. Roy, eds. *Perspectives on Plagiarism and Intellectual Property in a Postmodern World*. Albany: SUNY P, 1999.

Clark, Suzanne, and Lisa Ede. "Collaboration and Resistance." *The Right to Literacy*. Ed. Andrea A. Lunsford, Helene Moglen, and James Slevin. New York: MLA, 1990. 276–85.

"Collaborative Writing." Special issue of *Technical Communication: The Journal of the Society for Technical Communication* 38.4 (1991).

"Collaborative Writing in Business Communication." Special issue of *The Bulletin of the Association for Business Communication* 53.2 (1990).

Cook, Leonora (Leni), and Helen C. Lodge, eds. *Voices in English Classrooms: Honoring Diversity and Change*. Urbana, IL: NCTE, 1996.

Ede, Lisa, and Andrea Lunsford. "Collaboration and Concepts of Authorship." *PMLA* 116.2 (March 2001): 354.

———. *Singular Texts/Plural Authors: Perspectives on Collaborative Writing*. Carbondale and Edwardsville: Southern Illinois UP, 1990.

Forman, Janis, ed. *New Visions of Collaborative Writing*. Portsmouth, NH: Boynton/Cook, Heinemann, 1992.

LeFevre, Karen Burke. *Invention as a Social Act*. Carbondale and Edwardsville: Southern Illinois University Press for the Conference on College Composition and Communication, 1987.

Nunan, David, ed. *Collaborative Language Learning and Teaching*. Cambridge [England]; New York: Cambridge UP, 1992.

Peck, Elizabeth G., and JoAnna Stephens Mink, eds. *Common Ground: Feminist Collaboration in the Academy*. Albany: SUNY P, 1998.

Reagan, Sally Barr, Thomas Fox, and David Bleich. *Writing With: New Directions in Collaborative Teaching, Learning, and Research*. Albany: SUNY P, 1994.

Royster, Jacqueline Jones. *Traces of a Stream: Literary and Social Change Among African American Women*. Pittsburgh: U of Pittsburgh P, 2000.

———. "When the First Voice You Hear is Not your Own." *CCC* 47 (Feb. 1996): 29–40.

Semones, Lara. "Collaboration, Computer Mediation, and the Foreign Language Writer." *Clearing House* 74.6 (July/Aug. 2001): 308–13.

Spears, Karen. *Sharing Writing: Peer Response Groups in English Classes*. Portsmouth, NH: Boynton/Cook, Heinemann, 1988.

Speck, Bruce W. *Facilitating Students' Collaborative Writing*. San Francisco: Jossey-Bass, 2002.

Spigelman, Candace. *Across Property Lines: Textual Ownership in Writing Groups*. Carbondale: Southern Illinois UP, 2000.

Stewart Susan. *Crimes of Writing: Problems in the Containment of Representation*. New York: Oxford UP, 1991.

York, Lorraine Mary. *Rethinking Women's Collaborative Writing: Power, Difference, Property*. Toronto: University of Toronto P, 2002.

Community Service and Writing

Many writing programs have added a service learning component to their classes. This can take a variety of forms, and a brief bibliography that follows here will give you some resources if you wish to find out more. *Work in Progress* is ideally suited for such a project. Community service writing projects typically appear in two forms. First, students may write assignments for a specific community organization—pieces of writing such as brochures, newsletters, posters, or Web sites. Or, second, students may work as interns or volunteers in a community organization and write reflectively about their experiences.

In order to include a community service assignment in your class, you need to help set up a working arrangement between community resources and your students. Here, as guidelines you can provide your students, is a brief list of steps you might have them take. It will, of course, be useful if you already have a list of contacts with telephones and email addresses. Some communities have such a list already developed; or your campus may have a career center or central agency for community service with such a list.

Guidelines for Organizing Community Service Assignments

- First, contact and interview a representative of the group for which you will write.
- Second, develop a written proposal for your project that states clearly what you will do and how long you believe it will take—a work schedule.
- Third, develop a brief checklist that can serve as a basis for evaluation by the group's representative, and leave a little space for comments.
- Fourth, complete the project, and submit a copy to the instructor as well as to the group, together with the signed evaluation.

For information on setting up your writing class to include community service as a component, see:

Adler-Kassner, Linda, Robert Crooks, and Ann Watters. *Writing the Community.* Urbana, IL: AAHE/NCTE, 1997.

Eyler, Janet, Dwight Giles, and Angela Schmiede. *A Practitioner's Guide to Reflection in Service-Learning: Student Voices and Reflections.* Nashville: Vanderbilt UP, 1996. The National Service-Learning Clearinghouse in Minnesota will provide copies of the guide at cost. Contact: glass007@tc.umn.edu. Please include name, address, and phone number, and indicate whether you are a higher ed or K–12 practitioner.

Klooster, David, and Patricia Bloem. *The Writer's Community.* New York: St. Martin's, 1995.

National Council of Teachers of English. *The Service-Learning in Composition homepage.* <http://www.ncte.org/service/>.

Watters, Ann, and Marjorie Ford. *A Guide for Change: Resources for Implementing Community Service Writing.* New York: McGraw-Hill, 1995.

——— *Writing for Change: A Community Reader.* New York: McGraw-Hill, 1995.

Multilingual and Multicultural Writers

While the multilingual writer may have some real disadvantages in your classroom, what seems the most difficult problem may also be a great asset. Students who do not share majority assumptions, perspectives, and habits of mind—as well as the language itself—may be very much aware that knowledge is "situated." If you can develop a classroom in which differences can be talked about and integrated into discussions, the heightened awareness of distinctions that results will richly increase all students' critical thinking about writing and the rhetorical situation. Your valorization of differing perspectives will help multilingual students learn to understand the gaps between their assumptions and those of others. And it will help to improve the monocultural perspective of some students who have limited experience encountering other cultures and languages.

This does not mean that the academic writing you teach will be equally easy for all students to understand. Cultural assumptions can serve as a screen that prevents students from recognizing what they ought to do. For example, those whose home culture taught careful imitation rather than independent thought may feel confused by the very idea of speaking out or being critical.

You may even discover that the difficulties some multilingual students have are shared by local students. Some writers on multicultural issues in teaching believe that class differences are greater barriers to learning than linguistic differences. If cultural differences pose real difficulties, however, making use of them as part of the fabric of the class may solve some problems that would not have been seen as cultural. In current American universities the classroom is not a place where all agree, or even understand each others' differences, but rather a kind of "contact zone" where various languages and cultures of the world meet, mix, and perhaps reshape each other. The contact zone that is our classroom reinforces our need for an approach to writing that will enable students to understand their rhetorical situation. This means encouraging students to think flexibly about their strategies for writing, and to take an experimental and pragmatic perspective, trying more than one approach to see what works best for them. It means helping students not just to learn the rules of a new language and culture, but to think critically about writing options. For example, it may sometimes be best for students to write first in their home language, translating into English later as needed. To learn how to think better in another language, they may find it preferable at other times to compose directly in English. Students need to learn how to make such decisions for themselves, but you can provide guidance.

Here, then, are some general guidelines for adapting your teaching of writing to a classroom with multilingual students. Later, the Instructor's Notes will provide more specific suggestions in the chapter-by-chapter comments.

1. Think of ways to make good use of differences in language and culture. Instruction should be based on respect for the students' knowledge about their own language and culture, and should work to take advantage of that knowledge wherever possible and appropriate.

2. Since participation in class inquiry and group discussions is especially important, develop ways to foster participation that will be nonthreatening. For example, in the early days of the term, ask all students to hand in questions they'd like to ask, and read them out for class responses, rather than having them ask those questions orally. Gradually those students who might have been reluctant to speak will see that their questions were quite all right, that they prompted discussion; and perhaps they will begin to speak up themselves.

3. Offer multilingual students options for working in their first language, where appropriate, and assist them in thinking about these options. All Explorations in *Work in Progress* can be written in a native or home language first, and most will not need to be translated. For example, students might experiment with brainstorming in their first language, but then draft an essay in English. Students integrated into your writing class will usually have demonstrated a certain level of mastery in English, but that does not mean that using standard English will always be just as easy for them as using their first

language for many writing tasks. Even graduate students and professional writers can find that using their first language helps them clarify or work through writing issues that will eventually be written in a second language.

4. Be alert to problems associated with multiculturalism, even with students who speak English and seem to have "mainstream" cultural understandings. Class differences, for example, can sometimes create misunderstandings and differing expectations similar to those that international students experience in our classrooms. You may be surprised at the general accord among your students with the sense of disorientation that a multilingual writer expresses! Academic discourse is a foreign tongue to most, perhaps. This is not, however, to minimize the unique difficulties that may be felt by students with no previous experience of classrooms in the United States.

5. Don't make it the students' job to educate you about multilingual differences or the problems of multiculturalism. You can demonstrate that you are open to correction, however, and invite all students to keep you informed about issues generated by their diversity.

Here are some sources for further reading:

Ballister, Valerie M. *Cultural Divide: A Study of African-American College-Level Writers.* Portsmouth: Boynton/Cook, 1993.

Bizzell, Patricia. "'Contact Zones' and English Studies." *College English* 56.2 (February 1994): 163–69. Rpt. in *The Cultural Studies Reader.* 2nd ed. Ed. Simon During. New York: Routledge, 1999. 735–42

Boyarin, Daniel. *The Ethnography of Reading.* Berkeley: U of California P, 1993.

Calinescu, Matei. *Rereading.* New York: Yale UP, 1993.

Cushman, Ellen. *The Struggle and the Tools: Oral and Literate Strategies in an Inner City Community.* Albany: SUNY P, 1998.

Dubin, Fraida and Natalie A. Kuhlman, eds. *Cross-Cultural Literacy: Global Perspectives on Reading and Writing.* Englewood Cliffs, NJ: Prentice Hall, 1992.

Durgunoglu, Aydin Yucesan, and Ludo Verhoeven, eds. *Literacy Development in a Multilingual Context: Cross-Cultural Perspectives.* Mahwah, NJ: Erlbaum, 1998.

Fox, Helen. *Listening to the World: Cultural Issues in Academic Writing.* Urbana, IL: NCTE, 1994.

Friere, Paolo. *Education for Critical Consciousness.* New York: Continuum, 1973.

———. *Pedagogy of the Oppressed.* New York: Seabury Press, 1970.

Gilyard, Keith. *Let's Flip the Scrip: An African American Discourse on Language and Learning.* Detroit: Wayne State UP, 1996.

Lunsford, Andrea, Helene Moglen, and James Slevin. *The Right to Literacy.* New York: MLA, 1990.

Labov, William. *Language in the Inner City.* Philadelphia: U of Pennsylvania P, 1972.

Schaafsma, David. *Eating on the Street: Teaching Literacy in a Multicultural Society.* Pittsburgh: U of Pittsburgh P, 1993.

Schor, Ira, and Caroline Pari, eds. *Critical Literacy in Action: Writing Words, Changing Worlds.* Portsmouth, NH: Boynton/Cook, 1999.

Street, Brian. *Social Literacies: Critical Approaches to Literacy in Development, Ethnography and Education.* London: Longman, 1995.

Street, Brian V. *Cross-Cultural Approaches to Literacy.* Cambridge: Cambridge UP, 1993.

Handling the Paper Load

To make your responses to student writing more effective, communicate them *before* the final draft of an essay appears for grading. Students need readers in order to revise and to change. Comments on a final draft can seem irrelevant or nothing more than justifications for the grade unless there is a chance to put suggestions into practice in later drafts or future assignments. Instructors should also seek out alternative ways to increase the amount and kind of responses students receive before their final drafts. Instructors can talk with students about their writing in brief conferences and longer, more extensive sessions. Some instructors like to tape-record comments for students as they read. Brief, focused reading of certain sections can be more helpful than global corrections. Students can hand in drafts with those sections they particularly worry about marked for comment or with questions attached. In computer labs, instructors can answer questions as they arise in the process of revision. You can use email to comment on student drafts on a whole essay submitted or on small sections of it sent to you via email or on paper.

The fact is that students need to write much, much more than writing instructors can reasonably hope to evaluate, and instructors who try to micromanage their students' writing are probably wasting their time and being overdirective. Students do need wide-ranging responses to their writing; they can find other readers through the use of peer-response groups and through sharing their work with friends, family, roommates, and others. Instructors can greatly increase the focus and effectiveness of their evaluations by pressing students to draw on other resources such as writing centers for help and by expecting students to do their own correcting of mechanical problems. If students must read papers aloud—even tape them—they will rapidly improve their ability to correct many of their own problems of voice, syntax, style, diction, and even punctuation. But be sure that you direct students to help if they need it. Don't fail to circle, mark, or check errors that need to be brought to their attention. Errors that seem to be the result of widespread misunderstandings in your class can be the topic of an illustrated mini-lecture. Mechanics can also be explained for student reference as an attachment or link to a Web page for your class or your writing program. The many Guidelines in *Work in Progress* provide a tool for discussing student problems.

In response to the awareness that instructors of writing should focus on the writing process as well as on the written product, many instructors have reduced the number of final essays they require students to complete in a single term, while increasing the number of revisions and drafts. This change ensures that students will have time for planning activities, peer responses, and revision. By limiting the number of assignments, instructors have increased the time they can spend responding to the work in progress. But although this aspect of the paper load is perhaps improved, other problems quickly appear. How can instructors keep track of and give credit for the prewriting, drafting, and revising they require or encourage students to complete?

We suggest that instructors cope with the paper load created by multiple drafts by detailing in the clearest, most straightforward terms what they expect of students. A handout that specifies what students are to turn in for writing assignments will help both you and your students organize their work more efficiently. Note that you will provide a lengthier specification if you assign portfolios (see Chapter 2 for portfolio suggestions and the commentary on Chapter 2 in these Instructor's Notes). The following handout suggests the information you should provide to students.

A Note to Students about Writing Assignments

Because I want to provide numerous opportunities for you to revise your writing, I have limited your assignments to five essays—roughly one essay every other week. You will thus have time to engage in numerous planning activities, participate in peer-response groups, and revise your writing. You will have time to work with electronic technologies to learn about writing online. All of these activities are important to your improvement as a writer. Consequently, when you turn in the draft of an essay, I want to examine not just your final typed draft but all drafts that preceded it. I can study the process you used to write an essay only if you organize your work carefully. (Doing so will also help *you* keep track of work in progress.)

Whenever you hand in an assignment, please be sure to include *all* of the following items, arranged in the order listed below. Please paper-clip related items, such as invention and other planning materials. Turn in all material for an essay in a file folder or a pocket folder.

1. Invention and other planning materials—all the notes, diagrams, random jottings, lists, or other things that you wrote down to stimulate or collect your thinking before and during drafting

2. Rough drafts—all working drafts, numbered in order of completion (and also with pages numbered in each draft and in legible handwriting)

3. Peer-response form—indicating the name of the student who responded to your work

4. Your revision—typed, please, in a final draft with each page numbered

5. Statement from you (handwritten is fine) that answers the following questions:
   a. How did you write this essay?
   b. What aspect or aspects of this paper are you most satisfied with, and why?
   c. What aspect or aspects of this paper are you least satisfied with, and why?
   d. What did you learn about yourself as a writer by working on this essay?

Responding to Student Writing

The dialogue you establish with students through your responses to their writing plays a crucial role in determining your effectiveness as an instructor—and their likely success as students. Much has been written about instructors' comments on students' writing, so we limit our discussion to several important principles.

1. *Make your comments to students count.* Remember that your job is not to comment on every strength or weakness in a student's essay but to provide advice that students can *use* as they write and revise. Better to concentrate on a few salient points than to overwhelm them with a multitude of suggestions and corrections.

2. *Make comments that reflect your reading process.* Indicate when you're intrigued, confused, or puzzled. Ask questions. Respond to the content of the essay. Let students know that a person (not a grading machine) is reading their work.

3. *Be sure to find ways to tell students what they are doing well.* Write summarizing statements that say what worked, what was persuasive, what was accomplished.

4. *Comment on the rhetorical situation of the essay.* Frequently, an early draft of an essay will suffer from an incomplete or poorly developed sense of situation. Your comments about the situation that the paper implies can help the student think more clearly about this aspect of writing.

5. *When you make suggestions for revision, focus on strategies rather than on specific content.* For example, if a draft is rambling or incoherent, you might ask the student to write a descriptive outline or to summarize the essay and then to reflect on the degree to which it fulfills his or her controlling purpose. Be especially attentive to the need for multilingual students to fully understand the concept of revision.

6. *Help your students understand your comments by giving a public reading of one or more student papers, commenting as you go.* By showing students how you read their writing, you can demythologize the process and help students better interpret your comments as well. To engage in this process of commentary in class, you can also make a transparency of a student paper (with permission) or provide copies of student papers for comment via email. If you have access to a computer classroom, this is one of the benefits of shared access to papers.

7. *Check for plagiarism and proper documentation.*

8. *Publishing students' writing provides a wider audience for them.* You can easily produce a class publication. If you have no resources whatsoever, ask students to bring twenty-five copies of their best essay to class during the last week or so of the term. Perhaps you will want to provide copies of a title page. Often a student will contribute artwork, lettering, or a computer graphic for the cover. Desktop publishing expands the possibilities enormously. If you are assembling the volume yourselves, you can collate the copies by putting one page per desk in a circle around the room and letting students collect their own "books." Bring a stapler. Or you can have the whole thing copied and bound at a local copy center for a charge of about $5 or so a copy, if students want to pay the price. Classes are increasingly publishing student work online as well. If you do so, however, keep in mind that Web publication is public indeed. It may be more productive for your writing program to publish a Web selection of best papers.

The result is a collection of essays with histories the students may know very well, remembering the rough drafts and the struggles of composition from their groups. It is also a collection that provides a sort of reference, a cross-section of what one class of students produced—and that helps all of them to orient themselves in the academic world. Finally—not the least of its assets—publication gives students a reason to take the last step of editing seriously, as more than the personal crotchet of their group members or their instructors. Some instructors have classes buy packets of selected examples of student writing drawn from past terms. Finally, some programs, such as the Composition Program at the University of Arizona, publish books of essays selected from student submissions, together with comments and questions.

Using Writing Assignments

1. *Freewriting:* When you have students do freewriting assignments, be sure to keep them "free." The basic idea is that writers will not be held accountable for the kinds of problems or errors that would ordinarily discount the value of their efforts in the economy of the classroom. Freewriting has "use" value rather than "exchange" value: It doesn't count in the same way that final drafts count.

It sometimes helps to define freewriting by amounts of time spent. Ask students to write for five, ten, or fifteen minutes. You'll often find that in the first four or five minutes they write down everything that they are used to thinking or saying to themselves and that the next few sentences come more slowly, from less automatic responses. You might want to structure your freewriting assignments accordingly, asking students to spend at least seven to ten minutes on topics that they probably have rehearsed quite a bit already. Or have them freewrite for five minutes, pause, read some responses, and then go back for a second time to write for another five to ten minutes. Some multilingual students have difficulty with freewriting, especially in English. Suggest freewriting in the home language, and suggest other methods as well, such as making lists.

2. *Brainstorming:* Brainstorming is a form of listing that may be done by a group or by an individual. Given a topic or problem, students are to write down every idea that comes to mind, as quickly as possible. The only rules are (1) don't stop to elaborate and (2) don't censor the list.

We like to tell our classes that it's not a real brainstorming session unless they produce at least some ideas that are exotic, crazy, terrible, ridiculous, or reprehensible. The idea is to produce excess. When we do a brainstorming session in class, we sometimes ask students to go back and circle the items that are incredibly awful. If they have none, they need some.

Like freewriting, brainstorming works especially well as a mode of invention when it is detached from the critical judgments that will prune and restrain things later on for the final draft. Brainstorming encourages creativity—the production of a number of ideas. A Web search may produce results that look like a brainstorming session, and your students can use the variety in precisely the same way—to generate new ideas.

3. *Interviewing:* A number of the exercises in this book ask students to interview others—peers, family, tutors, older students, instructors—for various kinds of information about writing. These interviews serve collectively to help students construct a realistic idea of the rhetorical context within which they write. The interviews also help students to step out of their isolated writing habits and to think about asking others for information and help as a natural part of the writing process.

Most classes will benefit from guidance on the process of interviewing. Even if they have done "interviews" before, often they are still doing rather perfunctory research. To give them some direction and some sense of the possibilities of an interviewing assignment, instructors may have students role-play the interview first. For example, ask one student to play the role of an instructor in his field and another in the same field to interview him. List on the board or an overhead additional ideas for questions submitted by other class members. Ask all to take notes during the interview and check them against one another for the accuracy of their understanding. Instructors who invite speakers or panels into their classes can take advantage of the occasion to compare students' notes the next day. The hidden problem of interviewing will immediately become evident—that students often hear what they expect to hear rather than what is said, just as they also misinterpret what they read when they do research. Finding this out during the kind of informal interviewing suggested in this text will provide a low-anxiety entry into working on the problem.

In sum, students can improve their interviewing by setting up questions in advance to serve as guidelines, keeping careful notes about what was said, double-checking difficult or startling answers, and using quotes accurately.

4. *The writer's notebook:* The writer's notebook functions like a journal, a place where students are encouraged to write freely, explore ideas, reflect, or record messages to themselves. Where a writer's journal often contains extended pieces of writing and reflects the writer's desire to describe what she or he experiences, a writer's notebook might contain all sorts of things, including quotations, plans and schedules, clusters, or random thoughts, and might be more oriented to instrumental purposes. Perhaps an argument for calling this assignment a notebook rather than a journal might be that the journal has become associated with more personal, expressive writing. But you may wish just such expressive writing, and you should follow your own preferences in both title and suggestions for contents. The fundamental idea is to have students experiment and explore, using writing to learn and reflect—producing much more material than they eventually use in class essays.

If you wish to require students to keep the notebook, you may ask them to turn it in at the end of the term. It makes a logical part of a portfolio, if you are using that system. You don't, however, want to have students filling a notebook as a last-minute ordeal as our experience with assigning journals has sometimes provided. And giving credit for the notebook may be less important than giving notebook work attention as part of the class—not necessarily by responding in writing. (You probably don't have time.) Opportunities to use notebook material and to reflect on and discuss selected entries throughout the course of the term will help integrate using the notebook into the rest of students' writing. Or ask to see notebooks every other week or so, together with a comment from the student reflecting on the experience of keeping the notebook and notes about possible uses for the material. You can simply keep a checklist recording the fact that you have seen the notebook.

You will find that skimming notebook or journal entries frequently can be a valuable way of getting feedback about the progress of the class. If students are prewarned that you will be reading them, they can avoid unintended embarrassment. Or simply ask for the student's comment alone, without the bulk of the notebook (or the possible invasion of privacy).

The one thing you should not do with a notebook is to give it a grade or any other form of critical evaluation. It needs to be exploratory.

See Chapter 2 for an extended description of the writer's notebook and a list of possible uses.

5. *Essays:* Most writing classes base final grades on essays that have been developed into final drafts, handed in perhaps every other week (four or five per quarter, six or eight per semester). A length of two to four pages works well. If you wish to assign longer papers, you'll probably reduce the number accordingly. But you do not need to ask students to write only finished essays. You may want your students to try out many of the essay ideas prompted by assignments in the text and to choose just a few of the most promising to work into final draft form. Many instructors have students submit a *portfolio* of drafts and a certain number of essays chosen for revision as the basis for evaluation at the end of the term.

When you decide on the essays you would like students to write, whether you use suggestions from the text or other assignments, you can develop a more elaborate explanation of the essay assignment to help your students—together, perhaps, with samples of student work to serve as models. Sample essay assignments and student essays are collected at the end of these Instructor's Notes.

6. *Research:* Writing classes often must teach students how to think about research without specifically teaching the research methods of particular disciplines. This is not as impossible as it seems. Rhetorical inquiry provides a basis for all research, and you can help students take the first steps toward a responsible approach to the research projects they will be assigned in later classes. No matter what kind of research students might encounter, they must analyze the rhetorical situation (what is the exigency that prompts writing? who is the audience?) and the conventions that are necessary or appropriate. They must develop some form of argument. *Work in Progress* can help, not only when your students read Chapter 4, "Understanding the Research Process," but also through its emphasis on analyzing the rhetorical situation, its careful articulation of bridges between oral discussion and written projects, its attention to the place of conventions, and its opportunities for considering the differences and possible relationships between personal, informal writing and impersonal, formal writing.

7. *Online writing:* While you may specifically focus on online writing during the study of Chapter 7, you will find that *Work in Progress* provides a number of activities that use the Internet. Just as students may enter your class with habits in writing journals or letters or other quasi-personal writing that shouldn't carry over into their course writing, they may be used to an informal email style that you will want them to reconsider. Online writing will become another object of rhetorical reflection—a practice that *Work in Progress* will help them develop from the start.

Helping Students Plan and Manage Writing Time

Your syllabus will define the general schedule for the term, so students will know when assignments of reading and writing are due. However, many of your students may not have a clear idea of how to plan writing time effectively when they are doing most of their writing outside class. You might want to provide class time for groups to share advice about scheduling and completing writing projects, and you can also have students interview others about how much time writing takes (something they are not often realistic about). Here are two more suggested activities to improve time management:

- For your next writing assignment, establish a rough schedule detailing how you will manage your time planning, writing, and revising as you work on the assignment. Your schedule doesn't need to be elaborate, but do write it down. As you work on the assignment, note the changes you make (if any) in your schedule. After completing the assignment, take a few moments to reflect on this experience. Did you find it helpful to establish a schedule for your work? Would you follow this process in the future? If so, would you plan to balance your time any differently?

- Your instructor has probably either given you a written syllabus for your writing course or described the main assignments and indicated approximately when they will be due. Take half an hour to read and think about these writing assignments. If you are keeping a writer's notebook, copy these assignments into your notebook; otherwise, set up a separate manila folder or large envelope for each assignment. When ideas related to these assignments occur to you, write them in your notebook or add them to the appropriate folder or envelope. Simply copying your assignments and establishing a place to keep notes about them will start you thinking about possible topics and approaches. Now look at the due dates for each assignment. Compare these to the dates when you must turn in major projects or take tests in other classes. Try to formulate a general plan for accomplishing the work you need to do this term. You may want to use a calendar (or weekly charts with a section for each day) to note due dates and eventually to outline a work sequence. Finally, read and think about your first writing assignment. After realistically considering your academic schedule, family and social obligations, and the demands of the assignment, rough out a schedule that will provide reasonable time for planning, drafting, and revising. Your instructor may also ask you to write an essay describing the major academic challenges you face this term and explaining how you plan to meet them.

You might also ask students to try a writing schedule for an assignment they will have in another class. Often these aren't due until the last part of the term, and many students are not accustomed to planning so far ahead. Make a note to return to this assignment, perhaps even as part of a final analysis or final examination, asking students once again to think about the effects of planning and make changes, if appropriate. Meanwhile, for practice, have them concentrate on the first assignment due in your class. Don't be afraid to talk with your students about your own writing habits and rituals and what works for you. The testimony of many professional writers suggests that a regular turn at the writing desk is essential, whether one feels productive or not. Surprisingly, some of the students who have the most trouble with blocks and procrastination are people who don't allow themselves to *stop* writing once they have started. This kind of "must work until death" attitude leads them to put off writing. Sometimes it helps to suggest that such students keep *both ends* of a schedule—sticking to their planned quitting time even though they can imagine writing much, much more. One student found that it seemed revolutionary to go to bed at a reasonable hour the night before the paper was due, letting himself say that what he had completed was, if not perfect, nonetheless good enough. He had spent all the time he reasonably had available to work on the paper. Still, the next day when he turned his paper in, he was still not quite sure he had done the right thing: What if he could have moved the paper from a B to an A sometime between 2 and 4 A.M.?

Using Portfolios

If you have assigned portfolios for your class, you will need to define the portfolio's purpose, contents, format, due dates, and criteria for evaluation. If other students or other evaluators outside the class will be judging the portfolio, inform students how that will work. When you have students doing a great deal of writing that is ungraded—freewriting, drafts, lists, reflections, group work, and other activities—it makes sense to have them keep a portfolio of it so they can review the whole at the end of the term. Direct students to the section of the text on portfolios for help.

Evaluating Your Teaching

Teaching, like writing, takes place within a rhetorical situation. You will surely wish to assess in an ongoing way how your class is going and make adjustments to improve instruction during the term. The frequent sampling of students' experiences, ideas, drafts, and reflections that *Work in Progress* suggests will serve as an important means of keeping in touch with your class, so that these informal moments of evaluation can take place powerfully with no special structure beyond the dialogic form of instruction. Informal write-to-learn activities can also provide useful feedback. You might end a class period, for instance, by asking students to (1) write one thing they've learned as a result of class discussion or activities or (2) write one question they have or difficulty they're experiencing. Such comments can give you a good sense of your class.

Still, you will probably wish to provide for some more formalized kinds of evaluation. Your students may have plenty of opportunities to give you feedback about how they are doing and yet not take full advantage of the possibility. There may be misunderstandings about your aims and procedures that you need to address straightforwardly; students may believe that you expect them to be good students in terms defined by teacher-centered or lecture-dominated classrooms, for example. They may also expect you to be a good teacher according to such norms. Thus you may wish to take time periodically to explicitly evaluate the progress of the class. You can do this yourself by asking students for anonymous comments or soliciting comments and suggestions in an ongoing way—perhaps with a suggestion box or an email location.

You can also benefit from bringing others into your classroom to observe and comment. If your institution provides the opportunity, try midterm evaluation visits from an instructional center or from colleagues, whose interviews with your students can reveal trends you had not noticed and whose observations of the class can give you the benefit of a disengaged opinion. The benefits of such visits depend on the collegiality and shared understanding in your program. They should be "formative" rather than "summative" evaluations—that is, directed toward improving instruction rather than making judgments about your teaching ability. Such evaluations should begin with a conference before the visit when you discuss your goals and your concerns and a post-visit conference when you can hear the views of the evaluator and explore any changes you want to make.

When the class has finished, your teaching will be evaluated in a more conclusive way. Perhaps students will be asked to fill out an evaluation form or write brief comments. Many institutions that are paying more careful attention to teaching are asking for teaching portfolios. Your own notes and reflections about the class, together with the syllabus, sample papers, handouts, and even letters from students are items that may eventually contribute to a portfolio representing your teaching of that class in a final evaluation.

The following are questions often included in institutional evaluations. Although teaching evaluations may seem to assume a teacher-centered classroom, their components are also important functions for the teacher of a classroom using response groups and collaborative activities. Think about ways to determine how well your class is doing—and how well your students understand your approach.

1. *Did the instructor make this class interesting? Work in Progress* tries to show your students how to build their own sense of commitment to writing assignments rather than depending on teachers or on the contents of assignments. The frequent responses to their concerns and to their work that are a part of a collaborative classroom do, however, form a major component in generating interest. You can improve students' engagement in your writing class through the quality of their interactions with you and with other students. And you can teach them how to permanently improve the quality of their interactions in other classes and with other instructors by thinking in terms of building engagement rather than depending on instructors to make the course interesting.

2. *Is the instructor well-organized?* When you teach a writing course, all the recommendations made for organizing collaborative writing groups are appropriate. That is, it's

important to make goals clear, timelines definite, agreements explicit—and it's also important to attend to group process, to make sure everyone understands and has a chance to contribute, to ensure that disagreement has a place, to communicate what responsibilities they have. Unlike lecture-centered classrooms, whose success may seem to depend on the teacher's preparation alone, writing classrooms depend for their success on the students' participation as well. In particular, this may mean thoughtful attention to the organization of response groups and collaborative assignments. It also means organizing ways to keep track of the many kinds of writing and reading you ask them to do, whether graded or not. Online writing will add confusion, particularly if there are technical difficulties. While you cannot foresee all the problems that will arise with using the Internet, you can show students ways to cope with them. Do not count on everything working as predicted.

3. *Did the teacher give clear assignments? Were expectations clear?* Our experience suggests that students greatly appreciate explicit guidelines. The many Guidelines available in *Work in Progress* should help them know what to do step by step as they work through the process of writing. They will also appreciate explicit assignments from you (see the last section of these Instructor's Notes for samples) and help with understanding the grading system you will use. Students generally find essay writing and essay exams much less "clear" than "objective" measures. If you find this to be true for your students, you might want to talk with them about ways of evaluating the complexities of writing and collaborative work.

4. *Have you learned significantly from this course?* For a writing class, this question should not be translated as "Have you learned to write yet?" As we who are professionals in the field know well, writing is not a skill that can be mastered once and for all. Your class ought to help students plan and critically assess their own writing projects within a rhetorical situation that is appropriate. This sense of critical authority, this increasing self-confidence in learning more about how to write—and not learning to write in any final way—may be their most significant achievement in your class.

Further Reading in Composition Studies

The following bibliography does not attempt to list all the works that might be included in a basic bibliography of works on composition. Rather, we have included here those works that, by their broad scope or bibliographic emphasis, provide useful introductions to the field of composition studies. Should you wish to know more about the theoretical and research basis of *Work in Progress*, you may find useful the following essays on the teaching of writing by Lisa Ede: "Teaching Writing" in Lindemann and Tate's *Introduction to Composition Studies*, cited below, and "Methods, Methodologies, and the Politics of Knowledge" in Kirsch and Sullivan's *Methods and Methodologies in Composition Studies*, cited below.

Bartholomae, David, and Anthony Petrosky, eds. *Ways of Reading: An Anthology for Writers.* 4th ed. New York: St. Martin's, 1996.

Berlin, James. *Rhetorics, Poetics, and Cultures: Refiguring College English Studies.* Urbana: National Council of Teachers of English, 1996.

———, and Michael J. Vivion, eds. *Cultural Studies in the English Classroom.* Portsmouth: Boynton/Cook/Heinemann, 1992.

Brandt, Deborah. *Literacy as Involvement: The Acts of Writers, Readers, and Texts.* Carbondale: Southern Illinois UP, 1990.

Bullock, Richard, and John Trimbur. *The Politics of Writing Instruction: Postsecondary.* Portsmouth, NH: Boynton/Cook, Heinemann, 1991.

Clifford, John, and John Schilb. *Writing Theory and Critical Theory*. New York: Modern Language Association of America, 1994.

Corbett, Edward P. J., Nancy Myers, and Gary Tate, eds. *The Writing Teacher's Sourcebook*. 4th ed. New York: Oxford UP, 2000.

Crosswhite, James. *The Rhetoric of Reason: Writing and the Attractions of Argument*. Madison: U of Wisconsin P, 1996.

Crowley, Sharon. *Composition in the University: Historical and Polemical Essays*. Pittsburgh: U of Pittsburgh P, 1998.

Durst, Russel K. *Collision Course: Conflict, Negotiation, and Learning in College Composition*. Urbana: National Council of Teachers of English, 1999.

Elbow, Peter. *Writing with Power: Techniques for Mastering the Writing Process*. New York: Oxford UP, 1981.

Enos, Theresa. *A Sourcebook for Basic Writing Teachers*. New York: Random, 1987.

Faigley, Lester. *Fragments of Rationality: Postmodernity and the Subject of Composition*. Pittsburgh: U of Pittsburgh P, 1992.

Flower, Linda. *The Construction of Negotiated Meaning: A Social Cognitive Theory of Writing*. Carbondale: Southern Illinois UP, 1994.

Harkin, Patricia, and John Schilb. *Contending with Words: Composition and Rhetoric in a Postmodern Age*. New York: Modern Language Association of America, 1991.

Heilker, Paul, and Peter Vandenberg, eds. *Keywords in Composition Studies*. Portsmouth, NH: Boynton/Cook, Heinemann, 1996.

Jarratt, Susan, and Lynn Worsham, eds. *Feminism and Composition Studies: In Other Words*. New York: Modern Language Association of America, 1998.

Kirsch, Geza, and Patricia Sullivan. *Methods and Methodologies in Composition Studies*. Carbondale: Southern Illinois UP, 1992.

Lindemann, Erika, and Gary Tate. *An Introduction to Composition Studies*. New York: Oxford UP, 1991.

Lunsford, Andrea, and Robert Connors. *The New St. Martin's Handbook*. Boston: Bedford/St. Martin's, 1999.

McClelland, Ben W., and Timothy R. Donovan. *Perspectives on Research and Scholarship in Composition*. New York: Modern Language Association of America, 1985.

Rottenberg, Annette T. *Elements of Argument: A Text and Reader*. 6th ed. Boston: Bedford/St. Martin's, 2000.

Spellmeyer, Kurt. *Common Ground: Dialogue, Understanding, and the Teaching of Composition*. Englewood Cliffs, NJ: Prentice, 1993.

White, Edward M. *Teaching and Assessing Writing: Recent Advances in Understanding, Evaluating, and Improving Student Performance*. 2nd ed. San Francisco: Jossey-Bass, 1994.

3. SUGGESTIONS FOR TEACHING FROM *WORK IN PROGRESS*

Work in Progress draws on Kenneth Burke's idea of rhetoric as a conversation. Here is what he says:

> *Imagine that you enter a parlor. You come late. When you arrive, others have long pre-ceded you, and they are engaged in a heated discussion, a discussion too heated for them to pause and tell you exactly what it is about. In fact, the discussion had already begun long before any of them got there, so that no one present is qualified to retrace for you all the steps that had gone before. You listen for a while, until you decide that you have caught the tenor of the argument; then you put in your oar. Someone an-swers; you answer him; another comes to your defense; another aligns himself against you, to either the embarrassment or gratification of your opponent, depending upon the quality of your ally's assistance. However, the discussion is interminable. The hour grows late, you must depart. And you do depart, with the discussion still vigorously in progress.* —Kenneth Burke, *The Philosophy of Literary Form*

While the participants in the cultural conversation often sound as if they know exactly where it began and where it ought to end, students coming into academic settings are asked to begin writing before they feel anything like that sense of security. However, even aca-demic arguments are like Burkean conversations, although we often require that the be-ginner jump in without having the confidence he or she will later develop. *Work in Progress* is organized to help students begin to write with a rhetorical understanding of that process from the first.

Part One: Writing, Reading, and Research: An Introduction

In this first section of *Work in Progress*, your students will find an introduction to writing that leads them from personal situations to academic discourse, with illustrations of ver-nacular, online, and academic literacies. The chapters on writing, reading, and research provide basic elements for writing in academic situations that will be integrated later with strategies for writing and the analysis and argument forms of academic writing.

Chapter 1: On Writing

In This Chapter: Guidelines for Group Work (p. 18)

Chapter 1 of *Work in Progress* orients your students to their rhetorical situation in a writing class. It begins with a list of ways that people might use writing when it isn't assigned for a class: They write journals, notes, emails, proposals, postings on online bulletin boards, plans, family histories, and even academic essays. They are all ages, and some may write in a lan-guage other than English to start. Thus the chapter stresses a commonsense approach to writing, giving students credit for what they already know—their "rhetorical sensitivity"—and forecasting the factors and choices that may enter into learning to improve their writ-ing. In particular, this chapter counters some of the expectations about a writing class that many students bring with them. It stresses the interactive nature of writing, its complexity, and the need for students to use their judgment in making decisions. Rules and formulas are useful as guidelines, not as absolutes. The chapter speaks of writing as a process and focuses attention on that process as it is situated in cultures and in specific contexts. It asks students to reflect on their previous experiences with language and cultures and to see how much they already know about reading these rhetorically. It includes online writing and the use of visual texts as rhetorical issues from the beginning. Finally, Chapter 1 introduces students to the idea that writing is not necessarily a solitary activity but rather a set of processes that benefit from collaboration with others. The classroom can function as a writing community rather than an aggregate of isolated individuals.

This chapter can support several emphases. You might want to stress the conceptual, discussing the idea of *rhetoric*, the nature of writing, and the problem of describing effective writing with rules. You might want to stress the practical, setting your class up right away as a workshop and engaging students in the process of writing, reading, and exchanging responses. Students can use cultural texts to think about their rhetorical sensitivity. You can discuss the experience of the multilingual writer. If you are using additional reading material, you can use the commonsensical approach of this chapter to encourage your students to start right in on content-centered writing, making writing decisions rather than waiting to be told exactly what to do.

Concepts

1. *Writing as work in progress:* Chapter 1 asks students to begin thinking of writing not as a singular act, started and finished in one (perhaps stressful, last-minute) sitting, but as a complex process of choices involving their rhetorical sensitivity. As they begin to analyze their writing, they will find a number of ways to work on improvements rather than imagining they must work on everything at once.

2. *Rhetoric:* Students often have no idea what *rhetoric* means. They may have heard the expression "that's just rhetoric" used to complain about a political speech or an advertisement, and so they may think of writing as rhetorical when it wrongly values form over content.

Ironically, student papers also frequently suffer from being too rhetorical in this sense because they worry more about the effect (getting a good grade) than about their ideas. But you might want to point out to your students that rhetoric does not inherently necessitate this kind of imbalance. Rhetoric takes into account the *interaction* of reader, writer, text, and context. It overlaps with the study of communication, language, and discourse. In the medieval system of learning, the basic subjects in the lower division of the liberal arts, or the *trivium,* included logic, grammar, and rhetoric. Rhetoric was distinguished from the other two by its situational, practical nature.

Clearly, part of what rhetoric has to offer is a way to study the expressions and representations of culture. Thus you will find that this text's rhetorical approach allows you to easily integrate other cultural texts into your writing program. You will also find that the rhetorical approach helps students see the continuity between their own writing and the writing produced around them. Rhetorical study can apply equally to the freewriting produced by a freshman and the article she reads in *Harper's*, to the student's review, to the textbook for his psychology class, and to emails and Web sites.

You can begin right away to encourage your students to adopt a rhetorical way of thinking about all the texts they encounter. One way to do that is by asking students to consider how the various elements of rhetoric interact whenever they are looking at a piece of writing—whether written by one of them or by a professional writer. Who is the writer? What is the writer's *persona*? Who is the reader? What cultures and languages are involved? What is the context? How does the text reflect these considerations?

3. *Rhetorical sensitivity:* Students already have a commonsense knowledge about writing that they can both draw on and improve. They acquire this rhetorical sensitivity just as they acquire language—through experience. Of course, students in your classes vary widely in the amount of previous experience with written texts that they bring to this writing course, and you will want to take their different degrees of rhetorical sensitivity into account. What kinds of things have they read and written before? What experience have they had with the academic writing they will be doing in the future? Are many of your students better attuned to oral presentations than to written texts and thus more sophisticated about what "sounds right" than about how to arrange an essay? Do you have students who feel so uncertain about every detail of written language that they must approach it as a foreign discourse—who are, in fact, nonnative speakers?

You can help students translate some parts of their "rhetorical sensitivity" into their written work by asking them to explicitly identify what they know—not necessarily in particularly sophisticated vocabularies. When they explain what works, to you or to other students, they are making their knowledge conscious and accessible. Students already function as "readers" of culture, and they can already distinguish between being an uncritical and a critical audience.

Most students, for example, know quite a bit, perhaps even from watching television, about how a story should be structured, and they can apply that knowledge to narrative passages in each other's compositions. Most understand, tacitly, how devices that frame and structure a text help orient the reader: They can point out that they don't understand what an essay is about and that the writer needs to beef up the opening without needing much formal instruction on the topic of introductions.

On the other hand, students who have never read a persuasive essay or a critical review cannot understand what it should be like from a series of rules. If they have no prior experience with the kinds of texts you want them to write, students need plenty of examples and models to follow.

4. *Rules, formulas, and conventions:* Chapter 1 asks students to exercise judgment about what does and does not work in their particular rhetorical situation. It points out that general rules, such as "never use *I*," ought to be questioned and do not universally apply. Students begin to learn that conventions operate within constraints of writer, purpose, audience, and genre and that they must analyze the cultural context that determines the rhetorical situation. Rules of form, usage, and style imply specific contexts, so they are neither arbitrary nor universal. You may need to show students how to use a handbook effectively as a resource rather than as a straitjacket.

When they reconsider rules they perhaps once accepted, your students may feel liberated from arbitrary constraints, from the sense of being bound by rules that did not always seem reasonable. But you may find that students do not altogether welcome the end of dictatorship. Many continue to long for a tidy recipe that would enable them to cook up passable writing every time.

The problem is not that rules inevitably hamper creativity. After all, many sonnets illustrate how forms can stimulate creative solutions to their constraints. What damages the ability of students to learn how to write is an attitude of rigidity about the process that keeps them from thinking things through or having the confidence to change plans. Research on writing blocks (notably by Mike Rose) suggests that students who suffer from such blocks have a tendency to think about writing inflexibly, to follow rules or formulas as if they were absolute, and to stop writing rather than to try another approach that might better suit their subject or their audience or their aim. The point, then, is to help students to proceed flexibly, regarding rules as conventions or strategies rather than as directives. Asking students to examine rules critically and to use them as strategies rather than as scientific law should help students gain confidence, even when they run into problems with an assignment. At the same time that you question absolute rules in writing, be careful to provide simple, clear directions on your syllabus and in your classroom so students know what is expected of them.

With all of this said, we will of course go on supplying our students with handy hints, rules of thumb, guidelines, heuristics, and even useful recipes—all wonderful tools if used rhetorically rather than absolutely, as probabilities rather than mathematical certitudes. *Work in Progress* supplies students with a number of guidelines in each chapter to help them in this process. And for rhetorical reasons as well, we recognize the importance of adhering to the conventions of standard written English, particularly in academic writing. It will help your students if you simply make that expectation explicit.

To help focus students' anxiety about breaking rules, try this exercise. Ask them to write a paragraph that violates as many rules as possible. Run a contest for the worst paragraph in the class, if you like. You might then go on to point out that breaking grammatical rules is not the only way to write a perfectly terrible paragraph, as the Bulwer-Lytton Fiction Contest illustrates. By exaggerating the most banal clichés of the genre, such as variations on "it was a dark and stormy night," the winners are those who produce the worst samples of Gothic and romantic fiction. In writing, the most conventional can also be not the best but the worst.

5. *Writing processes:* The idea of writing processes is introduced here briefly and will be expanded in later chapters. By analogy with a number of other activities that you may wish to explore with your students, writing involves a performance of complex skills adapted to varying situations, requiring a great deal of practice and benefiting by setting goals and assessing progress. Here you might want to go on to specify the implications of this view of writing as a number of processes for the way you are organizing your class.

6. *Multilingual writers:* Notice the "Notes for Multilingual Writers" that you will find in this chapter and in each of the following chapter. Point out the notes in your class, if you think it appropriate. You may wish as well to pay specific attention to the relations of rhetoric and culture that are foregrounded by a diversity of linguistic backgrounds. Cultural ideas about who should speak and how, and cultural ideas about audience may affect the interactions of your students.

If you are encouraging students to write drafts in their native or home language, you may choose to introduce the idea of "code switching" at this point. To some degree, most students, not only multilingual students, do not feel at home yet in academic writing and must learn to some extent how to "code switch" from the vernacular, or the less formal English they may have used in earlier school experiences. Part of a rhetorical sensitivity involves learning when and how to code switch so that writing becomes appropriate to the rhetorical situation.

Notes and activities in this chapter ask multilingual writers to think about translation, or else about composing in English from the start. Some composition scholars, including Peter Elbow, have urged instructors to let students write first drafts in whatever vernacular seems most apt to free their expression and then change subsequent drafts to fit the academic occasion. Such issues of translation and interpretation are very interesting and rhetorically complex—well worth ongoing discussion in your class.

7. *The writing community:* If writing is not a series of algorithms to be memorized but rather a social process much like a conversation in its general structure, then the

collaborative model can help reformulate expectations about the way a classroom should work. *Work in Progress* will give you suggestions for group work and collaboration in each chapter, and Chapter 13 focuses specifically on strategies to improve writing with others. This chapter provides "Guidelines for Group Work" to help your students get started. There are a number of ways to organize a class as a writing community, with greater or lesser emphasis on using class time for learning groups. All have in common the attitude that students should be encouraged to exchange ideas at every stage of the writing process and that writing at best takes advantage of all social resources, rather than happening in isolation. Instead of concluding that *only* the writing class can be a "writing community," ideally students will use this approach to extend their roles in the academic community as they continue their education. Some commentators, including Greg Myers, have pointed out that group work does not automatically give students a chance to be heard: It may, in fact, increase the pressure on individuals to silence their disagreements. You can help by including disagreement and counterarguments as an important element in the rhetorical conversation. Keep in mind critiques of the ways collaboration might stifle student resistance or opposition as you set up your class, so you encourage debate and acknowledge tendencies to impose a normalizing consensus.

Section 2 of this manual ("Teaching Practices") offers additional suggestions for collaborative structures. There are many different forms of collaboration in contemporary writing practices. This book contains material on developing a rhetorical sensitivity to the collaborative nature of all writing and on using collaborative groups to help students learn to write as well as teaching students to work together on specific projects. For more information about the history of collaboration, current types of collaboration in business and industry as well as academic contexts, and a discussion of theory of collaborative writing, see Lisa Ede and Andrea Lunsford, *Singular Texts/Plural Authors: Perspectives on Collaborative Writing* (Carbondale: Southern Illinois UP, 1990).

8. *Freewriting:* Freewriting is a technique that can help students suspend attention to context, audience, and conventions to focus on developing ideas. It emphasizes one use of writing: Writing is a powerful tool in the production of thought. It's best if you have students do their first freewriting in class so they understand how to put everything aside and simply keep writing. Ten minutes is a workable length of time. If you occasionally take class time for freewriting and for reflecting on or responding to the writing, you encourage attention to the process and underline its importance. If you write along with the class, so much the better.

Activities

(p. 6) *For Exploration:* This Exploration asks students to list the kinds of writing they do. You might want to start this exercise on the first day of class because it immediately moves students into one step of the writing process, it affords an opportunity for students to share writing experiences, and it establishes the fact that students *are already writers*. If you want to help class members get to know one another and begin to establish the class as a community, put the responses up on the board or on an overhead transparency. The result will be an informal survey of the kinds of writing the students have done and their reasons for writing. You will establish the first evidence that you take them seriously as writers simply by the act of listening to their responses, some of which will probably be "I never write unless I have to" and other expressions of duress. Press them to define for themselves what they consider to be productive and satisfying writing experiences. This exercise concludes by asking them to write a paragraph or two that makes these differentiations. This activity is important in two ways. First, by doing this, students take their own experience seriously, and they take an analytical perspective toward those experiences. Second, it involves students in a workable model of a writing process—first listing and then drafting paragraphs. Finally, if you collect or record the responses, you have an informal inventory of your class.

(p. 7) *For Exploration:* This Exploration is to help students think methodically about writing. It asks students to examine the elements of a successful experience. Without previously discussing what criteria should define successful writing, you can use this Exploration to find out how they define *successful.* They will often be surprised by the variety of criteria other students bring to bear, if you give them a chance to talk about their responses with each other. (You may be surprised as well.) But more important, this exercise gives students the beginnings of a method for managing their own writing, discovering what works or does not work in their own practice. The discussion of what *successful* might mean will continue throughout the course, as more complex aspects of the rhetorical situation come into view. With luck, you can complicate the supposition that success means a good grade, as well as showing the various judgments that come into play in assigning grades.

(p. 10) *For Exploration:* This Exploration has students freewrite about their uses of vernacular language. Then they are asked to reflect about how the vernacular—both oral and written—seems to differ from academic discourse. You may want to invite them to include more than one language or dialect. You can mention, if you wish, the institutional contexts of academic writing and even its possible differences in other academic traditions—in China, France, Nigeria, or Mexico, for example. While it is both difficult and uncomfortable for many students to move from familiar uses of language to the unfamiliar and more distanced uses of academic writing, this Exploration starts from the assumption that students will take a problem-solving approach to learning what is new. You might want to have them think about their uses of language in communities other than home as well—for example, when writing to friends or sending email.

(p. 13) *For Exploration:* This Exploration asks students to demonstrate their understanding of *rhetoric* and *rhetorical sensitivity.* In discussing this assignment, you may fruitfully spend some class time exploring some different situations the students might describe: a job interview, a wedding, a sports event. What about situations that emphasize the difference between public and private discourses—for example, a family holiday, an appearance on television, a conversation between friends, the same story told to a newspaper reporter? Thinking about the doubleness of rhetorical conventions, ask students to decide how free and how limited their situation might be, from conventions of such things as dress to conventional expectations about how much you should know. When would they feel they needed to learn more about the conventions? Do they prefer writing tasks with specified conventions or writing that is very open-ended? What situations demand the use of a home or native language? When is the vernacular probably not to be used?

(p. 14) *For Exploration:* This exercise asks students to list rules that they have never understood or fully accepted and then to write a brief explanation about their reasons for questioning one of them. Tell them to look at a handbook or at a book about style if they are unsure about what kind of rules might be at issue. After this exercise, you may wish to have them look at documents from the history of rules and usage, such as the rules for rhetorical exercises that Shakespeare might have been taught or the rules imposed on American students in nineteenth-century one-room schoolhouses. The *McGuffey's Reader* reminds us, for example, that teachers once paid a good deal of attention to oral reading, and (in spite of admonitions to trust nature) they imposed rules for correct pronunciation that aimed to remedy the faults illustrated in a number of charts such as the following:

RULE II. Avoid the *omission* of unaccented vowels.

INCORRECT	CORRECT	INCORRECT	CORRECT
Sep'rate	Sep-a-rate	mem'ry	mem-o-ry
'pear	ap-pear	'pin-ion	o-pin-ion
'special	es-pe-cial	par-tic'lar	par-tic-u-lar

Can your students give any reasons that such rules would be valuable? Why they might not be?

(p. 14) *For Collaboration:* This exercise asks students to discuss in groups the rules they are questioning and to select one for further deliberation. The exercise suggests that you use groups to frame arguments against—and in favor of—a selected rule. Thus the students are asked to think rhetorically rather than grammatically, using judgment rather than correctness as a standard.

These discussions may usefully forecast topics that will be taken up later on in the course. As an example, a group may question whether paragraphs need topic sentences, by analogy with the rule about essays needing a thesis. There will perhaps be some contention in the class about certain rules: Many students feel strongly, for example, about academic rules against sentence fragments, which they encounter frequently in everyday prose. Most computer programs can check student papers for spelling and for grammatical correctness. As an additional exercise, have them run two or three samples of prose through their computer's grammar checker—something of their own but also some samples from textbooks or readers. Discuss whether they agree with the computer program's recommendations and what cannot be included in its checker. For example, how useful are comments about sentence length?

The exercise concludes with class discussion about conclusions. Students understandably want most of all to know about *your* list of necessary rules and how their developing common sense will connect to their grades. You might want to deal with this hidden agenda by pointing out that rules and grades don't have much to do with each other, since the point is that good writing requires the exercise of judgment and choice. However, you do have some assumptions for your course. What *are* some of the conventions that your writing assignments will require? Are they requirements for all class work, stated in the syllabus? Will there be conventions they must follow on specific assignments? You also can specify that certain errors of spelling and usage are not acceptable.

(p. 16) *For Exploration:* Students' opening responses to this Exploration can serve as a montage to jump start your next class meeting. Here are some samples from our students:

When I write, I feel like I'm in jail . . .

Writing means trouble . . .

Writing is like going into a long, dark tunnel . . .

(p. 18) *For Exploration:* If you assign students to interview a writing assistant at the writing center, you might forewarn the center about the date you choose. Freshmen in particular are often surprisingly shy about seeking out help, so it makes sense to encourage them to become familiar with what is available, especially if they have no other introduction to the services. Assigning an interview has the advantage of removing any imagined stigma from students' going to the writing center. Ask about how the center prefers to work with multilingual writers. Are there other resources on campus you could tell you students about?

(p. 21) *For Collaboration:* Even if you do not wish to establish ongoing groups in your class, you might want to help students form collaborative support groups to meet outside of class. Usually at least some students in a class will be interested in such a voluntary group. Once they get together and organize, they might meet once or twice a week to read and respond to each other's work, exchange ideas and discoveries, and make suggestions to each other. Support groups outside class, in other words, can serve the same kinds of functions that in-class groups serve. They do not really substitute for in-class groups, however, because without your help and modeling they sometimes have difficulty focusing, and without a required schedule, most students have trouble finding meeting time.

For Thought, Discussion, and Writing (p. 22)

You may wish to assign these activities as entries into a writer's notebook. Additionally, number 2 under this heading is a good starting point for an essay assignment.

Number 1: This activity asks students to write down concrete goals for themselves as writers. This paragraph can help show you how well students' expectations for the class articulate with your expectations. However, when you look at the goals your students write down, you may find that some students still have little conscious understanding of their writing and little knowledge of what a writing goal might be. Their goals may be vague rephrasings of something a former teacher told them they should do or guesses about what you want them to have as goals rather than anything they have a deep commitment to accomplish. One of the real achievements of the term's work on writing may finally show in the extent to which students are able to formulate concrete, realistic, attainable goals for their writing.

Number 2: This activity suggests an interview of other students and some form of a report on the results, either to the student's writing group or in the form of an essay.

A number of the exercises in this book ask students to interview others—peers, family, tutors, more advanced students—for various kinds of information about writing. These interviews serve collectively to help students construct a realistic idea of the rhetorical context within which they write. The interviews also help students to step out of their isolated writing habits and to think about asking others for information and help as a natural part of the writing process. *Work in Progress* offers several opportunities in later chapters to use interviewing as a means of researching writing. This exercise offers informal practice for an activity you may wish to teach more formally later. See "Guidelines for Conducting Interviews" (p. 130) and Section 2 of this manual for more on interviews.

Multilingual students may wish to interview a student who shares their first language. You may take one of two approaches to this:

- Recommend to them that they find someone with the same major. When they report to the class, they can include information particularly related to their linguistic and cultural needs on campus in addition to the information on the major.

- Or substitute the idea of interviewing a student who is also a native speaker for the interview with a major. While the disciplinary information will be missing, you may feel the information about language and culture—and resources—is more important at this point.

Interviewing other students will not necessarily inspire your students with positive reports about the worth of writing. Some of the technical majors at our university, for example, told Composition 121 students they didn't see much reason for anything but preparation for technical writing! This encounter with the realities of the rhetorical situation allowed, at least, for some exchange about what a beginning writing class should teach. We can, after all, argue with the technically oriented that there are defensible reasons for teaching versions of writing, such as the essay and most forms of argument, that are not oriented just to providing information. We can question the characterization of writing as merely a basic (remedial?) skill. And we can teach rhetoric as a means of inquiry that is central to learning, not peripheral or merely decorative or required.

Number 3: This exercise asks students to freewrite about their experiences doing collaborative activities. Like the individual writer, groups draw on rhetorical knowledge and context to function, and students will benefit by making assumptions and conventions explicit. The exercise can give you valuable information about your class. If you sense that students feel considerable awkwardness about working together, you may wish to work with them specifically on ways to improve the usefulness of group work, using the "Guidelines for Group Work" to help them.

Chapter 2: Understanding the Writing Process

Chapter 2 introduces your students to the writing process. Its purpose is to demystify the rituals of writing and the sense of isolation so that students will learn to regard their own writing practices as open to interaction, analysis, and change. In particular, the chapter emphasizes ways that expert as well as beginning writers may work to improve on raw inspiration. Students will learn some of the different forms planning, drafting, and revising may take in the experience of various kinds of writers. *Work in Progress* encourages students to think about how they can develop these composing processes in their own way through learning and practice. By opening up various possibilities to students, the text shows them how to develop more flexibility and more conscious decision making about writing habits that may have seemed as ineluctable as fate. Many students will find themselves changing their writing processes to accommodate various writing situations. Under the pressure of deadlines, for example, they may sometimes abbreviate planning or revising. Composing strategies presented in this text and in your classroom will help them make choices wisely about how they approach planning, drafting, and revision in changing circumstances.

Concepts

1. *Magical thinking and the students' histories as writers:* Many students believe writing requires a natural talent or inspiration and that hard work does not make much difference in how well one can write. Such a belief greatly influences their writing habits and discourages them from making the effort to change the way they write. Furthermore, writing is so complex and multiple that it probably most resembles learning a second language: It seems natural only once you've acquired considerable fluency, and is never acquired overnight in one extraordinary outburst of passionate scribbling. This process of naturalization, however, helps convince students that such magic exists.

You may want to take time to talk with your students about the way they think about writing. A useful technique is to ask them to brainstorm associations with the word *writer*. Typical responses include the following: genius, glasses, dead, brilliant, reclusive, creative, eccentric. Or ask them to do a freewrite beginning with the words "A writer is someone who. . . ." Many students think writers are in touch with some kind of magic—and out of touch with their everyday experience. Teachers find it productive to discuss some of their own writing processes with students, even if the students do not regard academic lives as particularly "everyday."

When you discuss revision and procrastination, you will find students especially full of mystical superstitions. Many of our students have stories about an essay they wrote at the last minute that received an A, while another essay was revised and revised but received only a C. As such folklore illustrates, students often seem to *want* to believe that the result of their writing is beyond their control. Of course, frequently those last-minute A papers worked well because the students tried nothing new and just repeated what they'd already mastered, and the much-revised papers may have represented some genuine learning, not fully assimilated or polished enough for an A. The shortest distance between an assignment and a finished paper is not the best direction to take for learning to write: Email efficiency may encourage a misleading haste. Students need rewards for choosing more difficult and risky paths to writing. You can use portfolio evaluation, organize your assignment grading to shield students from too-early grading of newly learned approaches, or let later drafts and papers compensate for early poorer grades.

This text is structured to interrupt the automatic and unconscious writing habits of your students. In Chapter 2 they will be asked to reflect on their experiences as writers and their representations of the craft. You may want to structure your classroom and requirements to resist the habits of magical thinking further.

2. *Composing strategies and narratives of literacy:* Chapter 2 asks students to identify the composing strategies that work best for them and to recognize differences among individuals in what works. The distinction between a strategy and a rule is exactly that criterion; if one strategy doesn't work, another one is called for. Students who think in terms of strategies rather than rules, Mike Rose's research suggests, are less apt to suffer from writing blocks. Students who think of writing as something they can pragmatically and systematically learn to do will be in a better position to put into practice the strategies that work. At the same time, the exercises in this chapter help to encourage your students to examine the ways writing is bound up with their own history and sense of identity. Thus strategic rhetorical choices are deeply involved as well with the development of an *ethos,* a sense of writing authority, and the ethical choices writers must make. If a rule seems merely technical, a matter of skills, rhetorical strategies are much more.

This chapter includes two essays reflecting on writing practices—one by a student, Mary Ellen Kacmarcik, and one by a professional writer, Burton Hatlen. It also includes follow-up letters from both writers about their writing life since. This insertion of the writing process into a life—into, that is, a narrative about learning a craft—emphasizes the agency of the writer at the same time that it demystifies what Hatlen decries as the myth of genius. We are also work in progress.

3. *The processes of writing: planning, drafting, revising:* Your students may be surprised to find significant variations in the way different people manage the writing process. Multicultural writers may have learned diverse approaches to the composing process, or a lack of emphasis and attention to process. Most of our students find it liberating to realize that individual writing processes might be different. They welcome the idea that heavy planners and heavy revisers and sequential composers might all have acceptable approaches even though they are apparently at odds. The situation often determines the best process, so no writer should depend on a single way of writing.

Since many of your students have probably not had much chance to experiment, they can try a new model if the one they use doesn't work very well, or deliberately exaggerate the opposite of their usual manner to develop flexibility.

Many students have never become aware of the writing process because they strongly dislike revising. They find heavy revising unimaginable: They are so used to squeezing out work one stingy word at a time to fulfill an assigned length that they just can't imagine ever revising anything voluntarily. To counteract this, try asking students to overwrite a draft— to bring in twice the number of pages that the finished essay will have—so they can discover the advantages and disadvantages of heavy revision. For example, since those pages are written with the expectation of heavy revision, students often find them quite a bit easier to write than usual. You can also combine freewriting with heavy revising to good effect. For further information, see Muriel Harris, "Composing Behaviors of One- and Multi-Draft Writers," *College English* 51.2 (Feb. 1984): 174–91.

4. *Procrastination:* You might find it useful and enlightening to take your students' intense desire to procrastinate seriously rather than letting it seem (unconsciously) a kind of

moral issue. Does it ever *really* work better to procrastinate? Our students have evolved some unusual theories—just waiting to be confirmed by research—to argue that it does. Meanwhile, most of us continue to draw distinctions between healthy amounts of planning and putting the draft off until the last minute out of less desirable (if understandable) motives. Some students who procrastinate are avoiding something that causes them anxiety. We tell them we understand. Writers almost universally agree that sitting down to write is *very hard*, even painful, certainly something that one would be willing to clean the house and weed the yard to avoid. You can lower the anxiety barrier, though, by encouraging students to write uncritically at first. John McPhee says he hates to write because he knows the first draft will inevitably be bad, less than what he wants. He hates having to produce bad writing to get to the good stuff. So do our students, especially since they feel far less confident than John McPhee about ever managing to revise the bad into the good.

A less acceptable motive for procrastination is simply that most college students don't make their writing class the first priority of their studies. You might want to discuss this frankly, letting students talk about their frustrations with requirements while pointing out that the writing course realistically requires rather large amounts of time. In our experience, most students really do want to become better writers—but they let themselves slip into a kind of resistance to the prescribed. When you are pragmatic rather than prescriptive, you make it harder for them to slide into such thinking. You may find that working with your class on scheduling writing time is helpful.

Finally, some students procrastinate because they are perfectionists, and putting things off until the last minute allows them to make choices that are pragmatic rather than ideal. Using the class as an audience can help to limit and particularize the abstract sense of a transcendental audience that often accompanies perfectionism.

5. *Monitoring and the composing inventory:* Monitoring is that cognitive function that supervises and directs the composing process, keeping watch and making strategic suggestions according to what's happening. The word comes from the Latin *monere*, "to warn," and the whole function may seem overly critical to some of your students. What you say and do as an instructor when you coach them can help model the monitoring, which your students internalize. You may also want to explicitly encourage students to change their ways of thinking about what they are doing when they write, putting aside, while they write a first draft, the critical perfectionist editor within in favor of a more flexible, practicing explorer.

6. *The writer's notebook:* See Section 2 of this manual for a more detailed discussion of planning assignments to use a writer's notebook or journal in your class.

7. *Writing with a computer:* This section of the text will be helpful to students throughout the term. You may find, as we have, that many students begin to make more extensive use of a computer's capabilities during the term as they find out its usefulness for moving from planning through draft to revision, using word processing, as well as for online writing and reading.

Activities

The first three activities in this chapter are coordinated to lead students from their response to reading to a collaborative task growing out of their own writing. It is a model as well, then, of ways you can integrate informal, personal writing with reading, collaboration, and discussion.

(p. 28) *For Exploration:* This exercise asks students to read essays by a student, Mary Kacmarcik, and a professional writer, Burton Hatlen, and then to respond to a list of questions about their own writing by freewriting or making a list. The questions may help them to be more specific and detailed about their reflections on writing and their history as a writer. Point out that even personal recollections can usefully be enlarged by such a list of pertinent issues.

(p. 29) *For Exploration:* This exercise asks students to use information generated by their lists to write a letter about themselves as a writer. The format encourages them to write informally and probably more personally than an essay, and you can make use of these letters in several ways. The next exercise brings them into a group activity. Later you may ask students to write an essay on their history as a writer, using Kacmarcik and Hatlen as models, or to write an essay comparing their own experience with writing to that of others. These "literacy narratives" usefully connect personal history to community as well as to writing.

(p. 29) *For Collaboration:* This important activity uses student letters about writing experiences as the basis for group discussion. You keep their exchange focused by asking them to report to the whole class after a certain amount of time. This discussion can be an important source of information for you as well as for your students about the general profile of the class. You might give groups twenty to twenty-five minutes to answer the questions and then take another ten minutes to hear reports of the results. Notice that students are asked to work toward a sense of group cohesiveness by identifying commonalities, then by noting differences, and finally by reporting common goals. Differences will often reflect context and situation. Multilingual students can usefully bring a recognition of cultural differences into the discussion. Many students have histories as writers that are really histories of the teachers they had—good and bad—and chronologies of grading dramas. Do you want to make time to discuss the experience of evaluation here—of being graded, and more generally, of having writing evaluated by others? Such concerns seem a digression, and yet the thought of the eventual audience obviously reaches into the apparently isolated writing process from the first.

How are your groups doing at this point? Do they feel reasonably comfortable with each other and with the idea of group tasks? If some are working with a great deal of awkwardness and inhibition, you might want to give some attention to group processes. See Section 2 of this manual for some more general suggestions.

(p. 36) *For Collaboration:* Students are to discuss "Guidelines for Analyzing Your Composing Process" to identify and describe their own characteristic style of composing. The exercise is important, leading them through guidelines they can use to examine thoroughly various aspects of their own composing practices and attitudes. This puts your students in the position of taking an analytic attitude, as if they were doing research about their own writing. Students usually very much enjoy figuring out their composing style. They may also enjoy talking about composing in the vernacular. A real willingness to change often seems to come out of this analysis: Many students start to experiment with writing processes and timing as they see composing increasingly as a matter of making choices that they can control. The assignment asks your students to decide for themselves which writing practices work well and also to decide on ways to do better. It makes a good entry for the writer's notebook, which they will more specifically think about later in this chapter.

You might have to limit time for talking about individual responses to the questions to get groups to move firmly toward making some statements about writing. Then, although it takes an extra ten to fifteen minutes, it's worth having groups report back the results of their thinking. If you record these on the board, on butcher paper, or on an overhead, you move the class from thinking mostly about their own work to making generalizations about the nature of the writing process that they can pursue.

(p. 38) *For Exploration:* This assignment asks your students to reflect on the writer's notebook and to look at it as a tool in furthering writing projects. If you are assigning such a notebook, you might also explicitly assign periodic reviews for reflecting and planning. If you ask students to hand in notebooks from time to time, you can ask students to hand in these comments as well. See Section 2 of this manual for further details. Even if you are not assigning a writer's notebook that you will check, this application invites your students to try it for themselves, an option you can reinforce simply by periodically calling attention to it.

For Thought, Discussion, and Writing (p. 47)

Number 1: This assignment encourages students to learn more about their own composing process and to do so by conducting a brief case study of themselves as they work on a writing project. Keeping a detailed process log is essential to the success of this assignment, for the process log enables students to get beyond vague generalities about their writing—generalities such as "coming up with ideas is hard" or "revising makes me nervous"—to more specific understandings of the strategies they employ (and the habits they draw on) when they write. Students are often surprised by what they discover when they analyze their process logs. Students sometimes overestimate how long they typically work on their writing, for instance. Recording when they start and end each work session helps them become more aware of the amount of time it can take to make significant progress in writing.

Depending on the nature and goals of your course, you can use this assignment in various ways. You may have students keep process logs and write an informal analysis of what they have learned by studying their own writing as a prelude to a class discussion of this activity. Or you may make the case study one of your course's major writing assignments.

Number 2: This assignment asks your students to write an essay about procrastinating. It's a subject that releases a great deal of pent-up energy. It's also a topic that allows most students to draw on extensive personal experience. I like to encourage students to take the fun seriously—that is, to imagine some attitude toward procrastination besides automatic responses of guilt and pleasure, to rethink and revise their first impressions. Procrastination is an especially important problem for your class because it forecloses the possibility of learning to revise. In other words, it may be a way of not learning much of what there is to be taught in a writing class.

Number 3: This assignment suggests that students read interviews and essays by professional writers about their work. One possible mode of organization for the class would use such a collection as a reader throughout the term. See Section 2 of this manual for detailed suggestions and plans. Or you might want to make some of these essays and interviews available to accompany this chapter. There are also a number of films and videotapes of interviews with writers. And, of course, there are increasing numbers of Web sites featuring authors, some of them with interviews appropriate for this particular question.

Ask students to respond in writing to what they read. In particular, ask them to point out whatever might have been unexpected. Do they find it surprising that best-selling author Anne Tyler speaks of herself as only a housewife who is "still just writing"? Do they agree with Alice Walker that a writer can't afford to risk having more than one child? Ask students to think about how the context affects the writer and how they themselves are affected and influenced *as writers* by the place they live, by their daily lives, by the people they know, by their favorite routines, by the weather, and by the past.

Number 4: This assignment puts students to work on a systematic ongoing project of self-examination and self-consciousness about their writing habits. You can assign this meta–analysis together with another writing assignment, and you can go on to use a version of such analysis for each assignment the student turns in for evaluation.

Chapter 3: Understanding the Reading Process

This chapter turns to the complexities of reading and shows how "reading" is a process of analysis and interpretation that applies to visual as well as to written texts. Even though reading and writing are fundamentals of literacy and basic in that sense, their apparent simplicity is deceptive. Just as advanced students need to keep on learning how to write, so do they need to keep on learning how to read. Both reading and writing involve students in a rhetorical process.

In Chapter 3, *Work in Progress* pays special attention to the kind of critical reading skills students will need in college and the rhetorical analysis that will help them to make connections between their reading and their writing. You will find a number of specific suggestions and examples to help students read a text more effectively. In particular, "Guidelines for Effective Reading" provide questions for analyzing the reading process and consider texts within a rhetorical situation. The chapter also provides help for previewing, annotating, outlining, summarizing, and analyzing. The chapter begins with the analysis of *Harper's* list and a comparative "reading" of two magazine covers. Short texts offer material to understand critical reading, including Jamaica Kincaid's "Girl" and an excerpt from Robin Lakoff's *Language and Woman's Place.* Then a portfolio of readings about cyberspace will enable students to carry out a more sustained rhetorical inquiry, so they can think about each reading in the context of larger arguments and in the discursive context of other kinds of texts that deal with related topics.

Concepts

1. *Reading:* Like writing, reading is a complex process, far from a basic skill, and, like writing, it occurs within a rhetorical situation. Furthermore, although it is frequently assumed that reading is a passive activity—no more than decoding a text—reading turns out, like writing, to involve the performance of all the student's linguistic and cultural problem-solving strategies. The reading analysis modeled in this chapter directs students to think about the author, the audience, and the text: elements of the rhetorical situation that will be further elaborated in Chapter 5. As the far-ranging research on literacy suggests, both reading and writing are deeply implicated in culture and in the interpretations that culture directs. Thus this chapter also directs students' attention to the rhetorical, social, and cultural contexts that shape their interpretations of both written and visual texts. Most students recognize that literature requires interpretation, and they may even see literary interpretation as a practice that requires a lengthy apprenticeship. But they generally have not extended the practice of critical reading to other kinds of texts. Once given the tools for analyzing their reading, students can consciously improve their critical thinking and their selection of materials, rather than relying solely on instructors for direction. The Internet poses additional issues for reading that this chapter will help to discuss.

2. *Writing and reading texts:* Writing results in a visible product; it is a physical activity. Students can easily see that they contribute to writing; they are producers; they *do actively*

write, even though they may not think of themselves as writers. Because of this, it is easier to make students critically aware of their writing processes than of their reading processes. The careful attention to their writing process in this class, however, has made students conscious of their own ability to manage, direct, and control complex processes in ways that will help them a great deal as they turn to thinking about reading and integrating their reading with their writing. What they have found out about the writing process will help the class overcome taking the reading process for granted too. See Robert Tierney and P. David Pierson, "Toward a Composing Process Model of Reading," *Perspectives on Literacy,* ed. Eugene R. Kintgen, Barry M. Kroll, and Mike Rose (Carbondale: Southern Illinois UP, 1988), 261–72.

3. *Genres:* "Genre" is a familiar idea in literature. Your students will probably recognize that a poem, a novel, a short story, and a play all have predictable conventions associated with the genre that help to govern their expectations and their readings. They may find it useful to sharpen their sensitivity to genre by noticing how a set of conventions also governs other written texts, and not only the written, but also familiar communications such as the commercial. Ask if they realize that they have a preference for certain genres of writing. Do their reading and writing preferences differ?

4. *A reading inventory:* The "Guidelines for Conducting a Reading Inventory" in this chapter lead students through a careful reflection on their reading as an experience that engages their feelings, their values, their memories, their sense of inquiry, their bodies, and their academic or nonacademic approach to the task.

5. *Visual texts:* This chapter helps students think about the rhetoric of visual texts by comparing two magazine covers, one from *Wired* and one from the *Thymes.* The discussion draws together the contextual information that one needs to read both visual and written texts from a periodical. Underscoring the ambiguities and suggestiveness of both images, this analysis guides the student through a situated reading and comparison at several levels that include the usual *ethos* of the magazine, audience, distribution, textual contents of this particular issue, and also other possible contexts for the analysis of images, including the history of art and the cultural conventions of representations of hunting. The image becomes a starting point for interrogation, analysis, and perhaps research. "Guidelines for Analyzing Visual Texts" begins with a formal or aesthetic reading as the basis for continuing into a rhetorical analysis. Students will learn more about appeals to *logos, ethos,* and *pathos* in the next chapter; here the point is to emphasize the rhetorical and persuasive aspect of visual texts, and their interaction with written texts. With the significant use of visual texts online and the improved technology permitting students to use visual elements in their work, rhetoric and composition scholars today are increasing their attention to visual texts.

6. *Difficult texts:* Academic work brings students into contact with difficult reading. Learning to read academic (and other) material that resists easy comprehension can challenge your students as much as academic writing. This chapter offers some strategies for reading difficult texts, such as trying to understand the reader's situation implied by the text and reading several times without expecting to understand on the first effort. Students can learn how to approach texts not to master them but to begin a process of reading and rereading that will not reach a conclusive end without years of study. For further reading, see David Bartholomae and Anthony Petrosky, eds., *Ways of Reading: An Anthology for Writers* (5th ed.) (Boston: Bedford/St. Martin's, 1999).

7. *Critical reading and the dialogue:* You may find yourself in all classes repeating the idea that *critical* does not mean "finding something wrong." When we assign a critical review essay, inevitably four or five papers will go through obviously *pro forma* rehearsals of

65

faults to prove they have fulfilled the requirement. This is true of first-year students as well as the more advanced, which suggests a widespread discursive habit at work, not just a misunderstanding about the meaning of the term.

Connecting critical reading with the idea of the dialogue may prove especially helpful to your students' understanding. Students think of the written text as the author's monologue, which they may either accept or reject. Thinking of their interaction with the text as a form of dialogue helps to encourage active understanding, analyzing, and evaluating instead. Classroom dialogue rather than the monologic lecture helps model critical thinking for them as well.

Elizabeth Flynn, in *Gender and Reading* (Baltimore: Johns Hopkins UP, 1986), outlines a way to think about this dialogue that may help students distinguish critical reading from habits of mind that block adequate response. She places readers on a continuum between the extremes of "submissive" and "dominant" responses. Extremely submissive readers lose themselves in the text, and their responses tend simply to amplify the way the text organized material, echoing even its very phrases and vocabulary. Students reading too submissively will frequently repeat phrases such as "then it says" or summarize plots rather than address ideas. Extremely dominant readers don't get beyond their own expectations, finding only what they already expected to learn or rejecting the text out of hand. Phrases such as "I could not relate to this article" obviously signal a failure of dialogue. They also signal a certain unwillingness or inability to analyze what might be causing the gap between reader and writer. Another mark of a dominant reading might be an aberrant interpretation that fails to take into account the apparent intentions of the writer. Between these two extremes comes dialogue, negotiating the differences between the reader's knowledge and expectations and the writer's work.

Using an online resource such as a chat room or a class listserv enables your students to respond to one another's ideas almost as immediately as in class. However, the idea of a critical reading may be lost in the process of hitting the reply button. Here are a couple of ideas to help students engage more fully in the reading part of this interaction. They can respond to material copied in their own email in quotes line by line instead of globally. If you are giving credit for online dialogue, you can require that a part of the reply demonstrate that other messages have been read, by summarizing or paraphrasing them before responding.

8. *Documentation:* Since reading notes, outlines, and summaries of reading materials are frequently used for research papers, they are also frequently the source of problems with documentation and plagiarism. Point out to students that they are obligated to give credit to the source for *ideas* they rephrase in notes as well as for sources of quotations. When they annotate, summarize, or otherwise take notes, they should also be careful to keep track of the reference. This is especially true with electronic texts that may be hard to relocate if no copy is made of them.

9. *Previewing:* The questions for previewing differentiate between print and electronic sources. It's harder to preview electronic texts, with their multiple or anonymous authors, no publisher, and their mutability. The guidelines in this chapter ask students to notice the publishing history of the text (the author, title, format, and organization) and to survey the text quickly to predict what it will include and what response the reader might have to it. Multilingual students will find it especially important to preview. It is, of course, much more difficult to skim texts in another language. Notice that some clues about the usefulness of a text can be uncovered just from entries in the library catalogue. Previewing extends from a decision about whether to read the book at all to organizing the reading work around appropriate questions. Students often imagine they must read everything and under-

stand everything in a text if they are to use it at all, a dangerous assumption when it prevents them from taking on reading that is difficult. Previewing ought to function as an active assessment of the material to be read. Previewing will be an important tool for the research strategies taken up in Chapter 4.

10. *Annotating:* Suggestions for more active ways of interacting with the text than simply underlining include the following:

- Asking questions

- Noting terms and vocabulary, identifying keywords

- Noting main ideas, passages, and points brought up in class

- Responding not only to ideas but also to style

- Using a reading journal for notes and comments

These are ideas worth assigning, for most students won't already have such habits in their repertoire of responses. You might also suggest that students try freewriting in response to reading, using "writing-to-learn" as a tool for critical reading. Occasional pauses in class for this kind of written response will give students an idea of how it might be used on their own.

Visual maps, from outlining to clustering, may also help students annotate and respond to a reading. Note that the logic of outlining is easier to learn when students use it to see the structure of reading than when they use it to make preliminary writing plans. Some students may benefit from other methods of visualizing the structure of readings. Just as many students find mapping or clustering a more accessible tool for organizing their own writing, they may also find a visual diagram easier than an outline for getting at the main points of written material. See Chapter 8's example of clustering for another use of visual representations.

11. *Summarizing:* Many students have difficulty writing a good summary. Since a summary involves finding the main ideas, it involves all the other aspects of critical reading as well. Ask students to write a number of brief summaries of things they have read, such as they might for general notes.

You can also help students work on determining the main idea. Have students do anti-summaries, or "vagaries," collecting divergent and supplementary sentences that they would *not* include in a summary. The object is to avoid clear references to a main idea. Challenge students to come up with the most incoherent or unexpected collage possible from the most rational and coherent discourse, perhaps from technical writing or from philosophy. Historical writing is fun but perhaps too easy. Strengthen the convergent thinking muscles by exercising the opposite as well. This exercise also shows students how well-knit texts work through redundancy and reference to lock all elements together.

12. *Analyzing the argument:* Students often are asked to analyze and evaluate material that does not appear to them to be an argument in the conventional sense because it is presented as a reasoned analysis. The questions in this chapter help make the significant structure visible for students, beginning with the major claim or thesis (whether explicit or implicit) and the appeals that the writer uses to argue in favor of the thesis—to *logos, ethos,* and *pathos.*

As the text notes, multilingual writers may find argument different in North American versions. While the idea of argument implied by a straightforward organization with claim or thesis plus support seems clear and obvious, many cultures would find such a direct approach unsubtle at the least, perhaps rude, and unpersuasive. For an extensive discussion of the way cultural traditions of indirect argument can create student resistance to North American conventions, see Helen Fox, *Listening to the World: Cultural Issues in Academic Writing.*

When students are asked to read and report or to do research, instructors expect them to get at the significance of what they have read. Yet most students have a hard time understanding how to do that. They do not know how to analyze arguments to discover what is at stake. Frequently they do not know enough about the field to be able to recognize what's at stake. And they very often do not read material as if it were an argument at all. Accustomed to reading to recall information, students are used to neglecting the significance of what they read—and furthermore, the context of academic work often requires them to read in this passive way. Students assume that their professor knows what's significant and what is not, and that by the time they reach graduate school, they may find out too. Unfortunately, it's hard for students to write unless they can find some way to figure out the important arguments before they graduate. They have to know enough—or read enough to learn—to get the point of the essay or article or book or story that they are reading. Only then can they write about it.

Students can learn how to be critically self-conscious about their reading. They need to know if they have gotten the point and why or why not. When they reflect about their reading processes, they come to know their own knowledge and experience and their limits. They learn to consider whether they know enough about psychology or computers to read the samples in the text. Some find it an enormous relief to realize that their reading skill is not a matter of raw talent and ability but rather something that is guaranteed to get better as they continue in their education.

13. *Reading online:* While all the strategies in this chapter apply to the reading of online texts, your students will encounter some issues that are specific to electronic technologies and the Internet. Email messages seem closer to speech than to writing, less formal, less decisive, and less permanent—but this is an illusion. Reading email with analytic, critical attention may seem as strange as a critical reading of letters or notes or memos, even though all these forms of pragmatic writing can have widespread practical effects. Yet mailing lists can be good resources for research projects, and email inquiries sometimes bring direct answers to questions. Students can refer to the work on rhetorical situation and email in Chapter 7 to think further about the implications of reading email messages for an academic research project.

Reading online can vary as widely as writing itself, since anything at all may be found on the Internet, from Shakespeare to graffiti. One characteristic of Internet reading should be noted, however. Internet links serve as a new kind of organizational element, different from outlines, tables of contents, or indexes. Links often send the reader beyond the text to a whole new document. The connections to other texts interrupt the linearity of print reading. Instead of a rhetorical organization with Aristotle's beginning, middle, and end, texts become infinite, extending through networks of possible connections in a digressive, associative form of logic. The pressure of this other logic may have interesting consequences in the future for cultural habits of reading. Right now the infinite potential for discovering related material imposes a new imperative on readers: They must impose closure or even refuse to follow up on connections. For example, even a student who chooses nothing more elaborate than checking a term in a Web dictionary must decide when to stop following links in search of an adequate definition.

14. *Portfolio of readings.* This chapter includes a number of readings about the Internet. Jonathan G. S. Koppell's "No 'There' There" provides the reading for analysis in chapter

activities. He introduces a range of questions about the Internet relating to the practice of thinking of it as a place, "cyberspace." The portfolio begins with "Lawrence Lessig, The 'Dinosaurs' Are Taking Over," an online *BusinessWeek* interview with the "Net's most famous freedom fighter." There is a tempering of excitement over technology in "Wow! Or Maybe Just Sort of" by George F. Will. In "How the Web Destroys the Quality of Student Research Papers," David Rothenberg argues that doing research on the Web is making the quality of students' writing decline. Rothenberg is not a technophobe, but rather argues for a reflective approach to writing that sounds very much like the *Work in Progress* project. A brief column fearing literacy decline gets even briefer with text messaging: "OMG, I've got s2pid dzs!" More than literacy may be at risk, warns David Brooks in "Time to Do Everything Except Think." A MasterCard ad, "Seven Days without Email: Priceless," suggests how the geewhiz technology of yesterday has already become the unwelcome pressure of work today. More welcome, obviously, is the chance to put personal opinions out for the world to read, a phenomenon traced in "Web + Log = Blog" by Christopher Elliott. As an example: the "Mister Crunchy" blog, Tuesday, December 31, 2002. The Internet is visual and provides an outlet for people who prefer to remain wordless, as "Picture Pages" by David F. Gallagher explains. Henry Jenkins wonders "Why are Online Personals so Hot?" and also writes in "Digital Land Grab" about the transfer of folk myth to corporate ownership on the Web. Two Dilbert cartoons finish the collection.

There are copies of Web-published documents in the portfolio; you may wish to add online sites you have found for your students to read. The readings offer many related issues for further discussion, reading, and research. They will prompt your students to think about the context for knowledge that electronic technologies introduce. How does their writing interact with cyberspace? These readings point to the rhetorical situations of students not only in a program of writing instruction but also in a culture of information.

Activities

(p. 52) *For Exploration:* This exercise has students freewrite in response to the items in a *Harper's* Index. When they reflect on the experience, perhaps they will see the reader's share in the composing process, as they detect patterns and themes and think about the habits and assumptions they bring to a text, and how facts generate interpretation.

(p. 54) *For Exploration:* Here the chapter provides two readings with extensive following questions to guide student responses. After they have answered the questions, students should reread the selections to note the process of revising in reading. Have students write out their answers to the questions to prepare for the group activity that follows. In each instance, ask them to be sure to think specifically about both differences and similarities in their reading. The first text, "Girl," by Jamaica Kincaid, is a very short story, while the second is an excerpt from Robin Lakoff's *Language and Woman's Place.*

The first question asks students about their expectations. They can discuss their differing responses to the literature and to the more scholarly prose. Perhaps they will notice the difference in genre. The second question asks them to reflect about how their own assumptions and values might have influenced their reading of two texts about women in society. Ask them to notice how the prediction of a kind of bias in the text corresponds to a bias in their responses, whether favorable or resistant. The third question asks them to look more closely at the process of reading to see if they detected shifts in their constructions as they read. The fourth question asks students to look at the roles of author and reader and to compare these in the two texts. The fifth asks what factors most influenced the difficulty of reading. And the sixth asks what kind of person might find the texts easy and pleasurable.

Or if they seemed easy and enjoyable reading, what are the reasons? After these questions, students are asked to reread and to list several ways the second reading was different. These questions focus on the process rather than on the content of the material. They ask students to think about how expectations, their knowledge of terms, values, and previous knowledge might influence reading. Be sure to tell students that the point is to monitor their experience, not to find a correct answer.

(p. 57) *For Collaboration:* Comparing responses to reading helps students see how individual reading processes differ and yet how certain commonalities arise as well. Students should begin to get a sense of how they read in comparison to their peers and perhaps even of ways they can improve their critical reading.

If you have many students who focus only on interest or on liking or not liking the material, try anticipating the rhetorical appeals presented in Chapter 5. Help them become sensitive to appeals that address their powers of critical reasoning, *logos,* as well as *ethos* and *pathos.* They will begin to be able to use the rhetorical terms and concepts as they practice thinking about these questions.

The activity also asks the group to discuss how their expectations and experiences affected their reading. It is a moment when they could usefully talk about both individual and cultural differences. There may be differences in writing practices that would strikingly affect reading—such as, for example, writing from right to left; writing in characters rather than phonetic alphabets. These graphic characteristics have been the object of fascinating speculation—Ezra Pound hoped that the Chinese written character served as an example of how language could more directly convey a concrete image.

(p. 67) *For Exploration:* This exercise asks students to apply the "Guidelines for Analyzing Visual Texts" to the advertisements at the end of Chapter 5 and then to reflect in writing on what they learned by this practice. The analysis and comparison of the two magazine covers from *Wired* and the *Thymes* should help by providing a model. However, analyzing visual texts may be both more familiar and intuitive and less customary in academic settings for many students. To help them develop a vocabulary for such analysis, you may wish to work through one of the advertisements in class first or to ask for students to report their conclusions after they write them.

(p. 72) *For Exploration:* This application asks students to preview the article "No 'There' There" It's important to have students write their answers down so you can compare the initial impressions gained by "skimming." Students who are prone to wildly divergent first impressions of their reading need to know what others see; students who worry about their mildly divergent first impressions need reassurance about the usual range of readings. Press students to make guesses about what they think the point and possible significance of the article will be.

(p. 76) *For Exploration:* This exercise asks students to annotate "No 'There' There" just as they would any reading in preparation to write an essay. Many students annotate only by highlighting; discuss the advantages and disadvantages of this. What might be the consequences (good and bad) for being able to respond verbally or for finding the main ideas?

(p. 77) *For Exploration:* This exercise asks students to write a brief summary of "No 'There' There"—say, half a page to a page. Advise students before they begin that summaries often start most effectively with a sentence naming the piece and stating its thesis or main idea. Summaries also follow the order of ideas and not necessarily the order of presentation in the original. Since the problems students have with summaries carry over into their research papers, try to go through the process thoroughly. Many students have severe problems distinguishing the most important ideas from the illustrations, examples, and evidence that they can safely omit. Discuss what is left out of the summaries as well as what is included. Do you want to discuss the problem of citations at this point? Our students admit learning to summarize for "reports" in elementary school and later by changing a few phrases in the original and leaving other phrases out. So it probably won't suffice to say "put it in your own words."

(p. 79) *For Exploration:* This exercise asks students to use the questions in the text to develop a critical reading of the argument in "No 'There' There," considering claims, the author's interests, evidence, key terms, emotional appeals, and their response as readers, conditioned by their own values and beliefs.

(p. 79) *For Collaboration:* Students need their written preview, annotations, summary, and analysis of argument from the previous activities. This group activity offers the chance for them to compare and contrast responses to "No 'There' There." Then they are to offer conclusions about critical reading that, if all goes well, will reflect both their recognition of the diversity of responses and the idea that there is considerable agreement about the main features of the reading. The most important conclusion they need to draw from this is that their reading is much richer, more complex, and more responsive after they use these critical reading strategies.

For Thought, Discussion, and Writing (p. 80)

Number 1: This exercise asks students to analyze two textbooks they are using for classes. You may want to do this as a specific writing assignment or as a group activity. You may also wish to encourage students in the habit of such analysis. Have them record their observations in their writer's notebooks, and invite them to do the same for other reading assignments. Give them an opportunity from time to time in small groups and in class discussions to focus on the context of their reading. Ask them frequently what makes the works they read effective or ineffective.

Number 2: This exercise asks students to do a critical reading of the materials on cyberspace included in the chapter. Then it provides a series of questions for them to answer as they reflect on their reading.

"Lawrence Lessig, The 'Dinosaurs' Are Taking Over," an online *BusinessWeek* interview, raises issues about the economy of the Internet. Do your students view the Internet as endangered by older institutions?

In "Wow! Or Maybe Just Sort of," George F. Will describes a generational difference about the use of the Internet. Perhaps students can think about how his tone affects their reading.

"How the Web Destroys the Quality of Student Research Papers" by David Rothenberg gives students a professor's view of evaluation. Do they agree with his standards for the papers he is reading?

"OMG, I've got s2pid dzs!" is about text messaging. They can probably agree or disagree knowledgeably.

David Brooks, in "Time to Do Everything Except Think," also worries about the negative effects of technology. With this reading, students should be able to understand a more complex critique of the Internet.

A MasterCard ad, "Seven Days without Email: Priceless," reflects a certain disaffection with the Internet. Is this a critique or does it assume agreement?

Christopher Elliott, in "Web + Log = Blog," describes a new Internet phenomenon. Students can ask whether this provides an answer to some of the other criticisms of the Internet.

Does the "Mister Crunchy" blog, Tuesday, December 31, 2002, refute these critiques? Is a "blog" a kind of vernacular, democratic culture—or an erosion of literacy?

David F. Gallagher explains in "Picture Pages" how people use the visual possibilities of the Internet.

Henry Jenkins interests himself in the democratic creativity of the Internet in "Why are Online Personals so Hot?" and also worries in "Digital Land Grab" about the silencing of vernacular inventions such as fan sites by corporations protecting copyrights.

With these selections, students have the resources to begin thinking about whether they are critical of the Internet's effects on their writing, or see it as a place for creativity, invention, and new possibilities.

The question to guide student responses ask them to make comparisons among these texts. They are to keep careful track of their expectations and impressions, first from skimming and then from a more analytic reading. In particular they are to think about the relationship of author and readers for each, their relationship to one another, and then to develop through answering the questions some responses to the ideas about education that emerge from their encounter.

Number 3: Next, students are asked to return to "No 'There' There" and to think about how subsequent readings might have altered their reading of this text. Ask them to identify explicitly juxtapositions of texts that alter their reading. Which readings seem to see the Web primarily as positive, an improvement in access to information, and which see it as the object of critique?

Number 4: Finally, the chapter closes with an essay assignment. Students are to write their own views on the subjects discussed in the readings. Alternatively, they might write an essay responding to one of the readings.

Suggestions for Further Activities

Number 1: Ask students to interview an expert or a more advanced student in their area about their reading. If you are teaching lower-division students, you might ask them to consult with upper-division students in their major; if undergraduates, ask them to interview graduate students or other knowledgeable sources. Multilingual students may benefit from interviewing a student who speaks their language. What do they typically read in classes in their field? Are they assigned online reading? How much reading is generally assigned? How difficult do they find this reading? Do their instructors discuss these readings extensively in class, or do they assume that students have assigned materials and discuss other subjects? What role do the readings typically play in these courses as a whole? Do they use the Internet extensively? What advice would these upper-class students give to a new student about the best way to approach the reading required in this field? (See Section 2 in this manual for a discussion of interviewing.) Ask students to report the results in class. This exercise offers the opportunity for students to research and describe the contribution of reading to their rhetorical situation in college, so it is well worth going on to assign an essay that summarizes their results.

Like most inquiry that aims to investigate genuinely interesting questions, your students' work will encounter real-life difficulties. When they report their findings to each other in groups and to the class as a whole, they may have wildly varying information. And some of their interviews may not be very reliable, either because the answers are superficial rather than considered or because the interviewees don't know everything they should about the reading they are expected to do. For example, juniors and seniors do not always know systematic ways to review the literature for a research project or what "the literature" might include in their discipline, even though they may be trying to do research projects. Since this exercise explores the realities of the academic writing and reading situation, you can usefully move to discussions that compare and contrast the ways you are handling reading material in this class to the various practices in other classes on campus. You may find the uses of online texts to be especially mixed. The opportunity to be pragmatic and descriptive will probably interest your students very much and be useful to them as well.

Number 2: There are a number of additional ways you might use this chapter's readings with your class. Students can do a limited research paper—limited, that is, to using only these sources, so that students don't do additional research. From their analysis of these readings, they might write a paper on the Internet. Or the readings can serve as the starting point for a more extended research project. Each reading opens up a different kind of question about cyberspace: You could assign groups to several of the topics suggested by the readings for a collaborative writing project, perhaps involving additional searches on the Web.

Chapter 4: Understanding the Research Process

Chapter 4 approaches research as a rhetorical process—an integral part of the reading and writing relationship, particularly in academic settings where learning is a primary goal. Your students will go step by step through the process of composing research projects, with a completed research paper as an example at the end of the chapter. Exercises for students involve them in research activities but not necessarily in writing a whole paper from first to last. Rather, this chapter should enable students to see research as a possible aspect of most of their academic writing and to integrate parts of the research process into reading and writing wherever it might be appropriate. The first two sets of guidelines help students assess the relevance of research to a project—whether it is a term paper, an oral presentation, a review, or any other writing assignment. Then the chapter gives guidelines for managing logistics—often the greatest difficulty for students with little research experience. These guidelines show students how to plan ahead and be systematic, making copies of the bibliographical information for cited material. This is part of a research process that might be integrated into most writing projects and not limited to the specific kind of assignment called a "research paper." Thinking of research as part of the productive or "creative" phase of invention helps to locate writing within a history of reading, of texts. An extensive discussion of plagiarism has been added in this edition. A certain level of plagiarism exists on writing projects that are not thought of as research projects because students use other sources to supplement their writing and simply don't keep track of them to give credit where credit is due. Adding "research" as a usual and conscious part of the writing process means that research should be included in planning and that the evaluation of sources is included in the invention process. There are separate guidelines for evaluating print sources and for evaluating online sources in this chapter. Finally, there is material on documentation, and a sample research essay with examples of MLA–style documentation.

Concepts

1. *Research:* This chapter defines research as part of a process of inquiry that might include print sources, online sources, interviews, or other field research, such as questionnaires. A clear idea of the project's goal and active evaluation of sources becomes increasingly important as the quantity of information increases. While online research may connect your students to endless links on a topic, they must as never before actively limit and select what interests them and what might be reliable. You can help them to discover that the more thoughtful, extended analysis available in print may make it easier to frame an idea or a topic purposefully. Seeing research as a process of inquiry and evaluation that connects both reading and writing, students may also come to see that the central aim goes

beyond piling up facts and printouts. They must exercise rhetorical judgment. This insight will be especially important to them in future writing tasks, for the testimony of professors increasingly points to student difficulties writing good research papers with materials gathered online. The abundance is apt to be overwhelming. This chapter emphasizes the variability of the research process, making a number of suggestions to enhance the discovery and elaboration of ideas. This reflects the principle that research is a type of *invention,* collaborative invention perhaps, not a matter of locating authorities to quote. The students must still behave as writers, actively determining their purpose and carrying out research accordingly.

Ask students to think about their knowledge of the library and freewrite for ten minutes about what they know. This can provide you with valuable information about your students' problems with the library. Either collect the freewrites or take oral reports. Your students' responses will give you some advance warning about problems with upcoming work on academic writing and reading. Since multilingual writers may need extra help with research, you might contact your library to learn how they prefer to work with such students. You may want to find out if your library has brochures, tours, or special introductory programs for students. They may need specific information about access to electronic databases and Internet resources at the library. Additionally, you might want to discuss research sources other than books, some of which may not be in the library: research on film or using videotapes, for example.

2. *Evaluating print resources:* Making evaluations for research is especially difficult for students and critical for success. The Guidelines offer multiple strategies for evaluating, with a series of specific questions to help students think about the library sources they have found. If you are working through a research topic with your class or intend to do so later in the term, you will want to have them bring sources to class so you can address these questions with as much detailed attention as you might give a written draft. Print sources have more well-established institutions of evaluation than online sources, but students may not be familiar with them.

3. *Evaluating Web sites and Web pages:* Issues of credibility, writing quality (or even correctness), bias, timeliness, and context become acute with online sources. After reading the analysis of a Web site in the chapter, using the Guidelines, you may wish to analyze one or two more sample Web sites in class. Comparing the evaluation of print sources and the evaluation of online sources can enable your class to discuss the issues of publication and access to publication that surround our use of sources. This will prepare for the later discussion of differing discourse communities in Chapter 6.

4. *Using sources by quoting, paraphrasing, and summarizing:* The chapter discusses the three ways of integrating source material into a piece of writing. Most students could benefit from practicing the ways to do this carefully (even graduate students misuse quotations and underuse summaries). The most common error in the use of sources is to quote too much. A paper littered with blocks of quotations has probably not integrated sources into the argument very well. Often students make the mistake of using the quotation to make the argument, rather than putting it in their own words, so that they lose the line of thought in their writing. The long quotation needs to be introduced by a sentence or a phrase. But quotations longer than three lines, requiring a block offset, should be used very sparingly in most student writing. On the other hand, keywords or phrases in quotations can become important terms in a discussion.

Paraphrasing and summarizing are important tools for incorporating research. You may want to assign class sessions to explaining these, practicing a model class paraphrase and summary and then discussing the students' work on the first exercise at the end of the chapter.

5. *Interviews, questionnaires, observations:* These and other sources of information in "field research" can be important as well. While disciplines that use these methods extensively (such as sociology, political science, and anthropology) have thoroughly considered protocols for them, students can also use them less formally (and social scientists would warn, with no right to claim scientific validity). The text provides a set of "Guidelines for Conducting Interviews" and "Guidelines for Designing and Using Questionnaires," as well as some suggestions for using close observation as a research tool. Ethnographic observation in particular has become a widely employed research method. Students gain considerable critical understanding of cultures through such observation. As anthropologists have been careful to warn us, however, the study of other people's behavior and values always needs to take account of the beholder's perspective as well, to make explicit the inevitable ethnocentrism and bias and correct it to the maximum extent possible.

6. *Plagiarism:* The "Guidelines for Understanding and Avoiding Plagiarism" advise your students to be very careful and accurate about making notes and keeping track of bibliographical information as they read. This need for care is not always what students think of in connection with the problem of plagiarism. Rather, they imagine that if they are not guilty of intentionally misrepresenting someone else's work as their own by using another student's paper or downloading a paper from the Internet, they will not need to worry about the increasingly strict consequences they might face for plagiarism. You may find that working with your students on note taking, with some amount of spot-checking, will help solve both kinds of plagiarism problems.

Activities

(p. 104) *For Exploration:* This activity asks students to freewrite about past experiences with research, both satisfying and difficult, to write a paragraph of reflection about the two, and to write two or three suggestions for making research more satisfying in the future. If they have had interesting and diverse experiences that others could benefit from knowing, you can have them discuss these in small groups. Multilingual writers will also be able to discuss differences in research methods and goals in such small groups.

(p. 124) *For Exploration:* This activity has students conduct a Web search, evaluate two sites (using the "Guidelines for Evaluating Web Sites and Web Pages"), and then write a paragraph or two about the results. The usefulness of this exercise depends in part on their having chosen a search term that might be involved in a research project, so you may want to ask them to think about the "conversation" their project might imply. You could have them try two or three searches to find out what, in fact, the conversation seems to be and to choose sites that have potential interest. The names of contemporary celebrities, for example, often yield numerous fan-based Web pages without much to evaluate, since they are largely epideictic. The "conversation" around them is celebratory or personal-biographical. An issue such as "sweatshops," on the other hand, might produce a number of sites that would be important to evaluate. The online "conversation" is implicated in several arguments, there is plenty of bias, and some sites are more credible than others.

For Thought, Discussion, and Writing (p. 154)

Number 1: This exercise asks students to paraphrase and summarize a paragraph from one of the Chapter 3 readings. Depending on how this seems to go, you may decide to expand the assignment to other readings that appear in Chapter 3 or that you bring into the class. If your class emphasizes a research paper, you will find this writing of summaries an especially important process, one that your students may come back to later. Some writing instructors devote a week or more of the term to summary writing, since it is so central to doing research.

Emphasize as you do this that summaries and paraphrases as well as quotes need documentation. You can ask them to provide that documentation as part of this exercise.

Number 2: This exercise has students conduct a search on the Web, refine the search and search again, and then write about the process. If you wish, ask them also which search engines they use and why. If you want to have them practice more searches, have them compare the results.

Number 3: This exercise asks students to evaluate two of the sites located through the search they carried out in the previous activity using the "Guidelines for Evaluating Web Sites and Web Pages." They should write a paragraph or two to record their thoughts. You might ask them to draw conclusions about whether they improved the quality of sites found when they refined search mechanisms.

Part Two: Rhetorical Situations

In Part Two of *Work in Progress*, students learn how to understand the concept of a rhetorical situation and how to build on their own rhetorical sensitivity to learn from a more explicit process of analysis. The section shows throughout how reading and writing are connected activities. Chapter 5 helps students situate themselves as writers; Chapter 6 helps them see reading as a situated process, in relationship to communities of discourse; and Chapter 7 addresses the particular situations of online writing.

Chapter 5: Analyzing Rhetorical Situations

In This Chapter: Guidelines for Analyzing Your Rhetorical Situation (p. 160)

Chapter 5 defines the concept of "rhetorical situation," showing how to analyze it and how a more acute sense of the relations among the elements of rhetoric and the world will enable your students to write more effectively. Your students have perhaps already learned to think about their readers when they write. They need to understand that the "reader" is both more and less specific and concrete than they think. To help them develop confidence in making judgments, you might stress that, just as the rules for writing are not absolute, so no magic or mathematical formulae exist for figuring out what the rhetorical situation is or how to address readers. A writing project involves making choices; taking the various factors into account helps point toward a solution, but it also helps to point out complexity that might come into play.

Greater complexity helps improve writing, but students sometimes resist acknowledging it: They want to intuit the rhetorical situation or reduce it to easily controlled dimensions so they can solve the writing problem expeditiously. Some say they feel blocked when there's too much to take into account. And of course most of us as teachers are used to hearing students say plaintively, "I don't know what you want," even when we think we've made an assignment crystal clear. To help students gain better control over defining their writing tasks, *Work in Progress* provides general Guidelines for analyzing the rhetorical situation in this chapter. For a list of workable criteria for academic writing, see the discussion of analyzing an assignment in Chapter 14.

Analyzing the rhetorical situation may seem fascinating if it is genuinely practical or demanding, and difficult if it is just an abstract exercise. In talking about the rhetorical situation, it helps to keep students thinking concretely about their actual situation as writers. Ask students for example, about how the geography and climate are shaping their prose, using regional writers for comparison with themselves. You might ask how their peer group or other groups they feel part of affect their writing. Furthermore, the classroom itself is always part of the rhetorical situation for students. For instance, students' essays are almost always, in some respect, an argument for a positive evaluation. (Don't you sometimes feel that argument as a subtext when you grade, as a demand for reasons if you don't give an A or B?) Keep on discussing your class itself as a rhetorical situation, using it as an ongoing, complex, rich, and concrete example.

Your own classroom is also likely to provide a multitude of examples of cultural diversity, whether economic, regional, linguistic, gendered, or other. Cultural assumptions, of course, are the often unspoken source of students' difficulties with any specific rhetorical situation. In this sense, the cultural situation is not the same as the rhetorical situation, even though it influences writer, reader, and text. Multicultural students are probably more conscious of differing cultural influences than most, and can perhaps help all your students become more conscious about the cultural assumptions they are making. All your students share to some degree the experience of entering into the new subculture of the academy and trying to understand its traditions and conventions.

Furthermore, too many choices, too much diversity or newness, and a hyperconsciousness of one's own assumptions will combine to be very disorienting. Thus multilingual and multicultural students will probably have a more complex understanding of the rhetorical situation, and at times more difficulty resolving the complexity by making choices. Help from you and perhaps from tutors will be important.

Concepts

1. *Rhetorical situation:* This chapter defines the concept of rhetorical situation in terms of the writer, the reader, and the text. If your course structure permits it, you may want to discuss the rhetorical situation more broadly as well. Critical theory has led many in English departments to conclude with Terry Eagleton that the discipline might best be described as rhetorical studies. Furthermore, much recent work in sociology, anthropology, psychology, political science, and philosophy has also demonstrated a turn to rhetoric, a sense that culture might be defined in terms of rhetorical situations. Inquiry like that of Clifford Geertz shows how rhetorical analysis could involve everything we know—our knowledge of culture (the way it works, its codes and conventions), our grammatical competence, our vocabulary, and our knowledge about the world (what it is and what it ought to be). Cultural studies are inherently rhetorical. The problem, then, is to separate out what is relevant and needed for a given writing project without being too reductive or egocentric.

The idea of the rhetorical situation explained in this chapter reflects a cultural tradition that comes down to us from Aristotle, through numerous interpretations. As one of the "Notes to Multilingual Writers" (p. 170) says, other cultures may not think easily in terms of three separate appeals to *ethos, logos,* and *pathos,* for example. You can teach the usefulness of these categories without assuming that they are universal, however. For a contemporary understanding of the "rhetorical situation," together with debates about how its cultural context might be addressed, see the bibliography below.

This chapter asks students to think about writing projects in several different situations. Using letter writing as a familiar form, the text begins by asking students to consider the rhetorical differences between, for example, personal correspondence and email. To provide an artificially limited rhetorical situation for students to focus on, ask students to write brief assignments from roles. You might use these exercises as in-class writing, perhaps for groups to do together. You can even give them suggestions—sometimes playful and then the more extreme and melodramatic the better (such as this: "Write a letter to the bank about an error—first as a well-known millionaire and then as a poor old semi-illiterate who has just lost his job"). Perhaps you can have them choose an unfamiliar role—asking the women to write as men and the men as women. Although you probably don't want to instill the ancient association of rhetoric with sophistry, or arguing both sides, you can exaggerate the theatricality and role playing in the classroom to help students see the significance of the rhetorical situation.

You can help your students develop their rhetorical sensitivity, their tacit, common-sense knowledge about rhetorical situations by encouraging them to ask again and again about different kinds of texts: What makes this writing work? What makes it effective—from the perspective of writer, reader, text?

This chapter connects analyzing the rhetorical situation specifically with planning to write, establishing intentions and goals. The "Guidelines for Analyzing Your Rhetorical Situation" (p. 160) will help students turn analysis into strategy.

For further discussion of the rhetorical situation, you might want to consult the following works, listed in chronological order:

Bitzer, Lloyd F. "The Rhetorical Situation." *Philosophy and Rhetoric* 1 (Jan. 1968): 1–14.

Vatz, Richard E. "The Myth of the Rhetorical Situation." *Philosophy and Rhetoric* 6 (Summer 1973): 154–61.

Consigny, Scott. "Rhetoric and Its Situations." *Philosophy and Rhetoric* 7 (Summer 1974): 175–86.

Jamieson, Kathleen M. Hall. "Generic Constraints and the Rhetorical Situation." *Philosophy and Rhetoric* 7 (Summer 1974): 162–70.

Brinton, Alan. "Situation in the Theory of Rhetoric." *Philosophy and Rhetoric* 14 (Fall 1981): 234–48.

Biesecker, Barbara A. "Rethinking the Rhetorical Situation from within the Thematic of Difference." *Philosophy and Rhetoric* 22 (1989): 110–30.

2. *The writer:* This chapter portrays the writer in terms of *persona, voice,* and *ethos.* To some extent, we choose an appropriate image of self and of character when we write. In other words, the writer is rhetorical, produced by the text, and writers need to change the *persona* representing themselves to suit different rhetorical situations. Students identify so closely with the *I* of their writing that they believe they always write simply as themselves. They may not notice how naturally they change registers when they move from informal to formal situations, for example. Try explaining this with an analogy: You change your *persona* in response to a situation, just as you change clothes—wearing jeans for one occasion and formal dress for another. You can probably help most students improve their control of the rhetorical situation by asking them to think about just how the writer needs to "sound" or "look" to be convincing. Students who have already internalized a good repertoire of successful approaches to writing will be able to write unselfconsciously, to simply feel "sincere" and also write well, but other students will be liberated if you encourage them to write parodies or play roles.

This analogy to theatricality has, of course, some limitations: Good writers seldom adopt more than a few roles or "personae." Instead, they develop authority, a "voice," made up of knowledge, experience, character, commitment, and a deep understanding of appropriate conventions. Student writers suffer because they haven't done this yet. Their recurring attention to the problem of "who is the writer here" will help them acquire strategies and devices that work for them.

When you have students consider the analysis of *ethos,* you can emphasize the important element of credibility, the relationship of *ethos* to ethics and to the standing of one's argument in the community. Thus while a certain playfulness and theatricality will improve their flexibility and open up possibilities for their position as a writer, the question of commitment to what they say is also part of analyzing the rhetorical situation.

3. *Readers:* Unlike an audience physically present at an oral presentation or performance, the rhetorical reader in a writing situation does not necessarily correspond to a single person or group of people. Instead, the reader holds a role or position in the discourse that the writer and the situation both help to define. For example, think about the readers of the public service announcements appearing at the end of Chapter 5. The writers of these examples didn't know more about the individual reader than information about the context could provide. In fact, these writers had an obligation not just to appeal to the reader but to create the reader as a participant. In a sense, then, the reader is anyone who might respond to the text's address. The writer develops a relationship with the reader, cuing the reader about the role to take.

For these reasons, students need to imagine their readers clearly and sympathetically, neither viewing them as the blank unknown nor limiting them to knowable persons such as instructors or the other members of their writing groups. Don't let your students get trapped by their tendency to think of readers too literally, as if they need a precise psychological profile of an individual or a demographic analysis of a crowd before they can think about the reader. The reader exists as a relationship and a role in the rhetorical situation. For further reading about the concept of reader and audience, see the following:

Ede, Lisa. "Audience: An Introduction to Research." *CCC* 35 (1984): 140–54.

Ede, Lisa, and Andrea Lunsford. "Audience Addressed/Audience Invoked: The Role of Audience in Composition Theory and Pedagogy." *CCC* 35 (May 1984): 155–70.

Ede, Lisa, and Andrea Lunsford. "Representing Audience: 'Successful' Discourse and Disciplinary Critique." *CCC* 47.2 (May 1996): 167–79.

4. *Text:* You might want to point out to your students that the word *text* in this book refers to all examples of writing and not just to a book required for a class. When students analyze a text, they need to consider the conventions of form, style, and logic that govern its presentation. Although rhetoric evolved from the study of speeches and students can benefit from analyzing the rhetorical situations of oral presentations on television and in classrooms, a written text differs from spoken language in ways that sometimes create difficulties for students. Texts operate according to conventions and codes of written language—and genres—that students frequently don't know or haven't yet mastered. Some students may not have read enough to develop firm common sense about academic writing. They will benefit by consistently thinking about the conventions of form and evidence that might apply in a given situation and by learning to seek out models to help them acquire these conventions. You might explore rhetorical conventions that they do know well—such as, for example, the Top Ten List that David Letterman uses—so they can see what kinds of tacit understandings might be included.

5. *Aristotle's appeals:* This chapter introduces the traditional Aristotelian categories for persuasive appeals: *logos, pathos,* and *ethos.* Your students may not be used to thinking about writing as an act of persuasion (or, indeed, as practical in any respect whatsoever), even though it's easy enough to point out the persuasive component of all writing. The analysis of *logos, pathos,* and *ethos* by Tova Johnson and Brandon Barrett should provide helpful examples. Even images, such as those in advertisements, work not as objective evidence but as means of persuasion, in ways your students can probably specify. Examples at the end of the chapter demonstrate the three appeals using images as well as text.

Later, when students look at academic writing, you can point out how more subtle forms of the same appeals work to make a text authoritative and convincing. Scholarly work in fields like women's studies often points out the persuasive aspect of even the most objective-seeming writing. See, for example, Evelyn Fox Keller's *Gender and Science.*

The appeal to *logos* is based on evidence and reasoning. So it is the most powerful appeal in most academic writing. Remind your students to consider the appeal to reason even in papers that they do not regard as objective, papers about issues or personal experiences. For example, their analyses of their own writing histories or processes go beyond an appeal to *pathos* or *ethos,* even though those are the primary appeals.

The appeal to *pathos* is based on emotion, or on values, beliefs, and desires. When students think about how to effectively address readers, they need to think about the readers' values and attitudes as well as more obvious kinds of feelings. What assumptions are the readers likely to accept? Aristotle lists certain commonplaces that human beings are likely to share or that apply commonsensically to large groups of people. For example, the old are likely to respond to appeals for greater security, the young to appeals for change. Through class discussions, you can elicit your students' contemporary understanding of what might seem commonsense knowledge. You can help students distinguish between more or less universal appeals such as those Aristotle describes and appeals that are culture-specific: for example, the appeal to explore new frontiers that is so familiar to North American audiences.

Many students have studied persuasion as part of units on propaganda and logical fallacies. Sometimes they have translated the idea of logical fallacy into a rule banning everything that is not *logos.* They may think you want them to write dry-as-dust informational prose, appealing to evidence alone. You can point out that sometimes a heavy emphasis on *logos* is inappropriate. Further, writers who rigorously segregate *pathos* from *logos* are apt to produce unmitigated sentiment or unmitigated fact. If students are encouraged to consider all three appeals carefully, they will find it easier to plan balanced papers that are well adapted to their purposes.

The third appeal, to *ethos,* turns to the good character of the writer—to the audience's willingness to believe what the writer says. The *persona* adopted by the writer helps convey the appeal to *ethos.* Because students are particularly vulnerable, writing from a position of little authority, they often struggle with angst about being convincing. This is not a problem that finding a personal voice can fully solve, and it is not easily resolved by imitating the *ethos* of another either (including the teacher). Since *ethos* is deeply involved with the interaction of individual, ethics, and rhetorical situation, it is an especially difficult but fruitful starting point for discussion.

Activities

(p. 159) *For Exploration:* This application asks students to apply their understanding of the elements of rhetoric to three letter-writing situations.

- The first, an application for an internship in the students' major fields, requires an academic/professional role and a limited purpose. Will they need to follow a set of specific forms or guidelines? Who could they ask about the requirements of such an application?

- The second, a letter to a friend whose parents have recently decided to divorce, poses its own difficulties. Some students will reply that they would never write such a letter. Ask them, perhaps, how they imagine the role and purpose of other writers of that letter.

- The third, a posting to the class Web site, asks students to integrate personal and academic roles in a quasi-public voice. Your students will be assessing the class's reception of Web postings.

Most students will find that they already have and will enjoy making explicit a considerable amount of tacit knowledge about rhetorical situations. Some students have difficulty doing this analysis but that difficulty may not always be a symptom of ineptitude. (At least one good student wished we would just get to the point and tell him the right way to do the letters.) These are students who need to understand that rhetorical reasoning doesn't involve a single right solution but requires them to make decisions based on ways of thinking about rhetorical situations.

It may help in such cases to give students sample materials by someone else to read and discuss first the kinds of choices other writers have made. If they are working in groups and exchanging the answers to this question, members of the group will be helped by hearing the variety of acceptable ways that others might handle the rhetorical situation.

(p. 166) *For Exploration:* This activity asks students to decide whether Annette Chambers's essay ("So, What Are You Doing This Weekend?") achieves the goals she has set for herself. This work allows them to rehearse the kind of careful analysis they should apply to each other's papers when they function as readers.

(p. 168) *For Exploration:* This activity asks students to read introductions from two articles about stress. They will talk about the differences between an article that tells a story and invites the reader's identification with a personal experience of stress and an article that summarizes information and invites the reader to think analytically about the relationship of stress to certain kinds of work. You might ask your students to look in particular at the pattern of common assumptions in the two introductions—what the writer *assumes* that the reader will already know or agree with or want to know. What do they assume about ordinary readers? Ask them as well to think about the stylistic cues—sentence length, complexity of syntax, diction. If you have time, you might also ask students if they think the way a text addresses them could change their minds. Can they see how the role of the reader might act as a means of persuasion or how the writer, by invoking the role of the reader, might direct the reader's response?

(p. 175) *For Exploration:* This activity asks students to apply their understanding of appeals—*logos, pathos,* and *ethos*—to student essays. Like the earlier analysis of a student essay, this practice will help students not only with their own writing but also with giving helpful responses to each other's papers. Tova Johnson and Brandon Barrett are describing their majors. These papers may allow your students to discuss the role of disciplinary interests in defining a rhetorical situation.

For Thought, Discussion, and Writing (p. 175)

Number 1: This exercise asks students to find an example of writing that fails to address the reader effectively, and to write an explanation. If you have students bring their examples to class for group discussion, you can ask them to find out whether other readers might be more responsive, and then to add a few sentences about how this extended inquiry did or did not change their minds about the rhetorical effectiveness of their examples.

Number 2: The chapter ends with three advertisements for students to analyze, using the categories of Aristotle's appeals to *ethos, pathos,* and *logos.*

- The first, an American Legacy Foundation advertisement against smoking, uses "handwritten" notes and an anguished photograph to personalize their message. It moves from the painful last thoughts of a dying mother and wife to the angry, assertive tone of the victim. How can she write that she is dying and in the same note underscore that "We will win"? Do your students believe this ad is primarily directed to smokers or to their families? In what way might it be directed to tobacco companies?
- The second, an American Century advertisement, has a photograph and a story about the founder's daily lunch of a peanut butter sandwich. This "institutional" advertising is about company values and "American Values," as the title says. Why would investment managers want to emphasize saving lunch money? Why would a marketing department choose *The New Yorker* for this message?
- The third, a Charles Schwab advertisement, has far more print copy than the others. What are the visual elements here? What is the answer to the question in the headline: "What Can I Do?" Are there in fact other questions being answered here as well?

Suggestions for Further Activities

Number 1: Ask students to write an analysis of their rhetorical situation for an essay or writing project on which they are currently working. If your next assignment *is* to do a rhetorical analysis of some kind (for instance, of the material at the end of Chapter 5), your students will encounter the metalinguistic nature of this kind of analysis: It can always comment on itself. Or you may wish to assign a persuasive essay like the examples used in the chapter. Frequently the "reader" in this analysis will be other class members and yourself—an interesting reason for general discussion.

Here are some brief suggestions for essay assignments:

a. Write a description of a place you particularly enjoy for readers of a travel magazine or for a brochure designed to inform tourists about your area. Choose a specific magazine, and analyze its likely readers, or interview a local travel agent or member of the Chamber of Commerce about the likely readers of a travel brochure.

b. Write a persuasive essay about an issue of importance to you, asking your readers to take some specific step as a consequence of your argument. Choose an issue and an audience that you know personally very well.

c. Write a response to an article or essay or advertisement. Begin by describing your experience as a reader. Then analyze its rhetorical situation and its appeals to the reader.

d. Write an essay examining the context of your writing, placing yourself in your region of the country, or as a member of a group or a historical period.

For Group Work: Exchange the above analyses, and discuss various responses. This activity offers students a chance to check their understanding of the rhetorical situation against the way a partner perceives it and to make suggestions to each other. If this is a good time for a group analysis of the way students see the rhetorical situation of your composition classroom, use one pair as a "model" exchange for class discussion after everyone has had a chance to talk. Whole-group discussion makes less sense here if the assignment is not the same for everyone.

Number 2: Ask students to draw up a plan for writing an essay (like Tova Johnson's or Brandon Barrett's) based on Aristotle's three appeals. This activity asks them to translate analysis into a plan for action, making decisions about their writing on the basis of thinking through how they will appeal to their readers.

This is a particularly important principle to rehearse, a process that you will want students to use every time they write. You might want to point this out and return to it from time to time during the term, asking again for explicit or written statements reflecting the results of students' rhetorical analysis. You might also point out that what seems like a somewhat artificial exercise right now will eventually, with practice, begin to seem a natural part of planning to write.

Number 3: Ask students to compare and contrast the rhetorical situations of two letters, one that was easy to write and one that was difficult. Then have them reflect about what makes writing easier and consider the ways that factors outside themselves might influence the difficulty of a writing task. It encourages them to consider their context as part of the job. This is particularly helpful if you have students who are having difficulty understanding the concept of the *rhetorical situation.*

Chapter 6: Thinking about Communities and Conventions

Chapter 6 introduces students to the role played by textual convention in changing rhetorical situations. It emphasizes the interconnectedness of literacy, showing how both reading and writing are acts of composing and how writing depends on knowledge gained from reading. It demonstrates how students may become more conscious about making connections between their reading and their writing, showing them how to read like a writer, rhetorically. This is a powerful means of access to understanding the various disciplinary conventions. The assumption that students can learn something about the available forms of writing by reading selections of rhetorical material is not new; it has, in fact, underwritten the long tradition of using rhetorical readers in composition classes. However, *Work in Progress* emphasizes the rhetorical situation of texts, directing students to pay attention to forms in specific contexts rather than forms artificially cut off from their connections to discursive communities and their intellectual and cultural history. This chapter pragmatically addresses the rhetorical situations of academic discourse and encourages students to become more critically aware of their variety. Specifically, by examining three articles by Deborah Tannen, students can see how she makes changes to suit the conventions of very different audiences.

Concepts

1. *Academic discourse:* Most rhetoric and composition theorists agree that the academic reading and writing tasks students will encounter taking classes belong to a rather specialized discourse. Part of what we are teaching is how to succeed in this academic discourse community, which may be alien indeed to some students and questionable to others. *Work in Progress* does not ask your students to master a specific form of writing; rather, it encourages them to develop a readerly, rhetorical approach to writing that will enable them to assess any discourse's possibilities and limits. You may wish to help them analyze, for example, the rather strict set of methods represented in scientific writing. Students get into trouble writing as if a single format and style were appropriate for any course. A piece of writing that makes the conventions strange or obvious can help: The chapter includes samples from a medieval guide, *The Principles of Letter Writing.* You may also wish to help them look for the cultural and social implications of discourses. Your students should learn not only to emulate but also to critique certain examples of academic writing. This chapter includes an exercise about textbooks. For an essay discussing the broader issues of academic discourse, see Peter Elbow, "Reflections on Academic Discourse: How It Relates to Freshmen and Colleagues," *College English* 53.2 (Feb. 1991): 135–55.

2. *Textual conventions:* This chapter directs students to pay attention to the functions of conventions ranging from the general to the specific: *persona,* genre, style, organization, and diction, among others. Rather than looking at these conventions formally, out of context, this chapter shows students how to analyze the ways the rhetorical situation might condition the choice of form and the ways that conventions shape reading. A letter from Monica Molina tells of her process learning to write grant proposals, using models of former proposals and consultation with her boss. Introductions to three different reports of research on argument by Deborah Tannen show how textual conventions shape the reader's experience and how some conventions—understood in the context of a professional journal—can even limit the ability of the uninitiated to understand at all. These textual conventions, bound to the rhetorical situation, are part of what students will learn about their disciplines. Students will improve their reading if they understand that they need to look for such

conventions, and they will improve their writing if they understand that textual conventions can give them accepted ways of organizing material. This understanding, in other words, will help demystify the reading as well as the writing process and alert students to recognize the role that textual conventions play in our construction and interpretation of texts. As they begin to look for such conventions, reading like a writer, they become a "noticing" reader, newly aware of what works and how it works.

Activities

(p. 182) *For Exploration:* In this activity, students use freewriting to open up a comparison of online writing and print writing. The next chapter includes more extended series of exercises to develop this line of inquiry with the new conventions being established by electronic technologies. For the moment, you might simply note that the changing status of online writing vividly demonstrates how dynamic the processes of textuality can be.

(p. 184) *For Exploration:* This exercise asks your students to write a paragraph about each of the introductions to three articles by Deborah Tannen. These analyses should reveal some of students' tacit assumptions about the meanings of forms, connecting conventions of writing with readers' resultant assumptions about an article's intention or purpose. Your students will probably vary widely in their ability to decode the formats of these introductions. Some will simply get stuck at saying the first one's easier than the others. To help improve the ability to analyze and decode conventions, discuss the results of the critical reading together with the comparison of these introductions *before* students do the next exercise.

(p. 194) *For Exploration:* The questions in this exercise lead students to examine further the differences and similarities among Deborah Tannen's three introductions.

1. This question asks students to examine the examples used in the excerpt from each article, and to consider their functions. The examples may serve, for instance, as a way to support the idea, or as ways to persuade the readers that the article is about something that interests them. You may wish to discuss what counts as an "example" with the students. Ask them to indicate the function of examples not only as evidence but also as illustrations for the various claims.

2. This question asks students to analyze the rhetorical situation of writer and reader in each of the articles, specifying the cues in each article that lead them to make these inferences. Suggest to your students that they think both about how the articles themselves situate the writer and reader, and what kinds of audiences the publication seems to be addressing. You can be playful about reconstructing an imaginary reader to try to discover how discursive cues operate—whether the cues appeal to psychological position, knowledge, economic status, or even gender. How in each case does Tannen adjust her argument to better address the interests of her reader?

3. This question asks students to think about style and the differences in style that Tannen has introduced in each article. Think about matters of syntax and diction with your students as well as changes of tone. What about length of sentences and the use of complex clause structures? How about specialized vocabulary? Students may talk about the difficulty of stylistic features and the effect style has on accessibility. Do stylistic changes make the articles seem more or less objective? More or less appealing? Why? Does style affect *logos*—what knowledge can be conveyed?

4. This question asks students to think about the reader again, discussing the assumptions that each article makes about what the reader knows. Point out that one of the problems for the general reader might be that these assumptions are not spelled out. Knowing

what has already been discussed among scholars of argument may be as important as the possession of facts. This is because reading puts the intertextuality of knowledge into play.

5. This question asks students to think about the author's *persona* and the appeal to *ethos*. As they describe the image of the author and the way it is developed in each article, students are considering factors that contribute to academic credibility, or authority. How do they find themselves reacting to Tannen's voice in each of these articles? She is making an argument about "argument"—does this put her in a particularly difficult position? Does she herself avoid the kind of over-polarization and oppositional rhetoric that she is criticizing? Does she provide a model for a different form of argument? You might have your students discuss the forms of argument they have encountered and compare Tannen's persona to that of others who are involved in making arguments.

(p. 196) *For Exploration:* This freewriting assignment invites students to characterize academic writing as they have experienced it so far. In particular, they should think about their own successes and failures and the differences among academic disciplines. Often students attribute these varying experiences to individual differences: their own talents or lacks and the personal decisions of instructors. They received a grade of A or C, but they do not know why, they may report. Look together at the "Characteristics of an Effective Academic Essay," and think about what kinds of writing might *not* meet these criteria and still be successful. Ask them how their work does and does not succeed, according to this list and according to the evaluations they have received. If they have done very little writing, ask them to answer in terms of the differences in reading. Multilingual students are asked to reflect on the differences introduced for them by multiple language communities.

(p. 197) *For Exploration:* This interview assignment asks students to write about their specific understanding of the writing demands in another course after asking questions of a teacher. Since this proactive approach to learning will be very helpful as they go on with their academic career, and it establishes contacts that will help beginning students to engage more fully with college experiences right now, it is probably worth the time to make sure students can effectively do this interview. If they are one of five hundred in a writing-intensive chemistry course, they may need to interview a teaching assistant rather than the professor. If all the students in writing courses carry out such interviews in the same week, they will flood teachers of entry-level courses. Some teachers will have circulated a description of their writing requirements. You might look at a few examples in class before students begin the interviews and ask them to examine their teacher's handouts closely so they can ask more focused questions. (See Section 2 of this manual for a discussion of interviewing.) Since this exercise explores the realities of the academic writing and reading situation, you can usefully move to discussions that compare and contrast the ways you are handling material in this class to the various practices in other classes on campus. The opportunity to be pragmatic and descriptive will probably interest your students very much and be useful to them as well.

Alternatively, you may wish to arrange for a panel of speakers from various disciplines to address composition students. Although students miss the opportunity to carry out an interview, this may solve logistical problems.

You may wish to use students' interview summary and two paragraphs of reflection about academic writing as the first draft of an essay assignment. The following group activity will help them develop their ideas.

(p. 197) *For Collaboration:* Students go on to collaborate by answering questions about their interview, comparing and contrasting the responses various group members found. This activity requires several rounds of discussion and writing. The process needs to include time for them to write down statements and examples. You will probably need to allow at least half an hour for individual groups and another fifteen minutes for their reports and class discussion.

For Thought, Discussion, and Writing (p. 198)

Number 1: This activity takes yet another step toward establishing connections between reading and writing, asking students to apply the "Guidelines for Analyzing Your Rhetorical Situation" in Chapter 5 to a selection they choose for its success. They are to imagine themselves as the writer. Here they are making explicit the conventions that characterize their preferred reading. Your remarks about their selection process will make a great deal of difference: They may choose pieces that they actually prefer, or they may choose pieces that represent what they imagine as excellence, perhaps far from their private choices of reading. What do you want them to analyze? Here is an opportunity to discuss the differences between the reading they are encountering in their classes and reading directed to another kind of audience.

Number 2: This exercise asks students to analyze two textbooks they are using for classes. You may want to work through this process either as a specific writing assignment or as a group activity. You may also wish to encourage students in the habit of such analysis. Have them record their observations in their writer's notebook, and invite them to do the same for other reading assignments they encounter in college. Give them an opportunity from time to time in small groups and in class discussions to orient their remarks in the context of reading they have done. Ask them frequently what makes the works they read effective—or not.

Number 3: This assignment of a collaborative essay asks students to work in a group to summarize and reflect about what they've learned from the interviews of teachers. They might begin with the answers they wrote earlier to questions on pp. 197–98. If you need to make sure everyone has heard a few good interviews, have the whole class take notes on those before they begin work in the smaller groups. Some group members will probably want to go back and ask the teachers further questions once they begin to make comparisons. You can help them resist oversimplifying or generalizing by asking them to compare and contrast: provide evidence that "academic writing" is not one single form of discourse as well as show similarities.

Suggestions for Further Activities

Number 1: Have students bring in examples of articles from publications that appeal to a specialized audience. Work in pairs or small groups to brainstorm lists that record the unfamiliar reader's first impressions. Discuss the approaches and the conventions of format and style that are at work. You are aiming to develop an awareness about the regularities of discourses and their relationships to readers. Your class may lead you to spend more time comparing a vernacular they prefer to unfamiliar academic argument or to concentrate on differences among academic discourses. Their heightened awareness of discursive conventions will help them orient their writing appropriately to the rhetorical situation. You may also wish to use this discussion of conventions and academic discourse to consider multicultural texts and to compare cultural assumptions about form and style.

Number 2: Conventions also occur online. As a way of moving from Chapter 6 to Chapter 7, ask students to bring in examples of Web writing they frequently read and spend some time enumerating conventions. For example, reviews of computer games tend to follow a stylized form that students who read them can specify.

Number 3: At this point in the term, you may wish to get some responses from the class about how well it is working. Have students use writing to evaluate what they have learned and the textbook's approach (so far) and to formulate questions—perhaps in the form of a letter. You may wish to add evaluation of other elements of the class—such as workload, pace, and group work, together with other readings and materials you have used.

Chapter 7: Negotiating Online Writing Situations

In This Chapter: Guidelines for Writing Email (p. 211)
Guidelines for Constructing a Web Site (p. 218)

Chapter 7 begins with a discussion of the cultural implications—both theoretical and pragmatic—of electronic technologies. It discusses the broad perspective of cultural literacies through history to suggest a flexible, work-in-progress approach to new ways of writing introduced by the Internet. It reinforces the commonsense approach to writing that students have learned so far, showing students how to build on what they already know—their "rhetorical sensitivity." In particular, this chapter helps students work through a specific assessment of their own rhetorical situation as they consider appropriate responses to new writing opportunities online. There are several kinds of online writing from one student, Matthew Johnston, including emails to his mother, to friends, on a listserv, and in a chat room and a Web site. Comparing a letter from a medieval student to a contemporary email message, this chapter shows students how they might also analyze a cultural situation. You can use this analysis as a model for how students can themselves use a combination of inquiry and informed judgment in making rhetorical choices for electronic writing situations. The chapter points out new implications for thinking about writing offered by common online situations: emails, discussion groups, Usenet newsgroups, chat rooms, MUDs, MOOs, and Web sites.

This chapter can help you approach writing and electronic technologies in several ways. You can emphasize the rhetorical: how the elements of a written rhetoric are both continued and changed in various online writing practices. You can emphasize the practical, particularly if your whole class can work together online in a computer classroom, a class listserv, or a discussion program. You can choose to have students construct a Web site. If you are using a reader, you can have students look at—and even participate in—online writing connected to your readings, from listservs and newsgroups to Web sites.

Concepts

1. *Online writing:* This chapter shows students how to think of online writing rhetorically, as work in progress that has continuities with what they already know about writing. Rather than seeking to explain electronic technologies in terms of specific instructions or technical knowledge, it encourages students to adopt an analytical attitude to the rapidly changing—and growing—Internet. Thinking rhetorically can help them both to learn about writing online and to see how their rhetorical common sense still applies. Using rhetorical sensitivity, they can begin to sort out the effects their online communications might have: They can avoid angry exchanges or unfortunate miscommunications. To keep this rhetorical focus, you might want to consider issues of access and technical skills before you begin, perhaps with a survey of the class. See Section 2 of this manual for general suggestions about planning for online writing assignments. The following books might also be helpful.

Branscomb, H. Eric. *Casting Your Net: A Student's Guide to Research on the Internet.* 2nd ed. Boston: Allyn, 2000.

Clark, Carol Lea. *The Harcourt Guide to the Internet.* Fort Worth: Harcourt, 2001.

Harnack, Andrew, and Eugene Kleppinger. *Online! A Reference Guide to Using Internet Sources.* 3rd ed. Boston: Bedford/St. Martin's, 2000.

Hawisher, Gail E., and Cynthia L. Selfe, eds. *Global Literacies and the World Wide Web.* New York: Routledge, 1999.

————. *Passions, Pedagogies, and Twenty-First-Century Technologies.* Logan: Utah State UP, 1999.
Williams, Robin, and John Tollett. *The Non-Designer's Web Book.* 2nd ed. Berkeley: Peachpit, 2003.

2. *Email:* You can use email in several ways for your writing class. Your students may use email for individual exchanges with you, and they may use email as a means to carry on discussion on a listserv set up just for your class. Email discussion groups on one of the many available for subscriptions are so useful that it is worth the effort to show your students how they work. However, remember that an email discussion group can add thirty or forty minutes' worth of reading time and can become a significant addition to the course requirements. On the other hand, without an explicit requirement, many students will not participate in online writing. Tailor your requirements so that students are given credit for posting on an email discussion group and yet the writing posted will be manageable.

Email is most likely to be part of your students' experience with online writing. Nevertheless, you cannot take even that level of electronic expertise for granted, particularly in the case of multilingual writers. Furthermore, students may have different kinds of email access. This diversity has several implications. Students who have access to email on their own computers can do sophisticated operations: They can screen and sort mail and save it for later review, incorporate URLs that link directly to Web sites, and send and receive attachments. Students who check email on shared computer systems (in computer labs, libraries, or computers shared with roommates) may be able only to send and receive current messages conveniently.

3. *Usenet groups:* Newsgroups can be fun, informative, or both. They provide an especially extensive sampling of writing conventions that are particular to writing online or even to specific groups. They also demonstrate the rapid specialization of online communications as audiences are assembled for more and more specific interests: from laptop computers to the diet of hedgehogs. Perhaps Web sites with discussion components will increasingly replace these newsgroups as a way for people to talk about such interests, but the principle of increasing specialization to suit readers' interests remains similar.

4. *World Wide Web:* Graphics, interactive animation, live sound, videos, and Internet communications that allow teleconferencing have fantastically expanded the capabilities of the Web. Many academics, however, argue that the most fantastic of all Web inventions is the increased access to the exchange of information and ideas in writing. You can explore others' ideas about teaching on the Web; your students can also find a great deal of information about writing. This chapter focuses specifically on the question of constructing Web sites. Other chapters, particularly Chapters 3 and 4, address the question of searching, reading, and evaluating Web sources.

5. *Textual conventions:* Online conventions are changing as the Internet becomes larger and more various, but you will find that following a few rules, such as those set out in the Guidelines of this chapter, will help smooth the way to better listserv and newsgroup exchanges. Posting an advertisement or violating a shared premise can provoke heated responses. The "Guidelines for Constructing a Web Site" in this chapter emphasize the importance of thinking about audience in organizing information using links.

6. *Technical and rhetorical knowledge, or e-literacies:* There may be very great differences in your students' experience with electronic technologies. However, though technologies seem daunting to some, the others—the most technically adept—are not necessarily able to translate their knowledge into effective writing online. It may help to think about the difference between writing conventions and technical issues. No matter how adept, most

students need help thinking about how to write effectively for online audiences. On the other hand, if some students in your class seem quite frustrated about writing online, technical issues may be interfering with their ability to think through the conventions they are also encountering. Students can analyze for themselves what the issues of email or Web sites or Internet discussions might include. For example, many students use email to communicate with parents and friends but find that they say things differently with email than they do with a personal letter or a phone call. One student reported a misunderstanding with a friend that resulted from the friend's joking insult: the tone of voice that would have communicated "joke" didn't get through on the email. Another student regretted the loss of a personal touch that came with handwritten letters, but another countered that email put them in touch with people whom they never found time to write letters to or call.

7. *Privacy:* As the chapter notes, most online writing is vulnerable to becoming public. Remind students (if it is the case) that their institution retains ownership of their email and rights of access to it and that erasing email does not delete it from system archives. Furthermore, Usenet and Web site entries may turn up in searches by anyone anywhere through online search engines. For these reasons, you may wish to consider privacy ramifications if you use online resources to post class information, student email addresses, or student work.

Activities

(p. 200) *For Exploration:* This activity uses freewriting to allow students to assess their online experience. Using this starting point, they may register their current hopes and fears about electronic technologies. You might ask students to read or report aloud what they have written, after they discuss the range of experiences and attitudes with which they begin (see For Collaboration, p. 209). Even if you decide not to spend class time for this survey, ask students to turn in their freewrites so you can use the information in your planning. (Remember to warn students ahead of time when you pick up freewrites so you don't get embarrassing language or doodles.)

(p. 209) *For Collaboration:* In this exercise, students can use their freewriting as a starting point to compare their own experience with electronic technologies to that of others in the class. The last question encourages students to look beyond their own experiences and to think critically about how electronic technologies are impacting our culture. When the groups have finished their work, you may have them report to the class as a whole for further discussion. Students typically have mixed feelings about technology, and some may very well express frustrations you had not imagined with their own problems in gaining access or figuring out how to make their computers work. Others may also surprise you with the advantages they perceive—such as being able to email you at 2 A.M. in their pajamas with a question about an assignment. This activity may give you and other students a chance to find student experts who can serve as resources.

(p. 218) *For Exploration:* This exercise asks students to analyze Web homepages, comparing the personal homepage of Farhan Ahmed with the institutional homepage for the student's college. As students write about the format and content of these two pages, they may begin to accumulate observations about how Web pages connect communities. You can discuss ways that identification with communities and organizations helps define a personal page and ways that an institutional page imagines the persons in its audience— and even works to define its audience.

Finally, use these homepages and others that students may find as ways to think through the items in the "Guidelines for Constructing a Web Site." What plans seem to be followed? Who is the audience? How is it inviting and well-organized? How well does it respond to the conditions of online viewing? What indications of the ongoing work in progress do you see?

(p. 244) *For Exploration:* This exercise asks students again to compare two Web sites, using the "Guidelines for Constructing a Web Site," and to write two paragraphs of analysis per Web page. This analysis will provide the opportunity for discussing elements of the Guidelines. Note that these Guidelines ask about the plan and considerations of the audience like other rhetorical analyses. Your students might particularly evaluate how these Web sites use a rhetorical element not so evident in analysis of print: the principles of design (alignment, proximity, repetition, contrast). What is the content theme? The visual theme? How easy or hard are these pages to read?

(p. 225) *For Collaboration:* This exercise has students discuss their analyses from the previous Exploration, using the Guidelines. It would be surprising if all students had the same level of expertise with making Web sites. You might take advantage of the differences by canvassing the class for "experts" and making sure each group has one or two students with considerable experience. Alternatively, put those students into a group together, and have them report back their findings to the entire class and perhaps respond to questions.

For Thought, Discussion, and Writing (p. 227)

Before you begin the first two activities in this section, you might consider how you want your students to focus their inquiry into email discussion groups and newsgroups. The site <www.groups.google.com> It has lists of both email discussion groups and newsgroups that your students might use for their analysis of online writing. To view an email group, students may be required to subscribe.

Warn students that even "public" mailing lists are nevertheless private exchanges within a small community. They'll need to respect that. Tell them to expect that they will receive email messages from the groups they have subscribed to. It is possible for them to be quite overwhelmed with messages if they subscribe to a particularly active group or to more than one or if they fail to check (and delete) their email frequently.

Newsgroups are more public and easier to view than mailing lists (and this greater ease of access may lead you to have students investigate newsgroups instead of email discussion groups). Are there certain subjects you'd particularly like your students to examine—or to avoid? Are entertainment topics all right with you—or would you rather they looked at more academic subjects? Mailing lists and newsgroups range from subjects such as finance or international politics to midwifery and animal husbandry.

If you are taking a cultural studies approach to writing, you may very well choose to make this series of activities an important assignment in your course work, opening out into an examination of how electronic technology is affecting cultural history as well as writing.

Number 1: The first activity asks students to subscribe to an email discussion group and perhaps write a contribution to it. You may assign particular email groups or make recommendations to your students, particularly if they have had no experience with such groups. Giving them the address and subscription directions for one or two groups will expedite their work, particularly if you have a number of inexperienced students. If you have one set up, you can use your own class listserv as a starting point. However, this exercise leads students to a process of discovering rhetorical conventions through inquiry, and for this an "outside" discussion group is also needed. Newsgroups are more open than mailing lists. If you decide to have students examine a newsgroup rather than subscribe to a mailing list, they will find the sense of community less obvious, and the posts may be more widely varied. It will be easier, on the other hand, to move quickly through a variety of newsgroups to see what kind of exchanges are going on.

This exercise will help students think through the "Guidelines for Writing Email." Their answers to the questions under Guideline 1, "Consider Your Online Rhetorical Situation," will enable them to write a detailed analysis that could develop later into an analytical essay. Finally, after students have completed this exercise, they will have material for further reflection on how electronic technologies are influencing the conventions of writing.

Number 2: The next activity in this process involves printing out for analysis five effective posts and five ineffective ones from an email discussion group or from a newsgroup, recording briefly the basis for each evaluation. As a next step, ask students to discuss these evaluations with others in a small group, referring to their understanding of the email discussion group's conventions. In particular, they should think through whether their evaluation might be shared by the usual audience for that group. I might evaluate the detail of a message about what to feed a pet hedgehog as unnecessary—unless I am wondering about how to feed my own hedgehog. One of the interesting phenomena related to online writing is the creation of virtual communities, with communal standards for writing that are certainly not academic and perhaps not even within general cultural norms. Using the lists they have found, students may want to look for a newsgroup that raises obvious rhetorical issues for them. If you can go to a computer lab as a class for part of this assignment, students can work effectively with one another to share leads on interesting groups to examine. Because the effectiveness of the activity depends on whether a mailing list or a newsgroup offers enough material during your work to discuss, you will probably want to have some way to make sure students can find good subjects, either by providing leads for them or by having them work together in a lab.

Number 3: Now students move for this activity to the analysis and evaluation of Web sites. Since they are exploring Web sites at random, the examples they choose are apt to be related to their own interests or knowledge. After they have composed their list of characteristics shared by the best sites, ask them to speculate about the way that the content of the site enters into their evaluations.

Number 4: To conclude the work on this chapter, this activity assigns an essay about the implications of electronic technologies. The careful and thorough analyses that students have carried out in previous activities may serve as a basis for their essay or will at least have given them some closely read experiences with the rhetoric of online writing.

If you want them to read further at this point, the readings at the end of Chapter 3 will suggest some common issues and themes. Online and library resources about the developments in electronic technologies are plentiful. There is a site with links to a number of magazines about the Internet at <http://www.techweb.com/>. However, students can certainly write an interesting essay relying simply on their reflections and analysis so far.

Suggestions for Further Activities

Number 1: Ask students to search for and list as many kinds of Web sites as they can find—that is, newspapers, company homepages, magazines, resource pages with links, class syllabi, advertising, reproduced books, reproduced art, and so forth. Which kinds of writing are specific to the Web? Which are changed by it? Which are simply print versions moved to the Internet?

Number 2: Web users have increasing opportunities to offer feedback to Web site sponsors. Some television networks provide a space for opinion exchanges on specific news topics;

newspapers provide electronic access for letters to the editor. Ask students to view one of these opinion exchanges about a contemporary issue and to evaluate the persuasive force of contributions. How much are they like written letters to the editor? In what ways do they seem closer to speech? What impact do deviations from correctness and standard English have, if any?

Number 3: Ask students to interview three or four students not in your writing class about their experiences with online writing.

Number 4: Find a Web site that may be of interest to others, and write a review of it, just as you might write a review of a film or a book. Take into account the following:

a. Who is the author or sponsor?

b. What is the purpose of the site? How well is that carried out?

c. What leads you to trust or not trust the claims made on this page?

d. Does the presentation enhance communication?

e. What does it offer that might interest the viewer?

Part Three: Practical Strategies for Writing

In Part Three of *Work in Progress,* Chapters 8, 9, 10, 11, 12, and 13 explain specific strategies your students can use to improve their composing processes. The chapters focus on one aspect at a time: inventing, planning and drafting, document design, global revising, local revising, and collaborating. Exercises ask students to try out the various strategies and to evaluate the results. These chapters emphasize the practical—what works to get the writing job done. You will find suggestions drawn from modern research on writing and from the older traditions of rhetoric as well. These six chapters may also function like a handbook, furnishing assistance to which your students will return again and again and supplying specific Guidelines that you may use as references throughout the term. Multilingual writers will find specific pragmatic suggestions as well.

Chapter 8: Strategies for Invention

In This Chapter: Guidelines for Group Brainstorming (p. 244)
Guidelines for Group Troubleshooting (p. 245)

Work in Progress urges students to take a writerly, pragmatic approach to these chapters, actively sorting through suggestions to select those to adopt for a given situation. Some students in the past may have been required to use certain procedures, such as outlining or clustering. These techniques themselves are fine, unless students treat them as algorithms rather than heuristics—as if they had to replace the power of judgment with mechanically applied procedures. You can help mitigate the sense of alienation or the tendency of students to shortcut engagement with the processes of writing. Keep specifically and concretely referring to the rhetorical situation of each writing project. And, on the other hand, give students time to experiment with the strategies in a playful or exploratory way. They ought to try most of the approaches sooner or later—and now is the time for them to try something unfamiliar.

Chapter 8 presents a number of strategies for invention. If you have students go through this chapter with a particular assignment in mind, you may want to have them be selective about the methods of invention they try—and ask them to come back to this chapter several times during the term with other assignments in mind. Or have students experiment with all the techniques, returning to use the most appropriate ones more extensively. Note that the process of research, which they have already encountered in Chapter 4, might be thought of as a strategy of invention as well.

Concepts

1. *Strategies for invention:* This chapter presents invention both as a matter of individual effort and as a matter of communal processes, giving students ways to tap into what they already know and suggesting ways to use dialogue and collaboration to add other resources. As you work through the strategies presented in the text, you may find it especially helpful to frame these tasks in two ways, as both an individual and a group effort.

When students come from widely differing discursive or cultural communities and have little experience negotiating among social differences in conventions, they often have difficulty with the process of invention. Past experience may not provide them naturally with successful ideas. To put it another way, extending the discourses they know or learning another discourse becomes part of the task of invention.

Students who are overly formulaic about invention may be freed to see new connections by informal processes like clustering. On the other hand, students who do not have much experience with North American academic discourse—at times the majority of our classes—may not think of using even very common patterns like cause and effect, or comparison and contrast. They may be especially helped by the traditional *topics,* since they do not know the kinds of questions that might conventionally be asked, or answered, in an argument.

2. *Informal methods:* These strategies may seem to work best for certain kinds of writing—for example, the informal, experience-based, or personal essay. However, they provide ways to get started on all kinds of writing, even if the writer is not "in the mood," as the selection from a student's journal suggests. Informal methods include freewriting, looping, brainstorming, and clustering. See Section 2 of this manual for comments on freewriting and brainstorming. Looping, the alternation of freewriting and analysis, helps students learn to read their work productively and develop a sense of purpose. You can also loop with a group: Have students freewrite for five or ten minutes and then write brief responses to each other's work. This kind of exercise creates a certain intensity and focus that may be especially helpful to get students started on a project. Clustering has a similar ability to generate commitment; many students prefer visual mapping of some kind, substituting the cluster for an outline and developing more and more elaborate graphics and figures as they plan. Encourage multilingual students to practice informal methods without worrying about correctness.

3. *Formal methods:* These strategies help guide students beyond informal methods, showing them some directions for systematic investigation. The text discusses journalists' questions, tagmemics, and the topical questions adapted from Aristotle. Many students like the systematic and comprehensive quality of the topics and find that having the list at hand can prompt an angle of thought that might have been otherwise ignored. Your students can enlarge their habits of invention as they become familiar with these conventions of analysis and argument, especially if they have tended to think of subjects only in terms of narratives or descriptions. A few enthusiasts may go overboard, perhaps putting their subjects diligently through all (or a number of) the topical paces with the hope of making a paper that is truly encyclopedic. In addition, students sometimes make the mistake of confusing invention and arrangement. Answering the questions doesn't solve the problem of order, as you might want to point out, though the topics do suggest some possibilities for later arrangement.

4. *Inventing collaboratively:* Collaborative invention means much more than working on a collaborative project. All writers, in a larger sense, necessarily work collaboratively since they draw on the language, research, and ideas of others. The strategies for "inventing collaboratively" in this chapter emphasize the social components of invention and show students how to look outside themselves for ideas. These collaborative strategies may also provide bridges from one form of discourse to another and thus help students who might flounder in isolation. Protect students against the coercive potential of group consensus-making by encouraging diversity and divergent reasoning. This chapter includes specific "Guidelines for Group Brainstorming" and "Guidelines for Group Troubleshooting."

If your students have not had much experience working in groups, you may want to pay special attention to troubleshooting. Hold a group troubleshooting session, and then have students freewrite for ten minutes about the experience. The freewriting evaluation is an important part of the introduction to troubleshooting that you will want to follow up on. Have groups list strengths and weaknesses and make some decisions about how to improve on problem areas. You may want to discuss common findings with the class as a whole. Work as a consultant with groups that seem to need further help—most frequently because members are reluctant to give firm advice or suggestions about problems. But note that the troubleshooting format helps a great deal with this because the writers ask specifically for the assistance they want.

Activities

(p. 236) *For Exploration:* This exercise asks students to use the process of looping on the topic of family or another topic they choose. It will help your students both to generate material and to focus on what is significant about it. Many of your students will find strong subjects for writing through looping and some will be enchanted when they discover their unknown resourcefulness. If you have assigned the essay on family as a possible writing project, your only problem may be getting students to set aside their looping to try other forms of invention before they complete their essays. Or you may want to arrange your schedule differently, letting students work through one project and then coming back to forms of invention appropriate to another.

(p. 237) *For Exploration:* This exercise shows students how to use brainstorming to develop ideas around a topic. Students sometimes use brainstorming and listing as an opening shotgun approach and then have trouble elaborating and developing their subject. Here they are integrating brainstorming with other modes of invention.

(p. 238) *For Exploration:* This exercise adds clustering to the methods of informal invention. If you have students who have not tried clustering before, you may be amazed at how liberating it seems for many of them. Students who respond well to visual representations may also want to try out more elaborate graphic schemes or maps for arranging their ideas.

(p. 239) *For Collaboration:* Here is a chance for students to evaluate together the informal modes of invention they have been exploring. The questions ask them to think about how different composing and learning styles as well as differences in situation might influence the effectiveness of these approaches. Since students are often used to thinking of themselves as individuals, most may feel very comfortable with the informal methods. It's reassuring to discover ways they can tap their own authority. (Multicultural students may have a different perspective, however.) After they have worked through the formal methods, you might ask students again to assess their effectiveness and to make comparisons with the group.

(p. 241) *For Exploration:* This exercise uses journalists' questions and tagmemics. Topics that are issue-oriented work best in trying out the strategies. If your students are working on the "family" essay, they may move into more general questions about families or perspectives on family issues, from changes in the nuclear family to the advent of "new" families with same-sex partners, and so forth. Many students find it rather difficult to negotiate the difference between private and public domains of discourse in a single essay, though the possibility of doing so is an interesting one. Private and public forms of writing may be associated with gender for some students. If you see a gendered preference in your class, you might want to discuss the issue.

(p. 243) *For Exploration:* This exercise continues the work on strategies of invention for the subject your students have chosen. Notice that the topics work as methods of *discovery* and will also work to suggest ways of *arranging* and *developing* the subject so that invention overlaps with drafting.

For Thought, Discussion, and Writing (p. 246)

Number 1: This activity puts the practice work on invention to use on an essay exploring family. Topics that draw on students' personal experiences help them make bridges from the familiar writing to the academic. But there is a danger: Such topics also tap a formidable store of stereotypes, clichés, and automatic responses. Informal methods of invention help bypass this ready banality, partly by generating so much material that students can get beyond it and also by allowing contradictions and complexities to be described before they are hidden by premature explanations. Going on to formal methods of invention will press students to engage the topic of family critically and place it in a larger cultural and historical context.

Number 2: This essay evaluating a group brainstorming or troubleshooting session has the merit of being grounded in empirical observation. Because it connects to improving a real-world activity, with consequences, it short-circuits the often hidden rhetorical situation of the classroom. If you decide to give your whole class the assignment, perhaps you will want to have groups exchange task and observer roles. Members can also collaborate on notes, brainstorm results, and discuss recommendations as a group.

Number 3: This assignment asks students to experiment with and evaluate a strategy not used before. It encourages students to use the strategies from this chapter again and again during the term and with various writing assignments. You might assign a new strategy of invention whenever the group seems to be lapsing into hasty invention or individual students need extra work.

Suggestions for Further Activities

Number 1: Research may be seen as one aspect of invention. Draw research into these strategies for invention by making it part of the exercise. For example, freewriting and looping can add the extra step of doing an Internet search or surveying library sources. Formal methods can include surveying sources or summarizing a reading. Integrating research into an essay topic such as "family" inserts it more persuasively into academic writing.

Chapter 9: Strategies for Planning and Drafting

In This Chapter: Guidelines for Planning an Essay (p. 248)
Guidelines for Evaluating Your Controlling Purpose (p. 250)
Guidelines for Drafting an Essay (p. 258)
Guidelines for Organizing and Developing Your Ideas (p. 262)

Chapter 9 discusses the design strategies of planning and drafting. It goes on from the work of Chapter 8, connecting planning and invention, emphasizing the different ways to plan, and grounding the concept of the controlling purpose in the rhetorical situation. Then the chapter suggests procedures for successful drafting. It discusses the shift from thinking about a subject to thinking about presenting ideas for readers.

Concepts

1. *Controlling purpose:* Students often have trouble finding a purpose because they try to invent one arbitrarily, in isolation. If writing is social and not the act of a solitary individual writing alone, then the goals of the writer develop out of the discursive community, not from acts of individual will alone. The sense of a purpose arises out of the individual writer plus the rhetorical situation—out of the potential readers, their concerns, the conventions of their discourse, and the additions the writer wants to make to the communal conversation. However, choosing an appropriate, interesting purpose doesn't always appear as a conscious, carefully articulated process but, rather, like other functions of language, as something that is tacitly understood. So planning must involve both conscious work and a kind of unconscious intuition or playfulness. This chapter suggests ways to evoke and determine a sense of purpose.

In this chapter, the controlling purpose is defined as "a capsulized or condensed summary of your rhetorical situation." The chapter suggests to multilingual writers that the idea of "controlling" may seem unfamiliar, and that it will be helpful to discuss differences in assumptions with other class members. When you ask students to think about their goals for a particular assignment, ask them to define their purpose in just this way—analyzing the rhetorical situation, describing it succinctly, and stating what they want to accomplish. This chapter provides "Guidelines for Evaluating Your Controlling Purpose," which may serve as a useful checklist for future projects. Recognize that a good deal of preliminary invention and even drafting may take place before the writer has a good sense of the controlling purpose. You don't necessarily want to insist that students submit a firm statement about controlling purpose before they begin drafting, for example, though making that effort and calling it tentative might help them. Defining the task at any stage brings the specific work that remains to be done into view.

2. *Planning:* A draft written without any plan at all may waste a good deal of a student's time—and yours because commenting helpfully on a loose collection of materials is hard. Define planning in an open-ended way, as part of an Exploration or inquiry into a question at issue so students can find a starting point that doesn't foreclose their options. Problems with invention, controlling purpose, and planning are related, so you can often help students work on all of them at once by referring them to work from Chapters 5 and 8 on the rhetorical situation and on invention.

Sometimes students have trouble with planning because they are exploring their topics—asking questions—and they imagine that they need to have reached conclusions or taken a stand before they can go on. You may want to remind these students that a plan can also consist of a series of questions, issues, or problems for the writer as well as the reader to raise. Many kinds of writing projects do not require conclusiveness. Rhetorical planning is a form of inquiry. Thinking about how to write is intimately connected with thinking about what to write. For this reason, multilingual writers may want to experiment with the advantages of planning either in English or in their home language. Remind students that planning may seem like cycles of work and play. A certain pragmatism arises from deciding on a controlling purpose. Guidelines will help students evaluate it.

Many students do very well using looping, freewriting, or discovery drafts, written without a plan to discover what the topic has to offer. Such processes combine invention and drafting. You usefully comment on such work by marking passages you find especially effective or interesting and pointing out connections as you notice them. If the whole draft seems coherent, you can summarize what it is about. Have students mark passages they find promising for your comments, or have them ask questions based on such a draft. Their plan may emerge inductively.

3. *Drafting:* The "Guidelines for Drafting an Essay" make specific recommendations to help students. You might want to talk about your own practices here—emphasizing differing practices for different kinds of writing. You might also want to address the tremendous gap students often experience between the ideal and the real situation of their writing. You may have many students who continue to procrastinate—often simply because they don't have much time and their writing is not a high priority or not high enough. Frequent attention to the work in progress keeps students from putting writing aside until the last minute. This *scheduling* of frequent attention is one of the advantages a writing class can offer. Talk about the impact of problems they are having. Is it hard to get time at a computer? The Guidelines include some suggestions for taking advantage of computer capabilities. Are students making good use of available resources? Are they giving themselves enough time per session to get going? Many students have unrealistic ideas about the amount of time they need to write, and they are simply not scheduling enough lengthy sessions until the last moment. At this point you may also see the cycles of writing and reflection giving results as students begin to have a sense of ownership about their writing, a sense that they understand how their own writing processes work rather than feeling dependent on their teachers.

This chapter includes some suggestions for overcoming resistance to drafting. These include using rituals, just getting started without trying for perfection, talking to others, and freewriting about the resistance itself. You might want to set aside some time in class for students to freewrite about their resistance, allowing volunteers to read their results to the class. Or discuss resistance, acknowledging that most writers experience it sooner or later. Other comments on resistance appear in Section 2 of this manual.

4. *Organizing and developing:* Some students think of drafting as nothing but a problem of organizing and developing their ideas, with little discovery involved. The more conventional and well rehearsed the topic, the more this is apt to be true. Drafting, in other words, may include varying amounts of invention and arrangement. This chapter provides separate Guidelines for the intermediate processes of organization, focusing on building strong connections between questions of content and questions of form, between the writer's ideas and the reader's expectations. It is here that students should concentrate on making their ideas explicit by unpacking code words, working on a thesis statement, and using conventional formats to signal organization. Here instructors may remind students of organizational formulas—problem solving, cause and effect, definition, comparison and contrast.

Activities

(p. 248) *For Exploration:* This freewriting exercise in effect asks students to explore their biases about planning before they begin to read. Discussing the variety of responses in the class might be helpful as well, particularly when you feel your class is especially worried or resistant to opening up their usual procedures.

(p. 251) *For Exploration:* This activity asks students to use the "Guidelines for Evaluating Your Controlling Purpose." You will want students to use these questions repeatedly as they develop a controlling purpose for subsequent essays. You may want to refer to the list of questions in comments you make on drafts, when it seems that students need more work on their controlling purpose. Students frequently, for example, choose a topic and describe it, as if their purpose were purely aesthetic or formal. Or they take on too large a task, so that the essay they write can't possibly succeed.

(p. 256) *For Exploration:* This exercise asks students to evaluate their methods of making plans and to think of ways to improve. Since some students seem especially resistant to internalizing planning, these questions may help them to start thinking purposefully about their usual strategies. Putting the practice into words makes it available for monitoring and change.

(p. 256) *For Collaboration:* Following up on the individual reflections about plans, this group activity summarizes planning practices and some conclusions about them. In the class discussion that follows, explore the variety of planning methods without prejudice, but also press students to make decisions about alternate methods with which they will experiment. This is an opportunity for multilingual writers to discuss the effect of their knowledge of multiple languages or dialects on planning. Since planning and drafting so often feel like a regimen being prescribed for students, their vows to do better can easily have no more long-term effect than vows to go on a diet. The only thing they really need to pledge is sufficient time and attention to practice so that they have a chance to internalize new approaches.

(p. 261) *For Exploration:* Like the above exercise, this Exploration of drafting habits will help students internalize explicit strategies.

(p. 261) *For Collaboration:* Like the group activity on planning, this exercise will help students to see the variety of drafting approaches available to them and, at the same time, press them to try new strategies that might improve their work.

For Thought, Discussion, and Writing (p. 265)

Number 1: Writing an essay about writers' block offers students a chance to have some fun, perhaps to make impassioned descriptions about the crisis they've been in because of writing blocks—in the past, of course—or the extreme measures taken for a cure. It encourages students to become analytical about resistance as well. This is an assignment that lends itself to collaboration too. They could describe some experiences they've had with the problem and then conclude with some group recommendations for solutions to writing block.

Number 2: This activity asks students to keep a record as they write. Comparing proposed and actual planning and drafting activities helps students to take a more extensive look into their actual writing processes. You might ask them to compare the results with the earlier descriptions of themselves they have written. Multilingual writers can keep this record either in their home language or in English, but note that it will prepare them better to discuss plans with the instructor and groups if they write in English.

Number 3: This assignment asks students to interview someone who is working in a field they might want to enter or even in a field they are simply curious about. (See Section 2 of this manual for notes on interviewing.) Students are to ask how their subjects plan writing, how they draft, whether they work collaboratively or alone, what technological aids they use, and whether the Internet has influenced their writing. This interview can serve not only to gather information but also to get advice: for example, on how the interviewee deals with writing blocks. Some students will interview spouses, relatives, and friends because they feel reluctant to approach strangers in their jobs. Unfortunately, they miss a wonderful opportunity to initiate conversation in the workplace and ask questions that will reveal much about the nature of the job. You may find the results interesting enough to warrant class discussion. Then students write an essay about their findings.

Suggestions for Further Activities

Number 1: As a variation on the second activity in the previous section, have students work in pairs to observe each other's composing process. This requires the composer to talk about what she or he is doing with planning and drafting while the other student observes and records. When both have done their work, they may compare notes about what they saw.

Chapter 10: Strategies for Document Design

In This Chapter: Guidelines for Effective Document Design (p. 271)

Chapter 10, new in this sixth edition, helps students take a rhetorical perspective on the issues of document design. This chapter integrates visual features into the rhetorical analysis of planning. Students now have many more choices available for how they will "publish" their papers, and even the most conservative presentation is likely to take advantage of elements such as bold and italic typefaces, bulleted lists, or columns and tables. Some writing assignments need illustrations; others may be enhanced by using photographs or artwork; and it is becoming increasingly easy to access such elements. Web design, of course, depends much more heavily than print on the visual and has no allegiance to traditional print formats. The influence of Web design on print texts may show up in your students' work as illustrations printed off the Web for papers. The "Guidelines for Effective Document Design" in this chapter emphasize the changing situation and provide questions to prompt a rhetorical analysis.

Concepts

1. *Document design from a rhetorical perspective:* Consider questions of *ethos, logos,* and *pathos.* Academic conventions are often very traditional and in general avoid calling attention to the design. Often professors will specify format requirements in the case of theses and dissertations. A visual presentation that is clear, unobtrusive, and conventional can make the writer more convincing. Design elements such as illustrations, charts, diagrams, maps, margin choices, columns, spacing, fonts, and color. become even more important for Web-based texts, discussed in Chapter 7. Your students may have thought about document design as part of the requirements for assignments rather than as one more rhetorical element over which they have a certain amount of strategic control.

2. *Elements of document design:* This chapter discusses the principles of alignment, proximity, repetition, and contrast as applied to many basic design decisions. Your students may want to experiment with elements such as font, color, visuals, and illustrations. A rhetorical approach to visual design helps them analyze whether these elements are necessary and integral to the overall purpose or simply distracting. The chapter includes three versions of a successful proposal to show the decision-making process in its drafting. If you wish to have students compare their own critical processes to Robertson's, you can make a transparency of his first draft to discuss in class before students read the chapter. Later you can ask them how his changes differed from what they would have suggested to him.

3. *Copyright law for visuals:* Just as students must document carefully the sources of citations, they should note sources of illustrations and photographs and pay careful attention to the question of copyright. When they are using this material in a print document submitted for class, they are, under "fair use," less likely to violate copyright than when they use visuals on Web sites.

4. *Document design and cultural differences:* Conventions of document design and the visual vary, sometimes considerably, across cultures. These differences play a role in "rhetorical sensitivity" and in the often unconscious judgments your students make. You might find it interesting to compare the design elements in documents from several cultures in class. If your classroom includes multilingual and multicultural students, you will have an even better reason for paying attention to these differences, and these students may have easy access to documents and publications from other languages and cultures that they can bring to class.

Activities

(p. 267) *For Exploration:* This exercise asks students to freewrite about their responses to visual elements in all their reading—not just academic reading. You might prompt them to be specific or to look first at some of the material they read and then freewrite. You can bring a variety of materials to class yourself, as an alternative, and have them respond to the various design elements. If you have access to the Internet in your classroom and a projector, you can examine some Web sites as a group.

(p. 270) *For Exploration:* This exercise asks students to write two or three paragraphs about the effectiveness of essay design, using the "Miscellany of Student Essays" in Chapter 17.

(p. 271) *For Collaboration:* After completing their individual analyses, students work in a group to compare their responses and then present two conclusions to the class. You may wish to reflect back on their earlier analysis of various reading materials as well, during the discussion that follows. Finally, do students want to reach some conclusions about the range of differences between academic writing and the magazines and Web sites they have examined?

(p. 274) *For Exploration:* This activity asks students to turn back to Brenda Shonkwiler's research paper on the Tacoma Narrows Bridge Catastrophe and evaluate its use of visuals—photographs, a diagram, a drawing, and a table—from a rhetorical perspective. In other words, they will need first to think again about the purpose and the controlling idea of the paper. This is an example for them of an academic paper with visual components, so it should help students see how visuals work within academic conventions of research. They should look at how copyright documentation is used here as well.

(p. 281) *For Exploration:* This exercise asks students to reread the changes made by Wayne Robertson as he drafted his proposal and to identify two of them not discussed in the text. How did these changes also improve the proposal? If the class discussed the first draft, did these changes respond to issues that they had raised for revising?

For Thought, Discussion, and Writing (p. 281)

Number 1: This exercise asks students to analyze the design elements of the articles presented in Chapter 5, using the "Guidelines for Effective Document Design" in this chapter. They can draw on their earlier work analyzing the changing rhetorical situation in the introductions to Deborah Tannen's argument, this time to see how visual and design elements interact with those rhetorical situations, particularly with the various audiences. Is it always the case that visual elements are used to address the broadest audiences? Can your students think of instances in which the visual elements of a text are quite narrowly directed to an expert audience?

Number 2: This activity asks students to evaluate the design of this textbook, *Work in Progress,* using the design principles they have learned in Chapter 10. Then they are to add suggestions for improvement. If you collect these and send them to us, we will be interested in what your students have to say. You can honestly tell them they could have an effect on future editions of the book.

Number 3: This activity suggests a community-based writing project—a flyer, brochure, newsletter, or Web page. You can develop this as a major assignment for the term, if such community-based learning interests you. Many students are already involved in volunteer work or in internships that might need such a project. For suggestions about including community service in your class, see Section 2 of this manual.

Number 4: This exercise asks students to evaluate visual representations from *Newsweek* that predict trends for the next decades. The analysis can serve as the basis of an essay if you choose to assign it. This is a particularly rich example of charts and diagrams used to present information. You might also think about using it as the basis for class analysis and then asking students to locate their own examples for an essay.

Suggestions for Further Activities

Number 1: This exercise asks students to analyze the design elements of the articles presented in Chapter 5, using the "Guidelines for Effective Document Design" in this chapter. They can draw on their earlier work analyzing the changing rhetorical situation in the introductions to Deborah Tannen's argument, this time to see how visual elements interact with those rhetorical situations, particularly with the various audiences. Is it always the case that visual elements are used to address the broadest audiences? Can your students think of instances in which the visual elements of a text are quite narrowly directed to an expert audience?

Number 2: After working through the various exercises on visual elements and design, ask students to analyze their own writing practices. What example of visual design appears in their own writing, and how does it vary with the audience? In online writing? Personal writing? Diaries, journals, memoires? In academic work? How do visual elements help or hinder their writing?

Chapter 11: Strategies for Managing the Revision Process

Chapter 11 addresses the larger questions of revision, asking students to think about revision as a time when they can look at their work as a reader, seeing it differently—perhaps more objectively—and bringing it to completion. The chapter provides suggestions for using feedback from various sources: from friends and family, from classroom groups, from peer tutors, from instructors. You will find two sample student papers included here as well. The first demonstrates how to use a descriptive outline for revision. The second shows rough and final drafts, together with commentary.

By now your students have probably accumulated a great deal of material to work on—and perhaps much longer rough drafts than they are used to revising. If so, you'll find this accumulation very helpful. Students are often stingy revisers because they so fear cutting out one hard-earned word. Many of your students have probably been amazed and gratified by the sheer number of pages of writing they can produce when they do freewriting and loops or apply Aristotle's topics. For the first time, they have too much, their drafts approach or exceed the page limits, and they must make choices about what to include.

The experience of *cutting things out* is so novel and so wonderful for some students that we frequently encourage them to overwrite their drafts for the first assignment that focuses on revising—that is, to make the rough draft perhaps twice as long as the final paper might be. Many students can hardly believe that they would write more than needed for a composition assignment or that it would feel so easy to do. Students who have suddenly discovered that they can invent more words easily are ready to enter a new economy of revision based not on scarcity but on abundance. Writing too much is also especially helpful if you have some students who still can't take the risk of making genuine changes in their papers.

Revising sometimes poses some difficult issues, nevertheless. For example, if students come to class with the kind of draft that we associate with automatic writing—something facile and acceptable that they've learned to produce without much risk—they may find it very hard to open the draft to inspection. Some work sounds good and says little. Revising may just make that more obvious. On the other hand, if students bring work that has come out of freewriting, has rough edges, but also has a lot of character, they sometimes seem prone to revise it into more stereotypical, less exciting forms. There's as much art to revising as to inventing, and perhaps as little guarantee that the result will be wonderful. But you can increase your students' chances of success by multiplying their options. If students know a number of people from whom to seek responses and a number of ways to try revising, they are not so apt to feel at a dead end. If they see revising as part of a process that they understand and can freely tap, they may extend their writing resourcefulness in ways that will make revising the most rewarding part of a project. Finally, as they learn to use a growing sense of audience, they can revise more firmly within a well-conceived rhetorical situation. This chapter shows them how to tap the resources of several audiences: family, friends, writing group, writing assistants, and, of course, instructors.

Concepts

1. *Revision:* This chapter emphasizes the larger dimensions of revision, giving examples of genuinely new visions or approaches to rough drafts that allow students to write a more successful version of their papers. This kind of global revision requires that the writers allow their dialogue with others to influence the way they read their own papers—that they take readers seriously. The chapter points out how this differs from editing, with its concern for correctness. To show them the difference, ask your students to read each others' drafts through quickly to determine the gist of what is said, so they could repeat it without the help of written pages in front of them. The problems they encounter getting at a gist and the differences of opinion about what it is and whether it suits the author's intention are matters for global revision. If you want them to experience proofreading, have them read the last paragraph of the paper, word by word, backwards from the end, checking for errors in spelling. Contrasting these two activities clarifies the point: Revision is concerned with the production of *meaning*.

Since meaning, forms, and style are not separable, however, revision also pushes students beyond the safe boundaries of what they already know how to say. Using new writing approaches may very well cause a momentary regression in the writer's mastery. As you press them to use conventions they have not practiced before and to use forms of academic discourse that do not yet seem integrated into their habitual *ethos*, part of their revising will be learning to integrate these new languages with their old successes. This happens at the level of revision rather than at the level of invention when students' first drafts have stayed on familiar ground. Multilingual writers should be encouraged to attend to global issues first, rather than to correctness. However, they may need to revise for correctness as well before they submit drafts to readers.

2. *Using responses to revise:* This chapter makes many suggestions about getting responses to a rough draft. You might want to ask the whole class to try some of them: for example, listening to a paper read aloud by someone else or asking every student to meet with a writing assistant at the writing center. The chapter has Guidelines for using each of these various kinds of responses.

The chapter also makes important, specific suggestions for using response groups as an integral part of revising. Many writing-across-the-curriculum programs have found that such response groups are helpful to students writing papers in content area classes. Teaching your students how to use a response group will help them greatly in the future, our students testify. Responses from peer groups and from the instructor are, of course, examples of variations in interpretation that students have already had to take into account. Frequently, however, students regard variations as some kind of error, either in the reader or in the writer, rather than as the inevitable differences that need to be negotiated to improve communication. Talking about reading each other's papers as a process will help them to see the dialogic nature of their understanding. This chapter gives some specific suggestions for the kinds of responses a group might use from Peter Elbow and Pat Belanoff's *A Community of Writers: A Workshop Course in Writing*, 3rd ed. (New York: McGraw-Hill, 2000). Peter Elbow does a good job of insisting on the contradictory-seeming nature of these response-group exchanges. He says that as a reader you are always 100 percent right about your response—but the writer is always 100 percent right about her intention as well. And it's a good idea to get both out in the open before the process of negotiation starts. See Chapter 13, Section 2, of this manual for further help with collaborative learning.

3. *Revising argumentative essays:* When your students are writing argumentative essays, they should pay close attention to the structure of claims, supports, and assumptions and

108

to their audience's likely response to these. Students should revise so they have a sharper idea of what is at stake in the paper and how the audience will see the question. The responses of future readers play an important part in revising argument. The writer must consider possible counterarguments. Elbow and Belanoff's "Believing and Doubting" strategy helps to clarify the shared assumptions and to raise unforeseen objections.

4. *How revising uses objectivity and distance:* This chapter lists a number of suggestions for building objectivity that will help students see their essays from a different perspective from that of the writer. Objectivity requires them to become the reader of their own work. Without claiming to rid themselves of all bias, they can still take on the analytic, critical attitude toward their own work that they have been adopting as a rhetorical reader of other work.

5. *Samples of student revisions:* Rosie Rogel's essay "Memories" provides an example of how descriptive outlining helps her revise a paper on the topic of family. You may wish to add samples from your own collection to show on an overhead transparency or make available in a class file on reserve. A student essay by Kira Wennstrom provides a model for responses to the papers of classmates.

Activities

(p. 287) *For Exploration:* This assignment asks your students to reflect on their experiences with revision, distinguishing it carefully from proofreading. Encourage them to share stories of disaster, triumph, and mistaken opinion, and try to get some sense of how much revision your class has done in the past, either by asking them to turn in written responses or by holding a class discussion. Don't be surprised if you have several students report that they ruin everything they revise: It's a common, self-serving superstition. Sometimes it may even be true. If they use all the writing skills they have mastered in the first draft, a revision can plunge them into new problems they haven't yet solved. Try to establish an atmosphere in which taking a risk looks worthwhile and trying something new that doesn't work will not ruin the writer's G.P.A.

(p. 293) *For Collaboration:* This exercise asks students to think about how they perceive peer responses and to understand what kinds of responses they prefer. Since this isn't necessarily something easily put into words, the collaborative part of the exercise helps students adapt or add to what they might have simply borrowed from the chapter. More important, it helps the group function more effectively. Often students say they want "tough" "critical" responses and don't get enough of them. As group members come to trust each other more, they are more willing to risk a critique that entails substantial revisions.

(p. 300) *For Exploration:* This exercise asks your students to work out a descriptive outline first for their own paper and then for another student's essay. Exchanging descriptive outlines allows them to compare their own readings of their essay to another's. This is also an important exercise for students to learn objectivity and forms of response, using Rosie Rogel's essay and descriptive outline as a model.

For Thought, Discussion, and Writing (p. 307)

Number 1: This assignment asks students to reflect on their revising practice in a way that may help promote their objectivity about their writing. At the same time you can also encourage them to have fun with their descriptions, to include all the relevant data (such as time taken out to watch a movie on television), and to try to find good metaphors for the process, such as building a wall out of a pile of bricks or encountering foggy weather. Analogies from the activity just below might be useful. If you have them write essays, they may be like Horatio Alger stories or like the confessions of revising sinners, perhaps with some repentance at the end. Most often, they will structure them as expositions of problem solving. Some students might want to write arguments advocating a better way of revising. Have collaborative writing groups keep a log of their meetings and records of their procedures—agreements, revising sessions, information networks, ground rules—as well as their decisions about writing goals and responsibilities. Asking questions about the effectiveness of the process is an ongoing necessity for such groups.

Number 2: This exercise asks students to use analogy as a way of describing and understanding the complicated processes of revision. Take the opportunity to point out how analogies structure a whole attitude into the comparison as well. If revising is like cleaning house, it's primarily a job of cutting and clearing out. What gets omitted are dirt and junk and disruption—with a premium on orderliness and clarity. If revising is like adjusting binoculars, it's primarily a matter of bringing the parts into focus so they all work together to form a single picture—just as the controlling idea establishes a single, clear image. If revising is like a forest fire, much valuable timber might be burned in the ruthless process of making room for new growth. Use these examples to help your students start thinking on their own.

Number 3: This assignment, like the first activity above, asks students to reflect on revising with some depth and thoroughness in a way that will improve their objectivity about the process. By interviewing other students about their revision strategies and by drawing comparisons, students may see how they can make some useful choices about their methods, and they may also develop some further understanding about the relationship between revising strategies and the kinds of writing that seem to result. If this is a class assignment or option, it makes some sense to have all the students doing this interviewing work together in groups of three. Perhaps this is a good opportunity for them to talk with people not in their usual response group. The resulting essays could be developed individually, or the group could collaborate on a single essay that summarizes the experiences of the group.

Suggestions for Further Activities

Number 1: Ask students to write their own personal guidelines for revision. Such an effort enables students to internalize what has been presented to them. Since this revision material takes time for assimilation and since students need quite a bit of experience with revising before they can formulate guidelines with much sense of authority, you may want to ask them to update their revising guidelines periodically or whenever they revise a new assignment. Don't judge their understanding of revision by the ability to produce guidelines. After all, that's not the point. Rather, urge them to keep an experimental attitude about revising processes.

Number 2: You might want to apply revision questions to composing online. Emails are notoriously unrevised—but is that really true? You could ask the class to brainstorm a list of ten reasons why one should revise an email. The difference between writing papers and putting together a Web site is more striking. How is revising a paper different from revising a Web site? Does the emphasis on *design* shift concern away from the conceptual or change our ideas of concept? What changes because a Web site can be continuously updated.

Chapter 12: Strategies for Revising Structure and Style

Chapter 12 continues the discussion of revision, moving on to consider matters of structure and style. The big issues—attention to focus, content, and organization—come first, complete with a checklist of questions to help guide analysis. Then the next step is to think about coherence. Finally, the chapter gives detailed advice about working on style. Texts by Ian Frazier provide a focus on stylistic possibilities.

Concepts

1. *Focus:* The controlling purpose gives focus, but this is not simply a matter of the writer's solitary will. It grows out of the rhetorical situation and the writer's clarity about what's at stake. A lack of focus shows up as a mismatch between the essay intended by the writer and the essay read by the reader. Focus, therefore, depends heavily on the relationship between the writer's goals and the writer's understanding of the rhetorical situation, conventions, and expectations at work.

2. *Content:* Content develops and elaborates the controlling purpose of the writer. Most students have heard a good deal about the need for more specifics and greater detail in their work, but to know what kind of elaboration is needed they need to have a strong sense of purpose, of what reader's questions they might be responding to.

3. *Organization:* Students revise organization by moving from the preliminary drafts on their subject to forms that will accommodate their readers. Writing has a beginning, a middle, and an end, in the reader's mind if not in the writer's text. So the writer needs to ask whether these elements all work suitably and whether more detailed organizational schemes are required. Some types of writing, for example, have highly conventionalized formats for their organization. While the introduction and conclusion are important, your students also need to rethink (with the reader in mind) how much evidence, definition elaboration, or reasoning is needed; how many other perspectives or other arguments they need to acknowledge; how much background or context must be included; and how much detail is too much.

4. *Coherence:* Many students are surprised to learn that specific techniques can improve coherence quickly in their work. The sense of coherence arises from the reader's ability to follow the connections between sentences and between paragraphs in a piece of writing. Transitions, pronouns, and the repetition of keywords and sentence structures are cuing devices that your students can quite consciously add to their work without changing it much, sometimes with a great increase in clarity.

5. *Style:* Style reflects all the choices of the writer about syntax, order, and diction. Nevertheless, some basic guidelines may help students develop a more effective style. This chapter analyzes some examples and explains some of the elements of good style, advising about how to work on sentence structure and variety, how to use concrete language, and how to reduce wordiness. An analysis of just how good style is effective may go further than such rules to illustrate the principle. Using the paragraph on pp. 323 from Ian Frazier's *Great Plains*, for example, ask students to decide which of a collection of dramatic sentences might contribute the most to the opening paragraph. We might start the discussion by admitting that we couldn't have decided on just one choice. Surely the first sentence is a good

candidate. It introduces "Away" as the anaphoric refrain that will structure all the explanations and sets up the doubleness repeated in the introduction. The Great Plains are both "immense . . . prairie" and "mostly plowed under." Some of your students will surely point out the unusual intensity of the syntax, with its repeated exclamations. Or they may tell you that these are not sentences. Style in this paragraph is unusually poetic. Why might Frazier have wished to use such an opening? Compare the effect of the later paragraph. Then comes matter for some good discussion. You might ask if students thought any of the sentences did *not* really contribute much. This is an analysis you could usefully do with the whole class to model the lines of discussion possible.

Edward P. J. Corbett has a very useful discussion of style and a set of guidelines for analyzing style in *Classical Rhetoric for the Modern Student,* 4th ed. (New York: Oxford UP, 1998), 380–426.

6. *Voice:* Although we use the term *voice* to talk about the sense of personal presence created by the writer, it's misleading and perhaps a bit mystifying to talk as if a writer had only a single way of sounding that was authentically the writer's own. A few students regard stylistic flexibility as hypocritical or unfaithful to their true selves, but nevertheless students need to develop several modes of personal and impersonal address for varying writing occasions. There are political and cultural implications in the voice a writer adopts, and furthermore, most of us can't just switch easily from one voice to another. Nevertheless, some students will face continuing problems with their writing because they cannot reconcile their sense of personal voice with the kind of objectivity demanded in academic writing. Aristotle's broader notion of the writer's *ethos* is a helpful corrective. You might want to offer some ways out of the impasse.

Here's a suggestion for students who are having trouble imagining themselves taking on a *persona* that seems alien. Have such students write a parody of the voice they find most objectionable or most difficult to imitate. Making fun of the voice removes the objections. When they don't have to be successful in the pretense, students can gain some experience practicing the *persona.*

This issue of "voice" is a different matter for multilingual students, some of whom may have a sense of voice only when they write in their home language. Reading in English will help.

Activities

(p. 313) *For Exploration:* This exercise asks students to read Todd Carpenter's paper on a national bottle law in the same way that they are reading each other's essays, both noting changes and making suggestions. Take this opportunity to double-check their perceptions by discussing the results with the whole class. Students should emerge with a better ability to gauge how much room there is for differences in reading and recommending and how much agreement there is on basic responses to revision. You might pay special attention to students who feel lost here. A few may continue to have severe problems with revising because they are unused to reading critically.

(p. 314) *For Exploration:* Using "Guidelines for Evaluating Focus, Content, and Organization," students now put these strategies to work on their own drafts. First they are to answer each question with respect to their draft, as fully as possible. Then they are to list goals for revision. This will be an extremely comprehensive analysis if carried through carefully. It might, for example, lead to their seeking out additional counterarguments and details, perhaps through research or trying a test outline or summary to judge their effectiveness with organization. It is, in other words, a time-consuming exercise, worth giving as much importance as you might give to peer revision.

(p. 318) *For Exploration:* To define *voice,* students are asked to find two passages from their current reading, one of them with a personal voice and the other with a public voice. The questions that follow are designed to help students make connections between their response to *persona* or voice and the rhetorical strategies that produce the effect of voice. The example in the text of a personal voice is from a Ken Kesey essay on the rodeo. The example of a public voice is from an article by Jeff Medkeff in *Sky & Telescope.* As students discuss these passages, ask them also to think about the different effects of authority and believability in these "voices," and how they are related to a rhetorical situation.

For Thought, Discussion, and Writing (p. 327)

Number 1: This exercise asks students to put into practice on their own draft suggestions for improving coherence. After they have tried out the suggestions, you can ask students to discuss the results. Remind them that coherence depends on the ability of the reader to follow their logic. Adding extra transitional words and phrases can help. But have them look again at "The Bike Messenger Look Goes High Fashion." This example shows how to build on logical relationships. You may want to make such intensive checks a regular part of the classroom routine for a while, at least until you think students are beginning to resolve their questions about coherence.

Number 2: Like the preceding exercise, this one asks students to apply the chapter's guidelines, this time for revising style.

Number 3: A list of questions direct students' reading of Ian Frazier's essay "To Mr. Winslow," asking them to focus on style and structure. Their first description of the style may take the form of vague impressions. Ask them to find a word or sentence in the essay itself that seems to represent its style. Ask them to talk about *persona* in terms not only of character but also as tone. When they find examples of effective prose style, they will surely fix on the use of concrete words and, perhaps, sentence variety. Ask them if the sentences that are *not* concrete seem excessive or what function they perform. What is the purpose of the following sentences?

"These words echoed in the media as reporters quoted and misquoted them."

"Finally, I found a wooden stake broken off about half an inch above the ground: the base of the memorial cross, probably—the only sign of the unmeasured sorrows that converge here."

As they compare the passages that they think are characteristic of the writer's *persona,* ask students to work on attending to the interaction of textual form and the production of meaning. You will need to discuss the results in groups or as a whole class. The exercise would work well for group collaboration. You can then take group reports to the class as a whole. Since many students feel less than authoritative about their reading analysis, you will need to have some form of closure for them—not necessarily total agreement but an opportunity for them to get the idea of how others are talking about style.

To get the discussion started, ask what the major connections are. What major elements are repeated? You might mention the idea of overdetermination. Many elements of a good essay function in several different ways at once. And important ideas get repeated several different ways.

Number 4: This exercise assigns students an essay on the relationship of style and content, using a reading list of essays by Frazier. It includes a research component: Students both look for the essays in copies of magazines and use reading approaches they worked on in Chapters 3 and 4 to examine the essays. This chapter has made use of several selections from Ian Frazier. As a way of extending this inquiry into style, you may wish to provide your students with other selections from Frazier's writing. Following the method of comparison and contrast afforded by a range of writing by the same writer, you could ask your students to discuss the effects of rhetorical situation on style. Here is an additional list of citations, this time of books by Ian Frazier rather than essays located in magazines:

Frazier, Ian. *Coyote v. Acme.* New York: Farrar, 1996.
———. *Dating Your Mom.* New York: Penguin, 1987.
———. *Family.* New York: Farrar, 1994.
———. *The Fish's Eye: Essays about Angling and the Outdoors.* New York: Farrar, Straus, and Giroux, 2001.
———. *Great Plains.* New York: Penguin, 1990.
———. *Nobody Better, Better Than Nobody.* New York: Lyons, 1997.
———. *On the Rez.* New York: Picador, 2000.
Zinsser, William, ed. *They Went: The Art and Craft of Travel Writing.* Boston: Houghton, 1991.

Chapter 13: Strategies for Successful Collaboration

In This Chapter: Guidelines for Effective Interpersonal and Group Skills (p. 335)
Guidelines for Collaborative Planning, Drafting, and Revising (p. 345)
Guidelines for Using Electronic Technologies in Collaborative Writing (p. 351)

Collaborative writing is an increasingly common practice. While most students will have had a certain amount of experience working in groups, they often have no idea how widespread the necessity of writing with others could be. They will probably not have carried collaborative writing all the way through a project to final publication, yet many will move into academic disciplines that make extensive use of team projects and into careers that ask employees to write jointly. Perhaps most will find themselves working collaboratively in their communities as citizens. Email has made collaborative work easier, and Web sites often necessitate a collaborative effort. This chapter helps students address ways to improve group functioning and ways to tailor the writing processes they have already been developing to the special demands of collaborative planning, drafting, and revising. You can have students think about a collaborative project assigned for the composition class or for other classes. You can build on their experiences with group work and use the materials in this chapter to improve that as well. An example of a collaborative report is included. For more suggestions about teaching students to write collaboratively, see Section 2 of this manual.

Concepts

1. *Collaboration:* As this chapter explains, collaboration can take many forms, and students may work together at several stages of the writing process. This chapter will help students learn how to use collaboration from start to finish—from idea to final draft. Many people first set about a collaborative writing task from necessity. But often they discover unforeseen benefits from writing with others. Your students will find that not only is it easier to come up with ideas for writing when several writers are brainstorming but that it is also easier to negotiate blocks and do research. Often a collaborative task goes more quickly, even with the extra time spent on working together. However, collaboration in fact requires that students take time to work out matters of schedule and organization that they might not have planned all by themselves. Whatever else happens, it requires an explicit, commonly understood set of plans and schedules for writing. Thus experience with a collaborative writing project will help your students to articulate the writing process and discover how others write. At the same time that they encounter difficulties because writing styles may be markedly different, they also become conscious of stylistic qualities in their writing that were previously not noticed. Collaboration also requires students to address differences and perhaps discover what's at stake in their own perspectives. If you mark the significance of such exchanges, students will increase their understanding of the interaction between author and audience in the rhetorical situation. In other words, collaboration provides a built-in opportunity to use highly effective comparative methods of analysis on writing processes.

2. *Interpersonal and group process skills for collaboration:* The chapter provides guidelines for collaborative groups, emphasizing the importance of developing both "task-conscious" and "interactive" roles. Successful groups acknowledge differences of culture and of opinion and find ways to make them productive. Productive conflict can be better than imposing consensus. John Trimbur in "Consensus and Difference in Collaborative Learning," *College*

English 51 (1989): 602–16, has advocated what he calls the "rhetoric of dissensus" as a dialogic way of thinking about such collaborative work. That is, to avoid silencing group members who might not share the dominant opinion in the group, students need to be taught not to rush to consensus but rather to solicit the various perspectives within the group, most particularly if they disagree. At the same time, students will need to somehow come to a consensus about their goals and their procedures. To sufficiently value differences, collaborative work above all requires time spent meeting together—even if the meeting is via electronic technologies. An extended note in this chapter from Rebecca Burnett's work may help multilingual writers in particular understand specific steps they might take to improve collaboration. These include acknowledging the collaborator's work or views; asking for clarification or elaboration; making direct suggestions; giving additional information; challenging or politely disagreeing; and synthesizing plans.

3. *Planning, drafting, and revising collaboratively:* Working collaboratively gives students less flexibility in exchange for the added power of group work. A set of Guidelines provides some specific questions for groups to use to open up discussion, emphasizes the importance of articulating and communicating shared understandings, advocates taking advantage of electronic technologies, and warns against using a cut-and-paste method. Collaborative writing works best, in other words, when the writers work on group processes as they go and is likely to run into trouble if writers simply split up the duties and go their separate ways. As you assign collaborative projects, build in time and place for these group exchanges, and check to make sure that students are genuinely collaborating on their effort.

4. *Collaborating electronically:* Your students can work together on projects in several ways using electronic technologies. Students can work collaboratively by email or by using a common Web site. Long-distance collaborations have been made much easier by such resources. The task of putting together a Web site itself is an excellent collaborative task for a group of students. If you want to emphasize writing in such a project, you can specify the task to include not only links, images, and brief texts but also more elaborate texts—for instance, in a site meant to describe some aspect of your university programs. Chapter 13 includes Guidelines to help students work together using electronic technologies.

Activities

(p. 334) *For Exploration:* This activity uses freewriting and brainstorming to help students reflect about their previous experiences, both positive and negative, with collaboration. Using the same processes that they have previously used to reflect on the rhetorical situation, here students reflect on a situation that is necessarily more complex because more than one writer is included. Point out that they need to think about both issues of interaction and the pragmatic matters of inventing, drafting, and revising. Ask them to think about details such as how meetings were planned, whether they seemed effective, how they kept track of drafts, and so forth.

(p. 344) *For Collaboration:* This activity asks students to share responses to the first two activities, to compare findings, and especially to examine problem areas, checking Guidelines for possible ways to address these. If they have thought of problems not mentioned in the chapter, they are also to think of ways those might be dealt with. You may decide to have them discuss their responses as a class, with the hope that you will hear even more solutions than problems. Nevertheless, students may have a few horror stories about unfair grades or about how a member of a previous group slacked off and left all the work to the others. There may be a benefit: Such a discussion could exert some pressure on students not to let others down. You will want to have thought through the grading issue so that your policy is clear to students.

For Thought, Discussion, and Writing (p. 353)

Number 1: This extended assignment asks students first to tape-record a group session and then to analyze the recording with an eye to improving the group's performance and productivity. It could be of considerable help to your students in reflecting on how collaborative processes are actually working. Questions prompt evaluative judgments about the problem solving of the group. They enlist students in a perspective on collaborative processes that is pragmatic and goal-oriented rather than social or personal—or therapeutic. Thus this exercise will provide students with a model for evaluating collaborative writing that is tough, specific, and workable.

Number 2: This assignment asks students to write an essay about collaborative writing, drawing either on their observations from the tape recording and questioning of the previous exercise or on their own notes and observations from a current collaborative project. It is to be an essay about personal experience and a self-evaluation. After the thorough examinations of collaboration provided by this chapter, students should be able to write with considerable and informative detail. Have them look back through the various Guidelines in this chapter to make sure their essays rely on specific description rather than generalizations.

Suggestions for Further Activities

Number 1: The extensive planning needed for collaborative writing to work well is not easy to fit into a class schedule. You can, of course, ask students to do this work on their own time. But to launch a successful first experience with collaborative writing, set aside a period of time in each class for a week. During this time you can sit in on groups briefly to make suggestions about their process. More important, students see both how much time collaborative sessions might need and (with luck) how much more fruitful collaboration is with some investment in communication.

Number 2: Finally, as the groups move into the final stages of a project, the need to coordinate carefully becomes even more pressing. When you teach students how to write together, you shift their attention from making isolated judgments to negotiating consensus about procedures and goals. As a number of commentators have pointed out (including the authors), the movement toward consensus that is required for a collaborative project offers a microcosm of the powerful forces that converge to influence students during their education. So, too, it offers an occasion when you can use your leverage as a teacher to support a fuller participation and attention to diversity of voices than a less self-conscious group might allow, maximizing "productive conflict." You can call attention, for example, to the possibility noted by feminist theorists that gender differences mean female students are less likely to assert their perspective. There may also be cultural differences that come into play. You can ask groups to compensate but also to recognize the increased productivity that full participation of all group members will allow. Furthermore, you might point out that moments of difficulty and resistance or loss of focus in groups mark problems not only with the functioning of the group but also with what is written.

Part Four: Analyzing and Writing Academic Arguments

Part Four of *Work in Progress* includes four chapters on academic writing and argument, together with a careful description of analysis and argument in student writing and a portfolio of academic writing by students. These chapters discuss the rhetorical situation of academic writing, drawing on the idea of textual conventions and the experience with reading analysis that students encountered in Chapters 3 and 5.

Chapter 14: Understanding Academic Audiences and Assignments

In This Chapter: Guidelines for Analyzing an Assignment (p. 364)
Guidelines for Gaining Commitment to an Assignment (p. 367)

Chapter 14 discusses the expectations students need to consider when their audience is academic, pointing out that academic discourse depends on reason, analysis, and argument. Because academic reasoning deals with complexities, it especially resists oversimplification.

Your students will find here a list of possible responses to their recurrent question: "What does the instructor want?" And they will find specific suggestions about academic writing assignments and how to develop plans to complete them successfully. Multilingual students should be invited to discuss with the instructor and fellow students the differences in expectations they may observe.

As they work through this chapter, students will find it helpful to have a current writing project in mind so they can put the suggestions into practice.

Concepts

1. *The academic audience:* What do members of an academic community look for, as readers of their students' writing? Not, perhaps, what some of your students may expect—that is, not just evidence that students have done the assignment or even that they learned what they were told. Students may improve their ability to assess academic writing situations if they see their instructors as people thinking about a certain body of knowledge rather than just as evaluators of student papers. That means that individual instructors evaluate papers within a set of disciplinary standards, and students will have to learn something about the discipline, not just about general writing, to succeed. Fortunately, the work on rhetorical situation that students have done will help them analyze academic assignments and understand what further inquiry is needed to get the job done.

Through a position of mutual inquiry and shared rationality, rather than the adversarial relationship of student to grader, students may be able to give instructors what they really do want: evidence of thought. On p. 360, the text lists criteria for effective writing. A sample essay written by Hope Leman for a take-home examination on politics and the media appears on p. 361.

2. *Analyzing academic writing assignments:* Although assignments range from the very broad and general to the very limited and specific, keywords, such as *define* or *evaluate*, point to appropriate strategies. You might ask students to note that these keywords suggest varying levels of complexity: An evaluation or a defense may include definition, analysis, and summary, for example. Students frequently mistake the intent of an assignment, responding with a simpler mode than the assignment requires or oversimplifying complexity.

For example, in critical reviews students may simply write summaries instead of including evaluation. Or they may include nothing but evaluative conclusions with no summaries of the contents or definitions of criteria.

3. *Identifying the assumptions inherent in the assignment:* Identifying assumptions requires students to ask: What is the rhetorical situation of this class? Students often rely heavily on carefully specified objectives, believing that they can understand only limited and explicit course objectives. When extensive objectives are listed, however, students may read them mechanically as simply a list of disconnected objects with coercive intention. And worse, they may fail to think any further about what purposes the class may have.

Since students need to learn what kinds of connections might be made in a given discipline and how assumptions might be examined critically, they should be encouraged to formulate and reformulate for themselves what they see as the directions and purposes of their classes. Then the questions on p. 362 will help to focus students' own inquiry, perhaps helping them to make suggestions as if they were the professor, or to guide group work. Chapter 15 will provide further help with appropriate methods for analysis.

4. *Building commitment:* Commitment to an assignment is not quite the same as interest, even though both are ways of describing what motivates writers. Most students will readily admit that finding a way to make a writing assignment interesting is a big part of their struggle. Working on strategies of invention in your class has probably already showed them ways to get started, whatever the academic writing project, without inspiration or even prior interest. A lack of engagement in writing assignments leads students to do them in a perfunctory or superficial way, skipping the process of thought that their professor expected—sometimes because the student does not understand the steps of inquiry that support the final piece of writing. In many disciplines this might include research through reading, but sciences and even social sciences might expect a careful description of experimental methodology as well. Students who work through assignments carefully are in a position to ask questions about methods and expectations they do not understand.

An especially good way to get involved in an academic topic—to enter into the conversation already going on in that field—is through reading. This may be seen as prewriting or even prereading, a preliminary step that may not involve taking any notes at all but rather making annotations and jotting down questions and remarks in the writer's notebook. Without your encouragement, many students regard this kind of reading as a waste of time because it does not seem to lead efficiently to the final product. Consequently, they fail to give themselves sufficient time for reading and thinking about the topic. Web searches can suggest some of the dimensions of a topic and serve as a starting point, though students need to be reminded that online sources are not the only possibilities and are often not the best resources. (See David Rothenberg's cautionary essay at the end of Chapter 3.)

Activities

(p. 359) *For Exploration:* If students have been exploring their writing situation frequently during the term, so that most of the stereotypical responses have already been exhausted, this opportunity to freewrite about the academic situation may produce insights and unforeseen questions. For multilingual writers, this is an occasion to compare, contrast, and explore differences in academic cultures.

Some students will probably raise questions about the seemingly arbitrary differences in expectations among classes and their regular mystification about what expectations are. If they do, it's a good lead right into the next section on criteria for effective academic writing.

119

(p. 362) *For Collaboration:* This exercise has students work together on four discussion points about Hope Leman's essay. If you wish, ask them to report the results of their discussion to the class.

- The first discussion question asks them to think about the abrupt beginning of the essay, which was written for a midterm. They can focus on the question of audience and just how and when to take wider audiences into account in academic writing. Here there is no need to interest the reader of the exam in what you have to say—but this may also be true of other kinds of academic writing.
- The second question brings up the question of the controlling purpose and the thesis. Students identify the thesis and then discuss why it is important to be explicit in this context.
- The third question helps students think about how reflection on the question itself (a kind of metacommentary) can make the difference between a satisfactory and an excellent response.
- The fourth question points to the use of a personal voice in Hope Leman's essay— while not dominant, it is nevertheless an effective part of the objective, academic answer.

After discussing these points, ask the students if they have changed their minds about the standards instructors might use to grade midterm essays. If they were to construct a grading rubric, what elements would they include?

(p. 368) *For Exploration:* Notice the two important steps of this exercise freewriting about a difficult or frustrating academic writing experience. If your students are likely to express fervent antipathies to some academic writing experiences or to present a formidable inability to deal with a lack of commitment, you might want to provide in-class time for writing about this. You can then explicitly divide this freewriting into two parts, asking students first to focus thoroughly on the way the problem felt and then asking them to turn to the way they now imagine themselves handling it. In any event, it's important not to leave them with the conviction of frustration and ineptitude.

For Thought, Discussion, and Writing (p. 368)

Number 1: Interviewing instructors can be important not only for giving students a chance to find out about matters they usually think of as secret or forbidden but also for prompting them to speak rationally about their classes and their major fields with members of the faculty. This ability to get precise understandings about assignments is crucial. Previous practice with interviews ought to give them some confidence in carrying this out. They need to be particularly careful to check their understanding of what is said and to report it accurately. What methods are assumed in the assignment, and what conventions must students have understood to write it?

You may wish to have a panel of instructors come to your class, either to supplement individual interviews or to provide an alternative way to interview faculty. Some situations make the logistics of individual interviews difficult. Your colleagues will not increase their friendliness toward writing classes if nine hundred freshmen seek interviews frantically during the same week.

The information students bring back may well be useful to other students who do not usually have the chance to ask faculty such questions. You can ask your students if they would like to spend class time hearing the results.

Occasionally students are intimidated or have difficulty understanding their instructors, and their reports seem vague and misleading. Faculty members may not always be accessible.

Faculty members do not always know just how many of their assumptions about disciplinary writing need to be made explicit for beginners. In any event, you will be able to tell quite a bit about how well students understand their academic situation from their ability to carry out this assignment. Chapter 15 offers further help with disciplinary differences.

The text gives an essay as the final step of the exercise. You might want to gauge the accuracy and depth of the interviews before you assign an essay summarizing and commenting on the results. If the interviews reveal difficulties, you might find that students will benefit from writing an essay about why they still do not understand the goals of undergraduate education or of a particular class or why they feel anxious and frustrated about the analytic and argumentative skills required. Most classes, after all, are mixed experiences, and students may not understand the goals of a great professor for years.

Number 2: This activity asks your students to put the suggestions from the chapter into practice. Students should follow the steps of analyzing their assignment, recognizing its assumptions, developing commitment, and creating a plan for writing. Then they should evaluate this planning process.

Do as you did with writing processes: Keep both the positive and the negative aspects of students' discoveries out in the open as matter for discussion. Students who labor through this planning in a perfunctory or distanced way may have trouble imagining themselves ever doing it again. Their genuine distance from understanding the assumptions of the disciplines they are studying is not remedied quickly. Can students write and plan in the absence of understanding? Your job is to persuade them that they can at least make a beginning and that such a beginning is itself the work of understanding.

Number 3: This exercise asks students to reflect on their experiences so far with academic writing. They are to freewrite about what kinds of assignments have been easier or harder. Then they are to compare a more successful essay with a less successful one. This will enable them to freewrite about their understanding of how the writing was evaluated. Even if they have not received differing grades, they can reflect on how their instructors might have been using the kinds of criteria for success that have been discussed in this chapter. It is possible that this will change a few minds about how "subjective" the grading of essays is as well as help students to think more productively about how to write well.

Chapter 15: Understanding Academic Analysis

Chapter 15, continuing the examination of academic writing begun in Chapter 14, shows students how academic argument is indeed a "conversation," involving the critical analysis of other texts as much as the writing of new ideas. The chapter discusses the idea of purpose in the light of the topic's broader significance, and directs students to consider what frameworks or methods are usual and appropriate for the discipline they are writing in. Students will examine analysis and its relationship to argument by using a paper written by a student, Jacob Agatucci. Leading readers through the process of analyzing academic arguments, the chapter shows them how first to determine the author's position and then to engage in a critical reading, using an article by Amitai Etzioni to demonstrate. Included are sections on the "Question at Issue," Aristotle's Three Appeals, Stephen Toulmin and his framework for analysis, and recognizing fallacies. The chapter concludes with sample essays for analysis.

Concepts

1. *Analysis is a group of skills:* In academic discourse or inquiry, analysis and argument are intimately related. In disciplines such as literary criticism, which students sometimes imagine as a matter of personal taste, unsupported appeals to emotions or beliefs (or both) are unacceptable. Reasoning is the process that needs to appear in academic writing. When your students understand that they need to include analysis to develop their immediate responses, they will not feel so frustrated about the problem of evidence. They will see that comparing, defining, categorizing, showing cause and effect, and evaluating are the work of reasoned inquiry, and that this work supports argument. Often our students have felt utterly blocked by needing to "support" a response such as "this poem seems sort of depressed." Because they want to imitate a scientific model, they go looking for "facts" to buttress a conclusion, instead of articulating their processes of analytic thinking.

You may also find that your students have trouble seeing how analysis and argument connect. A journal article on population, defining and explaining cause and effects, might seem to them to be purely factual with no argument. Watching for methods of analysis will help make the structure of reasoned argument visible.

2. *Purpose and significance:* Knowing what is significant and interesting in a field is part of what it means to be an expert. Nevertheless, students who write well understand how to develop a feeling for the significance of an argument. They have both the ability to focus on a manageable purpose and recognition of the wider implications, which they will not address directly. For instance, an essay on the plausibility of the fool in *King Lear* bears on the general discussion of the fool that the assignment evoked, and also on the question of effective characterization in drama. The significance of an argument is separate from its more specific purpose, and it is a mistake for a student writer to think he or she must draw conclusions about these larger issues as part of the local purpose. Note that significance often seems to arise at the intersection of two topics under discussion in a field, as a function of their relationship. Point out to students that one way to discover a worthwhile approach is to relate two well-discussed elements. In the case of Jacob Agatucci's essay on *King Lear,* he has brought together the interpretation of the relationships in the play and the visual staging of it.

3. *Methods for analysis:* Students have the tough but inevitable task of figuring out the preferred methods of analysis for the disciplines they study. This chapter recommends that they first use the instructor as a model, analyzing his or her methods, noticing the evidence and the kinds of questions asked. Then students might apply some of the approaches for critical reading, looking at written models.

You can help students use you as a model by pointing out the methods of analysis you yourself are using, or that you would use if you were approaching a topic they are discussing.

4. *Questions at issue:* Using John Gage's description of stasis theory, the chapter lists six types of questions at issue that students may find in their analysis of arguments: questions of fact, of definition, of interpretation, of value, of consequence, and of policy. What is the value of recognizing the type of question at issue? In large measure, whether or not the methods used by writers are appropriate may be determined by the type of question. If there is a question of *fact,* specific evidence is essential; but if there is a question of *consequence,* you might well expect *causal analysis,* for example. As your students think more carefully about the kinds of arguments they might be writing, they will learn to sort through evidence in terms of its relationship to their point, the question at issue.

Students may be greatly assisted by thinking about whether they are concerned with a question of *interpretation.* When writing arguments, students often fail to connect evidence to purpose. They may assume that facts speak for themselves, and that their only obligation is to accumulate a great stack of them. Student writers need to think about the principle of selection, and about how they and others might interpret those facts. Often they need to make their interpretive assumptions explicit. You can usefully comment on this when you read drafts.

Students also often fail to show the relationships among judgments, criteria, and examples. For instance, in evaluations or critical reviews, students may say that a play was "well done," but they do not explain their standards for good plays, or cite particular instances. Students may not know how to negotiate the difference between widely accepted standards and personal preferences, especially because entertainment values have encouraged them to think that raw response is enough. You might ask your class whether they think the Nielsen rating is good evidence for a question of value—for saying whether a television program is good or not; or you might ask or how they feel about the "sweeps" determining what may be on television next year.

Class discussion will also reveal interesting differences about what kinds of arguments seem acceptable. See if your class feels that these differences are based on gender, ethnicity, race, religion, politics, region, family conventions, or other factors. Does your class agree on the touchiest subject, the argument everyone would like to avoid? This is a discussion to which multicultural and multilingual students may have especially valuable contributions.

Finally, students may have problems with advocacy, perhaps in part because they think "everyone has the right to their own opinion," and also because they are influenced by the spectacle of public debate. As a result, they are apt to separate problem solving from a reasoned consideration of values. A student may, for example, examine a hot topic such as child abuse or drugs or teen pregnancy by collecting arguments as if they were facts, submitting a collage of problems and solutions rather than thinking through the various positions and their relative merit.

When students submit position papers, taking a stand against abortion or in favor of the rain forest, they may mistake passionate opinions and emotional revelations for an invitation to discuss issues. You may want to address directly the forms of public debate your students are used to hearing and reading and ask them to look at them critically. What kinds of models have influenced students' ideas of good arguments? Can they bring some examples to class? Should they be relying on these models? Do they differ from the models they are seeing in the academic world?

This chapter invites the class to discuss these issues in relation to the article titled "Less Privacy Is Good for Us (and You)" by Amitai Etzioni.

5. *The author's position and critical reading:* The chapter suggests that students engage in a "two-step" process of reading—first, to understand what the author's position is, and then to engage that position critically. You may find it helpful to work with the class as a whole on the "believing and doubting" game suggested by Peter Elbow. How does this essay look from a sympathetic reading, from the perspective of agreeing with the writer? What happens when you read more skeptically—which of his strategies seem vulnerable, less persuasive? If this is a kind of Burkean "conversation," who else might be participating, as sources or context for the writer, and as sources and contexts for your students? What do they bring to this reading? How hard is it to agree? How hard to read critically? Why? The "Guidelines for Critical Reading" on pp. 385 will help students analyze the reading systematically.

6. *Aristotle's appeals:* This chapter returns to the three appeals of Aristotle first discussed in Chapter 5, this time in order to help students evaluate arguments. The point is not only to decide which appeals the writer uses, but also to determine how effectively each appeal is used. Appeals to *logos* rest on a structure of reason that students have just been thinking about in this chapter—not only evidence drawn from facts, from primary and secondary sources, but also the methods of analysis. The chapter urges a certain skepticism, since academic arguments rely so heavily on the appeal to logos. *Pathos,* the appeal to emotion, values, and beliefs, depends very much on the writer's knowledge of the readers, both as individuals and in a cultural context. A vocabulary drawn from hip-hop might be more appealing to a young audience than a vocabulary from Aristotle. At the same time, such an appeal could suffer from the problems often encountered by *pathos*—its effectiveness is severely limited to a certain group in a particular time and place. Academic argument often strives for a more general, or even universal, audience. Finally, *ethos* is an appeal that depends upon how the writer is represented. What goes into creating the reader's confidence that the writer is sincere, truthful, reliable, equitable, thorough, and balanced? Why are these important qualities for the *ethos* of an academic argument? Are there other qualities in a writer that students like? How might the question of *ethos* be culturally determined or even belong to a specific discourse community?

7. *Toulmin argument:* This chapter summarizes the features of argument identified by Stephen Toulmin: claims, qualifiers, warrants, reasons, and evidence. The identification of *warrants* may particularly interest you, because students can learn to trace the chain of reasoning in an argument even where it is not explicit by describing the warrants that are invoked—assumptions and premises not stated. The personal, political, and cultural "unconscious" of an argument will rest in its warrants. John Gage has argued that reasoned inquiry proceeds not through syllogisms or formal logic but through the informal logic of *enthymemes,* similar to the idea of warrants in that the third premise in a syllogism is not expressed, but rather assumed. So an argument takes on the form of *x* because *y:* "The war was not justified because no weapons of mass destruction were found." Left out is the assumption that the only justification for the war was Iraq's possession of weapons of mass destruction. The response to this argument might not answer directly—"Such weapons will be found"—but rather respond to the unstated warrant: "There were many other reasons that the war was

justified." Analyzing arguments through the Toulmin features is another powerful tool for your students, a kind of discursive microscope that will reveal the internal structure of the argument as they classify its contents.

8. *Fallacies in argument:* Rather than a listing of prohibited methods and strategies, the description of fallacy presented here is based on the rhetorical situation, and the fallacies are grouped around Aristotle's appeals. They represent shortcuts that will seem obviously unfair, unjustified, invalid, and excessive if the underlying claims and warrants are analyzed and made explicit. However, since argument rests on informal logic and never makes everything explicit, such fallacies are a matter of degree. This chapter describes the following: (Fallacies of Ethos) *ad hominem, guilt by association;* (Fallacies of Pathos) *bandwagon appeal, slippery slope;* (Fallacies of Logos) *begging the question, hasty generalization, and non sequitur.* This is not an exhaustive list, and your students may enjoy thinking about others that are traditional as well, or even making up names for new varieties—for example, *flaming the listserv* or *Realityshow appeal.*

Activities

(p. 378) *For Exploration:* This exercise asks students to analyze Jacob Agatucci's essay carefully to determine how analysis is related to argument and how the analysis is developed. The argument that the visual component of a BBC film enhances Shakespeare's dialogue frames the analysis. This is not a debate about whether film is better than written texts, or vice versa—though it resonates with questions about the relationship of film and literature.

1. As students examine argument and analysis, they should notice how important the pointed detail of the analysis becomes. This sentence, for example, hovers between analysis and argument: "This cinematic technique neatly encapsulates the relationship among these three characters and calls attention to an important feature of the plot." Because it is convincing, the sentence seems closer to an observation than to an interpretation. It is convincing, however, because it depends on the additional detail given about the characters' relationships and the plot. How do the visual additions contribute to the argument/analysis?

2. What is made explicit, and how are ideas connected logically in this paper? Students may already have had experiences with academic writing for which they were not given the highest grade because of a failure to "support" their ideas. Jacob Agatucci's paper shows some ways to develop a point. What do you think about the use of visuals to supplement this? Do you want your students to use images in their papers? And do they have access to technologies that make it possible?

(p. 379) *For Exploration:* This activity asks students to freewrite in order to explore what they have experienced with academic arguments in the past. They are asked to think about the affective side of these experiences—their interests, positive and negative experiences, and possible relationships to their personal preferences or to cultural standards, traditions, and fashions. Multilingual and multicultural writers can usefully explore how language differences might have affected their experiences analyzing academic arguments and how cultural differences might have entered into their responses. You can ask how the difficulty of arguments might have affected their analysis, and if there are certain kinds of questions or methods that make arguments especially difficulty to follow. You can make use of these responses either to prompt class discussion, or—if you read over these freewrites—to shape your pedagogy.

(p. 384) *For Collaboration:* This group activity asks each student to identify two of the questions at issue in Etzioni's argument and then to discuss them with other students. In particular, they should explore the agreements and disagreements they found among the group members, perhaps with an eye to the assumptions they bring to the text. Then they are to agree on two stasis questions and present reasons why these are central to the rest of the class. Again, this may provide an opportunity to think about differences in readings. Multicultural students may have some very interesting things to say about differences in cultural assumptions about privacy, and so they may also offer some interesting perspectives on Etzioni's argument. Is Etzioni culturally limited in his assumptions?

(p. 386) *For Exploration:* This exercise applies the guidelines that the students have just read. Students are to answer the questions after rereading Etzioni's *The Limits of Privacy,* this time critically. They should answer with the entire essay in mind. For example, the first guideline asks what the purpose or agenda of the author might be. Did the students change their mind about this as they read? How much does the introduction match the student's final assessment of purpose? Perhaps you will want to encourage them to do a little research—online?—to find out more about Etzioni, in connection with the second guideline, and its questions about the author.

(p. 386) *For Collaboration:* This exercise asks students to discuss their answers in a group. They may have gathered a considerable amount of material, so give them adequate time for an exchange. They may need to select and/or summarize in order to present their findings to the entire class.

(p. 389) *For Exploration:* This activity asks students to analyze the appeals used by Etzioni and to evaluate their effectiveness. They should write comments for each of the kinds of appeals. Ask them to distinguish between what they said earlier about questions at issue and their comments about appeals. It may help if they think first of themselves as the readers and then of another audience.

(p. 389) *For Collaboration:* After the previous activity, students are to work together to discuss their responses about appeals in Etzioni's argument and to discover areas of agreement and disagreement. Then they are to forge a shared position, with a statement and examples from the Etzioni essay. The implications this exercise are interesting: Shared positions reflect the possibility that an argument may communicate a main idea in spite of differences in its readers' interpretations and analysis.

(p. 391) *For Exploration:* In this activity, students choose one part of Etzioni's argument and use Toulmin's system to analyze it. Since they have already worked on this argument, they may very well imagine they have been thorough. Their reports of what they have found that they did not see earlier will demonstrate the "microscope" effect of a Toulmin analysis. You can point out that such a detailed close reading of a text is an important method of analysis and can be significant evidence in arguments of many kinds.

(p. 398) *For Exploration:* In this activity, students read the analysis of Etzioni's argument provided by Stevon Roberts in the text. By now, they should be very familiar with Etzioni's essay, and even so, if they have not skipped ahead to read Roberts's essay, they should find some telling commentary in it—critical readings they had not considered. They are to identify and explain two or three examples of this in the essay. Then they are to do a critical reading of this essay that suggests improvements. They may be able to draw on their own previous analyses to point out aspects of Etzioni's argument that Roberts has overlooked, or to disagree with his conclusions. Or Roberts's essay may bring up new readings of Etzioni.

(p. 398) *For Collaboration:* The process of critical reading continues in this activity, as students bring the previous individual analyses together to discuss Roberts and Etzioni. At this point, they should write about the extent of their agreements and disagreements with Roberts and choose the best passage from the essay, and their recommendations for improvement, to share with the class. Many students could greatly improve their performance in academic writing through this kind of patient critical rereading. Showing them that their first reading leaves them only with vague impressions and not with the kind of precise understanding that further analysis will reveal can be a powerful help in their future work on writing their own academic arguments.

For Thought, Discussion, and Writing

Number 1: This exercise asks students to practice their critical reading skills on two of the readings from Chapter 3, assessing skills and weaknesses. If you are using a reader together with *Work in Progress,* you may wish to extend this practice to essays in the reader. In particular, having students go back to essays they have already "read" underscores the importance of rereading for analysis. The interdependence of close reading and critical reading will become increasingly apparent as your students return to texts for more precise analysis. Sometimes you can help them achieve the critical patience to do this by breaking your assignment into separate steps again, as this chapter has done. The habit of reading texts once and once only, a habit of apparent efficiency, will be hard to deter. If you find your students reporting that they find nothing new on the second reading, even when they are asked to find, for example, the kinds of appeals being used instead of the kinds of questions at issue, you may need to lead the whole class through a couple of exemplary readings and rereadings.

Number 2: This exercise asks students to interview a teacher about the methods of analysis that are especially important for his or her discipline and to write a brief summary about the understanding of the discipline they have gained. An interview with a history teacher may elicit, for example, the response that chronology and factual detail are the most important components of historical analysis. Does the student notice the teacher using other methods listed in this chapter? Probably and, if so, the student can prompt the teacher by asking specifically about some of these—what is the role of interpretation? Causal analysis? And so forth. If you wish, you may have students develop a list from this chapter of methods of analysis from which teachers could choose in order to create a mutual rhetorical vocabulary.

Number 3: This activity provides another reading for students to analyze: Nadine Strossen's "Everyone Is Watching You." Since both Etzioni and Strossen address the issue of privacy, you may wish to extend the theme, providing additional recent material or directing students to materials online. Ask students after they have analyzed Strossen to think about how their reading of Etzioni influenced their reading of Strossen. How does the "conversation" implied by arguments around such topics change the methods of critical reading they might apply? Do they find themselves developing a sort of collection of *warrants* on which they are willing to rely? Do criticisms of Etzioni alert them to problems in Strossen's essay?

Further Activities

Number 1: Ask students to bring in examples of arguments with unspoken warrants they might question. They can look for arguments they disagree with for reasons they cannot quite specify. These might include arguments they engage in with friends as well as written examples. Have them suggest one or more unspoken warrants that might be operating, and then analyze whether they agree or disagree with that warrant. If you wish, you can go on with this by having students work together to discuss the arguments and warrants they have identified. Other group members may be able to add ideas about hidden warrants.

Number 2: Analyzing newspaper editorials for a week provides practice in thinking about appeals, questions at issue, claims, and the warrants used in arguments. The object is not to find airtight distinctions among arguments, because most editorials will, in fact, mix questions of fact, value, policy, and so forth. Furthermore, your students, like all audiences, will read for the appeals that seem persuasive to them, and will tend to give them priority. Students will probably disagree about what the major questions of many editorials might be, so the exercise provides practice in identifying claims of different kinds.

When they bring the editorials to class, their discussion may reveal that different individuals or groups see the same editorial differently. There is a reader's share even in the structure of claims, reasons, warrants, and evidence. You might ask students what this discovery suggests for their own arguments. Ask them to consider how editorials work effectively—how claims prove anything—in spite of their various readers. Resist letting the discussion resort to "everyone to his or her own opinion," since that does not solve the puzzle of effective argument. As an alternative, use arguments from online publications, such as *Slate, Salon, Wired, Undercurrent,* or *Bad Subjects.* Of course, students may find interesting differences if they look into English-edition newspapers from non-English-speaking countries.

Number 3: Since advertising is an argument and operates almost entirely by the suggestiveness of hidden warrants, see if students can unpack the arguments in an advertisement or commercial.

Chapter 16: Understanding Academic Argument

This chapter addresses the contexts for academic argument and how it differs from other kinds of argument, particularly "debate." It points out the chief characteristic of academic discourse: Argument serves as a method of inquiry, not as a process of taking sides. It reviews Aristotle's appeals as they appear in academic discourse. As multilingual and multicultural students may recognize, academic argument in North America rests on disciplinary traditions that have a long history, but that may also differ from traditions elsewhere. The chapter discusses what makes it worthwhile to make an argument in academic disciplines, and how to determine what's at stake in order to form a thesis. Academic arguments must be based on good reasons, but they also include values and beliefs; this chapter helps students understand these relationships. Finally, it explains why academic arguments, as inquiry, must make use of counterarguments and how students should include "the other side" in their writing.

Concepts

1. *Academic argument:* Academic argument is most of all a method of *inquiry* to discover knowledge. To put it another way: The raw power struggle implied in the competition between opposing views should not be true of academic argument. However, some kind of struggle is implied, and reasons to argue are very dependent, of course, on academic disciplines. Thinking of academic argument in terms of the rhetorical situation helps to clarify what's at stake for students. What prompts an argument? A claim or fact that your student does not accept. Or a claim that your student wishes others would accept, but has reasons to think some may not. It is difficult for students to know enough to understand what disciplinary claims are credible, but they can learn to recognize a situation where argument might be appropriate. In other words, academic argument is generated out of a situation where a counterargument might be possible. The counterargument is very important because it is an integral part of the argument.

2. *Aristotle's three appeals in academic argument:* This chapter emphasizes that academic argument does not rest solely on an appeal to *logos*. The appeals to *ethos* and *pathos* may be conventional and traditional, and may include such matters as the style of presentation and even visual aspects. They may also, however, include the choice of vocabulary and, in particular, the judicious use of figurative language. A metaphor used by Edward P. J. Corbett illustrates how much influence figurative language can have.

Students who seek to use figurative language in their arguments should exercise caution (unless the metaphor is taken from a source text). Is figurative language an integral part of *logos* as well? Philosophers and literary theorists who explore the significance of figurative language or metaphor in the construction of knowledge include poststructuralists such as Jacques Derrida and American philosophers such as George Lakoff and Mark Johnson. A deconstructive argument might locate a hidden but foundational metaphor to show its hierarchical function, as Derrida reveals assumptions about the priority of voice over text in phenomenology in his *Speech and Phenomena*.

Appeals to *logos* in academic argument usually appear, however, as the logical and evidentiary requirements of disciplines—good reasons, acceptable evidence, the inclusion of counterarguments.

3. *Can this claim be argued?* As the Guidelines in this chapter suggest, arguments need to be about something that is at issue, and they need to persuade readers to believe in their claims, or to do something. Frequently students have a hard time understanding what the thesis of an essay ought to be because they do not think in terms of taking a position on a topic. They need to address an audience, and its array of positions, not just a topic. But the academic audience is unfamiliar. And peer response groups do not automatically provide a good sense of an audience that is committed to the ideas of a certain discipline. Ask group members to imagine what convictions might be unsettled or overthrown if the writer proves a certain point. Samples from newsgroups and mailing lists would be interesting texts for trying to decide what's at stake. In academic argument, "what's at stake" points not to opposing sides of an issue, but to the significance of the argument in the larger (perhaps disciplinary) conversation.

The argument must be stated as a *thesis*, meaning that the student must take a limited position. Even if they understand the idea of a thesis and can identify it in the papers of others, some students do not like asserting themselves in a position-taking stance. A resistance to position-taking can stem from their experience in what Tannen called "the argument culture," a desire not to offend others; or they may lack confidence in their ideas and feel a deep desire to avoid writing that takes such risks. Multicultural writers may find North American position-taking rude. Urge students to locate examples of a thesis that both states a position and avoids engaging in a confrontational *ethos*. Show them how taking counterarguments into account can help them develop balanced theses.

4. *The role of values, assumptions, and beliefs:* Even academic writing depends on a number of assumptions that remain unexamined. You might want to talk about these with your students, looking at some academic writing to decide what assumptions are made, what remains unexamined, and why. Show students how disciplines as interpretive communities have patterns of shared assumptions. A challenge to these assumptions is generally a major enterprise, a disciplinary revolution and not just a brief examination of assumptions. For example, a basic assumption in writing about literature has been the idea that literary texts are different from—and better than—other kinds of writing. Feminism, cultural studies, and poststructuralism have all challenged this assumption, generating considerable theoretical controversy. Scientific discourse also undergoes changes. However, a student's challenge to the theory of evolution is too major an enterprise for an academic paper.

Students often raise very interesting questions about disciplines because they do not know what is taken for granted. However, the truth is that students will seldom succeed in revolutionizing a discipline—their argument will fail instead to seem effective. Students need to be aware of these regular patterns of disciplinary assumptions or bases in order to write successfully. Even the challenges that appear as legitimate operate within discursive limits, or as arguments about limits.

Students also need to think about what their own arguments depend on and how they might be challenged. What do your students write about as if everyone agreed, or shared the experience, when they know that is not the case? Peer groups can help with this, pointing out assumptions that someone might challenge without the onus of a personal confrontation. Cultural diversity in your class helps ensure that provincialism will be challenged. You can help by making it clear that such questioning is valuable.

As students work through the "Guidelines for Analyzing Your Own Values and Beliefs," they may realize how much the goal of academic objectivity depends upon a relationship of *dialogue* with other writers and other texts. If academic inquiry progresses through argument, then writing that appears outside argument will also appear outside the interest of academic readers. Without defending some of the cultural limits of academic discourse that may be indefensible, you can show students various ways to deal with such limits other than assaulting a brick wall or giving up.

5. *Good reasons and evidence:* The analysis in this chapter demonstrates how the rhetorical situation might enter into students' reviews of their arguments as they use the tools discussed in Chapter 15: Aristotle's appeals, the question at issue, and Toulmin's categories. Students should not begin this review too early in the process of generating their arguments—rather, their critical analysis should take place after they have gone through the process of writing a first draft (alas for students who procrastinate). Then, in addition to the tools they have learned, students should turn to the chapter's "Guidelines for Evaluating Evidence." These guidelines recommend that students examine their examples, their statistics, and their use of authorities. You can talk to them about their use of sources at this point. Perhaps you will want to introduce the problem of choosing secondary sources with these guidelines in mind. What about using a source that is out of date? That is unacceptable within a discipline? That is biased?

6. *Counterarguments:* Students need to understand the importance of considering and including counterarguments in academic writing. Counterarguments may provide the stimulus for writing about a topic in the first place. Thinking of counterarguments will help students recognize and answer possible challenges to their assumptions. Considering counterarguments also will shift their reasoning from diatribe to dialogue. The counterarguments can serve as an important way of organizing an essay. And members of peer groups can learn to represent possible counterarguments, stimulating a more active consideration of writers' positions.

You can encourage students to assume critical roles even when they have limited knowledge, or do not feel critical. Use group work to dramatize the practice. Students need to learn to play the devil's advocate, raising counterarguments for themselves. You can have them argue one side and then the other without asking them to take up an *ethos* that could cynically argue both sides. Or take a few topics for general discussion and pass out pieces of paper assigning positions ("You are a logger in favor of cutting old-growth timber." "You are an environmentalist against cutting old-growth timber.") Ask students to write out slips of papers representing various positions on their topics to perform this exercise in their groups. Point out how learning to reason from the standpoint of the other is also an exercise in empathy, a recognition of our real inner ambivalence and the complexity of most arguments. It is important to be able to take a position, and also to suspend the argument in its favor long enough to hear other perspectives.

Activities

(p. 405) *For Exploration:* This activity asks students to reread the essay in Chapter 3 by Jonathan G. S. Koppell, "No 'There' There," examining his use of appeals to *ethos* and to *pathos* and looking for good reasons and evidence. Then they should write two or three responses that analyze how he uses *logos* together with the appeals to *ethos* and *pathos*, and provide passages that support their analysis. This is a step in the practice of close critical reading.

(p. 405) *For Collaboration:* Students bring previous responses to a meeting with their peer group and work toward a summary statement all can agree on to share with the whole class. Use a timekeeper and recorder for each group to ensure equal participation: It's too easy for groups to short-circuit this process and simply let one member's summary be the group's choice. You might ask them to go on to specify what difficulties they had in reaching an agreement, or whether there were disagreements they had to simply omit.

(p. 410) *For Exploration:* This exercise asks students to analyze their own values, assumptions, and beliefs about a possible writing topic. They are to list opposing arguments as part of their analysis. This not only helps them to imagine counterarguments they might address; it also will reveal much about their own commitments. Those in danger of being overinvolved in an issue are encouraged to think about their unexamined assumptions and whether they want to examine them. Those who habitually choose topics because they seem obvious or workable begin instead with a sense of commitment to an issue. Ask your students to repeat this freewriting and analysis for each essay topic they consider.

(p. 413) *For Exploration:* This activity asks students to answer three questions about the analysis of rhetorical situation, rough draft, and final draft of the essay "Why Isn't There a National Bottle Law?" that appeared in Chapter 12. First, they are to find the thesis statement ("The United States government should require every state to have a bottle law or constitute a national bottle law."). This enables the writer, Todd Carpenter, to argue for more than a change of attitude (the rough draft just said "What a shame."). Readers now find themselves asked to think about taking action—making a law. So the addition of a thesis shifts the way all the paper's reasons and evidence will be read. Ask your students to point to specific consequences in the paper. Are there sentences whose meaning or impact seem to change when viewed from the perspective of the added thesis?

Next, students analyze and list changes in the revised draft that make it a more effective academic argument. The second draft is more academic in a number of ways, from style to the specificity of evidence. Some students may nevertheless prefer the more relaxed tone of the first draft—if so, you can speculate about style and rhetorical situation. When they turn to the third question, students can imagine changes appropriate to the rhetorical situation implied by an ecological audience rather than an academic setting. Would such a group prefer a more relaxed tone? Wouldn't they want great precision about evidence? Would Todd need to add material about the impact of discarded bottles on all environmental efforts? Or comparisons with other environmental projects?

(p. 416) *For Exploration:* This exercise asks each student to develop a workable plan—thesis, claim, and appropriate evidence—for writing an argument. Since all the elements must mesh, you might encourage students to weigh their options carefully, perhaps rewriting the thesis after thinking about evidence and claims, or listing questions about claims and evidence for group discussion.

When students find that a number of the kinds of questions at issue can work for their arguments, have them arrange the claims in hierarchical order so they can see how to organize their evidence. Does the writer on teen pregnancy think that the most important claim is one of fact—for instance, arguing that teen pregnancy is a problem connected with poverty, disproportionately affecting girls from low-income families? Or is the most important a claim of policy—for instance, that the government ought to fund programs to prevent teen pregnancy because it increases poverty and all its accompanying problems? Should the writer, in other words, emphasize facts about the nature of teen pregnancy, examples of the problems faced by poor teen mothers, or an explanation of social programs to help teen mothers?

Often the emotions associated with a much-discussed public issue make the issue seem self-evident. Refusing to take the self-evident for granted can sometimes give a student a lead for his or her thesis. For example, the writer could observe that teen pregnancy seems a persistent problem despite mass education about sex and birth control, asking if there are other reasons why teens keep getting pregnant.

(p. 417) *For Collaboration:* This exercise asks your students to think of as many counterarguments to a thesis as possible, without pausing at this point to develop any of them, as a version of brainstorming. You may need to practice this assignment several times when you first assign it so that everyone gets a feeling for what counterarguments might be like. You might also bring a couple of statements to class on each of the next two or three days and challenge students to produce counterstatements, writing them down as a list or brainstorming aloud.

(p. 423) *For Exploration:* This activity provides another example of an academic argument, written by Stevon Roberts: "My Identity Crisis—and Yours." The exercise asks students to read and then reread, annotating the essay for its thesis, major claims, and reasons and evidence, and to evaluate the argument's effectiveness overall. They should then decide on its strengths and weaknesses. You might remind your students that this is not merely a formal evaluation; their response should be to the argument and not just to its status as an example, so they will need to decide whether they agree or disagree, and why. Does anyone find that they disagree even though they think the argument is "effective"?

(p. 423) *For Collaboration:* In this activity, students meet with a group to discuss their results. Their next step is to assess whether the group agreed or disagreed. Then students are to discuss how a critical reading helped them to understand the task of writing an academic argument. What did they see in Roberts's essay that they might apply to one of their own? These conclusions might be shared with the class as a whole.

For Thought, Discussion, and Writing

Number 1: This essay assignment pulls together the separate steps in preparing an argument that students have worked on through the chapter. Encourage students to refine their ideas as they develop their essays. If they have, indeed, worked their topic through the various exercises, they have probably found themselves with considerable material. The complexity now revealed will, in fact, make it a less familiar essay assignment. Most students have developed shortcuts that allowed them to write but also reduced their effectiveness in the long run. You may, in other words, find yourself at this point needing to reassure your students that the more sophisticated essay they are about to write will serve them better in their academic careers—and that such writing also takes practice to master.

Number 2: This activity asks students to interview a teacher about characteristics of a successful argument in his or her discipline and to write a summary. If they return to the same teacher they have interviewed before, they might think about how the idea of a successful argument is related to the disciplinary conventions and methods they have previously asked about. You can see the possibility of an interview essay here: Using all the material they have gathered over the term, students can discuss writing practices and what makes a good argument in a particular discipline.

Number 3: This activity asks students to select and bring to class two editorials or opinion columns from the school newspaper (or other source you can specify)—one that seems successful and one that seems "suspect." If you collect these ahead of time, you can put one or two of them on transparencies and discuss them with the whole class. You might also select the most interesting for smaller groups of students to analyze and evaluate. This is an opportunity for students to practice their critical reading skills in a very important context. The opinion pieces they select are not, however, academic arguments. As a final step, you might want to have them specify the ways these arguments do and do not work as "academic" arguments, and why.

Chapter 17: Putting It All Together: Analyzing and Writing Academic Arguments

Chapter 17 presents a case study of an argument. Tracing the development of the argument through a student's three drafts of an academic essay, the chapter provides an intimate analysis of the evolving paper. Following the case study, there is a sampler of academic writing by students.

Concepts

1. *Case study of an argument:* Beth Runciman, the writer, provides the notes she kept in a journal of the writing process and her analysis of the rhetorical situation: its *ethos, logos,* and *pathos.* Her first draft begins with a reading of the poem by Emily Dickinson she has selected. Analyzing the metaphorical structure, the rhythm, diction, and syntax, she develops an idea of the poem. In her second draft, she develops a thesis about the metaphorical structure and its allusions to the biblical story of Noah. This thesis makes an argument that connects the language of the poem to the cultural context of its writer and its readers—"A shared cultural story." Her final draft arises out of a return to her original analysis of the rhetorical situation. She decides that she wants to make clearer how critical and subversive of her culture Dickinson often was. In other words, she goes beyond arguing for a connection to culture and becomes more specific about what was at stake in that connection. In so doing, she not only shows how Dickinson's poem makes a kind of argument, but she also makes clearer that her own argument enters into some debates about poetry and culture that are more specific than the general claim about alluding to the story of Noah. She shows how Dickinson revised the cultural story. Her paper now enters into the "conversation" about revisionary narratives and about the possibility that literature might not only repeat but might also subvert cultural norms.

In each case, the drafts connect the conceptual argument to the analytic reading of the poem, adding evidence where it becomes necessary. The three drafts demonstrate the mutual interaction of argument and evidence. They also show how argument may emerge from analysis, through the process of making what's at stake increasingly explicit. Rather than adding an issue to a description, the argument comes out of clarifying the thetic element of the description, examining more fully how the poem itself participates in a rhetorical situation.

2. *Counterarguments and the academic conversation:* Note that counterarguments are engaged subtly in this argument. Once what's at stake is identified, more extensive possible counterarguments might be considered by thinking about the academic conversation she has entered. Has anyone argued that Dickinson is *not* subversive? Research could turn up such a position. What about theoretical counterarguments—about the speaker's identification with Noah, for example, or about the differences between subverting the reading norms of a nineteenth-century reading versus the status of a twentieth-century reading. In other words, the paper could become longer and the argument more substantial by a layered consideration of counterargument. Often undergraduate essays stop here, without engaging the counterargument of critics, and graduate writing differs from undergraduate by pushing on to thoroughly explore the critical situation.

3. *"A Miscellany of Student Essays":* This collection offers a range of different kinds of academic writing assignments. The following are included:

- An essay for a philosophy class by Stevon Roberts and Julie Baird
- A response to a scientific article by Hannah Grubb
- An essay for an art class by Michelle Fuller

- An application for a summer research fellowship by Tara Gupta
- A timed essay exam by Elizabeth Ridlington
- A personal narrative by Monica Molina
- A take-home essay exam by Eric Hill
- An analysis of a text by Chris Bowman
- A progress report on a long project by Brenda Shonkwiler

In particular, you might want to have students pay attention to the roles of analysis in these essays. They may also be used to review the various strategies studied in Part Three of *Work in Progress*. For further examples of assignments and student writing, see Section 4 of this manual.

Activities

(p. 435) *For Exploration:* This exercise asks students to find changes at the word or sentence level in the second and third drafts of Beth Runciman's essay. You may wish to hear what changes your students thought of as improvements and also, to go a step further, to have them try to specify why these changes improved the essay and even whether the changes seemed related to the increasing clarity of the thesis.

(p. 438) *For Exploration:* This exercise asks students to freewrite about the analytic techniques required by one genre of academic writing and about the kinds of writing ability called for by such techniques. This is, in other words, the first step of an inquiry into writing across the disciplines. While most students may feel comfortable doing one kind of writing, most students also feel some discomfort or unfamiliarity with others. Many of your students will declare themselves ambivalent about how confident they feel with forms that are familiar (since good students have done research papers in high school, they may choose them, for example, and yet also declare themselves not particularly expert). To underscore the disciplinary differences in writing, ask students to discuss writing by content area rather than by type.

(p. 438) *For Collaboration:* This exercise follows the previous one, asking students to answer questions that ask them to compare their experiences with academic writing. Each student should read the freewriting aloud to begin.

1. The group records the various kinds of writing they discussed. If you like, ask them to add other kinds of writing they have encountered as well.

2. The group records the kinds of analytic skills required by the various types and discusses the similarities among them. For example, do they require separating ideas into various parts? Describing organization or structure? Causes or effects? Definitions? Classifications? Evaluation? What kinds of details and evidence are relevant? What relationships among them? Refer students to "Guidelines for Developing an Appropriate Method for Analysis" in Chapter 15.

3. The group then discusses the differences in analytic skills demanded by the processes of writing different types of assignments, again referring back to Chapter 15 if needed.

(p. 463) *For Exploration:* This exercise asks students to freewrite about a specific analytic technique that they frequently use in the kind of academic writing they believe they have to some extent mastered. Then they are to think about what writing techniques they must use with this technique.

(p. 463) *For Collaboration:* This activity asks students in the group to compare their answers about individual mastery of various kinds of academic writing and the analytic techniques required. The group is directed to think about this systematically. First, thinking about the different kinds of writing included by their group may reveal a range students have not yet experienced firsthand. Second, comparing analytical skills may show how these are generalized across academic areas and genres of writing. Third, considering the different demands of academic writing genres may underscore the need for students to situate their writing carefully within the context of academic disciplines. This exercise will help students to think about writing in the content areas more broadly.

For Thought, Discussion, and Writing (p. 463)

Number 1: This question asks students to freewrite or brainstorm their observations about their work done so far. This reflective assessment asks them to consider both process and product. Perhaps you will want to give them a specific amount of time to do this so they will be pressed to generate thoughts beyond the first general impressions.

Number 2: The second question also asks students to reflect and then to freewrite or brainstorm, this time about future writing. They are to write both about what kinds of writing they will need to do and about how well they are prepared to do them, and then to list some steps they might take to improve their writing even further.

Number 3: The final question asks students to use the information they have generated in their freewriting or in their brainstorming to write a reflective essay about their writing— both what they have accomplished and what they will need to do in the future. Many instructors use such a reflective essay as the final one for a writing class or as the final examination. If you are interested in doing so, you should have students read over the portfolio or collection of the writing they have done so far. They may wish to use quotations or examples from that writing. They may also use information they have gathered in the course so far to be specific about the kind of writing in the disciplines they will face in the future. Did they interview an upperclassman or a professor in their major? Did they write earlier about the characteristics of the writing they will encounter in their major? This material will help them to write a fully developed essay reflecting on their current situation.

WRITERS' REFERENCES

Documentation Guidelines: In this appendix, *Work in Progress* provides your students with two commonly used systems of documentation; the MLA (Modern Language Association) Guidelines and the APA (American Psychological Association) Guidelines. The MLA documentation system is probably the most familiar to instructors, and offers a useful method of documenting quotations within papers that students can easily adopt for class work. The Web site does not post the handbook, but has current reports and responses to questions: <http://www.mla.org/>. The APA system highlights dates of publication, alerting readers and students when they are consulting sources that are seriously out of date. The APA Web site points out updates for the fifth edition and maintains an ongoing update of information about electronic technologies. It also features a section on "Removing Bias in Language" at <http://www.apastyle.org/elecref.html>.

Other important writing guidelines include the following:

The *Chicago Manual of Style,* 15th edition. University of Chicago Press, 2003. The press has a Web page for discussions and questions that your students may find useful and even interesting: <http://www.press.uchicago.edu/Misc/Chicago/cmosfaq/cmosfaq.html>.

The Council of Biology Editors, *Scientific Style and Format: The CBE Manual for Authors, Editors, and Publishers,* 6th edition. New York: Cambridge UP, 1994. The CBE maintains an extensive set of examples on its web site: <http://www.monroecc.edu/depts/library/cbe.htm>.

4. SAMPLE ASSIGNMENTS AND STUDENT ESSAYS

In the following pages we have collected sample assignments and student essays written for courses using *Work in Progress* as their text. Topics include the following:

Assignment for a critical review of an essay

Sample critical review of an essay

Assignment for a critical review of a reading from an academic area

Sample critical review of a reading from an academic area

Assignment for an argument

Sample argument

Assignment for a review

Sample review

Assignment for an analysis of a writing sample

Sample analysis of a writing sample

Assignment for an interview

Sample oral history

Assignment for an advanced class: Literacy narrative

Sample literacy narrative

Assignment for an advanced class: Rhetorical situation

Assignment for a Critical Review of an Essay

Writing a critical review is a basic step for most kinds of research. It involves not only reading for what the author intended to say but also reading "critically." Accordingly, your task for this essay will be twofold: You need to communicate the content of the original essay, and you also need to evaluate the essay.

Choose any one of the essays in our collection of readings as your subject, whether we have read it in class or not.

You may wish to start by writing a first-impression response, recording your reading experience before you go on with any analysis. After first reading the essay, freewrite whatever comes to mind—whatever strikes you, confuses you, or reminds you of something. Write down phrases that leap out without yet thinking about why. In this first response, your own initial prejudices and opinions may very well emerge, too. Again don't try to sort all this out yet. If you write this kind of first-impression response, you'll use it as a discovery draft, a way to think. In fact, you may use almost none of the text from a first response in a later critical essay. What the response does is to help you see what you thought.

Next go to work on trying to understand what the writer intends to say. What is the writer's rhetorical situation: Why is he or she writing? Who is the intended audience? Can you summarize the main points of the essay? How are the writer's most important themes developed? Are there certain phrases that seem to make the point especially well—phrases you might want to quote? In this work for understanding, you try to set your own feelings and opinions aside, even though your point of view will necessarily color what you see.

Finally, look at the essay "critically." Of course, that does not necessarily mean that you will say something negative; it means that you will interpret, analyze, and evaluate. Look at the essay from another point of view: Move away from your posture of unquestioning attention. Ask questions. Does the writer miss something that ought to have been taken into account? Does the writer "cheat" by making assumptions that ought to have been questioned? Why is the essay effective? How do style and arrangement contribute to its effectiveness? What are the implications of the writer's points? If an essay seems memorable, it is frequently because we can see many other examples supporting its claims or observations. What makes the essay interesting? Does it tell you something new? Does it say something you always thought but never could quite express? Do you agree or disagree—or both?

You may organize your review in two parts, with the summary coming first and the critical evaluation second. Or you may organize it around three to five main ideas, or sections, with each paragraph including both your summary and your critical commentary.

Use a bibliographical entry to head your review instead of a title. If you quote an entire sentence or passage, note the page number in parentheses at the end. Quotes longer than four lines must be indented five spaces. The finished length should be two to four pages, typed.

Sample Critical Review of an Essay

(Wrigley, Robert. "The Swing, the Snow, the Skull of a Hare." *Northwest Variety.* Ed. Lex Runciman. 1987. 138–44.)

In the essay, "The Swing, the Snow, the Skull of a Hare," Wrigley states, "I think that we are all regional writers, that we all carry with us the landscape we have come to call home" (Wrigley 140). The belief that a writer is or is not regional leaves much to be debated. A recent article in *Oregon Focus* magazine, titled "We Are the World," by Doug Marx does just that. Marx argues, "All this literary talk about regionalism is, if not pure bunk, at least artificial in the given text" (Marx 9). In contrast, Wrigley has strong feelings that there is something about the climate or the soil that inspires people to write.

Wrigley admits without shame that he was drawn to the Northwest and to Idaho by geography. His writing reflects the mountains and canyons, the wild, far-falling rivers, and the exhilaration he feels around them. Wrigley writes: "I was struck as I am again and again by the beauty of this irregular landscape, this dramatic unlevelness. It appeals to me, I think, for the same reasons swinging did when I was a child. It is up and down, it is rhythm on a dazzling vast scale" (Wrigley 140). He relates his love for the landscape to his enjoyable memory of swinging. Can this same simile be made in the far-flat Midwest? One of the distinctions of a well-written essay is that it introduces the reader to an idea that he or she would never have thought of otherwise. Could someone who has lived all of life in the Midwest make such an analogy? People who live in different regions may not think to associate the same things because they don't see the same scenery.

Wrigley, his wife, and his son borrowed a friend's cabin in the mountains near where they live and spent most of their Thanksgiving holiday there one year. He picturesquely describes how one morning he slipped into his skis for a trip through the woods and up onto a flat-topped knoll. Here is a sample of his vivid description: "From on top you can see across Hells Canyon, with the Seven Devils Mountains on one side and the Oregon Wallows on the other. The sky was clear; it would be a gorgeous and frigid dawn" (Wrigley 142). Wrigley is again describing a region of great inspiration to him. There is something about snow-covered mountains that amazes people and causes them to wonder. There is a feeling of a stimulation when people can stand at the top of a mountain and sense that they can see forever. Wrigley ponders the same excitability: "I thought to myself how in the seventy or eighty square miles of this little mountain range there were likely no more than six or seven people, and all of us had gotten here on skis or snowmobiles; there were no plowed roads here this time of year. It was that feeling, that exquisite melancholy, that silent, still exhilaration that the earth, and art, can bring on" (Wrigley 142).

As Wrigley proceeded on, he saw the tracks of a snowshoe hare. At the moment he saw the tracks, they reminded him of the summer before when he and his son went camping and found intact the skull of a hare. They took it home and boiled it in bleach. It is now on his son's dresser and is one of his most prized possessions. This experience inspired him to write the poem, "The Skull of a Snowshoe Hare." One of the lines in the poem has great significance because it relates nature to human understanding in a very subtle way: "If we relish the artifacts of death, it's for a sign that life goes on without us" (Wrigley 143). Thoughts like these can be understood by people, despite the region they live in, but it is the region that has created the images to bring on the thought. Wrigley explains, "It is a quieter poem than usual. Blame that on the tenderness of the subject, the landscape softened under snow" (Wrigley 143).

Marx states: "Are Homer, Shakespeare, Tolstoy, Balzac, and Dickens in any sense 'regional'? Probably—but the fact of our being able to locate their stories within this or that geographical boundary has little bearing on our appreciation of them" (Marx 10). Marx says that these authors are in a "sense" regional. Maybe their type of writing wasn't meant to be regional but was, in a sense, because it was unavoidable. Nevertheless, some writing displays more regionalism than others. Marx may be missing what Wrigley describes as "that feeling, that exquisite melancholy, that silent, still exhilaration that the earth, and art, can bring on" (Wrigley 142). The sensations described by Wrigley are ones that a reader can experience while reading his essay. Vividly describing the land can be almost as effective as actually seeing it, and more so if it is seen differently. Regionalism is very apparent in "The Swing, the Snow, the Skull of a Hare," as Wrigley gracefully meant it to be.

Assignment for a Critical Review of a Reading from an Academic Area

Your chief task in this essay will be to read an essay or article critically and then write an analysis of it, arguing for your understanding of its purpose.

For your reading, choose an essay from a field in which you may find yourself doing further academic work. Your selection process will be an important aspect of this assignment because you will need to consider very carefully the rhetorical situation of the essay you choose. The best selections will be sound arguments written in conventions that are accessible to you. Look carefully at the three articles written by Tannen in *Work in Progress*. If you were to begin with the version appearing in the *Journal of Pragmatics,* do you know enough about the discipline to read it critically? How about the version from *The Chronicle of Higher Education,* which is written for a wider audience, even though still professional? Finally, turn to the essay appearing in the *Washington Post,* written for the general public. Here your question changes: You no longer wonder if you know enough to read and write a review. Instead, you must ask if the essay contains enough academic "meat" for you to work on. In this case, the essay is an easier-to-read explanation of substantial, important research: It would be a good choice. Watch out for popular essays that are written by journalists, not experts, and may simply summarize a whole issue, or essays that are loose and speculative. As you can see, your ability to judge the integrity of material you might use for research is an important part of this assignment.

You will want to review the *Work in Progress* chapters on reading and on academic writing very carefully. Follow suggestions for a careful reading of your article, paying particular attention to the section of Chapter 15 on analyzing the argument and answering the questions there. Then turn to Chapter 17 and follow the suggestions for writing analysis and argument. Write a rough draft of your review from these reading and writing notes.

As you see your ideas about your review essay take shape, you will need to be ready to step back and consider its "frame" or context. You need to provide some sense of how this article or essay fits into the ongoing work of improving our knowledge. Be as concrete as you can. Your writer has some obligations to do this for you, but you also need to demonstrate your awareness of the rhetorical context in which this essay is appearing.

While your review will include evaluation, you do not need to say whether you liked or did not like the essay. The aim here is to enter into a dialogue of ideas, and your disagreements should take that form.

You may use quotations. Do not, however, let a quotation make your argument: Lead into it with your point or a paraphrase. Head your review with a bibliographical entry giving the author, title, source, and date of your essay. Include a copy of the essay you are reviewing with your paper.

Sample Critical Review of a Reading from an Academic Area
(Johnston, Jim. "Advertising." *Communication Arts* May/June 1987: 16, 18.)

After millions of dollars of research and audience testing, it appears that a trend among many major companies and their advertising agencies is to create commercials that rely on vivid, visual imagery, stunning music and cinematography. Yet, are these commercials serving their purpose, persuasive communications? In a short editorial essay in the May/June 1987 issue of *Communication Arts* magazine, Jim Johnston adamantly argues that many flashy, expensive commercials are fundamentally lacking central ideas.

Although he admits many advertising agencies are producing high-priced commercials that are entertaining and enjoyable, they are not presenting rational reasons for persuading their viewers to buy. Johnston presents his readers with the newest advertising campaign for Chevrolet. It's made up of what many commercials have borrowed from past hits from the Beatles, MTV, and *Miami Vice:* "Music without meaningful words. Flash without substance. Visual pyrotechnic without any real idea." He isn't saying that these devices weren't successful for the Beatles, MTV, and *Miami Vice,* but their use isn't intended to serve the same purpose. Advertising, in the true historical sense of the word, is to employ communication to persuade the masses or a target audience, not entertain you. "The Heartbeat of America is today's Chevrolet" is certainly impressed on our minds, but this isn't enough, even with its spectacular visual clips, to give a person a reason to buy a Chevy.

To defend his stance, Johnston says that audio/visual excitement and a strong central idea can coexist in a thirty-second spot, and he gives specific ad campaigns that successfully integrate both. Hal Riney's Bartles & James campaign is one of those that Johnston says is splendidly entertaining and also has an astonishingly clever idea. Riney's commercials aren't successful because a meaningless phrase like "The Night Belongs to Michelob" is flashed across a screen dozens of times, but because they present a simple persuasive message that even a sourpuss would chuckle at.

Johnston brilliantly makes a powerful statement about the current advertising world. He makes a point that is so eye-opening that many of his readers may very well reconsider the direction of the next commercial that they produce. This short essay could easily have been a powerful speech at the next Addy Awards, as he makes comments and observations that he might have expressed to any advertising colleague.

In a sense, Johnston is creating his own ad. And he is doing a very good job at that. He uses valid arguments and examples to create a persuasive ad for ideas to his target audience, the advertising community. He doesn't rely on dazzling clips from commercial spots to make his point but promotes it with witty, ironic undertones that are just as successfully entertaining. And no dummy could miss his central idea. He appears to have covered all the bases in his ploy to persuade us. Or has he?

Are these companies really washing millions of dollars down the drain in their idea-less, flashy hype? I doubt it. Johnston appears to overlook, maybe intentionally, that these companies initially incorporate thorough research and audience testing before ever deciding which method of persuasion to employ. Instead of giving us cold, hard facts about why we should buy their product, a large majority of television commercials purposefully appeal to our emotions. Are these trends toward focusing on emotional appeal in commercials implicitly telling us something? Have these corporations concluded that the general American public is comprised of mindless imbeciles who can't intelligently absorb rational reason but must rely on their emotions to guide their purchasing habits? It appears so. Johnston naively assumes in his assertions that there are rational reasons for buying anything. I have trouble finding rational reasons for buying a $50,000 Mercedes Benz over a $10,000 Ford Taurus when both have essentially identical functions. Are there really valid enough reasons for buying a Michelob beer over a Budweiser? I'm sure it must be because "The Night Belongs to Michelob."

Assignment for an Argument

As Corbett notes in his *Little Rhetoric and Handbook,* "Argument is that form of discourse in which the writer attempts to persuade an audience to adopt a certain position or to behave in a certain way." Argumentative writing, Corbett adds, "tries to achieve one or more of the following objectives":

142

To reinforce the reader's present position

To persuade readers to modify their present position

To persuade readers to reject their present position and to adopt another one

To persuade readers to act in a certain way

To dissuade readers from acting in a certain way (120)

This assignment asks you to create a rhetorical situation that involves argumentation, as defined above. To do so, you need to focus not only on a topic for this assignment—the importance of bicycle safety, the need to protect the remaining virgin forest in the coastal range, reasons that students should shop at the 1st Alternative Coop instead of supermarkets, or the need for students to become computer literate—but also on a particular rhetorical situation.

Suppose, for instance, that you decide you're interested in promoting bicycle safety. The following are just a few of the rhetorical situations you could create involving this general topic:

You could write a letter to the head of traffic safety urging him to enforce bicycle regulations on campus more strictly.

You could write a letter to the head of traffic safety urging him to revise the current bicycle regulations in some way.

You could write a letter to the local newspaper urging bicycle riders in your town to follow bicycle rules more closely. (This letter would be quite different from the previous one. Can you see why?)

You could write a letter to the student newspaper urging drivers and pedestrians to be more courteous to and observant of bicycle riders.

You could write a letter to the local newspaper urging drivers and pedestrians to be more courteous to and observant of bicycle riders. (Again, this letter would differ greatly from the preceding one.)

You could role-play as a member of the campus cycling club. (Does one exist?) As such, you could propose that the club sponsor events designed to encourage bicycle safety.

Although all these essays or letters would involve the same general subject, bicycle safety, they would vary in important ways because of the different rhetorical situations to which they respond.

Hints

- Be sure to choose a topic you know a lot about. Avoid such "large" issues as abortion, religion in the schools, handgun control, and so on unless you are particularly well informed (and concerned) about them.

- Be sure your topic is not too broad. Remember, you're going to have to persuade your audience, which means that you're going to have to marshal a lot of supporting evidence. If you try to deal with a topic that's too broad, you won't be able to be specific enough about any single aspect to be persuasive.

- Be sure to choose an audience with which you are to some degree familiar. You may choose to write to a specific person (your parents, your dorm counselor), a group (student government, the campus Environmental Task Force), or a larger audience (the readers of the student or the local newspaper). In each case, *your knowledge of and projections about your audience will play a critical role in the development of your argument.*

- Early in your planning you should develop a pro and con list of arguments related to your topic. This will help you think more concretely about your topic; it will also help you anticipate objections from your audience.

- Consider your purpose in writing—your persuasive intent—carefully. It might be more realistic, for instance, to attempt to argue that the library should establish a committee to consider the feasibility of longer hours than to argue that the library should offer longer hours. The latter commits you to proving that the library can do so—that it has the money, the staff, and so forth.

Sample Argument

Student's Statement of Intentions

My persona is myself—a college student who has worked through school as a waitress. I hope I've taken on a light tone, yet made a serious point.

After much soul-searching, I've decided that I'll put this in the *Oregonian* in the point-of-view section. Anyone reading the paper who has eaten at a restaurant will see the headline and possibly consider reading this. As this isn't a hard-news story, only the person who enjoys reading features in a newspaper will read this. I don't think one has to be a raging intellectual to enjoy the article; in fact, it's rather simply written. A person who enjoys lighter reading will perhaps enjoy reading this. The major constraint is that, as with most everything in life, the person who most needs to read this probably won't, i.e., the "insensitive customer."

I want to say that being a waitress is sometimes a difficult job, and customers should be sensitive to this fact, and tip accordingly (when the service merits it).

WAITRESSES ARE PEOPLE, TOO

The next time you eat at any kind of food-service establishment, please take time to notice the *person* who serves you your meal. I could have asked you to notice the food-service *employee* who serves you your meal, but I said "person" for a specific reason. Why? Because a food-service employee is a person too, an individual with feelings, dignity, and, quite possibly, tired feet.

How do I know? I speak from experience, especially in the tired-feet realm: I'm a waitress. Now waitressing isn't going to be my lifetime career, heaven forbid. I'm working part-time to put myself through college. But that isn't necessarily the case with all my colleagues. Some are single mothers who didn't have a chance for further education. Some are working because their husbands are disabled or unemployed. There are those who have taken the job just to help their families make ends meet. But whatever the reason, all of us have the task of ensuring that you have a satisfactory and enjoyable meal in a pleasant and relaxing atmosphere.

And that ain't always easy to do.

Now to the untrained eye, waitressing might look like a fairly uncomplicated chore. Take order, pour coffee, bring food, and presto! Job done. A coworker's husband recently echoed the "waitressing-is-easy" belief when he said to me, "It must be a relief to get there and lose yourself in some mindless work."

What his wife sees in him, I'll never know.

This "mindless work" includes keeping a constant eye on your section of tables so nobody creeps in unnoticed, taking orders while trying to remember who had what special with which salad dressing, trying to place the correct dinner in front of each member of a table of twenty without making a mistake—not to mention the six tables of customers who all sat down at the same time and who want their service all at the same time.

Now I can understand why we might end up mindless, but start out that way? I hardly think so. And those problems I mentioned are the tip of the iceberg. (And no, I'm not talking lettuce!) I didn't say a word about grouchy cooks, surly customers, screaming children, slippery floors, broken dishes, lazy coworkers, or those jolly folks who order three-course meals five minutes before closing time.

Now before I proceed much further let me note that, yes, I realize I haven't mentioned waiters. That's because, as a rule, the majority of men employed as waiters are working exclusively in more expensive restaurants. Let's be realistic: the day-to-day drudgery of the food-service profession is 99.9 percent borne by women. The fancy restaurant conjures up the image of a refined and intimate atmosphere where tips, those marvelously tangible tokens of appreciation for a job well done, are much more generously given. After all, who is going to leave fifty cents for a $50.00 meal? So the waiters have it pretty good. Besides, when was the last time anyone made a waiter dress in a polyester miniskirt uniform and wear heels?

But work in the everyday coffee shop or family restaurant differs drastically. There, the level of respect for waitresses and the difficulty of their job takes a nosedive. That's where the image of the nonentity—the unintelligent, gum-snapping bimbo—comes to mind. The waitress Vera, a character on the popular television show *Alice,* is giddy, scatterbrained, and not too bright: a typical (?) waitress. Vera seldom has any tables to wait on, but maybe that's how she keeps her job. In a real restaurant, she'd last a week, tops.

So what should customers expect of the average waitress? I'll tell you what I expect: a pleasant demeanor, a full coffee cup, prompt service, and a willingness to help if any problem comes up during the meal such as cold food, spilt milk, or an order change. I don't think that's unreasonable. But when customers expect the waitress to discipline their children, laugh at jokes that were new when Lincoln was president, or endure grouchiness that only the family dog is supposed to put up with, the line is drawn. I suppose what I'm trying to do is encourage you to treat your waitress like the person she actually is. No, I'm not suggesting that you invite her to sit down for a steak with you and your family; you don't even have to exchange names and birthdates. But do recognize that she too appreciates a *please* and a *thank you* just as much as the next human being. Emily Post aside, however, politeness isn't everything. If you don't leave your waitress a tip, no matter how nice you are, your name is mud. Seriously, if you "stiff" your waitress, don't expect marching bands, red carpet, and a key to the city when you eat at that restaurant again. Your reputation as a good customer will have been tarnished with the label of "cheapskate."

Now I'm not saying a tip is appropriate in every circumstance. I can still remember the tight-lipped waitress who earlier this month "waited" on my table in name only. I practically had to tackle her to get some more coffee, and then she looked like she would rather have poured it on me than serve it. I wanted to apologize for even coming into the restaurant. I still don't know what her problem was, but I didn't leave her a tip. She didn't deserve it in the least. However, for every unfriendly incompetent, there are five gracious professionals. These are the ones who merit the appreciation shown only by a generous tip.

Unfortunately, it's difficult to put those negative experiences with waitresses out of your mind. But remember, a pleasant restaurant meal is a two-way street. Human nature being what it is, a waitress will respond to customers the way she is treated. As a waitress,

I have vivid memories of some customers I would just as soon forget. For example, there was the man who berated me just for asking if he wanted cheese on his hamburger. "If I'd wanted cheese," he snapped, "I would've asked for it!" Then to his friend at the table he said, "Why do they always ask that stupid question?" At times like that, the phrase "grin and bear it" takes a personal meaning. But for every rude and arrogant customer, there are five courteous and gracious customers who show their appreciation by leaving generous tips while treating me like a human being.

The keys to a positive restaurant experience for both parties, then, are mutual respect and understanding of each other's needs. (My, this sounds like marriage!) As a waitress, I need to be both cordial and sensitive to customer necessities. As a customer, you need to give me credit for being an individual with thoughts, feelings, and a tough job on her hands. You may be surprised how the quality of your service will improve if the waitress knows you're going to treat her well. A waitress can bloom under the application of your courteous appreciation. Go ahead and try it next time you're in a restaurant—make someone's day!

Assignment for a Review

Reviews may inform, evaluate, persuade, and entertain. (Many reviews represent a subtle and complex mix of these purposes.) There is no standard or "formula" review: The exact shape of a review depends on a number of related factors such as audience, purpose, and means of publication.

Some reviews are largely informative. This would be appropriate, for instance, if you decided to write a review for the student newspaper comparing the three best-selling touring bikes in a certain price range to help students decide which is the best buy. Even here, however, there is an implicit argumentative edge to your review: If you're in the market for a touring bike, you should consider brand X; it's the best buy.

Some reviews are largely evaluative. After a brief rundown of the movie's plot and basic cinematic techniques, some critics focus almost entirely on evaluating a movie's script, acting, photography—its overall success. These reviews also have an implicit or explicit argumentative edge: You should (or shouldn't) see this movie.

Some reviews, though partly informative or evaluative in intent, also aim to entertain. When a writer reviews the ten best Sunday brunches in Oregon, as David Sarasohn recently did in *Oregon Magazine*, the best approach may be to treat the subject wittily and light-heartedly—to engage the reader as much with style and wit as with information or critical acumen. Even here, though, the writer's argumentative function as a reviewer holds true: Though his style is casual and witty, David Sarasohn is still telling readers—arguing— which restaurants have the kind of brunch worth spending hard-earned money on.

When you start to think about your review, don't just consider various subjects. Consider the rhetorical situation as a whole. You can review almost anything—movies; restaurants; places to ski, hike, fish, run, swim, play tennis, study, be alone, meet interesting people, or drink good coffee; all sorts of equipment such as stereos, bikes, calculators, food processors, fabrics, or tennis rackets. This list is endless. But when you decide what to review, you've just begun to define your topic. Who is your audience? How knowledgeable are readers about your subject? (You would write a very different review of this year's best running shoes if you were writing for the student newspaper versus *Runner's World*.) Are your readers already interested in your subject? (If you're writing about the best places to backpack in the Central Cascades for readers of the *Sierra Club Newsletter*, you can assume fairly strong interest. If you're writing about the same topic for readers of your local newspaper, you probably can't.) You also need to consider the image of yourself that you want to project in your writing—your *persona*. You may choose to adopt a serious, distanced *persona*. You may choose to be witty, sarcastic, casual, or whatever.

As the writer, it's your responsibility—and your freedom—to shape your review so that it best reflects your intentions, the needs and interests of your readers, your (hypothetical) means of publication, and your subject. Have fun!

Note: Be sure to remember the recommended length of two to four typed pages; choose a rhetorical situation that realistically calls for an essay of roughly that length.

Sample Review

Student's Statement of Intentions

I am writing a review of the movie *The Deer Hunter.* I'm not addressing my review to a specific audience; instead, I'm assuming an audience of intelligent readers, people who are already interested in and knowledgeable about films in general and Cimino's work in particular. I want to appear casual and yet knowledgeable.

THE DEER HUNTER

Focusing on a small Pennsylvania steel-mill town and the effects of the Vietnam conflict on some of the young men and women who live there, Michael Cimino's *The Deer Hunter* gives us a rich, tightly woven story. One of several made in the last few years that explore facets of the American involvement in Vietnam, this film presents the viewpoint of those small-town men who went off to fight in foreign jungles believing that America was still The Beautiful. Despite the horrors of a war that held no meaning for them, despite the painful losses that they suffered, the characters in this film still cling to that ideal.

I first viewed *Deer Hunter* right after its release, and its initial impact overwhelmed me. Cimino has masterfully created layer upon layer of cinematic reality. The first hour of the movie is a carefully crafted exposition of the town of Clairton, Pa., with all its grit and charm, and of the relationships between the major characters, forming a solid base for the more swiftly moving Vietnam footage and denouncement. This film is too lengthy, according to some, but I cannot think of a single shot that is not a necessary part of the whole; like an Altman film, it relies on the totality, gathering its effectiveness and strength from the sum of these parts.

Upon subsequent viewing, I have found that the film's impact is lessened by my knowledge of the plot. I think that this problem is accentuated by the intensity of the film's impact during my first viewing since after a year I still recalled much of it shot for shot. Even so, I continue to marvel at the texture and fullness that it has.

The violence that is a part of this story—a horrifying version of Russian roulette in which the Viet Cong pit one prisoner against another—is bloody and necessary to our understanding of the deep psychological anguish that the men undergo. It makes us realize that a superhuman control is needed by Michael (Robert De Niro) to save his buddies, Nick (Christopher Walken) and Steven (John Savage), from the mental and physical damage imposed by this terrifying game and from the war itself.

In many respects this is a buddy film. Three young men who grew up together, who work together and play together, end up going off to war together. Boisterous, daring types at home, they are confronted with a war that pounds at their minds, rips at their bodies, sends them back to the familiarity of their town as strangers. Through all of this, the unity of friends is what makes survival possible. I generally dislike buddy films because they tend to make women appear as peripheral adjuncts to men and portray men as one-sided good old boys, but *The Deer Hunter* manages to escape these pitfalls. The script itself can take much of the credit for this success since it allows the men to relate to each other in a caring, loving manner. The excellent acting by the cast members is also responsible for the wholeness of the characters they play. De Niro injects the part of Michael with all of the strength and control that it requires, with Walken and Savage superbly completing the triad of close friends. The women have smaller parts, but they have just as much reality for us. Meryl Streep (as Linda) is especially fine in giving life to a character that might otherwise have been overlooked.

One of the only real problems with *Deer Hunter* is that once in a while the cuts (exterior to interior, scene to scene) are confusing. In some instances this can be seen as effective—in the sequences of a disintegrating Saigon, for example—but in most cases it is merely disconcerting and annoying. Also bothersome is the insistence of the screenplay on some rather unbelievable coincidences such as the scene in which the hometown buddies are reunited in the middle of a field near a Vietnamese village. Sure it could happen, but . . .

Ah, but there are other coincidences, other miracles here. Is this actually a reality that we are presented with? More like a dream, it seems to me: a dream where you spend your paycheck over pool and beers at the local tavern, a dream where you are lifted from your home and a new bridge only to find yourself in a strange jungle with a gun, a dream—no, a nightmare—where you lose your closest friend, track him down beyond all possibility, and find him again, tell him that you love him, only to have his life blood slip through your fingers. It is the American Dream, a little the worse for wear.

Assignment for an Analysis of a Writing Sample

In your earlier essays, you've been focusing on writing in response to a particular rhetorical situation—one of your own making. In this essay, you are, in effect, to turn the process around: You are to study one or more samples of a particular genre of writing and analyze, among other things, the rhetorical situation to which it implicitly responds. This analysis is designed, of course, to help you become more sensitive to the constraints and options that all writers face.

Choose a specific kind of writing—generally, though not necessarily, one that you are either already somewhat familiar with or interested in learning about. Such kinds of writing might include the following:

Certain genres or subgenres of fiction (hard-boiled detective fiction, Harlequin romances, science fiction stories)

A magazine devoted to a particular subject or aimed at a limited audience (*Runner's World, Field and Stream, Oregon Magazine,* and so on)

A general news magazine (*Newsweek, Time,* and so on)

Professional writing in your field (one or more issues of a professional journal, a series of reports or memos)

A particular kind of writing published in newspapers or magazines (editorials, news stories, advice columns, and so on)

The writing of a specific columnist or writer (Ann Landers, George Will, Pauline Kael, and so on)

After you have decided on the kind of writing you want to analyze, choose a reasonable sample. Using the Guidelines in Chapter 15, analyze your sample. (As always, you'll

148

want to read the sample student essay very carefully as well.) The final step, of course, is to write your analysis. For this assignment, the general outline for your rhetorical situation is, quite simply, that you are writing an essay for this class with me, your instructor, as the intended reader. The general constraints of academic writing (that I am looking for a clearly organized, well-developed essay) would obviously obtain in this situation.

Sample Analysis of a Writing Sample

Student's Statement of Intentions

I have chosen to analyze Nancy Drew teenage detective stories because of my own familiarity with them as I grew up. I was always intrigued by the exciting, true-to-life episodes and characters from the mystery stories. My friends and I would make up our own mystery adventures, based on Nancy Drew stories, complete with hidden clues. Each of us would choose a character to portray, and I usually ended up being Nancy.

I am writing this as myself to an audience interested in the contents of teen mystery stories. This is a straight analysis format that could possibly be used as a guideline for writing such stories.

This Nancy Drew analysis could be part of a book that contains similar analyses of other teen detective stories (such as the Dana girls, the Hardy boys, Trixie Belden, and so on).

Parents could use this book as a guide to what their children could read. Educators might also benefit from such a book.

NANCY DREW: A MYSTERY TO SOLVE

As the structure—the old, creaky hanging bridge—swung around, Nancy clutched the railing for support, but it too was unsound. The decayed wood gave way, and the girl plunged violently forward to meet the turbulent waters of the swollen stream.

Eight- to fourteen-year-old girls are usually so engrossed in the Nancy Drew mystery story they are reading that they won't put the book down until they finish. As soon as they experience one exciting adventure with Nancy Drew and her friends, girls are eager to puzzle their way through another mystery. Carolyn Keene, the author of these teen detective novelettes, urges her readers through the series with a promotional line woven into the last few paragraphs of each book.

Again Bess smiled in admiration of her chum's cleverness. No matter how many mysteries Nancy solved, the Marvin girl never ceased to be amazed at each new one. She was to stand aghast at the solution of the next problem, The Clue of the Tapping Heels.

Young girls easily get caught up in the exciting, fast-paced Nancy Drew episodes. They can begin to frame the story through the setting, and they can anticipate a clue about the forthcoming mystery by the end of the first chapter. From there on, the plot of the mystery rapidly unfolds and sustains a quick pace throughout successive chapters.

Chapters vary from as little as four pages to a maximum of twelve pages in length. From one chapter to the next, transitional paragraphs leave the reader hanging for a split second—just long enough to prick the reader's curiosity—then quickly pick up the idea begun in the chapter before. For instance, the following paragraph shows how a new chapter carries through the action from a previous chapter, in this example the bridge collapse in the quotation opening this paper.

The current was swift, and before Nancy could battle her way to the shore she found herself carried far below the point where the haunted bridge had stood. Bedraggled,

*and with her clothes muddy and torn, she pulled herself out on the slippery bank and
sat there for a moment in the rain, trying to regain her breath.*

The paragraphs, each composed of no more than five sentences, flow naturally because the sentence structures vary and are just complicated enough to interest adolescent readers. Variation in sentence length prevents reading from becoming too tedious.

The vivid, descriptive language—the extensive use of action verbs, adjectives, and adverbs—of the omniscient narrator and the characters replaces illustrations; there are rarely more than three sketches in a Nancy Drew book. This induces the young reader to participate actively with her imagination and encourages her to envision the scenery and the action taking place.

The constant dialogue among Nancy Drew and the other supporting characters also draws young girls into the action and gives them a sense of being a part of the conversation, elevating the story to a personal level. It is at the personal level where girls wish to identify with the intelligent, eighteen-year-old amateur detective. Nancy Drew portrays a role model that younger girls look up to. She possesses many well-balanced characteristics, both physically and mentally. Being athletic and physically attractive does not detract from Nancy's feminine and well-mannered behavior. And despite her independence and ability to make her own decisions wisely, she readily accepts advice and guidance from her brilliant criminal-lawyer father, who taught her to think quickly and rationally. People's needs and feelings are important to the young sleuth's way of thinking; she demonstrates this by her friendly understanding and thoughtful attitude toward them.

Nancy's peaceful home environment contributes to her own well-being. A nice, comfortable, two-story house in a pleasant suburban neighborhood is her residence. Here she lives with her father, Carson Drew, and their housekeeper, Hannah Gruen, who frees Nancy from tedious domestic chores and occasionally gives her motherly advice. When the young detective is not busy solving a case (usually at the beginning of the story), she can be found at home adding to or improving her physical and mental skills. The varied interests of Nancy's reading audience are catered to by her wide range of abilities: drawing, skiing, riding, golfing, ad infinitum.

But to prevent young girls from envying Nancy's character, the author has taken care not to overdo Nancy's perfection and her comfortable station in life. Carolyn Keene has included a tragedy in the heroine's life—the death of her mother when she was only a four-year-old girl. Because of this tragic element, readers can empathize with Nancy. Her motherless life also explains her need to be independent and her ability to be compassionate with other characters who have their own woes.

The writer introduces the characters early in the reading so the reader can establish their relationship to the entire action of the mystery. Nancy's immediate family, her closest girlfriends Bess and George, and her boyfriend Ned Nickerson, constitute the supporting characters that round out Nancy's role and add fullness to the amateur detective stories. Bess is extremely timid and unsure of herself, whereas her cousin George, as her name implies, is tomboyish and impulsive. Ned always helps out when a young strong college man is needed for protection.

The importance of these primary characters could not be measured without the secondary characters: the protagonists and the antagonists. Without these actors there would be no mysteries for Nancy Drew to solve, no villains to outsmart, and no victims to rescue from disastrous circumstances.

As Nancy first probes her adversaries and then actively tests her cunning wits against them in each of her adventures, she exposes to her young readers the diverse personalities, values, and standards inherent in different people from all walks of life. In this capacity, Nancy Drew mystery stories not only provide exciting reading, but each story teaches its adolescent readers a valuable moral, ethical, or social lesson.

When each of Nancy's exciting cases is nearly solved, there is a heightened sense of drama when one more action comes into play, keeping the attention of young readers at the very end.

Each Nancy Drew mystery book puts Nancy and her readers in a different situation in a variety of settings across the country or around the world. A boy or girl can pick up and read just one book out of the whole numbered series without being confused about the identity of the Nancy Drew characters, or he or she can read the entire series without getting bored by repetitive plots.

Young readers enjoy sharing new secrets with Nancy Drew; it satisfies them to know that they were with her through every twist and turn, using valuable clues in unlocking mysteries and bringing villains to justice. The value of rational decision making, good attitudes, and manners is one thing that young readers can learn as they develop a familiarity with Nancy Drew. Nancy Drew is like an old friend whose exciting life readers can take part in.

Assignment for an Interview

The minimum requirement of this assignment is that you interview one or more persons and use the results of the interview (whether recorded in notes or on tape) as the data for an essay. As the following examples should indicate, the *form* and *purpose* of your essay may vary with the reason why you choose to interview someone. Possible reasons include the following:

- *To inform, to entertain, to illuminate.* We're all naturally curious about people. What was it like to live through the Great Depression? How do the janitors who work in the dorms feel about their jobs—and about students? What is the typical campus day of a disabled student like? Assuming that you choose appropriate readers, you can almost guarantee that you'll have an interested audience.

- *To make or support an argument.* Sometimes we interview people to prove a point, to search for answers that only someone in the know can provide. Such interviews can result in essays that *explicitly* attempt to persuade. Other interviews (for instance, an interview with a poor migrant worker) can also function as *implicit* arguments.

As always, in considering how best to respond to this assignment, be sure to consider the rhetorical situation in general, not just the person or people you'll interview. Going into each interview, you should have an idea not only of why you want to interview this person but also of what the general focus of the resulting essay will be. Who will read this? Why should they be interested? Where will the essay be published? What constraints will the means of publication provide?

In class, we'll talk about some of the formal considerations this essay raises. (What format should you follow? Should you include or delete your questions? What role should you as interviewer play?) We'll also discuss some questions of process. (Should you use a tape recorder or just take notes?) And we'll consider the ethics of interviewing. For now, though, here are a few closing suggestions:

- Don't assume that you need to find an unusual, exciting, or bizarre person to interview. Some of the best interviews simply reveal the richness inherent in even the most ordinary of people.

- Be sure to review the use of quotation marks.

- Save the notes or tape of your interview. Sometimes looking at notes or listening to the original interview can help solve problems that arise.

Sample Oral History

Student's Statement of Intentions

I am writing about my father's experience as a boy growing up on a farm in Nebraska. I want to try to recapture the event that he told about as best as I can, and I have tried to preserve the character of my father's speech when doing so.

The purpose of my paper is to record a piece of my family history in writing, to identify with a different way of life, and to learn more about my father.

My audience is myself and my brothers and sisters. I also plan to save this essay and let my children read it to give them a little knowledge about their family history. It may help them to know their grandfather better and may also enable them to get a feel for what their great-grandfather was like.

My paper may also be of interest to my cousins. Our families are scattered around the United States and have very little contact with each other. This paper is one piece of the history that unifies our family, so it would probably be interesting to them.

I don't have a means of publication in mind. This paper could, however, be an excerpt from a book on our family history.

I was a little apprehensive about interviewing my father at first. I was afraid that the artificial circumstances surrounding the interview would distort the character of his casual speech and inhibit his natural story-telling ability. It was difficult to decide exactly how to approach him about the interview, and finally I just sat down on the couch while he was reading the newspaper and began to ask him questions. He had to think awhile at first, but soon his past began streaming back through his mind, and his stories unravelled faster than I could record them.

He began by telling about the chores on the farm in Nebraska. "There was always something to be done, and we were just expected to do it—not for money or allowance or anything. I had to gather eggs and cobs. We used cobs in the stove for cookin' and heatin'. I'd have to go pick 'em up out of the hog yard after the hogs ate 'em clean. That was a messy job; boy, I hated it!

"My brothers had to milk the cows and water the livestock. All of us helped in separatin' the milk. We had a hand-turned separator that separated the cream from the milk.

"We had to shock the wheat; we'd put together seven or eight [shocks] in bundles to dry out. We'd let it sit and dry, then we'd come along with a hayrack pulled by horses or a tractor, pick up the bundles with pitchforks, and put 'em on the hayrack. Then we'd take 'em to the thrashin' machine to get grain. All the neighbors worked together for thrashin'; we'd move from farm to farm and help each other out. Usually only one family had a thrashin' machine, and everybody had to pay a charge to the owner to use it.

"We always had large dinners with lots of potatoes and gravy and platters piled with meat. Then after dinner—lunch was called dinner—we had lunch at about four o'clock in the afternoon. We'd have sandwiches, and we might have had a beer after shovelin' grain. I got to drink the bottom of the bottle.

"In the wintertime we didn't do too much except go to school. We went to school in a one-room country schoolhouse with all eight grades in the same room. We had to walk a half mile through the pasture in knee-deep snow.

"Of course, we still had to feed the animals in the winter. We fed the cows in the lots since we couldn't turn 'em out to pasture 'cause the grass was all dried off. Sometimes we turned 'em out into the cornfield and let 'em eat what was left. And we still had to milk 'em morning and night; 'course we all had our share of that. Everybody had more or less . . . oh, I don't know . . . things just had to be done.

"Then every Monday was wash day. We had a gasoline-powered washing machine. I used to fall asleep listening to it on the sofa. That was when I was just a little bitty fart and Mamma was still alive."

Dad stopped talking every once in a while, as if he had to probe his mind to remember some of the details. When there was a lag in the conversation, I would prompt him with another question. I was curious about how the death of his mother changed life on the farm, so I asked him about it.

"I was pretty young when Mom died; I didn't really understand everything that was going on," he started. "Mom died in 1942; I must've been about six years old. We had an aunt that stayed with us awhile—Claire Rooke was her name—but most of the time we had housekeepers. But us five boys were more than they could stand so most of 'em didn't last very long. Hazel Sickman was the longest one we had. She'd stick her head out the front door and holler whenever she wanted something. If she wanted eggs, she hollered, 'Eggs!' If she wanted cobs, she hollered, 'Cobs!' I can hear her yet. I mostly had to go get 'em for her because everyone else was busy with chores.

"We had one housekeeper with a son and daughter. Alice Ann was the daughter's name, and Freddie was the son. Alice Ann was spoiled, and she used to pick on her little brother. She was kind of fat, and she used to take his candy away from him. That's why Bob wired up the toilet; he didn't like the way Alice Ann used to pick on her little brother."

There was a sudden change in topic as Dad began to explain the reference to the toilet seat. "Bob charged up the outhouse seat with a magneto from the tractor and some wire," he said with a chuckle. "Then, when someone would sit down, he'd turn it on and shock 'em. Alice Ann wouldn't go out there after awhile, and she had to have a pot in the house. She kept saying that spiders were out there biting her. Anyway, one time Bob made the mistake of doing it while Dad was in there. I don't remember exactly whether Bob ran or what, but Dad came out with one suspender unhooked and hoppin' mad, and that was the end of the magneto and the toilet seat!"

By now my dad was really enjoying himself. He told numerous stories of mischievous antics performed by him and his brothers. I listened in amazement to some of these almost unbelievable tales and thought to myself how similar the experiences were to something that you might see on *The Little Rascals* television show.

"When the Kempsters [city slickers from Portland] used to drive back to Nebraska to visit," Dad recalled, "we used to play pranks on them. One time we put Loretta on the Shetland pony, Jerry went into the barn and shook the oats bucket, while we fixed the barn door so that the bottom was opened but the top was closed. The horse went running into the barn [for his food] under the top part of the door, and Loretta got knocked off." Dad thought back on this event and began to laugh out loud.

I asked my father how often he and his brothers were punished for their shenanigans. My dad answered, "There wasn't much Dad didn't know about. He used to use a razor strap to paddle our behinds."

Dad began another story. "I remember a time when brother Jerry and I pulled the car with a tractor to get it started. Dad had tried to start it but couldn't so he walked to the highway and hitched into town. We got it started and were racing around our driveway. (It was shaped like a semicircle and went up in front of our house and around.) We thought we were doin' Dad a favor by getting his car started—'course, we were having a little fun doin' it. Well the neighbors told Dad, and we both got the razor strap for that one!

"And then there was the time that my older brother John and I were riding our bicycles up to the main highway. He decided he was going to smoke a cigar. He'd take two or three puffs and stick it in the handle bar. Dad saw him smokin' it, and when John got back that night Dad said, 'I understand you like cigars.' John didn't know what to say. Then Dad made him sit down and smoke one cigar after another until he turned green."

From these and other episodes, I was beginning to picture my grandfather as a mean, unreasonable, and quick-tempered man, and I voiced this image to my father. He was quick to deny its validity, saying that his father wasn't all bad. Dad said that Grandpa was strict and strong willed, but that he was only doing what he thought was best for his boys. He also said that Grandpa was reluctant to accept new ways and illustrated this with the following story.

"One time Jim put a radio on a tractor," Dad said. "Dad didn't like it and told him to take it off. Well, one day Dad took the tractor out, and you could hear the radio playin' a half mile away. Then he told Jim he might as well leave it since he already had it on there."

I was interested in knowing how the economic conditions in the late thirties and early forties had affected my father's upbringing. I asked him whether his family had felt any of the effects of the Great Depression.

"The WPA built our outhouse for us," he began. "That was one of Franklin D. Roosevelt's job creators for gettin' through the depression.

"We didn't have to buy much because we raised mostly everything we needed. We had a garden and raised our own meat. We stored our salt pork in a barrel in the basement. There was no refrigeration, only an icebox.

"We never had a lot of stuff. For Christmas we usually only got one present. My clothes were hand-me-downs and so was my first bicycle. We had to go barefoot a lot—cut my foot one time and nearly bled to death. They had to pack it in flour to stop the bleeding. Well, anyway, I never felt deprived or anything; we just didn't expect much.

"The oldest boys went to boarding school in Missouri for a couple of years. Dad found it hard to get everyone to school in town during the winter, so he thought he'd send 'em to a Catholic boarding school to give 'em a good education. That's how he died—he was going down after 'em and got in an accident."

I had known that my grandfather had died in an automobile accident but had never known the circumstances. I waited for more.

"Nobody knows all the details, really," Dad continued. "He was driving in the rain and hit a drain in the highway. The tire blew out, and the car flipped end for end. He lived twenty-one days in the hospital before he died.

"After Dad died, I went to live with Aunt Monica on her farm in Giltner. We moved that summer to Hastings and lived in a basement apartment for a year or two. Then she bought a house, and we moved again.

"Aunt Monica was pretty strict. We had to be in the house by nine o'clock on week nights. She had a son by the name of John. I suppose there was some friction between us (John and I)—competition or whatever you want to call it."

It seemed Dad was implying that relations between Aunt Monica, John, and himself were a bit strained, but he volunteered little information on this subject when I asked about it. Maybe he didn't want me to get a bad impression of one of my favorite aunts. Whatever the reason, Dad changed the subject.

"I went to high school at St. Cecilia's. The nuns were pretty strict. I got my hand slapped with an eighteen-inch ruler for not filling a pew in church. There were only seven people in it, and there were supposed to be eight. My palm got slapped ten times, and I had to go to the principal's office. Another time I got whacked for polishing an apple on my pantleg in class. I thought I was paying attention, but the teacher didn't, so she whapped me.

"When graduation night came," Dad seemed to sigh with relief, "we had planned a big party. My brother Jerry had come back from Portland, but I didn't know it. Well, one of the other fellas, Don Webber, was supposed to tell me to go straight home after the graduation. He didn't, so I went to the party and got a 'little' inebriated. I had to climb in the window to get in that night, and Aunt Monica met me on the stairs and kicked me back out. I was told to leave—lock, stock, and barrel. I ended up sleeping in the porch swing that night.

"The next day, I got on my motor scooter and rode out to Aunt Irene's farm, and she was pretty understanding. She took me in for a while, but since Jerry was going back to Portland, I went and got my stuff and came out here with him. I was seventeen when I came out to Oregon."

Dad stopped here, and it seemed as though he was signaling the end of the interview. I guess he felt that this was where his growing up ended and a new phase of life began. I sat for a while, letting everything he had told me sift back through my mind, and tried to remember his expressions and tones in detail. I felt that I knew my father better now than I ever had before.

Assignment for an Advanced Class: Literacy Narrative
2. WR 416/516: Advanced Composition: Language, Literacy, and Community

In the broadest sense, this assignment asks you to reflect in some way upon the role that writing has played in your life—to consider, in other words, how you became the writer you are (and are still in the process of becoming) today. There are many ways that you might approach this assignment: so many, in fact, that I almost didn't list any here for fear of constraining you. Recognizing that examples can be helpful, however, I include the following. Please remember that they are suggestions only.

- Focus on one or more significant experiences in your development as a writer. In so doing, you could focus on a particular time period—early writing experiences, a specific time in your schooling, the present moment in your writing life, etc.; or you could discuss several different time periods. You could develop a theme or explore dissonances.

- Explore the relationship between schooling and literacy in your life. What emotions do you associate with various moments in your development as a schooled writer? Much schooling attempts to tame writing of what we might think of as its wildness: How did (and do) you respond to these efforts? Can you recall acts of resistance to schooled literacy, such as passing notes in class, writing graffiti, or deliberately neglecting writing assignments? As a student currently taking classes, what role or roles does writing play in your life?

- Another way of getting at a similar issue: Explore the relationship between the private and public uses of writing in your life. Our earliest literacy experiences are often private— listening to bedtime stories, half scribbling/half drawing stories for our family. Over time a shift occurs. What has that shift meant to you? Has it been a dramatic shift? Has it taken multiple turns? Followed a steady path? Left you with questions?

- Look at your development as a writer in relationship to the related literate acts of reading, speaking, and listening. How did (how do) these interact in your life?

- Reflect on social, cultural, or political influences on your writing or on your sense of yourself as a writer. How did your family view or value writing? Did claiming an identity as writer (if you have done that) connect you, or separate you, from your home or other communities? What does "claiming an identity as writer" mean to you, and what influences have caused you to feel as you do? What role did writing play as you established relationships with others at various points in your life? Has writing meant different things to you at different times of your life? What influences have others—a particular friend, coworker, teacher, etc.—had on your sense of yourself as a writer or on your writing?
- Focus on one or more moments of boundary crossing, moments when the relationship between your language and your intimate self seemed most at stake. (Amy Tan's "Mother Tongue" is such a reflection, as is Min Zhan-Lu's "Writing as Struggle.") Or look at the present moment in your life: As students, and as individuals with rich lives outside of school, you necessarily exist—and write—in many worlds. How do you negotiate these boundaries? What's at stake for you as you move from community to community? How do your present understandings and strategies connect with earlier experiences and emotions?

I hope that the multiplicity of questions just presented will give you a sense of how much freedom you have in this essay.

Here, in closing, are a few additional suggestions:

- Don't go for the obvious, and don't be afraid to invoke difficult or painful experiences. Some of the most powerful moments in our development (as humans as much as writers) are quiet moments, moments easily passed by, or moments of difficulty and struggle that we're tempted to forget precisely because they are painful.
- Another way of saying the same thing: Whatever prewriting strategies you use—freewriting, note taking, meditating, talking with friends (yes, these all can be prewriting, even when you're not writing)—go deep. Burrow into your memories. Call up concrete moments that provide access to emotional connections.
- And yet another way of saying the same thing: Look for dissonance, what you don't understand, what's always puzzled you, what still feels uncomfortable. Try to get beyond the "normal" story of literacy learning and education, the story that emphasizes that "natural" progression from first grade to high school or college graduation.
- Remember that however you organize and develop your essay, it is in an important way a narrative, and in narrative "showing" (rather than "telling") can be a particularly important and powerful means of connecting with your readers.
- Don't feel you have to tell a coherent "story" or that it has to result in a standard conclusion or summary. Traditional conclusions can, in fact, trivialize the complex issues that you may be considering. Your essay can be exploratory, open-ended. It can be experimental in form—though realize that if you employ a collage or other experimental structure you have to work harder and make your (implicit) structure clearer than when you rely on a more conventional linear structure. However you develop and organize your essay, when you consider structural and developmental issues, think about such holistic and goal-oriented issues as the point or interpretation you want to share with readers, the kind of experience you want readers to have as they move through your essay, and the *persona* you wish to create.

Please know that I'm always happy to discuss paper ideas—or to look at drafts of work in progress—with you.

POWELL'S
Jennifer Kollmer

"I'm so overwhelmed tonight. Just who the fuck do I think I am?"

I say it out loud, partially to see if I can milk an encouraging word from my friend, but mostly because I have a feeling it will sound dramatic enough to echo properly through the endless stacks of the largest bookstore in the hemisphere. Well, Powell's is certainly the largest bookstore *I* have ever seen; the building is so large they provide maps of the color-coded rooms for newcomers and regulars who find themselves lost. At the moment, we're standing in front of an enormous shelf of new books in the Green room, just by the front door. It seems as if half of the country has published something this month.

It is true: I am overwhelmed. The new arrivals are entirely too imposing, so I leave my friend to wander on her own as I retreat around the corner to the Blue room.

Literature, First Row on the Right: Austen to Beckett

The greats stare me down from every direction. I could never write beautifully like Jane Austen; I could never be prolific like Honoré de Balzac; I could never be brilliant like Samuel Beckett. I don't write in any outstanding fashion—my words come out clumsy, forced, wrong.

When I write I find myself staring at the blank page. Starting out in the same place as all the Masters, which would be encouraging, were it not for the fact that I'm confident that they had a blank page and an Idea, even if the inspiration was only that they had a burning desire to impress a chick or tell off a former friend or that they really needed to earn rent money for the week. I've got nothing but an inability to type and a blatant disregard for spelling and grammar rules. And here I am, cocky enough to even be concerned over the fact that I will never compare to the most amazing . . .

I banish myself from this section until more humility returns to my heart. I'll come back when I can do so with more reverence.

Reference: Dictionaries, Thesauruses, Encyclopedias

Miss Broadway was always telling us to look it up in the thesaurus, but vocabulary had never really been a problem for me. By the second grade, I wasn't sure I wanted to use reference books for choosing my words, and I found much more fun in thinking of a thesaurus as a prehistoric friend of the brontosaurus and triceratops. Miss Broadway took this to be a sign of creativity and made me promise to become a famous poet when I grew up. I didn't have other plans for adulthood, so I agreed wholeheartedly.

Entering the third grade, I was forced to learn cursive and all of a sudden everything I wrote was graded on my ugly letters and not what they said. My handwriting was consistently poor, so there wasn't much point in writing anymore. I gave up on my career in poetry and focused on paleontology for the next four years.

By the seventh grade—just as a realistic view of the potential monotony of digging through sand dunes with a toothbrush started to sink in—my teachers finally divorced penmanship from content, and again I considered myself a writer. I didn't really write anything without my teachers' prompting, but I was certain I could do it easily were I properly motivated. And once I found that motivation, what a life I would lead: terrifically cool, darkly clad friends, drinking and cigarettes until dawn, writing until my fingers hurt . . .

My concentration drifts back from these girlhood reflections to the stacks of reference books before me. I flip through a couple of the newest volumes of quotations: quotations by women, useful opening quips for speeches and essays, and the latest Bartlett's. After reading from Charlotte Brontë, Bob Dylan, and James Barrie, I note the $40 price tag and return the book to its place on the shelf. Reflecting on the value of public libraries, I head for the paperbacks in the Gold room.

Popular Fiction: Sci-Fi, Romance, Fantasy

I have to confess that when I try to write my every tenth thought comes forward sounding like an excerpt from one of those romance novels with the swirly airbrushed pink covers. *As she turned to storm out of the room, he grasped her arm, his eyes pleading with her not to leave him. Never to leave him alone again. Her fierce glare met his entreaty and suddenly melted. As she fell into his strong embrace, Lydia found herself determined to endure any hardship that life might thrust upon them* . . . Where does this come from?

I feel strangely drawn to and simultaneously repulsed by the romances. I mean, they're an easy read, and escapism has been my good friend for years. But honestly, I am not a pink, airbrushed kind of gal. I find myself resenting the romance novels for the time I waste thinking like them, time that could be spent scrawling my way to significance. How did so many empty, disconnected thoughts become so integral to my thinking process? These little snips might be useful if they connected; if I could hook them together somehow I could type the whole mess out and airmail the result to the editors at Harlequin. But these blurbs pop randomly into and out of my thoughts with no apparent connection, rendering them fairly useless. These thoughts are not only useless; they're sourceless as well. I've read perhaps eight romance novels in my entire life, and that was back in junior high when "reading" consisted of skimming through the book in search of the well-worn pages with the good parts.

I wonder if I should perhaps try to nudge my romance-like thoughts into some coherent order; maybe reading some of these novels would give my ideas some direction. Maybe if I pulled those flashes out of my head and onto paper, they'd go away and leave my mind open to deeper thinking, open to real writing. Or maybe writing a paperback romance would be fun. I reach for a novel covered with gold foil lettering and windswept hair before I remember where I am. Before I remember who I am. Certainly I am the sort of person who exits a hip scene like Powell's with Joyce and Yeats and Kerouac; I'll not be seen leaving with anything titled *Desert of Desire*. Maybe I'll pick up one at the supermarket later tonight, but now I continue empty-handed to the Rose room.

Science and Technology: Field Guides, Textbooks, Computer References

Sometimes I can force myself to feign an interest in my profession—from nine to five I'm a technical writer—but tonight I don't even bother to glance through *The Internet Yellow Pages* or *MS-DOS for Dummies*.

Work. Rent money. Beer money. Car payments.

Is my resistance to professional writing genuine? Can a job actually suck one's soul away? Did I have a soul before joining the corporate world? Wouldn't my intense sense of integrity have prevented me from entering a field that would jeopardize my nature?

Do I honestly believe that those forty to fifty hours each week are wasted? What would I do with the time if I didn't have to go to work? Would I just sleep? Would I write? Would I find that, with my last excuses removed, I cannot write? Would I find that I have no interest? Would I find that I have no talent? How long would it take before I accepted the truth? A month with no decent results? A year? Ten years?

What would qualify as decent results? A published short story? An acclaimed novel? The Nobel prize? A single page that I genuinely liked?

Clearly, I am not interested in checking up on the hottest technological wonders of the day. I think the Blue room is calling to me again.

Literature, Second Row (both sides): Hawthorne to Joyce

I could barely force myself to finish *The Scarlet Letter* when we had to read it in the tenth grade. With every torturous page, I wished more and more desperately for a sudden Indian raid or a hurricane to wipe out the entire town of Salem, to remove Hester Prynne, Arthur Dimmesdale, and the whole lot from sight once and for all. The hoped-for disaster never struck, and I could only be thankful for the fact that there weren't too many pages to go as I trudged through the novel. Hawthorne's plots and voice were, after all, no help in my own literary endeavors—as a sophomore I had undertaken my first voluntary writing projects. While my teachers and advisors were crying in unison, "Write what you know!" I chose instead to try to write something interesting. My first attempt at a novel was a spy story of sorts, except that the hero was a jumpy accountant who watched a lot of TV and preferred Pepto-Bismol to martinis. Through a case of mistaken identity, Chuck was drawn into the life of a suave double-agent. Action and hilarity ensued and fifteen pages and five months later I realized how ridiculous the whole setup was and threw my manuscript into the deep dark recesses of my closet, never to return. My second try at novel writing—a tale of intrigue that focused on the tension and passion of revolution—lasted for only three pages before I became thoroughly disgusted with my aspirations to become a writer. Reading became something I had to do to get to my more important homework: chemistry, physics, and algebra.

Four years later as a prematurely burned-out engineering major in my first college English class, I found a new interest in Goodman Brown and the veiled Parson Hooper. Compared to the three-page integrals and complex models of solid state physics that awaited me in my other homework, the Puritans were certainly welcome companionship. Reading became a legitimate way to avoid my tough homework. As the math got harder in my engineering curriculum, I developed a deeper love of reading. I took every chance to manipulate my schedule to work in another English course and developed an otherwise inexplicable appreciation for Ernest Hemingway, Washington Irving, and Henry James. Anything was better than calculus. I didn't fully understand the effects of my new reading habit, but I started to develop some peculiar practices. When I went with my roommates to the mall, I would lose myself in Waldenbooks while they rummaged for bargains at the Gap. I started writing simple essays for the yearbook. One summer—without warning—I turned off my TV and read *Dubliners* and *A Portrait of the Artist as a Young Man.* Twice.

I grab a copy of *Ulysses* as a voice chirps from the ceiling. The store will be closing in thirty minutes. I try to head straight for the cashiers in the Green room, but a hot pink book subtitled *Essays from a Feminist Hothead* distracts me. Surely a few more minutes among the shelves won't hurt anyone.

Feminist Studies: History, Anthologies, Essays

After picking up a copy of Kay Leigh Hagan's *Fugitive Information,* I glance over the shelves. From Wollstonecraft's *A Vindication of the Rights of Woman* to Kamen's *Feminist Fatale,* all of the titles seem so inviting.

My first understanding of feminism didn't strike me like a bolt of lightning, nor did it overwhelm me like a tidal wave; it didn't even consume me like a bonfire. My first sense of awareness was much more like a whisper—it was as if a passerby had leaned in my direction and said, "Oh, by the way, this is what you are."

Naturally, it seemed relatively insignificant at the time—who knew if she was even talking to me—but after a few more strangely significant encounters, I stated to pay attention. And I started to piece together the relationship between my buried admiration for my eighth-grade English teacher (I didn't really appreciate it when I was 14, but Ms. Elliott was Virginia Woolf reincarnated), my scorn for and mistrust of most women (especially myself), and my nine-year writing block. On a whim I enrolled in a Women's Studies class and learned there were official terms to describe my predicaments, terms like horizontal hostility and internalization.

Perhaps more significant was my realization that I wasn't by any means the only woman experiencing a tough time fitting into a preset notion of what and who I was supposed to be when I grew up. Sharing other women's experiences made mine seem more valid, and I started to reconcile and accept the numerous directions my mind and my life seem to simultaneously take. Just as I was beginning to credit my existence with a previously missing degree of validity, the course took a turn toward the literary. Instead of the typical sociological essays, the assigned reading for the last week was Ntozake Shange's *for colored girls who have considered suicide/when the rainbow is enuf*. Now here was an undeniable, uncompromising voice, an amazing sound resonating from an author who fit none of my "writer" stereotypes. If neither Shange, the artists we studied in class, nor my classmates had to fit into the mold, then why should I?

I can sit at the coolest coffee shops, wear a black beret and glasses, and snap my fingers until they bleed, but no matter how hard I try, I'm never going to grow a goatee. Obvious though this revelation may be, it called my entire image of myself as a writer into question. I finally stopped forcing my voice to sound as masculine as possible, stopped trying to only write stories about men. And as soon as I stopped pushing myself into this awkward role of translating my thoughts into man-speak, I started writing, writing a lot. Until recently, I had been so desperately trying to push myself into my image of a writer, I had never considered what a woman writer might actually be or that being simply a woman who is writing might be valid enough.

Around the corner in the second row of shelves I find my friend sitting on the floor. I slide down beside her and peer over her shoulder; she's absorbed in a bell hooks essay. We remain there, sharing the essay until the mysterious voice from above reminds us that the store will be closing in five minutes.

While we're standing in line for the cashier, Kate asks me what's on my mind. "I think I want to be a writer when I grow up," I answer her.

"I think you already are." She smiles as she says it, and unexpectedly I think I am a writer, too.

Assignment for an Advanced Class: Rhetorical Situation

2. WR 416/516: Assignment: essays 3 & 4
Suggested page limits: 3–5 pages undergrad/5–8 pages graduate

As the course syllabus indicates, you have considerable freedom in choosing the topic and approach for the final two essays in this class. The only requirement is that you situate your essays in the context of a specific rhetorical situation. Consequently, when you turn in each essay, you should *also* submit a written description of your rhetorical situation. To do so, simply answer the questions in "Guidelines for Analyzing Your Rhetorical Situation" presented in *Work in Progress* on p. 160. (Since I'm asking you to answer these questions when you write a proposal for each essay, the analysis you submit with your finished draft will probably represent a refinement of your proposal—unless you significantly revise your situation as you work on your essay.)

What kinds of options does this assignment provide you? An almost infinite number. Here are a few suggestions (meant to catalyze ideas, not limit possibilities) for you to consider. In many (but not all) of these cases, you could compose following traditional or alternate/experimental stylistic and generic conventions.

- You could write one of a number of popular or journalistic forms of writing: a movie, book, or restaurant review; a "how to" article; an evaluation of one or more products (CD players, cameras, camping equipment); a travel article; a humorous essay; an argument on a current political issue, and so on. In each case, your analysis of your rhetorical situation should include a potential means of publication and detailed consideration of the audience this publication assumes. (See Chapter 5, "Analyzing Rhetorical Situations," and in particular the "Guidelines for Analyzing Your Rhetorical Situation" (p. 160). Examples you might find helpful in *Work in Progress* include Annette Chambers's analysis of her rhetorical situation, pp. 166–63, and Beth Runciman's analysis of an academic rhetorical situation, pp. 426–37.

- You could write a traditional academic essay oriented toward a specific disciplinary situation. If you're an English major and you'd like to have more practice writing literary criticism, for instance, you could choose to analyze a literary text. You and I would need to agree on the text or texts you wish to analyze, and upon the disciplinary expectations. Are you writing a new critical essay, for instance, or an essay that reflects a particular theoretical orientation? You could also write an academic essay oriented toward disciplinary work in another field—but it would need to be one that I would feel comfortable evaluating.

- You could write a personal essay, one addressed to a general audience. That audience might be academic (in which case I and the other students in the class might most reasonably comprise your audience) or it might be nonacademic. Personal essays are published in a number of magazines and literary journals, for instance, and you could aim for such an audience.

- You could write an essay that in some way explores issues of writing and literacy that we have discussed in the class. This could focus primarily on self-introspection and analysis (remember the possible case study of one's own writing that we discussed in class). It could include traditional and field research. (Someone interested in the role of inspiration in writing might read a number of interviews with writers, as well as a few relevant research studies, and also talk with a variety of on-campus writers about this issue.) Or you could do a stylistic analysis of one or more texts—either ones we're reading for the class or ones of your choosing.

- Those who are current or aspiring teachers might want in some way to reflect upon their teaching. This could take a variety of forms—from an analysis of one or more texts of interest to you to traditional and/or field-based inquiry. A new TA, for instance, might interview experienced TA's to glean tips for successful practice, which could be written as a guide to be used in future TA training.

I'm sure that there are other options that I've not considered. This is an opportunity for you to gain experience with the kinds of writing that most interest and excite you, so if you have an idea that I've not included here don't hesitate to discuss it with me.